Bibliographies of New England History
Further Additions, to 1994

Bibliographies of New England History

Bibliographies of New England History
Further Additions, to 1994

Volume Nine of Bibliographies of New England History

Prepared by the

COMMITTEE FOR A NEW ENGLAND BIBLIOGRAPHY

Edited by
ROGER PARKS

UNIVERSITY PRESS OF NEW ENGLAND
Hanover and London

Ref
F
4
.B5
V.9

University Press of New England

Brandeis University
Dartmouth College
Middlebury College
University of New Hampshire
University of Rhode Island
Tufts University
University of Vermont
Wesleyan University
Salzburg Seminar

*This volume has been
made possible in part by a grant
from the Research Materials
Program of the National Endowment
for the Humanities*

OCLC# 32312000

Library of Congress Cataloging-in-Publication Data

Bibliographies of New England history. Further additions, to 1994 /
prepared by the Committee for a New England Bibliography ; edited
by Roger Parks.
    p.   cm. — (Bibliographies of New England history ; v. 9)
   Includes index.
   ISBN 0–87451–714–1 (alk. paper)
   1. New England—History—Bibliography—Union lists.
2. Catalogs, Union—United States. I. Parks, Roger. II. Committee for a
New England Bibliography. III. Series.
Z1251.E1N454 1995
[F4]
016.974—dc20   95-15340

JUN 1 6 1997

Sponsors

A-Copy, Inc.
Acorn Club of Connecticut
American Antiquarian Society
Amherst College Library
Ella F. Anderson Trust
Association for the Study of Connecticut History
Association of Historical Societies of New Hampshire
Bangor Public Library
Bates College
Bay State Historical League
Bennington Museum
Boston Athenaeum
Boston College
Boston Public Library
Boston University
Bowdoin College
Brown University Library
William F. Bryant Foundation
Helen P. Burns
Colby College Library
Colonial Society of Massachusetts
Randolph P. Compton
Friends of Connecticut College Library
Connecticut Historical Society
Connecticut Library Association
Connecticut State Library
Jere R. Daniell
Fred Harris Daniels Foundation, Inc.
Dartmouth College Library

Dexter Corporation Foundation
Frederick P. Elwert
Mr. and Mrs. Philip H. English
Faust and Louisa Fiore Memorial
Green Mountain Power Corporation of Vermont
Hartford Foundation for Public Giving
Stuart Higley
Historic Deerfield, Inc.
Cecil Howard Charitable Trust
Edward T. James
Janet Wilson James
David C. Libbey
Maine Historical Society
Maine Library Association
Maine State American Revolution Bicentennial Commission
Maine State Archives
Maine State Museum
Massachusetts Historical Society
Middlebury College
Mount Holyoke College
Mount Madison Volunteer Ski Patrol Trust
Museum of American Textile History
Museum of Our National Heritage
National Life Insurance Company of Vermont
National Society of the Colonial Dames of America in the State of Vermont
New England Historic Genealogical Society
New England Library Association
New Hampshire American Revolution Bicentennial Commission
New Hampshire Charitable Fund
New Hampshire Historical Society

New Hampshire State Library
Northeastern University
Norwich University
Old Sturbridge Village
John F. Page
Peabody Essex Museum
Mr. and Mrs. Hall J. Peterson
Phoenix Publishing
Portland Public Library
Providence College
Providence Heritage Commission
Providence Journal Company
Providence Public Library
Putnam Foundation
Rhode Island Bicentennial Commission
Rhode Island Committee for the Humanities
Rhode Island Foundation
Rhode Island Heritage Commission
Rhode Island Historical Society
Saint Anselm's College, Geisel Library
Shelburne Museum
The L. J. Skaggs and Mary C. Skaggs Foundation
Arthur H. Smith

Smith College
Society of the Cincinnati of Connecticut
Society of Colonial Wars in Connecticut
Society of Colonial Wars in Massachusetts
Ann F. Spencer
Abbott and Dorothy H. Stevens Foundation
Stoddard Charitable Trust
Dale Stultz
Torrington Historical Society
Trinity College Library, Hartford, Conn.
Tuttle Antiquarian Books, Inc.
United Technologies
University of Connecticut Foundation
University of Maine
University of Massachusetts
University of New Hampshire
University of Rhode Island Library
University of Southern Maine Library
University of Vermont Library
UpCountry Magazine
Vermont Bicentennial Commission
Vermont Department of Libraries
Vermont Historical Society
Vermont National Bank
Warren Brothers Company
Wellesley College Library
Wesleyan University
Williams College
H. W. Wilson Foundation
Woodstock Foundation
Mrs. Sidney Wright
Yale University Library
Yankee, Inc.

Officers and Directors

Committee for a New England Bibliography

Caroline F. Sloat American Antiquarian Society	*Chair*
A. L. Morris West Kennebunk, Maine	*First Vice Chairman*
Christopher P. Bickford Connecticut Historical Society	*Treasurer*
John B. Hench American Antiquarian Society	*Clerk*
Richard M. Candee Boston University	*Vice Chairman for Maine*
James W. Campbell New Haven Colony Historical Society	*Vice Chairman for Connecticut*
Ronald M. Potvin Newport Historical Society	*Vice Chairman for Rhode Island*
David R. Proper Keene, New Hampshire	*Vice Chairman for New Hampshire*
Michael Sherman Vermont Historical Society	*Vice Chairman for Vermont*
Conrad E. Wright Massachusetts Historical Society	*Vice Chairman for Massachusetts*
Brenda Howitson Massachusetts State Library	*Director*
Theresa Percy Old Sturbridge Village	*Director*

Contents

Introduction

This volume is a supplement to the *Bibliographies of New England History*, adding 4,231 entries to a series that now provides citations to nearly 66,000 books, dissertations, pamphlets, and magazine and journal articles. Readers can use the present work together with Volume 7 (1989; entry 101 in this volume) to obtain comprehensive and up-to-date listings of writings on the history of New England as a region that have been published since colonial times. Likewise, they can use it in conjunction with the six state volumes and Volume 8 (1989; entry 102 in this volume) to obtain comprehensive lists of published writings on any phase of New England state and local history.

As in Volume 8, additions and corrections to the earlier bibliographies have been included. Most of the entries in this volume, however, represent writings that have been published since the completion of Volumes 7 and 8 in 1989.

The series, as explained more fully in the introductions to earlier volumes, is inclusive, citing both scholarly and popular writings. Our goal is to identify as many writings as possible that fall within the editorial guidelines of the Committee for a New England Bibliography (CNEB) and to make those writings more accessible to scholars, students, and general readers than they otherwise would be.

Editorial Guidelines

Under the guidelines for the series, the writings listed here were produced as works of history or contain a significant historical dimension. To be considered as history, rather than current events, they must have been written at least a year after the events they describe. Also, they must deal primarily with people, places, and events within New England. Thus, the combat experiences of the region's units and soldiers in wars fought mainly in other places are excluded, whereas historical writings about political and social conditions in New England and any military events that may have occurred there during the same wars are included.

Certain categories of materials basically have been ruled out by our guidelines. These include almanacs, directories, and guidebooks; government documents; historical articles published in newspapers; genealogies; maps and atlases; works of fiction; and juvenile literature. Exclusions are not absolute, however, and although we do not systematically search any of these categories of materials, we do occasionally cite an item of historical substance from them that comes to our attention. In the case of newspapers, we list some historical articles, especially articles in a series.

Research Strategy and Procedures

From 1972 until 1989, the CNEB employed a full-time editor, based at Boston University. During that initial phase of the project, bibliographies of the six New England states were published, followed by one dealing with the history of the region as a whole (Volume 7) and another updating the state bibliographies to 1989 (Volume 8). With the completion of those last two volumes, the CNEB decided to continue updating the series. To do so, it retained the same editor who had been responsible for Volumes 5 through 8 to work on the bibliography approximately one day a week. The present volume was compiled on that basis over a period of nearly five years, from the fall of 1989 to the summer of 1994.

The majority of entries in Volume 9, as throughout the series, represent *magazine and journal articles*. As the focus here is on recent writings, most such entries were found through a systematic search of a large and selected list of current periodicals, supplemented by the use of a number of printed and electronic bibliographies. To the greatest extent possible, the editor used the extensive periodicals holdings of a number of libraries within a reasonable distance of his home in northeastern Connecticut and his primary place of work, Providence, Rhode Island. These libraries included the Connecticut Historical Society and Connecticut State Library in Hartford, the University of Connecticut in Storrs, Eastern Connecticut State University in Willimantic, Brown University and the Rhode Island Historical Society in Providence, the American Antiquarian Society in Worcester, Massachusetts, and the Old Sturbridge Village Research Library in Sturbridge, Massachusetts. Many other periodicals, not available in any of those repositories, were searched during visits to libraries in other parts of New England.

For the *books* cited in this volume, major collections, including those of most of the region's state historical societies and some universities, were searched in each state. So, too, were the holdings of a number of historical societies and other libraries that collect for geographical areas within their states. Among these were the New Haven Colony Historical Society in Connecticut, which focuses on the greater New Haven area; the Bethel Historical Society in Maine (western Maine); Historic Deerfield in Deerfield (western Massachusetts); the Berkshire Athenaeum in Pittsfield, Massachusetts (Berkshire County); and the Sturgis Library in Barnstable, Massachusetts (Cape Cod).

Most libraries gave the editor access to their recent accessions records and thereby made the task of identifying recent publications much easier than it otherwise would have been. Several, including the Vermont, New Hampshire, and Maine historical societies and the Massachusetts State Library, also sent monthly or occasional lists of their recent accessions.

In previous volumes, our book and pamphlet titles were checked against the *National Union Catalog*, which for recent years is available only on microfiche.

A symbol (+) was provided to indicate that further information about a particular title, including library locations in addition to those provided with our entry, could be found by consulting the NUC. For Volume 9, we have made similar use of listings on Online Computer Library Center (OCLC). OCLC is available in many university and other libraries, is easier to use than NUC, and appears to list recent publications much sooner. The majority of book titles in this volume have been verified as being listed on OCLC and are identified by an asterisk (*).

In Volumes 7 and 8, we began citing *doctoral dissertations* comprehensively and *masters' theses* selectively. We have continued to do so here, limiting the masters' theses to Vermont, the only New England state lacking a university with a Ph.D. program in history. Most of the dissertations cited in this volume were identified through a careful search of current issues of *Dissertation Abstracts International* (DAI), published monthly by University Microfilms of Ann Arbor, Michigan. Now available on CD-ROM as well as in print, DAI lists dissertations completed at most American universities and many foreign institutions. Wherever possible, we give the DAI citation so that readers can refer to the abstract for further information about the dissertation and for data needed to order a photocopy or microfiche copy of the dissertation.

Format and Citations

This volume, like seven of the other eight in the series, is organized geographically. (Volume 7, the New England regional bibliography, is arranged under broad subject headings.) A section of entries for New England is first, followed by each of the six states, in alphabetical order, with separate listings in each case for state, county, and local entries. Works pertaining to more than one town appear under the appropriate county; those relating to more than one county are included in the state sections. "See also" references at the end of many county and local listings serve as a guide to these boundary-spanning materials.

In this volume, the city and town sections list only those localities for which entries have been recorded. Similarly, the index lists only places that are the subjects of entries and "see also" references. Readers looking for complete listings of cities and towns and more complete listings of other geographical names should refer to the individual state volumes.

Under each geographical heading, entries are arranged alphabetically, by author. All works by a given author are listed in alphabetical order by title, followed by any titles by that author and a collaborator. A dash at the beginning of an entry means that the work was written by the author of the preceding entry. Authors' names are listed as they appear on title pages or in Library of Congress or OCLC cataloging. Thus, if the title page provides only a middle initial, and the middle name is later found in one of these other sources, we supply the middle name.

Author and corporate-author entries have been preferred in most cases to title entries. Edited and compiled works, however, are commonly given a title entry, unless it is clear from the text that a "compiler" should in fact be regarded as an author. Otherwise, the editor's or compiler's name follows the title.

Titles or imprints, when not shown on the title page or verso, appear in brackets. Where there is more than one edition, the most recent or best one is cited, and the date of the first edition, if known, appears in parentheses after the title. Pagination indicates the last numbered page; substantial unnumbered pages are shown in brackets.

In this volume we provide one library location for each book and pamphlet entry and for copies of dissertations and theses owned by libraries other than those of the universities and colleges at which they were written. We cite wherever possible a major in-state collection. Other collections cited, in order of preference, are local in-state collections; libraries in other New England states; the Library of Congress; and, in a few cases where a work is known to exist but is not known to be in any of the above collections, another non-New England library. Standard library symbols are used. For a list of those cited in this volume, see "Location Symbols."

Corrections

In cases where an entry in a previous volume contained erroneous information or has been superseded by a new and revised edition of a work, we provide a new entry. Along with the bibliographical data, we insert a note stating that the entry replaces a particular citation in the earlier volume.

Index

The index lists authors, editors, and compilers and also provides access to scores of different subjects. It lists place names that are the subjects of entries in this volume. Readers seeking additional information about local place names should consult the indexes of the six state volumes.

Acknowledgments

The staffs of the many libraries whose holdings were searched during the preparation of this volume were uniformly helpful. A grant from the National Endowment for the Humanities (NEH) supported the final two years of research and manuscript preparation; prior to that, the work had been supported by donations from a number of CNEB members and from various New England educational and cultural institutions. Special mention should be made of a grant from the Vermont Historical Society, which made possible a week-long research trip to libraries in that state. Thanks also are due the American Antiquarian Society, which administered the NEH grant, and that institution's assistant director, John B. Hench.

David Ruell, a contributor to Volume 8, again provided some New Hampshire-related entries. In the preparation of this volume, Elizabeth Stevens was very helpful as a proofreader. Karen Vogelaar of Providence Ad Associates converted the computer-generated data into final page form.

As one of those who attended the CNEB's formative meeting at Old Sturbridge Village in 1969, the present editor has seen a number of changes in the membership and leadership of the committee. Commitment to the project has always continued.

Many of the officers and members of the CNEB helped to make the completion of this volume possible, but special thanks should go to Caroline Sloat, who has led the committee for the past five years; to Al Morris, her predecessor, who has continued to give active support; to Christopher Bickford, who has served ably as treasurer for a number of years; to Michael Sherman and Conrad E. Wright, vice chairmen for Vermont and Massachusetts respectively, who have been particularly helpful in their fundraising efforts; and to Edward James, our longtime editorial vice chairman, who recently found it necessary to retire from the committee.

Future of the Project

With the publication of this volume, the updating of the *Bibliographies of New England History* series begins to approach the end of the century. We intend to continue into the next century, believing that that there is an ongoing need for the work we are doing. We are at present exploring various options for the future, including possibly an electronic format and additional bibliographic projects.

Pomfret Center, Connecticut   Roger Parks
October 1994

Serial Abbreviations

Only those titles for which abbrevations are used in this volume are listed. This is not a complete list of serials searched or cited.

AASP   *American Antiquarian Society. Proceedings*
ArcSocConB   *Archaeological Society of Connecticut. Bulletin*
ATQ   *ATQ (American Transcendental Quarterly)*
BDAM   *Biographical Dictionary of Architects in Maine*
C&N   *Concord and the North*
CCHSB   *Chittenden County [Vt.] Historical Society. Bulletin*
CEAIA   *Early American Industries Association. Chronicle*
CHSB   *Connecticut Historical Society. Bulletin*
CrHSN   *Cranston [R.I.] Historical Society. Newsletter*
DAI   *Dissertation Abstracts International*
DAR Magazine   *Daughters of the American Revolution Magazine*
DCI   *Dukes County [Mass.] Historical Society. Dukes County Intelligencer*
DCLB   *Dartmouth College Library Bulletin*
DubSemPr   *Dublin Seminar for New England Folklife. Annual Proceedings*
EIHC   *Essex Institute Historical Collections*
HF   *Stonington [Conn.] Historical Society. Historical Footnotes*
HJM   *Historical Journal of Massachusetts*
HN   *Nantucket [Mass.] Historical Association. Historic Nantucket*
HNH   *New Hampshire Historical Society. Historical New Hampshire*
IA   *IA: The Journal of the Society for Industrial Archeology*
JAMA   *JAMA: The Journal of the American Medical Association*
JSH   *Journal of Social History*
Kfari   *Kfari: The Jewish Magazine of Rural New England and Quebec*
MASB   *Massachusetts Archaeological Society. Bulletin*
MeArcSocB   *Maine Archaeological Society. Bulletin*
MeHSQ   *Maine Historical Society. Quarterly*
MHSC   *Massachusetts Historical Society. Collections*
MHSP   *Massachusetts Historical Society. Proceedings*
MtWObNB   *Mount Washington Observatory. News Bulletin*
NAWCCB   *National Association of Watch and Clock Collectors. Bulletin*
NEHGR   *New England Historic and Genealogical Register*
NEQ   *New England Quarterly*
NE-StLVGSPr   *New England–St. Lawrence Valley Geographical Society. Proceedings*
NH   *Newport [R.I.] Historical Society. Newport History*
NHArcheol   *New Hampshire Archeologist*
NHCHSJ   *New Haven Colony Historical Society [Conn.]. Journal*

NHPremier *New Hampshire Premier*
NHProfiles *New Hampshire Profiles*
Old RI *Old Rhode Island*
OSV *Old Sturbridge Village. Old Sturbridge Visitor*
RHSQ *Rutland [Vt.] Historical Society. Quarterly*
RIH *Rhode Island Historical Society. Rhode Island History*
RIJHN *Rhode Island Jewish Historical Notes*
S'liner *New York, New Haven and Hartford Railroad Historical and Technical Association. Shoreliner*
Spritsail *Spritsail: A Journal of the History of Falmouth [Mass.] and Vicinity*
VtH *Vermont Historical Society. Vermont History*
VtHN *Vermont Historical Society. Vermont History News*
WMQ *William and Mary Quarterly*

Location Symbols

Ct	Connecticut State Library, Hartford
CtB	Bridgeport [Conn.] Public Library
CtGu	Guilford [Conn.] Free Library
CtHi	Connecticut Historical Society, Hartford
CtHT	Trinity College, Hartford, Conn.
CtNbC	Central Connecticut State University, New Britain
CtNhHi	New Haven Colony Historical Society, New Haven, Conn.
CtPom	Pomfret [Conn.] Public Library
CtRK	Rockville [Conn.] Public Library
CtS	Ferguson Library, Stamford, Conn.
CtU	University of Connecticut, Storrs
CtW	Wesleyan University, Middletown, Conn.
CtWillE	Eastern Connecticut State University, Willimantic
CtY	Yale University, New Haven, Conn.
DLC	Library of Congress, Washington, D.C.
InND	University of Notre Dame, Notre Dame, Ind.
M	Massachusetts State Library, Boston
MA	Amherst College, Amherst, Mass.
MB	Boston Public Library
MBar	Sturgis Library, Barnstable, Mass.
MBAt	Boston Athenaeum
MBChM	Children's Museum Research Center, Boston
MBCo	Countway Medical Library, Harvard Medical School, Boston
MBE	Emerson College, Boston
MBNEH	New England Historical Genealogical Society, Boston
MBNU	Northeastern University, Boston
MBridT	Bridgewater State College, Bridgewater, Mass.
MBU	Boston University
MChB	Boston College, Chestnut Hill, Mass.
MDeeP	Pocumtuck Valley Memorial Association, Deerfield, Mass.
Me	Maine State Library, Augusta
MeB	Bowdoin College, Brunswick, Me.
MeBetHi	Bethel Historical Society, Bethel, Me.
MeHi	Maine Historical Society, Portland
MeLB	Bates College, Lewiston, Me.
MeP	Portland [Me.] Public Library

MeU	University of Maine, Orono
MeU-P	University of Southern Maine, Portland
MFal	Falmouth [Mass.] Public Library
MH	Harvard University, Cambridge, Mass.
MHi	Massachusetts Historical Society, Boston
MNanHi	Nantucket [Mass.] Historical Association
MNodS	University of Massachusetts, Dartmouth
MNS	Smith College, Northampton, Mass.
MPB	Berkshire Athenaeum, Pittsfield, Mass.
MS	Springfield [Mass.] City Library. (Local history collection is at Connecticut Valley Historical Society, Springfield.)
MShM	Mount Holyoke College, South Hadley, Mass.
MSou	Jacob Edwards Public Library, Southbridge, Mass.
MStuO	Old Sturbridge Village, Sturbridge, Mass.
MU	University of Massachusetts, Amherst
MW	Worcester [Mass.] Public Library
MWA	American Antiquarian Society, Worcester, Mass.
MWalB	Brandeis University, Waltham, Mass.
MWiW	Williams College, Williamstown, Mass.
Nh	New Hampshire State Library, Concord
NhAsh-DRuell	David Ruell, Ashland, N.H.
NhAsh-MRuell	Mary Ruell, Ashland, N.H.
NhD	Dartmouth College, Hanover, N.H.
NhHi	New Hampshire Historical Society, Concord
NhKe-Proper	David R. Proper, Keene, N.H.
NhMou	Moultonborough [N.H.] Public Library
NhPoA	Portsmouth [N.H.] Athenaeum
NhU	University of New Hampshire, Durham
NhWol	Wolfeboro [N.H.] Public Library
NhWolHi	Wolfeboro [N.H.] Historical Society
NhWonO	Wonalancet [N.H.] Outdoor Club Library
OU	Ohio State University, Columbus
R	Rhode Island State Library, Providence
RHi	Rhode Island Historical Society, Providence
RNHi	Newport [R.I.] Historical Society
RP	Providence [R.I.] Public Library
RPB	Brown University, Providence, R.I.
RPJ	Rhode Island Jewish Historical Association and Bureau of Jewish Education Libraries, Providence
RPPC	Providence College, Providence, R.I.
VtHi	Vermont Historical Society, Montpelier
VtU	University of Vermont, Burlington
WHi	Historical Society of the State of Wisconsin, Madison

Bibliographies of New England History
Further Additions, to 1994

New England

**Entries for the region as a whole
or pertaining to
more than one state**

---

1. ABATELLI, CAROL. "Ethics of reburial: two cases from southern New England." Man in the Northeast, No. 45 (Spring 1993), 87-100.
    Discusses the excavations of Indian burial sites in East Lyme, Conn., and North Kingstown, R.I.

2. ABBOTT, COLLAMER M. "John Theodore Child: dentist and jack-of-all-painting." VtHN, 44 (Jan.-Feb. 1993), 5-9.
    Of Boston and vicinity and West Fairlee, Vt. (1841-1893).

3. ABRAMOWITZ, MAYER S. Hakhme Yi'srael di-Nyu England: Chachmei Yisroel of New England: pictorial history of the New England orthodox rabbinate. Worcester, Mass.: Nathan Stolnitz Archives, 1991. xi, 114p. RPJ. *

4. AHEARN, MARIE L. The rhetoric of war: training day, the militia, and the military sermon. N.Y.: Greenwood Pr., 1989. vi, 217p. CtY. *
    In colonial New England.

5. ALLEN, MEL R. "The Aroostook County cowboy." Yankee, 57 (Jan. 1993), 82-86, 112-13, 115.
    The early life of contemporary country singer Dick Curless, who grew up in Caribou, Me., and Barre and Gilbertville, Mass.

6. _____. "The kid from Rowayton." Yankee, 53 (Dec. 1989), 76-81, 116-119.
    John R. Tunis (1889-1975), once well-known as the author of sports novels for juveniles.

7. ALLPORT, SUSAN. Sermons in stone: the stone walls of New England and New York. N.Y.: W. W. Norton, 1990. 205p. MB. *

8. AMERICAN BAPTIST CHURCHES OF VERMONT AND NEW HAMPSHIRE. Directory of founding churches: American Baptist Churches of Vermont and New Hampshire. Jean F. Blacketor and David J. Heim, eds. n.p., [1990]. 155p. NhHi.
    Includes historical sketches of individual churches.

9. AMERICAN Unitarianism, 1805-1865. Conrad Edick Wright, ed. Boston: Northeastern Univ. Pr., 1989. xiii, 272p. CtY. *

10. ANDERSON, ROBERT CHARLES. "The Great Migration Study Project." WMQ, 3 ser. 50 (July 1993), 590-593.
    Sponsored by the New England Historic Genealogical Society, Boston.

11. ANDERSON, VIRGINIA DeJOHN. New England's generation: the Great Migration and the formation of society and culture in the seventeenth century. N.Y.: Cambridge Univ. Pr., 1991. x, 232p. MB. *
    See also this author's Ph.D. dissertation on same subject (Harvard Univ., 1984; entry 321 in Vol. 7).

12. _____. "The origins of New England culture." WMQ, 3 ser. 48 (Apr. 1991), 231-237.
    Critique of one aspect of David Hackett Fischer's book, Albion's seed (1989).

13. ANDERSON, WILL. Beer New England: an affectionate look at our six states' past and present brews and breweries. Portland, Me., 1988. vii, 188p. CtHi. *

14. APESS, WILLIAM. On our own ground: the complete writings of William Apess, a Pequot. Barry O'Connell, ed. Amherst: Univ. of Massachusetts Pr., 1992. lxxxi, 344p. CtU. *
    19th-century reformer.

15. ARCH, STEPHEN CARL. "The edifying history of Edward Johnson's Wonder-working providence." Early American Literature, 28:1 (1993), 42-59.
    Johnson's work, first published in 1653, is listed in Vol. 7 (entry 395).

16. _____. "The Glorious Revolution and the rhetoric of Puritan history." Early American Literature, 27:1 (1992), 61-74.

17. _____. "Mastering history: Puritan historians in colonial America." Ph.D. dissertation, Univ. of Virginia, 1989. xvi, 368p.*
    Abstracted in DAI, 50:9A (1990), 2894.

* Online Computer Library Center (OLCC) listings for books and dissertations marked with this symbol may include additional library locations.

18   NEW ENGLAND

18.   ARCHER, RICHARD. "New England mosaic: a demographic analysis for the seventeenth century." WMQ, 3 ser. 47 (Oct. 1990), 477-502.

19.   ASSOCIATION OF FORMER INTELLIGENCE OFFICERS. DAVID ATLEE PHILLIPS NEW ENGLAND CHAPTER. Secret New England: spies of the American Revolution. Kennebunk, Me., 1991. 234p. VtHi. *

20.   ATLAS of historical county boundaries: New Hampshire, Vermont. Gordon DenBoer, comp.; John H. Long, ed. N.Y.: Simon & Schuster, 1993. xx, 216p. VtHi. *

21.   AUSTEN, BARBARA E. "Captured...never came back: social networks among New England female captives in Canada, 1689-1763." DubSemPr (1989), 28-38.

22.   BACHAND, ROBERT G. Northeast lights: lighthouses and lightships, Rhode Island to Cape May, New Jersey. Norwalk, Conn.: Sea Sports, 1989. xii, 422p. MU. *

23.   BAILEY, RONALD. "The slave(ry) trade and the development of capitalism in the United States: the textile industry in New England." Social Science History, 14 (Fall 1990), 373-414.

24.   BAKER, ANDREW H. "Premiums for ploughing." OSV, 30 (Fall 1990), 4-6.
       Early-19th-century fairs and cattle shows.

25.   BAKER, EMERSON W. "New evidence of the French involvement in King Philip's War." MeHSQ, 28 (Fall 1988), 85-91.

26.   BANKS, MARC. "Aboriginal weirs in southern New England." ArcSocConB, No. 53 (1990), 73-83.

27.   BARDWELL, JOHN D. The Isles of Shoals: a visual history. Portsmouth, N.H.: Portsmouth Marine Society, 1989. x, 198p. NhHi. *
       In Maine and New Hampshire.

28.   BARNES, FRANK T. Hooks, rings & other things: an illustrated index of New England iron, 1660-1860. Hanover, Mass.: Christopher Publishing House, 1988. 237p. MB. *

29.   BARON, DONNA KEITH, and CAROLINE FULLER SLOAT. "Cabinet furniture & chairs cheap: making & selling furniture in central New England, 1790-1850." OSV, 33 (Spring 1993), 4-6.

30.   BAUSCHINGER, SIGRID. Die Posaune der Reform: deutsche Literatur in Neuengland des 19. Jahrhunderts. Bern, Switzerland: Francke, 1989. 214p. VtU. *

31.   BEATTIE, BETSY. "Dutiful daughters: maritime-born women in New England in the late nineteenth century." Retrospection, 2:1 (1989), 16-31.

32.   BELL, MICHAEL M. "Did New England go downhill?" Geographical Review, 79 (Oct. 1989), 467-474.
       Considers the question of decline in New England farming during the 19th century.

33.   BENES, PETER. "Itinerant physicians, healers, and surgeon-dentists in New England and New York, 1720- 1825." DubSemPr (1990), 95-112.

34.   BERGAMASCO, LUCIA. "La religion populair en Nouvelle-Angleterre." Annales [France], No. 5 (Sept.- Oct. 1991), 1207-1214.
       Popular religion in New England. (Text in French.)

35.   BILLINGTON, LOUIS. "Northern New England sectarianism in the early nineteenth century." John Rylands University Library of Manchester [U.K.], Bulletin, 70 (Autumn 1988), 123-134.

36.   BLAKELY, JEFFREY A. "Xeroradiography of historic ceramics: four New England kilns." Historical Archaeology, 23:1 (1989), 107-112.
       The objects studied were from eighteenth- and nineteenth-century sites in Goshen and Woodstock, Conn.; Brimfield and Holland, Mass.

37   BLEJWAS, STANISLAUS A. "The inherited and the disinherited: the Polish peasant farmer in New England literature." Connecticut Review, 14 (Fall 1992), 49-60.
       A study of novels by Cornelia James Cannon and Edna Ferber.

38.   BLOW, RICHARD H. SR. A time to do: Barre, Vermont, 1938; Manchester, Conn., 1938-55; and points east-west. Barre, Vt.: Modern Printing, 1991. 257p. VtHi. *
       Autobiographical. See also entry 3934.

39.   BLUE HILL METEOROLOGICAL OBSERVATORY. Hurricane Bob, August 16-August 20, 1991: a brief history. William Elliott Minsinger and Charles Talcott Orloff, eds. [Milton, Mass], 1992. 80p. CtNhHi. *

40.   BLUESTONE, DANIEL. "Civic and aesthetic reserve: Ammi Burnham Young's 1850s federal customhouse designs." Winterthur Portfolio, 25 (Summer/Autumn 1990), 131-156.
       In New Hampshire and Vermont.

41.   BLUMENBERG, BENNETT, and DALE J. BUTTERWORTH. "Luther and Joseph Metcalf: two cabinetmakers/ planemakers of New England." CEAIA, 44 (June 1991), 37- 38.
       Of Franklin, Mass., and Winthrop, Me., respectively.

42.   BOND, CHARLES LAWRENCE. Native names of New England towns and villages: translating 199 names derived from Native American words. (1991) 2d ed. Topsfield, Mass.: C.L. Bond, 1993. vi, 78p. MeHi. *

43.   BONFIELD, LYNN A. "Diaries of New England quilters before 1800." American Quilt Study Group, Uncoverings (1988), 171-197.

44.   BORISH, LINDA JANE. "Farm females, fitness, and the ideology of physical health in antebellum New England." Agricultural History, 64 (Summer 1990), 17- 30.
      See also next entry and entry 652.

45.   _____. "'You must work quite too hard': farm women, work, and cultural perceptions of health." OSV, 33 (Fall 1993), 4-5.
      See also preceding entry.

46.   BOURNE, RUSSELL. The red king's rebellion: racial politics in New England, 1675-1678. N.Y.: Atheneum, 1990. xiv, 273p. CtU. *
      King Philip's War.

47.   _____. The view from Front Street: travels through New England's historic fishing communities. N.Y.: W. W. Norton, 1989. 282p. CtU. *

48.   BOZEMAN, THEODORE DWIGHT. To live ancient lives: the primitivist dimension in American Puritanism. Chapel Hill: Univ. of North Carolina Pr., 1988. xii, 413p. CtY. *

49.   BRAUN, ESTHER KAPLAN, and DAVID P. BRAUN. The first peoples of the Northeast. Lincoln, Mass.: Lincoln Historical Society, 1994. xv, 144p. MH. *

50.   BREITWEISER, MITCHELL ROBERT. American Puritanism and the defense of mourning: religion, grief, and ethnology in Mary White Rowlandson's captivity narrative. Madison: Univ. of Wisconsin Pr., 1991. viii, 223p. MB. *

51.   BREMER, FRANCIS JOHN. Congregational communion: clerical friendship in the Anglo-American Puritan community, 1610-1692. Boston: Northeastern Univ. Pr., 1994. 352p. MBNU. *
      See also next entry and entry 380.

52.   _____. Puritan crisis: New England and the English civil wars, 1630-1670. N.Y.: Garland Publishing, 1989. xix, 398p. CtU. *
      Published version of author's Ph.D. dissertation of same title (Columbia Univ., 1972; entry 596 in Vol. 7). See also previous entry.

53.   BROWN, DONA L. "The tourist's New England: creating an industry, 1820-1900." Ph.D. dissertation, Univ. of Massachusetts, 1989. x, 266p. *
      Abstracted in DAI, 50:12A (1990), 4072.

54.   BROWN, GAYLE KATHLEEN. "A controversy not merely religious: the anti-Catholic tradition in colonial New England." Ph.D. dissertation, Univ. of Iowa, 1990. iv, 342p. *
      Abstracted in DAI, 51:9A (1991), 3197.

55.   _____. "'Into the hands of Papists': New England captives in French Canada and the English anti-Catholic tradition, 1689-1763." Maryland Historian, 21 (Fall/ Winter 1990), 1-11.
      See also preceding entry.

56.   BURCHFIEL, RAE DEMLER. "The character of John Eliot: a study in the nurture of values." Ph.D. dissertation, Boston College, 1987. 225p.
      The Puritan missionary to the Indians. Abstracted in DAI, 53:9A (1993), 3344.

57.   BUSCH, BRITON COOPER. "Whaling will never do for me": the American whaleman in the nineteenth century. Lexington: Univ. of Kentucky Pr., 1994. xii, 265p. MeU. *

58.   BYRON, CARL R. "PA's & domes on the B&M." B&M Bulletin, 17:3 (1990), 6-11.
      Locomotives and train types on the Boston and Maine Railroad.

59.   CAHILL, ROBERT ELLIS. New England's mad and mysterious men. Peabody, Mass.: Chandler-Smith Publishing House, 1984. 48p. MB. *

60.   _____. New England's marvelous monsters. Peabody, Mass.: Chandler-Smith Publishing House, 1983. 48p. MB. *

61.   _____. New England's mountain madness. Peabody, Mass.: Chandler-Smith Publishing House, 1989. 48p. *
      On the subject of hauntings.

62.   _____. New England's pirates and lost treasures. Peabody, Mass.: Chandler-Smith Publishing House, 1987. 60p. *

63.   _____. New England's riotous revolution. Peabody, Mass.: Chandler-Smith Publishing House, 1987. 67p. *
      American Revolution.

64.   _____. New England's things that go bump in the night. Peabody, Mass.: Chandler-Smith Publishing House, 1989. 48p. *

65.   _____. New England's Viking and Indian wars. Peabody, Mass.: Chandler-Smith Publishing House, 1986. 56p. Meu-P. *

66.   _____. New England's visitors from outer space. Peabody, Mass.: Chandler-Smith Publishing House, 1985. 52p. *
      UFO sightings.

67   NEW ENGLAND

67. CAHILL, ROBERT ELLIS.. New England's war wonders. Peabody, Mass.: Chandler-Smith Publishing House, 1984. 48p. *

68. _____. New England's witches and wizards. Peabody, Mass.: Chandler-Smith Publishing House, 1983. 48p. MB. *

69. _____. The old Irish of New England. Peabody, Mass.: Chandler-Smith Publishing House, 1984. 48p. MB. *

70. _____. Olde New England's curious customs and cures. Peabody, Mass.: Chandler-Smith Publishing House, 1990. 48p. *

71. CALDWELL-HOPPER, KATHI. "A prescription for success." C&N, 2 (Dec. 1993), 44-45.
   Dr. Nathan Smith. See also entry 153.

72. CALLOWAY, COLIN GORDON. The Abenaki. N.Y.: Chelsea House Publishers, 1989. 111p. VtHi. *
   Abenaki Indians. See also entry 3747.

73. _____. "The Abenakis and the Anglo-French borderlands." DubSemPr (1989), 18-27.

74. _____. Indians of the Northeast. N.Y.: Facts on File, 1991. 96p. Me. *

75. _____. "Sentinels of the Revolution: Bedel's New Hampshire Rangers and the Abenaki Indians on the upper Connecticut." HNH, 45 (Winter 1990), 271-295.

76. CANDEE, RICHARD McALPIN. "First-period architecture in Maine and New Hampshire: the evidence of probate inventories." DubSemPr (1987), 97-120.

77. CANUP, JOHN LESLIE. Out of the wilderness: the emergence of an American identity in colonial New England. Middletown, Conn.: Wesleyan Univ. Pr., 1990. xiii, 303p. MWA. *
   See also this author's Ph.D. dissertation: "American nature, English culture: environmental thought and the emergence of a provincial mentality in New England" (Univ. of North Carolina, 1986; entry 348 in Vol. 7).

78. CARLSON, CATHERINE CARROLL. "The Atlantic salmon in New England prehistory and history: social and environmental implications." Ph.D. dissertation, Univ. of Massachusetts, 1992. xv, 298p. *
   Abstracted in DAI, 53:6A (1992), 1982.

79. _____. "The history and archaeological research potential of tree-ring studies in New England and their relationship to wetlands." Man in the Northeast, No. 43 (Spring 1992), 43-60.

80. CASH, FLORIS. "African American whalers: images and reality." Long Island Historical Journal, 2 (Fall 1989), 41-51.

81. CAVE, ALFRED A. "Indian shamans and English witches in seventeenth-century New England." EIHC, 128 (Oct. 1992), 239-254.

82. CAYTON, MARY KUPIEC. Emerson's emergence: self and society in the transformation of New England, 1800-1845. Chapel Hill: Univ. of North Carolina Pr., 1989. xiii, 307p. MB. *

83. CERNICH, CHRISTOPHER MICHAEL. "'Salvadge lande': the Puritan wilderness and the preservation of the world." Ph.D. dissertation, Univ. of Michigan, 1993. 197p.
   Literary history. Abstracted in DAI, 54:11A (1994), 4091.

84. CHAMBERLAIN, AVA. "The theology of cruelty: a new look at the rise of Arminianism in eighteenth-century New England." Harvard Theological Review, 85 (July 1992), 335-356.

85. CHARTIER, ARMAND B. Histoire des Franco-Américains de la Nouvelle-Angleterre, 1775-1990. Sillery, Que: Les éditions du Septentrion, 1991. 436p. MB. *

86. _____. Litterature historique populaire Franco-Américaine. Manchester, N.H.: National Materials Development Center for French and Creole, 1981. viii, 108p. MB. *

87. CHASE, THEODORE, and LAUREL K. GABEL. Gravestone chronicles: some eighteenth-century New England carvers and their work. Boston: New England Historic Genealogical Society, 1990. vi, 262p. MB. *

88. CHILTON, ELIZABETH S. "In search of paleo-women: gender implications of remains from paleoindian sites in the Northeast." MASB, 55 (Spring 1994), 8-14.

89. CHOQUETTE, LESLIE. "French and British emigration to the North American colonies: a comparative view." DubSemPr (1989), 49-57.
   New France and New England.

90. CLARK, EDIE. "A tale of two towns." Yankee, 54 (May 1990), 66-71, 74, 122-126.
   Recent efforts to deal with unsafe water supplies in Whatley, Mass., and Machias, Me.

91. CLINE, JUDITH ANN. "Margaret Ruthven Lang: her life and songs." Ph.D. dissertation, Washington Univ., 1993. iii, 225p. *
   "Prominent member of the Second New England School of composition" (late-19th and early-20th centuries). Abstracted in DAI, 54:7A (1994), 2376.

92. CLINE, LINDA, and ROBERT C. HAYDEN. A cultural guide to African-American heritage in New England. [Malden, Mass.]: Cline Transportation Service, 1992. 100p. RHi. *
   Includes historic sites.

93.   COBB, HUGH. "The siege of New England: hurricanes Carol and Edna come to call." Weatherwise, 42 (Oct. 1989), 262-266.
   1954.

94.   COGLEY, RICHARD W. "John Eliot in recent scholarship." American Indian Culture and Research Journal, 14:2 (1990), 77-92.

95.   COGLIANO, FRANCIS DOMINIC. "Nil desperandum Christo duce: the New England crusade against Louisbourg, 1745." EIHC, 128 (July 1992), 180-207.

96.   _____. "No king, no popery: anti-popery and revolution in New England, 1745-1791." Ph.D. dissertation, Boston Univ., 1993. xiii, 375p. *
   Abstracted in DAI, 53:12A (1993), 4447-4448.

97.   COHEN, DANIEL ASHER. Pillars of salt, monuments of grace: New England crime literature and the origins of American popular culture, 1674-1860. N.Y.: Oxford Univ. Pr., 1993. xi, 350p. MBAt. *
   See also next entry.

98.   _____. "Pillars of salt: the transformation of New England crime literature, 1674-1860." Ph.D. dissertation, Brandeis Univ., 1989. 582p. MWA. *
   Abstracted in DAI, 50:3A (1989), 779. See also preceding entry.

99.   COLEMAN, JACK. "Setting the stage for conflict." Middleborough [Mass.] Antiquarian, 29 (Spring 1991), 8-10, 12.
   Background of King Philip's War.

100.   COLLINGWOOD, DERYCK C. "William Pynchon (1590-1662), founder of Springfield, MA, and Thomas Hooker (1586-1647), founder of Hartford, Conn.: neighbors and friends in Essex, England." Connecticut Nutmegger, 23 (Dec. 1990), 388-398; (Mar. 1991), 626-635.
   See also entry 754.

101.   COMMITTEE FOR A NEW ENGLAND BIBLIOGRAPHY. New England: a bibliography of its history. Roger Parks, ed. Hanover, N.H.: University Pr. of New England, 1989. lvi, 259p. MWA. *
   Lists published historical writings and doctoral dissertations about the history of the region. Includes historiographical essay: "Reassessing the local history of New England," by David Hall and Alan Taylor, xix-xlvii.

102.   _____. New England: additions to the six state bibliographies. Roger Parks, ed. Hanover, N.H.: University Pr. of New England, 1989. xxiv, 776p. MWA. *
   This volume updates and expands the committee's published bibliographies of the histories of the six New England states through 1987, with additional entries for 1988 and early 1989. It adds doctoral dissertations and selected masters' theses to the series and expands biographical coverage for Massachusetts, Maine, and New Hampshire.

103.   CONFORTI, JOSEPH ANTHONY. "'Ice and granite': the New England character." MeHSQ, 28 (Fall 1988), 92-108.

104.   _____. "The invention of the Great Awakening, 1795-1842." Early American Literature, 26:2 (1991), 99-118.
   "Historical reification of the colonial revivals and of New England's religious experiences with a great, general, and transformative episode" during the period of the Second Great Awakening.

105.   CONNECTICUT HUMANITIES COUNCIL. The noblest of thoughts: literature and American history. Todd Levy and Betty Olson, eds. Middletown, Conn., 1987. 93p. CtU. *
   New England literature.

106.   CONNOR, SHEILA. New England natives: a celebration of people and trees. Cambridge, Mass.: Harvard Univ. Pr., 1994. xi, 274p. MStuO. *
   Trees in the history of New England.

107.   COOKE, BRIAN. "New England academy education in the early republic." HJM, 21 (Winter 1993), 74-87.

108.   COOLIDGE, GRACE. Grace Coolidge: an autobiography. Lawrence E. Wikander and Robert H. Ferrell, eds. Worland, Wyo.: High Plains, 1992. xvii, 120p. VtHi. *
   Wife of President Calvin Coolidge.

109.   COOPER-FORST, JULIANNE SIUDOWSKI. "To rend and teare the bodies of men: theology and the body in demonic possession; France, England and Puritan America, 1550-1700." Ph.D. dissertation, Univ. of New Hampshire, 1992. xi, 260p. *
   Abstracted in DAI, 53:11A (1993), 4049.

110.   CORBETT, WILLIAM. Literary New England: a history and guide. Boston: Faber and Faber, 1993. x, 206p. MBAt. *

111.   CORNWALL, L. PETER, and CAROL A. SMITH. Names first—rails later: New England's 700-plus railroads and what happened to them. Stamford, Conn.: Arden Valley Group, 1989. 132p. MWA. *

112   NEW ENGLAND

112.   CORRIGAN, JOHN. The prism of piety: Catholick congregational clergy at the beginning of the Enlightenment. N.Y.: Oxford Univ. Pr., 1991. x, 197p. MB. *

113.   COSTELLO, MARGARET F. "A child by any other name...." NEHGR, 147 (Jan. 1993), 68-70.
Naming practices in early New England.

114.   CRAIG, BEATRICE CHEVALIER. "Pour une approche comparative de létude des sociétès rurales nord-américaines." DubSemPr (1989), 135-149.
Reprinted from Histoire sociale/Social History [Canada], 23 (Nov. 1990), 249-270.

115.   CRANMER, LEON. "The New England frontier." Kennebec Proprietor, 5 (Summer 1988), 4-7.

116.   CRAWFORD, MICHAEL J. "New England and the Scottish religious revivals of 1742." American Presbyterians, 69 (Spring 1990), 23-32.
"Similarities in the religious contexts enabled the Scottish evangelists to bring New England's Great Awakening to Scotland." See also next entry.

117.   _____. Seasons of grace: colonial New England's revival tradition in its British context. N.Y.: Oxford Univ. Pr., 1991. xi, 354p. MB. *

118.   CRESSY, DAVID. "Letters home: old and New England in the seventeenth century." History Today, 37 (Oct. 1987), 37-41.

119.   CUNNINGHAM, EDWARD M. "My time with the Boston & Maine Railroad: from Worcester to Winnisquam." B&M Bulletin, 18:2 (1992), 8-13.
Recollections of trips between Worcester, Mass., and Winnisquam, N.H., during and after the 1930s.

120.   D'AMATO, DONALD A. "King Philip's War." Old RI, 1 (Dec. 1991), 33-35.

121.   DAME, BRIAN R. "Silent sentinels." B&M Bulletin, 18:2 (1991), 14-26.
Signals on the Boston and Maine Railroad.

122.   DANIEL Webster, "the completest man." Kenneth E. Shewmaker, ed. Hanover, N.H.: University Pr. of New England, 1990. xxxvii, 311p. MBAt. *
Essays.

123.   DANIELS, BRUCE COLIN. "Did the Puritans have fun?: Leisure, recreation and the concept of pleasure in early New England." Journal of American Studies [U.K.], 25 (Apr. 1991), 7-22.

124.   _____. The fragmentation of New England: comparative perspectives on economic, political, and social divisions in the eighteenth century. N.Y.: Greenwood Pr., 1988. xxi, 229p. CtY. *

125.   _____. "Frolics for fun: dances, weddings, and dinner parties in colonial New England." HJM, 21 (Summer 1993), 1-27.

126.   _____. "Opportunity and urbanism: population growth in New England's secondary cities, 1790-1860." Canadian Review of American Studies, 22 (Fall 1991) 173-193.

127.   _____. "Sober mirth and pleasant poisons: Puritan ambivalence toward leisure and recreation in colonial New England." American Studies, 34 (Spring 1993), 121-137.

128.   DARLINGTON, JAMES WILLIAM. "Down from the hills and into the nation: the migratory behavior of early nineteenth century New England college graduates." Ph.D. dissertation, Univ. of Kentucky, 1990. xi, 388p. *
Study of Dartmouth, Middlebury, and Williams College graduates. Abstracted in DAI, 51:4A (1990), 1345.

129.   DAUGHTERS OF THE AMERICAN REVOLUTION. NATIONAL SOCIETY. Minority military service: New Hampshire, Vermont, 1775-1783. [Washington], 1991. 17p. RHi. *

130.   DAVIS, LANCE EDWIN, ROBERT E. GALLMAN, and TERESA DUNN HUTCHINS. "The decline of U.S. whaling: was the stock of whales running out?" Business History Review, 62 (Winter 1988), 569-595.

131.   DAVIS, MARGARET HAIGLER. "'Thy maker is thy husband': the espousal metaphor in seventeenth century New England." Ph.D. dissertation, Univ. of Alabama, 1990. iv, 261p. *
Abstracted in DAI, 51:5A (1990), 1612.

132.   DAWNLAND encounters: Indians and Europeans in northern New England. Colin G. Calloway, ed. Hanover, N.H.: University Pr. of New England, 1991. xiii, 296p. VtHi. *

133.   DEETZ, JAMES J. F., and EDWIN STEWART DETHLEFSEN. "Death's head, cherub, urn and willow." Natural History, 76 (Mar. 1967) 29-37.
Anthropological analysis of early New England gravestone art.

134.   DICKASON, OLIVE PATRICIA. "The French and the Abenaki: a study in frontier politics." VtH, 58 (Spring 1990), 82-98.

135. DOHERTY, JOE. "Blackstone Canal diary." Old RI, 3 (June/July 1993), 30-31, 34-38; (Aug. 1993), 39-43; (Sept. 1993), 43-47; (Oct. 1993), 48-51; (Nov. 1993), 49-53; (Dec. 1993/Jan. 1994), 45-50; 4 (Feb. 1994), 50- 54; (Mar. 1994), 54-62.

The canal served as a link between Worcester, Mass., and Providence, R.I. Titles of installments vary.

136. DONOVAN, GRACE. "Immigrant nuns: their participation in the process of Americanization: Massachusetts and Rhode Island, 1880-1920." Catholic Historical Review, 77 (Apr. 1991), 194-208.

137. DORIANI, DANIEL. "The Puritans, sex, and pleasure." Westminster Theological Journal, 53 (Spring 1991), 125-143.

138. DOUGLAS, JIM. From farm to factory: the story of the New England textile industry in song. Sturbridge, Mass.: Pedlar Pr., 1988. 62p. CtHi. *

139. DUBLIN, THOMAS LOUIS. "Rural putting-out work in early nineteenth-century New England: women and the transition to capitalism in the countryside." NEQ, 64 (Dec. 1991), 531-573.

140. _____. Transforming women's work: New England lives in the industrial revolution. Ithaca, N.Y.: Cornell Univ. Pr., 1994. xix, 324p. VtHi. *

141. DUNBAUGH, EDWIN L. Night boat to New England, 1815-1900. N.Y.: Greenwood Pr., 1992. x, 370p. MBAt. *
Steamboat lines.

142. DUNN, JEROME P. "Squanto before he met the Pilgrims." MASB, 54 (Spring 1993), 38-42.

143. DURFEE, ROBERT. Robert Durfee's journal and recollections of Newport, Rhode Island, Freetown, Massachusetts, New York City and Long Island, Jamaica and Cuba, West Indies and Saint Simons Island, Georgia, ca. 1785-1810. Virginia Steele Wood, ed. Marion, Ga.: Belden Books, 1990. 131p. RHi. *

144. EARLY New England meditative poetry: Anne Bradstreet and Edward Taylor. Charles E. Hambrick- Stowe, ed. New York: Paulist Pr., 1988. vi, 270p. CtY. *

145. EBERWEIN, JANE DONAHUE. "'Harvardine quil': Benjamin Tompson's poems on King Philip's War." Early American Literature, 28:1 (1993), 1-20.

146. EGAN, JAMES FRANCIS. "Ideology and the study of American culture: early New England writing and the idea of experience." Ph.D. dissertation, Univ. of California, Santa Barbara, 1991. x, 181p. *
Study of the writings of Anne Hutchinson, Anne Bradstreet, and Jonathan Edwards. Abstracted in DAI, 52:11A (1992), 3927.

147. ERHARDT, JOHN G. A history of Rehoboth, Seekonk, Mass., Pawtucket & East Providence, R.I., 1692-1812. Vol. III. Seekonk, Mass., 1990. 1281p. RHi. *
Earlier titles in this series are listed in Vol. 7, entries 4111-4112.

148. ESTES, J. WORTH. "Samuel Thomson rewrites Hippocrates." DubSemPr (1990), 113-132.
Thomson, the well-known advocate of botanic medicine, published his New guide to health in 1822.

149. FANUZZI, ROBERT A. "'Be yourself': the public scheme and revolutionary politics of the New England abolition movement." Ph.D. dissertation, Northwestern Univ., 1993. 295p.
Abstracted in DAI, 54:5A (1993), 1803.

150. FELKER, CHRISTOPHER DANIEL. "Cotton Mather's 'Magnalia Christi Americana' and rehearsed spectacles of New England history, 1820-1862." Ph.D. dissertation, Univ. of New Hampshire, 1991. viii, 307p. *
Examines Mather's work and its effects on the writings of three 19th-century authors: Nathaniel Hawthorne, Harriet Beecher Stowe, and Elizabeth Drew Stoddard. Abstracted in DAI, 52:10A (1992), 3601.

151. FENSTERMAKER, J. VAN, and JOHN E. FILER. "The U.S. embargo act of 1807: its impact on New England money, banking, and economic activity." Economic Inquiry, 28 (Jan. 1990), 163-184.

152. FIELD, GREGORY. "Agricultural science and the rise and decline of tobacco agriculture in the Connecticut River Valley." HJM, 19 (Summer 1991), 155-174.

153. FIELD, WILLIAM W. The good Doctor Smith: life and times of Dr. Nathan Smith, 1762-1829, as seen through his letters, his lectures, and recollections of his students. New Haven, Conn.: Advocate Pr., 1992. iv, 156p. CtHi. *
Smith taught surgery and physics at Dartmouth, Yale, Bowdoin, and the University of Vermont.

154. FILIOS, ELENA LOUISE. "The end of the beginning or the beginning of the end: the third millennium B.P. in southern New England." Man in the Northeast, No. 38 (Fall 1989), 79-93.

155. _____. "Thresholds to group mobility among hunter-gatherers: an archaeological example from southern New England." Ph.D. dissertation, Univ. of Massachusetts, 1990. xix, 375p. *
Abstracted in DAI, 51:11A (1991), 3797.

156. FINKELSTEIN, BARBARA. "Perfecting childhood: Horace Mann and the origins of public education in the United States." Biography, 13 (Winter 1990), 6-20.

157   NEW ENGLAND

157.   FINNEGAN, KATHLEEN E., and TIMOTHY E.
HARRISON. Lighthouses of Maine and New Hampshire: a
pictorial tour of the lighthouses of Maine and New
Hampshire. Laconia, N.H.: Quantum Printing, 1991. 94p.
MeHi. *
    Includes historical information.

158.   FISH, JOHN PERRY. Unfinished voyages: a chronology of
shipwrecks in the northeastern United States. Orleans, Mass.:
Lower Cape Publishing, 1989. xii, 299p. MBAt. *

159.   "Seeing New Englandly: anthropology, ecology, and
theology in Thoreau's Week on the Concord and Merrimack
rivers." Centennial Review, 34 (Summer 1990), 381-394.

160.   FITTS, ROBERT K. "Gravestone inscriptions as a source for
colonial history: a case study of the transition from Puritan to
Yankee New England." Man in the Northeast, No. 41 (Spring
1991), 65-83.

161.   FLANDERS, TOM. "Afoot in central New England: the
history of the Wapack Trail." Appalachia, 49 (June 15, 1992),
41-51.
    Hiking trail in Massachusetts and New Hampshire.

162.   FLOYD, CANDACE. The history of New England. n.p.:
Portland House, 1990. 304p. Nh. *

163.   FORBES, HARRIETTE MERRIFIELD. "Symbolic
cemetery gates in New England." Markers VII (1990), 3-18.

164.   FOSTER, DAVID R. "Land-use history (1730-1990) and
vegetation dynamics in central New England, USA." Journal
of Ecology [U.K], 80:4 (1992), 753-771.

165.   FOSTER, DAVID R., P. ZEBRYK, P. SCHOONMAKER,
and A. LEZBERG. "Post-settlement history of human land
use and vegetation dynamics of a Tsuga canadensis
(hemlock) woodlot in central New England." Journal of
Ecology [U.K], 80:4 (1992), 773-786.

166.   FOSTER, GEORGE H., and PETER WEIGLIN. Splendor
sailed the Sound: the New Haven Railroad and the Fall River
Line. San Mateo, Calif.: Potentials Group, 1989. 384p. RHi. *

167.   FOSTER, STEPHEN. The long argument: English
Puritanism and the shaping of New England culture, 1570-
1700. Chapel Hill: Univ. of North Carolina Pr., 1991. xx,
395p. MB. *

168.   FOURNIER, CONSTANCE ANNE. "Undercurrents: the
experiences of New England maritime women, 1790-1912."
Ph.D. dissertation, Univ. of Hawaii, 1993. 441p.
    Abstracted in DAI, 54:12A (1994), 4491-4492.

169.   FRATTASIO, MARC, and JOEL ROSENBAUM. "The
McGinnis trains." S'liner, 19:2 (1988), 10-38; 19:3 (1988),
12- 29.
    Streamlined trains on the Boston-New York section of the
New Haven Railroad.

170.   FREUND, HUGH ALLEN. "Celebrating the American
Thanksgiving: an experience-centered approach to meaning
formation in a New England family." Ph.D. dissertation,
Univ. of Pennsylvania, 1991. xxvi, 362p. *
    Includes historical information. Abstracted in DAI, 52:3A
(1991), 1033.

171.   FRIEDMAN, RACHELLE ELAINE. "Writing the wonders:
Puritan historians in colonial New England." Ph.D.
dissertation, UCLA, 1991. 418p. *
    Abstracted in DAI, 52:9A (1992), 3402.

172.   FROST, ELIAS. The chronicle of Elias Frost, M.D. (1782-
1863): society and medicine in Uxbridge, Massachusetts, and
Meriden, New Hampshire. East Plainfield, N.H.: Lord
Timothy Dexter Pr., 1992. ix, 359p. MWA.

173.   FRY, RUSSELL RAYMOND. "Theological principles of
Isaac Backus and the move from Congregationalism to
Baptist leadership in New England." Ph.D. dissertation,
Drew Univ., 1988. viii, 256p. *
    Abstracted in DAI, 49:8A (1989), 2275.

174.   FULOP, CHARLES FRANK. "Elias Smith and the quest for
gospel liberty: popular religious and democratic radicalism in
early nineteenth-century New England." Ph.D. dissertation,
Princeton Univ., 1992. vii, 272p. *
    "Religious radical" (lived 1769-1848). Abstracted in
DAI, 53:6A (1992), 1964. See also entries 271-272.

175.   GALENSON, DAVID W. "Economic determinants of the
age of leaving home: evidence from the lives of nineteenth-
century New England manufacturers." Social Science
History, 11 (Winter 1987), 355-378.

176.   GANTER, MARY N. "The year there was no summer."
Early American Life, 23 (June 1992), 8-9, 64-66, 73.
    Summer of 1816 in New England.

177.   GARDNER, ERIC. "'This attempt of the sister': Harriet
Wilson's Our Nig from printer to readers." NEQ, 66 (June
1993), 226-246.
    The 1857 publication and distribution of a novel by a
black woman about white racism in the North. Wilson was a
resident of Milford, N.H.; the book was published in
Boston.

178.   GHERE, DAVID LYNN. "Abenaki factionalism, emigration
and social continuity, 1725 to 1765." Ph.D. dissertation,
Univ. of Maine, 1988. xii, 316p. MDeeP. *
    Abstracted in DAI, 50:2A (1989), 530.

179. GILCHRIST, JOHN H. "Latitude errors and the New England voyages of Pring and Waymouth." American Neptune, 50 (Winter 1990), 5-17.
Early-17th century.

180. GINSBURG, PHILIP E. The shadow of death: the hunt for a serial killer. N.Y.: Charles Scribner, 1992. x, 397, [16]p. VtHi. *
Seeks to establish a link between some 1980s murders in New Hampshire and Vermont.

181. GLEASON, SARAH C. Kindly lights: a history of the lighthouses of southern New England. Boston: Beacon Pr., 1991. xxi, 176p. MB. *

182. GODBEER, RICHARD. The devil's dominion: magic and religion in early New England. N.Y.: Cambridge Univ. Pr., 1992. x, 253p. MWA. *
See also next entry.

183. _____. "The devil's dominion: magic and religion in early New England." Ph.D. dissertation, Brandeis Univ., 1989. 340p. *
Abstracted in DAI, 50:8A (1990), 2620. See also preceding entry.

184. GOLDMAN, SHALOM. "Hebrew at the early colleges: orations at Harvard, Dartmouth, and Columbia." American Jewish Archives, 42 (Summer 1990), 23-26.

185. GOLDSACK, BOB. A century of fun: a pictorial history of New England amusement parks. Nashua, N.H.: Midway Museum Pub., 1993. 137p. NhHi. *

186. GORDON, BEVERLY. "Meanings in mid-nineteenth century dress: images from New England women's writings." Clothing and Textiles Research Journal, 10 (Spring 1992), 44-53.

187. _____. "Victorian fancy goods: another re- appraisal of Shaker material culture." Winterthur Portfolio, 25:2-3 (Summer/Autumn 1990), 111-129.
Articles produced and sold by Shakers in New England and New York State.

188. GORDON, SUZANNE. "Herstory in the making." Boston Globe Magazine (Jan. 31, 1993), 23, 33-39.
Historian Laurel Thatcher Ulrich's studies of the lives of ordinary women in early New England.

189. GORDON-GRUBE, KAREN. "Evidence of medicinal cannibalism in Puritan New England: 'mummy' and related remedies in Edward Taylor's 'Dispensatory.'" Early American Literature, 28:3 (1993), 185-221.

190. GOULD, PHILIP BENTON. "Virtuous Puritans: early national political culture and the historical romance of New England." Ph.D. dissertation, Univ. of Wisconsin, 1993. iii, 331p. *
Literary history. Abstracted in DAI, 54:6A (1993), 2150.

191. GRADY, CHARLES W. "High churchman in a low church: Frederic Henry Hedge's vision of the liberal church." Unitarian Universalist Historical Society, Proceedings, 21:1 (1987-1988), 1-12.
Unitarian minister in Massachusetts, Maine, and Rhode Island from 1829-1872.

192. GRAGG, LARRY D. "The early New England-Barbados trade." HJM, 17 (Summer 1989), 177-200.

193. GRAY, DAVID JUDSON. "History and insignia of United States naval harbor and coastal defense units in New England." Military Collector & Historian, 40 (Winter 1988), 165-168.
Naval reserve units (since ca. 1950s).

194. GREEN, BILL. The first line: air defense in the Northeast, 1952-1960. Fairview, Pa.: Wonderhorse Publications, 1994. 480p. VtHi.

195. GREENWOOD, RICHARD E. "Natural run and artificial falls: waterpower and the Blackstone Canal." RIH, 49 (May 1991), 51-62.

196. GRIFFIN, NANCY. The remarkable Stanley brothers and their amazing cars. Portland, Me.: Guy Gannett, 1987. 56p. Me. *
The Maine-born inventors worked in that state for many years but built Stanley Steamer automobiles in Newton, Mass.

197. GUICE, STEPHEN ANDREW. "The linguistic work of John Eliot." Ph.D. dissertation, Michigan State Univ., 1990. xi, 243p. *
The Puritan missionary's work with the Massachuset Indian language. Abstracted in DAI, 52:1A (1991), 150.

198. GURUSWAMY, ROSEMARY FITHIAN. "The sweet defender of New England." NEQ, 63 (June 1990), 294-302.
"David the psalmist" as a scriptural model for Puritan meditative writers and poets.

199. GUSSMAN, DEBORAH. "Remembering Plymouth Rock: the making of citizenship in nineteenth-century narratives of colonial New England." Ph.D. dissertation, Rutgers Univ., 1993. 204p.
Abstracted in DAI, 54:11A (1994), 4092-4093.

200   NEW ENGLAND

200.   GUSTAITIS, JOSEPH. "Samuel Slater: father of the American industrial revolution." American History Illustrated, 24 (May 1989), 32-33.

201.   GUTHMAN, WILLIAM H. Drums a'beating, trumpets sounding: artistically carved powder horns in the provincial manner, 1746-1781. Hartford: Connecticut Historical Society, 1993. 232p. CtHi. *

202.   _____. "Powder horns carved in the provincial manner, 1744-1781." Antiques, 144 (Oct. 1993), 494-500.

203.   HAFFENREFFER MUSEUM OF ANTHROPOLOGY. A bibliography for teaching about native Americans of southeastern New England. Joanna Foster Coppola, comp. Bristol, R.I., 1992. 40p. RHi. *

204.   HALE, JUDSON D. SR. "Vermont vs. New Hampshire." American Heritage, 43 (Apr. 1992), 47-55.
        Historical and contemporary differences between the two states.

205.   HALL, DONALD. "The darkened parlor." Yankee, 56 (Jan. 1992), 70-75.
        Traditions associated with New England parlors.

206.   HAMBRICK-STOWE, CHARLES EDWIN. "'An engaging sign': baptism in the history of American Congregationalism." Bulletin of the Congregational Library, 41 (Fall 1989), 4-15.

207.   HAMMOND, CHARLES A. "The dilemmas of domestic service in New England, 1750-1850." DubSemPr (1988), 58-67.

208.   HAMMOND, JEFFREY A. Sinful self, saintly self: the Puritan experience of poetry. Athens: Univ. of Georgia Pr., 1993. xiv, 305p. MBU. *

209.   HAND, SAMUEL BURTON. "Grace Coolidge and the historians." VtHN, 43 (Nov.-Dec. 1992), 98-103.
        Her ranking among First Ladies.

210.   HANDLER, MIMI. "Scenery on the walls." Early American Life, 22 (Aug. 1991), 54-63.
        Rufus Porter murals in houses in East Topsham, Vt., and North Haverhill, N.H.

211.   HANKINS, JEAN FITTZ. "Bringing the good news: Protestant missionaries to the Indians of New England and New York, 1700-1775." Ph.D. dissertation, Univ. of Connecticut, 1993. x, 600p. *
        Abstracted in DAI, 54:7A (1994), 2707.

212.   _____. "Solomon Briant and Joseph Johnson: Indian teachers and preachers in colonial New England." Connecticut History, No. 33 (Nov. 1992), 38-60.

213.   HANSEN, KAREN VYONNE. "The power of talk in antebellum New England." Agricultural History, 67 (Spring 1993), 43-64.
        The role of gossip in community life.

214.   _____. "Transcending the public/private divide: the social dimension of laborers' lives, 1810-1860." Ph.D. dissertation, Univ. of California, Berkeley, 1989. vii, 223p. *
        New England study. Abstracted in DAI, 51:6A (1990), 2167-2168. See also next entry.

215.   _____. A very social time: crafting community in antebellum New England. Berkeley: Univ. of California Pr., 1994. xiii, 262p. MBAt. *
        See also preceding entry.

216.   HANSON, CHARLES PARKER. "From the Quebec Act to the French alliance: the Catholic question in revolutionary New England." Ph.D. dissertation, Univ. of California, Berkeley, 1993. v, 487p. *
        Abstracted in DAI, 54:10A (1994), 3856.

217.   HARDING, VINCENT. A certain magnificence: Lyman Beecher and the transformation of American Protestantism, 1775-1863. Brooklyn, N.Y.: Carlson Publishing, 1991. xxxii, 573p. MChB. *
        Published version of author's Ph.D. dissertation. (See next entry.)

218.   _____. "Lyman Beecher and the transformation of American Protestantism, 1775-1863." Ph.D. dissertation, Univ. of Chicago, 1965. x, 696p. *
        See also preceding entry.

219.   HARMON, SANDRA D. "Colonial Puritan New England women, 1620-1750: a study and teaching unit in the history of American women." D.A. dissertation, Illinois State Univ., 1990. v, 337p. *
        Abstracted in DAI, 51:1A (1990), 277.

220.   HARTLEY, SCOTT. Guilford: five years of change. Piscataway, N.J.: Railpace, 1989. 112p. MeHi. *
        Guilford Transportation Industries, owner of the Boston and Maine and Maine Central railroads.

221.   _____. New Haven Railroad: the final decades. Piscataway, N.J.: Railpace, 1992. 160p. CtNhHi. *

222.   HASTINGS, SCOTT E. JR. Goodbye highland Yankee: stories of a North Country boyhood. Chelsea, Vt.: Chelsea Green Publishing, 1988. xiv, 165p. CtY. *
        Recollections of the 1920s and 1930s in the upper Connecticut River Valley. See also next entry.

223.   _____. The last Yankees: folkways in eastern Vermont and the border country. Hanover, N.H.: University Pr. of New England, 1990. xv, 143p. MWA. *
        Vermont and New Hampshire. See also preceding entry.

224. HAWTHORNE, NATHANIEL. Hawthorne's American travel sketches. Alfred Weber, ed. Hanover, N.H.: University Pr. of New England, 1989. xiii, 213p. MB. *
    Notes from a tour of New Hampshire, Vermont, and New York State in 1832.

225. HAYNES, LEMUEL. Black preacher to white America: the collected writings of Lemuel Haynes, 1774-1833. Richard Newman, ed. Brooklyn, N.Y.: Carlson Publishing, 1990. xxxviii, 251p. VtHi. *

226. HAZEN, MARIA. "The killer river." Portland, 4 (Oct. 1989), 28-31.
    Legend of an Indian curse on the Saco River of New Hampshire and Maine.

227. HEARD, JOSEPH NORMAN. The Northeastern woodlands. Metuchen, N.J.: Scarecrow Pr., 1990. [417]p. VtHi. *
    Vol. 2 of Handbook of the American frontier: four centuries of Indian-white relations.

228. HEARLE, KEVIN JAMES. "Regions of discourse: Steinbeck, Cather, Jewett and the pastoral tradition of American regionalism." Ph.D. dissertation, Univ. of California, Santa Cruz, 1991. viii, 216p. *
    Sarah Orne Jewett as a New England regional writer. Abstracted in DAI, 52:12A (1992), 4328-4329.

229. HEDRICK, JOAN D. Harriet Beecher Stowe. N.Y.: Oxford Univ. Pr., 1994. xviii, 507p. MBAt. *

230. HELFRICH, G. W. "An uncommonly misspent life." Down East, 36 (Nov. 1989), 74-77, 85, 88.
    The criminal career of Henry Tufts (1748-1831).

231. HENSLEY, PAUL B. "Time, work, and social context in New England." NEQ, 65 (Fall 1992), 531-559.
    Work practices and the use of time (17th-19th centuries).

232. HERN, MARY ELLEN W. "Picnicking in the Northeastern United States, 1840-1900." Winterthur Portfolio, 24 (Summer/Autumn 1989), 139-152.

233. HESLIP, COLLEEN COWLES. Between the rivers: itinerant painters from the Connecticut to the Hudson. Williamstown, Mass.: Sterling and Francine Clark Art Institute, 1990. 95p. M. *

234. HESSLER, MARK HUNT. "Providence lost: a study of epistemology and religious culture among New England Puritans, 1630-1730." Ph.D. dissertation, State Univ. of New York, Stony Brook, 1992. viii, 478p. *
    Abstracted in DAI, 53:6A (1992), 2074-2075.

235. HEYWOOD, AUGUSTA PIPKIN. "Walking 'fruitfully with God in the covenant': the origins of justified disobedience within the American social contract." Ph.D. dissertation, Fletcher School of Law and Diplomacy, Tufts Univ., 1992. 270p. *
    Examines the contributions of New England Puritans and the Massachusetts Bay Colony "to the foundations of the unique American social contract." Abstracted in DAI, 53:6A (1992), 2075.

236. HINES, BOB. "Remembering Rachel." Yankee, 55 (June 1991), 62-66.
    Rachel Carson in Maine and at Woods Hole, Mass.

237. HIRREL, LEO PHILLIP. "The ideology of antebellum reform within the New School Calvinist community." Ph.D. dissertation, Univ. of Virginia, 1989. xix, 411p. *
    Abstracted in DAI, 50:6A (1989), 1696.

238. "HISTORY of A.G.C. in New Hampshire and Vermont." New Hampshire Architect, 9 (Sept. 1957), 18, 20.
    Associated General Contractors of New Hampshire and Vermont (established 1950).

239. HOFFMAN, CURTISS. "The persistence of memory: Neville and Stark points in southern New England." ArcSocConB, No. 54 (1991), 23-53.
    On the radiocarbon dating of certain prehistoric artifacts.

240. HOGAN, DAVID. "Modes of discipline: affective individualism and pedagogical reform in New England, 1820-1850." American Journal of Education, 99 (Nov. 1990), 1-56.

241. HOLIFIELD, E. BROOKS. "Peace, conflict, and ritual in Puritan congregations." Journal of Interdisciplinary History, 23 (Winter 1993), 551-570.

242. HOMAGE to New England: selected essays on early New England history, 1937-1963. Peter Charles Hoffer, ed. N.Y.: Garland Publishing, 1988. viii, 312p. CtU. *
    See also entry 242.

243. HOOD, ADRIENNE D. "The gender division of labor in the production of textiles in eighteenth-century, rural Pennsylvania (rethinking the New England model)." JSH, 27 (Spring 1994), 537-561.

244. HOOPES, JAMES. Consciousness in New England: from Puritanism and ideas to psychoanalysis and semiotic. Baltimore: Johns Hopkins Univ. Pr., 1989. viii, 294p. CtU. *
    Psychological and intellectual history.

245. HOPPER, GORDON E. "The Fifteen Mile Falls Railroad." B&M Bulletin, 18:4 (1992), 30-39.
    In Vermont and New Hampshire.

246   NEW ENGLAND

246. HORVITZ, ELEANOR F., and GERALDINE S. FOSTER. "Jewish farmers in Rhode Island and nearby Massachusetts." RIJHN, 10 (Nov. 1990), 443-478.

247. HOVAIZI, FRAIDOON. "An analysis of structural change in residential utility demand in New England." Ph.D. dissertation, Univ. of Massachusetts, 1990. xi, 77p. *
Since ca. 1970. Abstracted in DAI, 51:7A (1991), 2468.

248. HOWARD, LEON. Essays on Puritans and Puritanism. James Barbour and Thomas Quirk, eds. Albuquerque: Univ. of New Mexico Pr., 1986. xiii, 221p. CtY. *
In England and New England.

249. HOY, JOAN McELROY. "The publication and distribution of books among New England Quakers, 1775- 1836." Ph.D. dissertation, Boston Univ., 1989. viii, 358p. RHi. *
Abstracted in DAI, 50:5A (1989), 1415.

250. HUMPHREY, CAROL SUE. "This popular engine": New England newspapers during the American Revolution, 1775-1789. Newark: Univ. of Delaware Pr., 1992. 204p. MBU. *
See also this author's Ph.D. dissertation of similar title (Univ. of North Carolina, 1985; entry 3547 in Vol. 7).

251. HURTH, ELISABETH. "The 'signs and wonders' of divinity: the miracles controversy in New England, 1836-1841." ATQ, 4 (Dec. 1990), 287-303.
Split among Unitarians.

252. HUSOCK, HOWARD. "Rediscovering the three-decker house." Public Interest, No. 98 (1990), 49-60.

253. HUTCHINS, TERESA DUNN. "The American whale fishery, 1815-1900: an economic analysis." Ph.D. dissertation, Univ. of North Carolina, 1989. 354p. *
Abstracted in DAI, 50:8A (1990), 2597.

254. THE ISLES of Shoals remembered: a legacy from America's first musicians' and artists' colony. With text by Caleb Mason. Rutland, Vt.: Charles E. Tuttle, 1992. Unp. Me. *

255. JACOBSEN, DOUGLAS. "American Puritanism observed: New England and New Jersey." New Jersey History, 110 (Spring/Summer 1992), 1-17.

256. JAFFE, DAVID. "The Village Enlightenment in New England, 1760-1820." WMQ, 3 ser. 47 (July 1990), 327- 346.
Examines the lives of publisher Robert Thomas, author-peddler Amos Taylor, and author-consumer Silas Felton "to explore changes in production, distribution, and consumption accompanying the commercialization of rural New England after the War for Independence." Emphasizes "the formation of a market for cultural commodities in printed form."

257. JAMES, WALTER H. Joys and sorrows of an automobilist: being an authentic account of the writer's experiences written for his own satisfaction but free to be read by anyone who wants to read. Jackson, N.H.: Earth Heart, 1992. 63p. NhHi. *
Author lived 1873-1963.

258. JOHNSON, ERIC SPENCER. "'Some by flatteries and others by threatenings': political strategies among Native Americans of seventeenth-century southern New England." Ph.D. dissertation, Univ. of Massachusetts, 1993. xi, 348p. *
Abstracted in DAI, 54:2A (1993), 571.

259. JONES, ROBERT WILLOUGHBY. Boston and Maine: three colorful decades of New England railroading. Glendale, Calif.: Trans-Anglo Books, 1991. 210p. MBAt. *
1940s-1970s.

260. JUSTER, SUSAN MARY. "Sinners and saints: the evangelical construction of gender and authority in New England, 1740-1830." Ph.D. dissertation, Univ. of Michigan, 1990. v, 457p. *
Study of Baptist churches between the first and second great awakenings. Abstracted in DAI, 51:7A (1991), 2499.

261. KAMENSKY, JANE NEILL. "Governing the tongue: speech and society in early New England." Ph.D. dissertation, Yale Univ., 1993. 518p.
Abstracted in DAI, 54:6A (1993), 2298.

262. _____. "'In these contrasted climes, how chang'd the scene': progress, declension, and balance in the landscapes of Timothy Dwight." NEQ, 63 (Mar. 1990), 80- 108.
On the subject of descriptions in Dwight's travel journal, published as Travels in New England and New York (entry 4043 in Vol 7).

263. KANE, NANCY FRANCES. Textiles in transition: technology, wages, and industry relocation in the U.S. textile industry, 1880-1930. N.Y.: Greenwood Pr., 1988. x, 190p. CtY. *
The movement of the industry from New England to the South.

264. KARR, RONALD DALE. Lost railroads of New England. Pepperell, Mass.: Branch Line Pr., 1989. 143p. MB. *

265. KATZ, SANDRA LEE. Elinor Frost: a poet's wife. Westfield, Mass.: Institute for Massachusetts Studies, Westfield State College, 1988. xiv, 193p. VtHi. *
See also next entry.

266. _____. "The subverted sunflower: the life of Elinor White Frost and her influence on the poetry of Robert Frost." Ph.D. dissertation, Univ. of Massachusetts, 1983. xi, 283p. *
Abstracted in DAI, 44:10A (1984), 3066. See also preceding entry.

267. KAWASHIMA, YASUHIDE. "Forest conservation policy in early New England." HJM, 20 (Winter 1992), 1-15.

268. KELLEHER, TOM. "The Yankee peddler." OSV, 33 (Fall 1993), 6-7.

269. KELLY, CATHERINE ELIZABETH. "Between town and country: New England women and the creation of a provincial middle class, 1820-1860." Ph.D. dissertation, Univ. of Rochester, 1992. viii, 423p. *
      Western Massachusetts and southern Vermont. Abstracted in DAI, 53:6A (1992), 2076.

270. KELLY, NANCY RITA. "Sarah Orne Jewett and spiritualism." Ph.D. dissertation, Univ. of Massachusetts, 1991. viii, 296p. *
      Abstracted in DAI, 52:9A (1992), 3283.

271. KENNY, MICHAEL G. "The democratic medicine of Dr. Elias Smith." DubSemPr (1990), 133-141.
      Advocate of botanic medicine. See also next entry and entry 174.

272. _____. The perfect law of liberty: Elias Smith and the providential history of America. Blue Ridge Summit, Pa.: Smithsonian Institution Pr., 1994. xvi, 328p. MH. *

273. KNIGHT, JANICE LYNN. "A garden enclosed: the tradition of heart-piety in Puritan New England." Ph.D. dissertation, Harvard University, 1988. 555p. *
      Abstracted in DAI, 50:2A (1989), 443. See also entry 1636.

274. KOLLER, ALAN M. "Mathematics education and Puritanism in colonial America: the colleges of Harvard and Yale." Ed.D. dissertation, Columbia Univ. Teachers College, 1990. 148p. CtWillE. *
      Abstracted in DAI, 51:7A (1991), 2290.

275. KONKER, ELIZABETH A. Colonial New England: the cashless society. Boston: Federal Reserve Bank of Boston, 1976. 75p. RHi. *

276. KONKLE, LINCOLN ERNEST. "Errand into the theatrical wilderness: the Puritan narrative tradition in the plays of Wilder, Williams, and Albee." Ph.D. dissertation, Univ. of Wisconsin, 1991. 579p. *
      20th century. Abstracted in DAI, 52:10A (1992), 3611.

277. KRAFT, HERBERT C. "Sixteenth and seventeenth century Indian/white trade relations in the Middle Atlantic and Northeast regions." Archaeology of Eastern North America, 17 (Fall 1989), 1-29.

278. KUPPERMAN, KAREN O. "Definitions of liberty on the eve of civil war: Lord Saye and Sele, Lord Brooke, and the American Puritan colonies." Historical Journal [U.K.], 32 (Mar. 1989), 17-34.
      English Civil War.

279. "LACKAWANNA Yankees: B&M's P-5 class Pacifics." B&M Bulletin, 18:2 (1991), 32-38.
      Locomotives on the Boston and Maine.

280. LaFANTASIE, GLENN W. "Roger Williams and John Winthrop: the rise and fall of an extraordinary friendship." RIH, 47 (Aug. 1989), 85-95.

281. LAIRD, MATTHEW W. "Nativist American humour: Sam Slick and the defense of New England Whig culture." Canadian Review of American Studies, 23:4 (1993), 71- 88.
      Fictional character, created by Thomas Chandler Haliburton.

282. LAMOREAUX, NAOMI R. "Bank mergers in late nineteenth-century New England: the contingent nature of structural change." Journal of Economic History, 51 (Sept. 1991) 537-557.

283. _____. "'No arbitrary discretion': specialisation in short-term commercial lending by banks in late nineteenth-century New England." Business History [U.K.], 33 (July 1991), 93-118.

284. LANGONE, KATHLEEN. "Discovering the dark days." NHProfiles, 4 (May 1993), 44, 46.
      The famous dark day of May 19, 1780.

285. LAPOMARDA, VINCENT ANTHONY. "The Jesuit missions of colonial New England." EIHC, 126 (Apr. 1990), 91- 109.

286. LARKIN, JACK. "Aspiration & respectability." OSV, 32 (Summer 1992), 4-6.
      Portraits as a key to understanding the lives of early-19th-century New Englanders. See also entry 326.

287. _____. "Holidays in 1830s rural New England." OSV, 34 (Summer 1994), 4-6.

288. _____. "Living and working in a sea of white faces." OSV, 31 (Summer 1991), 6-7.
      Blacks in rural New England (mid-19th century).

289. LAVIN, LUCIANNE. "Coastal adaptations in southern New England and southern New York." Archaeology of Eastern North America, 16 (Fall 1988), 101-120.
      See also entry 408.

290   NEW ENGLAND

290.   LAZEROW, JAMA. "Spokesmen for the working class: Protestant clergy and the labor movement in antebellum New England." Journal of the Early Republic, 13 (Fall 1993), 323-354.

291.   Le BEAU, BRYAN F. "Joseph Morgan's sermon at the ordination of Jonathan Dickinson and the clerical literature of colonial New England and New Jersey." New Jersey History, 109 (Spring/Summer 1991), 55-81.
    1709 ordination.

292.   LEWIS, GLADYS SHERMAN. "Message, messenger, and response: Puritan forms and cultural reformation in Harriet Beecher Stowe's 'Uncle Tom's cabin.'" Ph.D. dissertation, Oklahoma State Univ., 1992. vii, 486p. *
    Abstracted in DAI, 53:7A (1993), 2371.

293.   LIND, LOUISE. "If stone could talk." Old RI, 4 (Feb. 1994), 54-57.
    Historic stones and the uses to which stone was put in early New England.

294.   LITTON, ALFRED GUY. "'Speaking the truth in love': a history of the 'Christian Examiner' and its relation to New England Transcendentalism." Ph.D. dissertation, Univ. of South Carolina, 1993. v, 275p. *
    Abstracted in DAI, 54:11A (1994), 4094.

295.   MacFARLANE, LISA WATT. "The New England kitchen goes uptown: domestic displacements in Harriet Beecher Stowe's New York." NEQ, 64 (June 1991), 272-291.

296.   MacMULLEN, EDITH NYE. "Henry Barnard: a public life." Ph.D. dissertation, Columbia Univ., 1989. 476p.
    The well-known educational reformer (1811-1900). Abstracted in DAI, 52:5A (1991), 1657. See also next entry.

297.   _____. In the cause of true education: Henry Barnard and nineteenth-century school reform. New Haven, Conn.: Yale Univ. Pr., 1991. xiii, 378p. CtHi. *
    See also preceding entry.

298.   MADDEN, ETTA. "Resurrecting life through rhetorical ritual: a buried value of the Puritan funeral sermon." Early American Literature, 26:3 (1991), 232-250.

299.   MADSEN, DEBORAH L. "The sword or the scroll: the power of rhetoric in colonial New England." American Studies, 33 (Spring 1992), 45-61.
    The use of rhetoric by orthodox clergymen "in order to claim, if not to preserve, a share of political power in the evolving colonial government."

300.   MAIN, GLORIA LUND. "The distribution of consumer goods in colonial New England: a subregional approach." DubSemPr (1987), 153-168.

301.   _____. "Gender, work, and wages in colonial New England." WMQ, 3 ser. 51 (Jan. 1994), 39-66.

302.   _____. "An inquiry into when and why women learned to write in colonial New England." JSH, 24 (Spring 1991), 579-589.

303.   MAINE. UNIVERSITY. CANADIAN-AMERICAN CENTER. The Northeastern borderlands: four centuries of interaction. Stephen J. Hornsby, Victor A. Konrad, and James J. Herlan, eds. Orono, Me., 1989. 160p. MeHi. *

304.   MALLOY, MARY. African Americans in the maritime trades: a guide to resources in New England. Sharon, Mass.: Kendall Whaling Museum, 1990. 26p. RHi. *

305.   MALLOY, THOMAS A., and BRENDA MALLOY. "The disappearing Shaker cemetery." Markers IX [1992], 256-274.
    In New England and New York.

306.   MALONE, PATRICK MITCHELL. The skulking way of war: technology and tactics among the New England Indians. Lanham, Md.: Madison Books, 1991. 133p. CtW. *
    See also this author's Ph.D. dissertation: "Indian and English military systems in New England in the seventeenth century" (Brown Univ., 1971; entry 485 in Vol. 7).

307.   MARTIN, JOHN FREDERICK. Profits in the wilderness: entrepreneurship and the founding of New England towns in the seventeenth century. Chapel Hill: Univ. of North Carolina Pr., 1991. xiv, 363p. MBAt. *

308.   MARTIN-DIAZ, JAMES ROBERT. "Edward Johnson: the herald of New England." Ph.D. dissertation, State Univ. of New York, Buffalo, 1988. 180p.
    Abstracted in DAI, 48:9A (1988), 2660. Johnson wrote Wonder-working providence of Sions saviour in New England (1654; entry 395 in Vol. 7).

309.   MASUR, LOUIS P. "'Age of the first person singular': the vocabulary of the self in New England, 1780-1850." Journal of American Studies [U.K.], 25 (Aug. 1991), 189-211.
    Consciousness of self.

310.   MAVOR, JAMES W. JR., and BYRON E. DIX. Manitou: the sacred landscape of New England's native civilization. Rochester, Vt.: Destiny Books, 1989. viii, 390p. VtHi. *

311.   MAYNARD, MARY. Dead and buried in New England: respectful visits to the tombstones and monuments of 306 noteworthy Yankees. Camden, Me.: Yankee Books, 1993. x, 182p. VtHi. *

312.   McCAIN, DIANA ROSS. "Celebrating Valentine's Day." Early American Life, 23 (Feb. 1992), 12-15.

313.   _____. "Spinning matches." Early American Life, 21 (Aug. 1990), 6-11.

314.   _____. "What to name the baby." Early American Life, 20 (Apr. 1989), 11-13.
Naming practices in early New England.

315.   _____. "Women tavernkeepers." Early American Life, 21 (June 1990), 30-31, 61, 64.

316.   _____. "Yankee peddlers." Early American Life, 20 (Aug. 1989), 6-7, 12-15.

317.   McCALL, KENNETH F. "Boston & Maine's P-4 locomotives." B&M Bulletin, 17:3 (1990), 14-35.

318.   McCULLOUGH, ROBERT LAURENCE. "Cedar swamp and pine plantation: a history of communal forests in New England." Ph.D. dissertation, Cornell Univ., 1993. 897p.
Abstracted in DAI, 54:7A (1994), 2627.

319.   McDERMOTT, GERALD ROBERT. "One holy and happy society: the public theology of Jonathan Edwards." Ph.D. dissertation, Univ. of Iowa, 1989. iv, 337p. *
Abstracted in DAI, 50:11A (1990), 3626.

320.   McEWEN, ALEC. "Alden Partridge and the United States-Canada boundary." VtH, (Spring 1991), 59 97-110.
From Partridge's 1819 journal, which he kept while a member of an exploration and surveying party.

321.   McLOUGHLIN, WILLIAM GERALD. "Anne Hutchinson reconsidered." RIH, 49 (Feb. 1991), 13-25.

322.   _____. Soul liberty: the Baptists' struggle in New England, 1630-1833. Hanover, N.H.: University Pr. of New England, 1991. xiv, 341p. CtU. *

323.   McMAHON, SARAH FRANCIS. "'All things in their proper season': seasonal rhythms of diet in nineteenth century New England." Agricultural History, 63 (Spring 1989), 130-151.

324.   McMANUS, EDGAR J. Law and liberty in early New England: criminal justice and due process, 1620-1692. Amherst: Univ. of Massachusetts Pr., 1993. xiv, 279p. CtNhHi. *

325.   McREYNOLDS, SAMUEL A. "Rural life in New England." American Archivist, 50 (Fall 1987), 532-548.
"The major dimensions of 'rurality' and significant changes in the political, economic, and social composition of rural life."

326.   MEET your neighbors: New England portraits, painters, & society, 1790-1850. Caroline F. Sloat, ed. Sturbridge, Mass.: Old Sturbridge Village, 1992. 143p. MStuO. *
Includes essays by Jack Larkin, Elizabeth M. Kornhauser, and David Jaffee.

327.   MERCHANT, CAROLYN. Ecological revolution: nature, gender, and science in New England. Chapel Hill: Univ. of North Carolina Pr., 1989. xv, 379p. CtY. *
Covers the years 1600-1860.

328.   _____. "The theoretical structure of ecological revolutions." Environmental Review, 11:4 (1987), 265- 274.

329.   MERRITT, ROBERT ALLEN. "The socially constructed rhetorical categories of Protestant preaching in early nineteenth century New England." Ph.D. dissertation, Pennsylvania State Univ., 1991. vii, 239p. *
Based on a "study of the contents of early American periodicals." Abstracted in DAI, 52:12A (1992), 4146.

330.   MESERVE, ROBERT W. "Robert W. Meserve addresses the B&MRRHS." B&M Bulletin, 17:4 (1992), 6-13.
The address, about the "latter day" corporate history of the Boston and Maine Railroad, was presented to the Boston and Maine Railroad Historical Society.

331.   MEYER, WILLIAM E. H. JR. "Emerson vs. Freud: redefining the New England 'mind' (a study in visual- bias associationism)." Thought, 62 (1987), 369-387.

332.   MEYERS, PATRICIA RUTH. "Rhetoric of seventeenth-century New England Puritan occasional sermons." Ph.D. dissertation, Arizona State Univ., 1992. x, 312p. *
Abstracted in DAI, 53:11A (1993), 3910.

333.   MILLER, JOSHUA. "Direct democracy and the Puritan theory of membership." Journal of Politics, 53 (Feb. 1991), 57-74.
Examines "the political implications of 17th century American Congregationalism."

334.   MORRIS, ROBERT C. "From piracy to censorship: the admiralty experience." Prologue, 21 (Fall 1989), 187- 195.
Admiralty records in the National Archives pertaining to early New England.

335.   MROZOWSKI, STEPHEN A., and RICHARD A. GOULD. "Ethno-archaeology and historical archaeology: a comparative examination of marginality and farm abandonment." Northeast Anthropology, No. 46 (Fall 1993), 77-97.
Compares studies of 19th-century New England with studies of similar developments in Finland.

336   NEW ENGLAND

336.   MULLINEAUX, DONALD J. "Competitive monies and the Suffolk Bank System: a contractual perspective." Southern Economic Journal, 53 (Apr. 1987), 884-898.
    From the 1820s to the 1850s.

337.   MURPHY, TERESA ANNE. Ten hours' labor: religion, reform, and gender in early New England. Ithaca, N.Y.: Cornell Univ. Pr., 1992. xii, 231p. CtW. *
    "Religion and gender in the labor organization of New England mill towns." See also this author's Ph.D. dissertation, "Labor, religion and moral reform in Fall River, Massachusetts" (Yale Univ., 1982; entry 6310 in Vol. 8).

338.   NAEHER, ROBERT JAMES. "Dialogue in the wilderness: John Eliot and the Indian exploration of Puritanism as a source of meaning, comfort, and ethnic survival." NEQ, 62 (Sept. 1989), 346-368.

339.   NEW England rediscovered: selected articles on New England colonial history, 1965 to 1973. Peter Charles Hoffer, ed. N.Y.: Garland Publishing, 1988. viii, 352p. MB. *
    See also entry 242.

340.   NEW England's disastrous weather: hurricanes, tornadoes, blizzards, dark days, heat waves, cold snaps...and the human stories behind them. Benjamin Watson, ed. Camden, Me.: Yankee Books, 1990. xi, 228p. MB. *

341.   NEWELL, MARGARET ELLEN. "Economic ideology, culture and development in New England, 1620-1800." Ph.D. dissertation, Univ. of Virginia, 1991. 506p.
    Abstracted in DAI, 53:12A (1993), 4449-4450.

342.   NICHOLAS, GEORGE PETER. "Place and spaces: changing patterns of wetland use in southern New England." Man in the Northeast, No. 42 (Fall 1991), 75- 98.
    Prehistoric.

343.   NICKELS, CAMERON C. New England humor: from the Revolutionary War to the Civil War. Knoxville: Univ. of Tennessee Pr., 1993. xviii, 277p. CtU. *

344.   NICOLL, JESSICA. "Rainbow shapes & faint traceries." OSV, 30 (Winter 1990), 4-6.
    Quilts and quilting (early-19th century).

345.   NIMKE, R. W. Connecticut River railroads and connections. Walpole, N.H., 1991-1992. 5v. VtU. *

346.   "A NOBLE and dignified stream": the Piscataqua region in the colonial revival, 1860-1930. Sarah L. Giffen and Kevin D. Murphy, eds. York, Me.: Old York Historical Society, 1992. xiii, 241p. MBAt. *
    In Maine and New Hampshire. Deals with such subjects as literature, art, architecture, gardens, and historic preservation.

347.   NOONKESTER, MYRON C. "'God for its author': John Locke as a possible source for the New Hampshire Confession." NEQ, 66 (Sept. 1993), 448-450.
    Confession of faith, drafted in 1833 and adopted by New England Baptists.

348.   NORD, DAVID PAUL. "Teleology and news: the religious roots of American journalism, 1630-1730." Journal of American History, 77 (June 1990), 9-38.
    In Puritan New England.

349.   NORDBECK, ELIZABETH C. "Puritans go north: Massachusetts and the northern territories, 1630-1658." Bulletin of the Congregational Library, 40 (Spring/ Summer 1989), 4-16.
    Puritanism in Maine and New Hampshire.

350.   NORLING, LISA. "Captain Ahab had a wife: ideology and experience in the lives of New England maritime women, 1760-1870." Ph.D. dissertation, Rutgers Univ., 1992. 322p. *
    Abstracted in DAI, 54:3A (1993), 1071.

351.   _____. "Contrary dependencies: whaling agents and whalemen's families, 1830-1870." Mystic Seaport, Log, 42 (Spring 1990), 3-12.

352.   _____. "'How frought with sorrow and heartpangs': mariners' wives and the ideology of domesticity in New England, 1790-1880." NEQ, 65 (Sept. 1992), 422-446.

353.   NORTH country captives: selected narratives of Indian captivity from Vermont and New Hampshire. Colin G. Calloway, ed. Hanover, N.H.: University Pr. of New England, 1992. 160p. VtHi. *

354.   NYLANDER, JANE C. Our own snug fireside: images of the New England home, 1760-1860. N.Y.: Knopf, 1993. xiv, 317p. MBAt. *

355.   NYLANDER, ROBERT G. "Tales of a B&M railfan." B&M Bulletin, 17:1 (1990), 12-19.
    Autobiographical. See also entry 489.

356.   OLSON, ALISON G. "Rhode Island, Massachusetts, and the question of religious diversity in colonial New England." NEQ, 65 (Mar. 1992), 93-116.

357.   ONISHI, NAOKI. "Roja Uiriamuzu-Jon Koton ronso sai-saiko." Shakai Kagaku Janaru [Japan], 29 (Mar. 1991), 29-47.
    Roger Williams vs. John Cotton: a reconsideration of the controversy. (Text in Japanese.)

358.   OPENO, WOODARD DORR. The Sarah Mildred Long Bridge: a history of the Maine-New Hampshire interstate bridge from Portsmouth, New Hampshire, to Kittery, Maine. Portsmouth, N.H.: Peter E. Randall, 1988. xix, 130p. NhPoA. *

359.   O'TOOLE, JAMES MICHAEL. "Things of the spirit: documenting religion in New England." American Archivist, 50 (Fall 1987), 500-517.
       "Developments since the Second World War."

360.   OWENS, JAMES K. "Documenting regional business history: the bankruptcy acts of 1800 and 1841." Prologue, 21 (Fall 1989), 179-185.
       Discusses the types of information that can be extracted from New England federal court records in the National Archives.

361.   PAGE, ED. "Soldiers of the Revolution: two from New England." New England Journal of History, 47 (Winter 1990), 42-51.
       Joseph Plumb Martin and Seth Bullard.

362.   PALMER, WILLIAM PITT. New England: a poem...delivered before the society of alumni...at the University of Michigan, August 5th, 1846. Detroit: A.S. Williams, Printer, 1847. 27p. MH. *

363.   PANKRATZ, JOHN ROBERT. "New Englanders, the written word, and the errand into Ohio, 1788-1830." Ph.D. dissertation, Cornell Univ., 1988. xiii, 407p. *
       Literacy and reading as factors in the settlement of Ohio by New Englanders. Abstracted in DAI, 49:8A (1989), 2368.

364.   PENDERGAST, JOHN. The bend in the river: a prehistory and contact period history of Lowell, Dracut, Chelmsford, Tyngsborough, and Dunstable (Nashua, N.H.), Massachusetts, 17,000 BP to AD 1700. Tyngsborough, Mass.: Merrimac River Pr., 1991. xiv, 92p. NhHi. *

365.   THE PEQUOTS in southern New England: the fall and rise of an American Indian nation. Laurence M. Hauptman and James D. Wherry, eds. Norman: Univ. of Oklahoma Pr., 1990. xix, 268p. RHi. *

366.   PERLMANN, ARI JOEL, and DENNIS SHIRLEY. "When did New England women acquire literacy?" WMQ, 3 ser. 48 (Jan. 1991), 50-67.

367.   PETERSEN, JAMES BRANT. "Evidence of the Saint Lawrence Iroquoians in northern New England: population movement, trade, or stylistic borrowing?" Man in the Northeast, No. 40 (Fall 1990), 31-39.

368.   PETERSON, MARK ALLEN. "The lives of the churches in Puritan New England: from the Halfway Covenant to the Great Awakening." Ph.D. dissertation, Harvard Univ., 1993. 549p.
       Abstracted in DAI, 54:6A (1993), 2299-2300.

369.   PFEIFFER, JOHN E. "Radiometric dates from two cremation burial sites in southern New England." ArcSocConB, No. 52 (1989), 51-54.
       Indian sites.

370.   PHELPS, GEORGE. New England rail album: a traveling salesman remembers the 1930's. Glendale, Calif.: Trans-Anglo Books, 1989. 47p. WHi. *

371.   PISHA, LOUIS JOHN. "Library collections at Harvard, Yale, and Brown from the 1780's to the 1860's." D.L.S. dissertation, Columbia Univ., 1991. xiv, 814p. *
       Abstracted in DAI, 52:8A (1992), 2742-2743.

372.   PLANE, ANN MARIE. "Childbirth practices among Native American women of New England and Canada." DubSemPr (1990), 13-24.

373.   _____. "New England's logboats: four centuries of watercraft." MASB, 52 (Spring 1991), 8-17.

374.   PLUMMER, JOHN. "East Anglian immigration to New England in 1637: a hypothesis." National Genealogical Society Quarterly, 79 (June 1991), 123-127.

375.   PORTERFIELD, AMANDA. Female piety in Puritan New England: the emergence of religious humanism. N.Y.: Oxford Univ. Pr., 1991. x, 207p. MWA. *

376.   _____. "Women's attraction to Puritanism." Church History, 60 (June 1991), 223-246.
       See also previous entry.

377.   POST, CONSTANCE. "Old World order in the new: John Eliot and 'praying Indians' in Cotton Mather's Magnalia Christi Americana." NEQ, 66 (Sept. 1993), 416-433.

378.   PRESTON, JO ANNE. "Domestic ideology, school reformers, and female teachers: schoolteaching becomes women's work in nineteenth-century New England." NEQ, 66 (Dec. 1993), 531-551.

379.   PRINTS of New England. Georgia Brady Barnhill, ed. Worcester, Mass.: American Antiquarian Society, 1991. viii, 164p. MWA. *
       Papers presented at a 1976 conference.

380   NEW ENGLAND

380.   PURITANISM: transatlantic perspectives on a seventeenth-century Anglo-American faith. Francis J. Bremer, ed. Boston: Massachusetts Historical Society, 1993. xvii, 300p. CtU. *
    See also entries 51-52.

381.   PYNE, MARY A. "New England's gasholder houses." IA, 15:1 (1989), 55-62.

382.   RABINOWITZ, RICHARD ISAAC. The spiritual self in everyday life: the transformation of religious experience in nineteenth-century New England. Boston: Northeastern Univ. Pr., 1989. xxxi, 315p. CtY. *
    See also this author's Ph.D. dissertation on same subject: "Soul, character, and personality: the transformation of..." (Harvard Univ., 1977; entry 2191 in Vol. 7).

383.   RAMIREZ, BRUNO. On the move: French-Canadian and Italian migrants in the North Atlantic economy. Toronto: McClelland & Stewart, 1991. 172p. VtU. *
    Includes New England and Canada.

384.   RANDEL, WILLIAM PEIRCE. "Hawthorne and Sir William Pepperrell." EIHC, 126 (Jan. 1990), 37-51.
    Hawthorne's interest in and writings on Pepperrell.

385.   THE RECOVERY of meaning: historical archaeology in the eastern United States. Mark P. Leone and Parker B. Potter Jr., eds. Washington: Smithsonian Institution Pr., 1988. x, 490p. VtU. *

386.   REIS, ELIZABETH SARAH. "Satan's familiars: sinners, witches, and conflicting covenants in early New England." Ph.D. dissertation, Univ. of California, Berkeley, 1991. iv, 264p. *
    Abstracted in DAI, 52:8A (1992), 3049.

387.   _____. "Witches, sinners, and the underside of covenant theology." EIHC, 129 (Jan. 1993), 103-118.

388.   RENDA, LEX. "The polity and the party system: Connecticut and New Hampshire, 1840-1876." Ph.D. dissertation, Univ. of Virginia, 1991. xii, 1212p. *
    Abstracted in DAI, 53:3A (1992), 929-930.

389.   "THE REVEREND William Gordon's autumn 1776 tour of the Northeast." NEQ, 65 (Sept. 1992), 469-480.
    Malcolm Freiberg, ed. Gordon was the author of an early history of the American Revolution.

390.   REYNOLDS, DOUGLAS M. "Hardball paternalism, hardball politics: Blackstone Valley baseball, 1925- 1955." Labor's Heritage, 3 (Apr. 1991), 24-41.

391.   REYNOLDS, DOUGLAS M., and MARJORY MYERS. Working in the Blackstone River Valley: exploring the heritage of industrialization. [Woonsocket, R.I.: Rhode Island Labor History Society, 1991] xi, 187p. RHi. *
    In Massachusetts and Rhode Island.

392.   RICHARDSON, RALPH W. Historic districts of America: New England: Connecticut, Maine, Massachusetts, New Hampshire, Rhode Island, Vermont. (1989) Rev. ed. Bowie, Md.: Heritage Books, 1992. xv, 182p. RHi. *

393.   RIDER, CHRISTINE. "Early U.S. industrialization: a pre-industrial divide?" Review of Social Economy, 45 (Oct. 1987), 133-151.
    The New England textile industry (early-19th century).

394.   RING, BETTY. "New England heraldic needlework of the neoclassical period." Antiques, 144 (Oct. 1993), 484-493.

395.   ROBERT Durfee's journal and recollections of Newport, Rhode Island, Freetown, Massachusetts, New York City and Long Island, Jamaica and Cuba, West Indies and Saint Simons Island, Georgia, ca. 1785-1810. Virginia Steele Wood, ed. Marion, Ga.: Belden Books, 1990. xxi, 131p. RHi. *

396.   ROBERTS, DAVE. "The heroic landscape." New England Monthly, 7 (June 1990), 55-59.
    Rockwell Kent, the 20th-century painter.

397.   ROBINSON, PAUL ALDEN. "The struggle within: the Indian debate in seventeenth century Narragansett country." Ph.D. dissertation, State Univ. of New York, Binghamton, 1990. xix, 315p. *
    Abstracted in DAI, 51:6A (1990), 2068.

398.   ROBY, YVES. Les Franco-Américains de la Nouvelle-Angleterre, 1776-1930. Sillery, Que: Les éditions du Septentrion, 1991. 434p. MeU. *

399.   ROGERS, BRYAN, and SNOWDEN TAYLOR. "Eight day wood movement clocks: their cases, their movements, their makers." NAWCCB, Supplement No. 19 (Spring 1993), 1-60.

400.   ROLBEIN, SETH. "The hurricane nobody took seriously." Yankee, 56 (Aug. 1992), 64-68, 126-128.
    Hurricane Bob (1991).

401.   ROOTED like the ash trees: New England Indians and the land. Richard C. Carlson, ed. Rev. ed. Naugatuck, Conn.: Eagle Wing Pr., 1987. x, 86p. CtY. *

402. ROSS, RICHARD J. "The legal past of early New England: notes for the study of law, legal culture, and intellectual history." WMQ, 3 ser. 50 (Jan. 1993), 28- 41.

403. ROSSIER, ARTHUR. The preacher from Vermont: written in memory of John Colby, born Dec. 9th 1787. [St. Johnsbury, Vt.: Cowles Pr.], 1989. 28p. VtHi. *
    Free Will Baptist minister from Sutton, Vt. (died 1817), who preached in many New England localities.

404. SAILLANT, JOHN. "Lemuel Haynes and the revolutionary origins of black theology, 1776-1801." Religion and American Culture: a Journal of Interpretation, 2 (Winter 1992), 79-102.

405. SALISBURY, NEAL EMERSON. "Religious encounters in a colonial context: New England and New France in the seventeenth century." American Indian Quarterly, 16 (Fall 1992), 501-509.

406. SALTMARSH, JOHN A. Scott Nearing: an intellectual biography. Philadelphia: Temple Univ. Pr., 1991. xii, 337p. MB. *
    Nearing lived from 1883-1983.

407. SALWEN, BERT. "The development of contact period archaeology in southern New England and Long Island: from gee whiz!' to 'so what?'" Northeast Historical Archaeology, 18 (1989), 1-9.

408. SANGER, DAVID. "Maritime adaptations in the Gulf of Maine." Archaeology of Eastern North America, 16 (Fall 1988), 81-99.
    Prehistoric adaptations. The gulf extends from Cape Cod to Nova Scotia and New Brunswick. See also entry 289.

409. SARGENT, MARK L. "Thomas Hutchinson, Ezra Stiles, and the legend of the regicides." WMQ, 3 ser. 49 (July 1992), 431-448.
    See the Connecticut volume and volumes 7 and 8 for additional entries concerning the regicides.

410. SCHEICK, WILLIAM J. Design in Puritan American literature. Lexington: Univ. of Kentucky Pr., 1992. 167p. MBU. *

411. SCHNEIDER, JAN. "The Gulf of Maine case." American Journal of International Law, 79 (July 1985), 539-577.
    About a recent decision of the International Court of Justice on jurisdiction over Georges Bank. On the Gulf of Maine, see also entry 408.

412. SCHROCK, NANCY CARLSON. "Images of New England: documenting the built environment." American Archivist, 50 (Fall 1987), 474-498.
    Historic structures.

413. SCHULTZ, MARTIN. "Divorce patterns in nineteenth-century New England." Journal of Family History, 15:1 (1990), 101-115.

414. SCHWEITZER, IVY. The work of self-representation: lyric path in colonial New England. Chapel Hill: Univ. of North Carolina Pr., 1991. xi, 306p. CtU. *
    Literary history.

415. "SELECTED bibliography on aspects of house and home in New England and the Northeast before 1870." DubSemPr (1988), 116-131.
    Gerald W.R. Ward, comp.

416. SELIGMAN, ADAM. "Collective boundaries and social reconstruction in seventeenth-century New England." Journal of Religious History, 16 (June 1991), 260-279.

417. _____. "Inner-worldly individualism and the institutionalization of Puritanism in late seventeenth- century New England." British Journal of Sociology, 41 (Dec. 1990), 537-557.

418. SHEEHY, DONALD G. "(Re)Figuring love: Robert Frost in crisis, 1938-1942." NEQ, 63 (June 1990), 179-231.
    After the death of his wife Elinor.

419. SHEIDLEY, HARLOW ELIZABETH WALKER. "The Webster- Hayne debate: recasting New England's sectionalism." NEQ, 67 (Mar. 1994), 5-29.
    The debate took place in 1830.

420. SHERBURNE, MICHELLE. "Tracking the Underground Rail-road." Upper Valley, 7 (Mar./Apr. 1993), 25-31.
    In New Hampshire and Vermont.

421. SHORT, WILLIAM H. "New additions to a group of federal furniture." Antiques, 140 (Dec. 1991), 960-965.
    New England provenance.

422. SIEMINSKI, GREG. "The Puritan captivity narrative and the politics of the American Revolution." American Quarterly, 42 (Mar. 1990), 35-56.

423. SILVERTHORNE, ELIZABETH. Sarah Orne Jewett: a writer's life. Woodstock, N.Y.: Overlook Pr., 1993. 238, [16]p. MBAt. *

424. SIMPSON, LEWIS P. "Slavery and the cultural imperialism of New England." Southern Review, 25 (Jan. 1989), 1-29.

425. SIMPSON, MARC. "The early coastal landscapes of William Stanley Haseltine." Antiques, 142 (Aug. 1992), 204-213.
    Haseltine (1835-1900) "gained fame as an interpreter of both New England's shore line and Italy's most romantic sites."

426. SLOAT, CAROLINE FULLER. "The food, customs and etiquette of Thanksgivings long ago." On the Common (Sturbridge, Mass.), 2 (Nov. 1990), 25, 27.

427. _____. "Thanksgiving etiquette." OSV, 29 (Fall 1989), 4-6.
Early-19th century.

428. SMITH, DANIEL SCOTT. "All in some way related to each other: a demographic and comparative resolution of the anomaly of New England kinship." American Historical Review, 94 (Feb. 1989), 44-79.
Finds that the "operative" kinship ties in 18th- century New England were those between parents and their children.

429. SMITH, G. E. KIDDER. The Beacon guide to New England houses of worship: an architectural companion. Boston: Beacon Pr., 1989. xxii, 187p. MBU. *

430. SMITH, ROFF. "One more ride on The ghost train." Yankee, 58 (Aug. 1994), 76-81.
The Barnstormers, a summer theater company in New Hampshire and Maine, established in 1931.

431. SMITS, DAVID D. "'We are not to grow wild': seventeenth-century New England's refutation of Anglo-Indian intermarriage." American Indian Culture and Research Journal, 11 (1987), 1-31.

432. SMOLINSKI, REINER. "Israel redivivus: the eschatological limits of Puritan typology in New England." NEQ, 63 (Sept. 1990), 357-395.

433. SMYTH, GEORGE H. "The Scotch-Irish in New England." Magazine of American History, 9 (Mar. 1883), 153-167.

434. SPIESS, ARTHUR E. "On New England shell middens: response to Sanger's cautionary tale." American Antiquity, 53 (Jan. 1988), 174-177.
See also entry 1117.

435. SPURR, DICK, and GLORIA JORDAN. Wes Jordan: profile of a rodmaker, Cross-South Bend-Orvis. Grand Junction, Colo.: Centennial, 1992. 192p. VtHi. *
Jordan (1894-1975), a well-known maker of bamboo fishing rods, was associated successively with firms in Lynn, Mass., South Bend, Ind., and Manchester, Vt.

436. STACHIW, MYRON O., and FRANK G. WHITE. "'Heave 'er up. Heave 'er up.'" OSV, 30 (Spring 1990), 4-6.
House-frame raisings (early-19th century).

437. STANFORD, PETER. "Long Island Sound: introduction to a storied seaway." Sea History, 50 (1989), 15-18.

438. STEINBERG, THEODORE L. "Dam-breaking in the 19th-century Merrimack Valley: water, social conflict, and the Waltham-Lowell mills." JSH, 24 (Fall 1990), 25-45.
Conflict over water rights between the Massachusetts mill owners and residents of the valley farther upstream, in New Hampshire.

439. STEPHENS, CHARLENE. "'The most reliable time': William Bond, the New England railroads, and time awareness in 19th-century America." Technology and Culture, 30 (Jan. 1989), 1-24.

440. STERLING, DOROTHY. Ahead of her time: Abby Kelley and the politics of anti-slavery. N.Y.: W.W. Norton, 1991. 436p. MBAt. *
Lived 1810-1887.

441. STEVENS, CHERYL WHITMORE, and MARGARET PIATT. "Under a spell." OSV, 30 (Summer 1990), 4-6.
Storytelling in New England (early-19th century).

442. STILGOE, JOHN R. "The connective farm." New England Monthly, 7 (Mar. 1990), 49-51.
Connected farm buildings.

443. SWEENEY, KEVIN MICHAEL. "Meetinghouses, town houses, and churches: changing perceptions of sacred and secular space in southern New England, 1720-1850." Winterthur Portfolio, 28 (Spring 1993), 59-93.

444. SWEETLAND, DAVID R. New England rails, 1948-1968. Edison, N.J.: Morning Sun Books, 1989. 128p. Me. *

445. SYMMES, RICHARD W. "One woman's locomotives." B&M Bulletin, 18:4 [1992], 18-29.
Elizabeth S. Foley, recently deceased, a photographer and calendar maker.

446. TAWA, NICHOLAS E. The coming of age of American art music: New England's classical Romanticists. N.Y.: Greenwood Pr., 1991. x, 237p. MB. *
Study of six 19th-century composers.

447. TAYLOR, RICHARD H. The churches of Christ of the Congregational way in New England. Benton Harbor, Mich.: R.H. Taylor, 1989. vii, 308p. CtHi. *

448. TAYLOR, ROBERT. New England homefront, World War II. Camden, Me.: Yankee Books, 1992. xv, 208p. MBAt. *
Photographs and text.

449. TERRY, HENRY. American clock making: its early history. (1871) n.p., [1885]. 19p. CtHi. *

450.   TERRYBERRY, KARL JEFFREY. "New England cloister: cultural conformity and the concept of gender identity in the stories for and about children by Mary E. Wilkins Freeman." Ph.D. dissertation, Univ. of South Carolina, 1992. 180p.
       Abstracted in DAI, 53:11A (1993), 3913-3914.

451.   TEUSCHER, PHILIP T. "Riverman, shellerman." Sea History, 50 (1989), 18-19.
       Oystering and the collecting of oyster shells in the Long Island Sound area.

452.   THICKSTUN, MARGARET OLOFSON. Fictions of the feminine: Puritan doctrine and the representation of women. Ithaca, N.Y.: Cornell Univ. Pr., 1988. xi, 176p. RPB. *

453.   THISTLETHWAITE, FRANK. Dorset pilgrims: the story of West Country pilgrims who went to New England in the 17th century. London: Barrie & Jenkins, 1989. ix, 294p. MBAt. *

454.   THOMPSON, ROGER. "Attitudes towards homosexuality in the seventeenth-century New England colonies." Journal of American Studies [U.K.], 23 (Apr. 1989), 27- 40.

455.   _____. Mobility and migration: East Anglian founders of New England, 1629-1640. Amherst: Univ. of Massachusetts Pr., 1994. xv, 305p. MWA. *

456.   _____. "Social cohesion in early New England." NEHGR, 146 (July 1992), 235-253.

457.   THOMSON, ROSS. The path to mechanized shoe production in the United States. Chapel Hill: Univ. of North Carolina Pr., 1989. xii, 296p. MB. *
       Emphasizes the New England shoe industry.

458.   THRELFALL, JOHN BROOKS. Fifty Great Migration colonists to New England and their origins. Madison, Wis., 1990. vi, 554p. Ct. *

459.   TRACY, PATRICIA J. "Re-considering migration within colonial New England." JSH, 23 (Fall 1989), 93- 113.

460.   TRAVERS, CAROLYN. "The American Thanksgiving: the evolution of a tradition." New England Journal of History, 48 (Spring 1991), 30-32.

461.   "THE ULTIMATE clearcut." Forest Notes, No. 174 (Fall 1988), 3-7.
       Effects of the 1938 hurricane.

462.   UMBEL, WILLIAM THOMAS. "The making of an American denomination: Methodism in New England religious culture, 1790-1860." Ph.D. dissertation, Johns Hopkins Univ., 1991. vi, 258p. *
       Abstracted in DAI, 53:2A (1992), 602.

463.   "UNSOLVED mysteries." Upper Valley, 16 (May/June 1992), 11-12.
       Four unsolved murders of women in the upper Connecticut Valley (1984-1987).

464.   VALENTINE, DONALD B. JR. "B&M's G-11-a class Locomotives. B&M Bulletin, 18:4 (1992), 14-25.

465.   _____. "The Forest line." B&M Bulletin, 17:1 (1990), 6-11.
       Branch railroad between Hancock, N.H., and Windsor, Vt.

466.   VALERI, MARK. "The New Divinity and the American Revolution." WMQ, 3 ser. 46 (Oct. 1989), 741-769.

467.   VAN ANGLEN, KEVIN P. The New England Milton: literary reception and cultural authority in the early republic. University Park: Pennsylvania State Univ. Pr., 1993. xv, 255p. MU. *

468.   WALBRIDGE, J. H. "Haverhill, N.H.; Newbury, Vermont." Woodsville [N.H.] Weekly News (Feb. 19, 1897).
       Special supplement to the newspaper; includes historical articles.

469.   WALLACE, WILLIAM H. An agricultural renaissance in New England. Keene, N.H.: Keene State College, 1993. 25p. VtU. *

470.   WARTIK, NANCY. The French Canadians. N.Y.: Chelsea House, 1989. 111p. CtNbC. *
       Includes discussion of immigration to New England.

471.   WATERMAN, LAURA, and GUY WATERMAN. Forest and crag: a history of hiking, trail blazing, and adventure in the Northeast mountains. Boston: Appalachian Mountain Club, 1989. xxxviii, 888p. NhHi. *

472.   _____. Yankee rock & ice: a history of rock climbing in the Northeastern United States. Harrisburg, Pa.: Stackpole Books, 1993. xvi, 334p. MBAt. *

473.   WATSON, PATRICIA ANN. The angelical conjunction: the preacher-physicians of colonial New England. Knoxville: Univ. of Tennessee Pr., 1991. 187p. RPB. *
       See also next entry.

474.   _____. "The angelical conjunction: the preacher- physicians of colonial New England." Ph.D. dissertation, Johns Hopkins Univ., 1987. viii, 267p. *
       Abstracted in DAI, 48:7A (1988), 1802. See also preceding entry.

475.   _____. "The 'hidden ones': women and healing in colonial New England." DubSemPr (1990), 25-33.

476   NEW ENGLAND

476.   WATTERS, JAMES EDWARD. "The regulation of railroad technology between 1860 and 1920 and its effect on the New England carbuilding industry." Ph.D. dissertation, Clark Univ., 1989. v, 441p. *
   Abstracted in DAI, 50:11A (1990), 3718-3719.

477.   WEDDLE, MEREDITH BALDWIN. "Conscience or compromise: the meaning of the peace testimony in early New England." Quaker History, 81 (Fall 1992), 73-86.

478.   WEIL, FRANCOIS. Les Franco-Americains, 1860-1980. [Paris]: Belin, 1989. 249p. RHi. *

479.   WEINSTEIN-FARSON, LAURIE LEE. The Wampanoag. N.Y.: Chelsea House Publishers, 1988. 96p. CtB. *
   Wampanoag Indians.

480.   WEIR, DAVID ALEXANDER. "Church covenanting in seventeenth-century New England." Ph.D. dissertation, Princeton Univ., 1992. xviii, 393p. *
   Abstracted in DAI, 53:7A (1993), 2418.

481.   WEISS, JOANNE GRAYESKI. "The relationship between the 'Great Awakening' and the transition from psalmody to hymnody in the New England colonies." D.A. dissertation, Ball State Univ., 1988. iii, 208p. *
   Abstracted in DAI, 49:8A (1989), 2018.

482.   WELCH, WILLIAM L. "Lorenzo Sabine and the assault on Sumner." NEQ, 52 (June 1992), 298-302.
   Traces the 1856 assault on Sen. Charles Sumner of Massachusetts by Congressman Preston Brooks of South Carolina to anger over Sumner's use of anti-southern rhetoric taken from Sabine's pro-New England history of the American Revolution (1847).

483.   WESTBROOK, PERRY D. A literary history of New England. Cranbury, N.J.: Associated Univ. Presses, 1988. 362p. CtU. *

484.   WHITTAKER, ROBERT H. Land of lost content: the Piscataqua River basin and the Isles of Shoals: the people, their dreams, their history. [Dover, N.H.]: Alan Sutton, 1993. xi, 230p. MeHi. *

485.   WHITE, CHRISTIE. "'The roots & herbs of our own country.'" OSV, 29 (Summer 1989), 4-6.
   Samuel Thomson (1769-1863) and the use of medicinal herbs in New England.

486.   WHITE, FRANK G. "Pounding out a living." OSV, 31 (Fall 1991), 4-5.
   Basketmaking in early New England.

487.   WHITNEY, SCOTT J. "Conn. River bridges." B&M Bulletin, 17:1 (1990), 20-35.
   Railroad bridges in northern New England.

488.   WIGGIN, KATE DOUGLAS. "The littlest critic." Down East, 38 (Dec. 1991), 45, 57-58.
   Wiggin, a 19th-century writer, recalls a chance meeting with Charles Dickens during a train ride between Portland, Me., and Boston.

489.   WILDER, H. ARNOLD. "The saga of a New England railfan: Dana D. Goodwin." B&M Bulletin, 16:2 (1989), [3-7].
   1898-1982. See also entry 355.

490.   WILKIE, EVERETT C. JR. "Jonathan Carver, Oliver Wolcott, and Jedidiah Morse's American geography." CHSB, 54 (Summer/Fall 1989), 249-255.
   How Wolcott's criticism of a well-known travel book by Carver influenced Morse's writing.

491.   WILLIAMS, DANIEL E. "In defense of self: author and authority in the memoirs of Stephen Burroughs." Early American Literature, 25:2 (1990), 96-112.
   The memoirs of Burroughs (1765-1840) are cited in Vol. 8 (entry 2706).

492.   WILLIAMS, SUSAN REYNOLDS. "In the garden of New England: Alice Morse Earle and the history of domestic life." Ph.D. dissertation, Univ. of Delaware, 1992. xii, 390p. *
   Writings by Earle (1851-1911) on social life and customs in early New England are listed in Vol. 7 and other volumes in this series. Abstracted in DAI, 53:9A (1993), 3347.

493.   WITCH-hunting in seventeenth-century New England: a documentary history, 1638-1692. David D. Hall, ed. Boston: Northeastern Univ. Pr., 1991. 332p. MB. *

494.   WOOD, JOSEPH SUTHERLAND. "'Build, therefore, your own world': the New England village as settlement ideal." Association of American Geographers, Annals, 81 (Mar. 1991), 32-50.
   Assesses the idea of the New England village as a 19th-century invention.

495.   WOOD, JOSEPH SUTHERLAND, and MICHAEL STEINITZ. "A world we have gained: house, common, and village in New England." Journal of Historical Geography [U.K.], 18 (Jan. 1992), 105-120.
   The physical development of New England villages and its treatment by historians.

496.   WRIGHT, CONRAD EDICK. "'Multiplying the copies': New England historical societies and documentary editing." Documentary Editing, 11 (June 1989), 32-36.

497.   _____. The transformation of charity in postrevolutionary New England. Boston: Northeastern Univ. Pr., 1992. x, 330p. RHi. *

498.   WRIGHT, MEREDITH. Put on thy beautiful garments: rural New England clothing, 1783-1800. East Montpelier, Vt.: Clothes Pr., 1990. vi, 113p. VtHi. *

499.   YACOVONE, DONALD. Samuel Joseph May and the dilemmas of the liberal persuasion, 1797-1871. Philadelphia: Temple Univ. Pr., 1991. xii, 262p. MB. *
    Unitarian minister and social reformer. See also this author's Ph.D. dissertation on May (Claremont Graduate School, 1984; entry 2086 in Vol. 7).

500.   YOUNGS, JOHN WILLIAM THEODORE JR. The Congregationalists. N.Y.: Greenwood Pr., 1990. xvi, 376p. MB. *

501.   ZAKAI, AVIHU. Exile and kingdom: history and apocalypse in the Puritan migration to America. N.Y.: Cambridge Univ. Pr., 1992. x, 264p. CtU. *
    See also this author's Ph.D. dissertation of similar title (Johns Hopkins Univ., 1982; entry 3667 in Vol. 8).

502.   _____. "Orthodoxy in England and New England: Puritans and the issue of religious toleration, 1640- 1650." American Philosophical Society, Proceedings, 135 (Sept. 1991), 401-442.

503.   ZEA, PHILIP, and ROBERT C. CHENEY. Clock making in New England, 1725-1825: an interpretation of the Old Sturbridge Village collection. Caroline F. Sloat, ed. Sturbridge, Mass.: Old Sturbridge Village, 1992. 173p. MStuO. *

504.   ZIAC, DELCY C., and JOHN E. PFEIFFER. "Dry bone cremations from five sites in New England." ArcSocConB, No. 52 (1989), 55-60.
    Four of the Indian sites are in Connecticut, the other in Maine.

505.   ZONDERMAN, DAVID AARON. Aspirations and anxieties: New England workers and the mechanized factory system, 1815-1850. N.Y.: Oxford Univ. Pr., 1992. x, 357p. CtU. *
    See also this author's Ph.D. dissertation of same title (Yale Univ., 1986; entry 1604 in Vol. 7).

Connecticut

**Entries for the state as a whole
or pertaining to
more than one county***

506. ANDREWS, GREGORY E., and DAVID F. RANSOM. Historical survey report: the Connecticut Riverfront in the greater Hartford area. Hartford: Riverfront Recapture, 1989. 50, [10]p. CtHi. *

507. "AN ANNOTATED guide to sources for the story of African-American history in the museum and library collections of the Connecticut Historical Society." CHSB, special series, No. 1 [1994], 5-251.

508. ASHER, ROBERT. "Connecticut's first workmen's compensation law." Connecticut History, No. 32 (Nov. 1991), 25-50.

509. BAKER, MARY E. "A born antiquarian: George Dudley Seymour, 6 October 1859-21 January 1945." Connecticut Antiquarian, 41 (Winter 1990), 11-28.
    Seymour donated the Nathan Hale Homestead to the Antiquarian and Landmarks Society.

510. BAMBACH, CARMEN C. "Connecticut's historic theaters." Connecticut League of Historical Societies, League Bulletin, 41 (Sept. 1989), 9-13.

511. BANEY, TERRY ALAN. "Yankees and the city: struggling over urban representation in Connecticut, 1880 to World War I." Ph.D. dissertation, Univ. of Connecticut, 1989. xv, 444p. *
    Abstracted in DAI, 50:12A (1990), 4072. See also next entry.

512. _____. Yankees and the city: struggling over urban representation in Connecticut, 1880 to World War I. N.Y.: Garland, 1993. ix, 269p. CtHT. *
    See also preceding entry.

513. BARTOCCI, CLARA. "Puritans versus Pequots: four eye-witness reports of the first war in colonial New England." Storia Nordamericana [Italy], 4:1-2 (1987), 71-92.

514. BENDREMER, JEFFREY CAP MILLEN. "Late woodland settlement and subsistence in eastern Connecticut." Ph.D. dissertation, Univ. of Connecticut, 1993. xii, 429p. *
    Abstracted in DAI, 54:7A (1994), 2729.

515. BERDON, ROBERT I. "Connecticut equal protection clause: requirement of strict scrutiny when classifications are based upon sex or physical or mental disability." Connecticut History, No. 29 (Nov. 1988), 130-151.

516. BLEJWAS, STANISLAUS A. "The 'Polish' tradition in Connecticut politics." Connecticut History, No. 33 (Nov. 1992), 61-98.

517. BRANDT, CLARE. The man in the mirror: a life of Benedict Arnold. N.Y.: Random House, 1994. xxii, 360p. CtU. *
    See also entry 609.

518. BUCKLEY-VAN HOAK, SHARON. "Elective curricular enrollments in Connecticut urban schools before and after state graduation requirements." Ph.D. dissertation, Univ. of Connecticut, 1990. xii, 245p. *
    1984 and 1989. Abstracted in DAI, 51:8A (1991), 2699.

519. CALOGERO, BARBARA LOUISE ANDERSON. "Macroscopic and petrographic identification of the rock types used for stone tools in central Connecticut." Ph.D. dissertation, Univ. of Connecticut, 1991. xii, 280p. *
    Prehistoric tools. Abstracted in DAI, 52:3A (1991), 974.

520. CAMERON, KENNETH WALTER. Anglican experience in Revolutionary Connecticut and areas adjacent. Hartford: Transcendental Books, 1987. 320p. CtHi. *

521. CANNELLA, ANTHONY R. "When Connecticut got rocked." Connecticut, 54 (Dec. 1991), 56-61, 103.
    Early days of rock and roll in the state (1950s).

---

* Online Computer Library Center (OLCC) listings for books and dissertations marked with this symbol may include additional library locations.

522   CONNECTICUT

522.   CASSEDY, DANIEL FREEMAN. "Native American interaction patterns and lithic acquisition strategies in eastern New York and southern New England." Ph.D. dissertation, State Univ. of New York, Binghamton, 1992. 310p.
    Abstracted in DAI, 54:2A (1993), 570-571.

523.   CHATFIELD, JACK. "Connecticut Federalism and the Embargo: the politics and ideology of conservative dissent, 1807-1809." Connecticut History, No. 30 [i.e., 31] (Nov. 1990), 33-54.

524.   CHIPLEY, LOUISE. "Consociation and the Unitarian controversy in Connecticut." Unitarian Universalist Historical Society, Proceedings, 21:1 (1987-1988), 13- 32.
    Early-19th century.

525.   CLOUETTE, BRUCE ALAN, and MATTHEW ROTH. Connecticut's historic highway bridges. Wethersfield: Connecticut Department of Transportation, 1991. 101p. CtHi. *

526.   COHN, HENRY S., and WESLEY W. HORTON. Connecticut's four constitutions. n.p., [1988?]. 49p. CtHi. *

527.   COLLIER, CHRISTOPHER. "Sleeping with ghosts: myth and public policy in Connecticut, 1634-1991." NEQ, 65 (June 1992), 179-207.
    The "myth" is that of "New England town autonomy."

528.   _____. "William J. Hammersley, Simeon E. Baldwin, and the constitutional revolution of 1897 in Connecticut." Connecticut Law Review, 23 (Fall 1990), 31-97.
    Connecticut's belated establishment of a strong tradition of judicial review.

529.   CONNECTICUT. Public records of the State of Connecticut. Hartford, 1894-. CtHi. *
    15 volumes through 1991, extending the series through Oct. 1811. Charles J. Hoadly, Leonard Woods Labaree, Catherine Fennelly, Albert E. Van Dusen, Christopher Collier, Dorothy Ann Lipson, and Douglas M. Arnold, eds. Note: this item replaces entry 399 in the Connecticut volume. See also Public records of the Colony of Connecticut (entry 392 in the Connecticut volume).

530.   CONNECTICUT. HISTORICAL COMMISSION. Cultural resource survey of state-owned historic buildings in Connecticut. Marian Grabowicz, comp. [Hartford], 1989. 375p. CtWillE. *

531.   CONNECTICUT GALLERY. Charles Ethan Porter, 1847?-1923. Marlborough, 1987. 113p. CtHi. *
    Black artist.

532.   CONNECTICUT HUMANITIES COUNCIL. Connecticut case studies. Hartford, 1989. 10 packets. CtHi. *
    For teachers of the state's history.

533.   "CONNECTICUT historical and industrial archaeology bibliography." ArcSocConB, No. 55 (1992), 77-86.
    Robert R. Gradie III and David A. Poirier, comps.

534.   COWDEN, JOANNA DUNLAP. "Sovereignty and secession: peace Democrats and antislavery Republicans in Connecticut during the Civil War years." Connecticut History, No. 30 (Nov. 1989), 41-54.

535.   CROMLEY, ELLEN K. "Changing patterns of nursing home availability in Connecticut." NE-StLVGSPr, 17 (1987), 75-83.
    1970-1984.

536.   DALIN, DAVID G., and LOTHAR KAHN. "Connecticut's first Jewish Congressman: Herman P. Kopplemann." Connecticut Jewish History, 1 (Summer 1990), 55-68.
    Hartford resident, first elected in 1932.

537.   DANIELS, BRUCE COLIN. "Ratifying the past: historical influences on constitutional development in Connecticut." Connecticut History, No. 29 (Nov. 1988), 1-15.

538.   DAUGHTERS OF THE AMERICAN REVOLUTION. NATIONAL SOCIETY. Minority military service: Connecticut, 1775- 1783. [Washington], 1988. 17p. Ct. *

539.   DITZ, TOBY LEE. "Ownership and obligation: inheritance and patriarchal households in Connecticut, 1750-1820." WMQ, 3 ser. 47 (Apr. 1990), 235-265.
    Based on a larger study by the author, comparing conditions in the Connecticut River Valley town of Wethersfield with those in the upland communities of Bolton, Coventry, Union, and Willington. (See also entries 79-80 in Vol. 8.)

540.   DOWLING, WILLIAM C. Poetry and ideology in Revolutionary Connecticut. Athens: Univ. of Georgia Pr., 1990. xix, 167p. CtHi. *
    Poetry of the Connecticut Wits.

541.   DREYER, GLENN D. Connecticut's notable trees. 2d ed. New Haven: Connecticut Botanical Society, 1990. vi, 94p. CtHi. *

542.   DUCOFF-BARONE, DEBORAH. "Inventing tradition: the Connecticut Tercentenary medal and card of 1935." Connecticut History, No. 32 (Nov. 1991), 1-24.

543. FASSETT, JOHN D. UI: history of an electric company: a saga of problems, personalities and power politics. [New Haven? 1990] xvi, 764p. CtNhHi. *
United Illuminating Company.

544. FEDER, KENNETH L. "Late woodland occupation of the upland of northwestern Connecticut." MASB, 51 (Oct. 1990), 61-68.
Based on a study of Indian sites in the Peoples State Forest, Barkhamsted, and in Hartland.

545. FOX, ELIZABETH PRATT. "'Laid with Dutch tyles': the use of tin-glazed tiles in Connecticut." Connecticut Antiquarian, 40 (Winter 1989), 21-29.

546. _____, and LISA BROBERG QUINTANA. From pencil to palette: landscapes by George Edward Candee (1837- 1907). New Haven: New Haven Colony Historical Society, 1992. 16p. CtHi.

547. FREE men: the Amistad revolt and the American anti-slavery movement. [New Haven, 1989] [16]p. CtNhHi.
Catalog of an exhibition at the New Haven Colony Historical Society and the Connecticut Historical Society. See also entries 574, 589, and 601.

548. FUSSCAS, HELEN K. Fannie C. and Jennie M. Burr: Connecticut artists. Marlborough: Connecticut Gallery, 1990. 40p. *
Late-19th and 20th centuries.

549. _____. Frederick Lester Sexton, 1889-1975: Connecticut regionalist. Marlborough: Connecticut Gallery, 1987. 20p. *
Painter.

550. GERARDI, DONALD F. "Zephaniah Swift and the Connecticut Standing Order: skepticism, conservatism, and religious liberty in the early republic." NEQ, 67 (June 1994), 234-256.
Swift was Connecticut's chief justice from 1815-1819 and the author of the nation's first law text.

551. GERMAN, ANDREW W. "Connecticut's changing relationship with Long Island Sound." Long Island Historical Journal, 2 (Fall 1989), 76-89.

552. GRAHAM, KENNETH A. "Issues of federalism in Connecticut in the twentieth century." Connecticut History, No. 29 (Nov. 1988), 116-129.

553. GRANT, ELLSWORTH STRONG. "Connecticut: a state of genius." Connecticut Humanities Council News (Summer 1993), 1, 3-4.

554. _____. The miracle of Connecticut. Oliver Jensen, ed. Hartford: Connecticut Historical Society, [1992?]. xi, 328p. CtHi. *

555. _____. "Wilbur Cross." Connecticut, 53 (Nov. 1990), 50, 52, 54, 57-58, 60, 62, 64.
Governor from 1931-1939.

556. GRASSO, CHRISTOPHER DANIEL. "Between awakenings: learned men and the transformation of public discourse in Connecticut, 1740-1800." Ph.D. dissertation, Yale Univ., 1992. vii, 458p. *
Abstracted in DAI, 54:1A (1993), 291.

557. GREENBERG, IVAN. "Class, culture and generational change: immigrant families in two Connecticut industrial cities during the 1930s." Ph.D. dissertation, City Univ. of New York, 1990. ix, 430p. CtWillE. *
Bridgeport and New Britain. Abstracted in DAI, 51:11A (1991), 3879.

558. GROSSBART, STEPHEN REED. "The Revolutionary transition: politics, religion, and economy in eastern Connecticut, 1765-1800." Ph.D. dissertation, Univ. of Michigan, 1989. xii, 391p. *
Abstracted in DAI, 51:1A (1990), 270.

559. _____. "Seeking the divine form: conversion and church admission in eastern Connecticut, 1711-1832." WMQ, 3 ser. 46 (Oct. 1989), 696-740.

560. HALL, PETER DOBKIN. "Organizational values and the origins of the corporation in Connecticut, 1760-1860." Connecticut History, No. 29 (Nov. 1988), 63-90.

561. HEPBURN, KATHERINE. Me: stories of my life. N.Y.: Knopf, 1991. viii, 420p. CtHi. *
Autobiography of the well-known actress (born 1909).

562. HERDEG, J. A. "A lower Housatonic River Valley shop tradition: an analysis of six related dressing tables." CHSB, 56 (Winter/Spring 1993), 39-56.

563. HOKE, DONALD R. Ingenious Yankees: the rise of the American system of manufactures in the private sector. N.Y.: Columbia Univ Pr., 1990. 345p. MWA. *
Case studies of developments in the clock, watch, axe, and typewriter industries.

564. HOLLANDER, STACY C. "Revisiting Ammi Phillips." Antiques, 145 (Feb. 1994), 266-275.
Artist (lived 1788-1865).

565   CONNECTICUT

565. HORTON, WESLEY W. "Annotated debates of the 1818 constitutional convention." Connecticut Bar Journal, 65 (Jan. 1991), SI3-SI104.

566. HUBBARD, IAN. Crossings: three centuries from ferry boats to the New Baldwin Bridge. Lyme: Greenwich Publishing Group, 1993. 104p. CtHi. *

567. IFKOVIC, JOHN W. "Pierpont Edwards and the constitutional convention of 1818." Connecticut History, No. 29 (Nov. 1988), 46-62.

568. "INTERVIEW: Judge Louis Shapiro." Connecticut Jewish History, 1 (Summer 1990), 45-53.
    Former state supreme court justice.

569. "INTERVIEW: Milton and Gertrude Koskoff." Connecticut Jewish History, 1 (Summer 1990), 29-43.
    Both were state legislators, representing Plainville from 1938-1946 and 1953-1959 respectively.

570. JANICK, HERBERT F. JR. "Connecticut: the suburban state." Connecticut Humanities Council News (Fall 1993), 7-9.

571. JIMERSON, RANDALL C. "The Connecticut Labor Archives." Labor History, 31 (Winter-Spring 1990), 39- 43.
    At the Univ. of Connecticut.

572. JODZIEWICZ, THOMAS W. "Charters and corporations, independence and loyalty." Connecticut History, No. 29 (Nov. 1988), 27-45.
    Connecticut Colony's early constitutional history.

573. JOHN Warner Barber's views of Connecticut towns, 1834-36. Christopher P. Bickford and J. Bard McNulty, eds. [Hartford]: Acorn Club, 1990. xxix, 123p. CtHi. *
    See also entry 87 in the Connecticut volume.

574. JOHNSON, CLIFTON H. "The Amistad case and its consequences in U.S. history." NHCHSJ, 36 (Spring 1990), 3-22.
    1839 incident. See also entries 547, 589, and 601; note at entry 76 in the Connecticut volume, and additional listings there and in Vol. 8.

575. JONES, MARY JEANNE ANDERSON. The Fundamental Orders of Connecticut. Hartford: U.S. Constitution Bicentennial Commission of Connecticut, 1988. viii, 64p. CtHi. *
    Adopted in 1638/1639. The text of this booklet was extracted from the author's book, Congregational commonwealth... (1968; entry 1000 in the Connecticut volume).

576. KAFER, PETER K. "The making of Timothy Dwight: a Connecticut morality tale." WMQ, 3 ser. 47 (Apr. 1990), 189-209.
    On Yale president Dwight (lived 1752-1817), see also entry 262.

577. KATZ, STEVEN T. "The Pequot War reconsidered." NEQ, 64 (June 1991), 206-224.

578. KLING, DAVID WILLIAM. A field of divine wonders: the New Divinity and revivals in northwestern Connecticut, 1792-1822. University Park: Pennsylvania State Univ. Pr., 1993. xvi, 296p. CtU. *
    See also this author's Ph.D. dissertation, on the Second Great Awakening in Connecticut (Univ. of Chicago, 1985; entry 160 in Vol. 8).

579. KORNHAUSER, ELIZABETH MANKIN. "Artist for the new nation." American History Illustrated, 27 (May/June 1992), 44-51.
    Portrait painter Ralph Earl (lived 1751-1801).

580. _____. "Ralph Earl: art for the new nation." Antiques, 140 (Nov. 1991), 794-805.

581. _____. "Ralph Earl: artist-entrepreneur." Ph.D. dissertation, Boston Univ., 1988. xxv, 470p. CtHi. *
    Abstracted in DAI, 49:12A (1988), 3534. See also next entry.

582. _____. Ralph Earl: the face of the young republic. New Haven: Yale Univ. Pr., 1991. xiii, 258p. CtHi. *
    See also preceding entry.

583. _____, and HAROLD SPENCER. Connecticut masters, Connecticut treasures: the collection of the Hartford Steam Boiler Inspection and Insurance Company. Hartford: Wadsworth Atheneum, 1989. 110p. CtHi. *
    Art collection.

584. KUMOR, BOLESLAW. "Koscielne dzieje Polonii w Connecticut (1870-1986): wybrane zagadnienia." Nasza Przeszlosc [Poland], 73 (1990), 192-289.
    Ecclesiastical history of the Polish community in Connecticut, 1870-1986: select issues. (Text in Polish.)

585. LACEY, BARBARA ELLISON. "Gender, piety, and secularization in Connecticut religion, 1720-1775." JSH, 24 (Summer 1991), 799-821.

586. _____. "Sarah Kemble Knight's journey across Connecticut, 1704." Connecticut History, No. 34 (Spring 1993), 1-17.
    Knight's travel journal is listed in Vol. 7 (entry 4057).

587. LANGE, ROLAND H. American Red Cross: 85 years of service: the Greater Hartford Chapter. [Farmington]: The Chapter, 1989. 50p. CtHi. *

588. MANN, WILLIAM JOHN. "Wild West." Connecticut, 54 (Nov. 1991), 46, 48-52.
Actress Mae West as a performer in Connecticut theaters.

589. MARTIN, B. EDMON. All we want is make us free: La Amistad and the reform abolitionists. Lanham, Md.: University Pr. of America, 1986. xvi, 131p. CtHi. *
See also entries 547, 574, and 601.

590. McBRIDE, KEVIN ALLEN. "Prehistoric and historic patterns of wetland use in eastern Connecticut." Man in the Northeast, No. 43 (Spring 1992), 10-24.

591. McCAIN, DIANA ROSS. "The Acadians." Connecticut, 54 (Jan. 1991), 51-53.
Exiled to Connecticut and other English colonies in 1755.

592. _____. "The Connecticut apprentices." Early American Life, 20 (Dec. 1989), 6-7, 13-14.
Reprinted in NAWCCB, 33 (Aug. 1991), 411-414.

593. _____. "The greening of Connecticut." Connecticut, 53 (Mar. 1990), 128-131.
Reaction to Irish immigration (19th century).

594. _____. "The hardships of worship." Early American Life, 20 (Oct. 1989), 8, 10-11.
Physical conditions in early Connecticut meetinghouses.

595. _____. "Life before Lotto." Connecticut, 52 (Sept. 1989), 117-119.
Early Connecticut lotteries.

596. MEYER, DAVID R. "The national prominence of Connecticut's industrial centers in the nineteenth century." CHSB, 55 (Winter/Spring 1990), 68-80.

597. MILKOFSKY, BRENDA. "Connecticut tobacco farming." Connecticut League of Historical Societies, League Bulletin, 40 (July 1988), 6-10.

598. MILLER, DANIEL TIMOTHY. "Fire from the hearth: Connecticut, irregular warfare, and national identity, 1754-1783." Ph.D. dissertation, Indiana Univ., 1993. viii, 336p. *
Abstracted in DAI, 54:4A (1993), 1518.

599. MORAN, ANTONIA C. "Expenditure control: balancing the constitutional powers in Connecticut." Connecticut Law Review, 20 (Summer 1988), 953-1028.
Historical.

600. _____. "The period of peaceful anarchy: constitutional impasse, 1890-1892." Connecticut History, No. 29 (Nov. 1988), 91-115.

601. MOTLEY, CONSTANCE. "The legal aspects of the Amistad case." NHCHSJ, 36 (Spring 1990), 23-31.
See also entries 547, 574, and 601.

602. MOYNIHAN, RUTH BARNES. "Coming of age: four centuries of Connecticut women and their choices." CHSB, 53 (Winter/Spring 1988), 5-112.

603. PAGOULATOS, PETER. "The functional uses of eastern Connecticut quartzite." ArcSocConB, No. 54 (1991), 65-75.
I.e., artifacts from prehistoric sites.

604. _____. "Terminal archaic 'living areas' in the Connecticut River Valley." ArcSocConB, No. 53 (1990), 59-72.

605. _____. "Terminal archaic settlement and subsistence in the Connecticut River Valley." Ph.D. dissertation, Univ. of Connecticut, 1986. xiii, 320p. *
Abstracted in DAI, 47:9A (1987), 3464.

606. "THE PAPERS of Dr. Ernest Caulfield on Connecticut carvers and their work." Markers VIII [1991], entire issue.
Gravestone carvers. James A. Slater, ed. Issue includes a biographical sketch (pp. 1-8) of Caulfield (1893-1972), whose writings on the subject are listed individually in the Connecticut volume. See also entry 623.

607. PECHIN, S. P. "The Connecticut marines." NAWCCB, 31 (Oct. 1989), 387-398.
Marine clocks.

608. RAI, KUL B., and JOHN W. CRITZER. "Affirmative action in Connecticut: a comparison of Connecticut State University and the University of Connecticut." Connecticut Review, 13 (Spring 1991), 55-68.
Comparison of policies of the state's two public university systems.

609. RANDALL, WILLARD STERNE. Benedict Arnold: patriot and traitor. N.Y.: Morrow, 1990. 667, [24]p. CtHi. *
See also entry 517.

610. RANSOM, DAVID F. "One hundred years of Jewish congregations in Connecticut: an architectural survey." Connecticut Jewish History, 2 (Fall 1991), 7-147.

611. READ, ELEANOR B. "String of pearls." HF, 27 (May 1990), 1, 9.
Early textile mills in eastern Connecticut.

612. RIBICOFF, ABRAHAM. "Autobiographical sketch." Connecticut Jewish History, 1 (Summer 1990), 15-28.
Ribicoff served as governor from 1955-1961 and as a U.S. senator from 1963-1981.

613   CONNECTICUT

613.   RIPLEY, DAVID B. "Amos Bronson Alcott: Transcendental educator." Vitae Scholasticae, 6:1 (1987), 125-140.
    Alcott's early teaching experiences in Bristol and Cheshire (1823-1827).

614.   ROETGER, ROBERT WEST. "New Haven's charter quest and annexation by Connecticut." Connecticut History, No. 29 (Nov. 1988), 16-26.
    New Haven Colony.

615.   ROHRER, JAMES RUSSELL. "The fields at home: Connecticut evangelism, the Connecticut Missionary Society, and republican culture, 1774-1818." Ph.D. dissertation, Ohio State Univ., 1991. v, 322p. *
    Abstracted in DAI, 52:8A (1992), 3049-3050.

616.   ROWLAND, JOHN T. "Down the Sound in an old two-sticker." Sea History, 50 (1989), 45-48.
    Memories of a 1910 voyage along the Connecticut coast in an old type of schooner.

617.   RUTLIN, LEN. "The story of the American wood works clock industry, 1790-1841." NAWCCB, 33 (June 1991), 249-250.
    Primarily Connecticut.

618.   SCOPINO, ALDORIGO JOSEPH JR. "The Social Gospel in Connecticut, 1893-1929." Ph.D. dissertation, Univ. of Connecticut, 1993. v, 346p. *
    Hartford and New Haven (1893-1929). Abstracted in DAI, 54:9A (1994), 3570.

619.   SELESKY, HAROLD EDWARD. War and society in colonial Connecticut. New Haven: Yale Univ. Pr., 1990. 288p. CtY. *
    See also this author's Ph.D. dissertation: "Military leadership in an American colonial society: Connecticut, 1635-1785" (Yale Univ., 1984; entry 278 in Vol. 8).

620.   SHARON, MICHAEL R. "Transcending the earthplane": the life, travels and artistic achievements of Gustave Adolph Hoffman. Vernon: Historical Society of Vernon, 1991. 77p. CtHi. *
    Lived 1869-1945.

621.   SHERER, THOMAS E. JR. The Connecticut atlas: a graphic guide to the land, people and history. West Hartford: Kilderatlas Publishing, 1990. 102p. CtHi. *

622.   SIEMIATKOSKI, DONNA HOLT. "Connecticut's early Welsh community; or Connecticut Yankees from King Arthur's court." Connecticut Nutmegger, 25 (Mar. 1993), 552-566.

623.   SLATER, JAMES A. "Ernest Joseph Caulfield (1893-1972)." Markers VIII, (1991), 1-8.
    Caulfield, a physician, studied and wrote widely about Connecticut gravestones and gravestone carvers. This issue of Markers contains reprints of a number of his writings on the subject. The original publications are listed in the Connecticut volume. See also entry 606.

624.   SMITH, ANDREW F. "The great tomato pill war of the late 1830s." CHSB, 56 (Winter/Spring 1991), 91-107.
    Controversy over claims that tomatoes had medicinal powers.

625.   SMITH, MATTHEW M. "Interpretations of a Connecticut conflict: Pequots vs. settlers." Concord Review, 1 (Fall 1988), 84-93.
    Pequot War.

626.   SNYDER, K. ALAN. Defining Noah Webster: mind and morals in the early republic. Lanham, Md.: University Pr. of America, 1990. viii, 421p. CtHi. *

627.   SNYDER, STEPHEN H. Lyman Beecher and his children: the transformation of a religious tradition. Brooklyn, N.Y.: Carlson Pub., 1991. xviii, 179p. CtU. *
    On the Beecher family and its members, including Catharine, Harriet, Henry Ward Beecher, and Harriet Beecher Stowe, see also additional entries in this volume, the Connecticut volume, and Vols. 7 and 8.

628.   STARK, BRUCE PURINTON. "'A factious spirit': constitutional theory and political practice in Connecticut, c. 1740." WMQ, 3 ser. 47 (July 1990), 391- 410.
    On the significance of the colonial election of 1740.

629.   STAVE, BRUCE M., and MICHELE PALMER. Mills and meadows: a pictorial history of northeast Connecticut. Virginia Beach, Va.: Donning Co. Publications, 1991. 191p. CtU. *

630.   STAVE, BRUCE M., and JOHN F. SUTHERLAND. From the old country: an oral history of European migration to America. N.Y.: Twayne Publishers, 1994. xx, 281p. CtHi. *
    Based primarily on Connecticut sources.

631.   STONE, DAVID T., and FRANK ANDREWS STONE. The legal foundations of Connecticut education. Storrs: Isaac N. Thut World Education Center, Univ. of Connecticut, 1988. 28p. CtHi. *

632.   STONE, FRANK ANDREWS. African American Connecticut: African origins, New England roots. Storrs: Isaac N. Thut World Education Center, Univ. of Connecticut, 1991. vii, 388p. CtHi. *

633. VAN BEEK, ELIZABETH TUCKER. "Piety and profit: English Puritans and the shaping of a godly marketplace in the New Haven Colony." Ph.D. dissertation, Univ. of Virginia, 1993. xi, 507p. *
Abstracted in DAI, 54:8A (1994), 3181.

634. WARD, BARBARA McLEAN. "Women's property and family continuity in eighteenth-century Connecticut." DubSemPr (1987), 74-85.

635. WEAVER, GLENN. "Elisha Williams: the versatile Puritan." CHSB, 53 (Summer/Fall 1988), 119-238.
Minister in Newington; president of Yale from 1726-1739; legislator, merchant, and soldier.

636. WEBSTER, NOAH. The autobiographies of Noah Webster: from the letters and essays, memoir, and diary. Richard M. Rollins, ed. Columbia, S.C.: Univ. of South Carolina Pr., 1989. xvi, 378p. CtHi. *
Webster lived 1758-1843.

637. WEINSTEIN-FARSON, LAURIE LEE. "Land politics and power: the Mohegan Indians in the seventeenth and eighteenth centuries." Man in the Northeast, No. 42 (Fall 1991), 9-16.

638. WHITE, JOHN. People, power, progress: a brief history of Northeast Utilities. Hartford: Northeast Utilities, 1991. [48]p. CtHi. *
Electric utility company.

639. WILKIE, EVERETT C. JR. "Some Connecticut land company publications." CHSB, 56 (Winter/Spring 1991), 108-130.

640. WORCESTER, WAYNE. "Three songs and it was over." Yankee, 54 (July 1990), 52-57, 102, 104-105.
1989 tornado in western Connecticut.

641. ZAIMAN, JACK. "Recollections of a political writer." Connecticut Jewish History, 1 (Summer 1990), 11-12.

SEE ALSO entries 6,14, 44, 152,166, 212, 221, 296-297, 342, 365, 369, 388, 399, 409, 437, 449, 451, 456, 490.

Connecticut

Entries for Counties†

FAIRFIELD COUNTY

642. CHASE, JEANNE. "L'Organisation de l'espace économique dans le nord-est des Etats-Unis après le guerre d'independance." Annales: Economies, Sociétés, Civilisations [France], 43 (July-Aug. 1988), 997-1020.
New York and southwestern Connecticut.

643. CHASE, W. THAYER. "Recollections." New Canaan Historical Society Annual, 11 (1990-1991), 1-7.
Author was landscape architect of the Merritt Parkway.

644. CORNWALL, L. PETER. In the Shore Line's shadow: the six lives of the Danbury & Norwalk Railroad. Littleton, Mass.: Flying Yankee Enterprises, 1987. [132]p. CtHi. *

645. CRUSON, DANIEL. The prehistory of Fairfield County. Newtown: Newtown Historical Society, 1991. ii, 103p. CtB. *

646. DiGIOVANNI, STEPHEN MICHAEL. The Catholic Church in Fairfield County, 1666-1961. New Canaan: William Mulvey, 1987. xxix, 296p. CtY. *

647. HASLAM, PATRICIA L. "Deaths untimely: Fairfield County, Connecticut, Superior Court inquests." NEHGR, 144 (Jan. 1990), 39-47.

648. LYNN, CATHERINE. "The Merritt Parkway—a road in a park." New Canaan Historical Society Annual, 11 (1990-1991), 24-49.

† See the Connecticut volume in this series (1986) for a complete list of counties.

* Online Computer Library Center (OLCC) listings for books and dissertations marked with this symbol may include additional library locations.

31

649   FAIRFIELD COUNTY

649.   MORTON, CHARLES P. "The Merritt Parkway scandal."
        New Canaan Historical Society Annual, 11 (1990-1991),
        17-23.
            Acquisition of land for the road.

650.   RADDE, BRUCE. The Merritt Parkway. New Haven: Yale
        Univ. Pr., 1993. xii, 135p. CtHi. *

651.   STRAZDINS, SALLY. "The Cyrus Sherwood Bradley
        collection: a preliminary study of the prehistoric native
        American presence in Fairfield County, Connecticut."
        ArcSocConB, No. 55 (1992), 1-20.
            Assembled between 1888 and ca. 1895.

652.   YACHER, LEON. "Population change in Fairfield County,
        Connecticut, 1940-1980." NE-StLVGSPr, 17 (1987), 84-97.

        SEE ALSO entries 543, 562.

        HARTFORD COUNTY

653.   BORISH, LINDA JANE. "'The lass of the farm': health,
        domestic roles, and the culture of farm women in Hartford
        County, Connecticut, 1820-1870." Ph.D. dissertation, Univ.
        of Maryland, 1990. ix, 602p. MStuO. *
            Abstracted in DAI 51:11A (1991), 3795.

        SEE ALSO entry 44.

        LITCHFIELD COUNTY

654.   NICHOLAS, GEORGE PETER. "The archaeology of early
        place: early postglacial land use and ecology at Robbins
        Swamp, northwestern Connecticut." Ph.D. dissertation, Univ.
        of Massachusetts, 1990. xvii, 264p. CtHi. *
            The swamp is in Canaan and North Canaan. Abstracted in
        DAI, 51:11A (1991), 3797-3798.

        SEE ALSO entry 578.

        MIDDLESEX COUNTY

655.   CONNIFF, RICHARD. "The towns that ivory built." Yankee,
        53 (Nov. 1989), 66-74, 146-148, 150, 152.
            Deep River and Ivoryton.

        NEW HAVEN COUNTY

656.   HOGAN, NEIL. The lower Naugatuck Valley: a rich and
        beautiful prospect. Chatsworth, Calif.: Windsor Publications,
        1991. 128p. CtNhHi. *
            History.

657.   LEE, WILL. "Post-Civil War soldiers' monuments in New
        Haven County, Connecticut." NHCHSJ, 36 (Fall 1989),
        25-51.

658.   STEVENS, JOHN R. "A piece of the true cross: the Derby
        Horse Railway's 'electrical line motor' of 1888." Railroad
        History, No. 157 (Autumn 1987), 65-84.
            Street railroad between Ansonia and Derby.

659.   YELLIG, MARTHA FINDER. Alice F. Washburn, architect.
        Hamden: Eli Whitney Museum, 1990. 32p. CtNhHi. *
            Of New Haven and Hamden (1870-1958).

        SEE ALSO entry 543.

        NEW LONDON COUNTY

660.   COLBY, BARNARD LEDWARD. Whaling captains of New
        London County, Connecticut: for oil and buggy whips.
        Mystic: Mystic Seaport Museum, 1990. xvi, 203p. CtHi. *

661.   _____. "Whaling from southeastern Connecticut,
        1647-1909." Mystic Seaport, Log, 41 (Fall 1989/Winter
        1990), 75-90.

662.   CONROY, DAVID W. "The defense of Indian land rights:
        William Bollan and the Mohegan case in 1743." AASP, 103
        (Oct. 1993), 395-424.

663.   JOHNSON, J. MYRON. A history of Catholics in Lyme and
        Old Lyme, Connecticut, from colonial time to the present.
        Old Lyme: Christ the King Church, 1990. 42p. CtHi. *

664.   JULI, HAROLD D. "Late prehistory of the Thames River:
        survey, landscape, and preservation along a Connecticut
        estuary." Northeast Anthropology, No. 47 (Spring 1994),
        21-44.

665.   PETERSON, WILLIAM N. Mystic built: ships and shipyards
        of the Mystic River, Connecticut, 1784-1919. Mystic: Mystic
        Seaport Museum, 1989. xv, 254p. CtHi. *

666. PFEIFFER, JOHN EDWARD. "Late and terminal archaic cultural adaptations of the lowest Connecticut Valley." Ph.D. dissertation, State Univ. of New York, Albany, 1992. iv, 344p. *

   Archaeological sites in Lyme and Old Lyme. Abstracted in DAI, 53:10A (1993), 3575.

SEE ALSO entry 637.

WINDHAM COUNTY

667. DOMNARSKI, WILLIAM. "The country lawyer remembered." American Scholar, 58 (Spring 1989), 283-288.

   Windham County lawyers of the 1930s.

SEE ALSO entries 629, 961.

Connecticut

Entries for Cities and Towns †

ANDOVER (TOLLAND CO.)

668. BRASS, PHILIP D. The history of Andover, Connecticut. Andover: Andover Historical Society, 1991. 58p. CtHi. *

ASHFORD (WINDHAM CO.)

669. ASHFORD, CONN. 275TH ANNIVERSARY COMMITTEE. Ashford, 1714-1989, moments from history: a chronology reflecting the history of Ashford, Connecticut. Barbara B. Metsack, research director. Ashford, 1990. 165p. CtHi. *

BARKHAMSTED (LITCHFIELD CO.)

670. FEDER, KENNETH L. "Legend of the Barkhamsted Lighthouse." Archaeology, 47 (July/Aug. 1994), 46-49.
   See also following entries.

671. _____. "The Lighthouse: history and archaeology of an outcast village." Northeast Anthropology, No. 46 (Fall 1993), 39-59.

† See the Connecticut volume in this series (1986) for a complete list of cities and towns.

* Online Computer Library Center (OLCC) listings for books and dissertations marked with this symbol may include additional library locations.

672. MARLATT, ANDREW. "Sanctuary." Connecticut, 56 (Jan. 1993), 40, 42-43.
   The Lighthouse. (See also preceding entries.)

SEE ALSO entry 544.

BERLIN (HARTFORD CO.)

673. BERLIN: other times, other voices. Doris Vroom Meyers, comp. Berlin: Berlin Free Library, [1986]. 110p. CtHi. *
   Extracts of articles from the Berlin News.

BETHLEHEM (LITCHFIELD CO.)

674. BETHLEHEM, CT. FIRST CHURCH (Congregational). 250 years of the First Church of Bethlehem, United Church of Christ. Marshall Linden and Linton E. Simerl, eds. Bethlehem, [1989?]. vii, 304p. CtS. *

675. "CAROLINE Woolsey Ferriday (1902-1990): donor of Bethlehem's Bellamy Manse." Antiquarian and Landmarks Society, The Landmark (Fall 1991), 5-8.
   Historic house.

676   BETHLEHEM

676.   LINDEN, MARSHALL E. "In and beyond Joseph Bellamy's shadow: a life of Azel Backus (1765-1816)." Bulletin of the Congregational Library, 42 (Fall 1990/ Winter 1991), 4-17.
    Bellamy's successor as Congregational minister in Bethlehem.

BRIDGEPORT (FAIRFIELD CO.)

677.   ANDRENYAK, GAIL M. An epidemiologic study of demographic factors associated with infant mortality in Bridgeport, Connecticut, 1981-1984. N.Y.: Garland, 1990. iii, 150p. MB. *

678.   BANIT, THOMAS. "A city goes to war: Bridgeport, Conn., 1914-1917." New England Journal of History, 46 (Spring 1989), 29-53.

679.   BUCKI, CECELIA FRANCES. "The pursuit of political power: class, ethnicity, and municipal politics in interwar Bridgeport, 1915-1936." Ph.D. dissertation, Univ. of Pittsburgh, 1991. xi, 537p. *
    Abstracted in DAI, 52:10A (1992), 3701-3702.

680.   EMBARDO, ROBERT J. "'Summer lightning,' 1907: the Wobblies in Bridgeport." Labor History, 30 (Fall 1989), 518-535.
    Industrial Workers of the World.

681.   GREENWOOD, JANET KAE DALY. The University of Bridgeport: celebrating sixty years of excellence. N.Y.: Newcomen Society of the U.S., 1987. 24p. CtHi. *

682.   SAXON, A. H. "Olympia Brown in Bridgeport: 'acts of injustice.'" Unitarian Universalist Historical Society, Proceedings, 21:1 (1987-1988), 55-65.
    Controversial minister of the Universalist Church of Bridgeport (1869-1875).

683.   WITKOWSKI, MARY K. "Sources for business and labor history in the Bridgeport Public Library." Labor History, 31 (Winter-Spring 1990), 44-47.

    SEE ALSO entry 557.

BRISTOL (HARTFORD CO.)

684.   BRISTOL PUBLIC LIBRARY. Images of Bristol. West Kennebunk, Me.: Phoenix Publishing, 1993. viii, 109p. CtHi. *

685.   BRUNDAGE, LARRY. "Yankee ingenuity: starting from scratch." CEAIA, 44 (Dec. 1991), 99-100.
    Samuel Monce and the development of glass-cutting technology (late-1860s and 1870s).

686.   DOMONELL, WILLIAM G. "A history of copper mining in Bristol." CHSB, 56 (Winter/Spring 1991), 5-37.

687.   EDWARDS, ROBERT S. "Birge & Ives eight-day wood movement OG clock." NAWCCB, 31 (Apr. 1989), 109-113.
    Ca. 1830s.

    SEE ALSO entry 613.

BROOKFIELD (FAIRFIELD CO.)

688.   BROOKFIELD CRAFT CENTER. Brookfield Mills/ Brookfield Craft Center: a continuing heritage, 1780- 1976. Brookfield, 1976. [32]p. CtHi. *

CANAAN (LITCHFIELD CO.)

689.   FELTON, HAROLD W. Canaan: a small Connecticut town during the American Revolutionary War. Falls Village: Bramble, 1990. 162p. DLC. *

    SEE ALSO entry 654.

CANTERBURY (WINDHAM CO.)

690.   STRANE, SUSAN. A whole-souled woman: Prudence Crandall and the education of black women. N.Y.: W.W. Norton, 1990. 278p. CtHi. *
    See additional entries on Crandall in the Connecticut volume and Vol. 8.

    SEE ALSO entry 499.

CANTON (HARTFORD CO.)

691.   SEALAND, EVANS F. JR. "Portrait of a faithful pastor: Jairus Burt (1795-1857)." Bulletin of the Congregational Library, 38 (Fall 1986/Winter 1987), 4- 14.
    Served the Congregational church in Canton Center from 1826-1857.

CHESTER (MIDDLESEX CO.)

692.   DELANEY, EDMUND THOMAS. St. Joseph's Parish: more than a century of faith, Chester and Deep River, Connecticut. Chester: St. Joseph's Church, 1991. 63p. CtHi. *
   Roman Catholic.

CLINTON (MIDDLESEX CO.)

693.   ALLEN, RICHARD SANDERS. "Connecticut iron and steel from Black Sea sands." IA, 18:1-2 (1992), 129- 132.
   On an experiment performed by the Rev. Jared Eliot (ca. 1760).

694.   GRASSO, CHRISTOPHER DANIEL. "The experimental philosophy of farming: Jared Eliot and the cultivation of Connecticut." WMQ, 3 ser. 50 (July 1993), 502-528.
   Eliot (1685-1763), Congregational minister and scientist, was the author of an Essay on field husbandry in New England.

COLCHESTER (NEW LONDON CO.)

695.   GUDRIAN, FRED W. "The Salmon River rock shelter." ArcSocConB, No. 54 (1991), 57-64.
   Prehistoric site.

CORNWALL (LITCHFIELD CO.)

696.   GANNETT, MICHAEL ROSS. The distribution of the common land of Cornwall, Connecticut, 1738-1887. Cornwall: Cornwall Historical Society, 1990. 36p. CtHi. *

COVENTRY (TOLLAND CO.)

697.   WILLIAMS, MARTHA. The history of Boynton's Mill of Coventry, Connecticut. n.p., [1987?]. Unp. Ct. *

CROMWELL (MIDDLESEX CO.)

698.   DECKER, ROBERT OWEN. Cromwell, Connecticut, 1650-1990: the history of a river port town. West Kennebunk, Me.: Phoenix Publishing, 1991. xi, 525p. CtHi. *

DANBURY (FAIRFIELD CO.)

699.   GOLEMBESKI, DEAN J. "Blood brothers." Connecticut, 53 (May 1990), 67-68, 70-75.
   James and John Pardue, remembered for a bank robbery and bombings in 1970 and the latter's failed attempt to escape from jail in 1971.

700.   GREENWALD, RICHARD A. "Work, health and community: Danbury, Connecticut's struggle with an industrial disease." Labor's Heritage, 2 (July 1990), 4-21.
   The disease, among hat workers (ca. 1920s and 1930s), was caused by exposure to a mercury compound.

701.   JANICK, HERBERT F. JR. "From union town to open shop: the decline of the United Hatters of Danbury, Connecticut, 1917-1922." Connecticut History, No. 30 [i.e., 31] (Nov. 1990), 1-20.

702.   SCHLING, DOROTHY T. The untold story: Danbury's unsung role in the Revolution. Danbury: Danbury Tricentennial Committee, 1985. [34]p. CtHi. *

SEE ALSO entry 644.

DEEP RIVER (MIDDLESEX CO.)

703.   SHAYT, DAVID H. "Elephant under glass: the piano key bleach house of Deep River, Connecticut." IA, 19:1 (1993), 37-59.

SEE ALSO entries 713, 655.

EAST HADDAM (MIDDLESEX CO.)

704.   PARKOS, JOSEPH. "The M.R. site: a preliminary report." ArcSocConB, No. 54 (1991), 77-86.
   Prehistoric site in Moodus.

EAST HAMPTON (MIDDLESEX CO.)

705.   FOSTER, SHERRILL. "Reverend Samuel Buell of East Hampton: tastemaker in the Connecticut Valley tradition." CHSB, 54 (Summer/Fall 1989), 189-211.
   18th century.

706   EAST HAVEN

EAST HAVEN (NEW HAVEN CO.)

706.   TOWNSHEND, DORIS B. The streets of East Haven: the origin of their names. [East Haven]: East Haven Historical Society, 1992. 158p. CtNhHi.

EAST LYME (NEW LONDON CO.)

707.   CHENDALI, OLIVE TUBBS. The East Lyme hornbook—the abc's of East Lyme history. (1976) East Lyme: East Lyme Century and a Half Committee, 1989. [84]p. CtHi. *

708.   _____. East Lyme: our town and how it grew. Mystic: Mystic Publications, 1989. x, 184p. CtHi. *

709.   PFEIFFER, JOHN EDWARD, and DONALD MALCARNE. "An investigation into the ancient burial ground at Crescent Beach, Niantic, Connecticut." ArcSocConB, No. 52 (1989), 61-69.
    Prehistoric site. See also entry 1.

EAST WINDSOR (HARTFORD CO.)

710.   MINKEMA, KENNETH PIETER. "Hannah and her sisters: sisterhood, courtship, and marriage in the Edwards family in the early eighteenth century." NEHGR, 146 (Jan. 1992), 35-56.

ENFIELD (HARTFORD CO.)

711.   GWOZDZ, JOHN P. A place of their own: a history of Saint Adalbert Church, Enfield, Connecticut. 1915- 1990. Manchester: Cross Media Publications, 1990. ix, 71p. CtHi. *
    Roman Catholic.

712.   "THE HAZARD Powder Company." Museum of the Fur Trade Quarterly, 27:1-2 (1991), 25-32.
    19th-century manufacturer of gunpowder.

ESSEX (MIDDLESEX CO.)

713.   CONNECTICUT RIVER MUSEUM. From combs to keyboards: the development of a Connecticut River industry. Essex, 1990. 20p. CtHi. *
    Ivory.

SEE ALSO entries 655, 703.

FAIRFIELD (FAIRFIELD CO.)

714.   CIGLIANO, JAN. Southport: the architectural legacy of a Connecticut village. Southport: Southport Conservancy, 1989. 214p. CtHi. *

715.   FARNHAM, THOMAS J. The Oak Lawn Cemetery. Fairfield: Oak Lawn Cemetery Association, 1993. 22p. CtNhHi.

FARMINGTON (HARTFORD CO.)

716.   DAVIS, NANCY, and BARBARA FINLAY DONAHUE. Miss Porter's School: a history. Farmington: Miss Porter's School, 1992. 125p. CtHi. *
    Private school.

717.   DONAHUE, BARBARA FINLAY. Farmington: New England town through time. Farmington: Farmington Land Trust, 1989. 160, [14]p. CtHi. *

718.   McCAIN, DIANA ROSS. "Reconsidering the Stanley-Whitman House." Early American Life, 23 (June 1992), 28-35, 78.
    The house is now thought to have been built ca. 1720 instead of 1660.

719.   STARBUCK, DAVID R. "The Lewis-Walpole site (6-HT-15)." NHArcheol, 32:1 (1991), 73-86.
    Prehistoric site.

720.   WHITE, FRANK G. "The unturning of a screw manufactory." CEAIA, 44 (Sept. 1991), 77-78.
    The "short-lived" Patent Wood Screw Manufacturing Company, of Unionville (1830s).

SEE ALSO entries 212, 547, 574, 589.

FRANKLIN (NEW LONDON CO.)

721.   ROBBINS, MARJORIE B. Franklin bicentennial history, 1786-1986. [Franklin: Bicentennial Committee, 1986] 25p.CtHi. *

GLASTONBURY (HARTFORD CO.)

722.   COOKE, DAVID G. "Adena related burials: Glastonbury, Connecticut." ArcSocConB, No. 52 (1989), 7-16.
    Indian site.

723. DOHERTY, THOMAS E. History of St. Augustine's Church, South Glastonbury, Connecticut, 1877-1977. South Glastonbury: St. Augustine Church, 1977. [12]p. CtHi. *
    Roman Catholic.

724. HOUSLEY, KATHLEEN L. The letter kills but the spirit gives life: the Smiths: abolitionists, suffragists, Bible translators. Glastonbury: Historical Society of Glastonbury, 1993. 234, [4]p. CtHi. *
    Julia and Abby Smith.

725. JODZIEWICZ, THOMAS W. "'A curious soaking rain to night (thanks be to God)': Gershom Bulkeley's 1710 diary." CHSB, 56 (Winter/Spring 1991), 57-88.
    Weather observations in the diary.

726. RICKARD, TIMOTHY J. "Town efforts to preserve agricultural land: a case study in Hartford's urban fringe." NE-StLVGSPr, 17 (1987), 17-26.
    1980s.

GOSHEN (LITCHFIELD CO.)

727. GOSHEN, CONN. QUADRIMILLENNIUM EDITORIAL COMMITTEE. Goshen, Connecticut: a town above all others. West Kennebunk, Me.: Phoenix Publishing, 1990. xii, 274p. CtHi. *

SEE ALSO entry 36.

GRANBY (HARTFORD CO.)

728. LAUN, CAROL, and GLADYS GODARD. Centennial: Frederick H. Cossitt Library, 1891-1991. [North Granby]: Friends of the Cossitt Library, 1991. 52p. CtHi. *

GREENWICH (FAIRFIELD CO.)

729. HISTORICAL SOCIETY OF THE TOWN OF GREENWICH. Greenwich: an illustrated history. A celebration of 350 years. Robert G. Atwan, ed. Cos Cob, 1990. xvi, 193, [7]p. CtHi. *

730. MEAD, EDGAR THORN. Greenwich grows up. Cos Cob: Historical Society of the Town of Greenwich, 1990. 103p.CtHi. *

731. RAY, DEBORAH WING, and GLORIA P. STEWART. Loyal to the land: the history of a Greenwich, Connecticut family. West Kennebunk, Me.: Phoenix Publishing, 1990. xii, 181p. CtHi. *
    Reynolds family.

SEE ALSO entry 649.

GRISWOLD (NEW LONDON CO.)

732. PFEIFFER, JOHN EDWARD. "Hopeville Pond: archaeological evidence of a middle woodland Jack's Reef component in eastern Connecticut." ArcSocConB, No. 56 (1993), 101-114.

GROTON (NEW LONDON CO.)

733. JONES, STEPHEN. Noank: the ethereal years. Noank: Noank Historical Society, 1988. 64p. CtHi. *

734. McCAIN, DIANA ROSS. "Bloody Fort Griswold." Connecticut, 53 (Oct. 1990), 122, 124-127.
    Site of the alleged massacre in 1781 of American defenders after they tried to surrender to an attacking British force under Benedict Arnold.

735. PARNES, STUART L. "The art of Reynolds Beal in Mystic at last." Mystic Seaport, Log, 42 (Summer 1990), 31-36.
    Marine artist (1866-1951), who summered in Noank from 1902-1907.

736. WYLIE, EVAN McLEOD. "'I can't land the plane.'" Yankee, 53 (Apr. 1989), 68-73, 118-119.
    Betty Mohr's safe landing of a private plane in 1987, following the sudden death of the pilot, her husband.

SEE ALSO entry 665.

GUILFORD (NEW HAVEN CO.)

737. ANDERSON, BEVERLY. Foundations: contribution to the design origins of the Henry Whitfield House. n.p., 1991. [11]p. CtHi. *
    17th century.

738. _____. Guilford roots. n.p., 1990. 75, [10]p. CtGu.

739. COMMITTEE FOR GUILFORD ORAL HISTORY. Taking time to remember: an oral history of Guilford. Guilford: Guilford Free Library, 1988. xi, 174p. CtHi. *

740   GUILFORD

740.   GUILFORD, CONN. ELISABETH C. ADAMS MIDDLE
SCHOOL. Guilford's 350th anniversary road ramble.
[Guilford], 1989. 52p. CtGu.
    Historical sketches.

741.   GUILFORD FREE LIBRARY. A Guilford bibliography.
Nona Bloomer, comp. Guilford, 1990. 19p. CtGu.

742.   KAHN, NAOMI. Untold tales of old Guilford. [Guilford:
Guilford 350 Committee, 1989?] [16]p. CtGu.

743.   ST. GEORGE, ROBERT BLAIR. "Bawns and beliefs:
architecture, commerce, and conversation in early New
England." Winterthur Portfolio, 25 (Winter 1990), 241- 287.
    A bawn was a "defensive structure." The article considers
evidence of a plan for an enclosed farm, "drawn and built
by Bray Rossiter in Guilford...between 1652 and...1660."

HADDAM (MIDDLESEX CO.)

744.   JOHNSON, TIMOTHY LEONARD. "Focusing attention on
the 'Mission Friends' heritage of the Haddam Neck Covenant
Church." D.Min. dissertation, Hartford Seminary, 1991. 80p. *
    Evangelical Covenant church. Abstracted in DAI, 51:5A
(1990), 1772.

HAMDEN (NEW HAVEN CO.)

745.   LAHEY, JOHN L. Quinnipiac College: an educational leader
in business, health and liberal arts. N.Y.: Newcomen Society
of the U.S., 1991. 20p. CtHi. *

SEE ALSO entry 659.

HAMPTON (WINDHAM CO.)

746.   ROBERTSON, JAMES OLIVER, and JANET C.
ROBERTSON. All our yesterdays: a century of life in an
American small town. N.Y.: Harper-Collins Publishers, 1993.
512p. CtS. *

HARTFORD (HARTFORD CO.)

747.   BANNER, JAMES M. JR. "A shadow of secession?: the
Hartford Convention, 1814." History Today, 38 (Sept. 1988),
24-30.

748.   BAROL, BILL. "The army Colt." American Heritage, 41
(Mar. 1990), 28.
    Colt revolver, used by the Union army during the Civil
War.

749.   BERMAN, AVIS. "Mr. Wadsworth's museum." American
Heritage, 43 (Sept. 1992), 100-103.
    Daniel Wadsworth and the Wadsworth Atheneum.

750.   CIMINO, D. C. (Architects/Planners). Development plan:
Connecticut State Capitol, June, 1983. Hartford, [1983?]. 86,
7, 7, 3p. CtWillE.
    Includes historical information.

751.   CLOUETTE, BRUCE ALAN. "'Getting their share': Irish
and Italian immigrants in Hartford, Connecticut, 1850-1940."
Ph.D. dissertation, Univ. of Connecticut, 1992. xvi, 379p.
CtHi. *
    Abstracted in DAI, 53:8A (1993), 2950.

752.   _____. "Irish-Americans in Hartford city politics,
1850-1900." Connecticut History, No. 34 (Spring 1993),
36-51.

753.   COHN, HENRY S., and DAVID BOLLIER. The great
Hartford Circus Fire: creative settlement of mass disasters.
New Haven: Yale Univ. Pr., 1991. xxi, 207p. CtU. *
    1944 disaster and its legal aftermath.

754.   COLLINGWOOD, DERYCK C. "Growing towards
greatness—Thomas Hooker." Connecticut Nutmegger, 23
(June 1990), 4-15; (Sept. 1990), 196-207.
    Hooker's early years in England. See also entry 100.

755.   CONNECTICUT. GENERAL ASSEMBLY. The State
Capitol: Hartford, Connecticut, 1879-1988. Hartford, 1988.
[24]p. CtHi.

756.   CONNECTICUT HUMANITIES COUNCIL. Twain/Stowe
sourcebook: curriculum resource materials for the study of
Mark Twain and Harriet Beecher Stowe. Elaine Cheesman
and Earl French, eds. Middletown, 1989. 157p. CtB. *

757.   "THE CONNECTICUT captivity of Major Christopher
French." CHSB, 55 (Summer/Fall 1990), 125-232.
    During the American Revolution.

758.   DARDENNE, ROBERT WARD. "Newstelling: story and
themes in 'The Courant' of Hartford from 1765 to 1945."
Ph.D. dissertation, Univ. of Iowa, 1990. viii, 534p. *
    Newspaper. Abstracted in DAI, 52:3A (1991), 721.

759.   DUFFY, JOSEPH W. "Images of Hartford's Irish-Catholic
community: 1827-1867." Connecticut History, No. 30 [i.e.,
31] (Nov. 1990), 21-32.

760. EDWARDS, ROBERT LANSING. Of singular genius, of singular grace: a biography of Horace Bushnell. Cleveland: Pilgrim Pr., 1992. xi, 405p. CtHi. *

The noted Congregational minister and theologian (lived 1802-1876).

761. GALE, NAHUM. Memoir of Rev. Bennet Tyler, D.D., late president and professor of Christian theology in the Theological Institute of Connecticut. Boston: J.E. Tilton, 1860. 149p. CtHi. *

762. HALL, ELTON W. "Edwin Valentine Mitchell." CHSB, 52 (Spring 1987), 103-111.

Mitchell (1890-1960), an author and publisher of New England antiquarian books, was also the proprietor of a Hartford bookstore.

763. HARTFORD PUBLIC LIBRARY. Hartford Public Library: 100 years. [Hartford, 1993]. [44]p. CtHi. *

764. HODDER, ALAN D. "In the glasse of God's word: Hooker's pulpit rhetoric and the theater of conversion." NEQ, 66 (Jan. 1993), 67-109.

The Rev. Thomas Hooker.

765. JANSEN, RAYMOND A. The Hartford Courant: older than a nation. N.Y.: Newcomen Society of the U.S., 1992. 24p. CtHi. *

Newspaper.

766. JONES, TRUDY K. "'Give the tramp a chance!'" Antiquarian and Landmarks Society, The Landmark (Fall 1992), 5-9.

The Rev. John James McCook and his late-19th-century studies of homeless men.

767. _____. "Hartford's Bushnell Park: antidote to urban ills." Connecticut Antiquarian, 41 (Fall 1990), 11-21.

The park was renamed for Horace Bushnell in 1876.

768. KAPLAN, JUSTIN. "Mr. Clemens at home: the curious house that Mark Twain built." Art & Antiques (Apr. 1989), 62-67.

769. LAZARUS, BARRY A. "The practice of medicine and prejudice in a New England town: the founding of Mount Sinai Hospital, Hartford, Connecticut." Journal of American Ethnic History, 10 (Spring 1991), 21-41.

770. MAHONEY, MARGARET WARD. "Catharine Beecher: champion of female intellectual potential in nineteenth-century America." Ph.D. dissertation, Drew Univ., 1993. 284p.

Educator and reformer (lived 1800-1878). Abstracted in DAI, 54:6A (1993), 2198.

771. MAKOWSKI, LEE JOSEPH. "Horace Bushnell: a study of his sermons from the perspective of his Christian anthropolgy." Ph.D. dissertation, Catholic Univ. of America, 1992. ii, 235p. *

Abstracted in DAI, 53:10A (1993), 3570.

772. MARK Twain's Hartford connections: the inaugural exhibition of the Mark Twain Memorial program at Trinity College, October 7, 1991-January 31, 1992, in the Watkinson Library. Hartford: Watkinson Library, 1991. 19p. CtHi. *

773. MARLATT, ANDREW. "Huck Finn wouldn't have come near it." Yankee, 56 (Oct. 1992), 34-39.

Mark Twain House.

774. McCAIN, DIANA ROSS. "Spreading the news." Early American Life, 21 (Oct. 1990), 6-8, 16-17.

Early years of the Connecticut Courant (newspaper).

775. MURPHY, JANET T. "Union for Home Work: a study of nineteenth-century Hartford philanthropy." CHSB, 55 (Winter/Spring 1992), 83-114.

Women's organization.

776. PALM, CHRISTINE. Eyes in the mind: a century at Oak Hill School. [Hartford]: Connecticut Institute for the Blind/Oak Hill, 1993. 99p. CtHi. *

School for the blind.

777. PETERSON, KARIN E. "Butler-McCook talent: four generations of artists." Connecticut Antiquarian, 40 (Summer 1989), 12-16.

See also next entry.

778. _____. "A survey of the paintings in the Butler- McCook Homestead." Connecticut Antiquarian, 40 (Summer 1989), 3-10.

See also preceding entry.

779. PRATT AND WHITNEY COMPANY. In the company of Eagles: 65 years in the forefront of flight propulsion. Hartford, 1990. 63p. CtHi. *

780. RAMSEY, GORDON CLARK. "Skinner's organ, opus 793: a unique masterpiece." Connecticut Antiquarian, 41 (Fall 1990), 3-9.

The organ was installed in the Second Church of Christ, Scientist, in 1930; restoration was begun in 1989.

781. RANSOM, DAVID F. "Biographical dictionary of Hartford architects." CHSB, 54 (Winter/Spring 1989), 9- 160.

782. STANKAITIS, ALFONSAS P. "A short history of Holy Trinity Church." Lituanus, 37 (Fall 1991), 82-93.

Roman Catholic (Lithuanian parish).

783   HARTFORD

783.   STEINWAY, KATE. "The Kelloggs of Hartford: Connecticut's Currier & Ives." Imprint, 13 (Spring 1988), 2-12.
        19th-century lithographers.

784.   STRONG, LEAH A. Joseph Hopkins Twichell: Mark Twain's friend and pastor. Athens: Univ. of Georgia Pr., 1966. x, 182p. CtHi. *
        Congregational minister (lived 1838-1918).

785.   TALCOTT, MARY DUDLEY VAILL. The Hartford diaries of Mary Dudley Vaill Talcott (Mrs. Charles Hooker Talcott) from 1896-1919. Avon, 1990. 4v. CtHi. *

786.   TIPSON, BAIRD. "Samuel Stone's 'discourse' against requiring church relations." WMQ, 3 ser. 46, (Oct. 1989), 786-799.
        Stone opposed the requirement of a "'personall & publick confession, & declaration of Gods maneur of working upon the soul'" as a prerequisite for church membership. Stone lived 1602-1663.

787.   UNION SETTLEMENT OF HARTFORD. Serving for 75 years: the Union Settlement of Hartford, 1872-1947. Hartford, 1947. 12p. CtHi.
        Social settlement.

788.   VALENTINE, PHYLLIS KLEIN. "A nineteenth-century experiment in education for the handicapped: the American Asylum for the Deaf and Dumb." NEQ, 64 (Sept. 1991), 355-375.

789.   WAIT, GARY ERNEST. "Julia Brace." Dartmouth College Library Bulletin, 33 (Nov. 1992), 2-10.
        Brace (1807-1884), "the first deaf-blind person in America to receive instruction," was a student and a longtime resident at the Hartford (now American) Asylum for the Deaf and Dumb.

790.   _____. Lydia Sigourney: philanthropist. Hartford, 1993. 16p. CtHi. *
        The poet and author lived 1791-1865.

791.   WALTMAN, IRVING. "Nathan Mayer: 19th century surgeon and drama critic." Connecticut Jewish History, 1 (Summer 1990), 69-78.
        Lived 1838-1912.

792.   WATSON, ALEXANDER M. The treasure which is ours: a cultural and historic perspective on the Imanuel Congregational Church building, Hartford, Connecticut. Hartford: Imanuel Congregational Church, 1990. vi, 35p. CtHi. *

793.   WEAVER, GLENN, and J. BARD McNULTY. An evolving concern: technology, safety and the Hartford Steam Boiler Company, 1866-1991. Hartford: Hartford Steam Boiler Inspection and Insurance Co., 1991. 168p. CtHi. *
        Note: this item replaces entry 4942 in the Connecticut volume.

794.   WELLES, GIDEON. "Gideon Welles's diary—1854." CHSB, 55 (Winter/Spring 1990), 5-67.
        Gary E. Wait, ed. Welles, who would later serve as secretary of the navy during the Civil War, was a newspaperman when the diary was written.

795.   WILSON, TRACEY MORGAN. "From assembly line to steno pool: women workers at Colt's Firearms and the Travelers Insurance Company, 1910-1955." Ph.D. dissertation, Brown Univ., 1993. 282p.
        Abstracted in DAI, 54:10A (1994), 3859.

        SEE ALSO entries 100, 506, 536, 540, 561, 587.

HEBRON (TOLLAND CO.)

796.   HEBRON TRICENTENNIAL COMMISSION. Hebron's historic heritage: a selection of historic sites. Hebron, 1992. [15]p. CtHi. *

KENT (LITCHFIELD CO.)

797.   POWERS, RON. Far from home: life and loss in two American towns. N.Y.: Random House, 1991. xi, 317p. CtU. *
        Contemporary life in Kent and in Cairo, Ill. Includes historical information.

LEBANON (NEW LONDON CO.)

798.   WEEKS, CHRISTOPHER. "Revolutionary village." American Heritage, 40 (Apr. 1989), 80-90.
        As the hometown of Gov. Jonathan Trumbull, Lebanon was the scene of much governmental activity during the American Revolution.

LEDYARD (NEW LONDON CO.)

799.   CLARK, JANET W. Geer Hill School: a history of the smallest one room school in Connecticut. Storrs: I. N. Thut World Education Center, School of Education, Univ. of Connecticut, 1983. 23p. CtHi. *

800. OLIVER, SANDRA L. "The Burrows brothers and johnny cake." Mystic Seaport, Log, 46 (Summer 1994), 21-22.
  See also entry 945.

LITCHFIELD (LITCHFIELD CO.)

801. SIZER, THEODORE, and NANCY SIZER. To ornament their minds: Sarah Pierce's Litchfield Female Academy, 1792-1833. Catherine Keene Fields and Lisa C. Kightlinger, eds. Litchfield: Litchfield Historical Society, 1993. 132p. CtNhHi. *

SEE ALSO entries 217-218, 494, 627.

LYME (NEW LONDON CO.)

802. CAVE, ALFRED A. "Who killed John Stone?: a note on the origins of the Pequot War." WMQ, 3 ser. 49 (July 1992), 509-521.

SEE ALSO entries 663, 666.

MANCHESTER (HARTFORD CO.)

803. SUTHERLAND, JOHN F. "'One loom or no looms!': the Cheney velvet weavers' strike of 1902 and the limits of paternalism." Connecticut History, No. 33 (Nov. 1992), 1-37.

SEE ALSO entry 38.

MANSFIELD (TOLLAND CO.)

804. SMITH, ROBERTA K. The Constant years: the life of Constant Southworth. [Mansfield]: Mansfield Historical Society, 1990. 68p. CtHi. *
  Lived 1730-1813.

SEE ALSO entry 608.

MARLBOROUGH (HARTFORD CO.)

805. FOWLER, JANET. A history of education in a small Connecticut town: Marlborough, Connecticut. Storrs: I. N. Thut World Education Center, School of Education, Univ. of Connecticut, 1984. iv, 38p. CtHi. *

MERIDEN (NEW HAVEN CO.)

806. BLEJWAS, STANISLAUS A. St. Stanislaus B. & M. Parish, Meriden, Connecticut: a century of Connecticut Polonia, 1891-1991. New Britain: Central Connecticut State Univ., 1991. xvi, 215p. CtNbC. *
  Roman Catholic.

MIDDLETOWN (MIDDLESEX CO.)

807. HARRINGTON, KARL POMEROY. A history of the Xi chapter of the Psi Upsilon fraternity. Middletown: Xi Corporation, 1935. 203p. CtHi. *
  At Wesleyan Univ.

808. HOSLEY, WILLIAM. "The Wetmore parlor and eighteenth-century Middletown, Connecticut." Antiques, 139 (Mar. 1991), 586-597.
  Parlor from the Seth Wetmore House, now in the Wadsworth Atheneum, Hartford.

809. KRUEGER, GLEE. "Mary Wright Alsop, 1740-1829, and her needlework." CHSB, 53 (Summer/Fall 1987), 125-137.
  Article is followed by exhibition catalog (pp. 140-223).

810. POTTS, DAVID BRONSON. Wesleyan University, 1831-1910: collegiate enterprise in New England. New Haven: Yale Univ. Pr., 1992. xvii, 383p. CtHi. *

811. SHERROW, DORIS. "Murder in Middletown: lower-class life in Connecticut in 1815." DubSemPr (1988), 38-47.
  Murder of Lucy Kelley Lung by her husband, Peter.

812. SILVESTRINI, MARC. "Nightmare on Main Street." Connecticut, 56 (June 1993), 64-69.
  Public reaction to the 1989 killing of a local child by an escaped mental patient.

813. WARNER, ELIZABETH ANN. A pictorial history of Middletown. Norfolk, Va.: Donning, 1990. 200p. CtHi. *

814. THE WESLEYAN tradition: four decades of American poetry. Michael Collier, ed. Hanover, N.H.: University Pr. of New England, 1993. xxxix, 276p. CtU. *
  Wesleyan Univ. poetry program.

815   MILFORD

MILFORD (NEW HAVEN CO.)

815.   ONLY in Milford: an illustrated history. Volume One.
DeForest W. Smith, ed. Milford: George J. Smith & Son,
1989. 189p. CtHi. *

MONTVILLE (NEW LONDON CO.)

816.   GRANDJEAN, PAT. "The elder." Connecticut, 55 (Aug.
1992), 92-97.
Biographical sketch of Gladys Tantaquidgeon (born
1899), "cultural guardian and spiritual leader of the
Mohegan nation."

817.   VOIGHT, VIRGINIA FRANCES. Mohegan chief: the story
of Harold Tantaquidgeon. N.Y.: Funk & Wagnalls, 1965.
192p. Ct. *
20th-century tribal leader. This item was reprinted in
1983.

NEW BRITAIN (HARTFORD CO.)

818.   LARSON, KENNETH A. In the spirit of the Nightingale: the
history of the New Britain General Hospital School of
Nursing. New Britain: New Britain General Hospital School
of Nursing Alumni Association, 1992. 126p. CtHi. *

SEE ALSO entry 557.

NEW CANAAN (FAIRFIELD CO.)

819.   HUIDEKOPER, PETER G. "Weed & Duryea update." New
Canaan Historical Society Annual, 10 (1988-1989), 27- 28.
Dealer in building materials and other retail items.

820.   KING, MARY LOUISE. "New Canaan and the Merritt
Parkway." New Canaan Historical Society Annual, 11
(1990-1991), 10-16.
See also related articles under heading of Fairfield
County.

821.   _____. "One hundred years, 1889-1989." New Canaan
Historical Society Annual, 10 (1988-1989), 2-10.
Centennial of the historical society.

822.   MERRITT, MARGARET C. "Jelliff Mill." New Canaan
Historical Society Annual, 10 (1988-1989), 11-16.
Reprint of an article in the New Canaan Advertiser
(1933). See also entry 824.

823.   SWEET, JOSEPH C. "Johnson's carriage works and garage."
New Canaan Historical Society Annual, 10 (1988-1989),
29-39.

824.   WAGNER, KATHY. "Jelliff Mill update." New Canaan
Historical Society Annual, 10 (1988-1989), 17-19.
Currently used for carpentry and mill work. See also
entry 822.

NEW FAIRFIELD (FAIRFIELD CO.)

825.   NEW FAIRFIELD HISTORICAL SOCIETY. Pictorial
history of New Fairfield, Connecticut, 1740-1990. New
Fairfield, 1990. 96p. CtHi. *

NEW HAVEN (NEW HAVEN CO.)

826.   ANNUNZIATO, FRANK R. "'Made in New Haven':
unionization and the shaping of a clothing workers'
community." Labor's Heritage, 4 (Winter 1992), 20-33.

827.   BASS, PAUL. "Hidden history: New Haven finds a new
past." Progressive, 54 (July 1990), 28-29.
History of women garment workers in New Haven.

828.   BRODY, LISA R. "Yale College in the 19th century: an
archaeological perspective." ArcSocConB, No. 56 (1993),
3-24.

829.   BROPHY, WILLIAM S. Marlin Firearms: a history of the
guns and the company that made them. Harrisburg, Pa.:
Stackpole Books, 1989. viii, 696p. CtNhHi. *

830.   BROWN, CHANDOS MICHAEL. Benjamin Silliman: a life
in the young republic. Princeton, N.J.: Princeton Univ. Pr.,
1989. xvi, 377p. CtHi. *
The noted scientist lived 1779-1864. See also this
author's Ph.D. dissertation of same title (Harvard Univ.,
1987; entry 601 in Vol. 8).

831.   CAMPBELL, JAMES W. "We are not the first to sail these
waters": incidents in the maritime history of New Haven.
New Haven, 1993. 24p. CtNhHi.

832.   CAPPEL, ANDREW J. "A walk along Willow: patterns of
land use coordination in pre-zoning New Haven." Yale Law
Journal, 101 (Dec. 1991), 617-642.

833.   CASSAGNERES, EVERETT. Tweed-New Haven Airport:
60th anniversary celebration, Sept. 8, 1991. [New Haven],
1991. [16]p. CtNhHi.

834.   DAVENPORT, JOHN BRIAN. "'Yours unfeignedly in the Lord': the theology of John Davenport (1597-1670) and its context." Ph.D. dissertation, Univ. of Minnesota, 1994. viii, 274p. *
    Puritan minister. Abstracted in DAI, 54:12A (1994), 4562.

835.   DOBROW, JOE. "A farewell to arms: Winchester Repeating Arms Company and New Haven, Connecticut." NHCHSJ, 39 (Spring 1993), 20-64.

836.   EMMEL, STEPHEN. "Antiquity in fragments: a hundred years of collecting papyri at Yale." Yale University Library Gazette, 64 (Oct. 1989), 38-58.

837.   FAHLMAN, BETSY. "Art displays in New Haven: Edward Sheffield Bartholomew and Yale's exhibition of 1858." NHCHSJ, 38 (Fall 1991), 27-45.

838.   _____. "The city beautiful in the city of elms: the Bennett Memorial Fountain by John Ferguson Weir." NHCHSJ, 39 (Spring 1993), 3-19.
    The fountain, designed in 1906-1907, is on the New Haven Green.

839.   FARNHAM, THOMAS J. Southern Connecticut State University: a centennial history, 1893-1993. New Haven: Southern Connecticut State Univ., 1993. xiv, 278p. CtNhHi. *

840.   GALLUP, DONALD CLIFFORD. "Pigeons is people." Yale University Library Gazette, 63 (Oct. 1988), 54-70.
    See also next entry.

841.   _____. Pigeons on the granite: memories of a Yale librarian. New Haven: Beinecke Rare Book and Manuscript Library, Yale Univ., 1988. 353p. CtY. *
    Gallup was curator of the American literature collection.

842.   GALPIN, VIRGINIA M. New Haven's oyster industry, 1638-1987. New Haven: New Haven Colony Historical Society, 1989. 78p. CtHi. *

843.   _____. "New Haven's seascape, 1815-1900, and the relationship between steam packets and trains." NHCHSJ, 37 (Fall 1990), 25-48.

844.   GIBSON, ROBERT A. "A deferred dream: the proposal for a Negro college in New Haven, 1831." NHCHSJ, 37 (Spring 1991), 22-29.

845.   HARROLD, MICHAEL C. "The New Haven watch of S.T.J. Byam." NAWCCB, 33 (Oct. 1991), 499-509.
    Manufactured during the 1880s.

846.   HEGEL, RICHARD. "Veterans and war memorials and monuments in the city of New Haven, Connecticut." NHCHSJ, 37 (Spring 1991), 31-43.

847.   HERMAN, BARRY E. "New Haven's Maier Zunder: nineteenth-century educational and community leader." NHCHSJ, 39 (Fall 1992), 25-32.
    1829-1901.

848.   "THE HILL Health Center: two decades—and growing." Yale Medicine, 23 (Summer 1989), 4-7.

849.   HOGAN, NEIL. "The actual enumeration: New Haven and the U.S. Census." NHCHSJ, 38 (Fall 1991), 2-17.
    On census counts in New Haven through the years.

850.   _____. Wearin o' the green: St. Patrick's Day in New Haven, 1842-1992. [New Haven?]: Connecticut Irish-American Historical Society, 1992. 234p. CtHi. *

851.   HUMPHREY, DANIEL CRAIG. "Teach them not to be poor: philanthropy and New Haven school reform in the 1960s." Ed.D. dissertation, Columbia Univ. Teachers College, 1992. 238p.
    Abstracted in DAI, 54:8A (1994), 2918.

852.   KAGAN, MYRNA. Vision in the sky: New Haven's early years, 1638-1783. [Hamden]: Linnet Books, 1989. xiii, 161p. CtNhHi. *

853.   KING, CAROL. "Two New Haven Loyalists: Abiathar Camp, Sr., and Abiathar Camp, Jr." NHCHSJ, 39 (Fall 1992), 3-12.
    American Revolution.

854.   KOEL, OTTILIA. A guide to the manuscripts and archives in the Whitney Library of the New Haven Colony Historical Society. New Haven: New Haven Colony Historical Society, 1988. 90p. CtNhHi. *

855.   KUTZ, CHRISTOPHER. Democracy in New Haven: a history of the Board of Aldermen, 1638-1988. New Haven: Office of Legislative Services, 1988. 77, [8]p. CtHi. *

856.   LANTUCH, KATHERINE A. "The origin of New Haven's Nine Squares." NHCHSJ, 37 (Spring 1991), 7-21.

857.   LEBOW, KATHERINE A. "Education and the immigrant experience: an oral history of working women and men of New Haven." NHCHSJ, 40 (Fall 1993), 14-46.

858.   LEVY, FRANK. "Confidence in post-Revolutionary New Haven." NHCHSJ, 36 (Fall 1989), 3-24.

859   NEW HAVEN

859.   LOWET, JONATHAN G. "The elms of the Elm City."
NHCHSJ, 38 (Fall 1991), 47-63.

860.   MININBERG, MARK J. Saving New Haven: John W.
Murphy faces the crisis of the Great Depression. New Haven:
Fine Arts Publications, [1988]. 92p. CtHi. *
      Longtime mayor, first elected in 1931.

861.   MORRIS, WILLIAM SPARKES. "The young Jonathan
Edwards." Ph.D. dissertation, Univ. of Chicago, 1955. xxxvii,
906p. *
      Study of Edwards's intellectual development between
1720 and 1726, during much of which time he was at Yale,
first as a graduate student and later as a tutor. See also next
entry.

862.   _____. The young Jonathan Edwards: a reconstruction.
Brooklyn, N.Y.: Carlson Pub., 1991. xvi, 688p. CtU. *
      See also preceding entry.

863.   NEW HAVEN, CONN. POLICE DEPARTMENT. SPECIAL
PROJECTS COMMITTEE. Brief history of law enforcement
in New Haven. [New Haven, 1989] [26]p. CtNhHi.

864.   PURMONT, JON EMMETT. "Student protest in Connecticut
colleges and universities, 1701-1870: Yale College as a case
study." Ed.D. dissertation, Columbia Univ. Teachers College,
1988. ii, 153p.
      Abstracted in DAI, 49:9A (1989), 2559.

865.   RIEKE, ALISON. "Stevens in Corsica, Lear in New Haven."
NEQ, 63 (Mar. 1990), 35-59.
      Wallace Stevens's borrowing from nineteenth-century
travel writings by Edward Lear in his 1949 poem, "An
ordinary evening in New Haven."

866.   SCHMITT, DALE J. "Community and the spoken word: a
seventeenth-century case." Journal of American Culture, 13
(Summer 1990), 51-55.
      Court case involving a charge of slander.

867.   SEWALL, RICHARD B. "An unofficial tour of Yale."
American Heritage, 42 (Mar. 1991), 88-102.
      Includes historical information.

868.   SHEN, XIAO HONG. "Yale's China and China's Yale:
Americanizing higher education in China, 1900-1927." Ph.D.
dissertation, Yale Univ., 1993. 373p.
      Abstracted in DAI, 54:12A (1994), 4492.

869.   SHUMWAY, E. J., FLOYD MALLORY SHUMWAY, and
DORIS B. TOWNSHEND. The First Church of Christ in
New Haven: a membership album. New Haven: [First
Church of Christ], 1993. 57p. CtNhHi. *

870.   SHUMWAY, FLOYD MALLORY. "The founders of New
Haven." Connecticut Nutmegger, 22 (Mar. 1990), 580-592.

871.   _____. "What Benjamin Franklin did for New Haven."
NHCHSJ, 38 (Fall 1991), 19-26.
      Franklin's ownership of a printing office.

872.   _____, and RICHARD HEGEL. "The first century of the
Greater New Haven Chamber of Commerce, 1794-1894."
NHCHSJ, 40 (Spring 1994), 3-29.

873.   _____. "The Mary Wade Home: the first 125 years."
NHCHSJ, 38 (Spring 1992), 3-42.
      Founded in 1866 as the "Home for the Friendless."

874.   _____. "New Haven's two creeks." NHCHSJ, 37 (Fall 1990),
13-23.
      East Creek and West Creek.

875.   _____. "On the campaign trail: Abraham Lincoln's visit to
New Haven." NHCHSJ, 39 (Fall 1992), 13-24.
      March 1860.

876.   SUMMERS, MARY E., and PHILIP A. KLINKNER. "The
Daniels election in New Haven and the failure of the
deracialization hypothesis." Urban Affairs Quarterly, 27
(Dec. 1991), 202-215.
      Election of black candidate John Daniels as mayor in
1989.

877.   SUTTON, WILLIAM R. "Benevolent Calvinism and the
moral government of God: the influence of Nathaniel W.
Taylor on revivalism in the Second Great Awakening."
Religion and American Culture: a Journal of Interpretation, 2
(Winter 1992), 23-47.
      Theologian Taylor (lived 1786-1858) and the New Haven
theology.

878.   TODD, GILLIEN. "School desegregation and the decline of
liberalism: New Haven, Connecticut, in 1964." Connecticut
History, No. 30 (Nov. 1989), 1-40.

879.   TROUT, AMY L., and JULIE PONESSA SALATHE. "A
brief introduction to the maritime history of New Haven."
NHCHSJ, 37 (Fall 1990), 3-12.

880.   WARREN, LINDSEY DAVIS. "Invention in the Lyman
Beecher Lectures on Preaching, 1958-1988." Ph.D.
dissertation, Univ. of Oklahoma, 1991. viii, 246p. *
      Lectures at Yale. Abstracted in DAI, 52:10A (1992),
3477-3478.

881.   WIEDERSHEIM, WILLIAM A. "The Harugari Singing
Society: German-American ethnicity in New Haven."
NHCHSJ, 39 (Fall 1992), 33-42.
        Founded in 1875.

882.   WILLIAMS, GRAY JR. "The Center Church crypt of New
Haven, Connecticut." Markers IX [1992], 79-103.

883.   WILLIAMS, MEREDITH M., and GRAY WILLIAMS JR.
"Md. by Thos. Gold: the gravestones of a New Haven
carver." Markers V [1988], 1-59.

884.   WITTEN, LAURENCE C. II. "Vinland's saga recalled."
Yale University Library Gazette, 64 (Oct. 1989), 11-37.
        The author's involvement in the 1965 publication by Yale
of the Vinland Map.

        SEE ALSO entries 71, 153, 237, 274, 371, 409, 509, 517,
543, 546, 547, 659, 574, 576, 589, 609, 614, 618, 633, 635,
2050.

NEW LONDON (NEW LONDON CO.)

885.   CALABRETTA, FRED. "The picture of Antoine DeSant:
focusing on New London's black maritime history." Mystic
Seaport, Log, 44 (Spring 1993), 93-95.
        DeSant (ca. 1815-1886), a Cape Verdean, was a
whaleman and later a New London businessman.

886.   GONZALEZ, JOSE B. "Homecoming: O'Neill's New
London in Long day's journey into night." NEQ, 66 (Sept.
1993), 450-457.
        Eugene O'Neill.

887.   GORDINIER, GLENN S. "Autonomy, politics, and embargo
in New London, Connecticut, 1807-1809." American
Neptune, 52 (Summer 1992), 180-186.

888.   JULI, HAROLD D., and MARC A. KELLEY. "The
excavation of a human burial along the Thames River,
southeastern Connecticut." ArcSocConB, No. 54 (1991),
3-11.
        Prehistoric site.

889.   MENDENHALL, THOMAS CORWIN. The Harvard-Yale
boat race, 1852-1924, and the coming of sport to the
American college. Mystic: Mystic Seaport Museum, 1993.
xi, 371p. MBAt. *
        Most of the races in the series have been held at New
London.

890.   STOUT, BRYAN C. "Giles George Hempstead—lost at sea."
Connecticut Antiquarian, 41 (Winter 1990), 3-9.
        Lived 1826-1846.

        SEE ALSO entries 660-661.

NEW MILFORD (LITCHFIELD CO.)

891.   KORNHAUSER, ELIZABETH MANKIN. "'By your
inimitable hand': Elijah Boardman's patronage of Ralph
Earl." American Art Journal, 23:1 (1991), 5-19.

        SEE ALSO entries 579-582.

892.   LAVIN, LUCIANNE, and LAURIE MIROFF. "Aboriginal
pottery from the Indian Ridge site, New Milford,
Connecticut." ArcSocConB, No. 55 (1992), 39-61.

893.   PECK, HOWARD. Howard Peck's New Milford: memories
of a Connecticut town. James E. Dibble, ed. West Kennebunk,
Me.: Phoenix Publishing, 1991. xii, 189p. CtHi. *

NEWINGTON (HARTFORD CO.)

894.   BUTTERWORTH, KENNETH W. The Loctite story. N.Y.:
Newcomen Society of the U.S., 1988. 24p. CtHi. *
        Manufacturer of chemicals. See also entry 7629 in the
Connecticut volume.

NEWTOWN (FAIRFIELD CO.)

895.   HERZOG, ARTHUR. The woodchipper murder. N.Y.: Henry
Holt, 1989. viii, 274p. CtHi. *
        1986 murder of Helle Crafts, for which her husband
stood trial.

896.   WISMAR, GREGORY JUST. "A parish portrait: Christ the
King Lutheran Church." D.Min. dissertation, Hartford
Seminary, 1990. 144p. *
        "First thirty years." Abstracted in DAI, 52:6A (1991),
2171.

        SEE ALSO entry 562.

897   NORFOLK

NORFOLK (LITCHFIELD CO.)

897.   ROBINSON, GLYNNE. "A town that looked just so."
American Heritage, 40 (July/Aug. 1989), 92-99.
    Marie Kendall's photographs of Norfolk (late-19th
century).

NORTH HAVEN (NEW HAVEN CO.)

898.   GERMAN, JAMES DALE. "The preacher and the New
Light revolution in Connecticut: the pulpit theology of
Benjamin Trumbull, 1760-1800." Ph.D. dissertation, Univ. of
California, Riverside, 1989. vii, 315p. *
    Abstracted in DAI, 50:8A (1990), 2620.

NORWALK (FAIRFIELD CO.)

899.   BOAS, NORMAN FRANCIS. "The wreck of the
Lexington." HF, 28 (May 1991), 1, 10-11.
    1840 steamboat disaster off Eaton Neck.

900.   LAST drift: oral histories of Connecticut's last commercial
windship sailors. Norwalk: Seaport Association, [1988?]. 8v.
CtHi. *
    Transcripts of interviews.

901.   RAYMOND, FRANK E. Rowayton on the half shell: the
history of a Connecticut coastal village. West Kennebunk,
Me.: Phoenix Publishing, 1990. xi, 221p. CtHi. *

    SEE ALSO entries 6, 644, 649.

NORWICH (NEW LONDON CO.)

902.   FITCH, JOHN T. Puritan in the wilderness: a biography of
the Reverend James Fitch, 1622-1702. Camden, Me.: Picton
Pr., 1993. xvi, 319p. CtNhHi. *

903.   JOHANESSEN, TED. "Thanksgiving at the front." Tidings
(Nov./Dec. 1992), 842-851.
    For Connecticut troops (1864), provided by Norwich
residents.

    SEE ALSO entries 517, 609.

OLD LYME (NEW LONDON CO.)

904.   ELY, SUSAN H., and ELIZABETH B. PLIMPTON. The
Lieutenant River. Old Lyme: Lyme Historical Society, 1991.
71p. CtHi. *

    SEE ALSO entries 663, 666.

PLAINFIELD (WINDHAM CO.)

905.   McCAIN, DIANA ROSS. "Perkins' amazing tractors."
Connecticut, 53 (May 1990), 143-147.
    Dr. Elisha Perkins (1741-1799) claimed that his invention
could cure many diseases.

PLYMOUTH (LITCHFIELD CO.)

906.   BAROL, BILL. "The pillar-and-scroll clock." American
Heritage, 40 (Apr. 1990), 24-25.
    Made by Eli Terry.

POMFRET (WINDHAM CO.)

907.   DAYTON, CORNELIA HUGHES. "Taking the trade:
abortion and gender relations in an eighteenth-century New
England village." WMQ, 3 ser. 48 (Jan. 1991), 19-49.
    1742 incident.

908.   PEARSON, BRAD. The spirit that is Pomfret. Emerson
Stone, executive ed. n.p.: Kashino Design Enterprises, 1993.
xii, 324p. CtPom.
    Centennial history of Pomfret School (private school).

RIDGEFIELD (FAIRFIELD CO.)

909.   BEDINI, SILVIO A. "A skirmish in America: a rare etching
and the battle of Ridgefield." CHSB, 52 (Spring 1987),
61-102.
    The etching, by an unknown artist, was published in
London in 1780, three years after the battle.

910.   BIAGIOTTI, ALDO P. Impact: the historical account of the
Italian immigrants of Ridgefield, Connecticut. Ridgefield:
Romald Pr., 1990. 345p. CtHi. *

911.   NAUMANN, FRANCIS M. "Man Ray and America: the
New York and Ridgefield years: 1907-1921." Ph.D.
dissertation, City Univ. of New York, 1988. 856p.
    The noted photographer (lived 1890-1976). Abstracted in
DAI, 52:10A (1992), 3461.

ROCKY HILL (HARTFORD CO.)

912.   BELLANTONI, NICHOLAS FRANK. "Two prehistoric human skeletal remains from the Morgan site, Rocky Hill, Connecticut." ArcSocConB, No. 54 (1991), 13-20.

913.   LAVIN, LUCIANNE, and FRED W. GUDRIAN. "Prehistoric pottery from the Morgan site, Rocky Hill, Connecticut." ArcSocConB, No. 56 (1993), 63-100.

SALISBURY (LITCHFIELD CO.)

914.   DORSEY, GARY. "Death of a Raggy." New England Monthly, 7 (Sept. 1990), 44-50.
    Incidents of arson and murder (1985 and 1986), related to social-class tensions in the town.

SCOTLAND (WINDHAM CO.)

915.   CUNNINGHAM, JANICE POTE. The history and architecture of Scotland, Connecticut: from an architectural survey, 1988-1989. Scotland: Town of Scotland Historic District Study Committee, 1989. 19, [98]p. CtWillE.

916.   LYMAN ALLYN ART MUSEUM. The Devotion family: the lives and possessions of three generations in eighteenth-century Connecticut. Lance Mayer and Gay Myers, eds. New London, 1991. 64p. CtHi. *

SHELTON (FAIRFIELD CO.)

917.   BARKER, WILLIAM V. H., MARY UNGER, and JANET WELLS. Shelton Congregational Church history, 1892-1992: a century of memories, a promising future. Shelton: Shelton Congregational Church, 1992. 86p. CtNhHi. *

SIMSBURY (HARTFORD CO.)

918.   PETKE, STEPHEN. "A chronological survey of gravestones made by Calvin Barber of Simsbury, Connecticut." Markers X [1993], 1-51.

919.   WHITLOCK, REVERDY. By grit and grace: the first one hundred years of Westminster School. Simsbury: Westminster School, 1988. 330p. CtNhHi.
    Private school.

SOMERS (TOLLAND CO.)

920.   HAMMOND, RANSOM. "Children and youth in the annals of a Connecticut congregation: (Somers, 1729- 1839)." Bulletin of the Congregational Library, 41 (Winter-Spring/Summer 1990), 4-14.

SOUTH WINDSOR (HARTFORD CO.)

921.   BENDREMER, JEFFREY CAP MILLEN, ELIZABETH A. KELLOGG, and TONYA BAROODY LARGY. "A grass-lined maize storage pit and early maize horticulture in central Connecticut." North American Archaeologist, 12:4 (1991), 325-349.

SOUTHINGTON (HARTFORD CO.)

922.   GUDRIAN, FRED W. "Southington rock shelters." ArcSocConB, No. 55 (1992), 21-37.
    Indian sites.

STAMFORD (FAIRFIELD CO.)

923.   KOENIG, SAMUEL. An American Jewish community, 50 years, 1889-1939: the sociology of the Jewish community in Stamford, Connecticut. (1940) Stamford: Stamford Historical Society, 1991. xxv, 175p. CtS. *

924.   MAJDALANY, JEANNE. The early settlement of Stamford, Connecticut, 1641-1700. Bowie, Md.: Heritage Books, 1990. xi, 211p. CtHi. *

925.   SHAPIRO, BRUCE. "Framed." Connecticut, 54 (Oct. 1991), 33-37, 112-118.
    Benjamin Franklin Miller Jr. spent some 18 years in a mental hospital as the supposed murderer of five women in the Stamford area between 1968 and 1971.

926.   STAMFORD HISTORICAL SOCIETY. Delos Palmer (1890- 1960), Stamford artist. Stamford, 1991. 32p. CtHi. *

STONINGTON (NEW LONDON CO.)

927.   BAILEY, ANTHONY. "Village people." Connecticut, 59 (Sept. 1992), 42-44.
    Reactions to the author's 1971 book about Stonington, In the village.

928   STONINGTON

928.   "THE BATTLE of Stonington." HF, 30 (Feb. 1993), 1, 6-7, 9.
As described in an 1814 letter. Mary M. Thacher, ed.

929.   BOAS, NORMAN FRANCIS. Stonington during the American Revolution. Mystic: Seaport Autographs, 1990. ix, 195p. CtHi. *

930.   CAMPBELL, GEORGE L. "Lighthouse Museum column." HF, 27 (Feb. 1990), 6-7.
History of the lighthouse.

931.   CHESBRO, SAMUEL H. "1850 map of north part of Stonington Borough." HF, 40 (Nov. 1993), 1, 8.
Written in 1897.

932.   "CLARK Greenman's true colors." Mystic Seaport, Log, 42 (Fall 1990), 67-69.
Documenting the painting history of the Clark Greenman House in Mystic (built in 1841 and altered during the 1870s).

933.   DAVIDSON, CARLA. "Stonington." American Heritage, 44 (October 1993), 22, 24.

934.   De KAY, JAMES TERTIUS. The battle of Stonington: torpedoes, submarines, and rockets in the War of 1812. Annapolis, Md.: Naval Institute Pr., 1990. xi, 216p. CtU. *

935.   FAVRETTI, RUDY J. "My friend Grace Denison Wheeler." HF, 29 (Feb. 1992), 1, 5-7, 11.
"Stonington's unofficial historian."

936.   FISH, STEVEN. "A center of dance, sport and fun." HF, 28 (Feb. 1991), 1, 9-11.
Wequetequock Casino, in operation from 1906-1940. See also entry 940.

937.   GERMAN, ANDREW W. "The Oceanic Base Ball Club." Mystic Seaport, Log, 45 (Winter 1993), 78-82.
Early baseball club in Mystic.

938.   GOODMAN, MARY P. "Pequot Trail." HF, 27 (Feb. 1990), 2-3, 10.
Stonington section of an Indian trail that became "the principal route from Newport to New London for over a hundred years" (17th and 18th centuries).

939.   GORDON, BERNARD LUDWIG. "Ellery Franklin Thompson: fisherman, author, and marine painter." Mystic Seaport, Log, 41 (Fall 1989/Winter 1990), 100-104.
20th century.

940.   GOULD, DOROTHEA. "A dance at the casino." HF, 28 (Feb. 1991), 1, 7.
Wequetequock Casino. See also entry 936.

941.   HINSHAW, JOHN V. "Third Stonington: the Afro-American Baptist church on Water Street." HF, 29 (May 1992), 1, 5-7, 10.
Third Baptist Church, in existence from 1846-ca. 1924.

942.   LYNCH, EMILY H. "More from the Davis Homestead." HF, 26 (Aug. 1989), 1, 10; (Nov. 1989), 2-3, 5.
See also John L. Davis, The Davis Homestead (1986; entry 790 in Vol. 8).

943.   LYONS, SHEILA. "Stonington schoolboys in the Spanish-American War." HF, 27 (May 1990), 4-5, 11.
Request from a local school to President William McKinley for "guns and equipage."

944.   MEYERS, MINOR SR. "Upjohn's church in Stonington." HF, 30 (May 1993), 1, 7, 9; (Aug. 1993), 2-3, 7; (Nov. 1993), 2, 7.
Calvary Church (Episcopal), designed ca. 1847-1848 by architect Richard Upjohn.

945.   PEABODY, ANN F. "The life and times of 'Winty' Burrows." Mystic Seaport, Log, 46 (Summer 1994), 13-20.
Retailer in Mystic (lived 1825-1899). See also entry 800.

946.   SIMM, STANTON WHITNEY JR. "The dam at Wequetequock." HF, 26 (May 1989), 1, 11.

947.   THACHER, MARY M. "1827 map of Stonington." HF, 27 (May 1990), 2-3, 11.

948.   _____. "The 1850 census of the town." HF, 29 (Feb. 1992), 2, 9.

949.   _____. "History of the Arcade Building." HF, 28 (Aug. 1991), 2-3, 7, 11.

950.   _____. "Huldah Hall, heroine of 1814." HF, 31 (May 1994), 1, 7, 9.
Biographical sketch of woman who stayed with her dying mother while the town was being bombarded by the British.

951.   _____. "The Stonington Arsenal, 1809-1878." HF, 29 (Nov. 1992), 2, 9-10.
U.S. government arsenal.

952.   _____. "Stonington's salt works, 1826-1857." HF, 27 (Aug. 1990), 2, 11.

953. _____. "Temperance and the Steamboat Hotel." HF, 29 (Aug. 1992), 2-3.
    19th century.

954. _____. "The wetlands of Stonington Borough." HF, 30 (Aug. 1993), 1, 5-6.
    As shown on 1827 map.

955. "THE VELVET mill." HF, 29 (Nov. 1992), 1, 7.
    American Velvet Company (since 1892). Article signed "V.T.B."

SEE ALSO entry 665.

SUFFIELD (HARTFORD CO.)

956. BOWEN, JOANNE VICKIE. "A study of seasonality and subsistence: eighteenth century Suffield, Connecticut." Ph.D. dissertation, Brown Univ., 1990. x, 211p. *
    Abstracted in DAI, 51:8A (1991), 2789.

957. LOOMIS, ROGER C. "The King House." Connecticut Antiquarian, 37 [i.e., 39] (Summer 1988), 21-25.
    See also next entry.

958. _____. The King House Museum, 1764. [Suffield: The Museum, 1986]. [16]p. CtHi. *

959. PETERSON, KARIN E. "From farm to suburb: two centuries of life at the Hatheway House." Connecticut Antiquarian, 37 [i.e., 39] (Summer 1988), 4-19.
    Built ca. 1761.

THOMPSON (WINDHAM CO.)

960. McGEE, DONALD J. Towers of brick, walls of stone: a history of the textile industry in New England, with Thompson, Connecticut, as a prism of the factory town. N.Y.: Vantage Pr., 1991. 291p. CtWillE. *

961. WYATT, DONALD W. "The lady was an historian." Old RI, 3 (Oct. 1993), 15-18; (Dec. 1993/Jan. 1994), 39-41.
    Ellen D. Larned of Thompson (1825-1912), known for her history of Windham County (entry 2202 in the Connecticut volume).

TOLLAND (TOLLAND CO.)

962. CREZNIC, JEAN. "The old Babcock Tavern." Early American Life, 20 (Feb. 1989), 58-63.

TORRINGTON (LITCHFIELD CO.)

963. HODGES, THEODORE B. Erastus Hodges, 1781-1847: Connecticut manufacturer, merchant, entrepreneur. West Kennebunk, Me.: Phoenix Publishing, 1994. x, 360p. CtHi. *

TRUMBULL (FAIRFIELD CO.)

964. SMITH, CLAUDE CLAYTON. Quarter-acre of heartache. Blacksburg, Va.: Pocahontas Pr., 1985. xiv, 168p. CtHi. *
    Paugussett Indian reservation.

VERNON (TOLLAND CO.)

965. VERNON HISTORICAL SOCIETY. Vernon, our town. Jean Luddy, chair. 2d ed. Vernon, 1989. xii, 112p. CtHi. *
    Note: this item replaces entry 9101 in the Connecticut volume.

WARREN (LITCHFIELD CO.)

966. GRAY, FRANCINE DU PLESSIX. "Warren, Conn." New York, 26 (June 28, 1993), 46-48, 53.

WATERBURY (NEW HAVEN CO.)

967. BISAILLON, ROBERT R. Saint Anne Parish and its people: centenaire de la paroisse Sainte Anne, 1886- 1986. Waterbury: St. Anne Church, 1986. 144p. CtHi. *
    Roman Catholic.

968. FASCE, FERDINANDO. "Gli italiani di Waterbury. Un percorso di ricerce." Altreitalie [Italy], 1 (Nov. 1989), 46-56.
    See also next entry.

969. _____. "The Italian American Catholic parish in the early twentieth century: a view from Waterbury, Connecticut." Studi Emigrazione [Italy], 28 (1991), 342-350.

970. MOLONEY, DEIRDRE M. "Waterbury's working women, 1900-1920." Connecticut History, 34 (Spring 1993), 18- 35.

971. ROTH, MATTHEW W. Platt Brothers and Company: small business in American manufacturing. Hanover, N.H.: Wesleyan Univ. Pr., 1994. x, 256p. CtHi. *
    Non-ferrous metals.

972   WATERBURY

972.   VERNON, STEVEN K. "The Terry Clock Company's fishing reels." NAWCCB, 34 (Dec. 1992), 713-716.

WATERFORD (NEW LONDON CO.)

973.   WEIR, WILLIAM. "Nightmare in Waterford." Connecticut, 53 (Feb. 1990), 70, 72-74, 84-86, 135.
    1980 killing of George Patterson, for which two men were convicted.

WATERTOWN (LITCHFIELD CO.)

974.   LOVELACE, RICHARD H. Mr. Taft's school: the first century, 1890-1990. Watertown: Taft School, 1989. x, 198p. CtHi. *
    Taft School (private school).

WEST HARTFORD (HARTFORD CO.)

975.   BUCK, MARGARET F. One hundred years of the Woman's Exchange. West Hartford: The Exchange, [1989]. 39p. CtHi. *
    Consignment sales shop.

976.   FAIRBAIRN, JOHN B. The history of Sunny Reach. n.p., [199?]. var. p. CtHi. *
    Real estate subdivision.

977.   FERNANDEZ, RONALD. Los Macheteros: the Wells Fargo robbery and the violent struggle for Puerto Rican independence. N.Y.: Prentice Hall Pr., 1987. xiv, 272p. Ct. *
    1983 robbery.

978.   MARION Houghton Hepburn Grant, 1918-1986: a biography. Katharine Houghton Grant, ed. West Hartford: Fenwick Publications, 1989. 245p. CtHi. *
    Author of books and articles on Connecticut history and co-author of a history of Hartford (1986; entry 511 in Vol. 8).

WEST HAVEN (NEW HAVEN CO.)

979.   JOHNSON, GIL. The West Shore and its heritage: featuring official West Shore history, by Bennett W. Dorman; West Shore Fire Department, 1918-1989. [West Haven? 1989] 166p. CtNhHi. *

WESTPORT (FAIRFIELD CO.)

980.   FOSTER, JOANNA. Stories from Westport's past. Westport: J. Foster, 1985-1988. 3v. Ct. *
    Articles from the Westport News. Note: this item replaces entry 829 in Vol. 8.

981.   SCHLOSBERG, JEREMY. "Pop till you drop: the story of Newman's Own." Connecticut, 55 (Jan. 1992), 60-63, 107.
    Actor Paul Newman and Newman's Own products.

WETHERSFIELD (HARTFORD CO.)

982.   KENDALL, DOUGLAS. "Wallace Nutting at Wethersfield: the Colonial Revival and the Joseph Webb House." Connecticut Antiquarian, 40 (Winter 1989), 7-19.

983.   SWEENEY, KEVIN MICHAEL. "Using tax lists to detect biases in probate inventories." DubSemPr (1987), 32-40.
    Study of early Wethersfield records.

    SEE ALSO entries 539, 635.

WILLINGTON (TOLLAND CO.)

984.   WEIGOLD, ISABEL B. A glimpse of Willington's past. Willington: Willington Historical Society. 1991. 139p. Ct. *

    SEE ALSO entry 539.

WILTON (FAIRFIELD CO.)

985.   WINSLOW, JOYCE. "George Washington undone." Yankee, 54 (Feb. 1990), 62-67, 124-126.
    Gifford Proctor's 50-year effort to complete a statue of Washington.

WINDHAM (WINDHAM CO.)

986.   BEARDSLEY, THOMAS R. Willimantic industry and community: the rise and decline of a Connecticut textile city. Willimantic: Windham Textile & History Museum, 1993. xx, 244p. CtHi. *

987.   _____. Willimantic women: their lives and labors. Willimantic: Windham Textile and History Museum, 1990. 21p. CtHi. *

988.   EXCELSIOR HOOK AND LADDER COMPANY, NO. 1, WILLIMANTIC. Souvenir and history of Excelsior Hook and Ladder Co., No. 1, Willimantic, Connecticut. Willimantic: Redman Pr., 1908. 95p. CtHi.

989.   GLASSER, IRENE. More than bread: ethnography of a soup kitchen. Tuscaloosa: Univ. of Alabama Pr., 1988. x, 180p. CtHi. *
       In Willimantic (1980s).

990.   [SWIFT, RUTH]. A history of the village and the First Congregational Church, Windham, Connecticut: 275th anniversary, 1700-1975; December 19, 1975. n.p., [1975?]. 65p. CtWillE.

991.   WILLIMANTIC, CONN. ST. PAUL'S EPISCOPAL CHURCH. St. Paul's Episcopal Church, Willimantic, Connecticut, 1865-1965. n.p., [1965?]. [24]p. CtWillE.

992.   "WILLIMANTIC—the thread city." State of Connecticut Labor Department Monthly Bulletin, 17 (Feb. 1952), 5-7.

WINDSOR (HARTFORD CO.)

993.   McCLURE, DAVID. "Settlement and antiquities of the town of Windsor, in Connecticut." MHSC, 5 (1798), 166-171.

WOLCOTT (NEW HAVEN CO.)

994.   WOLCOTT HISTORICAL SOCIETY. Wolcott facts and legends. Wolcott, n.d. 16p. CtHi. *

995.   _____. Wolcott on parade. Wolcott, n.d. 16p. CtHi. *

WOODBURY (LITCHFIELD CO.)

996.   HULL, BROOKS B., and GERALD F. MORAN. "A preliminary time series analysis of church activity in colonial Woodbury, Connecticut." Journal for the Scientific Study of Religion, 28 (Dec. 1989), 478-492.

997.   THOMPSON, DAVID H. "The Susquehanna horizon as seen from the summit of Rye Hill (6LF100), Woodbury, Connecticut." ArcSocConB, No. 52 (1989), 17-50.
       Prehistoric site.

WOODSTOCK (WINDHAM CO.)

998.   PERKINS, CHARLENE. "The gardens at Roseland Cottage." Early American Life, 22 (June 1991), 48-53.
       Historic house.

999.   WOODSTOCK, CONN. FIRST CONGREGATIONAL CHURCH. Woodstock parish observer. 3d ed. Woodstock, 1990. 12p. CtHi.
       Includes historical sketches.

SEE ALSO entries 36, 2091, 2846.

Maine

**Entries for the state as a whole
or pertaining to
more than one county***

1000. ADAMS, HERBERT. "The saga of Nature Man." Yankee, 52 (Oct. 1988), 82-87, 166-168.
Joe Knowles, who claimed to have spent two months alone and naked in the Maine woods in 1913 as a publicity stunt for a Boston newspaper.

1001. ALLEN, E. JOHN B. "'Skeeing' in Maine: the early years, 1870's to 1920's." MeHSQ, 30 (Winter-Spring 1991), 146-165.

1002. ALLEN, KENNETH C. The Cumberland Oxford Canal, 1830-79: traces on the land. n.p., 1991. 41p. MeHi.

1003. AMERICAN FRIENDS SERVICE COMMITTEE. The Wabanakis of Maine and the Maritimes: a resource book about Penobscot, Passamaquoddy, Maliseet, Micmac, and Abenaki Indians. Bath: New England Regional Office, Maine Indian Program, 1989. [497]p. MeU. *

1004. ANDERSON, MARK W. "Images of nineteenth century Maine farming in the prose and poetry of R.P.T. Coffin and C.A. Stevens." Agricultural History, 63 (Spring 1989), 120-129.

1005. ANDERSON, WILL. Good old Maine: 101 past and present pop delights. Portland: Will Anderson, 1993. 106p. MeHi. *

1006. _____. Was baseball really invented in Maine?: a lively look at the history of professional baseball in Maine and at every Mainer who's ever played in the Majors. Portland: Will Anderson, 1992. viii, 180p. MeHi. *

1007. ARNDT, JOHN CHRISTOPHER. "Maine in the Northeast boundary controversy: states' rights in antebellum New England." NEQ, 62 (June 1989), 205-223.

1008. BAKER, EMERSON W. "A scratch with a bear's paw: Anglo-Indian land deeds in early Maine." Ethnohistory, 36 (Summer 1989), 235-256.

1009. BANFIELD, ALFRED T. "The padrone, the sojourners, and the settlers: a preface to the 'little Italies' of Maine." MeHSQ, 31 (Winter-Spring 1992), 114-141.
The padroni were labor recruiters and facilitators of emigration.

1010. BARRY, WILLIAM DAVID. "James Healy, we hardly knew you." Portland, 9 (May 1994), 9, 11-15, 17.
20th-century philanthropist.

1011. _____. "Maine & the remarkable Elizabeth Ring." Portland, 9 (Apr. 1994), 9, 11-14.
Maine historian. (See, for example, entry 1330.)

1012. BEACH, CHRISTOPHER STONE. "Conservation and legal politics: the struggle for public water power in Maine, 1900-1923." MeHSQ, 32 (Winter-Spring 1993), 150-173.

1013. _____. "Pulpwood province and paper state: corporate reconstruction, underdevelopment and law in New Brunswick and Maine, 1890-1930." Ph.D. dissertation, Univ. of Maine, 1991. 303p. *
Abstracted in DAI, 53:1A (1992), 272.

1014. BEEM, EDGAR ALLEN. "The art of island Maine." Island Journal, 10 (1993), 72-79.

1015. BENNETT, PAUL E. Sardine carriers and seiners of the Maine coast. Freeport, 1992. 69p. MeHi. *
Boats.

* Online Computer Library Center (OLCC) listings for books and dissertations marked with this symbol may include additional library locations.

1016   MAINE

1016.   BERMAN, ANN E. "Maine plein air painting: capturing the coastal beauty of northern New England." Architectural Digest, 50 (Aug. 1993), 154-158.
        19th and 20th centuries.

1017.   BIBBER, JOYCE K. A home for everyman: the Greek Revival and Maine domestic architecture. Lanham, Md.: University Publishing Associates, 1989. xi, 209p. MeU. *

1018.   "A BIBLIOGRAPHY of recent writings in Maine history." MeHSQ, 30 (Summer 1990), 48-61.

1019.   BLANK, JOHN S. III. "Steaming up to Bangor." Down East, 39 (June 1993), 52-55, 73-77.
        Steamboating on the Penobscot River.

1020.   BROWN, ELSPETH. "Gender and identity in rural Maine: women and the Maine Farmer, 1870-1875." MeHSQ, 33 (Fall 1993), 120-135.
        The Maine Farmer was a periodical.

1021.   CABOT, THOMAS D. Avelinda: the legacy of a Yankee yachtsman. Rockland: Island Institute, 1991. 154, [16]p. MeHi. *
        Autobiographical. The author sailed along the Maine coast for many years.

1022.   _____. "Cruising the Gulf of Maine." Island Journal, 7 (1990), 17-20; 8 (1991), 35-40.

1023.   CARTER, MICHAEL D. Converting the wasteplaces of Zion: the Maine Missionary Society (1807-1862). Wolfeboro, N.H.: Longwood Academic, 1990. xx, 169p. MeHi. *
        Congregational missions in Maine.

1024.   CAYFORD, JOHN E. Maine's hall of fame. Vol. 1. Brewer: Cay-Bel Publishing, 1987. viii, 202p. MeHi. *
        Biographical sketches of some famous Mainers.

1025.   CHAMBERLAIN, JOSHUA L. "Do it! That's how." Bowdoin, 64 (Spring/Summer 1991), 2-12.
        From an autobiographical account written by the Civil War general and Bowdoin College president. See also entry 1134.

1026.   CHANGING Maine. Richard Barringer, ed. [Portland]: Univ. of Southern Maine, 1990. vii, 204p. MeHi. *

1027.   CHURCHILL, EDWIN A. "Evolution of Maine place names." MeHSQ, 29 (Fall 1989), 66-90.

1028.   _____. Hail Britannia: Maine pewter and silver plate: an exhibition of Maine Britannia ware and silverplate, 1829-1941, in the collections of the Maine State Museum, May 15, 1992-May 15, 1993. Augusta: Maine State Museum, 1992. viii, 69p. MeHi. *

1029.   CLARK, JEFF. "Harkan was here!" Down East, 36 (Oct. 1989), 61-63, 74, 76.
        Geographer George Carter on evidence of early visits by Northmen and other Europeans to the Maine coast.

1030.   _____. "The roaring eighties." Down East, 37 (Jan. 1991), 24-25, 52-57.
        Population growth and immigration from other states during the 1980s.

1031.   _____. "They took to the woods." Down East, 39 (1993 Annual), 51-53, 60-61, 63.
        Maine's "summer camp tradition."

1032.   _____, MICHAEL BROSNAN, ELLEN MacDONALD WARD, and BETH CRICHLOW. "Voices of Maine." Down East, 35 (1989 Annual), 49-71.
        Excerpts from oral history interviews with a number of state residents about changes in Maine during the previous 35 years.

1033.   COGLIANO, FRANCIS DOMINIC. "'To obey Jesus Christ and General Washington': Massachusetts, Catholicism, and the eastern Indians." MeHSQ, 32 (Fall 1992), 108- 133.
        Indians of eastern Maine.

1034.   CONDON, RICHARD H. "Nearing the end: Maine's rural community, 1929-1945." MeHSQ, 31 (Winter-Spring 1992), 142-173.
        Depression and war years.

1035.   CONKLING, PHILIP W. "The great Maine lobster war." Island Journal, 10 (1993), 56-60.
        1957.

1036.   COWIE, ELLEN. "Recent archaeological investigations in the southern Androscoggin River Valley, Maine." MeArcSocB, 30 (Spring 1990), 1-14.

1037.   CROCK, JOHN G. "Recent archaeological investigations in the Messalonskee portion of the central Kennebec River drainage." MeArcSocB, 32 (Spring 1992), 45-62.

1038.   CUMMING, NAN. "Collecting nineteenth-century costumes at the Maine Historical Society." MeHSQ, 30 (Spring 1991), 6-11.

1039.   CURTIS, WAYNE. "Maine's golden decade." Down East, 38 (Jan. 1992), 22-23.
        Social life during the 1890s.

1040.   DAUGHTERS OF THE AMERICAN REVOLUTION. NATIONAL SOCIETY. Minority military service: Maine, 1775-1783. [Washington, D.C.], 1990. 24p. Me. *

1041. DAVENPORT, LINDA GILBERT. "Maine's sacred tunebooks, 1800-1830: divine song on the northeast frontier." Ph.D. dissertation, Univ. of Colorado, 1991. xiv, 629p. *
Abstracted in DAI, 52:6A (1991), 1934-1935.

1042. DeMERRITT, DAVID. "Cuban annexation, slave power paranoia, and the collapse of the Democratic Party in Maine, 1805-1850." MeHSQ, 29 (Summer 1989), 2-29.

1043. DOTY, C. STEWART. "Rudy Vallée: Franco-American and man from Maine." MeHSQ, 33 (Summer 1993), 2-19.
The well-known singer and band leader (died 1986).

1044. DUNCAN, ROGER. Coastal Maine: a maritime history. N.Y.: W.W. Norton, 1992. 573p. MeHi. *

1045. EASTMAN, JOEL W. "Pitching in." Portland Monthly, 4 (Winterguide 1990), 22-25, 28-29.
Maine in World War II.

1046. _____. "U-Boats off the coast of Maine." Portland Monthly, 4 (Winterguide 1990), 14.
World War II.

1047. ELDRIDGE, STUART ALLYN. "Ceramic period occupation of the central Maine coast: hunter-gatherer estuarine adaptations in the St. George River drainage." Ph.D. dissertation, Univ. of Pennsylvania, 1990. xii, 315p. *
Abstracted in DAI, 51:12A (1991), 4166-4167.

1048. ELLSWORTH, ME. STUDENTS OF ELLSWORTH HIGH SCHOOL. Voices on Vietnam: interviews. Ellsworth, 1989. 97p. MeU. *

1049. EVES, JAMIE H. "'Shrunk to a comparative rivulet': deforestation, stream flow, and rural milling in 19th-century Maine." Technology and Culture, 33 (Jan. 1992), 38-65.

1050. _____. "'The valley white with mist': a Cape Cod colony in Maine." MeHSQ, 32 (Fall 1992), 74-107.
The movement of settlers from Cape Cod to the Penobscot River Valley (ca. 1770-1810).

1051. FAULKNER, ALARIC. "Gentility on the frontiers of Acadia, 1635-1674: an archaeological perspective." DubSemPr (1989), 82-100.
Fort Pentagoet, the settlement at Pemaquid, and sites in New Brunswick and Nova Scotia.

1052. FLANAGAN, JAMES M. Builders of Maine. Mt. Desert: Windswept House, 1994. 331, [8]p. MeHi. *

1053. FLANAGAN, TERESA M. Mourning on the Pejepscot. Lanham, Md.: University Pr. of America, 1992. xv, 115p. Me. *
Funeral and burial customs.

1054. FRASER, RICHARD, and NANCY FRASER. A history of Maine built automobiles, 1834-1934. East Poland, 1991. 292, [4]p. Me. *

1055. GHERE, DAVID LYNN. "The 'disappearance' of the Abenaki in western Maine: political organization and ethnocentric assumptions." American Indian Quarterly, 17 (Spring 1993), 193-207.

1056. GOLD, DAVID M. The shaping of nineteenth-century law: John Appleton and responsible individualism. N.Y.: Greenwood Pr., 1990. xiv, 229p. MeU. *
Appleton, chief justice of the state supreme court, was a member of the court from 1852-1883.

1057. GOLDSTEIN, JUDITH S. Crossing lines: histories of Jews and gentiles in three communities. N.Y.: William Morrow, 1992. 320p. MeHi. *
Bangor, Calais, and Mount Desert Island.

1058. GOULD, ALBERTA. First lady of the senate: a life of Margaret Chase Smith. Mt. Desert: Windswept House Publishers, 1990. 79p. MeU. *
U.S. senator from 1950-1973.

1059. GRANT, GAY. "W. Clark Noble: Maine sculptor." Kennebec Proprietor, 6 (Summer 1989), 20-25.
Lived 1858-1938.

1060. GROWING up in Maine: recollections of childhood from the 1780s to the 1920s. Charles Shain and Samuella Shain, eds. Camden: Down East Books, 1991. viii, 264p. MeHi. *

1061. HILL, TOM. "The little war that wasn't." Down East, 35 (Mar. 1989), 54-58.
Aroostook War.

1062. HOKANSON, KIMBERLY. "The changing status of fraternities at northeastern, liberal arts colleges: case studies of Bowdoin and Colby." Ed.D. dissertation, Harvard Univ., 1992. vi, 240p. *
1980s. Abstracted in DAI, 53:2A (1992), 420.

1063. HOUDETTE, ELIZABETH M. "Home, sweet (mail-order) home." Down East, 35 (Feb. 1989), 76-79.
Examples of architect George Palliser's designs built in Maine (late-19th century).

1064. HUTCHINSON, DOUG. The Rumford Falls & Rangeley Lakes Railroad. Louise M. Korol, ed. Dixfield: Partridge Lane Publications, 1989. vii, 129p. MeU. *

1065. IGLEHEART, ELIZABETH. "Frederick Law Olmsted, 1822-1903." BDAM, 5:16 (1988), [1-10].
The noted landscape architect had a number of commissions in Maine.

1066   MAINE

1066.   IVES, EDWARD D. George Magoon and the Down East game war: history, folklore, and the law. Urbana: Univ. of Illinois Pr., 1988. xiv, 335p. MeU. *
     Late-19th century.

1067.   JOHNSON, RON. The best of Maine railroads. South Portland: Ron Johnson, 1985. 144p. MeB. *

1068.   JONES, JACQUELINE. "Men and women in northern New England during the era of the Civil War." MeHSQ, 33 (Fall 1993), 70-87.

1069.   JONES, ROBERT C., and DAVID L. REGISTER. Two feet to tidewater: the Wiscasset, Waterville & Farmington Railway. Boulder, Colo.: Pruett Publishing, 1987. xviii, 269p. MeU. *

1070.   JUDD, RICHARD W. "The coming of the clear waters acts in Maine, 1941-1961." Environmental History Review, 14 (Fall 1990), 50-73.

1071.   _____. "Grass roots conservation in eastern coastal Maine: monopoly and the moral economy of weir fishing, 1893-1911." Environmental Review, 12 (Summer 1988), 80-103.

1072.   _____. "Saving the fisherman as well as the fish: conservation and commercial rivalry in Maine's lobster industry, 1872-1933." Business History Review, 62 (Winter 1988), 596-625.

1073.   KARMEN, ABBE L. "Keeping the house in order: women's cooperative extension work in the early twentieth century." MeHSQ, 32 (Summer 1992), 30-50.

1074.   KATRA, JOSEPH R. JR. "Clocks & clockmaking in southern Maine, 1770-1870." NAWCCB, Bulletin Supplement No. 17 (Summer 1989), 3-80.

1075.   LARSON, ANDERS. "Franco-Americans and the International Paper Company strike of 1910." MeHSQ, 33 (Summer 1993), 40-60.
     In Livermore Falls and Rumford.

1076.   LAWRY, NELSON H. "The Kennebec defended through a dozen wars." Periodical: Journal of the Council on America's Military Past, 13:2 (1984), 3-20.

1077.   LEAMON, JAMES S. Revolution downeast: the war for American independence in Maine. Amherst: Univ. of Massachusetts Pr., 1992. xviii, 302p. Me. *

1078.   LEGAULT, L. H. "A line for all uses: the Gulf of Maine boundary revisited." International Journal [Canada], 40 (Summer 1985), 461-477.
     International boundary.

1079.   LEMKE, WILLIAM. The wild, wild east: unusual tales of Maine history. Camden: Down East Books, 1990. 180p. MeHi. *

1080.   LEWIS, GEORGE H. "The Maine lobster as regional icon: competing images over time and social class." Food & Foodways, 3:4 (1989), 303-316.

1081.   LOVELL, JOHN. "Death's door." Yankee, 56 (Sept. 1992), 63-65, 120, 122.
     Airline pilot's near brush with death during a 1987 flight.

1082.   LOWREY, NATHAN S. "Tales of the northern Maine woods: the history and traditions of the Maine guide." Northeast Folklore, 28 (1989), 69-110.

1083.   MacWILLIAMS, DON. "Summer Olympians." Portland Monthly, 3 (July/Aug. 1988), 25.
     Maine athletes who participated in the early renewals of the Olympic Games.

1084.   MADDEN, JOAN C., and MARGARET E. SLATTERY. Thompson Lake book: a narrative history. Oxford: Thompson Lake Environmental Association, 1991. 74p. Me. *
     In Androscoggin, Cumberland, and Oxford counties.

1085.   MAINE. COMMISSION TO CELEBRATE THE BICENTENNIAL OF THE UNITED STATES CONSTITUTION. A rising sun: Maine commemorates the bicentennial of the United States Constitution. Neal W. Allen, comp. n.p., 1988. ix, 74p. MeHi. *

1086.   MAINE. STATE ARCHIVES. Maine's historical records: a guide to collections of original, unpublished materials. Augusta, 1992. ix, 126p. Me. *

1087.   MAINE HISTORICAL SOCIETY. Maine in the age of discovery: Christopher Levett's voyage, 1623-1624, and a guide to sources. Portland, 1988. 96p. MeHi. *

1088.   MAINE HUMANITIES COUNCIL. The land of Norumbega: Maine in the age of exploration and settlement: an exhibition by Susan Danforth. [Freeport: Village Pr.], 1988. 276p. MeHi. *
     See also preceding entry.

1089. "MAINE or bust." Down East, 37 (Jan. 1991), 32- 33, 62-69.
Excerpts from selected accounts by immigrants to Maine (17th-20th centuries).

1090. MAINE: the Pine Tree State from prehistory to the present. Richard W. Judd, Edwin A. Churchill, and Joel W. Eastman, eds. Hanover, N.H.: University Pr. of New England, 1994. 586p. Me. *

1091. MAY, STEPHEN. "Pioneer painters of Maine." Down East, 36 (Nov. 1989), 58-61.
Landscape painter Frederic Church and the Maine wilderness (19th century).

1092. McBRIDE, BUNNY. "Last of the Pequawkets." Down East, 36 (July 1990), 79-84.
"Indian doctress" Molly Ockett (died 1816).

1093. _____. Our lives in our hands: Micmac Indian basketmakers. Gardiner: Tilbury House, 1990. x, 85p. MeU. *

1094. McEWEN, CRAIG A., and RICHARD J. MAIMAN. "Coercion and consent: a tale of two court reforms." Law & Policy [U.K.], 10 (Jan. 1988), 3-24.
Relating to small-claims judgments in Maine (1980s).

1095. McLANE, CHARLES B. Islands of the mid-Maine coast. Volume II: Mount Desert to Machias Bay. Falmouth: Kennebec River Pr., 1989. xvii, 406p. MeHi. *
See also entry 1087 in Vol. 8.

1096. MUNDY, JAMES H. Hard times, hard men: Maine and the Irish, 1830-1860. Scarborough: Harp Publications, 1990. xiv, 201p. MeP. *

1097. O'BRIEN, KERRY A. "'So monstrous smart': Maine women and fashion, 1790-1840." MeHSQ, 30 (Spring 1991), 13-43.

1098. O'LEARY, WAYNE M. "Fish and politics in Jacksonian Maine." NEQ, 67 (Mar. 1994), 92-114.
On the strength of the Democratic Party in Maine fishing communities (1830s and 1840s).

1099. _____. "Who were the Whigs and Democrats?: the economic character of second-level party leadership in tidewater Maine, 1845-53." MeHSQ, 28 (Winter 1989), 146-169.

1100. PALMER, KENNETH T., and MARCUS A. LiBRIZZI. "Development of the Maine Constitution: the long tradition, 1819-1988." MeHSQ, 28 (Winter 1989), 126-145.

1101. PALMER, KENNETH T., G. THOMAS TAYLOR, and MARCUS A. LiBRIZZI. Maine politics and government. Lincoln: Univ. of Nebraska Pr., 1992. xxviii, 240p. MeU. *
Includes historical information.

1102. PELADEAU, MARIUS B. "Brother Moses Johnson, 1752-1842." BDAM, 5:11 (1988), [1-4].
Shaker architect, who designed Shaker meetinghouses in Alfred and Sabbathday Lake.

1103. _____. "Harry H. Cochrane, 1860-1946." BDAM, 5:6 (1988), [1-6].
His architectural designs in Maine included buildings in Monmouth.

1104. PENOBSCOT MARINE MUSEUM. Goodly ships on painted seas: ship portraiture by Penobscot Bay artists. Andrew German, ed. Searsport, 1988. 52p. MeHi. *
Paintings by William P. Stubbs, James G. Babbidge, and Percy A. Sanborn.

1105. PRINS, HARALD E. L. "A romantic poet touring 19th-century Maine: William Cullen Bryant's trip on the Kennebec River in 1847." Kennebec Proprietor, 5 (Summer 1988), 18-19.

1106. _____, and BUNNY McBRIDE. "A social history of Maine Indian basketry." Kennebec Proprietor, 6 (Winter 1990), 18-21.

1107. REED, ROGER G. A delight to all who know it: the Maine summer architecture of William R. Emerson. Augusta: Maine Historic Preservation Commission, 1990. 144p. MeHi. *
Boston architect (lived 1833-1917).

1108. _____. "Francis W. Chandler, 1844-1926." BDAM, 5: 4 (1988), [1-6].
Boston architect, who designed "lifesaving stations [in Maine] and three stylish summer cottages on North Haven Island."

1109. _____. "William R. Miller, 1866-1929." BDAM, 5:14 (1988), [1-6].
Architect, of Lewiston and Portland. See also entry 1435.

1110. RICHARDS, DAVID. "Medicine and healing among the Maine Shakers." DubSemPr (1993), 142-153.

1111. RIVARD, PAUL E. Lion: the history of an 1846 locomotive engine in Maine. Augusta: Maine State Museum, 1988. 63p. MeLB. *
On exhibit in the museum.

1112   MAINE

1112.   RIVARD, PAUL E. Maine sawmills: a history. Augusta: Maine State Museum, 1990. xii, 62p. MeU. *

1113.   ROBINSON, BRIAN S., and JAMES BRANT PETERSEN. "Perceptions of marginality: the case of the early holocene in northern New England." Northeast Anthropology, No. 46 (Fall 1993), 61-75.

1114.   ROLDE, NEIL. Maine: a narrative history. Gardiner: Harpswell Pr., 1990. xii, 361p. Me. *

1115.   RUMMEL, JACK. "Maine's WPA." Portland Monthly, 4 (Dec. [1989]), 27-33, 46.
         Works Progress Administration (1930s).

1116.   SANGER, DAVID. "Five thousand years of contact between Maine and Nova Scotia." MeArcSocB, 31 (Fall 1991), 55-61.

1117.   _____. "Unscrambling messages in the midden." Archaeology of Eastern North America, 9 (Fall 1981), 37-42.
         See also entry 434.

1118.   SCHRIVER, EDWARD OSWALD. "Reluctant hangman: the State of Maine and capital punishment, 1820-1887." NEQ, 63 (June 1990), 271-287.

1119.   SCONTRAS, CHARLES A. "Maine lobstermen and the labor movement: the Lobster Fishermen's International Protective Association, 1907." MeHSQ, 29 (Summer 1989), 30-51.
         See also this author's article of same title in Labor's Heritage, 2 (Jan. 1990), 50-63.

1120.   _____. The origins of Labor Day in Maine and historical glimpses of labor on parade in early nineteenth century Maine. Orono: Bureau of Labor Education, Univ. of Maine, 1989. 53p. MeHi.

1121.   SCOTT, GERALDINE TIDD. Isaac Simpson's world: the collected works of an itinerant photographer. Falmouth: Kennebec River Pr., 1990. xxiii, 183p. MeU. *
         Lived 1874-1957.

1122.   SEWALL, ABBIE. Message through time: the photographs of Emma D. Sewall, 1836-1919. Gardiner: Harpswell Pr., 1989. xvi, 104p. MeHi. *
         Of Bath and Phippsburg.

1123.   SHERMAN, JANANN MARGARET. "Margaret Chase Smith: the making of a senator." Ph.D. dissertation, Rutgers Univ., 1993. 370p.
         Smith served in Congress from 1940-1973. Abstracted in DAI, 54:7A (1994), 2710.

1124.   SHETTLEWORTH, EARLE GREY JR. "Gershom Flagg, 1705-1771." BDAM, 5:9 (1988), [1-6].
         Architect.

1125.   SHIPMAN, WILLIAM D. "Samuel Melcher III, 1775-1862." BDAM, 5:13 (1988), [1-6].
         "Leading builder in the Brunswick-Topsham area" (early-19th century).

1126.   "SIX rivers, twelve towns, one bay." Bowdoin, 63 (Summer 1990), 3-9.
         History of the area surrounding Merrymeeting Bay.

1127.   SPIESS, ARTHUR E. "Two isolated paleoindian artifacts from Maine." Archaeology of Eastern North America, 18 (Fall 1990), 65-74.

1128.   STAKEMAN, RANDOLPH. "The black population of Maine, 1764-1900." New England Journal of Black Studies, No. 8 (1989), 17-35.

1129.   STEINHAUER, DALE R. "'A class of men's': United States Army recruits in Maine, 1822-1860." MeHSQ, 30 (Fall 1990), 92-119.

1130.   STONE, JASON. "Flu!" Down East, 35 (Apr. 1989), 45-47.
         The 1918 epidemic in Maine.

1131.   TAYLOR, ALAN SHAW. Liberty men and great proprietors: the revolutionary settlement on the Maine frontier, 1760-1820. Williamsburg, Va.: Institute of Early American History and Culture, 1990. xiv, 381p. MeHi. *
         See also this author's Ph.D. dissertation of similar title (Brandeis Univ., 1986; entry 1245 in Vol. 8).

1132.   _____. "Regulators and white Indians: forms of agrarian resistance in post-Revolutionary New England." Storia Nordamericana [Italy], 4:1-2 (1987), 157-171.

1133.   THOMPSON, ELLIE R. The history of broadcasting in Maine: the first fifty years. Augusta: Maine Association of Broadcasters, 1990. 112p. MeHi. *

1134.   TRULOCK, ALICE RAINS. In the hands of providence: Joshua L. Chamberlain and the American Civil War. Chapel Hill: Univ. of North Carolina Pr., 1992. xxii, 569p. MeHi. *
         Chamberlain (1828-1914), the Civil War general, taught at Bowdoin College before the war and served in later years as governor of Maine and president of Bowdoin.

1135.   VERDE, THOMAS A. Maine ghosts and legends: 26 encounters with the supernatural. Camden: Down East Books, 1989. 126p. MeHi. *

1136.   "VOICES of a Maine childhood." Down East, 39 (1993 Annual), 20-29, 54-55.
   Childhood memories of a number of adult Mainers. See also entry 1060.

1137.   WEBSTER, EDWARD GLEN. "The impact of the Maine Educational Reform Act of 1984 on curriculum development in the Maine public schools." Ed.D. dissertation, West Virginia Univ., 1989. iv, 243p. *
   Abstracted in DAI, 51:3A (1990), 735.

1138.   WELCH, WALLY. The lighthouses of Maine. [Apopka, Fla.]: W. Welch, 1985. 66p. Me. *

1139.   WELLS, WILLIAM W. "John Appleton: through his own words." MeHSQ, 31 (Summer 1991), 205-220.
   See also entry 1956.

1140.   WESCOTT, RICHARD ROLLINS. "The transformation of farming in Maine, 1940-1985." MeHSQ, 28 (Fall 1988), 66-84.

1141.   WHITTEN, MAURICE M. The gunpowder mills of Maine. Gorham, 1990. x, 324p. MeU. *

1142.   WILSON, DEBORAH B., and ARTHUR E. SPIESS. "Study unit 1: fluted point paleoindian." MeArcSocB, 30 (Spring 1990), 15-31.

1143.   WINGATE, GORDON. "R.B. Hall and the community bands of Maine." Ph.D. dissertation, Univ. of Maine, 1993. 460p.
   Hall lived 1858-1907. Abstracted in DAI, 54:5A (1993), 1583-1584.

1144.   WORCESTER, FRANK. "Crossing by ferry on the Androscoggin." Bethel Courier, 3 (June 1979), 1-2.

   SEE ALSO entries 19, 27, 73, 76, 157, 178, 191, 220. 226, 230, 303, 320, 349, 358, 367, 384, 396, 408, 411, 430, 434, 504.

Maine

Entries for Counties†

AROOSTOOK COUNTY

1145. THE COUNTY: land of promise: a pictorial history of Aroostook County, Maine. Anna Fields Mcgrath, ed. Norfolk, Va.: Donning, 1989. 223p. MeHi. *

1146. CRAIG, BEATRICE CHEVALIER. "Agriculture and the lumberman's frontier in the upper St. John Valley, 1800-70." Journal of Forest History, 32 (July 1988), 125-137.

   The article, primarily about lumbering in the Canadian side of the valley, refers to areas of what is now Aroostook County.

1147. _____. "Kinship and migration to the upper St. John Valley, 1785-1842." Quebec Studies, 25 (Spring 1986), 230-247.

1148. _____. "Land transmission practices among nineteenth-century northern Maine French Canadians." DubSemPr (1989), 69-81.

1149. DOTY, C. STEWART. Acadian hard times: the Farm Security Administration in Maine's St. John Valley, 1940-1943. Orono: Univ. of Maine Pr., 1991. xiv, 184p. MeU. *

1150. ENO, R. D. "Clinging to the fringes in northern Maine: the Jews of Aroostook County." Kfari, 3 (Nov. 1989), 8-10.

1151. FEATHERSTONEHAUGH, GEORGE WILLIAM, and RICHARD ZACHARIAH MUDGE. In search of the highlands: mapping the Canada-Maine boundary, 1839: the journals of Featherstonehaugh and Mudge, August to November 1839. Alec McEwen, ed. Fredericton, New Brunswick: Acadiensis Pr., 1988. 120p. MeHi. *

1152. FREEBERG, ERNIE. "Voice of the valley." Down East, 36 (Nov. 1989), 78, 95-96.

   Ida Roy and the preservation of Acadian ballads of the St. John Valley.

1153. JUDD, RICHARD W. Aroostook: a century of logging in northern Maine. Orono: Univ. of Maine Pr., 1989. xiii, 351p. MeHi. *

1154. PRINS, HARALD E. L. "Tribulations of a border tribe: a discourse of the political ecology of the Aroostook band of Micmacs (16th-20th centuries)." Ph.D. dissertation, New School for Social Research, 1989. vi, 358p. MeU. *

   Abstracted in DAI, 49:10A (1989), 3072.

1155. SCOTT, GERALDINE TIDD. "Fortifications on Maine's northeast boundary, 1828-1845." MeHSQ, 29 (Winter-Spring 1990), 118-141.

1156. _____. Ties of common blood: a history of Maine's northeast boundary dispute with Great Britain, 1783- 1842. Bowie, Md.: Heritage Books, 1992. xviii, 445p. Me. *

SEE ALSO entry 5.

CUMBERLAND COUNTY

1157. BARRY, WILLIAM DAVID. "The handsome span." Greater Portland, 32 (Fall 1988), 50-51, 53-55.

   The Portland Bridge, between Portland and South Portland (built in 1916).

---

† See the Maine volume in this series (1977) for a complete list of counties.

* Online Computer Library Center (OLCC) listings for books and dissertations marked with this symbol may include additional library locations.

1158.   FRAPPIER, WILLIAM J. Steamboat days on Casco Bay: the steamboat era in Maine's Calendar Island region. Toronto: Stoddard, 1993. 196p. Me. *

1159.   MILLINGER, JIM. The Nellie G.s on Casco Bay. Yarmouth: Yarmouth Printing and Graphics, 1993. vii, 72p. MeHi. *
        Two passenger boats, both named Nellie G.

        SEE ALSO entry 1084.

FRANKLIN COUNTY

1160.   MOHNEY, KIRK F. "Daniel Beedy, 1810-1889." BDAM, 5:1 (1988), [1-4].
        Architect, known for his suspension bridges at Kingfield and Strong.

HANCOCK COUNTY

1161.   CROCK, JOHN G., JAMES B. PETERSEN, and ROSS ANDERSON. "Scalloping for artifacts: a biface and plummet from eastern Blue Hill Bay, Maine." Archaeology of Eastern North America, 21 (Fall 1993), 179-192.
        Prehistoric artifacts.

1162.   JELLISON, CONNEE. Hancock County, a rock-bound paradise: a bicentennial pictorial. Richard A. Horwege, ed. Norfolk, Va.: Donning, 1990. 216p. MeU. *

1163.   ROBERTS, ANN ROCKEFELLER. Mr. Rockefeller's roads: the untold story of Acadia's carriage roads and their creator. Camden: Down East Books, 1990. ix, 166p. MeHi. *
        John D. Rockefeller, Jr.

1164.   SANGER, DAVID, and HARALD E. L. PRINS. An island in time: three thousand years of cultural exchange on Mount Desert Island: essays. Ann McMullen and Diane Kopec, eds. Bar Harbor: Robert Abbe Museum, 1989. 36p. MeHi.

1165.   WILMERDING, JOHN. The artist's Mount Desert: American painters of the Maine coast. Princeton, N.J.: Princeton Univ. Pr., 1994. 195p. DLC. *

1166.   _____. "Thomas Cole in Maine." Record of the Art Museum, Princeton Univ., 49:1 (1990), 3-23.
        The painter's work on Mount Desert Island (1840s

KNOX COUNTY

1167.   CAREY, GEORGE. "Family island: Graffam anchors four generations." Island Journal, 5 (1988), 38-41.
        One of the Muscle Ridge islands.

LINCOLN COUNTY

1168.   McCARRON, EDWARD THOMAS. "The world of Kavanagh and Cottrill: a portrait of Irish emigration, entrepreneurship, and ethnic diversity in mid-Maine, 1760-1820." Ph.D. dissertation, Univ. of New Hampshire, 1992. xii, 397p. *
        Abstracted in DAI, 53:4A (1992), 1256-1257.

OXFORD COUNTY

1169.   HOWE, STANLEY RUSSELL. "Bethel-Fryeburg connections through the years." Bethel Courier, 12 (Winter 1988), 1-5.

        SEE ALSO entry 1084.

PENOBSCOT COUNTY

1170.   VICKERY, JAMES B. III. "Orono: the great sachem." MeHSQ, 32 (Fall 1992), 134-139.
        Joseph Orono (died 1801), Penobscot chief.

WASHINGTON COUNTY

1171.   IVES, EDWARD D. "The poacher as hero: the Graves case as exemplar." Forest & Conservation History, 35 (Jan. 1991), 24-28.
        A series of incidents in 1886 resulted in the killing of game wardens.

YORK COUNTY

1172.   CHANEY, MICHAEL P. White pine on the Saco River: an oral history of river driving in southern Maine. Orono: Maine Folklife Center, 1993. vii, 88p. Me. *
        Vol. 19 of Northeast Folklore.

1173.   CUMMINGS, OSMOND RICHARD, and EDWARD D. LEAVITT. Street cars to Old Orchard Beach: the Biddeford & Saco Railroad and connecting lines. Forty Fort, Pa.: Harold E. Cox, 1989. 63p. MeB. *

1174.   GERRIER, ARTHUR J. "Thomas Eaton (active 1794-1831)." BDAM, 5:8 (1988), [1-8].
        Architect.

        SEE ALSO entry 346.

Maine

Entries for Cities and Towns†

ADDISON (WASHINGTON CO.)

1175. LOWE, SUE DAVIDSON. "Marin's Maine: glimpses of the great American painter at home and work." Art & Antiques (Apr. 1989), 68-75, 115.
Recollections of a visit to John Marin in 1947.

ANDOVER (OXFORD CO.)

1176. POOR, AGNES BLAKE. Andover memorials. (1883) Andover, 1968. 125p. MeBetHi.

AUBURN (ANDROSCOGGIN CO.)

1177. FREDERIC, PAUL B. "Protecting farmland protection: the case of Auburn, Maine." NE-StLVGSPr, 17 (1987), 27-32.
1980s.

AUGUSTA (KENNEBEC CO.)

1178. ADAMS, JAY. "Material culture at Fort Western." Kennebec Proprietor, 6 (Summer 1989), 14-19.

1179. BALLARD, MARTHA MOORE. The diary of Martha Ballard, 1785-1812. Robert R. McCausland and Cynthia MacAlman McCausland, eds. Camden: Picton Pr., 1992. xiv, 972p. Me. *
See also entry 1185.

1180. BANWELL, ELIZABETH. "New look for Blaine House." Down East, 37 (Oct. 1990), 41, 59-60.
On the preservation of the house as the governor's mansion.

1181. CRANMER, LEON E. "Cushnoc: an example of non-traditional 17th-century New England architecture." Kennebec Proprietor, 5 (Winter 1988), 4-12.
See also next entry.

1182. _____. Cushnoc: the history and archaeology of the Plymouth Colony traders on the Kennebec. Augusta: Maine Historic Preservation Commission, 1990. 125p. Me. *

1183. JACKSON, BARTLEY. "Edward Charles Allen: publisher of mail order magazines in Augusta." Kennebec Proprietor, 5 (Winter 1988), 24-25.
Lived 1849-1891.

1184. ULRICH, LAUREL THATCHER. "Derangement in the family: the story of Mary Sewall, 1824-1825." DubSemPr (1990), 168-184.
Case of mental illness.

1185. _____. A midwife's tale: the life of Martha Ballard, based on her diary, 1785-1812. N.Y.: Knopf, 1990. x, 444p. MeU. *
Ballard lived in what was then a part of Hallowell. See also entry 1179.

1186. WARD, ELLEN MacDONALD. "The midwife's tale." Down East, 37 (Apr. 1991), 35, 50-53.
See also preceding entry.

---

† See the Maine volume in this series (1977) for a complete list of cities and towns.

* Online Computer Library Center (OLCC) listings for books and dissertations marked with this symbol may include additional library locations.

1187. YOUNG, DAWN K. "Martha Ballard's apothecary."
Kennebec Proprietor, 5 (Summer 1988), 23-25.
   Late-18th and early-19th centuries. See also entry 1185.

BANGOR (PENOBSCOT CO.)

1188. ALLIN, LAWRENCE CARROLL. "Telos, the last American
brig and Bangor River's 'class of '83.'" American Neptune,
49 (Winter 1989), 29-33.
   "Last commercial sailing vessel built in Bangor" (1883).

1189. BANGOR, ME. CONGREGATION BETH ISRAEL.
Congregation Beth Israel, Bangor, Maine: 1888-1988. James
Adam Emple, ed. Bangor: Bacon Printing & Paper, 1988.
MeU. *
   Synagogue.

1190. BROWN, JAMES P. "The house that axes built." Down
East, 40 (Aug. 1993), 71, 92-94.
   Snow and Nealley, hardware manufacturers.

1191. COLE, GALEN L. The Cole family of businesses: serving
Maine and New England for 72 years. N.Y.: Newcomen
Society of the U.S., 1989. 28p. MeHi. *

1192. TEIXEIRA, ELIZABETH. "The history of St. John's
School." "Paper Talks," Greater Bangor ed. ([Apr.] 1990),
77-78, 80-81, 86.
   Church school (Roman Catholic).

1193. TOLLES, BRYANT FRANKLIN JR. "Early architecture and
campus planning at the Bangor Theological Seminary."
MeHSQ, 29 (Fall 1989), 92-108.

1194. TONER, CAROL N. "Franklin Muzzy: artisan entrepreneur
in nineteenth-century Bangor." MeHSQ, 30 (Fall 1990),
70-91.
   Muzzy (1806-1873) owned a large machine shop and
iron foundry.

1195. _____. "Persisting traditions: the artisan community of
Bangor, Maine, 1820-1860." Ph.D. dissertation, Univ. of
Maine, 1989. ix, 218p. *
   Abstracted in DAI, 51:4A (1990), 1365.

1196. VERDE, THOMAS A. "Oscar Wilde in America?" Down
East, 36 (Oct. 1989), 64, 70-72.
   Wilde visited Bangor in 1882 during a lecture tour.

1197. ZELZ, ABIGAIL EWING, and MARILYN ZOIDIS.
Woodsmen and Whigs: historic images of Bangor. Norfolk,
Va.: Donning, 1991. 192p. MeHi. *

SEE ALSO entries 1019, 1057.

BAR HARBOR (HANCOCK CO.)

1198. BROSNAN, MICHAEL. "Teeing off down memory lane."
Down East, 37 (July 1991), 63-66.
   Kebo Valley Club.

1199. HELFRICH, G. W. "Bar Harbor's prize Pulitzer." Down
East, 40 (Aug. 1993), 53, 85-89.
   Publisher Joseph Pulitzer was a late-19th and early-
20th-century summer resident.

1200. HORNSBY, STEPHEN J. "The Gilded Age and the making
of Bar Harbor." Geographical Review, 83 (Oct. 1993),
455-468.

1201. LINCOLN, NAN. "Bertie vamps Bar Harbor." Down East,
38 (Jan. 1992), 50-54, 80.
   Heiress Huybertie Pruyn and social life in Bar Harbor
(1892).

1202. _____. "In search of 'lost' Bar Harbor." Down East, 39 (Mar.
1993), 50-53, 82-83.

1203. _____. "Safe haven." Down East, 38 (Aug. 1991) 48-51, 78,
80.
   German luxury liner, which reached safety in Bar Harbor
at the beginning of World War I.

1204. MOORE, RUTH. High clouds soaring, storms diving low:
the letters of Ruth Moore. Sanford Phippen, ed. Nobleboro:
Blackberry Pr., 1993. 524p. MeU. *
   Novelist (lived 1903-1989).

SEE ALSO entries 1163-1164.

BATH (SAGADAHOC CO.)

1205. BARRY, WILLIAM DAVID. "Fires of bigotry." Down East,
36 (Oct. 1989), 44-47, 77-78.
   1854 incident in which a mob burned the Old South
Meetinghouse, where Catholic masses were held.

1206. "CITY of ships." American Heritage, 42 (Sept. 1991), 28, 30.

1207. LACEY, PETER. "The magnificent 'J.'" Portland, 4
(July/Aug. 1989), 59-63.
   Interview with Olin J. Stephens II, one of the designers of
the Bath-built yacht "Ranger," which successfully defended
the America's Cup in 1937.

1208. SHETTLEWORTH, EARLE GREY JR. "Elegant
Elmhurst." Down East, 37 (May 1991), 43-45, 63.
   Mansion (1913), built by shipbuilder John S. Hyde.

1209. TROTMAN, JULIA. "City of ships." American Heritage, 42
(Sept. 1991), 28, 30.

1210   BATH

1210.   WEBB, ROBERT LLOYD. "Tragic homecoming." Down East, 36 (Dec. 1989), 66-68.
    Shipwreck (1849).

SEE ALSO entries 1053, 1122.

BELFAST (WALDO CO.)

1211.   EARLY histories of Belfast, Maine: Annals of Belfast for half a century, by William George Crosby; Sketches of the early history of Belfast, by John Lymburner Locke; History of Belfast from its first settlement to 1825, by Herman Abbot; A history of Belfast with introductory remarks on Acadia, by William White. Camden: Picton Pr., 1989. xiv, 298p. MWA. *

SEE ALSO entries 2255, 2269, and 2271 in the Maine volume.

BETHEL (OXFORD CO.)

1212.   BENNETT, RANDALL H. Bethel, Maine: an illustrated history. Bethel: Bethel Historical Society, 1991. xii, 242p. MeHi. *

1213.   BROWN, ARLENE G., and DONALD S. BROWN. "History of the Bethel United Methodist Church." Bethel Courier, 17 (Winter 1993), 1-4, 6-9.

1214.   DAVIS, LESLIE E. "Reflections of a half century." Bethel Courier, 10 (Winter 1986), 6-8; 11 (Spring 1987), 3, 6-8; (Summer 1987), 3, 10; (Fall 1987), 8; (Winter 1987), 1, 4-5; 12 (Spring 1988), 5; (Summer 1988), 1, 3-6; (Fall 1988), 6-7; (Winter 1988), 6, 8; 13 (Spring 1989), 8; (Summer 1989), 2, 4, 7; (Fall 1989), 5; (Winter 1989), 7-8; 14 (Spring 1990), 8; (Summer 1990), 2-4; (Winter 1990), 7; 15 (Spring 1991), 2-3; (Summer 1991), 3-5, 7-8; (Fall 1991), 2-3; (Winter 1991), 4-5; 16 (Spring 1992), 3-4; (Summer 1992), 9; (Fall 1992), 8.
    Author lived 1892-1961. To be continued.

1215.   DAVIS, PAULINE P. "Bethel's Bridge Street/Cross Street/Riverside Lane: a history." Bethel Courier, 17 (Summer 1993), 1-4; (Fall 1993), 5-6.

1216.   "THE DR. Moses Mason House 175 years old in 1988." Bethel Courier, 12 (Summer 1988), 1-2.

1217.   FREEMAN, MARY TIBBETTS. "Old-time gardens and some Bethel gardeners." Bethel Courier, 13 (Spring 1989), 1, 6-7.

1218.   HALL, RALPH S. "Brief history of the Bethel Fire Department." Bethel Courier, 16 (Spring 1992), 1, 5.

1219.   HOWE, GERALDINE S. "Highlights of the history of three Bethel streets: Crescent, Kilborn and Tyler." Bethel Courier, 12 (Spring 1988), 1-3.

1220.   _____. "Railroad Street through the years." Bethel Courier, 14 (Spring 1990), 1-3.

1221.   HOWE, STANLEY RUSSELL. "Centenary of the Cole Block." Bethel Courier, 15 (Winter 1991), 1, 3-4.

1222.   _____. "Lucy Larcom's poetic vision of Bethel." Bethel Courier, 14 (Summer 1990), 1-2.
    The 19th-century poet and author.

1223.   KENISTON, MARY C. "Highlights of Mill Hill history." Bethel Courier, 13 (Fall 1989), 1-4, 7-9.

1224.   "PORTRAIT of a patriarch: Dr. Moses Mason." Bethel Courier 13 (Summer 1989), 1-2.
    Born 1789.

1225.   SAUNDERS, LINDA. "The last of the Twentieth Maine: Collins F. Morgan." Bethel Courier, 17 (Fall 1993), 1-2.
    Civil War veteran (died 1939).

1226.   "SOCIETY marks first decade." Bethel Courier, 1 (Dec. 1976), 1-2.
    Bethel Historical Society.

1227.   TIBBETTS, MARGARET JOY. "Paradise Road: a brief history." Bethel Courier, 16 (Summer 1992), 1-4, 7; (Fall 1992), 1-4, 7-8.

1228.   WANGER, JOYCE. "19th century medicine in Bethel, Maine." Bethel Courier, 14 (Fall 1990), 1-7; (Winter 1990), 1, 4-6; 15 (Spring 1991), 8-10; (Summer 1991), 1-3.

SEE ALSO entries 1092, 1169.

BIDDEFORD (YORK CO.)

1229.   THOMAS, DAVIS. "Old and new at Biddeford Pool." Down East, 35 (July 1989), 38-45.
    Development of the resort area.

SEE ALSO entry 1173.

BLUE HILL (HANCOCK CO.)

1230.   BLUE HILL HISTORICAL SOCIETY. Blue Hill, Maine: a bibliography. Robert Sweetall, comp. Blue Hill, 1989. 32p. MeU. *

1231. SHAW, LESLIE C. "A biocultural evaluation of the skeletal population from the Nevin site, Blue Hill, Maine." Archaeology of Eastern North America, 16 (Fall 1988), 55-77.

1232. STEWART, TOM. "Blue Hill." Yankee, 54 (June 1990), 52-60, 108-112, 114.

1233. WOOD, ESTHER E. Deep roots: a Maine legacy. Camden: Yankee Books, 1989. ix, 279p. MeHi. *

BRIDGTON (CUMBERLAND CO.)

1234. BRIDGTON HISTORICAL SOCIETY. History of Bridgton, Maine, 1768-1794. (1968) 2d ed. Camden: Picton Pr., 1993. 966p. MeHi.

BRISTOL (LINCOLN CO.)

1235. DASH, C. WESTON. Bristol meeting houses, their cemeteries, and some of the people in them. Bristol, 1988. 11p. MeHi.

1236. KELLOGG, DOUGLAS CARLTON. "Prehistoric landscapes, paleoenvironments, and archaeology of western Muscongus Bay, Maine." Ph.D. dissertation, Univ. of Maine, 1991. 341p. *
    Abstracted in DAI, 53:1A (1992), 195.

    SEE ALSO entry 1051.

BROOKLIN (HANCOCK CO.)

1237. RUSSELL, ISABEL. Katharine and E.B. White: an affectionate memoir. N.Y.: W. W. Norton, 1988. 269p. MeU. *
    Editor and author, respectively. (E.B. White lived 1899-1985.)

BROOKSVILLE (HANCOCK CO.)

1238. CLARK, JEFF. "Summing up the good life." Down East, 38 (Apr. 1992), 30-33, 52.
    Author Helen Nearing at age 88. (Article includes biographical information.)

    SEE ALSO entry 406.

BRUNSWICK (CUMBERLAND CO.)

1239. ANDERSON, PATRICIA McGRAW. "Donors and patrons: the building of Bowdoin." Bowdoin, 61 (Fall 1988), 12- 15.
    Bowdoin College.

1240. BEEM, EDGAR ALLEN. "Evolution of the Bowdoin man." Down East, 40 (Nov. 1993), 54-57, 72-75.

1241. "A BOWDOIN miscellany: glimpses of the college in the 19th century." Bowdoin, 62 (Summer 1989), 2-19.

1242. BRUNSWICK, ME. Brunswick, Maine: 250 years a town, 1739-1989. Paul Downing, comp. Brunswick, 1989. 208p. MeHi. *

1243. CALHOUN, CHARLES C. A small college in Maine: two hundred years of Bowdoin. Brunswick: Bowdoin College, 1993. xviii, 294p. MeHi. *

1244. FLANAGAN, JAMES W. "Fly boys in the blueberry fields: the making of Brunswick Naval Air Station, 1942." Portland Monthly, 4 (Winterguide 1990), 16-20.

1245. GAFFNEY, JOHN. "The day John Masefield came to Bowdoin." Bowdoin, 65 (Spring 1993), 30-31.
    The poet visited Bowdoin as a guest lecturer in 1933.

1246. HUDSON, KATHARINE B. "Brunswick's French connection." Bowdoin, 62 (Winter 1988), 21-25.
    The town's Franco-Americans.

1247. OEHMIG, JULIA. "John Calvin Stevens' Brunswick." Bowdoin, 64 (Fall 1991), 9-13.
    The architect's buildings at Bowdoin and elsewhere in Brunswick.

1248. SHIPMAN, WILLIAM D. "Jim Abrahamson remembered." Bowdoin, 62 (Winter 1988), 16-20.
    Abrahamson was the first Jewish instructor at Bowdoin (1928), a longtime economics professor there, and at one time a New Deal administrator.

    SEE ALSO entries 71, 153, 1004, 1025, 1053, 1062, 1125.

CALAIS (WASHINGTON CO.)

1249. CANTON, DONALD R. "Champlain slept here." Down East, 35 (June 1989), 64-65, 92-95.
    St. Croix settlement (1604).

    SEE ALSO entry 1057.

1250   CAMDEN

CAMDEN (KNOX CO.)

1250.   BROWN, JAMES P. "The great doughnut debate." Down East, 38 (Dec. 1991), 50-51, 61-63.
    Lighthearted debate in national media (ca. 1940) over a claim that doughnut holes originated in Camden.

CAPE ELIZABETH (CUMBERLAND CO.)

1251.   CAPE ELIZABETH HISTORICAL SOCIETY. Cape Elizabeth: past to present. Cape Elizabeth, 1991. iv, 102p. MeHi. *

1252.   CLARK, JEFF. "Disaster in Casco Bay." Down East, 38 (Nov. 1991), 48-49, 71-72.
    1864 wreck of the transatlantic steam bark Bohemian: "the worst disaster in the history of Casco Bay."

CARATUNK PLANTATION (SOMERSET CO.)

1253.   McALLISTER, DONNA L. The sesquicentennial history of Caratunk, Maine. David Rosenberg, ed. North Anson: Carrabassett Printers, [1990]. 76p. MeU. *

CASCO (CUMBERLAND CO.)

1254.   KLUGE, MELISSA JILL. The history of Casco, Maine: in honor of Casco's sesquicentennial birthday in 1991. State College, Pa.: Jostens Printing and Publishing, 1991. x, 536p. MeHi. *

COLUMBIA FALLS (WASHINGTON CO.)

1255.   BEDARD, RICHARD N. 1910 census and historical sketch of Columbia Falls, Maine. Cherryfield: Narraguagus Printing, 1990. 31p. MeHi.

CRANBERRY ISLES (HANCOCK CO.)

1256.   DWELLEY, HUGH L., and ELLEN MacDONALD WARD. "The strange case of the K-14." Down East, 40 (July 1994), 65-66.
    Wreckage of a U.S. Navy dirigible, thought to have been shot down by a German submarine in 1944.

1257.   LITTLE, CARL. "'La grande poétesse du Maine...': Hortense Flexner of Sutton Island." Island Journal, 7 (1990), 66-67.
    Poet (lived 1885-1973).

1258.   PEARSON, ARN H., and MARY LOU WENDELL. "Solstice on Baker's Island." Island Journal, 9 (1992), 60-62.
    Year-around life on the island, past and present.

CUMBERLAND (CUMBERLAND CO.)

1259.   PLATT, DAVID W. "Growing up on Chebeague: an interview with Donna Miller Damon." Island Journal, 10 (1993), 80-83.
    Damon was born in 1950.

DAMARISCOTTA (LINCOLN CO.)

1260.   BARRY, WILLIAM DAVID, and STEPHEN G. BOOTH. "A country love-hate story." Portland, 8 (Summerguide 1993), 39-45.
    Poet Robert Lowell and his wife, who moved to Damariscotta Mills in 1945.

DEXTER (PENOBSCOT CO.)

1261.   BLANCHARD, DOROTHY A. "Into the heart of Maine: a look at Dexter's Franco-American community." MeHSQ, 33 (Summer 1993), 20-39.

1262.   BURKE, MICHAEL D. "Who killed John Wilson Barron? " Down East, 36 (June 1990), 73-79.
    1878 murder.

DURHAM (ANDROSCOGGIN CO.)

1263.   NELSON, SHIRLEY. Fair, clear and terrible: the story of Shiloh, Maine. Lathem, N.Y.: British American Publishing, 1989. x, 447p. MeHi. *
    Shiloh was the religious community begun by Frank W. Sandford (late-19th and early-20th centuries).

1264.   STONE, JASON. "Till Shiloh come." Down East, 36 (Mar. 1990), 44-48, 56.
    See also preceding entry.

ELIOT (YORK CO.)

1265.   GREEN ACRE BAHAI SCHOOL COUNCIL. Green Acre
on the Piscataqua: a centennial celebration. Eliot, 1991. xiii,
132p. MeHi.
        Piscataqua River.

ELLIOTTSVILLE PLANTATION (PISCATAQUIS CO.)

1266.   SAWTELL, WILLIAM R. Onawa revisited. [Milo: Paper
Pusher], 1989. 144p. MeHi. *

EMBDEN (SOMERSET CO.)

1267.   PETERSEN, JAMES BRANT. "The Dennison site: a deeply
stratified site on the Kennebec River." MeArcSocB, 31 (Fall
1991), 27-54.
        Indian site.

FALMOUTH (CUMBERLAND CO.)

1268.   HAMILTON, NATHAN DONNE. "Test excavation of the
Walker site, Presumpscot River drainage, Falmouth."
MeArcSocB, 30 (Fall 1990), 1-24.

FARMINGTON (FRANKLIN CO.)

1269.   GREGOR, SANDY. "Upcountry diva." Down East, 37 (Dec.
1990), 48-50, 57-58.
        Opera soprano Lillian Norton (died 1914), whose life and
career are commemorated at the Nordica Homestead.

1270.   THE LAST 100 years: a glimpse of the Farmington we have
known. Richard P. Mallett, comp. Wilton: Wilton Printed
Products, 1991. iii, 161p. MeHi. *

1271.   MALLETT, RICHARD P. Two centuries of Farmington
schools. Wilton: Wilton Printed Products, 1992. vi, 56p.
MeHi. *

SEE ALSO entry 1069.

THE FORKS PLANTATION (SOMERSET CO.)

1272.   ADAMS, AZEL. Creative survival: a narrative history of
Azel Adams, The Forks, Maine. Sally K. Butcher, comp.
Brunswick: Old Bess Publishing, [1991?]. 201p. MeHi. *

FORT KENT (AROOSTOOK CO.)

1273.   McDONALD, SHEILA. "The war after the war: Fort Kent
blockhouse, 1839-1842." MeHSQ, 29 (Winter-Spring 1990),
142-168.
        After the Aroostook War.

FRANKFORT (WALDO CO.)

1274.   "THE FRANKFORT Congregational Church." "Paper
Talks," Greater Bangor ed. ([Apr.] 1988), 70, 72-75, 77.

SEE ALSO entry 1050.

FREEPORT (CUMBERLAND CO.)

1275.   BARRY, WILLIAM DAVID, and BRUCE KENNETT. "The
world according to Foster." Down East, 35 (Mar. 1989),
50-53.
        Romantic artist William Foster, who summered and
worked in South Freeport from 1908-1941.

FRYEBURG (OXFORD CO.)

1276.   BARRY, WILLIAM DAVID. "The Rembrandt of sugaring
off." Down East, 38 (Apr. 1992), 34-37, 51.
        Painter Eastman Johnson (lived 1824-1906), a native of
Fryeburg.

1277.   FRYEBURG, ME. MAINE STREET '90 COMMITTEE.
"Old Pequawket Days," Fryeburg, Maine: a celebration of
Maine Street '90, July 7-July 14, 1990. [Fryeburg: Hurricane
Pr., 1990.] 25p. MeBetHi.
        Cover title. Includes historical sketches.

1278.   FRYEBURG HISTORICAL SOCIETY. The reminiscences
of Samuel Wiley, 1883. Fryeburg, 1991. 17p. MeBetHi.
        Recollections of some of the town's early settlers.

SEE ALSO entry 1169.

1279   GARDINER

GARDINER (KENNEBEC CO.)

1279.   "BUILDING a whaleship on the Kennebec." Nautical
Research Journal, 35:3 (1990), 120-138.
   Construction in 1850 of a vessel named the Hunter.
Includes Richard C. Kugler, "Historical background,"
120-125; Erik A. R. Ronnberg, Jr., "Design and construction
aspects of ship Hunter," 125-138.

1280.   SMITH, DANNY D. Gardiner's yellow house: a tribute to
the Richards family upon the occasion of the centennial
birthday of Laura Elizabeth Richards Wiggins—our dear
Betty. Gardiner: Friends of Gardiner, 1988. 58p. MeHi. *
   Includes biographical sketch of author Wiggins.

GILEAD (OXFORD CO.)

1281.   HEATH, EMELINE V. "Gilead memories." Bethel Courier, 5
(Dec. 1981), 1-5.

GORHAM (CUMBERLAND CO.)

1282.   BIBBER, JOYCE K. "Isaac Gilkey, 1768-1814." BDAM,
5:10 (1988), [1-4].
   Housewright.

GRAFTON TOWNSHIP (OXFORD CO.)

1283.   TIBBETTS, MARGARET JOY. "Grafton, Maine: a
historical sketch." Bethel Courier, 12 (Fall 1988), 1- 4.

GRAND ISLE (AROOSTOOK CO.)

1284.   BALDWIN, ROBERT. "Donald Cyr's magnificent
obsession." Down East, 36 (Apr. 1990), 49-51.
   Preservation of the Church of Notre Dame du Mont-
Carmel, in Lille.

GREENVILLE (PISCATAQUIS CO.)

1285.   RITCHIE, MRS WALLACE. "History of the Charles A.
Dean Memorial Hospital." "Paper Talks," Penquis ed.
([Aug.] 1988), 8, 11, 13-14, 16-19, 24, 26, 28-30, 33- 35.

HALLOWELL (KENNEBEC CO.)

1286.   JAEGER, A. ROBERT. "Lawrence B. Valk, 1838-1924."
BDAM, 5:20 (1988), [1-6].
   Designer of Hallowell's Old South Church

SEE ALSO entries 1179, 1185-1187.

HANCOCK (HANCOCK CO.)

1287.   LINCOLN, NAN. "Remembering the 'Maine.'" Down East,
37 (Aug. 1990), 67-71.
   Recounts a disaster that occurred during a celebration of
the first anniversary of victory in the Spanish-American War
(1899).

1288.   PHIPPEN, SANFORD. "The maestro of Taunton Bay."
Pierre Monteux and the Pierre Monteux School for
Conductors and Orchestra Musicians, which he founded
during the 1940s.

HANOVER (OXFORD CO.)

1289.   HANOVER, Maine, settled in 1774, incorporated in 1843.
n.p., [1976?]. 36p. MeBetHi.
   Title is as it appears on cover.

HARPSWELL (CUMBERLAND CO.)

1290.   CLARK, TIM. "The prisoner of Eagle Island." Yankee, 53
(Mar. 1989), 74-79, 82, 122-124, 126-128.
   Arctic explorer Robert E. Peary.

1291.   GOFF, JOHN V. "Mann & MacNeille." BDAM, 5:12,
(1988), [1-6].
   New York architects (early-20th century), who designed
Library Hall and MacNeille's cottage on Bailey Island.

1292.   SNOW, RICHARD F. A history of Birch Island, Casco Bay,
Maine. Topsham: S'no Hill Publications, 1992. 298p. MeHi. *

HEBRON (OXFORD CO.)

1293.   BEDFORD, RICHARD E. Hebron then to now. [Hebron]:
Hebron Bicentennial Committee, 1991. 47p. MeBetHi.

1294. DAVIDSON, HELEN T. Bicentennial celebration of the founding of Hebron Community Baptist Church, 1791-1991: a commemorative booklet including a program of events for August 23, 24, and 25, 1991. Hebron, 1991. 42p. MWA.

HIRAM (OXFORD CO.)

1295. COTTON, RAYMOND C. Split, rive and whittle: the story of Lemuel Cotton's axe handle shop. Hiram: Hiram Historical Society, 1989. 23p. MeHi. *

HODGDON (AROOSTOOK CO.)

1296. DICKINSON, FLORENCE GRANT. History of East Hodgdon, Maine: facts and fiction. n.p., [1983]. 83p. MeHi.

HOPE (KNOX CO.)

1297. HARDY, ANNA SIMPSON. History of Hope, Maine. Camden: Penobscot Pr., 1990. xvi, 528p. MeHi. *

INDIAN TOWNSHIP STATE INDIAN RESERVATION (WASHINGTON CO.)

1298. COX, STEVEN L. "Site 95.20 and the Vergennes phase in Maine." Archaeology of Eastern North America, 19 (Fall 1991), 135-161.
    Prehistoric site.

ISLE AU HAUT (KNOX CO.)

1299. BELCHER, WILLIAM R. "Prehistoric fish exploitation in East Penobscot Bay, Maine: the Knox site and sea-level rise." Archaeology of Eastern North America, 17 (Fall 1989), 175-191.
    On Pell Island.

1300. MURPHY, KEVIN D. "Ernest W. Bowditch, 1850-1918." BDAM, 5:3 (1988), [1-4].
    Engraver and landscape architect, who developed the plan for Point Lookout on Isle au Haut.

ISLEBORO (WALDO CO.)

1301. SHETTLEWORTH, EARLE GREY JR. The summer cottages of Isleboro, 1890-1930. Isleboro: Isleboro Historical Society, 1989. 124p. MeHi. *

KENNEBUNK (YORK CO.)

1302. ARMENTROUT, SANDRA S. "Eliza Wildes Bourne of Kennebunk: professional fancy weaver, 1800-1820." DubSemPr (1988), 101-115.

1303. BARRY, WILLIAM EDWARD (1846-1932). William E. Barry's Sketch of an old river; with an illustrated essay: Shipbuilding on the Kennebunk, by Joyce Butler. West Kennebunk: Phoenix Publishing, 1993. x, 74p. Me. *
    See also entry 3404 in the Maine volume.

1304. DAGGETT, KENDRICK PRICE. Fifty years of fortitude: the maritime career of Captain Jotham Blaisdell of Kennebunk, Maine, 1810-1860. Mystic, Conn.: Mystic Seaport Museum, 1988. xiv, 173p. MeU. *

1305. SARGENT, COLIN. "Heralds of freedom: St. Anthony's Franciscan Monastery." Portland Monthly, 5 (Apr. [1990]), 36-37.
    Founded by Lithuanian priests in 1947.

KENNEBUNKPORT (YORK CO.)

1306. BALES, JACK. "The irascible Mr. Roberts." Down East, 38 (Aug. 1991), 39, 70-74.
    See also next entry.

1307. _____. Kenneth Roberts: the man and his works. Metuchen, N.J.: Scarecrow Pr., 1989. xxii, 312p. MeU. *
    Historical novelist Kenneth Roberts (lived 1885- 1957).

1308. CLARK, JEFF. "The house that Bert built." Down East, 36 (Aug. 1989), 43-45, 96,98-99.
    The summer home of President George Bush, built by his grandfather, George Herbert Walker, in 1903.

1309. _____. "Last of the lightkeepers." Down East, 36 (July 1990), 48-51.
    Goat Island Light, the last lighthouse in the state to be automated.

1310   KENNEBUNKPORT

1310.   DOWNS, JACQUES M. Whence we came: a history of the
        South Congregational Church in Kennebunkport.
        Kennebunkport: South Congregational Church, 1990. 63p.
        MBAt. *

1311.   SARGENT, COLIN. "The Kennebunk River Indians."
        Portland Monthly, 3 (June/July 1988), 21-23, 36.
            Type of sailboat, dating from ca. 1929.

KITTERY (YORK CO.)

1312.   BARRY, WILLIAM DAVID. "The lady—and the painter."
        Down East, 38 (Jan. 1992), 41-44.
            Poet Celia Thaxter's friendship with and influence on the
        impressionist painter Childe Hassam, a visitor to Appledore
        Island (1890s). See also next entry and entry 1315.

1313.   KAGELEIRY, JAMIE F. "Celia's garden." Yankee, 58 (Aug.
        1994), 56-70, 104-105.
            Celia Thaxter. See also preceding entry and entry 1315.

1314.   LA VO, CARL. "Last dive of the 'Squalus.'" Down East, 35
        (May 1989), 50-53, 64-69.
            U.S. submarine, sunk off Kittery in 1939.

1315.   MAY, STEPHEN. "Island garden." Historic Preservation, 43
        (Sept./Oct. 1991), 38-45, 95.
            Celia Thaxter's garden, "celebrated in her charming
        classic, An island garden, and immortalized" in the
        paintings of Childe Hassam. See also entries 1312-1313.

1316.   WARD, ELLEN MacDONALD. "Living in a landmark."
        Down East, 36 (June 1990), 45-49, 90-91.
            Private ownership of the Lady Pepperrell House after its
        deaccessioning by the Society for the Preservation of New
        England Antiquities.

1317.   _____. "Only a memory." Down East, 39 (Feb. 1993), 53-54.
            Sparhawk Hall, at Kittery Point, built in 1742 and
        demolished in 1967.

        SEE ALSO entries 27, 254, 346, 358, 484.

LEBANON (YORK CO.)

1318.   JONES, SAMUEL WINGATE. A history of the town of
        Lebanon, Maine, with a short biographical sketch of some of
        its first settlers. Lebanon: Lebanon Historical Society, 1992.
        iv, 149, [5]p. MeHi. *
            Written ca. 1873; published from a manuscript belonging
        to the Maine Historical Society.

LEE (PENOBSCOT CO.)

1319.   LEE ACADEMY ALUMNI ASSOCIATION. A history of a
        frontier school: Lee Academy. Deanna Lathrop House, ed.
        Lee, 1989. 264p. MeHi. *

LEWISTON (ANDROSCOGGIN CO.)

1320.   ELDER, JANUS GRANVILLE (1835-1907). A history of
        Lewiston, Maine: with genealogical register of early families.
        David Young and Elizabeth Keene Young, eds. Bowie, Md.:
        Heritage Books, 1989. ix, 481p. MeU. *
            Note: this item replaces entry 1981 in Vol. 8.

1321.   FRENETTE, YVES. "La genese d'une communaute
        canadienne-française en Nouvelle-Angleterre; Lewiston,
        Maine, 1800-1880." Historical Papers [Canada] (1989),
        75-99.
            The birth of the French-Canadian community in
        Lewiston.

1322.   _____. "Lewiston's ethnic majority: the Francos." Bates: the
        Alumni Magazine, 86th ser., No. 4 (May 1988), 3-9.

1323.   HOOGEVEEN, JULIE M. "The first four presidents." Bates:
        the Alumni Magazine [Special Issue, 1989], 23-24.
            Presidents of Bates College.

1324.   _____. "Gleaned from the archives: inaugurations in Bates
        history." Bates: the Alumni Magazine, 88th ser., No. 4
        (Spring 1990), 14-19.
            See also preceding entry.

1325.   KUJAWA, RICHARD STEPHEN. "Local social relations
        and urban revitalization: the case of Lewiston, Maine." Ph.D.
        dissertation, Univ. of Iowa, 1990. viii, 216p.
            Downtown revitalization (mid-1970s). Abstracted in DAI,
        52:3A (1991), 1034.

1326.   MERRILL, CHARLES E. "The Reynolds years." Bates:
        Alumni Magazine [Special Issue, 1989], 2-6.
            Thomas Hedley Reynolds, president of the college from
        1967-1989. See also next entry.

1327.   "RECALLING the Reynolds years." Bates: the Alumni
        Magazine [Special Issue, 1989], 7-13.
            See also preceding entry.

1328.   SPILLER, LEE. "Life in the snow lane." Bates: the Alumni
        Magazine, 91st series, No. 2 (Winter 1993), 3-4.
            The author and other Bates students were hired to help
        clear a railroad after a 1920s blizzard.

1329. STAPLES, SARAH L. "Bates in the Nineties." Bates: the Alumni Magazine, 86th ser., No. 4 (May 1988), 19- 23.
1890s.

SEE ALSO entry 1109.

LIMINGTON (YORK CO.)

1330. RING, ELIZABETH. The McArthurs of Limmington, Maine, 1783-1917: the family in America a century ago. Falmouth: Kennebec River Pr., 1992. xv, 87p. MeHi. *

SEE ALSO entry 230.

LINCOLN (PENOBSCOT CO.)

1331. "LONGFELLOW School." "Paper Talks," Northern Penobscot ed. ([Jan.] 1988), 33, 42, 45.

LISBON (ANDROSCOGGIN CO.)

1332. WATKINS, AMBRA. The birth, being and burning of Worumbo Mill. Norway: The Oxford Group, 1987. 50p. Me. *
19th-century woolen mill, burned in 1987.

LITTLETON (AROOSTOOK CO.)

1333. SWEET, GEORGE ALLISON. "General history of Littleton." "Paper Talks," "The County" ed. ([Jan.] 1988), 11, 14, 16, 20-21, 25, 28, 35, 37, 40, 42, 45, 48-49.

LIVERMORE (ANDROSCOGGIN CO.)

1334. WEBB, THEODORE A. "Westward from Maine: a study of the Washburns as classic American myth." MeHSQ, 30 (Winter-Spring 1991), 126-145.
Washburn family.

SEE ALSO entry 1336.

LIVERMORE FALLS (ANDROSCOGGIN CO.)

1335. "REPORT on archeological dig at Norlands." Pray Pioneers, 2 (Spring 1984), 1, 4.
Otis Pray homesite.

1336. ROYS, OZRO. History, Oriental Star Lodge Number Twenty-one, Free and Accepted Masons, Livermore Falls, Maine. 5th ed. [Livermore Falls: The Lodge, 1933] 66p. MeHi.
Includes the early history of the lodge in Livermore.

SEE ALSO entry 1075.

LONG ISLAND (CUMBERLAND CO.)

1337. FAVORITE, FELIX. The steamboat era on Casco Bay: with special reference to Cleaves Landing, Long Island. [Seattle, Wash.]: Favorite Creations, 1989. 21p. MeHi. *

LONG ISLAND PLANTATION (HANCOCK CO.)

1338. BOURGEAULT, CYNTHIA. "Frenchboro, Maine." Yankee, 54 (Jan. 1990), 56-62, 108-110, 112-113.
Results of a recent attempt to attract year-round residents.

MACHIAS (WASHINGTON CO.)

1339. MANCKE, ELIZABETH. "Two patterns of New England transformation: Machias, Maine, and Liverpool, Nova Scotia, 1760-1820." Ph.D. dissertation, Johns Hopkins Univ., 1990. vii, 388p. VtU. *
Abstracted in DAI, 51:2A (1990), 611.

1340. NAULT, MARC A. "A report on the founding of the University of Maine at Machias and origin of the model school agreement." "Paper Talks," Washington County ed. ([Jan.] 1988), 11-15, 17, 20-21, 23-26, 28, 30-31.

SEE ALSO entry 90.

MACHIASPORT (WASHINGTON CO.)

1341. BROSNAN, MICHAEL. "Place of wonder." Down East, 36 (July 1990), 63-65, 67.
Children's author Robert McCloskey as a summer resident of an island in Penobscot Bay since ca. 1946.

1342   MACHIASPORT

1342.   HEDDEN, MARK H. "A new group of early petroglyphs
        from Machias Bay." MeArcSocB, 29 (Fall 1989), 17-36.
            On Hog Island.

MADAWASKA (AROOSTOOK CO.)

1343.   CRAIG, BEATRICE CHEVALIER. "Migrant integration in a
        frontier society: the Madawaska settlement, 1800-1850."
        Histoire sociale/Social History [Canada], 38 (Nov. 1986),
        277-298.

1344.   STEVENSON, MICHAEL DONALD, and GRAEME S.
        MOUNT. "The Roman Catholic diocesan boundary and
        American Madawaska, 1842-1870." MeHSQ, 32
        (Winter-Spring 1993), 174-187.

MATINCUS ISLE PLANTATION (KNOX CO.)

1345.   ROGERS, DONNA K. Tales of Matincus Island: history, lore
        and legend. n.p.: Offshore Publishing, 1990. 63p. MeU. *

MECHANIC FALLS (ANDROSCOGGIN CO.)

1346.   PETERSONS, ERIKS. A history: Mechanic Falls,
        1795-1893: in commemoration of this town's 100th year.
        Mechanic Falls: Mechanic Falls Centennial Committee,
        1993. xii, 54, 80p. MeHi. *

MONHEGAN PLANTATION (LINCOLN CO.)

1347.   MAY, STEPHEN. "George Bellows: the power and the
        glory." Down East, 38 (July 1992), 44-48, 60-61.
            The 20th-century painter and Monhegan Island.

1348.   SAUNDERS, LAURA S., and JOHN A. SAUNDERS.
        "Carrying the mail by sail." Down East, 36 (Oct. 1989),
        68-69.
            Capt. William Humphrey (from 1883-1908).

MONSON (PISCATAQUIS CO.)

1349.   WHITNEY, ROGER A. The Monson Railroad. Westbrook:
        Robertson Books, 1989. 88p. Me. *
            Between Monson Junction and Monson Village.

MOUNT DESERT (HANCOCK CO.)

1350.   DALFONSO, DEBORAH. "Summering with the
        Peabody's." Down East, 37 (Aug. 1990), 49, 77-81.
            Recollections of a summer job (1969).

1351.   HARLOW, JIM. "Beth's Fancy: oldest house on Mount
        Desert Island, Maine." Pray Pioneers, 2 (Summer 1984), 1-3.
            In Pretty Marsh.

1352.   MAY, STEPHEN. "Two geniuses and a paintbrush." Down
        East, 41 (Aug. 1994), 67, 86-88.
            Painter Thomas Eakins and his subject, physicist Henry
        A. Rowland (1897).

1353.   MORGAN, KEITH N. "Charles A. Platt, 1861-1933."
        BDAM, 5:17 (1988), [1-4].
            Designed the Theodore Dunham House in Northeast
        Harbor (1902).

        SEE ALSO entries 1163-1164.

MOUNT VERNON (KENNEBEC CO.)

1354.   MOUNT VERNON BICENTENNIAL LITERARY
        COMMITTEE. Mount Vernon Historical Review:
        bicentennial edition, 1792-1992. Mount Vernon, 1992. 82p.
        MeHi. *

MT. KATAHDIN TOWNSHIP (PISCATAQUIS CO.)

1355.   HILL, TOM. "The old man and the mountain." Southern
        Vermont Magazine, 1 (Spring 1986), 10-12.
            Augustus Aldrich, an elderly Vermonter, who vanished
        while climbing Mt. Katahdin in 1974.

NEW GLOUCESTER (CUMBERLAND CO.)

1356.   NEW GLOUCESTER HISTORICAL SOCIETY.
        Universalist Meeting House, New Gloucester, Maine. New
        Gloucester, 1989. 6p. MeHi.

        SEE ALSO entry 1102.

NEWCASTLE (LINCOLN CO.)

1357.   SPIESS, ARTHUR E. "The Ann Hilton site: a case of archaeological site management." MeArcSocB, 29 (Fall 1989), 13-16.
        Indian site, "possibly dating as late as the French and Indian wars." See also entry 1359.

1358.   _____, and MARK H. HEDDEN. "Archaeology at Dodge Point for the Land for Maine's Future Board." MeArcSocB, 30 (Fall 1990), 25-52.

1359.   WILL, RICHARD, and REBECCA COLE-WILL. "A preliminary report of the Ann Hilton site." MeArcSocB, 29 (Fall 1989), 1-11.
        See also entry 1357.

NOBLEBORO (LINCOLN CO.)

1360.   BARNES, KATE. "Chimney Farm revisited." Down East, 38 (May 1992), 24-27, 50.
        Author's recollections of life there with her writer-parents, Henry Beston and Elizabeth Coatsworth, beginning in 1930s.

NORRIDGEWOCK (SOMERSET CO.)

1361.   CALVERT, MARY R. Black robe on the Kennebec. Monmouth: Monmouth Pr., 1991. 292p. MeHi. *
        Father Sébastian Rale (lived 1652-1724).

NORTH HAVEN (KNOX CO.)

1362.   ALLEN, MEL R. "The man who broke North Haven's heart." Yankee, 53 (Sept. 1989), 52-57, 142, 144-146.
        Fred Demara, an impostor who taught school on the island during the 1950s.

1363.   BARBIAN, LENORE T., and ANN L. MARGENNIS. "Variabililty in late archaic human burials at Turner Farm, Maine." Northeast Anthropology, No. 47 (Spring 1994), 1-19.

1364.   CHAFEE, RICHARD. "William Y. Peters, 1858-1938." BDAM, 5:19 (1988), [1-6].
        Boston architect, who designed five summer cottages on North Haven.

1365.   DAY, JANE. "A family tradition: North Haven's J.O. Brown boatyard is launched on its second century." Island Journal, 9 (1992), 37-40.

1366.   REED, ROGER G. Summering on the thoroughfare: the architecture of North Haven, 1885-1945. Portland: Maine Citizens for Historic Preservation, 1993. 104p. MeHi. *

1367.   RICHARDSON, ELEANOR MOTLEY. North Haven summers: an oral history. Andover, Mass.: Catharine Little Motley, 1992. 256p. Me. *

        SEE ALSO entry 1108.

NORTH YARMOUTH (CUMBERLAND CO.)

1368.   COOKE, NYM. "William Billings in the District of Maine, 1780." American Music, 9 (Fall 1990), 243-259.
        The composer taught a singing school.

NORTHPORT (WALDO CO.)

1369.   MITCHELL, HARBOUR III. "The Carr site (41:66): a middle ceramic period site in Northport, Maine." MeArcSocB, 33 (Fall 1993), 33-44.

NORWAY (OXFORD CO.)

1370.   BRADBURY, OSGOOD N. Norway in the forties. Don L. McAllister, ed. Norway: Twin Town Graphics, 1986. xxv, 733p. MeHi. *
        First published as a series of articles in the Norway Advertiser (1866-1897). An index, compiled by "Mrs. Haines," was published by Heritage Books in 1991. Note: this item replaces entry 2120 in Vol. 8.

1371.   GEORGE L. Noyes, 1863-1945, Norway, Maine. Norway: Bruce B. Richards, 1989. [304]p. MeHi. *
        Artist and naturalist.

1372.   McALLISTER, DONNA L. Bound by memories' ties: a pictorial history of Norway, Maine. n.p., [1988]. 236p. MeHi.

        SEE ALSO entry 1004.

1373   ORONO

ORONO (PENOBSCOT CO.)

1373.   LIBBY, WINTHROP C. "Under no condition will the university close." Maine, 70 (Fall 1989), 25-27.
    Libby was president of the Univ. of Maine during the Vietnam War years.

1374.   PHIPPEN, SANFORD. "The student King." Maine, 70 (Fall 1989), 18-24.
    Novelist Stephen King as a student at the Univ. of Maine (class of 1970).

OXFORD (OXFORD CO.)

1375.   OXFORD HISTORICAL SOCIETY. A pictorial history of Oxford, Maine. Oxford, 1990. 118p. MeBetHi.

PARIS (OXFORD CO.)

1376.   DIBNER, MARTIN. Portrait of Paris Hill: a landmark village. Paris: Paris Hill Pr., 1990. 213p. Me. *

1377.   PARIS CAPE HISTORICAL SOCIETY. A pictorial history of Paris, Maine: a small New England shiretown. [Paris], 1987. 96p. MeBetHi.

PENOBSCOT (HANCOCK CO.)

1378.   PENOBSCOT HISTORICAL SOCIETY. Penobscot bicentennial, 1787-1987. Penobscot, 1987. 101p. MBNEH. *

PHILLIPS (FRANKLIN CO.)

1379.   PHILLIPS HISTORICAL SOCIETY. Phillips: 175 years, 1812-1987. Phillips, 1987. iv, 90p. MeU. *

1380.   "THE STORY of Greenwood Inn, Phillips, Maine, 1946-1971." "Paper Talks," Western Maine ed. ([June] 1988), 5, 10-11, 19, 23, 25, 27.

PHIPPSBURG (SAGADAHOC CO.)

1381.   CRICHLOW, BETH. "The house that Charlie built." Down East, 37 (Sept. 1990), 46-51, 79.
    On an island (1980s).

1382.   HAGGETT, ADA M. "Community continuity and change: Phippsburg's town hall." Maine History News, 25 (Spring 1989), 4-7.

SEE ALSO entry 1122.

POLAND (ANDROSCOGGIN CO.)

1383.   CLARK, JEFF. "Leisure in the grand tradition." Down East, 38 (Jan. 1992), 34-39, 60-62.
    Resort life at the Poland Spring House (1890s).

1384.   TURLEY, TOM. "Babe in the woods." Down East, 57 (June 1993), 92.
    The author once caddied for Babe Ruth at a golf course in Poland Spring (1940).

1385.   WARD, ELLEN MacDONALD. "A chip off the old block." Down East, 39 (Nov. 1992), 50-51.
    The Maine State Building at Poland Spring, originally built for the Chicago World's Fair of 1892-1893.

PORTLAND (CUMBERLAND CO.)

1386.   BABCOCK, ROBERT H. "The decline of artisan republicanism in Portland, Maine, 1825-1850." NEQ, 63 (Mar. 1990), 3-34.

1387.   BARNES, JACK. "Little Armenia." Portland Monthly, 3 (June/July 1988), 16-17, 19, 25.

1388.   _____. "Portland's Greek community." Portland Monthly, 5 (Apr. [1990]), 26-31.

1389.   BARRY, WILLIAM DAVID. "Antoine Dorticos, 1848-1906." BDAM, 5:7 (1988), [1-6].
    "During the 1880s and 1890s, [he] designed a series of five Queen Anne and Shingle Style cottages and pioneered the Casco Bay islands as a fashionable summer retreat for local families."

1390.   _____. "Henry & me." Down East, 35 (Apr. 1990), 52-54, 61-63.
    "Arthur Charles Jackson (1858-1919), one of Portland's most curious and storied eccentrics, proved himself remarkably adept at ingratiating himself with the rich and famous." The article traces his efforts to preserve Henry Wadsworth Longfellow's birthplace.

1391. _____. "John Neal, 'the man who knew everything else.'" Portland, 9 (July/Aug. 1994), 9, 11-17.
Lived 1793-1876.

1392. _____. "The Munjoy Hill caper." Down East, 36 (May 1990), 40-41, 60-63.
Riot (1849), resulting from an incident in which a black man, "attempting to defend his house against a band of rowdy sailors, killed another man."

1393. _____. "New works discovered by Portland's early modernist, William Wallace Gilchrist, Jr." Portland Monthly, 3 (Oct. 1988), 20, 22.
Lived 1879-1926.

1394. _____. "Nothing succeeds like failure." Down East, 37 (May 1991), 33, 58-61.
"Squire" Jonathan Morgan (1778-1871), a lawyer, author, and inventor.

1395. _____. "Portland's merchant prince." Down East, 39 (Oct. 1992), 55-57.
Asa Clapp (1762-1848).

1396. _____. "Portland's wackiest Fourth." Down East, 40 (July 1994), 47, 72-74.
July 4, 1873.

1397. _____. "The redoubtable Miss Clapp." Down East, 40 (June 1994), 56-58, 75.
The reclusive Mary Jane Emerson Clapp (died 1921) ordered that most of her property be destroyed after her death.

1398. _____. "There goes the neighborhood!" Down East, 40 (Aug. 1993), 72-73, 95-98.
Collapse of the Munjoy Reservoir (1893).

1399. _____, and RANDOLPH DOMINIC. "Who were those Deering people, anyway?" Portland Monthly, 5 (Feb./Mar. [1990]), 15-16.
Portland's Deering family.

1400. BIBBER, JOYCE K. "Charles Q. Clapp, 1799-1868." BDAM, 5:5 (1988), [1-6].
Architect.

1401. BRAHMS, ANN ALLEN. "The neighborhood." Greater Portland, 33 (Summer 1989), 79, 81-82.
Spruce Street (ca. 1944).

1402. _____. "24 May Street." Greater Portland, 34 (Spring 1990), 50-51, 53-54.
Autobiographical recollections of Portland life (ca. 1945).

1403. BURNS, CONNIE. "Margaret Jane Mussey Sweat and the expanding female sphere." MeHSQ, 33 (Fall 1993), 106-119.
19th century.

1404. BUTLER, JOYCE. "The 'single-parent' households of Portland's Wadsworth-Longfellow House." DubSemPr (1988), 28-37.
Late-18th and early-19th centuries.

1405. BUTTERWORTH, DALE J., and BENNETT BLUMENBERG. "Abel Sampson: Maine privateer turned planemaker." CEAIA, 45 (June 1992), 35-37.
In business ca. 1820s and 1830s.

1406. CONNOLLY, MICHAEL COLEMAN. "The Irish longshoremen of Portland, Maine, 1880-1923." Ph.D. dissertation, Boston College, 1988. 276p. MeU. *
Abstracted in DAI, 49:10A (1989), 3116.

1407. CURTIS, WAYNE. "Portland's modest Medici." Down East, 35 (May 1989), 39-43.
Mayor James Phinney Baxter (1831-1921), "one of Portland's greatest benefactors and most cultivated citizens."

1408. DERMAN, LISA. "Ten years on the real estate rollercoaster." Greater Portland, 33 (Spring 1989), 29- 30, 32-34.

1409. FELKER, TRACIE. "Charles Codman: early nineteenth-century artisan and artist." American Art Journal, 22 ([Summer] 1990), 60-86.

1410. FERGUSON, DONALD. "The massacre of 1692." Portland Monthly, 4 (Dec. [1989]), 14-17.
Capture of Fort Loyall by French and Indians.

1411. GARSON, SANDRA. "When the eating was good." Down East, 38 (Apr. 1992), 42-43, 49.
The popularity of "charity" cookbooks (late-19th century).

1412. GERRIER, ARTHUR J. "Parkside." Landmarks Observer, 16 (Fall 1990), 5-9.
Portland neighborhood.

1413. GRIBBIN, PETER E. The first century of Portland High School football. Portland: Dale Rand Printing, 1989. [125]p. MeHi. *

1414. GRIMES, SEAMUS, and MICHAEL COLEMAN CONNOLLY. "The migration link between Cois Fharraige and Portland, Maine, 1880s to 1920s." Irish Geography [Ireland], 22:1 (1989), 22-30.
Irish emigration.

1415   PORTLAND

1415.   HAMILTON, NATHAN DONNE. "Maritime adaptation in western Maine: the Great Diamond Island site." Ph.D. dissertation, Univ. of Pittsburgh, 1985. xxvii, 582p. Me. *
     Prehistoric site. Abstracted in DAI, 47:5A (1986), 1787.

1416.   JEROME, STEPHEN. "Richard Bond, 1798-1861." BDAM, 5:2 (1988), [1-4].
     Boston architect, who designed the Merchants Exchange and other buildings in Portland.

1417.   JORDAN, CHET. "Remembering the Gate: a mission on Main Street." Greater Portland, 33 (Spring 1989), 52-64.
     Mission for young people, in operation from 1965-1973.

1418.   JORDAN, WILLIAM B. JR. "Mr. Asa Clapp, entrepreneur extraordinary (1762-1848)." Portland Monthly, 5 (Feb./Mar. 1990), 8-9.

1419.   KING, DONALD C. "The theatres of Portland, Maine." Marquee, 23:1 (1991), 3-13.

1420.   KOBBINS, RHEA J. COTE. "'Down the plains': three generations of Franco-American women." Portland Monthly, 5 (Apr. [1990]), 20-25.

1421.   KULAWIEC, E. P. "Polish echoes." Greater Portland, 5 (Apr. [1990]), 32-35.

1422.   LANNIN, JOANNE. "Smokey was a natural." Yankee, 57 (Apr. 1993), 96-99.
     Florence Irene "Smokey" Woods, an outstanding pitcher on men's baseball teams (early-20th century), who later became a nun.

1423.   LUISE, PAUL J. "Portland's little Italy." Portland Monthly, 5 (Apr. [1990]), 14-20.

1424.   MacWILLIAMS, DON. "Franklin Simmons, sculptor." Portland Monthly, 2 (Dec./Jan. 1988), 46-47.
     Maine-born sculptor of Portland's Longfellow statue and its Soldiers and Sailors Monument.

1425.   MARCIGLIANO, JOHN. All aboard for Union Station. South Portland: Pilot Pr., 1991. viii, 154p. MeHi. *
     History of the building, which was demolished in 1961.

1426.   McCUE, JULIA. "'...For the building of model homes for working men.'" Landmarks Observer, 15 (Summer 1988), 1, 8-9.
     In 19th-century Portland.

1427.   MOULTON, JOHN K. An informal history of four islands: Cushing, House, Little Diamond, Great Diamond. Yarmouth, 1991. 91p. MeHi. *

1428.   _____. Peaks Island: an affectionate history. Yarmouth, 1993. 109p. Me. *

1429.   NELSON, DEREK. "The Dave Astor Show." Portland Monthly, 3 (June/July 1988), 8-13, 15.
     Local television show (1956-1971), which featured high school students.

1430.   NILSEN, KENNETH E. "Thinking of Monday: the Irish speakers of Portland, Maine." Eire-Ireland, 25 (Spring 1990), 6-19.

1431.   PEAVEY, ELIZABETH. "Bomb shelter interiors." Portland, 7 (Apr. 1992), 32-34.
     Ca. 1960s.

1432.   PORTER, DORIS AMBLER. A history of the Longfellow Garden. n.p., 1983. 28p. MeP. *
     At Henry Wadsworth Longfellow House.

1433.   "PORTLAND's historic districts: recognition at last." Landmarks Observer, 16 (Winter 1990), 3-11.

1434.   PUTNAM, ARNOLD. "Portland's Civil War Monitor." Portland, 7 (July/Aug. 1992), 12-17.
     One of the Union navy's ironclad vessels, built in Portland.

1435.   PUTNAM, ROGER A. Verrill & Dana: faith in the future, pride in the past. N.Y.: Newcomen Society of the U.S., 1987. 20p. Me. *
     Law firm. See also entries 1443-1444.

1436.   REED, ROGER G. "Miller and Mayo." BDAM, 5:15 (1988), [1-6].
     Architectural partnership (early-20th century).

1437.   SHERBO, ARTHUR. "On the ethics of reprinting: Thomas Mosher vs. Andrew Lang." NEQ, 64 (Mar. 1991), 100-112.
     1895 lawsuit.

1438.   SHETTLEWORTH, EARLE GREY JR. "George B. Pelham, 1831-1889." BDAM, 5:18 (1988), [1-6].
     Architect, responsible for three churches and two houses in Portland.

1439.   STEVENS, JOHN CALVIN II, and EARLE GREY SHETTLEWORTH JR. John Calvin Stevens: domestic architecture, 1890-1930. Scarborough: Harp Publications, 1990. 223p. MeU. *

1440.   STORER, ALLYN. "Brown Thurston's year, Portland, Maine, 1855." MeHSQ, 33 (Fall 1993), 136-153.
     Diarist.

1441. UMINOWICZ, GLENN. "Portland's monuments: beautiful and not merely useful." Landmarks Observer, 16 (Fall 1990), 1, 3-4.

1442. _____. "The statue in Portland's front hall." Greater Portland, 6 (Apr./May 1991), 20-22.
       Henry Wadsworth Longfellow statue.

1443. VERRILL AND DANA (attorneys). Verrill & Dana: counsel, partners and associates, 1987. [Portland]: Printed by Penmor Lithographers, [1988?]. [48]p. MeHi.
       Biographical sketches. See also next entry.

1444. _____. Verrill & Dana: the first 125 years. [Portland]: Printed by Penmor Lithographers, [1988?]. [40]p. MeHi.
       See also preceding entry and entry 1435.

1445. WAGNER, DAVID, and MARCIA B. COHEN. "The power of the people: homeless protesters in the aftermath of social movement participation." Social Problems, 38 (Nov. 1991), 543-561.
       Effects on homeless participants of a 1987 "tent city" protest.

1446. WALLACE, ALEXANDER. "The life of a house." Greater Portland, No. 4 (June/July 1991), 22-25.
       McClellan House, a Federal-style structure on High Street.

1447. WARD, ELLEN MacDONALD. "A landmark to remember." Down East, 38 (July 1992), 56-58.
       Union Station.

1448. WELCH, ED. "The furniture revolution of Portland, Maine." Portland, 7 (Dec. 1991), 26-29.
       Walter Corey Furniture Company (19th century).

1449. WHITNEY, DONALD PATRICK. Portland Fire Department: a historian's view. [Portland]: Guy Gannett Publishing, [1991?]. 119p. MeHi. *

1450. WOODFORDS CLUB. Woodfords Club and the Woman's Woodford's Club: "from the beginning to now": the historical record, 1913-1988. Portland, 1988. 34p. MeHi. *

       SEE ALSO entries 488, 1046, 1109, 1157.

PRESQUE ISLE (AROOSTOOK CO.)

1451. HOLMES, MARGARET LOUISE. "The analysis of enrollment patterns and student profile characteristics at a small rural New England university, 1978-1988." Ed.D. dissertation, Univ. of North Carolina, Greensboro, 1990. xii, 400p. *
       Univ. of Maine, Presque Isle. Abstracted in DAI, 51: 11A (1991), 3643-3644.

       SEE ALSO entry 1150.

RANGELEY (FRANKLIN CO.)

1452. BOYNTON, MIA. "A gift of native knowledge: the history of Russell's Motor Camps in Rangeley, Maine." Northeast Folklore, 28 (1989), 1-68.

1453. CLARK, TIM. "The doctor who made it rain." Yankee, 53 (Sept. 1989), 72-79, 130-132, 134.
       Psychiatrist Wilhelm Reich and his reputation as a "mad scientist."

RAYMOND (CUMBERLAND CO.)

1454. LANGLOIS, ALMA HANSEN. "What made Edgar run?" Down East, 38 (June 1992), 67-69.
       Distance runner Edgar Welch (lived 1849-1903).

RICHMOND (SAGADAHOC CO.)

1455. LIMANNI, ANTHONY M. "Life at Fort Richmond, District of Maine: from the account book of John Minot, truckmaster, 1737-1742." Kennebec Proprietor, 5 (Winter 1988), 13-19.
       Indian trading post.

ROCKLAND (KNOX CO.)

1456. GLASER, ED. "Captain Ed Glaser of Rockland, Maine: nobody in my family liked boats." Kfari, 1 (Aug. 1988), 8-10.
       Operator of a charter schooner. Based on an oral history interview by R.D. Eno.

1457. MAY, STEPHEN. "The day FDR toured Rockland." Down East, 38 (Sept. 1991), 43, 62.
       President Franklin D. Roosevelt (Aug. 16, 1941).

1458   ROCKLAND

1458.   MERRIAM, PAUL G., THOMAS J. MOLLOY, and
THEODORE W. SYLVESTER JR. Home front on Penobscot
Bay: Rockland during the war years, 1940-1945. Rockland:
Rockland Cooperative History Project, 1991. vi, 330p. MeHi. *

RUMFORD (OXFORD CO.)

1459.   STONE, JASON. "Chisholm's 'folly.'" Down East, 38 (Jan.
1992), 55-59.
Hugh J. Chisholm's promotion and development of
Rumford as an industrial center (1890s).

SEE ALSO entries 1064, 1075.

SACO (YORK CO.)

1460.   FAIRFIELD, ROY P. New compass points: twentieth century
Saco. Saco: Bastille Books, 1988. viii, 256p. MeU. *

SEE ALSO entry 1173.

SANFORD (YORK CO.)

1461.   PAQUETTE, WILLIAM ARTHUR. "Educational
opportunity, social mobility, and assimilation among the
Québécois: a comparative case study of St. Georges de
Windsor, Quebec, Sanford, Maine, and the Paquette family in
each, 1870-1970." Ph.D. dissertation, Emory Univ., 1993.
381p.
Abstracted in DAI, 54:12A (1994), 4374.

1462.   PROSSER, ALBERT L. Nasson: the seventy years. West
Kennebunk: Phoenix Publishing, 1993. ix, 297p. Me. *
Nasson College. Includes an epilogue by Richard
D'Abate.

SCARBOROUGH (CUMBERLAND CO.)

1463.   PROVOST, PAUL RAYMOND. "Winslow Homer's The fog
warning: the fisherman as heroic character." American Art
Journal, 22 ([Spring] 1990), 21-27.
Homer's 1885 painting was done at Prout's Neck.

1464.   SHETTLEWORTH, EARLE GREY JR, and WILLIAM
DAVID BARRY. "'Brother artists': John Calvin Stevens and
Winslow Homer." Bowdoin, 61 (Fall 1988), 16-19.
Stevens (1855-1940) designed three houses in
Scarborough for Homer and members of his family.

1465.   WINSLOW Homer in the 1890s: Prout's Neck observed.
N.Y.: Hudson Hills Pr., 1990. 154p. MeU. *
Essays by Philip C. Beam, Lois Homer Graham, Patricia
Junker, David Tatham, and John Wilmerding.

SEARSPORT (WALDO CO.)

1466.   WILEY, CAROLYN. "Meats, grains, groceries: F.L. Perkins,
prop." Maine History News, 25 (Fall 1989), 8- 9, 11.
World War I era and later.

SEBEC (PISCATAQUIS CO.)

1467.   ROBERTS, GWILYM R. Sebec, Maine, before, during, and
after the Civil War. n.p., 1991. 20p. MeHi. *

SHERMAN (AROOSTOOK CO.)

1468.   IVES, EDWARD D. "'The teamster in Jack MacDonald's
crew': a song in context and its singing." Folklife Annual
(1985), 74-85.
Folk song about a man from Sherman Mills.

SIDNEY (KENNEBEC CO.)

1469.   SIDNEY, ME. BICENTENNIAL COMMITTEE. History of
Sidney, Maine, 1792-1992. Camden: Picton Pr., 1992. ix,
273p. Me. *

SMITHFIELD (SOMERSET CO.)

1470.   FERM, DEANE WILLIAM, and DEBRA CAMPBELL.
Smithfield 150, 1840-1990: Maine's only leap year town.
Smithfield: Town of Smithfield, 1990. 68p. VtHi. *

SOLON (SOMERSET CO.)

1471.   SPIESS, ARTHUR E., and MARK H. HEDDEN. "The
Evergreens: archaeology and an alluvial landform on the
Kennebec." MeArcSocB, 33 (Fall 1993), 1-21; 34 (Spring
1994), 1-37.

SOUTH BERWICK (YORK CO.)

1472. WARD, ELLEN MacDONALD. "Romancing the past."
Down East, 36 (Sept. 1989), 53-56, 89, 92-93.
    Restoration and preservation of the 18th-century
Hamilton House.

SOUTH PORTLAND (CUMBERLAND CO.)

1473. EASTMAN, JOEL W. "Ships for liberty: World War II
shipbuilding in South Portland." Portland, 9 (July/Aug.
1994), 19-23, 25-27, 29, 31.

1474. SOUTH PORTLAND HISTORY COMMITTEE. History of
South Portland, Maine. [South Portland: Brownie Pr.], 1992.
iii, 69p. MeHi. *

SEE ALSO entry 1157.

SOUTHPORT (LINCOLN CO.)

1475. STICKNEY, ALDEN P. "The hometown fleet of Southport,
Maine." Steamboat Bill, 46 (Summer 1989), 98-101.

1476. STINNETT, CASKIE. "The legacy of Rachel Carson."
Down East, 38 (June 1992), 39-42.
    Carson was a summer resident. The article was
occasioned by the 30th anniversary of the publication of her
well-known book, Silent spring.

SOUTHWEST HARBOR (HANCOCK CO.)

1477. MacDONALD, D. S. "The year the Russians came to town."
Down East, 35 (June 1989), 78-99.
    A detachment of Russian sailors spent the summmer of
1878 in Southwest Harbor while waiting for the completion
of some warships under construction in Philadelphia.

ST. ALBANS (SOMERSET CO.)

1478. ST. ALBANS, ME. St. Albans 175th anniversary,
1813-1988. Pittsfield: Printed by Valley Graphics, 1988. 84p.
MeHi. *

ST. GEORGE (KNOX CO.)

1479. McLANE, CHARLES B. "A single-family island." Island
Journal, 9 (1992), 78-81.
    Teel Island.

STANDISH (CUMBERLAND CO.)

1480. SEARS, ALBERT JOHNSON. The founding of
Pearsontown (Standish), Maine. Bowie, Md.: Heritage
Books, 1991. xiii, 223p. Me. *

STONINGTON (HANCOCK CO.)

1481. ETCHISON, CRAIG. Maine man: the life and times of a
Down Easter; an oral history of the life of Ray Rice. Santa
Barbara, Calif.: Fithian Pr., 1989. 207p. MeHi. *

SULLIVAN (HANCOCK CO.)

1482. A BICENTENNIAL history of Sullivan, Maine. S. Josephine
Cooper, ed. Camden: Picton Pr., 1989. 328p. MeHi. *

SWANS ISLAND (HANCOCK CO.)

1483. BOURGEAULT, CYNTHIA. "How the State Ferry Service
came to Swans Island." Island Journal, 10 (1993), 48- 52.
    To be continued.

1484. HEDDEN, MARK H. "A winged figure incised on a slate
pebble." MeArcSocB, 31 (Spring 1991), 41-50.
    Petroglyph, found on Pond Island.

THOMASTON (KNOX CO.)

1485. WHITE, JONATHAN. "Maine's last hanging." Portland, 4
(July/Aug. 1989), 23-24, 27-28.
    Daniel Wilkinson was executed in 1885 for a murder
committed in Bath.

TOPSHAM (SAGADAHOC CO.)

1486.   COX, STEVEN L., and DEBORAH B. WILSON. "4500 years on the lower Androscoggin: archaeological investigation of the Rosie-Mugford site complex." MeArcSocB, 31 (Spring 1991), 15-40.

1487.   CRANMER, LEON E. "The Purinton House: colonial and federal archaeology in Topsham." MeArcSocB, 33 (Spring 1993), 1-55.

SEE ALSO entries 1053, 1125.

TRENTON (HANCOCK CO.)

1488.   LITTLE, CARL. "A life in pictures." Down East, 38 (Nov. 1991), 56-60.
George Daniell, a noted contemporary photographer.

UNION (KNOX CO.)

1489.   HOLMES, RAYNOLD R. "The Gerald Hall site (site #27.66): a single component Susquehanna site." MeArcSocB, 34 (Spring 1994), 39-45.

UPTON (OXFORD CO.)

1490.   BUTTERWORTH, DALE J., and BENNETT BLUMENBERG. "E.S. Lane: a Maine rule maker and scaler." CEAIA, 46 (Mar. 1993), 15-16.
Hand tool maker (lived 1877-1945).

VASSALBORO (KENNEBEC CO.)

1491.   TRAUTMAN, ELIZABETH, and ARTHUR E. SPIESS. "The Cates Farm: archaic and woodland occupation at China Lake outlet." MeArcSocB, 32 (Spring 1992), 1-44.
Archaeological site in East Vassalboro.

VEAZIE (PENOBSCOT CO.)

1492.   LAGERBOM, CHARLES H. "Jonathan Lowder's truckhouse: an American Revolutionary War trading post on the Penobscot River." MeArcSocB, 31 (Spring 1991), 1-14.

VINALHAVEN (KNOX CO.)

1493.   BROWN, JAMES P. "Rebirth of an island." Down East, 38 (Sept. 1991), 30-35, 70-71.
Hurricane Island as a site for Outward Bound operations. Article includes historical information about the island. See also entry 1495.

1494.   HOLMES, EDWARD M. "Vinalhaven Lobstermen's Co-operative, 1938." MeHSQ, 29 (Summer 1989), 52-57.

1495.   RICHARDSON, ELEANOR MOTLEY. Hurricane Island: the town that disappeared. Rockland: Island Institute, 1989. xviii, 124p. MeHi. *

WALLAGRASS PLANTATION (AROOSTOOK CO.)

1496.   STADIG, RITA. The St. John Valley story and the Wallagrass story, 1830-1920. [Soldier Pond], 1989. 128p. MeU. *

WARREN (KNOX CO.)

1497.   OVERLOCK, LELAND. Windships of Warren, Maine: writings and records pertaining to the history of shipbuilding and related matters, 1770 to 1867. Brewer: Cay-Bel Publishing, 1988. xiii, 306p. MeHi. *

WASHINGTON (KNOX CO.)

1498.   OVERLOCK, CLARA S. Washington, Maine, facts. E. Burnell Overlock, ed. Winter Haven, Fla., 1988. 2v. MeHi.

WATERFORD (OXFORD CO.)

1499.   BOWERS, Q. DAVID. The Waterford water cure: a numismatic inquiry. Wolfeboro, N.H.: Bowers and Merena Publications, 1992. 221p. MeBetHi. *
19th-century health resort.

1500.   SAWYER, MARGARET MERRY. Reaching for the summit. Gardiner: Steele Publishing, 1992. viii, 190p. MeHi. *
Autobiographical (author was born in 1914).

WATERVILLE (KENNEBEC CO.)

1501.   "ATHLETICS at Colby." Colby, 77 (Fall 1988), 44- 49.
    Colby College.

1502.   CAMPBELL, DEBRA. "The Baptists and the founding of
    Colby College." Colby, 77 (Fall 1988), 14-16.
    1813.

1503.   COCKS, J. FRASER III. "Colby's special collections."
    Colby, 77 (Fall 1988), 54-55.

1504.   GINZ, THOMAS. "A tour of the old campus." Colby, 77
    (Fall 1988), 18-24.

1505.   HUDSON, YEAGER. "The philosophy of J. Seelye Bixler."
    Colby, 78 (Winter 1989), 12-14.
    Former president of Colby.

1506.   JOSEPH, JOYCE. "The Joseph years in the Spa." Colby, 77
    (Fall 1988), 50-52.
    The Joseph family and the Colby student Spa (1947-
    1985).

1507.   MICHAELS, HARRIETTE. "A visit from 'Mrs. President.'"
    Colby, [80] (Jan. 1991), 22-23.
    Michaels was the wife of an English instructor at Colby
    in the late 1940s; "Mrs. President" was Mrs. J. Seelye
    Baxter.

1508.   SMITH, EARL H. "The old that's worth saving." Colby, 77
    (Fall 1988), 36-41.
    Objects saved from Colby's old campus when the new
    one was opened in 1946.

    SEE ALSO entries 1062, 1069.

WAYNE (KENNEBEC CO.)

1509.   SPIESS, ARTHUR E. "A red paint effigy from Wayne,
    Maine." Archaeology of Eastern North America, 19 (Fall
    1991), 163-170.

WELLS (YORK CO.)

1510.   "THE ARTISTIC legacy." Down East, 36 (Sept. 1989),
    42-45.
    In Ogunquit.

1511.   RIDDLE, LYN. "Having a wonderful time!" Down East, 36
    (Sept. 1989), 39-41, 80-82.
    Ogunquit artists' colony (late-19th and 20th centuries).

1512.   THOMAS, DAVIS. "Bold legacy of an Ogunquit
    Bohemian." Down East, 40 (July 1994), 60-64.
    Painter Henry H. Strater (20th century).

    SEE ALSO entry 346.

WEST GARDINER (KENNEBEC CO.)

1513.   BUTTERWORTH, DALE J., and BENNETT
    BLUMENBERG. "David Fuller, rural planemaker of West
    Gardiner, Maine." CEAIA, 43 (Sept. 1991), 112-113.
    1850s.

WESTBROOK (CUMBERLAND CO.)

1514.   SEVERNS, MARTHA. "Waldo Peirce and the $700 'jack.'"
    Down East, 39 (Apr. 1993), 44-48.
    Mural, painted for the Westbrook Post Office (1937),
    depicting lumbering in the North Woods.

WINSLOW (KENNEBEC CO.)

1515.   CRANMER, LEON E. "Blockhouses and cellars: the 1989
    and 1990 archaeological work at Fort Halifax." MeArcSocB,
    21 (Fall 1991), 1-26.

1516.   _____. "Fort Halifax archaeological excavations, 1991."
    MeArcSocB, 33 (Fall 1993), 23-31.

1517.   "FORT Halifax National Historic Landmark: a preliminary
    master plan." Kennebec Proprietor, 6 (Winter 1990), 22-29.
    Includes historical information.

1518.   HORNE, HOPE BRALEY. Winslow: our town, our people.
    [Decorah, Iowa: Anundsen Printing, 1991] xii, 600p. MeHi. *

WISCASSET (LINCOLN CO.)

1519.   WARD, ELLEN MacDONALD. "Captain Nickels' folly."
    Down East, 40 (Sept. 1993), 45-47, 73-74.
    Nickels-Sortwell House (early-19th century).

WOODSTOCK (OXFORD CO.)

1520.   EMERY, RUBY C. Hamlin's Gore, 1816-1973. [Bryant
    Pond], 1985. 115, 14, [11]p. Me. *
    Place in Woodstock.

1521   WOODSTOCK

1521.   EMERY, RUBY C. Woodstock schools, 1815-1983. [Bryant Pond], 1983. 195p. Me. *

1522.   WOODSTOCK HISTORICAL SOCIETY. Pictorial Woodstock, Maine, 1815-1920. Bryant Pond: Inman Printing, 1988. 92p. Me. *

WOOLWICH (SAGADAHOC CO.)

1523.   BRADLEY, ROBERT L. "Was the plantation despicable?: the archaeology of the Phips site, ca. 1646-1676." Kennebec Proprietor, 6 (Winter 1990), 11- 17.

YORK (YORK CO.)

1524.   BEAL, CLIFFORD. "Candlemas Day massacre." Down East, 39 (Dec. 1992), 52, 62-63.
    Destruction of York by Abenakis in 1692.

    SEE ALSO entry 346.

Massachusetts

**Entries for the state as a whole
or pertaining to
more than one county**

1525. AARON, PAUL GASTON. "From 'bleeding heart' to 'bottom line': routinization of reform in Massachusetts youth services." Ph.D. dissertation, Brandeis Univ., 1988. x, 321p. *
Study of the Massachusetts Department of Youth Services from 1969-1985. Abstracted in DAI, 49:11A (1989), 3520.

1526. ABBOTT, GORDON JR. Saving special places: a centennial history of the Trustees of Reservations, pioneer of the land trust movement. Ipswich: Ipswich Pr., 1993. xi, 334p. M. *

1527. ABEL, MARJORIE, and NANCY RUSSELL FOLBRE. "A methodology for revising estimates: female market participation in the U.S. before 1940." Historical Methods, 23 (Fall 1990), 167-176.
Based on a study of 1880 census data for Easthampton and Montague.

1528. ADAMS, JOHN W., and ALICE BEE KASAKOFF. "Estimates of census underenumeration based on genealogies." Social Science History, 15 (Winter 1991), 527-543.
Uses censuses and genealogies to identify and locate descendants, living in 1850, of some immigrants to Massachusetts in 1650.

1529. ADAMSON, JEREMY ELWELL. "The Wakefield Rattan Company." Antiques, 142 (Aug. 1992), 214-221.
Late 19th-century manufacturer of rattan furniture, in Boston and South Reading.

1530. AICHELE, GARY J. Oliver Wendell Holmes, Jr.: soldier, scholar, judge. Boston: Twayne Publishers, 1989. 212p. MB. *
Holmes lived 1841-1935.

1531. ALCOTT, LOUISA MAY. The journals of Louisa May Alcott. Joel Myerson and Daniel Shealey, eds. Boston: Little, Brown, 1989. xxviii, 356, [16]p. MB. *

1532. ALLEN, MEL R. "The education of Doug Flutie." Yankee, 53 (Nov. 1989), 76-80, 126-128, 130, 132, 134.
Boston College quarterback and later a member of the New England Patriots football team (1980s).

1533. ALMEIDA, DEIDRE ANN. "The role of western Massachusetts in the development of American Indian education reform through the Hampton Institute's summer outing program (1878-1912)." Ed.D. dissertation, Univ. of Massachusetts, 1992. ix, 179p. *
Abstracted in DAI, 53:10A (1993), 3460.

1534. ALTSCHULER, ALAN. "Massachusetts Governor Sargent: Sarge in charge." Journal of State Government, 62 (July/Aug. 1989), 153-160.
Gov. Frank Sargent (served from 1969-1975).

1535. THE ANTINOMIAN controversy, 1636-1638: a documentary history. David D. Hall, ed. (1968) 2d ed. Durham, N.C.: Duke Univ. Pr., 1990. xxi, 453p. MB. *
Note: this item replaces entry 748 in the Massachusetts volume.

1536. ARMSTRONG, SUSAN OUELETTE. "The legacy of Everett Titcomb." D.M.A. dissertation, Boston Univ., 1990. xiii, 245p. *
Composer, choral director, and teacher (20th century). Abstracted in DAI, 51:2A (1990), 334.

1537. BALF, TODD. "The longest-running story in Boston." Yankee, 56 (Apr. 1992), 66-71, 124-126.
Runner Johnny Kelley, who ran the Boston Marathon many times, retiring after the 1992 race.

1538. BARISH, EVELYN. Emerson: the roots of prophecy. Princeton, N.J.: Princeton Univ. Pr., 1989. xv, 267p. MB. *
Biographical study of Ralph Waldo Emerson's early life.

* Online Computer Library Center (OLCC) listings for books and dissertations marked with this symbol may include additional library locations.

1539   MASSACHUSETTS

1539.   BARNEY, ROBERT KNIGHT. "To breast a storm: Nathaniel Topliff Allen and the demise of military drill as the physical education ethic in the public schools of Massachusetts, 1860-1870." Canadian Journal of the History of Sport, 18:2 (1987), 1-14.

1540.   BARNHILL, GEORGIA BRADY. "'Extracts from the journals of Ethan A. Greenwood': portrait painter and museum proprietor." AASP, 103 (Apr. 1993), 91-178.
Lived 1779-1856.

1541.   BARROW, CLYDE W. "Unions and community mobilization: the 1988 Massachusetts prevailing wage campaign." Labor Studies Journal, 14 (Winter 1989), 18- 39.

1542.   BEATTY, NOELLE BLACKMER. Literary byways of Boston & Cambridge. Washington: Starrhill Pr., [1991]. 79p. M. *

1543.   BERMAN, PAUL. "Medical practice in the Connecticut River Valley." HJM, 18 (Winter 1990), 27- 36.

1544.   _____. "Obstetrical practice in south central Massachusetts from 1834 to 1845." DubSemPr (1990), 185-190.

1545.   A BIBLIOGRAPHIC listing of materials pertaining to the following towns: Ashfield, Buckland, Charlemont, Colrain, Hawley, Heath, Plainfield, Rowe, Shelburne; which comprise the Mohawk Trail Regional School District; as well as material related to western Massachusetts, especially Franklin County, the Hoosac Tunnel and the works of author Mary P. Wells Smith. Susan B. Silvester, comp. [Buckland: Mohawk Trail Regional School District, 1986.] Unp. MDeeP.

1546.   BOGLE, LORI. "Paradox of opportunities: Lucy Stone, Alice Stone Blackell, and the tragedy of reform." HJM, 22 (Winter 1994), 17-33.
The mother and daughter (lived 1818-1893 and 1857-1950) were feminists, suffragists, and advocates of other social reforms.

1547.   BOROWSKI, CAROL H. "The modern Renaissance commune." Society, 25 (Jan./Feb. 1988), 42-46.
The contemporary Renaissance movement in rural Massachusetts.

1548.   BROOKE, JOHN L. "To the quiet of the people: revolutionary settlements and civil unrest in western Massachusetts, 1774-1789." WMQ, 3 ser. 46 (July 1989), 425-462.

1549.   BROWN, CHARLES A. "Trolley freight and express in southern New England: eastern Massachusetts." S'liner, 19:3 (1988), 6-11.
See also next entry.

1550.   _____. "Trolley freight and express in southern New England: eastern Massachusetts: Boston Elevated Rwy.—Boston & Worcester St. Rwy." S'liner, 19:2 (1988), 6-9.
See also preceding entry.

1551.   BROWN, RICHARD DAVID, ROSS W. BEALES JR., RICHARD B. LYMAN JR., and JACK LARKIN. Farm labor in southern New England during the agricultural-industrial transition. Charlottesville, Va.: University Pr. of Virginia, 1990. [113]p. MWA. *
All of the studies are of localities in Massachusetts.

1552.   BROWNING, DEBORAH FAIRMAN. "Toilers within the home: servants' quarters in nineteenth-century New England." Journal of American Culture, 15 (Spring 1992), 93-98.
Study of servants' quarters in several middle-class houses in the Springfield-Holyoke area.

1553.   BRYNNER, ROCK. "'Fire beneath our feet': Shay's Rebellion and its constitutional impact." Ph.D. dissertation, Columbia Univ., 1993. vii, 320p. *
Abstracted in DAI, 54:3A (1993), 1068.

1554.   BURKA, EDWARD R. "Uniforms and equipment of the ambulance corps, Massachusetts Volunteer Militia, 1890-1900." Military Collector & Historian, 40 (Fall 1988), 120-124.

1555.   BURRELL, BARBARA. "The presence of women candidates and the role of gender in campaigns for the state legislature in an urban setting: the case of Massachusetts." Women & Politics, 10:3 (1990), 85-102.
1980s campaigns.

1556.   BUSH, SARGENT JR. "John Wheelwright's forgotten Apology: the last word on the antinomian controversy." NEQ, 64 (Mar. 1991), 22-45.

1557.   CAHN, MARK D. "Punishment, discretion, and the codification of prescribed penalties in colonial Massachusetts." American Journal of Legal History, 33 (Apr. 1989), 107-136.

1558.   CAPPER, CHARLES HERBERT. Margaret Fuller: an American romantic life. N.Y.: Oxford Univ. Pr., 1992. 432p. MH. *
The writer and reformer lived 1810-1850. See also next entry.

1559.   _____. "Margaret Fuller: the early years." Ph.D. dissertation, Univ. of California, Berkeley, 1984. x, 629p. *
Abstracted in DAI, 50:4A (1989), 1065. See also preceding entry.

1560. CARLSON, STEPHEN P., and THOMAS W. HARDING. From Boston to the Berkshires: a pictorial review of electric transportation in Massachusetts. Boston: Boston Street Railway Association, 1990. 160p. M. *
    Street railroads.

1561. CASH, PHILIP. "The phoenix and the eagle: the founding of the Boston and Massachusetts medical societies in 1780 and 1781." New England Journal of Medicine, 305 (Oct. 29, 1981), 1033-1039.

1562. CHANNING, WILLIAM ELLERY (1817-1901). "The selected letters of William Ellery Channing the younger." Studies in the American Renaissance (1989), 115-218; (1990), 159-214; (1991), 257-343; (1992), 1- 75.
    Edited by Francis B. Dedmond.

1563. CHI, CHRISTOPHER YONG-MIN. "Diffusing early knowledge in Worcester and Concord: the early lyceum movement in two Massachusetts towns." Ph.D. dissertation, Harvard Univ., 1993. 50p. MWA.

1564. CLARK, CHRISTOPHER. The roots of rural capitalism: western Massachusetts, 1780-1860. Ithaca, N.Y.: Cornell Univ. Pr., 1990. xii, 339p. MWA. *

1565. COHEN, DANIEL ASHER. "'The Female marine' in an era of good feelings: cross dressing and the 'genius' of Nathaniel Coverly, Jr." AASP, 103 (Oct. 1993), 359-393.
    Fictional account of a "young woman from rural Massachusetts," published after the War of 1812.

1566. COLONIAL SOCIETY OF MASSACHUSETTS. The Glorious Revolution in Massachusetts: selected documents, 1689-1692. Robert Earle Moody and Richard Clive Simmons, eds. Boston, 1988. xxviii, 647p. MWA. *

1567. CONNORS, ROBERT LYLE. "The history and development of the Office of Religious Education/CCD of the Archdiocese of Boston from 1962 to 1982." Ph.D. dissertation, Catholic Univ. of America, 1988. vii, 388p. *
    Abstracted in DAI, 49:9A (1989), 2558.

1568. COOPER, CAROLYN C. Shaping invention: Thomas Blanchard's machinery and patent management in nineteenth-century America, 1820-1870. N.Y.: Columbia Univ. Pr., 1991. xii, 326p. MWA. *
    Inventor of lathes and other industrial machinery.

1569. _____. "Visualizing invention: from tools to machines in the career of Thomas Blanchard (1788-1864)." CEAIA, 44 (Mar. 1991), 3-6.

1570. COOPER, JAMES FENIMORE JR. "Enthusiasts or democrats?: separatism, church government, and the Great Awakening in Massachusetts." NEQ, 52 (June 1992), 265-283.
    See also this author's Ph.D. dissertation on church government in colonial Massachusetts (Univ. of Connecticut, 1987; entry 2772 in Vol. 8).

1571. COQUILLETTE, DANIEL R. "Radical lawmakers in colonial Massachusetts: the 'countenance of authoritie' and the Lawes and liberties." NEQ, 67 (June 1994), 179- 211.

1572. CRANBERRY harvest: a history of cranberry growing in Massachusetts. Joseph D. Thomas, ed. New Bedford: Spinner Publications, 1990. 224p. M. *

1573. CULLEN, KEVIN. "The quiet man." Boston Globe Magazine (Feb. 4, 1990), 16, 24, 26, 28-40.
    Darin Nino Bufalino, accused of serving as a hit man in a 1984 murder.

1574. CUMBLER, JOHN T. "The early making of an environmental consciousness: fish, fisheries commissions, and the Connecticut River." Environmental History Review, 15:4 (1991) 73-91.
    Background of an 1869 act.

1575. DAUGHTERS OF THE AMERICAN REVOLUTION. NATIONAL SOCIETY. Minority military service: Massachusetts, 1775-1783. [Washington], 1989. 34p. RHi. *

1576. DAVIS, THOMAS J. "Emancipation rhetoric, natural rights, and revolutionary New England: a note on four black petitions in Massachusetts, 1773-1777." NEQ, 62 (June 1989), 248-263.

1577. DAVIS-FULLER, ETHLYN ANITA. "An historical and analytical study of the Massachusetts Board of Regents: 1965 to 1987." Ph.D. dissertation, Boston College, 1988. xvi, 163p. *
    Higher education. Abstracted in DAI, 49:12A (1989), 3460.

1578. DAWSON, HUGH J. "John Winthrop's rite of passage: the origins of the 'Christian charitie' discourse." Early American Literature, 26:3 (1991), 219-231.
    Winthrop delivered the discourse in 1630.

1579. DERDERIAN, THOMAS. Boston Marathon: the history of the world's premier running event. Champaign, Ill.: Human Kinetics Publishers, 1994. xxvi, 606p. MBAt. *

1580   MASSACHUSETTS

1580. DONAHUE, MARTIN. "The history of administrative law in Massachusetts, 1639-1932." Journal of Legal History [U.K.], 8:3 (1987), 330-366.

1581. DUKAKIS, KITTY. Now you know. N.Y.: Simon & Schuster, 1990. 315, [16]p. M. *
Autobiography of the wife of Gov. Michael S. Dukakis.

1582. ECKERT, RICHARD SCOTT. "The gentlemen of the profession": the emergence of lawyers in Massachusetts, 1630-1810. N.Y.: Garland Publishing, 1991. iv, 556p. MB. *
Published version of author's Ph.D. dissertation (Univ. of Southern California, 1981; entry 2855 in Vol. 8).

1583. EDUCATION in Massachusetts: selected essays. Michael F. Konig and Martin Kaufman, eds. Westfield: Institute for Massachusetts Studies, Westfield State College, 1989. xi, 244p. M. *

1584. EMIRBAYER, MUSTAFA. "The shocking of a virtuous citizenry: educational reform in Massachusetts, 1830-1860." Studies in American Political Development, 6 (Fall 1992), 391-419.

1585. ERLICH, MARK. Labor at the ballot box: the Massachusetts prevailing wage campaign of 1988. Philadelphia: Temple Univ. Pr., 1990. xiv, 219p. M. *

1586. ESTES, J. WORTH. "The practice of medicine in eighteenth-century Massachusetts: a bicentennial perspective." New England Journal of Medicine, 305 (Oct. 29, 1981), 1040-1047.

1587. FARRELL, JAMES MICHAEL JR. "John Adams and the Ciceronian paradigm." Ph.D. dissertation, Univ. of Wisconsin, 1988. vi, 247p. *
Examines "the influence of Cicero's life and eloquence on the public and private discourse" of Adams. Abstracted in DAI, 49:12A (1988), 3549.

1588. _____. "John Adams's autobiography: the Ciceronian paradigm and the quest of fame." NEQ, 62 (Dec. 1989), 505-528.

1589. FEER, ROBERT A. Shay's Rebellion. N.Y.: Garland Publishing, 1988. vi, 597p. MB. *
Published version of author's Ph.D. dissertation (Harvard Univ., 1958; entry 2879 in Vol. 8).

1590. FERLING, JOHN. John Adams: a life. Knoxville: Univ. of Tennessee Pr., 1992. x, 535p. MBU. *

1591. FIELD, ALEXANDER JAMES. Educational reform and manufacturing development in mid-nineteenth century Massachusetts. N.Y.: Garland Publishing, 1989. 346p. MB. *
Published version of author's Ph.D. dissertation (Univ. of California, Berkeley, 1974; entry 2888 in Vol. 8).

1592. FIELD, PETER S. "The crisis of the standing order: a history of Congregational ministers in Massachusetts, 1790-1833." Ph.D. dissertation, Columbia Univ., 1993. 360p.
Abstracted in DAI, 54:12A (1994), 4563.

1593. FISCHER, DAVID HACKETT. Paul Revere's ride. N.Y.: Oxford Univ. Pr., 1994. xviii, 445p. MBAt. *

1594. FISHER, MATHEW DAVID. "A selected, annotated edition of the letters of George Ripley, 1828-1841." Ph.D. dissertation, Ball State Univ., 1992. viii, 215p. *
Ripley, the Unitarian minister and transcendentalist, lived 1802-1880. Abstracted in DAI, 53:4A (1992), 1158.

1595. FOLBRE, NANCY RUSSELL. "Women on their own: residential independence in Massachusetts in 1880." Continuity and Change [U.K.], 6:1 (1991), 87-105.

1596. _____. "Women's informal market work in Massachusetts, 1875-1920." Social Science History, 17 (Spring 1993), 135-160.

1597. FONES-WOLF, KENNETH. "Labor history sources at the University of Massachusetts, Amherst." Labor History, 31 (Winter-Spring 1990), 31-38.
Sources for the study of Massachusetts labor.

1598. FOX, JOHN W. "Irish immigrants, pauperism, and insanity in 1854 Massachusetts." Social Science History, 15 (Fall 1991), 315-336.

1599. FRANK, STEPHEN M. "'Rendering aid and comfort': images of fatherhood in the letters of Civil War soldiers from Massachusetts and Michigan." JSH, 26 (Fall 1992), 5-31.

1600. FREELAND, RICHARD M. Academia's golden age: universities in Massachusetts, 1945-1970. N.Y.: Oxford Univ. Pr., 1992. xii, 532p. MChB. *

1601. FREIBERG, MALCOLM. Prelude to purgatory: Thomas Hutchinson in provincial Massachusetts politics, 1760-1770. N.Y.: Garland Publishing, 1990. viii, 357p. MB. *
Published version of author's Ph.D. dissertation (Brown Univ., 1951; entry 2909 in Vol. 8).

1602. GABLER, EDWIN. "Gilded Age labor in Massachusetts and Illinois: statistical surveys of workingmen's families." Labor's Heritage, 4 (Fall 1992), 4-21.

1603. GAMES, ALISON FRAZIER. "Venturers, vagrants and vessels of glory: migration from England to the colonies under Charles I." Ph.D. dissertation, Univ. of Pennsylvania, 1992. xvi, 533p. *
    Migration to Massachusetts and other English colonies. Abstracted in DAI, 53:5A (1992), 1642.

1604. GELLES, EDITH B. Portia: the world of Abigail Adams. Bloomington: Indiana Univ. Pr., 1992. xviii, 227p. MBAt. *

1605. GERO, ANTHONY. "A light infantry cap for the Massachusetts Volunteer Militia: ca. 1805-1820, a possibility." Military Collector & Historian, 42 (Summer 1990), 52-55.

1606. GOLDEN, HILDA H. Immigrant and native families: the impact of immigration on the demographic transformation of western Massachusetts, 1850-1900. Lanham, Md.: University Pr. of America, 1994. 259p. MH. *

1607. GOODHEART, LAWRENCE B. Abolitionist, actuary, atheist: Elizur Wright and the reform impulse. Kent, Ohio: Kent State Univ. Pr., 1990. xiii, 282p. MB. *
    Wright (1804-1885) served as state commissioner of life insurance from 1858-1867.

1608. THE GOSNOLD discoveries in the north part of Virginia, 1602: now Cape Cod and the islands, Massachusetts; according to the relations by Gabriel Archer and John Brereton, arranged in parallel for convenient comparison. Lincoln A. Dexter, ed. Brookfield, 1982. vi, 66p. MB. *

1609. GRAHAM, JULIE, and ROBERT J. S. ROSS. "From manufacturing-based industrial policy to service-based employment policy?: industrial interests, class politics and the 'Massachusetts miracle.'" International Journal of Urban and Regional Research [U.K.], 13 (Mar. 1989), 121-136.
    1970s and 1980s.

1610. GREEN, JAMES R. "Workers, unions, and the politics of public history." Public Historian, 11 (Fall 1989), 11-38.
    The Massachusetts History Workshop (since 1978).

1611. HALL, JULIE ELIZABETH. "Sophia Peabody Hawthorne: the woman behind the man." Ph.D. dissertation, Univ. of North Carolina, 1993. x, 193p. *
    Wife of Nathaniel Hawthorne. Abstracted in DAI, 54:4A (1993), 1364.

1612. HALL, MAX. "Seeds of history: the arboretum and two forests." Harvard Magazine, 93 (Sept./Oct. 1990), 42-45.
    Botanical research at various Harvard Univ. facilities since the 19th century.

1613. HANSON, EDWARD WILLIAM. "'A sense of honor and duty': Robert Treat Paine (1731-1814) of Massachusetts and the new nation." Ph.D. dissertation, Boston College, 1992. 421p. *
    Abstracted in DAI, 53:9A (1993), 3345. See also entry 1681.

1614. HENDERSON, JAMES M. "Taxation and political culture: Massachusetts and Virginia, 1760-1800." WMQ, 3 ser. 47 (Jan. 1990), 90-114.

1615. HERBERT, THOMAS WALTER JR. Dearest beloved: the Hawthornes and the making of the middle-class family. Berkeley: Univ. of California Pr., 1993. xx, 331p. MBAt. *
    Nathaniel and Sophia Hawthorne.

1616. _____. "Divine childhood in the Hawthorne family." EIHC, 125 (Jan. 1989), 45-54.

1617. HIGGINBOTHAM, DON. "Fomenters of revolution: Massachusetts and South Carolina." Journal of the Early Republic, 14 (Spring 1994), 1-3.
    American Revolution and Civil War.

1618. HIRSCH, ADAM JAY. "From pillory to penitentiary: the rise of criminal incarceration in the new republic." Ph.D. dissertation, Yale Univ., 1987. xv, 563p. *
    Massachusetts study. Abstracted in DAI, 48:11A (1988), 2964.

1619. HISTORICAL atlas of Massachusetts. Richard W. Wilkie and Jack Tager, eds. Amherst: Univ. of Massachusetts Pr., 1991. 152p. MB. *

1620. HOBERMAN, MICHAEL BRIAN. "Back up on brushey: folk regional identity in the Sawmill Valley of western Massachusetts, 1890-1920." Ph.D. dissertation, Univ. of Massachusetts, 1993. xviii, 245p. *
    Abstracted in DAI, 54:10A (1994), 3481.

1621. HOFFMAN, CURTISS R. "The Cedar Swamp Archaeological District: a model for conservation archaeology." MASB, 53 (Spring 1992), 1-17.
    In Westborough and Hopkinton.

1622. HOFFMANN, RICHARD EUGENE. "Ralph Waldo Emerson: his reasons for leaving the ministry." Ph.D. dissertation, Bowling Green State Univ., 1989. vii, 222p. *
    Emerson left in 1832. Abstracted in DAI, 50:11A (1990), 3589.

1623   MASSACHUSETTS

1623.   HOWE, CHARLES A. "He lives tomorrow: Clinton Lee Scott, revitalizer of Universalism." Unitarian Universalist Historical Society, Proceedings, 21:2 (1989), 7-25.
         Superintendent of the Massachusetts Universalist Convention (1946-1956).

1624.   IN debt to Shays: the bicentennial of an agrarian rebellion. Robert A. Gross, ed. Charlottesville: University Pr. of Virginia, 1993. xiv, 418p. M. *

1625.   INDRISANO, LINDA. "A history of state-level testing in Massachusetts." Ed.D. dissertation, Boston College, 1989. 367p.
         Educational testing. Abstracted in DAI, 51:3A (1990), 763.

1626.   JENSEN, RONALD L. "A religious and historical study of Horace Mann." Ph.D. dissertation, Univ. of Iowa, 1991. 276p.
         The educational reformer (lived 1796-1859). Abstracted in DAI, 53:1A (1992), 85-86.

1627.   JOHNSON, ERIC SPENCER. "Bifurcate base projectile points in eastern and central Massachusetts: distribution and raw materials." MASB, 54 (Fall 1993), 46-55.

1628.   JONES, DANIEL CHARLES LLOYD. "Elias Mann: reform-era Massachusetts psalmist." American Music, 11 (Spring 1993), 54-89.

1629.   _____. "Elias Mann (1750-1825): Massachusetts composer, compiler, and singing master." Ph.D. dissertation, Univ. of Colorado, 1991. 343p. *
         Abstracted in DAI, 53:2A (1992), 343.

1630.   KANAI, KOTARO. "Masachusettsu no gun-seifu to Amerika kakumei: Shakai, ho, kakumei." Nenpo Seijigaku [Japan] (1990), 81-110.
         The county court in Massachusetts and the American Revolution: community, law, and revolution. (Text in Japanese.)

1631.   KENNEDY, ANNE MARGARET. "Louisa May Alcott: culture, family, fiction." Ph.D. dissertation, Bowling Green State Univ., 1990. 144p. *
         Abstracted in DAI, 52:3A (1991), 972.

1632.   KERBER, LINDA K. "The paradox of women's citizenship in the early republic: the case of Martin vs. Massachusetts, 1805." American Historical Review, 97 (Apr. 1992), 349-378.
         The case was argued on the question of a married woman's responsibilities as a citizen. (The property of the plaintiff's Loyalist mother had been confiscated when she left the state with her husband during the Revolution.)

1633.   KERSHAW, GORDON E. James Bowdoin II: patriot and man of the Enlightenment. Lanham, Md.: University Pr. of America, 1991. xi, 327p. M. *
         Bowdoin (1726-1790) was governor from 1785-1787.

1634.   KEYES, LANGLEY. "The shifting focus of neighborhood groups: the Massachusetts experience." Policy Studies Journal, 16 (Winter 1987), 300-306.
         Community action groups (1960s-1980s).

1635.   [KINGSBURY, ANNA]. [Series of articles on Quinton Pray, an iron founder and an early settler of Lynn and Braintree.] Pray Pioneers, No. 3 (Autumn 1983), 1-2; No. 4 (Winter 1983-1984), 1-2; No. 5 (Spring 1984), 2-3.

1636.   KNIGHT, JANICE LYNN. Orthodoxies in Massachusetts: rereading American Puritanism. Cambridge: Harvard Univ. Pr., 1994. ix, 301p. MH. *
         See also entry 273.

1637.   KONEFSKY, ALFRED S. "'As best to subserve their own interest': Lemuel Shaw, labor conspiracy, and fellow servants." Law and History Review, 7 (Spring 1989), 219-239.
         Compares two decisions written by Justice Shaw in 1842, one of which "appeared to expand workers' rights to collective action"; the other "appeared to restrict workers' rights to compensation from workplace injuries."

1638.   KUEHNE, DALE STANWAY. "The design of heaven: Massachusetts Congregationalist political thought, 1760-1790." Ph.D. dissertation, Georgetown Univ., 1993. vii, 269p. *
         Abstracted in DAI, 54:10A (1994), 3782.

1639.   LABOR in Massachusetts: selected essays. Kenneth Fones-Wolf, Martin Kaufman, and Joseph Carvalho III, eds. Westfield: Institute for Massachusetts Studies, Westfield State College, 1990. viii, 293p. MWA. *

1640.   LANDMAN, RONALD D. "From normal schools to state colleges: a political, social, and economic history of normal schools in Massachusetts." Ed.D. dissertation, Boston College, 1992. 166p.
         Abstracted in DAI, 53:1A (1992), 86.

1641.   LANDON, DAVID BACHENHEIMER. "Zooarchaeology and urban foodways: a case study from eastern Massachusetts." Ph.D. dissertation, Boston Univ., 1991. xvii, 510p. *
         Based on faunal evidence from sites in downtown Boston, Marshfield, and Newbury.

1642. LEVINSON, DAVID L. "High technology's influence upon higher educational policy in Massachusetts." Ph.D. dissertation, Univ. of Massachusetts, 1987. xi, 334p. *
Since World War II. Abstracted in DAI, 49:3A (1988), 636.

1643. LEWINSON, VICTOR A. "Sam Crocker, boat designer." American Neptune, 48 (Summer 1988), 182-185.
Crocker (1890-1964) worked in Boston and Manchester.

1644. LI, YAN. "The transformation of the constitution of Massachusetts, 1780-1860." Ph.D. dissertation, Univ. of Connecticut, 1991. v, 388p. *
Abstracted in DAI, 53:3A (1992), 908.

1645. LINDGREN, JAMES M. "'A constant incentive to patriotic citizenship': historic preservation in Progressive-era Massachusetts." NEQ, 64 (Dec. 1991), 594-608.

1646. LITTLE, CRAIG B. "The criminal courts in 'young America': Bucks County, Pennsylvania, 1820-1860, with some comparisons to Massachusetts and South Carolina." Social Science History, 15 (Winter 1991), 457-478.

1647. LOSCHKY, DAVID. "Mid-XIX century military spending patterns." Journal of European Economic History [Italy], 17 (Spring 1988), 127-130.
Massachusetts (1860-1861).

1648. LOWENTHAL, LARRY. "Railroad rivalry in the Connecticut River Valley." HJM, 20 (Summer 1992), 109-132.

1649. LYMAN, CHARLES PEIRSON. The Massachusetts Society for Promoting Agriculture: the years 1942-1992. Ipswich: Ipswich Pr., 1992. 119, [12]p. MBAt. *

1650. MAAS, DAVID EDWARD. The return of the Massachusetts Loyalists. N.Y.: Garland Publishing, 1989. 592p. MB. *
Published version of author's Ph.D. dissertation (Univ. of Wisconsin, 1972; entry 3200 in Vol. 8).

1651. MANDELL, DANIEL RICHARD. "Behind the frontier: Indian communities in eighteenth-century Massachusetts." Ph.D. dissertation, Univ. of Virginia, 1992. 296p. *
Praying Indian communities. Abstracted in DAI, 53:8A (1993), 2954.

1652. MARCHALONIS, SHIRLEY. "Lucy Larcom (1824-1893)." Legacy, 5 (Spring 1988), 45-52.
Biographical sketch. See also next entry.

1653. ____. The worlds of Lucy Larcom, 1824-1893. Athens, Ga.: Univ. of Georgia Pr., 1989. x, 326p. MWA. *
Poet, author, and editor.

1654. MARSH, ROGER ALAN. "Diminishing respect for the clergy and the first Great Awakening: a study of the antecedents of revival among Massachusetts Congregationalists, 1630-1741." Ph.D. dissertation, Baylor Univ., 1990. xiv, 477p. *
Abstracted in DAI, 51:4A (1990), 1268.

1655. MASSACHUSETTS. HISTORICAL COMMISSION. Bibliography of archaeological survey and mitigation reports: Massachusetts. Stephen A. Cole, comp. (1981) [Boston], 1986. Unp. MH. *

1656. MASSACHUSETTS. STATE ARCHIVES. Guide to the records of the secretary of state in the Massachusetts Archives. Boston, 1987. iii, 81p. M. *

1657. MASSACHUSETTS. SECRETARY OF STATE. "It wasn't in her lifetime, but it was handed down": four black oral histories of Massachusetts. Eleanor Wachs, ed. [Boston], 1989. v, 40p. MW. *

1658. MASSACHUSETTS HISTORICAL SOCIETY. Massachusetts and the new nation. Conrad Edick Wright, ed. Boston, 1992. xiv, 296p. MH. *

1659. THE MASSACHUSETTS miracle: high technology and economic revitalization. David R. Lampe, ed. Cambridge: MIT Pr., 1988. xii, 367p. MB. *
1970s and 1980s.

1660. MASTROMARINO, MARK. "Elkanah Watson and early agricultural fairs, 1790-1860." HJM, 17 (Summer 1988), 105-118.
Watson was an advocate of improvements in agriculture.

1661. MATTERN, DAVID BRUCE. "A moderate revolutionary: the life of Major General Benjamin Lincoln." Ph.D. dissertation, Columbia Univ., 1990. ii, 479p. *
Revolutionary War general. Abstracted in DAI, 52:4A (1991), 1491.

1662. McADOW, RON. The Concord, Sudbury and Assabet rivers: a guide to canoeing, wildlife, and history. Marlborough: Bliss Publishing, 1990. xv, 223p. MW. *

1663. McCLYMER, JOHN F. "How to read Wright: the equity of the wage system and the morality of spending." Hayes Historical Journal, 8 (Winter 1989), 37-43.
Carroll D. Wright's Sixth annual report of the Massachusetts Bureau of the Statistics of Labor (1875).

1664   MASSACHUSETTS

1664.   McDEVITT, JOSEPH LAWRENCE JR. The house of Rotch: whaling merchants of Massachusetts, 1734-1828. N.Y.: Garland Publishing, 1986. 641p. MB. *
Of Nantucket and New Bedford. This is a published version of the author's Ph.D. dissertation (American Univ., 1978; entry 3186 in Vol. 8).

1665.   McGAHAN, JANE A. "History of the Norwottuck chapter." MASB, 50 (Oct. 1989), 52-53.
Chapter of the Massachusetts Archaeological Society in the Connecticut River Valley.

1666.   McLAIN, GUY A. Pioneer Valley: a pictorial history. Virginia Beach, Va.: Donning, 1991. 151p. MS. *
In western Massachusetts.

1667.   McLAUGHLIN, JANE A. "Baldwin Coolidge, photographer, 1845-1928." Spritsail, 1 (Summer 1987), 5-25.

1668.   MESSER, STEPHEN C. "Individual responses to death in Puritan Massachusetts." OMEGA: the Journal of Death and Dying, 21:3 (1990), 155-163.

1669.   MICHAELSEN, SCOTT. "John Winthrop's 'modell' covenant and the company way." Early American Literature, 27:2 (1992), 85-100.

1670.   MILLER, JEROME G. Last one over the wall: the Massachusetts experiment in closing reform schools. Columbus: Ohio State Univ. Pr., 1991. xv, 279p. M. *
Beginning ca. 1969.

1671.   MOIR, ROB, and JACKSON PARKER. "Massachusetts waterfowl decoys." Antiques, 136 (Sept. 1989), 516-527.

1672.   MORGAN, EDMUND SEARS. "An address to the Colonial Society of Massachusetts, on the occasion of its centennial." NEQ, 66 (Sept. 1993), 355-365.

1673.   MOSELEY, JAMES G. John Winthrop's world: history as a story; the story as history. Madison: Univ. of Wisconsin Pr., 1992. ix, 192p. MWA. *
Biography of Winthrop (lived 1588-1649).

1674.   MOWER, CHARLES H. "Early canals on the Merrimack River." Towpath Topics, 29 (Mar. 1992), 11-15.

1675.   MULKERN, JOHN RAYMOND. The Know-nothing Party in Massachusetts: the rise and fall of a people's movement. Boston: Northeastern Univ. Pr., 1990. ix, 236p. MB. *
See also this author's Ph.D. dissertation of similar title (Boston Univ., 1963; entry 3287 in Vol. 8).

1676.   MYERSON, JOEL, and DANIEL SHEALY. "The sales of Louisa May Alcott's books." Harvard Library Bulletin, n.s. 1 (Spring 1990), 47-86.

1677.   NATIONAL GALLERY OF ART. Paintings by Fitz Hugh Lane. John Wilmerding, ed. N.Y.: Harry N. Abrams, 1988. 163p. MWA. *
Lane lived 1804-1865.

1678.   NATIVE writings in Massachusett. Ives Goddard and Kathleen J. Bragdon, eds. Philadelphia: American Philosophical Society, 1988. 2v. MWA. *
Vol. 185 of the society's Memoirs. See also Bragdon's Ph.D. dissertation on writings in the Massachusett Indian language (Brown Univ., 1981; entry 2670 in Vol. 8).

1679.   O'CONNOR, THOMAS HENRY, and ALAN ROGERS. This momentous affair: Massachusetts and the ratification of the Constitution of the United States. Boston: Trustees of the Public Library of the City of Boston, 1987. 116p. MWA. *

1680.   PAGOULATOS, PETER. "Edge alteration study for Attleboro red felsite tools." MASB, 53 (Fall 1992) 53- 63.

1681.   PAINE, ROBERT TREAT. The papers of Robert Treat Paine. Stephen T. Riley and Edward W. Hanson, eds. Boston: Massachusetts Historical Society, 1992-. MBNEH. *
Two vols. to date, covering the years 1746-1774. Paine (1731-1814) was a signer of the Declaration of Independence. See also entry 1613.

1682.   PATKUS, RONALD D. The Archdiocese of Boston: a pictorial history. Boston: Quinlan Pr., 1989. x, 198p. MB. *

1683.   PENCAK, WILLIAM. "The humorous side of Shays' Rebellion." HJM, 17 (Summer 1989) 160-176.

1684.   PERSON, LELAND S. JR. "Inscribing paternity: Nathaniel Hawthorne as a nineteenth-century father." Studies in the American Renaissance (1991), 225-244.

1685.   PESTANA, CARLA GARDINA. Quakers and Baptists in colonial Massachusetts. N.Y.: Cambridge Univ. Pr., 1991. xii, 197p. MB. *
See also this author's Ph.D. dissertation: "Sectarianism in colonial Massachusetts" (UCLA, 1987; entry 3369 in Vol. 8).

1686.   PETRIN, RONALD ARTHUR. French Canadians in Massachusetts politics, 1885-1915: ethnicity and political pragmatism. Philadelphia: Balch Institute Pr., 1990. 234p. M. *

1687. "THE PHILOSOPHER and the activist: new letters from Emerson to Wendell Phillips." NEQ, 62 (June 1989), 280-296.
Irving H. Bartlett, ed.

1688. PICCARELLO, LOUIS JOSEPH. "Poverty, the poor, and public welfare in Massachusetts: a comparative history of four towns, 1643-1855." Ph.D. dissertation, Brandeis Univ., 1991. ix, 507p. MWA. *
Danvers, Deerfield, Greenfield, and Salem. Abstracted in DAI, 52:2A (1991), 660.

1689. PLANE, ANN MARIE, and GREGORY BUTTON. "The Massachusetts Indian Enfranchisement Act: ethnic contest in historical context, 1849-1869." Ethnohistory, 40 (Fall 1993), 587-618.

1690. PONTE, SUSAN E. "Religious opposition to the Massachusetts State Lottery." HJM, 20 (Winter 1992), 53-63.

1691. PORTER, CATHARINE CROW. "Earning income in the home: an historical perspective prefacing a profile of home-based business owners in Franklin and Berkshire Counties in Massachusetts." Ph.D. dissertation, Univ. of Massachusetts, 1992. viii, 235p. *
Abstracted in DAI, 53:2B (1992), 806-807.

1692. "PUBLIC education in Plymouth Colony and Massachusetts Bay." Mayflower Quarterly, 56 (Feb. 1990), 28-29; (Aug. 1990), 244-245.
Second installment by Daniel S. Parkinson.

1693. PUGLISI, MICHAEL J. Puritans besieged: the legacies of King Philip's War in the Massachusetts Bay Colony. Lanham, Md.: University Pr. of America, 1991. xii, 244p. MBAt. *
See also this author's Ph.D. dissertation of similar title (College of William and Mary, 1987; entry 3395 in Vol. 8).

1694. PURDY, VIRGINIA CARDWELL. Portrait of a Know-nothing legislature: the Massachusetts General Court of 1855. N.Y.: Garland Publishing, 1989. ix, 289p. MA. *
Published version of author's Ph.D. dissertation (George Washington Univ., 1970; entry 3396 in Vol. 8).

1695. RAPOZA, ANDREW V. "The trials of Phillip Reade, seventeenth-century itinerant physician." DubSemPr (1990), 82-94.

1696. RAWSON, DAVID A. "A Massachusetts perspective on the income tax amendment." HJM, 18 (Summer 1990), 190-207.
The legislature's actions in regard to the proposed amendment to the U.S. Constitution, which was adopted in 1913.

1697. RICKETSON, WILLIAM F. "To be young, poor, and alone: the experience of widowhood in the Massachusetts Bay Colony, 1675-1676." NEQ, 64 (Mar. 1991), 113-127.
Based on a sampling of women, widowed in King Philip's War, who petitioned the legislature.

1698. ROBIE, CURT DOUGLAS. "The Massachusetts state colleges: an unsupported past, an uncertain future." Ed.D. dissertation, Univ. of Massachusetts, 1991. xi, 207p. *
Abstracted in DAI, 52:6A (1991), 2046.

1699. ROGERS, ALAN. "'Under sentence of death': the movement to abolish capital punishment in Massachusetts, 1835-1849." NEQ, 66 (Mar. 1993), 27-46.

1700. ROSEGRANT, SUSAN, and DAVID R. LAMPE. Route 128: lessons from Boston's high-tech community. [N.Y.]: Basic Books, 1992. xvi, 240p. M. *

1701. ROSTON, CAROLINE HOPE. "To make a better spirit: community and history at the hill town fairs of western Massachusetts." Ph.D. dissertation, Univ. of Pennsylvania, 1993. 676p.
Country fairs, still in existence, in Blandford, Chester, Cummington, and Middlefield. Abstracted in DAI, 54:3A (1993), 1050.

1702. ROTHENBERG, WINIFRED BARR. From market-places to a market economy: the transformation of rural Massachusetts, 1750-1850. Chicago: Univ. of Chicago Pr., 1992. xiv, 275p. MWA. *
See also this author's Ph.D. dissertation on same subject (Brandeis Univ., 1985; entry 3437 in Vol. 8).

1703. RUSSELL, PETER EDMUND. His majesty's judges: provincial society and the superior court in Massachusetts, 1692-1774. N.Y.: Garland Publishing, 1990. ix, 318p. MB. *
Published version of author's Ph.D. dissertation (Univ. of Michigan, 1980; entry 3443 in Vol. 8).

1704. RYERSON, RICHARD ALAN. "The limits of a vicarious life: Abigail Adams and her daughter." MHSP, 100 (1988), 1-14.
Abigail and her daughter, Abigail Amelia Adams.

1705. SABEL, CHARLES F., GARY B. HERRIGEL, RICHARD DEEG, and RICHARD KAZIS. "Regional prosperities compared: Massachusetts and Baden-Württemberg in the 1980s." Economy and Society [U.K.], 18 (Nov. 1989), 374-404.
Baden-Württemberg is in what was formerly West Germany.

1706   MASSACHUSETTS

1706.   SACCO, EDWARD FRANK. "An analysis of the reading programs in ten Massachusetts communities that participated in the right to read effort from 1973 to 1980." Ph.D. dissertation, Univ. of Lowell, 1988. iv, 171p. *
Abstracted in DAI, 49:9A (1989), 2527.

1707.   SACK, HAROLD. "The bombé furniture of Boston and Salem, Massachusetts." Antiques, 135 (May 1989), 1178-1189.
18th century.

1708.   SARGENT, MARK L. "William Bradford's 'dialogue' with history." NEQ, 65 (Sept. 1992), 389-421.
Bradford's history of Plymouth Plantation.

1709.   _____. "The witches of Salem, the angel of Hadley, and the Friends of Philadelphia." American Studies, 34 (Spring 1993), 105-120.
Discusses the treatment in romantic literature of the Salem judges and the English regicide judge William Goffe—the "angel of Hadley."

1710.   SCHEICK, WILLIAM J. "'An allegorical description of a certain island and its inhabitants': eighteenth- century parable or satire?" NEQ, 63 (Sept. 1990), 468- 478.
The title refers to a brief prose work, published in The Massachusetts Magazine in 1790.

1711.   SCHERR, ARTHUR. "John Adams, provincial rhetoric, and party warfare: a note on Massachusetts politics in the late 1790s." Mid-America, 73 (Jan. 1991), 7-27.

1712.   SCHULDINER, MICHAEL JOSEPH. "The doctrine of spiritual growth and church polity in early America." Ph.D. dissertation, Kent State Univ., 1979. vi, 247p. *
Abstracted in DAI, 40:7A (1980), 4108. See also next entry.

1713.   _____. Gifts and works: the post-conversion paradigm and spiritual controversy in seventeenth- century Massachusetts. Macon, Ga.: Mercer Univ. Pr., 1991. xii, 180p. RPB. *
See also preceding entry.

1714.   SECHANDICE, ARISTIDE. "The negotiation of power in a Puritan settlement." HJM, 22 (Summer 1994), 121- 140.

1715.   SEHR, TIMOTHY JEROME. Colony and commonwealth: Massachusetts Bay, 1649-1660. N.Y.: Garland Publishing, 1989. 313p. MB. *
Published version of author's Ph.D. dissertation (Indiana Univ., 1976; entry 3471 in Vol. 8).

1716.   SELIGSON, SUSAN V. "How they found the Portland." Yankee, 53 (Dec. 1989), 68-75, 120-125.
Successful search in 1989 for the wreckage of a steamship sunk in Massachusetts Bay in 1895.

1717.   SHAYS' Rebellion: selected essays. Martin Kaufman, ed. Westfield: Institute for Massachusetts Studies, Westfield State College, 1987. xviii, 104p. MB. *

1718.   SHEA, MARION E. "Nathaniel Gorham: signer of the U.S. Constitution." Daughters of the American Revolution Magazine, 121 (Oct. 1987), 684-688, 711, 760.

1719.   SHEALY, DANIEL. "'A fuller record to offer': Louisa May Alcott's life in her private writings." Documentary Editing, 15 (Dec. 1993), 81-85.

1720.   SHEIDLEY, HARLOW ELIZABETH WALKER. "Sectional nationalism: the culture and politics of the Massachusetts conservative elite, 1815-1836." Ph.D. dissertation, Univ. of Connecticut, 1990. xvi, 556p. *
Abstracted in DAI, 51:11A (1991), 3881.

1721.   SHERIDAN, CLARE M. "Labor material in the collections of the Museum of American Textile History." Labor History, 31 (Winter-Spring 1990), 25-30.
The museum is in North Andover. Collection includes records of firms in that area.

1722.   SIDEN, DOROTHY RYAN. "Comparative analysis of the disappearance of functional distinctions in law and in practice between banks and thrifts in Massachusetts since deregulation." Ph.D. dissertation, Northeastern Univ., 1990. v, 281p. *
Study covers the years 1982-1988. Abstracted in DAI, 52:2A (1991), 635.

1723.   SIMMONS, RICHARD CLIVE. Studies in the Massachusetts franchise, 1631-1691. N.Y.: Garland Publishing, 1989. vi, 130p. MB. *
Published version of author's Ph.D. dissertation (Univ. of California, Berkeley, 1965; entry 3490 in Vol. 8).

1724.   SIMON, BRONA G. "Prehistoric land use and changing paleoecological conditions at Titicut Swamp in southeastern Massachusetts." Man in the Northeast, No. 42 (Fall 1991), 63-74.
In Bridgewater and Raynham.

1725.   SKEMP, SHEILA L. "The Judith Sargent Murray papers." Journal of Mississippi History, 53 (Aug. 1991), 241-250.
Murray (1751-1820), author, poet, and wife of the Rev. John Murray, founder of the Universalist Church in America, lived most of her life in Gloucester and Boston.

1726.   SKLAR, KATHRYN KISH. "The schooling of girls and changing community values in Massachusetts towns, 1750-1820." History of Education Quarterly, 33 (Winter 1993), 511-542.
On this subject, see also "Erratum" in ibid., 34 (Spring 1994), 69-71.

1727. SLOAT, CAROLINE FULLER. "'A great help to many families': straw braiding in Massachusetts before 1825." DubSemPr (1988), 89-100.

1728. SMITH, DANIEL SCOTT. "Continuity and discontinuity in Puritan naming: Massachusetts, 1771." WMQ, 3 ser. 51 (Jan. 1994), 67-91.
  Naming practices.

1729. SPEZIALE, MARCIA JEAN. "The Puritan pariah or a citizen of somewhere else: defamation in Massachusetts, 1642 to 1850." Ph.D. dissertation, Harvard Univ., 1992. 117p. *
  Abstracted in DAI, 53:5A (1992), 1563.

1730. SPORTS in Massachusetts: selected essays. Ronald Story and Martin Kaufman, eds. Westfield: Institute for Massachusetts Studies, Westfield State College, 1991. xi, 172p. MB. *

1731. STALOFF, DARREN MARCUS. "The making of an American thinking class: intellectuals and intelligentsia in Puritan Massachusetts." Ph.D. dissertation, Columbia Univ., 1991. xvii, 375p. *
  Abstracted in DAI, 52:11A (1992), 4065.

1732. STEPHENS, CARLENE E. "Partners in time: William Bond & Son of Boston and the Harvard College Observatory." Harvard Library Bulletin, 35 (Fall 1987), 351-384.
  Relations between the chronometer manufacturer and the observatory (mid-19th century).

1733. STERN, MADELEINE B. The life of Margaret Fuller. (1942) Rev. ed. Westport, Conn.: Greenwood Pr., 1991. xxvii, 402p. MB. *
  Note: this item replaces entry 3520 in Vol. 8.

1734. STRAIGHT, STEPHEN. "Diversion of streams to furnish power for water wheel mills." MASB, 51 (Spring 1990), 43-47.
  Examines the Congamond lakes in Southwick and the Mother Brook Canal, Dedham, as examples.

1735. SULLIVAN, GERALD, and MICHAEL KENNEY. The race for the Eighth: the making of a congressional campaign: Joe Kennedy's successful pursuit of a political legacy. N.Y.: Harper and Row, 1987. xiv, 288p. MB. *
  1986 election.

1736. SWANN, CHARLES. Nathaniel Hawthorne: tradition and revolution. N.Y.: Cambridge Univ. Pr., 1991. ix, 284p. MB. *

1737. SWEENEY, KEVIN MICHAEL. "Mansion people: kinship, class, and architecture in western Massachusetts in the mid eighteenth century." Winterthur Portfolio, 19 (Winter 1984), 231-256.

1738. SYLVA, ALAN J. "Rituals of empowerment: politics and rhetoric in the Puritan election sermon." Ph.D. dissertation, Univ. of California, Davis, 1993. xiii, 303p. *
  Massachusetts study. Abstracted in DAI, 54:10A (1994), 3751-3752.

1739. TAGER, JACK. "The Massachusetts miracle." HJM, 19 (Summer 1991), 111-132.
  The state's economic "miracle" (from "late 1970s to 1988").

1740. TOMLINS, CHRISTOPHER L. "A mysterious power: industrial accidents and the legal construction of employment relations in Massachusetts, 1800-1850." Law and History Review, 6 (Fall 1988), 375-438.

1741. ____. "The ties that bind: master and servant in Massachusetts, 1800-1850." Labor History, 30 (Spring 1989), 193-237.
  Legal aspects of employer-employee relationships.

1742. TRASK, KERRY ARNOLD. In the pursuit of shadows: Massachusetts millennialism and the Seven Years War. N.Y.: Garland Publishing, 1989. viii, 362p. MB. *
  Published version of author's Ph.D. dissertation (Univ. of Minnesota, 1971; entry 3570 in Vol. 8).

1743. TRAVIS, ANTHONY S. "From Manchester to Massachusetts via Mulhouse: the transatlantic voyage of aniline black." Technology and Culture, 35 (Jan. 1994), 70-99.
  Dyestuff used in the printing of textiles.

1744. TUCKER, RALPH L. "The Lamson family gravestone carvers of Charlestown and Malden, Massachusetts." Markers X [1993], 151-217.

1745. VALENTI, PATRICIA DUNLAVY. "Sophia Peabody Hawthorne: a study of artistic influence." Studies in the American Renaissance (1990), 1-21.
  Wife of Nathaniel Hawthorne.

1746. VARG, PAUL A. Edward Everett: the intellectual in the turmoil of politics. Selinsgrove, Pa.: Susquehanna Univ. Pr., 1992. 251p. MWalB. *
  Everett (1794-1865) served as both governor of Massachusetts and president of Harvard.

1747. VECCHIONE, NANCY JANE. "A longitudinal study of secondary school suspensions: an analysis of reasons for secondary school suspensions as recorded in the discipline logs of Massachusetts secondary schools during the 1979-80 and the 1989-90 school year." Ed.D. dissertation, Northeastern Univ., 1991. xx, 415p. *
  Abstracted in DAI, 52:9A (1992), 3150-3151.

1748   MASSACHUSETTS

1748.   VOLMAR, MICHAEL A. "Effigy pestles from Massachusetts." MASB, 55 (Spring 1994), 15-23.

1749.   WALL, ROBERT EMMET JR. The membership of the Massachusetts Bay General Court, 1630-1686. N.Y.: Garland Publishing, 1990. ix, 613p. MB. *
    Published version of author's Ph.D. dissertation (Yale Univ., 1965; entry 3603 in Vol. 8).

1750.   WARREN, ROLAND L. "Whittier and the Quaker 'argonauts.'" EIHC, 128 (Apr. 1992), 67-141.
    Poet John Greenleaf Whittier on the persecution of Quakers in 17th-century Massachusetts.

1751.   WASMUS, J. F. An eyewitness account of the American Revolution and New England life: the journal of J.F. Wasmus, German company surgeon, 1776-1783. Helga Doblin, translator; Mary C. Lynn, ed. N.Y.: Greenwood Pr., 1990. xxxiii, 311p. MStuO. *
    Wasmus, captured at the battle of Bennington in 1777, spent the next four years as a paroled prisoner of war in various Massachusetts towns, including Brimfield, Hardwick, Holden, Rutland, and Westminster.

1752.   WATSON, DAVID. Margaret Fuller: an American romantic. N.Y.: Berg, 1988. xvi, 127p. RPB. *

1753.   WE will rise in our might: workingwomen's voices from nineteenth-century New England. Mary H. Blewett, ed. Ithaca, N.Y.: Cornell Univ. Pr., 1991. xii, 220p. M. *
    The study is focused on the "shoemaking industry of eastern Massachusetts."

1754.   WESTERKAMP, MARILYN J. "Anne Hutchinson, sectarian mysticism, and the Puritan order." Church History, 59 (Dec. 1990), 482-496.

1755.   WHITE, G. EDWARD. Justice Oliver Wendell Holmes: law and the inner self. N.Y.: Oxford Univ. Pr., 1993. xii, 628p. MBAt. *
    The biography includes Holmes's Massachusetts background.

1756.   WHITING, GEORGE C. "Horace Mann: a comparison of a traditional and a revisionist biography." Ed.D. dissertation, College of William and Mary, 1989. 115p. *
    Compares Bruce A. Hinsdale's Horace Mann and the common school revival in the United States (1900) with Jonathan Messerli's biography of Mann (1972; entry 3257 in Vol. 8). Abstracted in DAI, 50:7A (1990), 1966-1967.

1757.   WHITMAN, JULIE. "Cotton Mather and Jonathan Edwards: philosophy, science, and Puritan theology." Ph.D. dissertation, Indiana Univ., 1993. xi, 212p. *
    Abstracted in DAI, 54:9A (1994), 3441.

1758.   WINSHIP, MICHAEL PAUL. "Behold the bridegroom cometh!: marital imagery in Massachusetts preaching, 1630-1730." Early American Literature, 27:3 (1992), 170-184.

1759.   _____. "A theater of God's judgments: providentialism and intellectual change in early Massachusetts orthodoxy." Ph.D. dissertation, Cornell Univ., 1992. vii, 453p. *
    Abstracted in DAI, 52:12A (1992), 4453.

1760.   WRIGHT, CONRAD. "Unitarian beginnings in western Massachusetts." Unitarian Universalist Historical Society, Proceedings, 21:2 (1989), 27-40.

1761.   WRIGHT, W. REDWOOD. "Completing a peaceful revolution." Spritsail, 2 (Winter 1988), 16-18.
    The state's ratifying convention of 1788.

1762.   ZEA, PHILIP. "The emergence of neoclassical furniture making in rural western Massachusetts." Antiques, 142 (Dec. 1992), 842-851.

1763.   ZEKAN, DONALD LOUIS. "Mergers in public higher education in Massachusetts." Ed.D. dissertation, Univ. of Massachusetts, 1990. viii, 139p. *
    1964-1985. Abstracted in DAI, 51:7A (1991), 2288.

    SEE ALSO entries 18, 68, 81, 94, 108, 122,135-136, 144, 146, 152, 156, 159, 166, 191, 197, 200, 212, 221, 225, 230, 233, 235, 246, 269, 299, 321, 336, 342, 345, 350, 390, 391, 404, 419, 432, 438, 440, 443, 479, 491, 501, 1033, 1131-1132, 3312, 4164.

Massachusetts

Entries for Counties†

BARNSTABLE COUNTY

1764. BAISLY, CLAIR. Cape Cod architecture: featuring the author's illustrated index of architectural terms. Orleans: Parnassus Imprints, 1989. xvii, 210p. MB. *

1765. BOSSARD, TIMOTHY DEAN. "'Cape Cod': Thoreau's experiment in human culture." Ph.D. dissertation, Lehigh Univ., 1994. 223p.
Thoreau's book of that title. Abstracted in DAI, 54: 12A (1994), 4439-4440.

1766. DOBBYN, ALICE, BARBARA WATERS, LESLEY SAGE, and MARILYN CRARY. "History of the Cape Cod chapter." MASB, 50 (Oct. 1989), 37-39.
Massachusetts Archaeological Society.

1767. FARSON, ROBERT H. Cape Cod railroads: including Martha's Vineyard and Nantucket. Yarmouth Port: Cape Cod Historical Publications, 1990. ix, 318p. MWA. *

1768. FAWSETT, MARISE. Cape Cod annals. Bowie, Md.: Heritage Books, 1990. 184p. M. *

1769. FRIEDMAN, RUTH LYNN. "Governing the land: an environmental history of Cape Cod, Massachusetts, 1600-1861." Ph.D. dissertation, Brandeis Univ., 1993. xii, 337p. *
Abstracted in DAI, 54:4A (1993), 1514.

1770. QUINN, WILLIAM P. The saltworks of historic Cape Cod: a record of the nineteenth century economic boom in Barnstable County. Orleans: Parnassus Imprints, 1993. viii, 247p. MWA. *

1771. "UPPER Cape delegates." Spritsail, 2 (Winter 1988), 19-25.
Delegates to the state's ratifying convention of 1788.

1772. ZAPATKA, FRANCIS E. "Melville and Cape Cod." Journal of American Culture, 12:4 (Winter 1989), 105- 109.
Herman Melville.

SEE ALSO entries 1050, 1572, 1608, 2102.

BERKSHIRE COUNTY

1773. THE BERKSHIRE reader: writings from New England's secluded paradise. Richard Nunley, ed. Stockbridge: Berkshire House Publishers, 1992. xiii, 530p. MPB. *
Includes writings on historical subjects.

1774. CARR, DENNIS J. "The Spanish influenza of 1918 and Berkshire County." HJM, 19 (Winter 1991), 43-62.

1775. CHAPMAN, GERARD. "The Berkshire County Historical Society's ventures into historic preservation." Berkshire History, 7 (Fall 1987), 11-16.

1776. _____. Eminent Berkshire women. Great Barrington: Attic Revivals Pr., 1988. 32p. M. *

1777. COOGAN, TIMOTHY CHRISTOPHER II. "The forging of a new mill town: North and South Adams, Massachusetts, 1780-1860." Ph.D. dissertation, New York Univ., 1992. 580p. *
Adams and North Adams. Abstracted in DAI, 53:8A (1993), 2950.

† See the Massachusetts volume in this series (1976) for a complete list of counties.

e Computer Library Center (OLCC) listings for and dissertations marked with this symbol may include additional library locations.

95

1778   BERKSHIRE COUNTY

1778.   DREW, BERNARD ALGER. "Favorite events in Berkshire's past." Berkshire History, 7 (Fall 1987), 2- 10.

1779.   _____. Spanning Berkshire waterways: a personal excursion into the history of metal truss highway bridge construction in western Massachusetts, 1865- 1905. Great Barrington: Attic Revivals Pr., 1990. 32p. M. *

1780.   GRIEVE, ALAN B. Berkshire bands: a pictorial review from 1884 to 1984. Pittsfield: Peter Drozd Graphic Arts, 1992. 247p. MPB. *

1781.   HICKEY, MAUREEN JOHNSON, and WILLIAM T. OEDEL. A return to arcadia: nineteenth century Berkshire County landscapes. Pittsfield: Berkshire Museum, 1990. 85p. MWalB. *

1782.   KELLEY, MARY. "Negotiating a self: the autobiography and journals of Catharine Maria Sedgwick." NEQ, 66 (Sept. 1993), 366-398.
        See also next entry.

1783.   MACDONALD, LINDA ROBERTS. "The discarded daughters of the American Revolution: Catharine Sedgwick, E.D.E.N. Southworth, and Augusta Evans Wilson." Ph.D. dissertation, Univ. of Colorado, 1992. v, 228p. *
        Literary history (19th century). Abstracted in DAI, 53:10A (1993), 3529-3530. On novelist Sedgwick (1789-1867), see also preceding entry.

1784.   PARRISH, LILA H. "When the Sioux came in summer." Great Barrington Historical Society Newsletter, No. 21 (Winter 1993), [1].
        Indian students from the Hampton Institute in Virginia came to work on Berkshire County farms during the late 19th century. On this subject, see also entry 1533.

        SEE ALSO entries 1560, 1660, 1691, 2622.

BRISTOL COUNTY

1785.   GEORGIANNA, DANIEL. The strike of '28. New Bedford: Spinner Publications, 1993. 160p. MBAt. *
        In the mills of New Bedford and Fall River.

        SEE ALSO entries 246, 2336-2337.

DUKES COUNTY

1786.   BAYLIES, HENRY. "A running account of matters & things." DCI, 34 (May 1993), 206-212; 35 (Aug. 1993), 40-48; (Nov. 1993), 88-96.
        Serialized diary of Baylies (1822-1893), a Methodist minister. To be continued.

1787.   DRUETT, JOAN. "Partners in history: the Bay of Islands and Martha's Vineyard." DCI, 33 (Nov. 1991), 67-87.
        Links between New Englanders and New Zealanders as a result of whaling and other activities.

1788.   _____. "Rough medicine: doctoring the whalemen." DCI, 30 (Nov. 1988), 3-15.

1789.   _____. "Vineyarders catch the 1849 gold bug." DCI, 31 (Aug. 1989), 3-19.

1790.   GARDNER, RUSSELL HERBERT. "A rare aboriginal artifact from Martha's Vineyard Island, with a living family history." MASB, 54 (Spring 1993), 3-10.

1791.   GUDE, JOHN. "The whip-poor-will and James Thurber." DCI, 32 (May 1991), 151-163.
        Thurber as a summer resident of Martha's Vineyard.

1792.   HOLLAND, JACQUELINE L. "The African-American presence on Martha's Vineyard." DCI, 33 (Aug. 1991), 3-26.

1793.   HUNTINGTON, GALE. "The character and life style of the Indians." DCI, 31 (May 1990), 194-200.

1794.   "THE LAPWING and other 'small tokens of respect.'" DCI, 30 (Nov. 1988), 31-34.
        Schooner given to Daniel Webster in 1849 by members of the Forbes family of Martha's Vineyard. See also entry 1796.

1795.   MacKENZIE, CLYDE L. SR. "Shellfisheries on Martha's Vineyard." DCI, 34 (Aug. 1992), 3-34.

1796.   MONAGHAN, E. JENNIFER. "'She loved to read in good books': literacy and the Indians of Martha's Vineyard, 1643-1725." History of Education Quarterly, 30 (Winter 1990), 493-521.

1797.   RAILTON, ARTHUR R. "Daniel Webster, fisherman, on the Vineyard." DCI, 30 (Nov. 1988), 16-31.
        1849 visit. See also entry 1793.

1798.   _____. "The hallucinations of Rev. John Adams." DCI, 32 (Feb. 1991), 121-141.
        Methodist circuit rider (1820s).

1799.   _____. "The Indians and the English on Martha's Vineyard." DCI, 31 (May 1990), 163-193; 32 (Nov. 1990), 43-80; 33 (Aug. 1991), 27-63; (Feb. 1992), 135-163; 34 (Feb. 1993), 109-164.

1800.   RATHBONE, CHARLES H. "An 1894 Vineyard visitor: painter N.A. Moore." DCI, 35 (May 1994), 166-179.
        Nelson Augustus Moore (1824-1902), a Connecticut painter.

1801. SCOTT, JONATHAN F. "Historic ship drawings found on boards in early houses." DCI, 33 (Feb. 1992), 115-128.

1802. THAXTER, JOSEPH. "The island in the 1800s: its economy and life style." DCI, 35 (May 1994), 155-165.
   Martha's Vineyard as described in two letters of Thaxter's, written in 1814 and 1824.

1803. "THE VISIT by the New York Yacht Club in 1895, with Herreshoff's Defender of America's Cup." DCI, 34 (May 1993), 197-200.

1804. "WHEN the island's biggest employer was a London missionary society: from the receipt book of Samuel Sewall, 1708-1719." DCI, 34 (May 1993), 184-196.

SEE ALSO entries 1608, 17767.

ESSEX COUNTY

1805. BROWN, MARY LEY M. "A tribute to Anne Dudley Bradstreet, first recognized British-American authoress, 1612-1672/3." DAR Magazine, 120 (Jan. 1986), 22-24.
   See also entries 1808, 1810.

1806. DEXTER, RALPH WARREN. "Essex County and the development of American marine biology." American Neptune, 49 (Winter 1989), 34-38.

1807. NORTHEY, RICHARD P. "A brief history of the Essex Railroad." B&M Bulletin, 19:2 [1993], 12-15.

1808. RICHTER, PAULA BRADSTREET. "Following the footprints of the past: the shoe collection of the Essex Institute." EIHC, 127 (Apr. 1991), 115-137.
   Primarily shoes made in Essex County.

1809. ROSENMEIER, ROSAMOND. Anne Bradstreet revisited. Boston: Twayne Publishers, 1991. xvi, 174p. MB. *
   The poet. See also entry 1810.

1810. TAGNEY, RONALD N. The world turned upside down: Essex County during America's turbulent years, 1763- 1790. West Newbury: Essex County History, 1989. vi, 504p. MWA. *

1811. WINEBRENNER, KIMBERLY COLE. "Anne Bradstreet: the development of a Puritan voice." Ph.D. dissertation, Kent State Univ., 1991. iv, 253p. *
   Abstracted in DAI, 52:3A (1991), 1334. See also entry 1808.

SEE ALSO entry 2703.

FRANKLIN COUNTY

1812. FIELD, JOSEPH. Historical sketches, or the spirit of orthodoxy, illustrated by the records and transactions of Franklin Association from August 1810 to the present time; being the second part of Clerical discipline, by the same author. Springfield: Wood & Lyman, 1823. 71p. MDeeP. *
   Ministerial association (Congregational).

1813. GARRISON, JOHN RITCHIE. Landscape and material life in Franklin County, Massachusetts, 1770-1860. Knoxville: Univ. of Tennessee Pr., 1991. 320p. MA. *

1814. NUTTER, KATHLEEN BANKS. "'This Greenback lunacy': third party politics in Franklin County, 1878." HJM, 22 (Summer 1994), 106-120.

1815. YNGVESSON, BARBARA. After the law: virtuous citizens, disruptive subjects: order and complaint in a New England court. N.Y.: Routledge, 1993. xii, 168p. MDeeP. *
   Franklin County Court.

SEE ALSO entry 1691.

HAMPDEN COUNTY

1816. GREENE, J. R. "Historical notes on the Hampden RR: 1909-1912." B&M Bulletin, 19:1 [1993], 12-17.
   Railroad.

SEE ALSO entry 1552.

HAMPSHIRE COUNTY

1817. CONUEL, THOMAS. Quabbin: the accidental wilderness. (1981) Rev. ed. Amherst: Univ. of Massachusetts Pr., 1990. xx, 66p. M. *
   Quabbin Reservoir. Note: this item replaces entry 3924 in Vol. 8.

1818. EMERY, DEBORAH DAY. "The monarch of Hampshire: Israel Williams." HJM, 17 (Summer 1989), 119-136.
   See also entry 1822.

1819. FERRIS, MARC. "The Working Men's Party of Hampshire County, 1811-1835." HJM, 18 (Winter 1990), 37-60.

1820. FIVE colleges: five histories. Ronald Story, ed. Amherst: Five Colleges, 1992. x, 137p. MWA. *
   Amherst, Hampshire, Mount Holyoke, and Smith colleges; Univ. of Massachusetts.

1821   HAMPSHIRE COUNTY

1821.   GURA, PHILIP F. "Early nineteenth-century printing in rural Massachusetts: John Howe of Greenwich and Enfield, ca. 1803-45, with a transcription of the 'printer's book,' ca. 1832." AASP, 101 (Apr. 1991), 25- 62.

1822.   LOWENBERG, CARLTON. Hampshire County textbooks, 1812-1850. Territa A. Lowenberg and Carla L. Brown, eds. Lafayette, Calif., 1988. 145, [47]p. MWA. *

1823.   MERRIAM, GEORGE HENRY. "Israel Williams, monarch of Hampshire, 1709-1788." Ph.D. dissertation, Clark Univ., 1961. v, 165p. M. *
   Abstracted in DAI, 22:9 (1962), 3178. Note: this item replaces entry 3937 in Vol. 8.

1824.   SHATTUCK, DEBRA A. "Bats, balls, and books: baseball and higher education for women at three eastern women's colleges, 1866-1900." Journal of Sport History, 19 (Summer 1992), 91-109.
   Including Mount Holyoke and Smith.

1825.   WALKER, WILLIAM H. (1857-1934). Ez, or, lovemaking, horsetrading, and fighting in Swift River Valley. Athol: Millers River Publishing, 1984. 160p. MWA. *

MIDDLESEX COUNTY

1826.   DONAHUE, BRIAN. "'Dammed at both ends and cursed in the middle': the 'flowage' of the Concord River meadows, 1798-1862." Environmental Review, 13 (Fall/ Winter 1989), 47-67.

1827.   MIDDLEBROOK, DIANE WOOD. Anne Sexton: a biography. Boston: Houghton Mifflin, 1991. xxiii, 488p. MBAt. *
   Poet (lived 1928-1974).

1828.   STEINBERG, THEODORE L. Nature incorporated: industrialization and the waters of New England. N.Y.: Cambridge Univ. Pr., 1991. xv, 284p. MB. *
   See also next entry.

1829.   _____. "Nature incorporated: the Waltham-Lowell mills and the waters of New England." Ph.D. dissertation, Brandeis Univ., 1989. v, 570p. *
   Abstracted in DAI, 50:6A (1989), 1783. See also preceding entry.

1830.   WOLKOVICH-VALKAVICIUS, WILLIAM LAWRENCE. "The Ku Klux Klan in the Nashoba Valley." HJM, 18 (Winter 1990), 61-80.

   SEE ALSO entries 1662, 1674, 1735.

NORFOLK COUNTY

1831.   HOFFMAN, CURTISS R. "A brief history of the South Shore chapter." MASB, 50 (Oct. 1989), 56-58.
   Chapter of the Massachusetts Archaeological Society.

PLYMOUTH COUNTY

1832.   HOFFMAN, CURTISS R. "North River chapter history." MASB, 50 (Oct. 1989), 50-51.
   Massachusetts Archaeological Society.

WORCESTER COUNTY

1833.   BARON, DONNA KEITH. "Furniture makers and retailers in Worcester County, Massachusetts, working to 1850." Antiques, 143 (May 1993), 784-795.
   Includes an alphabetical list.

1834.   BROOKE, JOHN L. The heart of the Commonwealth: society and political culture in Worcester County, Massachusetts, 1713-1861. N.Y.: Cambridge Univ. Pr., 1990. xxi, 446p. MWA. *
   See also this author's Ph.D. dissertation on same subject: "Society, revolution and the symbolic uses of the dead..." (Univ. of Pennsylvania, 1982; entry 3996 in Vol. 8).

1835.   CUMMINGS, PAMELA J. "Worcester County soldiers in the Civil War." HJM, 20 (Winter 1992), 32-52.

1836.   DAUPHINAIS, PAUL RAYMOND. "Structure and strategy: French-Canadians in central New England, 1850-1900." Ph.D. dissertation, Univ. of Maine, 1991. 307p. *
   Fitchburg and Worcester. Abstracted in DAI, 53:1A (1992), 281.

1837.   HAAKER, MARY. "W. Elmer Ekblaw chapter." MASB, 50 (Oct. 1989), 42-47.
   Central Massachusetts chapter of the Massachusetts Archaeological Society.

1838. LANCE, MARTHA BLANCHARD. "'The fathers lived in the forests: their children live off them'; rural New England sawmilling and the timber trade, 1730-1870." Ph.D. dissertation, Univ. of Pennsylvania, 1993. 355p.
    Southbridge and Sturbridge. Abstracted in DAI, 54:6A (1993), 2198.

1839. RICHARDS, KENNETH G. Memories of a small-town Yankee. Athol: Millers River Publishing, [1985]. 128p. MDeeP. *
    In Athol and Petersham (autobiographical).

1840. WHITE, FRANK G. "Make a specification of a patent." CEAIA, 46 (Sept. 1993), 68, 86-88.
    Article based on 19th-century diary extracts.

1841. WHITNEY, JEANNE ELLEN. "'An art that requires capital': agriculture and mortgages in Worcester County, Massachusetts, 1790-1850." Ph.D. dissertation, Univ. of Delaware, 1991. xi, 284p. MWA. *
    Abstracted in DAI, 52:9A (1992), 3409.

    SEE ALSO entries 29, 135, 164-165, 195, 1551, 1544, 1751.

Massachusetts

Entries for Cities and Towns †

AMESBURY (ESSEX CO.)

1842. KEISTER, KIM. "Rowing against the tide." Historic Preservation, 43 (July/Aug. 1991), 38-45, 73.
    Lowell's Boat Shop, "founded circa 1793...the country's oldest manufacturer of boats.

    SEE ALSO entry 1536.

AMHERST (HAMPSHIRE CO.)

1843. ACKMANN, MARTHA. "The matrilineage of Emily Dickinson." Ph.D. dissertation, Univ. of Massachusetts, 1988. xii, 309p. *
    Norcross family. Abstracted in DAI, 49:5A (1988), 1141.

1844. AMHERST, MASS. FIRST CHURCH. 250 years at First Church in Amherst, 1739-1989. Amherst, 1990. 328p. MDeeP. *
    Congregational.

1845. CARY, HAROLD WHITING. The church in North Amherst, Massachusetts, 1826-1976. Amherst: North Congregational Church of Amherst, 1976. 41p. MDeeP.

1846. DICKINSON HOMESTEAD. The Dickinson Homestead, Amherst, Mass. [Amherst, 1977] [14]p. MDeeP. *

1847. GOLDEN, DANIEL. "Rebels without a cause." Boston Globe Magazine (Mar. 7, 1993), 10, 19-21.
    Recollections of high school days in Amherst (late 1960s).

1848. GROSS, ROBERT ALAN. "The machine-readable Transcendentalists: cultural history on the computer." American Quarterly, 41 (Sept. 1989), 501-521.
    The use of computers to analyze 1850 census records in a course taught by the author at Amherst College (1980s).

† See the Massachusetts volume in this series (1976) for a complete list of cities and towns.

* Online Computer Library Center (OLCC) listings for books and dissertations marked with this symbol may include additional library locations.

1849.   HALL, DONALD. "The poet of Fort Juniper." Yankee, 53
(June 1989), 53, 80-83, 116.
Robert Francis (1901-1987).

1850.   IVES, PHILIP T. A brief history of South Congregational
Church in Amherst, organized 1824; 1969 revision.
[Amherst: South Congregational Church in Amherst, 1969]
[4]p. MDeeP.

1851.   LONGSWORTH, POLLY. The world of Emily Dickinson.
N.Y.: W.W. Norton, 1990. viii, 136p. MB. *
Primarily pictorial.

1852.   MASSACHUSETTS. UNIVERSITY. A research guide to the
history of the University of Massachusetts. Robert
Gabrielsky, comp. Amherst, 1989. 116p. MU. *

1853.   THOMPSON, LaVERNE ELIZABETH THOMAS. "A
study of influence in liberal education and liberal educational
thought: presidents Alexander Meikeljohn and Charles W.
Cole of Amherst College." Ph.D. dissertation, Univ. of
Toledo, 1991. viii, 194p. *
The two served from 1912-1924 and 1946-1960,
respectively. Abstracted in DAI, 52:8A (1992), 2840- 2841.

1854.   VARNUM, ROBIN R. "A maverick writing course: English
1-2 at Amherst College, 1938-1968." Ed.D. dissertation,
Univ. of Massachusetts, 1992. viii, 331p. *
Abstracted in DAI, 53:12A (1993), 4232.

1855.   WALKER, ALICE MOREHOUSE. Mary Mattoon and her
hero of the Revolution. Amherst: [Pr. of Carpenter &
Morehouse], 1902. 83p. MDeeP. *
Gen. Ebenezer Mattoon.

SEE ALSO entries 1597, 1600, 1820.

ANDOVER (ESSEX CO.)

1856.   ABBOT, ELINOR. "Transformations: the reconstruction of
social hierarchy in early colonial Andover, Massachusetts."
Ph.D. dissertation, Brandeis Univ., 1990. iv, 279p. *
Abstracted in DAI, 51:5A (1990), 1740.

1857.   FAGAN, CHARLES W. IV. "Charles Bulfinch, Peter Banner,
and Andover Hill." EIHC, 125 (Apr. 1989), 177-195.
The architecture of Phillips Academy.

1858.   GRANQUIST, MARK. "The role of 'common sense' in the
Hermeneutics of Moses Stuart." Harvard Theological
Review, 83 (July 1990), 305-319.
Hebrew scholarship at Andover Theological Seminary.

1859.   VICKERS, DANIEL. "Competency and competition:
economic culture in early America." WMQ, 3 ser. 48 (Jan.
1991), 3-29.
Caleb Jackson Jr. (born 1786) and his efforts to gain
economic "competency" by farming and shoemaking.

ASHBURNHAM (WORCESTER CO.)

1860.   VON DECK, JOSEPH F. "Party and politics: Ashburnham in
the 1850s." HJM, 21 (Winter 1993), 33-54.

ASHBY (MIDDLESEX CO.)

1861.   DAWSON, SUSANNE M., and M. SUSAN BARGER.
"'Painted on Frances' copy': profiles of Ruth Henshaw
Bascom." DAR Magazine, 120 (Oct. 1986), 692-693, 706,
710, 725.
Artist (lived 1772-1848).

ASHFIELD (FRANKLIN CO.)

1862.   ASHFIELD, MASS. ST. JOHN'S CHURCH. One hundred
years at Saint John's Church, Ashfield, Massachusetts,
1828-1928. [Greenfield: E.A. Hall, 1932] 45p. MDeeP.
Episcopal.

1863.   COONEY, BLANCHE. "Back to the land: 1941." New
England Monthly, 6 (May 1990), 48-52, 102.
Autobiographical.

1864.   FESSENDEN, RUSSELL. The first 25 years: a history of the
Ashfield Historical Society, 1961-1986. [Ashfield: Ashfield
Historical Society, 1986] [28]p. MDeeP. *

1865.   GRAY, FRANCIS A. Commemorating 150 years: St. John's
Church, Ashfield, Massachusetts. n.p., [1978?]. [16]p.
MDeeP.
Episcopal.

1866.   GREENFIELD RECORDER-GAZETTE (newspaper).
Ashfield anniversary, 1765-1965, Section A supplement.
[Greenfield, 1965] 24p. MDeeP.

1867.   GULICK, BETTY, and EDWARD GULICK. Charles Eliot
Norton and the Ashfield Dinners, 1879-1903. [Ashfield]:
Ashfield Historical Society, 1990. 36p. MDeeP.
Intellectual life in Ashfield.

1868.   PAINE, WILLIAM POMEROY. "Ashfield Centennial
address." Greenfield Courier (July 17, 1865).

1869. SHEPARD, THOMAS. A ministry of fourteen years: a discourse preached at Ashfield, Mass., June 16, 1859; being the fortieth anniversary of his ordination in that town. Providence [R.I.]: Knowles, Anthony, 1859. 24p. MDeeP. *
Shepard served the First Congregational Church from 1819-1833.

SEE ALSO entry 1545.

ATHOL (WORCESTER CO.)

1870. CHAISSON, KATHRYN A. Athol's historic buildings and places: a partial inventory. Roderick H. McColl, ed. [Athol]: Athol Historical Commission, 1986. 63p. MDeeP.

1871. STARRETT, L. S., COMPANY. The Starrett story: a brief account of the origin and development of the L.S. Starrett Company, Athol, Massachusetts, and how it became the "world's greatest toolmakers." [Athol], 1948. 32p. MDeeP.

SEE ALSO entry 1839.

ATTLEBORO (BRISTOL CO.)

1872. WAIT, JAMES. "The Massachusetts Archaeological Society museum: past, present and future of the Robbins Museum of Archaeology." MASB, 50 (Oct. 1989), 61-64.

SEE ALSO entry 246.

AUBURN (WORCESTER CO.)

1873. EDDY, WANDA JEAN CRIGER. "Joseph Stone (1758-1837): an early American tunesmith." D.M.A. dissertation, Univ. of Oregon, 1987. xii, 214p. *
Abstracted in DAI, 49:4A (1988), 652.

BARNSTABLE (BARNSTABLE CO.)

1874. BODENSIEK, FRED. Commemorative booklet of the town of Barnstable, 1639-1989. Marion Vuilleumier, ed. Barnstable: Barnstable 350th Committee, 1989. 48p. MBar. *

1875. CARPENTER, DELORES BIRD. The early days of Cape Cod Community College. West Barnstable: Cape Cod Community College, 1989. xi, 220p. M. *

1876. CHESBRO, PAUL L. Osterville: a history of the village. Taunton: William S. Sullwold Publishing, 1988- 1989. 2v. MB. *
Note: this item replaces entry 4117 in Vol. 8.

1877. HERBERGER, CHARLES F. Three centuries of Centerville scenes: vignettes of a Cape Cod village. [Centerville]: Centerville Historical Society, 1989. 180p. MWA. *

BARRE (WORCESTER CO.)

1878. CONNINGTON, HELEN WEBBER. History of Barre: windows into the past. Barre: Barre Historical Commission, 1992. 290p. MWA. *

SEE ALSO entries 5, 1841.

BECKET (BERKSHIRE CO.)

1879. UNDERWOOD, SHARRY TRAVER. "Ted Shawn's summer oasis, 1942: Pillow talk." Dance Magazine, 63 (July 1989), 28-31.
The noted modern dancer, at Jacob's Pillow.

BELMONT (MIDDLESEX CO.)

1880. HILL, TERESA LYNNE. "Religion, madness, and the asylum: a study of medicine and culture in New England, 1820-1840." Ph.D. dissertation, Brown Univ., 1991. viii, 313p. *
Medical and religious views of "religious insanity" and its treatment at the McLean Asylum. Abstracted in DAI, 52:9A (1992), 3404.

1881. SUTTON, S. B. Crossroads in psychiatry: a history of the McLean Hospital. Washington, D.C.: American Psychiatric Pr., 1986. xii, 372p. MB. *

BERNARDSTON (FRANKLIN CO.)

1882. GREENFIELD RECORDER-GAZETTE (newspaper). Bernardston 220th anniversary: Section A, B; anniversary edition. [Greenfield, Aug. 15, 1962] 22, 16p. MDeeP.

1883   BEVERLY

BEVERLY (ESSEX CO.)

1883.   BENNEWITZ, KATHLEEN MOTES. "John F. Kensett at Beverly, Massachusetts." American Art Journal, 21 (Winter 1989), 46-65.
    Kensett painted in Beverly between 1859 and 1872.

1884.   HARRIS, MARGUERITE L., MILES F. HARRIS, ELEANOR V. SPILLER, and MARY CARR. John Hale, a man beset by witches: his book, A modest enquiry into the nature of witchcraft, Boston in N.E.; with an introduction and articles on his life, his church, his house and some of his illustrious descendants. Beverly: Wilkscraft Creative Printing, 1992. xvi, 230p. DLC. *
    Hale was the town's first minister (late-17th century).

    SEE ALSO entries 1653, 2498.

BOLTON (WORCESTER CO.)

1885.   WHITCOMB, ESTHER KIMMENS. About Bolton. Bowie, Md.: Heritage Books, 1988. xi, 463p. MWA. *

1886.   _____, and DOROTHY O. MAYO. Bolton soldiers & sailors in the American Revolution. Bowie, Md.: Heritage Books, 1985. vii, 90p. MB. *

BOSTON (SUFFOLK CO.)

1887.   ABBOTT, RICHARD H. Cotton & capital: Boston businessmen and antislavery reform, 1854-1868. Amherst: Univ. of Massachusetts Pr., 1992. x, 294p. MBU. *

1888.   ALLSTON, WASHINGTON. The correspondence of Washington Allston. Nathalia Wright, ed. Lexington: Univ. of Kentucky Pr., 1993. xix, 682p. MBAt. *
    Painter (lived 1779-1843). See also entry 2199.

1889.   AMBLER, LOUISE TODD. Katharine Lane Weems: sculpture and drawings. Boston: Boston Athenaeum, 1987. xv, 111p. MBAt. *
    20th century.

1890.   AMORY, HUGH. "Under the Exchange: the unprofitable business of Michael Perry, a seventeenth- century Boston bookseller." AASP, 103 (Apr. 1993), 31- 60.

1891.   ANDERSON, PETER. "Roslindale remembered." Boston Globe Magazine (Mar. 18, 1990), 21, 76-82, 84.

1892.   ANDREWS, WAYNE. "Martin Brimmer: the first gentleman of Boston." Archives of American Art Journal, 30:1-4 (1990), 4-7.
    Brimmer (1829-1896) was the first president of the Museum of Fine Arts.

1893.   ARATON, HARVEY, and FILIP BONDY. The selling of the green: the financial rise and moral decline of the Boston Celtics. N.Y.: Harper Collins, 1992. xvi, 271p. MB. *
    Basketball.

1894.   ARCHITECTURE of Boston: journal articles, 1979-1986. Mary A. Vance, comp. Monticello, Ill.: Vance Bibliographies, 1987. 14p. MB. *

1895.   ARMSTRONG, RODNEY. "The Boston Athenaeum and its furnishings." Antiques, 136 (Aug. 1989), 302-315.

1896.   BAKER, LIVA. The justice from Beacon Hill: the life and times of Oliver Wendell Holmes. N.Y.: Harper Collins, 1991. xiv, 783p. MBAt. *
    The noted Supreme Court justice (lived 1841-1935). See also entry 2101.

1897.   BANKS, HENRY H. A century of excellence: the history of Tufts University School of Medicine, 1893- 1993. Boston: Tufts Univ., 1993. viii, 338p. MBAt. *

1898.   BEATTY, JACK. The rascal king: the life and times of James Michael Curley, 1874-1958. Reading: Addison-Wesley, 1992. x, 571p. MBAt. *

1899.   BEISEL, NICOLA KAY. "Class, culture, and campaigns against vice in three American cities, 1872-1892." American Sociological Review, 55 (Fall 1990), 44-62.
    See also next entry.

1900.   _____. "Upper class formation and the politics of censorship in Boston, New York, and Philadelphia, 1872-1892." Ph.D. dissertation, Univ. of Michigan, 1990. 301p. *
    Abstracted in DAI, 52:1A (1990), 300.

1901.   BIRD, LARRY. Drive: the story of my life. N.Y.: Doubleday, 1989. xii, 259p. MB. *
    Starred for Boston Celtics from 1979-1992.

1902.   BISSON, WILFRED JOSEPH. Countdown to violence: the Charlestown Convent Riot of 1834. N.Y.: Garland Publishing, 1989. iii, 151p. MB. *
    Published Ph.D. dissertation (Michigan State Univ., 1974; entry 4271 in Vol. 8).

1903.   BLACK, FREDRICK R. Charlestown Navy Yard, 1890- 1973. Boston: Boston National Historical Park, National Park Service, U.S. Department of the Interior, 1988. 2v. MB. *

1904. BLACKWELL, ALICE STONE. Growing up in Boston's Gilded Age: the journal of Alice Stone Blackwell, 1872-1874. Marlene Deahl Merrill, ed. New Haven, Conn.: Yale Univ. Pr., 1990. xx, 270p. MB. *
See also entry 1546.

1905. BLOOMFIELD, ZACHARY STEWART. "Baptism of a 'deacon's' theatre: audience development at the Boston Museum, 1841-1861." Ph.D. dissertation, Univ. of Missouri, 1991. vi, 360p. *
Abstracted in DAI, 53:3A (1992), 666.

1906. BLOUNT, ROY JR. "October 21, 1975." Sports Illustrated, 79 (July 19, 1993), 39.
The sixth game of the 1975 World Series, between the Red Sox and Cincinnati Reds, as the "greatest game" the author had seen. See also entry 1996.

1907. BORDMAN, MARCIA BETH. "Dear old golden rule days: a study in the rhetoric of separate-but-equal in Roberts v. City of Boston (1849), Plessy v. Ferguson (1896), and Brown v. Board of Education (1954)." Ph.D. dissertation, Univ. of Maryland, 1993. xiv, 119p. *
Abstracted in DAI, 54:10A (1994), 3685.

1908. BORIS-SCHACTER, SHERYL. "The Boston Public Schools' decision whether to institute school-based health services." Ed.D. dissertation, Harvard Univ., 1989. vi, 187p. *
1986. Abstracted in DAI, 50:9A (1990), 2715.

1909. BOSTON, MASS. ST. CECELIA'S CHURCH. Saint Cecelia's Church, 1888-1988, Boston, Massachusetts. Boston, 1988. 16p. MB. *
Roman Catholic.

1910. BOSTON ATHENAEUM. Change and continuity: a pictorial history of the Boston Athenaeum. Being selections from an exhibition held in December, 1976. Boston, 1976. 32p. MBAt. *
Includes essay by Jane S. Knowles.

1911. THE BOSTON personalist tradition in philosophy, social ethics, and theology. Paul Deats and Carol Robb, eds. Macon, Ga.: Mercer, 1986. xxiv, 295p. MB. *

1912. BOSTONIAN SOCIETY. The last tenement: confronting community and urban renewal in Boston's West End. Sean M. Fisher and Carolyn Hughes, eds. Boston, 1992. 112p. MChB. *

1913. BOULTON, ALEXANDER ORMOND. "Behind the federal facade." American Heritage, 40 (May/June 1989), 69-75.
Harrison Gray Otis, Charles Bulfinch, and federal architecture in Boston.

1914. BOWDOIN COLLEGE MUSEUM OF ART. The legacy of James Bowdoin III. Brunswick, Me., 1994. xix, 247p. MeHi. *
Bowdoin (1752-1811) was Bowdoin College's "first patron."

1915. BOWEN, JANET WOLF. "Architectural envy: 'a figure is nothing without a setting' in Henry James's The Bostonians." NEQ, 65 (Mar. 1992), 3-23.
1886 novel.

1916. BRADLEY, MICHAEL. "New York vs. Boston: 1978." Sport, 84 (Oct. 1993), 70-71.
American League playoff game (baseball). See also entry 1996.

1917. BRAVERMAN, WILLIAM ALAN. "The ascent of Boston's Jews, 1630-1918." Ph.D. dissertation, Harvard Univ., 1990. iii, 450p.
Abstracted in DAI, 51:3A (1990), 974.

1918. BREEN, LOUISE A. "Cotton Mather, the 'angelical ministry,' and inoculation." Journal of the History of Medicine and Allied Sciences, 46 (July 1991), 333-357.

1919. BRODZINS, DEAN DAVID. "Theodore Parker and Transcendentalism." Ph.D. dissertation, Harvard Univ., 1993. 470p. *
Parker lived 1810-1860. Abstracted in DAI, 54:5A (1993), 1923-1924. See also entry 1984.

1920. BROWN, ALEX, and LAURIE SHERIDAN. "Pioneering women's committee struggles with hard times." Labor Research Review, 11 (1988), 62-77.
Women's Committee, Local 201, International Union of Electrical, Salaried, Machine and Furniture Workers, and its dealings with General Electric (since 1978).

1921. BROWN, JOSEPH E. "Some notes on Simon Willard and his trapezoids." NAWCCB, 35 (Aug. 1993), 420-425.
Clockmaker.

1922. BROWN, KATHERINE HEMPLE. "The cavalier and the syren: Edgar Allan Poe, Cornelia Wells Walter, and the Boston Lyceum incident." NEQ, 66 (Mar. 1993), 110-123.
1845.

1923. BROWN, THOMAS W. "The African connection: Cotton Mather and the Boston smallpox epidemic of 1721-1722." JAMA, 260 (Oct. 21, 1988), 2247-2249.

1924. BROYLES, MICHAEL. "Music and class structure in antebellum Boston." Journal of the American Musicological Society, 44 (Fall 1991), 451-493.

1925   BOSTON

1925.   BROYLES, MICHAEL. Music of the highest class: elitism and populism in antebellum Boston. New Haven, Conn.: Yale Univ. Pr., 1992. ix, 392p. MWA. *

1926.   BUCHHEIM, GUNTHER. "Two miniature maps of Boston found." Map Collector [U.K.] (1992), 24-27.
        The 1775 maps were found at the John Carter Brown Library, Brown Univ.

1927.   BUCKLEY, STEVE. "A postcard from my brother." Yankee, 56 (Oct. 1992), 68-71, 114, 116.
        Memories associated with the clinching of the American League pennant in 1967 by the Red Sox.

1928.   BUTTERFIELD, REBECCA CODMAN. "Rebecca Codman Butterfield's reminiscences of Brook Farm." NEQ, 65 (Dec. 1992), 603-630.
        The author was part of the community from 1843-1847; her recollections date from ca. 1890s. Joel Myerson, ed.

1929.   CABOT, ELIZABETH ROGERS MASON. More than common powers of perception: the diary of Elizabeth Rogers Mason Cabot. P.A.M. Taylor, ed. Boston: Beacon Pr., 1991. xiv, 357p. MB. *
        Cabot lived 1834-1920.

1930.   CAMERON, JEAN ELIZABETH. "John Cotton's role in the trials of Anne Hutchinson." Ph.D. dissertation, Univ. of Minnesota, 1991. iii, 229p. *
        1637-1638. Abstracted in DAI, 53:1A (1992), 193.

1931.   CAMPBELL, ROBERT, and PETER VANDERWARKER. Cityscapes of Boston: an American city through time. Boston: Houghton Mifflin, 1992. xi, 220p. MBAt. *

1932.   CAPUTO, JOHN PAUL. "Boston High School, as an at-risk intervention program, 1968-1979." Ed.D. dissertation, Univ. of Massachusetts, 1988. xiii, 233p. *
        Abstracted in DAI, 49:11A (1989), 3235-3236.

1933.   CASH, PHILIP. "Setting the stage: Dr. Benjamin Waterhouse's reception in Boston, 1782-1788." Journal of the History of Medicine and Allied Sciences, 47 (Jan. 1992), 5-28.

1934.   CATALOGUS librorum: the library of Thomas Paine of Boston (1694-1757)." MHSP, 100 (1988), 100-127.
        John D. Cushing, ed.

1935.   CAVANAUGH, JACK. "The Celtics' music man." Sports Illustrated, 76 (Mar. 23, 1992), 90, 95.
        Tony Lavelli, who played for the Celtics in 1949-1950, entertained crowds at halftime by playing the accordion.

1936.   CHADWICK, BRUCE. The Boston Red Sox: memories and mementoes of New England's team. N.Y.: Abbeville Pr., 1992. 131p. M. *
        Baseball.

1937.   CHASE, THEODORE, and LAUREL K. GABEL. "Seven initial carvers of Boston, 1700-1725." Markers V (1988) 210-232.
        Gravestone carvers.

1938.   CLARK, CHARLES E. "Boston and the nurturing of newspapers: dimensions of the cradle, 1690-1741." NEQ, 64 (June 1991), 243-271.

1939.   CLIFFORD, DEBORAH PICKMAN. Crusader for freedom: a life of Lydia Maria Child. Boston: Beacon Pr., 1992. viii, 367p. MBAt. *
        Lived 1802-1880. See also entries 2046, 2085-2086.

1940.   COHEN, DANIEL ASHER. "The murder of Maria Bickford: fashion, passion, and the birth of a consumer culture." American Studies, 31 (Fall 1990), 5-30.
        Social implications of the journalistic sensationalism and public reaction associated with the 1845 murder of a prostitute.

1941.   COLLINS, JIM. "Still Spaceman after all these years." Yankee, 57 (Aug. 1993), 74-82, 116-118.
        Former Red Sox pitcher Bill Lee.

1942.   CONWAY, ANN CATHERINE. "Organizational symbolism in the Peter Bent Brigham Hospital, 1913-1938: a cultural history." Ph.D. dissertation, Brandeis Univ., 1993. 365p. *
        Abstracted in DAI, 54:4A (1993), 1547.

1943.   CORRIGAN, JOHN. The hidden balance: religion and the social theories of Charles Chauncy and Jonathan Mayhew. N.Y.: Cambridge Univ. Pr., 1987. xiv, 161p. MWA. *
        18th century.

1944.   COURAGE and conscience: black & white abolitionists in Boston. Donald M. Jacobs, ed. Bloomington: Indiana Univ. Pr., 1993. xiv, 237p. MBAt. *

1945.   CRAKER, WENDEL DEAN. "Cotton Mather's wrangle with the devil: a sociological analysis of the fantastic." Ph.D. dissertation, Univ. of Georgia, 1990. xi, 479p. *
        Abstracted in DAI, 52:1A (1991), 300.

1946.   CRANDALL, RALPH J., and JULIE HELEN OTTO. "The New England Historic Genealogical Society." Mayflower Quarterly, 55 (Nov. 1989), 298-303.
        Includes a historical sketch.

1947.   CREAMER, ROBERT W. "When New York and Boston played 74 years ago." Sports Illustrated, 65 (Oct. 27, 1986), 27.
Giants and Red Sox in 1912 World Series.

1948.   CROMWELL, ADELAIDE M. The other Brahmins: Boston's black upper class, 1750-1950. Fayetteville: Univ. of Arkansas Pr., 1994. xii, 284p. M. *

1949.   CUNNINGHAM, BILL, and DANIEL GOLDEN. "Malcolm X: the Boston years: retracing the emergence of a black leader." Boston Globe Magazine (Feb. 16, 1992), 16-19, 24-30, 35-36, 39-42.

1950.   CUSHING, GEORGE M. JR. Great buildings of Boston: a photographic guide. N.Y.: Dover Publications, 1982. 130p. MB. *
Includes historical text.

1951.   DAVISON, GRAEME. "Cities and ceremonies: nationalism and civic ritual in three new lands." New Zealand Journal of History, 24:2 (1990), 97-117.
Includes revolutionary-era Boston.

1952.   DAVISON, PETER. "The hub of the solar system." American Heritage, 40 (Apr. 1989), 54-56, 58-60, 64-65.
Boston landmarks that reflect the city's literary heritage.

1953.   De ZEGO, FRANK. "Edmund Kean in New York and Boston: the 1820s." Ph.D. dissertation, City Univ. of New York, 1988. xvi, 598p. MBE. *
Actor. Abstracted in DAI, 49:8A (1989), 2024-2025.

1954.   DEAN, ANDREA OPPENHEIMER. "Urban alchemist." Historic Preservation, 42 (July/Aug 1990), 12, 14-15.
Contemporary architect Benjamin Thompson and historic preservation in Boston.

1955.   DEARINGER, DAVID BERNARD. "American Neoclassic sculptors and their private patrons in Boston." Ph.D. dissertation, City Univ. of New York, 1993. 801p.
First half of the 19th century. Abstracted in DAI, 54:6A (1993), 1980.

1956.   DEESE, HELEN R. "Alcott's conversations on the Transcendentalists: the record of Caroline Dall." American Literature, 60 (Mar. 1988), 17-25.
Bronson Alcott (1851).

1957.   _____. "Caroline H. Dall: recorder of the Boston intellectual scene." Documentary Editing, 12 (Dec. 1990), 83-86.
Author, reformer, and diarist (lived 1822-1912).

1958.   DePLASCO, JOSEPH. "The university of labor vs. the university of letters in 1904." Labor's Heritage, 1 (Apr. 1989), 52-65.
Harvard president Charles W. Eliot's address to an audience of Boston workers, sponsored by the Boston Central Labor Union.

1959.   DESMOND, CHARLES FRANK. "An historic analysis of the development and implementation of equal opportunity educational programs at the University of Massachusetts at Boston, 1964-1990." Ed.D. dissertation, Univ. of Massachusetts, 1992. xi, 126p. *
Abstracted in DAI, 53:6A (1992), 1821.

1960.   DEUTSCH, SARAH. "Learning to talk more like a man: Boston women's class-bridging organizations, 1870- 1940." American Historical Review, 97 (Apr. 1992), 379- 404.

1961.   DICKENS, CARRIE NELL. "The history of continuing education for black people in the Roxbury community, 1900-1980." Ed.D. dissertation, Boston Univ., 1984. xi, 218p. *
Abstracted in DAI, 52:9A (1992), 3154.

1962.   DIMAGGIO, DOM. Real grass, real heroes. N.Y.: Kensington Publishing, 1990. 240p. MB. *
Former Red Sox star's recollections of the 1941 season.

1963.   DODSON, JAMES. "The crumbling conscience of Boston." Yankee, 57 (Feb. 1993), 60-67, 122-124, 126.
The Arlington Street Church and its history of political activism.

1964.   DOMOSH, MONA. "Controlling urban form: the development of Boston's Back Bay." Journal of Historical Geography [U.K.], 18 (July 1992), 288-306.

1965.   _____. "Shaping the commercial city: retail districts in nineteenth-century New York and Boston." Association of American Geographers, Annals, 80 (June 1990), 268-284.

1966.   DREIER, PETER, and BRUCE EHRLICH. "Downtown development and urban reform: the politics of Boston's linkage policy." Urban Affairs Quarterly, 26:3 (Mar. 1991), 354-375.
See also next entry.

1967.   _____, and W. DENNIS KEATING. "The limits of localism: progressive housing policies in Boston, 1984- 1989." Urban Affairs Quarterly, 26 (Dec. 1990), 191- 216.

1968   BOSTON

1968.   DRISCOLL, JOHN. "George Curtis: coming to light." Peabody Essex Museum Collections, 129 (Oct. 1993), 372-393.
    Marine painter (lived 1816-1881). See also entries 1993, 2219.

1969.   DUBROW, GAIL LEE. "Claiming public space for women's history in Boston: a proposal for preservation, public art, and public historical interpretation." Frontiers: a Journal of Women History, 13:1 (1992), 111-148.

1970.   DUFFY, TIMOTHY PATRICK. "The gender of letters: the man of letters and intellectual authority in nineteenth-century Boston." Ph.D. dissertation, Univ. of Virginia, 1993. 389p.
    Abstracted in DAI, 54:8A (1994), 3175.

1971.   _____. "Intellectual authority and gender ideology in nineteenth-century Boston: the life and letters of Oliver Wendell Holmes, Sr." HJM, 22 (Winter 1994), 1-16.

1972.   DUNNE, WILLIAM MATTHEW PATRICK. "An Irish immigrant success story." NEQ, 52 (June 1992), 284-290.
    Irish immigrants in the "Boston market" fisheries and related trades. See also next entry.

1973.   _____. "An Irish immigration success story: Thomas Francis McManus (1856-1938)." Ph.D. dissertation, State Univ. of New York, Stony Brook, 1990. xiv, 505p. *
    McManus was a Boston-born naval architect. Members of his parents' generation migrated to Massachusetts during the 1840s and soon "captured a monopoly of the...market fishery." Abstracted in DAI, 51:9A (1991), 3197-3198.

1974.   ECKARDT, ALLISON M. "A collection of American neo-classical furnishings on the East Coast." Antiques, 131 (Apr. 1987), 858-863.
    Collection of Boston and New York furnishings.

1975.   EDWARDS, RALPH. "How Boston selected its first black superintendent of schools." Ed.D. dissertation, Harvard Univ., 1989. iii, 223p. *
    Laval Wilson (1985). Abstracted in DAI, 51:1A (1990), 130-131.

1976.   EDWARDS, ROBERT S. "Watches and clocks in Boston, 1760-1831." NAWCCB, 32 (Apr. 1990), 156-161.
    Ownership of same.

1977.   ETHINGTON, PHILIP J. "Recasting urban political history: gender, the public, the household, and the political participation in Boston and San Francisco during the Progressive Era." Social Science History, 16 (Summer 1992), 301-333.

1978.   ETMEKJIAN, LILLIAN K. "The reaction of the Boston press to the 1909 massacre of Adana." Armenian Review, 40 (Winter 1987), 61-74.
    In Turkey.

1979.   FAIRBROTHER, TREVOR J. "Edmund C. Tarbell's paintings of interiors." Antiques, 131 (Jan. 1987), 224-233.
    Painted between 1903 and 1914.

1980.   FARRELL, BETTY G. Elite families: class and power in nineteenth-century Boston. Albany: State Univ. of New York Pr., 1993. viii, 229p. MStuO. *

1981.   FERTIG, WALTER LONGLEY. "John Sullivan Dwight: Transcendentalist and literary amateur of music." Ph.D. dissertation, Univ. of Maryland, 1952. v, 366p. *

1982.   FINLAY, NANCY. "The graphic art of Thomas Buford Meteyard." Harvard Library Bulletin, n.s. 1 (Summer 1990), 50-66.
    Late-19th and early-20th centuries.

1983.   FINNEY, CHARLES GRANDISON. "Another winter in Boston." Christian History, 7:4 (1988), 10-12.
    Concerning Finney's spiritual growth in 1843-1844, while preaching in Boston; taken from his memoirs.

1984.   FITZGIBBONS, JOHN PATRICK. "Theodore Parker's man-making strategy: a study of his professional ministry in selected sermons." Ph.D. dissertation, Loyola Univ. of Chicago, 1993. iv, 245p. *
    Abstracted in DAI, 54:5A (1993), 1803. See also entry 1919.

1985.   FLOYD, MARGARET HENDERSON. Architectural education and Boston: centennial publication of the Boston Architectural Center, 1889-1989. Boston: Boston Architectural Center, 1990. xii, 177p. MBU. *
    On the training of architects in Boston during that time.

1986.   FORMISANO, RONALD P. Boston against busing: race, class, and ethnicity in the 1960s and 1970s. Chapel Hill: Univ. of North Carolina Pr., 1991. xvi, 323p. MB. *

1987.   FOUNTAIN, CHARLES. Another man's poison: the life and writing of columnist George Frazier. Chester, Conn.: Globe Pequot Pr., 1984. ix, 355p. MB. *
    Nationally known columnist (died 1974), who wrote for the Boston Herald and Boston Globe.

1988.   FOWLER, WILLIAM M. JR. "Sloop of war/sloop of peace: Robert Bennet Forbes and the USS Jamestown." MHSP, 98 (1986), 49-59.
    Use of a naval vessel by Boston residents to provide relief from the Irish potato famine.

1989. FREEBERG, ERNEST. "'An object of peculiar interest': the education of Laura Bridgman." Church History, 61 (June 1992), 191-205.
On the philosophical implications that 19th-century Unitarians found in the education of Bridgman, a deaf, mute, and blind student taught by Dr. Samuel Gridley Howe.

1990. FRIEDLANDER, WALTER J. "The Bigelow-Simpson controversy: still another early argument over the discovery of anesthesia." Bulletin of the History of Medicine, 66 (Winter 1992), 613-625.
The contributions of some Boston physicians.

1991. FRIENDS OF THE PUBLIC GARDEN AND COMMON. The Public Garden, Boston. Boston, 1988. 80p. MBAt. *

1992. FRYER, JUDITH. "What goes on in the ladies' room? Sarah Orne Jewett, Annie Fields, and their community of women." Massachusetts Review, 30 (Winter 1989), 610- 628.

1993. GABOSH, KARL. "George Curtis and his work: a chronology." Peabody Essex Museum Collections, 129 (Oct. 1993), 394-415.
19th-century marine painter. Article followed by "Chrolonogical listing of illustrations" (416-420), and fifty-three plates. See also entries 1968, 2219.

1994. GAMBER, WENDY. "A precarious independence: milliners and dressmakers in Boston, 1860-1890." Journal of Women's History, 4 (Spring 1992), 60-88.

1995. GAMM, GERALD H. The making of New Deal Democrats: voting behavior and realignment in Boston, 1920-1940. Chicago: Univ. of Chicago Pr., 1989. xii, 277p. MB. *

1996. GAMMONS, PETER. "October 2, 1978." Sports Illustrated, 79 (July 19, 1993), 43.
The 1978 playoff game between the Red Sox and New York Yankees as the "greatest game" the author had seen. See also entries 1906, 1916.

1997. GAMST, FREDERICK C. "The context and significance of America's first railroad, on Boston's Beacon Hill." Technology and Culture, 33 (Jan. 1992), 66-100.
Argues that the Beacon Hill Railroad (1805) was technologically the first American railroad.

1998. GELLER, CLINT B. "E. Howard & Company watch dials." NAWCCB, 35 (Aug. 1993), 387-419.
Ca. 1858-1904.

1999. GIBBS, NORMAN B., and LEE W. GIBBS. "Charles Chauncy: a theology in two portraits." Harvard Theological Review, 83 (July 1990), 259-270.
Chauncy lived 1705-1787.

2000. A GLIMPSE into the shadows: forgotten people of the eighteenth century. Barbara McLean Ward, ed. Winterthur, Del.: Henry Francis du Pont Winterthur Museum, 1987. 47p. MWA. *
The poor of Boston.

2001. GOLENBOCK, PETER. Fenway: an unexpurgated history of the Boston Red Sox. N.Y.: Putnam's 1992. 464p. MBAt. *

2002. GOLLIN, RITA K. "'Pegasus in the pound': the editor, the author, their wives, and the Atlantic Monthly." EIHC, 125 (Jan. 1989), 104-122.
James. T. Fields, Nathaniel Hawthorne, Annie Adams Fields, and Sophia Peabody Fields.

2003. GOUGEON, LEN. "1838: Ellis Gray Loring and a journal for the times." Studies in the American Renaissance (1990), 33-47.
The brief journal includes notes on a conversation between Loring and Ralph Waldo Emerson.

2004. GREEN, MARTIN BURGESS. The Mount Vernon Street Warrens: a Boston story, 1860-1910. N.Y.: Scribner's, 1989. xvi, 270p. MB. *

2005. ____. "Mrs. Fiske Warren's husband." New England Monthly, 7 (May 1990), 51-53.
Warren (died 1938) is described as a "nudist, radical, vegetarian, and wearer of gloves on his feet."

2006. GREENE, DAVID L. "Samuel G. Drake and the early years of the New England Historical and Genealogical Register, 1847-1861." NEHGR, 145 (July 1991), 203-238.
Periodical.

2007. GRIFFIN, KATHERINE H., and PETER DRUMMEY. "Manuscripts of the American China trade at the Massachusetts Historical Society." MHSP, 100 (1988), 128-139.

2008. GURA, PHILIP F. "Theodore Parker and the South Boston ordination: the textual tangle of A discourse on the transient and permanent in Christianity." Studies in the American Renaissance (1988), 149-178.
1841 discourse.

2009. GUSTAITIS, JOSEPH. "Elizabeth Peabody: pioneer educator and intellectual." American History Illustrated, 25 (Nov./Dec. 1990), 42-43.
Lived 1804-1894.

2010. HALL, DONALD. "That swing, in 1941." Yankee, 55 (July 1991), 70-73, 116.
Ted Williams's 1941 season, in which he batted .406 for the Red Sox. See also entries 2028, 2064, 2157, 2178, 2187.

2011   BOSTON

2011.   HANNA, WILLIAM F. "The Boston draft riot." Civil War History, 36 (Sept. 1990), 262-273.
    1863.

2012.   HANNAN, NANCY H. Doctors, carpenters, builders, chiefs: women of Hyde Park. Hyde Park: Albert House Publishing, 1986. vi, 120p. M. *

2013.   _____. The whole cloth: a history of the Greater Boston Council of Girl Scouts, 1913-1969. Hyde Park: Albert House Publishing, 1987. var. p. M. *

2014.   HANSEN, DEBRA GOLD. "Bluestockings and bluenoses: gender, class, and conflict in the Boston Female Anti-Slavery Society, 1833-1840." Ph.D. dissertation, Univ. of California, Irvine, 1988. xii, 257p. *
    Abstracted in DAI, 50:1A (1988), 240.

2015.   HARPER, GEORGE WALTER. "Changing patterns of pastoral ministry in the Congregational churches of mid-eighteenth century Boston." Ph.D. dissertation, Boston Univ., 1992. xi, 350p. *
    Abstracted in DAI, 53:3A (1992), 848.

2016.   _____. "Manuductio ad ministerium: Cotton Mather as pastoral innovator." Westminster Theological Journal, 54 (Spring 1992), 79-97.

2017.   HAYDEN, ROBERT C. The African Meeting House in Boston: a sourcebook. Boston: Museum of Afro American History, 1990. viii, 50p. M. *

2018.   _____. African-Americans in Boston: more than 350 years. Boston: Trustees of the Public Library of the City of Boston, 1991. 187p. M. *

2019.   _____. Boston's NAACP history, 1910-1982. Boston: Boston Branch, NAACP, 1982. 26p. MB. *
    National Association for the Advancement of Colored People.

2020.   HAYDEN, SARA ELAINE. "Twenty-three years of 'Our bodies, ourselves': individualism, community, and social change in the work of the Boston Women's Health Book Collective." Ph.D. dissertation, Univ. of Minnesota, 1994. 209p. *
    Abstracted in DAI, 54:12A (1994), 4305-4306.

2021.   HENIGMAN, LAURA. "Coming into communion: pastoral dialogue in eighteenth century New England." Ph.D. dissertation, Columbia Univ., 1991. xii, 245p. *
    The "pastoral relationship" between Jane Colman Turell (1708-1735) and her father, the Rev. Benjamin Colman, which "shows that the laywoman contributed in a substantial way to a two-sided conversation, and therefore had a hand in shaping religious culture." Abstracted in DAI, 52:4A (1991), 1329-1330.

2022.   HERMANSON, JOHN BRADFORD. "The Shirley-Eustis House, Roxbury, Massachusetts." Antiques, 140 (Aug. 1991), 206-217.

2023.   HEWITT, JOHN H. "A black New York newspaperman's impressions of Boston, 1883." Massachusetts Review, 32 (Fall 1991), 445-463.
    T. Thomas Fortune, editor of the New York Globe, a black newspaper.

2024.   HINKS, PETER B. "'Frequently plunged into slavery': free blacks and kidnapping in antebellum Boston." HJM, 20 (Winter 1992), 16-31.

2025.   HIRSHLER, ERICA EVE. "Lilian Westcott Hale (1880-1963): a woman painter of the Boston school." Ph.D. dissertation, Boston Univ., 1992. 393p. *
    Abstracted in DAI, 52:10A (1992), 3460-3461.

2026.   HOLLERAN, MICHAEL. "'Changeful times': preservation, planning, and permanence in the urban environment, Boston, 1870-1930." Ph.D. dissertation, Massachusetts Institute of Technology, 1991. 346p. *
    Abstracted in DAI, 53:21 (1992), 639.

2027.   HOLLORAN, PETER C. Boston's wayward children: social services for homeless children, 1830-1930. Rutherford, N.J.: Fairleigh Dickinson Univ. Pr., 1989. 330p. MB. *
    See also this author's Ph.D. dissertation of same title (Boston Univ., 1982; entry 4726 in Vol. 8).

2028.   HOLWAY, JOHN. The last .400 hitter: the anatomy of a .400 season. Dubuque, Iowa: William C. Brown Publishers, 1992. viii, 360p. MBridT. *
    Ted Williams of the Red Sox (1941 season). See also entries 2064, 2157, 2178, 2187.

2029.   HONIG, DONALD. The Boston Red Sox: an illustrated history. Englewood Cliffs, N.J.: Prentice-Hall, 1990. xi, 292p. MB. *

2030.   HORAN, CYNTHIA. "Organizing the 'new Boston': growth, policy, governing coalitions & tax reform." Polity, 22 (Spring 1991), 489-510.
    From 1945-1959.

2031.   HOWE, CHARLES A. "How human an enterprise: the story of the First Universal Society in Boston during John Murray's ministry." Unitarian Universalist Historical Society, Proceedings, 22:1 (1990-1991), 19-34.
    1793-1815.

2032.   HUDDLE, THOMAS S. "Looking backward: the 1871 reforms at Harvard Medical School reconsidered." Bulletin of the History of Medicine, 65 (Fall 1991), 340-365.

2033. HUSOCK, HOWARD. "The lives of a house." New England Monthly, 7 (Jan. 1990), 30-37.
Number Seven Bowdoin Avenue, in Dorchester (built ca. 1868).

2034. HUX, ROGER K. "Lillian Clayton Jewett and the rescue of the Baker family, 1899-1900." HJM, 19 (Winter 1991), 13-23.
An anti-lynching campaign in the North was focused on the plight of a black South Carolina family, two members of which had been killed by a mob; the family came to Boston and remained there.

2035. HYND, NOEL. "If outfield play's the thing, this cast from Boston was a smash hit." Sports Illustrated, 64 (June 30, 1986), 81-82.
Red Sox outfielders Tris Speaker, Harry Hooper, and Duffy Lewis (ca. 1910-1915).

2036. IRIZARRY, MARIA R. "Bilingual education and the law: effectiveness of bilingual/bicultural program implementation in the Boston public schools." Ed.D. dissertation, Univ. of Massachusetts, 1992. xii, 351p. *
Includes historical background. Abstracted in DAI, 53:2A (1992), 360-361.

2037. ISENBERG, MICHAEL T. John L. Sullivan and his America. Urbana, Ill.: Univ. of Illinois Pr., 1988. xii, 465p. MB. *
The well-known prizefighter (lived 1858-1918).

2038. JACOBS, WILBUR R. Francis Parkman, historian as hero: the formative years. Austin: Univ. of Texas Pr., 1991. xvii, 237p. MWA. *
Parkman lived 1823-1893.

2039. JOBE, BROCK W. "A Boston desk-and-bookcase at the Milwaukee Art Museum." Antiques, 140 (Sept. 1991), 412-419.
18th-century.

2040. JOHNSON, RICHARD D. John Nelson: merchant adventurer: a life between empires. N.Y.: Oxford Univ. Pr., 1991. xii, 194p. MB. *
Died 1734.

2041. JOHNSON, VIOLET MARY-ANN. "The migration experience: social and economic adjustment of British West Indian immigrants in Boston, 1915-1950." Ph.D. dissertation, Boston College, 1993. 246p.
Abstracted in DAI, 54:1A (1993), 292.

2042. JORDAN, PAT. "The game according to Red." Yankee, 53 (May 1989), 70-75, 120-124.
Red Auerbach and Boston Celtics basketball.

2043. KATZ, HARRY L., and RICHARD CHAFEE. A Continental eye: the art and architecture of Arthur Rotch. Boston: Boston Athenaeum, 1985. xi, 48p. MBAt. *
Lived 1850-1894.

2044. KAUFMAN, POLLY WELTS. "Building a constituency for school desegregation: African-American women in Boston, 1962-1972." Teachers College Record, 92 (Summer 1991), 619-631.

2045. _____. "Julia Harrington Duff: an Irish woman confronts the Boston power structure, 1900-1905." HJM, 18 (Summer 1990), 113-137.
First woman from the Irish Catholic community to be elected to the Boston School Committee."

2046. KELLOW, MARGARET RIVERS. "Duties are ours: a life of Lydia Maria Child, 1802-1880." Ph.D. dissertation, Yale Univ., 1992. 681p.
Author and reformer. Abstracted in DAI, 54:11A (1994), 4232. See also entries 1939, 2085-2086.

2047. KELSO, GERALD K., and MARY C. BEAUDRY. "Pollen analysis and urban land use: the environs of Scottow's Dock in 17th, 18th, and early 19th century Boston." Historical Archaeology, 24:1 (1990), 61-81.

2048. KENNEDY, LAWRENCE. Planning the city upon a hill: Boston since 1630. Amherst: Univ. of Massachusetts Pr., 1992. xi, 314p. MBAt. *

2049. _____. "Thomas Brattle and the scientific provincialism of New England, 1680-1713." NEQ, 63 (Dec. 1990), 584-600.
See also next entry.

2050. KENNEDY, RICK. "Thomas Brattle, mathematician-architect in the transition of the New England mind, 1690-1700." Winterthur Portfolio, 24 (Winter 1989), 231-245.
See also preceding entry.

2051. KILGORE, KATHLEEN. Transformations: a history of Boston University. Boston: Boston Univ., 1991. xi, 479p. MB. *

2052. KINDLE, MILLICENT. The Ford Hall Forum: 75 years of public discourse. [Boston: Ford Hall Forum, 1983?] 65p. M. *

2053. KNIGHTS, PETER R. Yankee destinies: the lives of ordinary nineteenth-century Bostonians. Chapel Hill: Univ. of North Carolina Pr., 1991. xxv, 281p. MB. *

2054. KOHEI, KAWASHIMA. "The forging of a new upper class at Boston's Back Bay, 1850-1941." Ph.D. dissertation, Brown Univ., 1992. 421p.
Abstracted in DAI, 53:11A (1993), 4057.

2055   BOSTON

2055.   KRUH, DAVID. Always something doing: a history of
        Boston's infamous Scollay Square. Boston: Faber and Faber,
        1990. xiv, 162p. MB. *
            See also entry 2150.

2056.   LAPOMARDA, VINCENT ANTHONY. "A Catholic in a
        Puritan society." American Benedictine Review, 41:2 (1990),
        192-208.
            Ann Glover, hanged as a witch in 1688.

2057.   LENK, WALTER E. "Boston and Maine's Haymarket
        Depot." B&M Bulletin, 18:1 (1991), 8-16.

2058.   _____. "Boston's Causeway Street depots." B&M Bulletin,
        17:2 (1990), 6-15.

2059.   LEVERNIER, JAMES A. "Phillis Wheatley and the New
        England clergy." Early American Literature, 26:1 (1991),
        21-38.
            The black poet.

2060.   LEVINE, HILLEL, and LAWRENCE HARMON. The death
        of an American Jewish community: a tragedy of good
        intentions. N.Y.: Free Pr., 1991. xii, 370p. MB. *
            Blue Hill Avenue (1960s and 1970s).

2061.   LINCOLN GROUP OF BOSTON. The Lincoln Group of
        Boston: fiftieth anniversary publication. Sylvia B. Larson, ed.
        Boston, 1988. 51p. WHi. *
            Abraham Lincoln study group.

2062.   LINENTHAL, ARTHUR J. First a dream: the history of
        Boston's Jewish hospitals, 1896 to 1928. Boston: Beth Israel
        Hospital, 1990. xxii, 734p. MB. *

2063.   LINN, EDWARD. The great rivalry: the Yankees and the Red
        Sox, 1901-1990. N.Y.: Ticknor & Fields, 1991. xxiii, 359p.
        MB. *
            New York Yankees and Boston Red Sox.

2064.   _____. Hitter: the life and turmoils of Ted Williams. N.Y.:
        Harcourt Brace, 1993. 437p. MBAt. *
            Former Red Sox star. See also entries 2028, 2157, 2178,
        2187.

2065.   LIPSEY, ELLEN J. "Boston's historic burying grounds."
        APT Bulletin, 21:2 (1989), 6-9.
            Recent preservation problems.

2066.   LOFTUS, PATRICK J. That old gang of mine: a history of
        South Boston. South Boston, 1991. xxiv, 632p. MBAt. *

2067.   LOWANCE, MASON IRA JR. "Hawthorne and Brook
        Farm: the politics of the Blithedale romance." EIHC, 125
        (Jan. 1989), 65-91.

2068.   LUPICA, MIKE. "George Frazier, baby." Yankee, 56 (July
        1992), 65-67, 110-111.
            See also entry 1987.

2069.   MacCARTHY, ESTHER. "The Home for Aged Colored
        Women, 1861-1944." HJM, 21 (Winter 1993), 55-73.

2070.   MacDOUGALL, ROBERT ELLIOTT. "Mr. Garrison and the
        mob." American History Illustrated, 22 (Feb. 1988), 42- 45.
            Attack on William Lloyd Garrison (1835).

2071.   MASSA, MARK. "On the uses of heresy: Leonard Feeney,
        Mary Douglas, and the Notre Dame football team." Harvard
        Theological Review, 84 (July 1991), 325- 341.
            Feeney and the "Boston heresy case" of the 1940s and
        1950s. See also entry 2116.

2072.   MASSACHUSETTS COMMITTEE FOR THE
        PRESERVATION OF ARCHITECTURAL RECORDS.
        Boston architects and builders: compiled from the Boston
        directory, 1789-1846. Christopher Hail, comp. Cambridge,
        1989. 347p. MWA. *

2073.   MASSACHUSETTS HISTORICAL SOCIETY. Witness to
        America's past: two centuries of collecting by the
        Massachusetts Historical Society. Boston, 1991. 207p. MB. *

2074.   MATHEWS, JAMES W. "Dr. Gamaliel Bradford, early
        abolitionist." HJM, 19 (Winter 1991), 1-12.

2075.   MAY, PETER. The Big Three. N.Y.: Simon & Schuster,
        1994. 288p. MBAt. *
            Celtics stars Larry Bird, Kevin McHale, and Robert
        Parish, who played together through most of the 1980s and
        the early 1990s.

2076.   McCARRISTON, WILLIAM THOMAS. "An extended case
        study in planning in a human services agency: a history of
        human services of Morgan Memorial Goodwill Industries,
        Inc." Ed.D. dissertation, Univ. of Massachusetts, 1991. vii,
        272p. *
            Abstracted in DAI, 52:6A (1991), 2243.

2077.   McDOWELL, PEGGY. "Martin Milmore's Soldiers' and
        Sailors' Monument on the Boston Common: formulating
        conventionalism in design and symbolism." Journal of
        American Culture, 11 (Spring 1988), 63-85.
            1870s.

2078.   McFADDEN, MARGARET. "Boston teenagers debate the
        woman question, 1837-1838." Signs, 15 (Summer 1990),
        832-847.
            Correspondence between Ednah Dow Littlehale (later
        Ednah Cheney) and Caroline Wells Healey (later Caroline
        Dall) on the subject of women's rights.

2079. McFARLAND, GEORGE KENNEDY. "Clergy, lay leaders, and the people: an analysis of 'faith and works' in Albany and Boston, 1630-1750." Ph.D. dissertation, Bryn Mawr College, 1992. 346p. *
Abstracted in DAI, 53:4A (1992), 1257.

2080. McGRATH, SUSAN MARGARET. "Great expectations: the history of school desegregation in Atlanta and Boston, 1954-1990." Ph.D. dissertation, Emory Univ., 1992. vi, 523p. M. *
Abstracted in DAI, 53:4A (1992), 1246.

2081. McLAUGHLIN, LORETTA. "Dr. Rock and the birth of the pill." Yankee, 54 (Sept. 1990), 72-77, 152, 154- 155.
Gynecologist John Rock and the development of the oral contraceptive (late-1950s and early-1960s).

2082. MERRIFIELD, SUSAN RUTH. "Readin' and writin' for the hard-hat crowd: the introductory curriculum at the University of Massachusetts, Boston, 1965-85." Ed.D. dissertation, Harvard Univ., 1989. iv, 224p. *
Abstracted in DAI, 50:4A (1989), 866.

2083. MILLER, DAVID MICHAEL. "The beginnings of music in the Boston schools: decisions of the Boston School Committee in 1837 and 1845 in light of religious and moral concerns of the time." Ph.D. dissertation, Univ. of North Texas, 1989. v, 398p. *
Abstracted in DAI, 50:9A (1990), 2823.

2084. MILLER, NAOMI, and KEITH N. MORGAN. Boston architecture, 1975-1990. Munich, Germany: Prestel, 1991. 248p. M. *

2085. MILLS, BRUCE EDWARD. Cultural reformations: Lydia Maria Child and the literature of reform. Athens: Univ. of Georgia Pr., 1994. 216p. DLC. *
See also next entry.

2086. _____. "Cultural reformations: the literary and social worlds of Lydia Maria Child." Ph.D. dissertation, Univ. of Iowa, 1990. 265p. *
The 19th-century author and reformer. Abstracted in DAI, 51:12A (1991), 4123. See also preceding entry and entries 1939, 2046.

2087. MINETT, TERRY. "The execution of a Quaker." Old RI, 2 (Jan. 1992), 45.
Mary Dyer (1660).

2088. MONTVILLE, LEIGH. "Beantown: one tough place to play." Sports Illustrated, 75 (Aug. 19, 1990), 40-46.
The problems that black professional athletes have had in Boston.

2089. MOORE, BARBARA W., and GAIL WEESNER. Beacon Hill: a living portrait. Boston: Centry Hill Pr., 1992. 120p. MBAt. *

2090. MORRIS, JANET LEE. "School desegregation and student self-concept: a study of three middle schools in Boston." Ed.D. dissertation, Harvard Univ., 1990. vii, 106p. *
Abstracted in DAI, 51:9A (1991), 2931.

2091. MOSS, RICHARD J. "Republicanism, liberalism, and identity: the case of Jedidiah Morse." EIHC, 126 (Oct. 1990), 209-236.
Morse, whose conservative social and religious values had been shaped in rural Woodstock, Conn., was the pastor of the First Church of Charlestown from 1789-1819 and the author of The American universal geography.

2092. MURPHEY, KATHLEEN. "Gender barriers to forming a teachers union in Boston." HJM, 21 (Summer 1993), 60- 86.

2093. MURPHY, FRANCIS STEPHEN JR. "A history of teacher training in the city of Boston and the role of the laboratory school as an integral part in the preparation of teachers." Ed.D. dissertation, Univ. of Massachusetts, 1989. xii, 106p. *
Abstracted in DAI, 50:8A (1990), 2461.

2094. MURPHY, KEVIN D. "Ernest W. Bowditch and the practice of landscape architecture." EIHC, 125 (Apr. 1989), 162-176.
Lived 1850-1918.

2095. MUSURACA, MICHAEL. "The 'celebration begins at midnight': Irish immigrants and the celebration of Bunker Hill Day." Labor's Heritage, 2:3 (July 1990), 48-61.

2096. NELLIS, ERIC GUEST. "The working poor of pre-revolutionary Boston." HJM, 17 (Summer 1989), 137-159.

2097. NELSON, CARLA ANN. "The Shepard-Gill School of Practical Nursing of Massachusetts General Hospital, 1918-1984." Ph.D. dissertation, Boston College, 1987. v, 210p. *
Abstracted in DAI, 48:11A (1988), 2819.

2098. NORD, DAVID PAUL. "Tocqueville, Garrison and the perfection of journalism." Journalism Quarterly, 13 (Summer 1986), 56-63.
Alexis de Tocqueville and William Lloyd Garrison.

2099. NORWOOD, STEPHEN H. "From 'white slave' to labor activist: the agony and triumph of a Boston Brahmin woman in the 1910s." NEQ, 65 (Mar. 1992), 61-92.
Lois Burnett Rantoul.

2100   BOSTON

2100.   NOORWOOD, STEPHEN H. Labor's flaming youth: telephone operators and worker militancy, 1878-1923. Urbana: Univ. of Illinois Pr., 1990. xii, 340p. MB. *
    Has strong emphasis on the history of the Boston Telephone Operators Union.

2101.   NOVICK, SHELDON. Honourable justice: the life of Oliver Wendell Holmes. Boston: Little, Brown, 1989. xxi, 522p. MB. *
    See also entry 1896.

2102.   O'CONNELL, SHAUN. Imagining Boston: a literary landscape. Boston: Beacon Pr., 1990. xvi, 405p. MB. *
    Literary landmarks.

2103.   O'CONNOR, THOMAS HENRY. Building a new Boston: politics and urban renewal, 1950-1970. Boston: Northeastern Univ. Pr., 1993. xvi, 351p. M. *

2104.   O'GRADY, THOMAS B. James Jeffrey Roche: Irishman, islander, and Boston man of letters." Island Magazine [Canada], 27 (1990), 31-37.
    Roche, a native of Prince Edward Island, edited the Boston Pilot, a Catholic newspaper.

2105.   O'TOOLE, JAMES MICHAEL. Militant and triumphant: William Henry O'Connell and the Catholic Church in Boston, 1859-1944. Notre Dame, Ind.: Notre Dame Univ. Pr., 1992. viii, 324p. MBAt. *
    Archbishop of Boston. See also this author's Ph.D. dissertation on O'Connell (Boston College, 1987; entry 5036 in Vol. 8).

2106.   _____. "'The newer Catholic races': ethnic Catholicism in Boston, 1900-1940." NEQ, 65 (Mar. 1992), 117-134.

2107.   _____. "The role of bishops in American Catholic history: myth and reality in the case of Cardinal William O'Connell." Catholic Historical Review, 77 (Oct. 1991), 595-615.

2108.   OSGOOD, ROBERT LINCOLN. "History of special education in the Boston Public Schools to 1945." Ph.D. dissertation, Claremont Graduate School, 1989. x, 417p. *
    Abstracted in DAI, 50:5A (1989), 1274.

2109.   OSTERMAN, PAUL. "Welfare participation in a full employment economy: the impact of neighborhood." Social Problems, 38 (Nov. 1991), 475-491.
    Study of female single parents (1988-1989).

2110.   PARRISH, STEPHEN MAXFIELD. Currents of the nineties in Boston and London: Fred Holland Day, Louise Imogen Guiney, and their circle. N.Y.: Garland Publishing, 1987. 350p. MB. *
    See also next entry.

2111.   _____. "Currents of the nineties in Boston and London: Fred Holland Day, Louise Imogen Guiney, and their circle." Ph.D. dissertation, Harvard Univ., 1954. 5, 350, [18]p. *
    1890s. See also preceding entry.

2112.   PAUL, OGLESBY. The caring physician: the life of Dr. Francis W. Peabody. Boston: Francis A. Countway Library of Medicine, 1991. xi, 220p. MA. *
    Lived 1881-1927.

2113.   PAUL REVERE MEMORIAL ASSOCIATION. Paul Revere: artisan, businessman, and patriot: the man behind the myth. Boston, 1988. 191p. MWA. *
    Essays.

2114.   PEASE, JANE H., and WILLIAM H. PEASE. Ladies, women & wenches: choice & constraint in antebellum Charleston and Boston. Chapel Hill: Univ. of North Carolina Pr., 1990. xiii, 218p. MB. *
    Charleston, S.C.

2115.   PENDERY, STEVEN ROGER. "Probing the Boston Common." Archaeology, 43 (Mar./Apr. 1990), 42-47.
    Findings of an archaeological investigation on the site.

2116.   PEPPER, GEORGE B. The Boston heresy case in view of the secularization of religion: a case study in the sociology of religion. Lewiston, N.Y.: Edwin Mellen Pr., 1988. xix, 209p. MB. *
    The case involved the teachings of Father Leonard J. Feeney and the St. Benedict Center (1940s and 1950s).

2117.   PERKINS, ANGELA LOUISE. "The Boston African American National Historic Site: an interpretation using interactive multimedia." Dr.D.E.S. dissertation, Harvard University Graduate School of Design, 1993. 270p. *
    Abstracted in DAI, 54:5A (1993), 1571.

2118.   PESTANA, CARLA GARDINA. "The Quaker executions as myth and history." Journal of American History, 80 (Sept. 1993), 441-469.
    See also entry 1685.

2119.   PETERSON, MARK ALLEN. "'Ordinary' preaching and the interpretation of the Salem witchcraft crisis by the Boston clergy." EIHC, 129 (Jan. 1993), 84-102.

2120.   PETERSON, MICHAEL L. "The Church cryptogram: to catch a spy." American History Illustrated, 24 (Dec. 1989), 36-42.
    See also entry 2176.

2121.   PIERCE, SALLY. Whipple and Black: commercial photographers in Boston. Boston: Boston Athenaeum, 1987. x, 121p. MB. *
    Active from 1840s to 1870s.

2122.   _____, and CATHARINA SLAUTTERBACK. Boston lithography, 1825-1880: the Boston Athenaeum collection. Boston: Boston Athenaeum, 1991. 191p. MWA. *

2123.   PITTMAN, PAMELA TURNER. "The Ramist rhetoric of Samuel Willard: a rhetorical analysis of three sermons." Ph.D. dissertation, Univ. of Southwestern Louisiana, 1993. xiv, 281p. *
        Late-17th century. Abstracted in DAI, 54:11A (1994), 4095.

2124.   PITTS, MARY E. Hyde Park, Massachusetts, this modern Canaan: a history written for the centennial of the Hyde Park Historical Society, 1887-1987. Hyde Park: Albert House Publishing, 1988. viii, 91p. M. *

2125.   PODMANICZKY, MICHAEL S., and PHILIP D. ZIMMERMAN. "Two Massachusetts bombé desk-and-bookcases." Antiques, 145 (May 1994), 724-731.
        18th century.

2126.   POINTER, STEVEN R. Joseph Cook, Boston lecturer and evangelical apologist: a bridge between popular culture and academia in late nineteenth-century America. Lewiston, N.Y.: Edwin Mellen, 1991. 265p. OU. *
        Lived 1838-1901.

2127.   PROCESS ARCHITECTURE (periodical). Boston by design: a city in development, 1960 to 1990. Tokyo: Process Architecture Publishing, 1991. 145, [15]p. *
        August 1991 issue (No. 97) of the periodical. Text in English and Japanese.

2128.   READVILLE: a mysterious providence. Hyde Park: Albert House Publishing, [1990?]. [87]p. M. *
        Site of Civil War encampment.

2129.   REEVES, W. G. "Newfoundlanders in the 'Boston states': a study in early twentieth-century community and counterpoint." Newfoundland Studies [Canada], 6 (Spring 1990), 34-55.

2130.   REMER, ROSALIND. "Old lights and new money: a note on religion, economics, and the social order in 1740 Boston." WMQ, 3 ser. 47 (Oct. 1990), 566-573.

2131.   REYNOLDS, BILL. Lost summer: the '67 Red Sox and the impossible dream. N.Y.: Warner Books, 1992. viii, 293p. MS. *

2132.   RICHARDS, PHILLIP M. "Phillis Wheatley and literary Americanization." American Quarterly, 44 (June 1992), 163-191.

2133.   RING, BETTY. "Heraldic embroidery in eighteenth- century Boston." Antiques, 141 (Apr. 1992), 622-631.

2134.   ROBERG, NORMAN. "Internal medicine in the 1930s." JAMA, 260 (Dec. 23, 1988), 3645-3646.
        At Boston City Hospital.

2135.   ROBERTS, DAVID. "American history at Boston's Vose Galleries." Architectural Digest, 45 (Mar. 1988), 68, 74, 84.

2136.   ROBINSON, RAYMOND HENRY. The Boston economy during the Civil War. N.Y.: Garland Publishing, 1988. 435p. MB. *
        Published version of author's Ph.D. dissertation (Harvard Univ., 1958; entry 5143 in Vol. 8).

2137.   ROCK, MARY DESMOND. Museum of Science, Boston: the founding and formative years: the Washburn era, 1939-1980. Boston: Museum of Science, 1989. 224p. DLC. *
        Director Bradford Washburn.

2138.   ROGERS, ALAN. "'A dangerous sport': a Boston boy's life at sea, 1820-1837." American Neptune, 50 (Summer 1990), 211-218.
        Moses Adams.

2139.   _____. "The founders of the Boston Bar Association: a collective analysis." HJM, 22 (Summer 1994), 93-105.
        1876.

2140.   ROMAN, JUDITH A. Annie Adams Fields: the spirit of Charles Street. Bloomington: Indiana Univ. Pr., 1990. x, 191p. MB. *
        Fields (1834-1913), an author and editor, was the wife of publisher James T. Fields.

2141.   ROSEN, CHRISTINE M. "After the fire: politics and the rebuilding of Boston's public works." Essays in Public Works History, 15 (1987), 3-20.
        1872 fire.

2142.   ROSENMEIER, JESPER. "John Cotton on usury." WMQ, 3 ser. 47 (Oct. 1990), 548-565.

2143.   RYAN, BOB. The Boston Celtics: the history, legends & images of America's most celebrated team. Reading: Addison-Wesley Publishing, 1990. 224p. MB. *

2144.   SALTERO, PAUL WILLIAM. One name, one family: an Italian-American's search for continuity. N.Y.: Vantage Pr., 1987. xiv, 147p. MB. *

2145   BOSTON

2145.   SAXTON, MARTHA PORTER. "Being good: moral standards for Puritan women, Boston: 1630-1730." Ph.D. dissertation, Columbia Univ., 1989. 349p. *
        Abstracted in DAI, 50:10A (1990), 3341.

2146.   SCHABERT, TILO. Boston politics: the creativity of power. N.Y.: Walter de Gruyter, 1989. xii, 361p. MB. *

2147.   SCHAMA, SIMON. Dead certainties (unwarranted speculations). N.Y.: Knopf, 1991. xiv, 333p. MB. *
        Explores the battlefield death of Gen. James Wolfe in 1759 and the murder of Dr. George Parkman (Boston, 1849).

2148.   SCHARNHORST, GARY. "William Rounsville Alger and the legacy of Emerson." Unitarian Universalist Historical Society, Proceedings, 21 (1987-1988), 43-54.
        Alger (1822-1905) was a Unitarian minister and friend of Ralph Waldo Emerson.

2149.   SCHNEIDER, ERIC C. In the web of class: delinquents and reformers in Boston, 1810s-1930s. N.Y.: New York Univ. Pr., 1992. xiii, 260p. MWA. *
        See also this author's Ph.D. dissertation of similar title (Boston Univ., 1980; entry 5193 in Vol. 8).

2150.   SCHULTZ, CHRISTINE. "Can't get enough of Scollay Square." Yankee, 55 (June 1991), 86-90, 122.
        On author David Kruh's interest in the history of what was once "the liveliest part of Boston." See also entry 2055.

2151.   SCHWENINGER, LEE. John Winthrop. Boston: Twayne Publishers, 1990. xiv, 144p. MB. *
        Lived 1588-1649.

2152.   SEABURG, ALAN. At the fair: the Boston immigrant experience. Medford: Anne Miniver Pr., 1990. vii, 83p. MBAt. *
        Swedish Americans.

2153.   THE SEARCH for missing friends: Irish immigrant advertisements placed in the Boston Pilot. Ruth-Ann M. Harris and Donald M. Jacobs, eds. Boston: New England Historic Genealogical Society, 1989-1991. 2v. MBNEH. *

2154.   SEARS, ELIZABETH ANN. "The art song in Boston, 1880-1914." Ph.D. dissertation, Catholic Univ. of America, 1993. xii, 303p. *
        Abstracted in DAI, 54:3A (1993), 731.

2155.   SEASCHOLES, NANCY STEIN. "Landmaking and the process of urbanization: the Boston landmaking projects, 1630s-1888." Ph.D. dissertation, Boston Univ., 1994. 578p.
        Abstracted in DAI, 54:12A (1994), 4495-4496.

2156.   SEDGWICK, ELLERY. The Atlantic Monthly, 1857-1909: Yankee humanism at high tide and ebb. Amherst: Univ. of Massachusetts Pr., 1994. 352p. M. *

2157.   SEIDEL, MICHAEL. Ted Williams: a baseball life. Chicago: Contemporary Books, 1991. xvi, 400p. MB. *
        See also entries 2028, 2064, 2178, 2187.

2158.   SHAUGHNESSY, DAN. The curse of the Bambino. N.Y.: Dutton, 1990. 210p. MB. *
        Red Sox history.

2159.   _____. Ever green: the Boston Celtics: a history in the words of their players, coaches, fans, and foes, from 1946 to the present. N.Y.: St. Martin's Pr., 1990. x, 259p. MB. *

2160.   _____. "Nobody won." Boston Globe Magazine (Sept. 30, 1990), 12-15, 29-30, 32, 34-36.
        Darryl Williams, a black high school football player, was shot and left permanently paralyzed at a high school game in Charlestown in 1979. The unsolved shooting is thought to have been racially motivated.

2161.   SHEA, PRESTON TUCKERMAN. "The rhetoric of authority in the 'New-England Courant.'" Ph.D. dissertation, Univ. of New Hampshire, 1992. 514p. *
        Newspaper (1721-1726), published by James and Benjamin Franklin. Abstracted in DAI, 53:7A (1993), 2519-2520.

2162.   SHELLEY, FREDERICK. "George M. Stevens & Company tower clocks." NAWCCB, 36 (Apr. 1994), 131-150.
        Late-19th and early-20th centuries.

2163.   SHIELDS, DAVID S. "Nathaniel Gardner, Jr., and the literary culture of Boston in the 1750s." Early American Literature, 24:3 (1989), 196-216.
        Poet.

2164.   SICILIA, DAVID B. Boston Edison centennial, 1886-1986: history of the Boston Edison Company. n.p., [1986?]. 107p. MB. *
        See also next entry.

2165.   _____. "Selling power: marketing and monopoly at Boston Edison, 1886-1929." Ph.D. dissertation, Brandeis Univ., 1991. 651p. *
        Abstracted in DAI, 51:2A (1991), 637.

2166.   SLAWSON, DOUGLAS J. "'The Boston tragedy and comedy': the near-repudiation of Cardinal O'Connell." Catholic Historical Review, 77 (Oct. 1991), 616-643.
        Archbishop William O'Connell (1921). See also entry 2105.

2167. SMITH, MARGARET SUPPPLEE, and JOHN C. MOORHOUSE. "Architecture and the housing market: nineteenth century row housing in Boston's South End." Society of Architectural Historians, Journal, 52 (June 1993), 159-178.

2168. SMITH, MARION WHITNEY. Colonel Robert Gould Shaw, a pictorial history: his family, background, and Shaw's brave Massachusetts 54th Volunteer Infantry. N.Y.: Carlton Pr., 1990. 206p. MB. *
The well-known Civil War officer.

2169. SOUTHWICK, ALBERT B. "'Boston is burning up—send help.'" Boston Sunday Globe (Nov. 8, 1992), A22.
Great fire of 1872.

2170. STANBURY, JOHN B. A constant ferment: a history of the thyroid clinic and laboratory at the Massachusetts General Hospital, 1913-1990. Ipswich: Ipswich Pr., 1991. 209p. MNS. *

2171. STAPP, CAROL BUCHALTER. Afro-Americans in antebellum Boston: an analysis of probate records. N.Y.: Garland Publishing, 1993. xxiii, 309p. M. *
See also next entry.

2172. _____. "Afro-Americans in antebellum Boston: an analysis of probate records." Ph.D. dissertation, George Washington Univ., 1990. xxxviii, 867p. MA. *
Abstracted in DAI, 51:3A (1990), 966. See also preceding entry.

2173. STEVENS, JAY. "The riddle of Joseph Warren." Yankee, 57 (July 1993), 52-57, 126-130.
The Revolutionary-era physician.

2174. _____. "When Hodgson spoke from the grave." Yankee, 53 (Jan. 1989), 76-81, 114, 116.
William James's investigation of a possible psychic phenomenon (ca. 1906).

2175. STEWART, JAMES BREWER. William Lloyd Garrison and the challenge of emancipation. Arlington Heights, Ill.: Harlan Davidson, 1992. xiv, 213p. MH. *

2176. STOLLER, MARGARET G. "Benjamin Church: Son of Liberty, Tory spy." American History Illustrated, 24 (Nov./Dec. 1989), 28-35.
Physician, convicted in 1775. See also entry 2120.

2177. STONE, CHRISTIAN. "No hits, but no history." Sports Illustrated, 77 (Fall 1992), 8.
A 1917 Red Sox game, in which Babe Ruth was the starting pitcher, was later disallowed as a no-hitter.

2178. STOUT, GLENN. Ted Williams: a portrait in words and pictures. Dick Johnson, ed. N.Y.: Walker, 1991. xiv, 225p. MBAt. *
See also entries 2028, 2064, 2157, 2187.

2179. STREITMATTER, RODGER. "Maria W. Stewart: the first female African-American journalist." HJM, 21 (Summer 1993), 44-59.
Lived 1803-1879.

2180. SULLIVAN, GEORGE. "Hugh Duffy." Old RI, 2 (Oct. 1992), 41-45.
Duffy, a native of Rhode Island, was an outfielder for the Boston Beaneaters baseball team during the 1890s and a longtime employee of the Red Sox.

2181. SULLIVAN, ROBERT F. Shipwrecks and nautical lore of Boston Harbor: a mariner's chronicle of more than 100 shipwrecks, heroic rescues, salvage, treasure tales. Chester, Conn.: Globe Pequot Pr., 1990. xii, 164p. M. *

2182. TAGER, JACK. "Urban renewal in Boston: municipal entrepreneurs and urban elites." HJM, 21 (Winter 1993), 1-32.
After World War II.

2183. TALBOTT, PAGE. "The furniture trade in Boston, 1810-1835." Antiques, 141 (May 1992), 842-844.
Following the article is a checklist of Boston cabinetmakers during that period (pp. 845-855).

2184. _____. "Seating furniture in Boston, 1810-1835." Antiques, 139 (May 1991), 956-969.

2185. TAYLOR, KAREN A. "Gentled words and battered families: a comparative study of Australia and America, 1850-1910." Ph.D. dissertation, Duke Univ., 1988. 282p. *
Case studies of Melbourne and Boston. Abstracted in DAI, 50:4A (1989), 1069-1070.

2186. TAYLOR, ROBERT. "The journey of Howling Wolf." Boston Globe Magazine (Apr. 11, 1993), 10-17.
"In 1877 a Cheyenne warrior traveled from his Florida prison to Boston, where he became something of a local sensation. But it is through his paintings that his story endures."

2187. THE TED Williams reader. Lawrence Baldassaro, ed. N.Y.: Simon & Schuster, 1991. 299p. MB. *
See also entries 2028, 2064, 2157, 2178.

2188. THEROUX, ALEXANDER. "Yin and Yankees." Boston Globe Magazine (July 2, 1989), 22-25, 31, 34-41.
The rivalry between the Red Sox and New York Yankees.

2189   BOSTON

2189.   THORNTON, TAMARA PLAKINS. Cultivating gentlemen: the meaning of country life among the Boston elite, 1785-1860. New Haven, Conn.: Yale Univ. Pr., 1989. xii, 244p. MWA. *
        See also this author's Ph.D. dissertation of similar title (Yale Univ., 1987; entry 5319 in Vol. 8).

2190.   TINORY, EUGENE. Journey from Ammeah: the story of a Lebanese immigrant. Brattleboro, Vt.: Amana Books, 1986. vii, 146p. MB. *
        Delia Ann Tinory (1894-1984).

2191.   TOBIN, LAD. "A radically different voice: gender and language in the trials of Anne Hutchinson." Early American Literature, 25:3 (1990), 253-270.
        See also entry 1930.

2192.   TONELI, EDITH A. "The avant-garde in Boston: the experiment of the WPA Federal Art Project." Archives of American Art Journal, 30:1-4 (1990), 41-47.
        1930s.

2193.   TRAVERS, LEONARD. "'The brightest day in our calendar': Independence Day in Boston and Philadelphia, 1777-1826." Ph.D. dissertation, Boston Univ., 1992. vi, 280p. *
        Abstracted in DAI, 53:3A (1992), 860.

2194.   _____. "Hurrah for the Fourth: patriotism, politics, and Independence Day in Federalist Boston, 1783-1818." EIHC, 125 (Apr. 1989), 129-161.

2195.   TUCKER, LOUIS LEONARD. Clio's consort: Jeremy Belknap and the founding of the Massachusetts Historical Society. Boston: Massachusetts Historical Society, 1989. xii, 149p. MWA. *

2196.   TURNER, CHUCK. "Sharing the pie: the Boston Jobs Coalition." Labor Research Review, 7:2 (1988), 80-87.
        Late 1970s and 1980s.

2197.   TWO Mather biographies: Life and death, and Parentator. William J. Scheick, ed. Bethlehem [Pa.]: Lehigh Univ. Pr., 1989. 241p. MWA. *
        Increase Mather's biography of Richard Mather and Cotton Mather's study of Increase Mather.

2198.   UNO, HIROKO. Emily Dickinson visits Boston. Kyoto, Japan: Yamaguchi Publishing House, 1990. 93p. MBAt. *

2199.   VIOLA, MARY JO. "Washington Allston and his Boston patrons: the exhibition of pictures in 1839." Ph.D. dissertation, City Univ. of New York, 1992. 285p.
        Abstracted in DAI, 54:3A (1993), 716. See also entry 1888.

2200.   VOGEL, MARY ELIZABETH. "Courts of trade: social conflict and the emergence of plea bargaining in Boston, Massachusetts, 1830-1890." Ph.D. dissertation, Harvard Univ., 1988. 191p. *
        Abstracted in DAI, 49:10A (1989), 3176.

2201.   VOGEL, ROBERT M. Vertical transportation in old Back Bay: a museum case study—the acquisition of a small residential hydraulic elevator. Washington: Smithsonian Institution Pr., 1988. iii, 41p. MB. *

2202.   VonHOFFMAN, ALEXANDER. "An officer of the neighborhood: a Boston patrolman on the beat in 1895." JSH, 26 (Winter 1992), 309-330.
        Based on a patrolman's diary.

2203.   WACH, HOWARD M. "Unitarian philanthropy and cultural hegemony in comparative perspective: Manchester and Boston, 1827-1848." JSH, 26 (Spring 1993), 539-557.
        Manchester, England.

2204.   WALTER, CARL W. "Finding a better way." JAMA, 263 (Mar. 23, 1990), 1675-1678.
        Peter Bent Brigham Hospital.

2205.   WALTON, EDWARD H. Red Sox triumphs and tragedies: a continuation of day by day listings and events in the history of the Boston American League baseball team. N.Y.: Stein and Day, 1980. 380p. MB. *

2206.   WARD, BARBARA McLEAN. "Hierarchy and wealth distribution in the Boston goldsmithing trade, 1690-1760." EIHC, 126 (July 1990), 129-147.

2207.   _____. "Medicine and disease in the diary of Benjamin Walker, shopkeeper of Boston." DubSemPr (1990), 44-54.
        18th century.

2208.   WARNER, MARGARET HUMPHREYS. "Vindicating the minister's medical role: Cotton Mather's concept of the nishmath-chajim and the spiritualization of medicine." Journal of the History of Medicine and Allied Sciences, 36 (July 1981), 278-295.

2209.   WEBSTER, SALLY. William Morris Hunt (1824-1879). N.Y.: Cambridge Univ. Pr., 1991. vii, 244p. MBAt. *
        Artist.

2210.   WEHTJE, MYRON FLOYD. "Controversy over the legal profession in post-revolutionary Boston." HJM, 20 (Summer 1992), 133-142.

2211.   _____. "Fear of British influence in Boston, 1783-1787." HJM, 18 (Summer 1990), 154-163.

2212. WELCH, CLAUDE E. A twentieth-century surgeon: my life in the Massachusetts General Hospital. Boston: Massachusetts General Hospital, 1992. xx, 392p. MBCo. *
The author became affiliated with the hospital during the 1930s.

2213. WENTWORTH, MICHAEL. Conger Metcalf: a retrospective. Boston: Boston Athenaeum, 1990. 100p. MBAt. *
Painter (born 1914).

2214. _____. "'There sat Dr. Harris in his customary chair....'" Athenaeum Items, No. 101 (Jan. 1993), 4-8.
Nathaniel Hawthorne wrote of seeing the ghost of the Rev. Thaddeus Mason Harris (1768-1842) a number of times in the reading room of the Boston Athenaeum.

2215. WEST ENDER (periodical). Commemorative issue, Oct. 1992. Somerville, 1992. 16p. M.
Includes historical articles about Boston's West End.

2216. WHITWELL, DAVID. The Longy Club: a professional wind ensemble in Boston. Northridge, Calif.: WINDS, 1988. 198p. MBU. *
In existence from 1900-1917.

2217. WIDER, SARAH. "'Most glorious sermons': Anna Tilden's sermon notes, 1824-1831." Studies in the American Renaissance (1988), 1-93.
Summaries of sermons heard at the Federal Street Church.

2218. WILKINSON, DORIS Y. "The 1850 Harvard Medical School dispute and the admission of African American students." Harvard Library Bulletin, n.s. 3 (Fall 1992), 13-27.

2219. WILMERDING, JOHN. "George Curtis: a rediscovery in the New England marine tradition." Peabody Essex Museum Collections, 129 (Oct. 1993), 367-371.
Painter. See also entries 1968, 1993.

2220. WINSHIP, MICHAEL PAUL. "Cotton Mather, astrologer." NEQ, 63 (June 1990), 308-314.

2221. _____. "Prodigies, Puritanism, and the perils of natural philosophy: the example of Cotton Mather." WMQ, 3 ser. 51 (Jan. 1994), 92-105.

2222. WINSSER, JOHAN. "Mary Dyer and the 'monster' story." Quaker History, 79 (Spring 1990), 20-34.
Dyer, executed as a Quaker in 1660, had earlier gained notoriety for giving birth to a severely malformed, stillborn child.

2223. WOODALL, GUY R. "Convers Francis, the Transcendentalists, and the Boston Association of Ministers." Unitarian Universalist Historical Society, Proceedings, 21:2 (1989), 41-48.
Francis (1795-1863) was a Unitarian minister and professor of divinity at Harvard.

2224. WORTHAM, THOMAS. "Did Emerson blackball Frederick Douglass from membership in the Town and Country Club?" NEQ, 52 (June 1992), 295-298.

2225. WYLIE, EVAN McLEOD. "Night air raid on Boston." Yankee, 54 (May 1990), 76-81, 120-121.
Alfred J. Hunter's bizarre attack on parts of the city from a private plane in May 1989.

2226. _____. "The night they robbed the Gardner." Yankee, 56 (Oct. 1992), 63-67, 123-124, 126-127.
The 1990 theft of art works from the Isabella Stewart Gardner Museum.

2227. YASTRZEMSKI, CARL MICHAEL, and GERALD ESKENAZI. Yaz: baseball, the Wall, and me. N.Y.: Doubleday, 1990. xv, 300p. MB. *
Autobiography of Yastrzemski, longtime Red Sox star.

2228. YELLIN, VICTOR FELL. Chadwick, Yankee composer. Washington, D.C.: Smithsonian Institution, 1990. xvi, 238p. MB. *
George Whitefield Chadwick (1854-1931), longtime director of the New England Conservatory of Music.

2229. YIN, XIAO-HUANG. "The population pattern and occupational structure of Boston's Chinese community in 1940." Maryland Historian, 20 (Spring-Summer 1989), 59-69.

2230. ZSHOCHE, SUE. "Dr. Clarke revisited: science, true womanhood, and female collegiate education." History of Education Quarterly, 29 (Winter 1989), 545-569.
Edward H. Clarke, late-19th-century physician, who used medical reasons to advocate a "separate system of female higher education."

SEE ALSO entries 2, 112, 169, 174, 177, 217-218, 271-272, 321, 423, 488, 780, 1000, 1107-1108, 1364, 1529, 1531, 1536, 1538, 1540, 1542, 1546, 1560, 1567-1568, 1594, 1600, 1612-1613,1622, 1632-1633, 1660, 1667, 1673, 1681-1682, 1707, 1720, 1725, 1732, 1735, 1744, 1750, 1800, 1935, 2739, 3170.

2231   BOURNE

BOURNE (BARNSTABLE CO.)

2231.   BOURNE, MASS. HISTORICAL COMMISSION. Bourne
        Village: an oral history. Michael Bradley, ed. Bourne, 1993.
        xiii, 146p. MWA.

2232.   _____. Memories of Monument Beach: an oral history.
        Michael Bradley, ed. Bourne, 1992. iii, 153p. MWA.

BREWSTER (BARNSTABLE CO.)

2233.   STRAUSS, ALAN E., and ROBERT GOODBY. "The
        Slough Pond site, Brewster, Mass." MASB, 54 (Spring
        1993), 25- 37.
            Indian site.

BROCKTON (PLYMOUTH CO.)

2234.   BERNOTAVICZ, JOHN W. "My salute to the Lithuanians of
        Brockton, Massachusetts." Lituanus, 36 (Fall 1990), 44-53.

2235.   CARROLL, WALTER F. Brockton: from rural parish to
        urban center: an illustrated history. Northridge, Calif.:
        Windsor Publications, 1989. 152p. MWA. *

2236.   NACK, WILLIAM. "The Rock." Sports Illustrated, 79 (Aug.
        23, 1993), 52-56, 58-62, 64, 66-68.
            The boxing career and private eccentricities of Rocky
        Marciano. See also next entry.

2237.   SKEHAN, EVERETT M. Rocky Marciano: biography of a
        first son. Boston: Houghton Mifflin, 1977. 369p. MChB. *
            The former heavyweight boxing champion (died 1969).

BROOKLINE (NORFOLK CO.)

2238.   BERG, SHARY PAGE. "Fairsted: documenting a historic
        landscape." APT Bulletin, 20:1 (1988), 40-49.
            Home of Frederick Law Olmsted.

2239.   GARRETT, WENDELL. "Nina Fletcher and Bertram
        Kimball Little." Antiques, 144 (Oct. 1993), 504-512.
            Nina Fletcher Little. The recently deceased couple were
        well-known collectors and antiquarians.

2240.   KENWORTHY, RICHARD G. "Bringing the world to
        Brookline: the gardens of Larz and Isabel Anderson." Journal
        of Garden History [U.K.], 11 (Oct.-Dec. 1991), 224-241.
            Early-20th-century formal gardens.

2241.   KRAMER, JEAN. Brookline, Massachusetts: a pictorial
        history. Boston: Historical Publishing, 1989. xi, 199p. M. *

2242.   McNAMARA, EILEEN. Breakdown: sex, suicide, and the
        Harvard psychiatrist. N.Y.: Pocket Books, 1994. ix, 289p. M. *
            Background of medical student Paul Lozano's suicide in
        1991. Dr. Margaret Bean-Bayog later relinquished her
        license to practice.

        SEE ALSO entry 1929.

BUCKLAND (FRANKLIN CO.)

2243.   BUCKLAND, MASS. BICENTENNIAL COMMITTEE.
        Buckland, Franklin County, Massachusetts: a bicentennial
        souvenir, 1779-1979. [Buckland, 1979.] 47p. MDeeP. *

2244.   CROSS, BEULAH MARY SCOTT. The history of
        Buckland, vol. II, 1935-1979. Bicentennial ed. Thomas M.
        McDonald, ed. Buckland: Town of Buckland, 1979. 312p.
        MDeeP.
            See also entry 6206 in the Massachusetts volume.

        SEE ALSO entry 1545.

CAMBRIDGE (MIDDLESEX CO.)

2245.   AMORY, HUGH. Steven Day's first type: Cambridge,
        Massachusetts, 1639-1989. Cambridge: Houghton Library,
        1989. [8]p. MBAt. *
            Printing history.

2246.   AYOOB, KENNETH PAUL. "An annotated bibliography of
        original works for band commissioned for the Massachusetts
        Institute of Technology Concert Band between 1952 and
        1987." D.A. dissertation, Univ. of Northern Colorado, 1988.
        vii, 218p. *
            Abstracted in DAI, 50:3A (1989), 567.

2247.   BIG-time football at Harvard, 1905: the diary of coach Bill
        Reid. Ronald A. Smith, ed. Urbana: Univ. of Illinois Pr.,
        1994. xxxviii, 354p. MH. *

2248.   BLACKS at Harvard: a documentary history of
        African-American experience at Harvard and Radcliffe.
        Werner Sollors, Caldwell Titcomb, and Thomas A.
        Underwood, eds. N.Y.: New York Univ. Pr., 1993. xxxiv,
        548p. MU. *

2249.   BUCKLEY, STEVE. "Barry's Corner forever." Yankee, 58
        (July 1994), 82-86, 108, 110-111.
            Tip O'Neill and Barry's Corner.

2250. BURTON, JOHN D. "Crimson missionaries: the Robert Boyle legacy and Harvard College." NEQ, 67 (Mar. 1994), 132-140.

The college's use of an early legacy for the support of missions to the Indians.

2251. CAMBRIDGE, MASS. HISTORICAL COMMISSION. East Cambridge. (1965) Rev. ed. Cambridge: Cambridge Historical Commission, 1989. 256p. MB. *

Architectural. Authorship attributed to Susan Maycock and the commission. Note: this item replaces entry 6310 in the Massachusetts volume.

2252. CARLSON, W. BERNARD. "Academic entrepreneurship and engineering education: Dugald C. Jackson and the MIT-GE cooperative engineering course, 1907-1932." Technology and Culture, 29 (July 1988), 536-567.

Massachusetts Institute of Technology and General Electric.

2253. THE CATHOLICS of Harvard Square. Jeffrey Wills, ed. Petersham: Saint Bede's Publications, 1993. vii, 212p. MChB. *

St. Paul's Parish.

2254. CEDARBAUM, JONATHAN. "Clement Garnett Morgan." Harvard Magazine, 94 (May-June 1992), 36.

One of the first black graduates of Harvard (class of 1890), who later practiced law and served in various elected offices in Cambridge.

2255. COTTRELL, DEBORA LYNN. "Women's minds, women's bodies: the influence of the Sargent School for Physical Education." Ph.D. dissertation, Univ. of Texas, 1993. 575p.

Private normal school for women (1881-1929). Abstracted in DAI, 54:12A (1994), 4562.

2256. DENNIS, MICHAEL AARON. "A change of state: the political cultures of technical practice at the MIT Instrumentation Laboratory and the Johns Hopkins Applied Physics Laboratory, 1930-1945." Ph.D. dissertation, Johns Hopkins Univ., 1991. 451p. *

Abstracted in DAI, 51:1A (1990), 281.

2257. DIMMICK, LAURETTA. "Thomas Crawford's monument for Amos Binney in Mount Auburn Cemetery: 'a work of rare merit.'" Markers IX [1992], 158-195.

Ca. 1847-1849.

2258. ELLIOTT, CLARK A. "The history of Harvard astronomy: a view from the archives." Journal for the History of Astronomy [U.K.], 21 (Feb. 1990), 3-8.

2259. EVANS, CATHERINE. Cultural landscape report for Longfellow National Historic Site. Boston: National Park Service, North Atlantic Region, Division of Cultural Resources Management, Cultural Landscape Program, 1993. xxiii, 138p. MWA. *

2260. FARNUM, RICHARD ALBERT JR. "Prestige in the Ivy League: meritocracy at Columbia, Harvard and Penn, 1870-1946." Ph.D. dissertation, Univ. of Pennsylvania, 1990. xii, 369p. MH. *

Abstracted in DAI, 51:5A (1990), 1517.

2261. FITZGERALD, JOHN M., and OTEY M. SCRUGGS. "A note on Marcus Garvey at Harvard, 1922: a recollection of John M. Fitzgerald." Journal of Negro History, 63 (Apr. 1978), 157-160.

Garvey addressed a black students' club.

2262. GALLUP, DONALD CLIFFORD. "The Eliots and the T.S. Eliot collection." Harvard Library Bulletin, 36 (Summer 1988), 233-247.

2263. GENUTH, SARA SCHECHNER. "Blazing stars, open minds, and loosened purse strings: astronomical research and its early Cambridge audience." Journal for the History of Astronomy [U.K.], 21 (Feb. 1990), 9-20.

At Harvard (17th-19th centuries).

2264. GINGERICH, OWEN. "Through rugged ways to the galaxies." Journal for the History of Astronomy [U.K.], 21 (Feb. 1990), 76-88.

Harlow Shapley's long research career as director of the Harvard College Observatory, beginning in 1921.

2265. HAPGOOD, FRED. Up the infinite corridor: MIT and the technical imagination. Reading: Addison-Wesley, 1993. xii, 203p. M. *

2266. HEGGESTAD, MARTIN. "State of the art: defeating Harvard's anti-union campaign." Radical America, 21:5 (1987), 42-45.

Culmination of a 15-year campaign to unionize the university's clerical and technical workers.

2267. HERSHBERG, JAMES G. James B. Conant and the birth of the nuclear age: from Harvard to Hiroshima. N.Y.: Knopf, 1993. ix, 948, [16]p. MBAt. *

Conant was president of Harvard from 1933-1953.

2268. "THE HISTORY of preservation at Harvard." Harvard Library Bulletin, n.s. 2 (Summer 1991), 18-21.

Preservation of library materials.

2269.   LECUYER, CHRISTOPHE. "The making of a science-based technological university: Karl Compton, James Killian, and the reform of MIT, 1930-1957." Historical Studies in the Physical and Biological Sciences, 23:1 (1992), 153-180.

2270.   LENTRICCHIA, FRANK. "Philosophers of modernism at Harvard, ca. 1900." South Atlantic Quarterly, 89 (Fall 1990), 787-834.

2271.   LESLIE, STUART W. The Cold War and American science: the military-industrial-academic complex at MIT and Stanford. N.Y.: Columbia Univ. Pr., 1993. xiii, 332p. MU. *

2272.   LINDEN-WARD, BLANCHE. "'The fencing mania': the rise and fall of nineteenth-century funerary enclosures." Markers VII [1990], 35-58.
    Mount Auburn Cemetery.

2273.   _____. Silent city on a hill: landscapes of memory and Boston's Mount Auburn Cemetery. Columbus: Ohio State Univ. Pr., 1989. xi, 403p. MB. *

2274.   MACK, PAMELA E. "Strategies and compromises: women in astronomy at Harvard College Observatory." Journal for the History of Astronomy [U.K.], 21 (Feb. 1990), 65-75.

2275.   McCARL, MARY RHINELANDER. "Thomas Shepard's record of relations of religious experience, 1648-1649." WMQ, 3 ser. 48 (July 1991), 432-466.
    See also entry 2277.

2276.   McGIFFERT, MICHAEL. "The church on the square and the church on the common: Puritan foundations, 1636." Bulletin of the Congregational Library, 42:3/43:1 (Spring/Summer 1991), 4-14.
    First Church.

2277.   McGILL, CARLA ANN. "Thomas Shepard's 'Confessions': conversion and modes of expression." Ph.D. dissertation, Univ. of California, Riverside, 1993. 215p.
    Puritan minister. Abstracted in DAI, 54:12A (1994), 4442-4443.

2278.   METCALF, KEYES DeWITT. My Harvard Library years, 1937-1955. Edwin E. Williams, ed. Cambridge: Harvard Univ. Pr., 1988. xvii, 285p. MB. *
    Director of the library.

2279.   MOORE, MAUREEN T. "Andrew Jackson: 'pretty near a treason' to call him doctor." NEQ, 62 (Sept. 1989), 424-435.
    Political controversy over the awarding of an honorary degree to the U.S. president by Harvard in 1833.

2280.   O'CONNELL, CHARLES THOMAS. "Social structure and science: Soviet studies at Harvard." Ph.D. dissertation, UCLA, 1990. x, 523p. *
    Abstracted in DAI, 51:2A (1990), 641.

2281.   OLSEN, MARK, and LOUIS-GEORGES HARVEY. "Reading in Revolutionary times: book borrowing from the Harvard College Library, 1773-1782." Harvard Library Bulletin, n.s. 4 (Fall 1993), 57-72.

2282.   PFITZER, GREGORY M. Samuel Eliot Morison's historical world: in quest of a new Parkman. Boston: Northeastern Univ. Pr., 1991. xxii, 367p. MB. *
    The noted historian and Harvard faculty member.

2283.   PLOTKIN, HOWARD. "Edward Charles Pickering." Journal for the History of Astronomy [U.K.], 21 (Feb. 1990), 47-58.
    Director of the Harvard College Observatory from 1877-1919.

2284.   "RALPH Waldo Emerson's report on the Harvard College Library." Harvard Library Bulletin, n.s. 1 (Spring 1990), 6-12.
    1868. Kenneth E. Carpenter, ed.

2285.   ROBINSON, FORREST GLEN. Love's story told: a life of Henry A. Murray. Cambridge: Harvard Univ. Pr., 1992. xi, 459p. MBAt. *
    Murray was director of the Harvard Psychological Clinic (1930s) and a Melville scholar.

2286.   ROBINSON, LEIF. "Enterprise at Harvard College Observatory." Journal for the History of Astronomy [U.K.], 21 (Feb. 1990), 89-103.
    The observatory's involvement with the American Association of Variable Star Observers (established in 1911) and the magazine Sky and Telescope (established in 1941).

2287.   ROSSELL, CHRISTINE H., and CHARLES L. GLENN. "The Cambridge controlled choice plan." Urban Review, 20 (Summer 1988), 75-94.
    Parental choice in selection of public schools (since ca. 1965).

2288.   ROTHENBERG, MARC. "Patronage of Harvard College Observatory, 1839-1851." Journal for the History of Astronomy [U.K.], 21 (Feb. 1991), 37-46.

2289.   SCIENCE at Harvard University: historical perspectives. Clark A. Elliott and Margaret W. Rossiter, eds. Bethlehem, Pa.: Lehigh Univ. Pr., 1992. 380p. MU. *

2290. SIEGEL, THOMAS JAY. "Governance and curriculum at Harvard College in the eighteenth century." Ph.D. dissertation, Harvard Univ., 1990. 515p.
Abstracted in DAI, 51:7A (1991), 2291.

2291. SIMMONS, LOVIE SUE. "A critique of the stereotype of current-traditional rhetoric: invention in writing instruction at Harvard, 1875-1900." Ph.D. dissertation, Univ. of Texas, 1991. xi, 310p. *
Abstracted in DAI, 52:4A (1991), 1241.

2292. SLOAN, JULIE L., and JAMES L. YARNALL. "John LaFarge and the stained-glass windows in Memorial Hall at Harvard University." Antiques, 141 (Apr. 1992), 642- 651.

2293. " 'STATESMAN and warrior.' " Harvard Magazine, 96 (Sept-Oct. 1993), 19-22.
Winston Churchill, honored at Harvard in 1943. Article signed "J.T.B." (John T. Bethell).

2294. STEPHENS, CARLENE E. "Astronomy as public utility: the Bond years at the Harvard College Observatory." Journal for the History of Astronomy [U.K.], 21 (Feb. 1990), 21-36.
The facility served from 1839-1865 "as the de facto national observatory." William Cranch Bond was the director.

2295. STODDARD, ROGER. "How Harvard didn't get its rare books and manuscripts." Harvard Library Bulletin, n.s. 3 (Winter 1992-1993), 12-17.

2296. TRAUTMAN, PATRICIA. "Dress in seventeenth-century Cambridge, Massachusetts: an inventory-based reconstruction." DubSemPr (1987), 51-73.

2297. VARNUM, ROBIN R. "Harvard's Francis James Child: the years of the rose." Harvard Library Bulletin, 36 (Summer 1988), 291-319.
Professor of English literature (late-19th century).

2298. WARSH, DAVID. "The odd couple." Boston Globe Magazine (Dec. 1, 1991), 16-19, 36-39, 42-43.
Harvard and MIT. Article includes historical information about the relationship between the two universities.

2299. WHELAN, MICHAEL. "Albert Bushnell Hart and history education, 1854-1907." Ed.D. dissertation, Columbia Univ. Teachers College, 1989. vi, 196p. *
Historian at Harvard. Abstracted in DAI, 50:8A (1990), 2048.

SEE ALSO entries 1350, 1542, 1600, 1612, 1732, 2050.

CANTON (NORFOLK CO.)

2300. CARTY, FREDERICK M., and ARTHUR E. SPIESS. "The Neponset paleoindian site in Massachusetts." Archaeology of Eastern North America, 20 (Fall 1992), 19-37.

2301. GALVIN, EDWARD D. A history of Canton Junction. Brunswick, Me.: Sculpin Publications, 1987. iv, 99p. MH. *
Railroad junction.

CHARLEMONT (FRANKLIN CO.)

2302. GREENFIELD RECORDER-GAZETTE (newspaper). Charlemont anniversary, 1765-1965: section A supplement, Friday, August 6, 1965. [Greenfield, 1965] [28]p. MDeeP.

2303. LEAVITT, WILLIAM H. A sketch of the life and character of Rev. Jonathan Leavitt, the first minister of Charlemont, Mass. Waterloo, Iowa: John H. Leavitt, 1904. [12]p. MDeeP. *

SEE ALSO entry 1545.

CHARLTON (WORCESTER CO.)

2304. CHARLTON HISTORICAL SOCIETY. A glance back: Charlton photographic history. Charlton, 1992. 60p. MWA.

CHATHAM (BARNSTABLE CO.)

2305. McGLAMERY, PATRICK. "George Eldridge: the Chatham chartmaker." Meridian, No. 3 (1990), 23-27.
Eldridge prepared hydrographic surveys and nautical charts (late-19th century).

2306. NICKERSON, JOSHUA ATKINS II. Days to remember: a Chatham native recalls life on Cape Cod since the turn of the century. Chatham: Chatham Historical Society, 1988. 277p. M. *

SEE ALSO entry 2685.

CHELSEA (SUFFOLK CO.)

2307. LaCELLE-PETERSON, MARK WALTER. "The roots of curriculum differentiation: the context, contours, and content of school knowledge in Chelsea, Massachusetts, 1847 to 1930." Ed.D. dissertation, Harvard Univ., 1991. ii, 180p. *
Abstracted in DAI, 52:6A (1991), 2046.

2308   CHESHIRE

CHESHIRE (BERKSHIRE CO.)

2308.   CHESHIRE, MASS. BICENTENNIAL COMMITTEE.
History of Cheshire, Massachusetts, 1793-1993. Cheshire,
1993. 77p. M. *

CHICOPEE (HAMPDEN CO.)

2309.   CHICOPEE, MASS. CHICOPEE FALLS UNITED
METHODIST CHURCH. 150th anniversary. [Chicopee,
1974] 32p. MDeeP.

CHILMARK (DUKES CO.)

2310.   RAILTON, ARTHUR R. "Tom Benton: Chilmarker." DCI,
31 (Nov. 1989), 51-78, 86.
Thomas Hart Benton (1889-1975), the well-known
painter, was a longtime summer resident.

2311.   SCOTT, JONATHAN F. "The 300-year evolution of a
Chilmark homestead." DCI, 32 (Aug. 1990), 12-31.
The Barn House.

COLRAIN (FRANKLIN CO.)

2312.   COLRAIN, MASS. Colrain voices: a souvenir booklet
commemorating the 225th anniversary of the founding of
Colrain, Massachusetts, June 30, 1761. Colrain, 1986. 49p.
M. *

2313.   DAVENPORT, ELMER F. The puzzle of Catamount Hill:
being a report of pioneer life in Franklin County,
Massachusetts, during the century after the War of
Independence, 1780-1880. n.p., 1969. [46]p. MDeeP. *

SEE ALSO entry 1545.

CONCORD (MIDDLESEX CO.)

2314.   ADAMS, STEPHEN, and BARBARA ADAMS. "Thoreau's
diet at Walden." Studies in the American Renaissance (1990),
243-260.
Henry David Thoreau.

2315.   BAILEY, WILLIAM M. The history of the West Concord
Union Church, 1891-1991. Concord: West Concord Union
Church, 1991. iii, 149p. M. *

2316.   BIRCH, THOMAS D., and FRED METTING. "The
economic design of Walden." NEQ, 65 (Dec. 1992), 587-602.
Thoreau's book, Walden.

2317.   BROOKS, PAUL. The people of Concord: one year in the
flowering of New England. Chester, Conn.: Globe Pequot Pr.,
1990. 228p. MB. *
1846.

2318.   BURKHOLDER, ROBERT E. "Emerson and the West:
Concord, the historical discourse, and beyond." Nineteenth
Century Studies, 4 (1990), 93-103.
Ralph Waldo Emerson.

2319.   FINK, STEVEN SCOTT. "Prophet in the marketplace:
Thoreau's development as a professional writer." Ph.D.
dissertation, Univ. of Washington, 1981. iv, 470p. *
Abstracted in DAI, 42:6A (1981), 2674. See also next
entry.

2320.   _____. Prophet in the marketplace: Thoreau's development
as a professional writer. Princeton, N.J.: Princeton Univ. Pr.,
1992. xii, 321p. MH. *
See also preceding entry.

2321.   GOUGEON, LEN. "Emerson, Carlyle, and the Civil War."
NEQ, 62 (Sept. 1989), 403-423.

2322.   _____. Virtue's hero: Emerson, antislavery, and reform.
Athens: Univ. of Georgia Pr., 1990. xiii, 408p. MB. *

2323.   GRAHAM, ROBERT D. "Domestic archeology in Concord:
Thoreau and the Hunt House." CEAIA, 43 (Mar. 1990), 7-8;
(June 1990), 33-35.
Thoreau as historical archaeologist.

2324.   HEGARTY, PAMELA P. "A light in Concord." Early
American Life, 23 (June 1992), 54-59.
A glimpse of Concord history and historic houses.

2325.   JARVIS, EDWARD. Traditions and reminiscences of
Concord, Massachusetts, 1779-1878; or A contribution to the
social and domestic history of the town, 1779-1878. Sarah
Chapin, ed. Amherst: Univ. of Massachusetts Pr., 1993. xliv,
254p. MWA. *

2326.   LOJEK, HELEN. "Thoreau's bog people." NEQ, 67 (June
1994), 279-297.
His opinion of the Irish.

2327.   LORING, HILARY. Tales of a village bookshop: the first
fifty years. Concord: Estabrook Pr., 1991. 30p. M. *
Concord Bookshop.

2328.   McGREGOR, ROBERT KUHN. "Historic preservation at Walden." Organization of American Historians, OAH Newsletter, 18:1 (Feb. 1990), 8-9.

2329.   SATTELMEYER, ROBERT. "'When he became my enemy': Emerson and Thoreau, 1848-49." NEQ, 62 (June 1989), 187-204.

2330.   WILSON, JOHN S. "Purchase delay, pricing factors, and attribution elements in gravestones from the shop of Ithamar Spauldin." Markers IX [1992], 104-131.

2331.   "WITH Hawthorne in wartime Concord: Sophia Hawthorne's 1862 diary." Studies in the American Renaissance (1988), 281-359.
   Edited by Thomas Woodson, James A. Rubino, and Jamie Barlowe Kayes.

   SEE ALSO entries 82, 331, 494, 1531, 1562-1563, 1593, 1615-1616, 1622, 1631, 1684, 1719, 1745, 1818, 2102.

CONWAY (FRANKLIN CO.)

2332.   CONWAY SAVINGS BANK. Conway Savings Bank. [Conway], 1973. [14]p. MDeeP. *
   Includes historical sketch.

2333.   GREENFIELD RECORDER (newspaper). Celebrating Conway's 200th anniversary, 1767-1967: a special supplement prepared and published by Greenfield Recorder, Friday, June 16, 1967, Section B1. [Greenfield], 1967. 18p. MDeeP.

CUMMINGTON (HAMPSHIRE CO.)

2334.   CHAPMAN, GERARD. William Cullen Bryant: the Cummington years. [Milton: Trustees of Reservations, 1980?] [33]p. MDeeP. *
   The poet was a native of Cummington (born 1794).

   SEE ALSO entry 1701.

DARTMOUTH (BRISTOL CO.)

2335.   McLOUGHLIN, WILLIAM GERALD. "The Dartmouth Quakers' struggle for religious liberty, 1692-1734." Quaker History, 78 (Spring 1989), 1-23.

2336.   NEUSTADT, KATHERINE D. "For want of a nail (or how a study of Allen's Neck clambake leads to the demise of western epistemological imperialism)." Ph.D. dissertation, Univ. of Pennsylvania, 1990. xii, 474p. *
   Local Quaker tradition since late-19th century. Abstracted in DAI, 50:11A (1990), 3703. See also next entry.

2337.   _____. A history and celebration of an American tradition. Amherst: Univ. of Massachusetts Pr., 1992. x, 227p. MBU. *
   See also preceding entry.

2338.   PUTNEY, MARTHA S. "John Albert Mashow: shipbuilder." Afro-American Historical and Genealogical Society, Journal, 8 (Summer 1987), 57-60.
   Lived 1805-1872.

2339.   ROSE, GREGORY S. "Reconstructing a retail trade area: Tucker's General Store, 1850-1860." Professional Geographer, 39 (1987), 33-41.

DEDHAM (NORFOLK CO.)

2340.   AVRICH, PAUL. Sacco and Vanzetti: the anarchist background. Princeton, N.J.: Princeton Univ. Pr., 1991. x, 265p. MB. *
   The two were tried for murder in Dedham in 1921; they were executed in 1927.

2341.   HANDLER, MIMI. "Puncheons, lamb's tongues, and chickerings." Early American Life, 22 (Feb. 1991), 24- 29.
   Preservation of an early-18th-century house.

2342.   PENCAK, WILLIAM. "Nathaniel Ames, Sr., and the political culture of provincial New England." HJM, 22 (Summer 1994), 141-158.
   The well-known compiler of almanacs (18th century).

2343.   WRIGHT, CONRAD. "The Dedham case revisited." MHSP, 100 (1988), 15-39.
   Legal case (1818), resulting from a dispute between Unitarians and orthodox Congregationalists in Dedham's First Church.

   SEE ALSO entry 1734.

DEERFIELD (FRANKLIN CO.)

2344.   BOWEN, ROGER. "Frank Boyden: dean of the headmasters." Yankee, 32 (June 1968), 68-71, 139-142, 145.
   See also entry 2355.

2345   DEERFIELD

2345.   CONWAY SCHOOL OF LANDSCAPE DESIGN. Deerfield's agricultural lands. [Deerfield?] 1989. 66, xxvi p. MDeeP.
     Authors: Ali Crolius and Sarah Drew Reeves.

2346.   DEERFIELD, MASS. COMMUNITY ACTIVITIES COMMITTEE. The old Deerfield meeting house, 1838-1958. [Deerfield, 1958] 28p. MDeeP.
     Congregational.

2347.   DEERFIELD, MASS. ORTHODOX CONGREGATIONAL CHURCH. Directory and history of the Orthodox Congregational Church, Deerfield, Mass. Lewis G. Spooner, comp. [Deerfield, 1915] 16p. MDeeP.

2348.   DEERFIELD, 1704-1984: 280 years ago, the massacre at Deerfield. Hyde Park: Albert House Publishing, 1984. 48p. M. *
     See also next two entries.

2349.   DEMOS, JOHN. "The Deerfield massacre." American Heritage, 44 (Feb./Mar. 1993), 82-89.
     1704. See also next entry.

2350.   _____. The unredeemed captive: a family story from early America. N.Y.: Alfred A. Knopf, 1994. xiii, 315p. MBAt. *
     Eunice Williams, captured by Indians in 1704.

2351.   FLYNT, SUZANNE LASHER. Ornamental and useful accomplishments: schoolgirl education and Deerfield Academy, 1800-1830. Deerfield: Pocumtuck Valley Memorial Association, 1988. 63p. MWiW. *

2352.   HAYES, GEORGE WARREN. Linden Hill: the first ten years. [Northfield, 1990] 58p. MDeeP.
     Private school.

2353.   [LEAVITT, JOSHUA]. The redeemed captive: a narrative of the captivity, sufferings, and return of the Rev. John Williams, minister of Deerfield, Massachusetts, who was taken prisoner by the Indians on the destruction of the town, A.D. 1704; for Sabbath schools. N.Y.: S.W. Benedict, 1833. 116p. MDeeP. *

2354.   McCAIN, DIANA ROSS, and DIONE LONGLEY. "Visiting the past." Early American Life, 20 (June 1989), 26-31, 66.
     Furnishings in the Wells-Thorn House.

2355.   McPHEE, JOHN. The headmaster: Frank L. Boyden, of Deerfield. N.Y.: Farrar, Straus and Giroux, [1966]. 149p. MDeeP. *
     Deerfield Academy.

2356.   MELVOIN, RICHARD IRWIN. New England outpost: war and society in colonial Deerfield. N.Y.: W.W. Norton, 1989. 368p. MWA. *
     See also next entry.

2357.   _____. "New England outpost: war and society in colonial frontier Deerfield, Massachusetts." Ph.D. dissertation, Univ. of Michigan, 1983. 384p. MA. *
     Abstracted in DAI, 44:10A (1984), 3143. See also preceding entry. Note: this item replaces entry 6172 in Vol. 8.

2358.   MILLS, PETER R. "The pursuit of a regional context: understanding an Indian burial near Steam Mill Road, Deerfield, Massachusetts." MASB, 52 (Fall 1991), 50-58.

2359.   PROPER, DAVID R. "Lucy Terry Prince: 'singer of history.'" Contributions in Black Studies, Nos. 9/10 (1990-1992), 186-214.
     Prince (died 1821), once a slave in Deerfield, wrote a poem about the last Indian raid on the town.

2360.   SMOLLAR, DAVID JOHN. The rural trolley through Deerfield, Mass., and its impact, 1901-1924. [Deerfield], 1971. [16]p. MDeeP. *

2361.   SOUTH DEERFIELD, MASS. ROTARY CLUB, DISTRICT 789. Fiftieth anniversary, Saturday, March 21, 1987. [South Deerfield, 1987] [13]p. MDeeP.
     Includes historical sketch.

2362.   SOUTH DEERFIELD, MASS. ST. JAMES ROMAN CATHOLIC CHURCH. Golden jubilee, 1895-1945: Church of St. James, South Deerfield, Massachusetts. [Deerfield, 1945] 48p. MDeeP.

2363.   SOUTH DEERFIELD, MASS. ST. STANISLAUS ROMAN CATHOLIC CHURCH. 75th anniversary. [Greenfield: E.A. Hall, 1984] [118]p. MDeeP.

2364.   STILLINGER, ELIZABETH. Historic Deerfield: a portrait of early America. N.Y.: Dutton Studio Books, 1992. viii, 206p. MB. *

     SEE ALSO entry 1688.

DUDLEY (WORCESTER CO.)

2365.   HAAS, MARY M. "A granite Cape." Early American Life, 21 (Aug. 1990), 30-35, 56.
     Preservation of a Cape Cod-type house.

EASTON (BRISTOL CO.)

2366.   EASTON HISTORICAL SOCIETY. Easton's past as shown through maps. Easton, 1988. 8, [42]p. MBNEH. *

2367.   KOWSKY, FRANCIS R. "H.H. Richardson's Ames Gate Lodge and the romantic landscape tradition." Society of Architectural Historians, Journal, 50 (June 1991) 181- 188.
        In North Easton.

EDGARTOWN (DUKES CO.)

2368.   BAYLIES, HENRY. "Edgartown schools in the 1830s." DCI, 34 (Nov. 1992), 98-104.
        Originally published as a newspaper article in 1876.

2369.   "THE 1828 meetinghouse: it was almost turned down." DCI, 33 (May 1992), 233-235.
        Congregational church.

2370.   GOLDWYN, ALVIN J. "The adventurous life, on land and sea, of Capt. LaRoy Lewis of Edgartown." DCI, 34 (May 1993), 167-183.
        Lived 1839-1916.

2371.   "THE HARBOR View Hotel, now 100 years old." DCI, 32 (May 1991), 172-180.

2372.   HOWLAND, JOHN A. "Family tragedy at Cape Pogy Light." DCI, 30 (Feb. 1989), 47-56.
        After the death of one of her children, a lighthouse keeper's wife left and divorced her husband because of the loneliness and isolation of their lives.

2373.   JERNEGAN, PRESCOTT F. "Growing up in Edgartown in the 1870s." DCI, 30 (May 1989), 95-111.
        Part of an autobiographical account written during the 1920s.

2374.   KAPPELL, KENNETH. Chappaquiddick revealed: what really happened. 2d ed. N.Y.: Shapolsky Publishers, 1989. viii, 310p. MS. *
        The 1969 accident and drowning in which Sen. Edward M. Kennedy was involved.

2375.   KERN, FLORENCE. "Customs collectors at Edgartown, 1842-1855." DCI, 31 (Feb. 1990), 115-146.

2376.   _____. "Customs collectors at Edgartown, 1855-1861." DCI, 32 (Feb. 1991), 99-120.

2377.   _____. "Customs collectors at Edgartown: John Presbury Norton (1830-1842)." DCI, 30 (Feb. 1989), 57-75.

2378.   _____. "Customs collectors at Edgartown: John Vinson, 1861-1870." DCI, 34 (Nov. 1992), 71-84.

2379.   _____. "The last of the Vineyard's customs collectors." DCI, 35 (Nov. 1993), 51-65.

2380.   _____, and ARTHUR R. RAILTON. "The slandering of Jeremiah Pease." DCI, 31 (Feb. 1990), 147-153.
        A newspaper in 1832 charged that he had failed to properly maintain the Edgartown Lighthouse.

2381.   NEVIN, ANNA JOSEPHA SHIVERICK. "Imaginative Edgartown widow turns a house into a mansion." DCI, 35 (May 1994), 180-190.
        Shiverick House. Written ca. 1933.

2382.   RAILTON, ARTHUR R. "The first 30 ministers of the First Church (1642 to 1878)." DCI, 33 (May 1992), 171-222.
        Congregational.

2383.   _____. "Richard L. Pease goes job hunting after the panic of 1837." DCI, 30 (Feb. 1989), 76-86.
        Pease tried unsuccessfully to get the appointment as collector at Edgartown following the 1840 election.

2384.   _____. "The tribulations of Reverend Thaxter." DCI, 34 (Aug. 1992), 35-68.
        The Rev. Joseph Thaxter, Jr., minister of the Congregational Church from 1780-1827. See also entry 2386.

2385.   _____. "The Vineyard's opening shot in the American Revolution." DCI, 30 (May 1989), 112-121.
        Capture of the captain of a British supply ship en route to Boston (1776), after the ship had run aground off Nantucket.

2386.   "REV. Joseph Thaxter and his politics." DCI, 34 (Nov. 1992), 85-97.
        See also entry 2384.

2387.   VANCOUR, STEVE. "The Edgartown Engine Company and the fires it fought, 1836-1906." DCI, 35 (Aug. 1993), 3-29; (Nov. 1993), 68-85.

        SEE ALSO entries 1786, 1797.

ERVING (FRANKLIN CO.)

2388.   ERVING, MASS. The history of Erving, Massachusetts, 1838-1988; this book is published in observance of the 150th anniversary of the incorporation of the town, 1838-1988. Pearl B. Care, Anastacia Burnett, and Doris A. Felton, comps. [Erving, 1988] 275p. MDeeP. *

2389   ESSEX

ESSEX (ESSEX CO.)

2389.   STORY, DANA A. Building the Blackfish. Gloucester: Ten Pound Island Book, 1988. ix, 172p. MB. *
    The schooner yacht, launched in 1938, was one of the last wooden vessels built in Essex.

2390.   _____. Growing up in a shipyard: reminiscences of a shipbuilding life in Essex, Massachusetts. Mystic, Conn.: Mystic Seaport Museum, 1991. xviii, 139p. MH. *
    Autobiographical.

EVERETT (MIDDLESEX CO.)

2391.   Di FELICE, GOETO. The Italians in Everett: from the first immigrant to today's generation. Everett, 1992. M. *

2392.   O'BRIEN, ESTHER M. Everett: our city. Everett: Everett High School, Vocational Division, 1992. [50]p. M. *

FALL RIVER (BRISTOL CO.)

2393.   BEEM, EDGAR ALLEN. "Did Lizzie Borden really take an ax and give her mother 40 whacks?" Yankee, 56 (Aug. 1992), 83-86, 117-119.
    The famous 1892 murder.

2394.   BRISTOL COMMUNITY COLLEGE. Proceedings: Lizzie Borden conference, Bristol Community College, Fall River, Massachusetts, August 3-5, 1992. Jules R. Ryckebusch, ed. Portland, Me.: King Philip Publishing, 1993. xi, 373p. MNodS. *

2395.   BROWN, ARNOLD. Lizzie Borden: the legend, the truth, the final chapter. Nashville, Tenn.: Rutledge Hill Pr., 1991. 382p. MB. *

2396.   CARLISLE, MARCIA R. "What made Lizzie Borden kill?" American Heritage, 43 (July-Aug. 1992), 66-72.
    Speculates on sexual abuse as a factor in the officially unsolved murder.

2397.   KENT, DAVID. Forty whacks: new evidence in the life and legend of Lizzie Borden. Emmaus, Pa.: Yankee Books, 1992. xvi, 231p. MS. *

2398.   THE LIZZIE Borden sourcebook. David Kent, ed. Boston: Branden Publishing, 1992. iii, 353p. MH. *

2399.   ROSA BORGES, ALUISIO MEDEIROS DA. "The Portuguese working class in the Durfee Mills of Fall River, Massachusetts: a study of the division of labor, ethnicity, and labor union participation, 1895-1925." Ph.D. dissertation, State Univ. of New York, Binghamton, 1990. xii, 340p. *
    Abstracted in DAI, 51:6A (1990), 2165-2166.

2400.   SCHERZER, KENNETH A. "The politics of default: financial restructure and reform in Depression Era Fall River, Massachusetts." Urban Studies [U.K.], 26 (Feb. 1989), 164-176.

2401.   SCHOFIELD, ANN. "Lizzie Borden took an axe: history, feminism and American Culture." American Studies, 34 (Spring 1993), 91-103.

2402.   SEWELL, TOM. "In praise of peggyball." Yankee, 53 (July 1989), 56-59.
    Locally popular game (20th century).

2403.   VICTORIAN vistas: Fall River, 1886-1900: as viewed through its newspaper accounts. Philip T. Silvia, Jr., ed. Fall River: R. E. Smith Publishing, 1988. xix, 777p. MB. *
    See also next entry and entry 6326 in Vol. 8.

2404.   VICTORIAN vistas: Fall River, 1901-1911: as viewed through its newspaper accounts. Philip T. Silvia, Jr., ed. Fall River: R. E. Smith Printing, 1992. xxvi, 948p. MB. *
    See also preceding entry.

    SEE ALSO entries 337, 1785.

FALMOUTH (BARNSTABLE CO.)

2405.   CLAPP, PAMELA. "Cornelia Clapp and the earliest years of the MBC." Spritsail, 2 (Summer 1988), 4-15.
    Marine Biological Laboratory, Woods Hole.

2406.   CRAIG, EDGAR HENRY, and MOLLY CRAIG RICE. "Molly Dodd Craig showed Falmouth women the way." Spritsail, 6 (Summer 1992), 20-30.
    Elected to the school committee in 1914.

2407.   DYER, ARNOLD W. Hotels & inns of Falmouth: a survey of 17th, 18th and 19th century accommodations. [Falmouth]: Falmouth Historical Society, 1993. 73p. MWA. *

2408.   FUGLISTER, JAYNE, and ROBERT BLOOM. "Accounting records of Quakers of West Falmouth, Massachusetts (1796-1860)." Accounting Historians Journal, 18:2 (1991), 133-154.

2409. HATCH, RUTH ANNA. The diary of Ruth Anna Hatch, 1886. Mary Lou Smith, ed. Woods Hole: Woods Hole Historical Collection, 1992. 141p. MFal. *

2410. JANNEY, MARY DRAPER. "Maria Mitchell—stellar scientist." Spritsail, 2 (Summer 1988), 16-29.
       19th-century astronomer.

2411. JENKINS, CANDACE. "The development of Falmouth as a summer resort, 1850-1900." Spritsail, 6 (Winter 1992), 2-34.

2412. LOVELL, HOLLIS. "Merchant on Main Street." Spritsail, 4 (Summer 1990), 18-29.
       Autobiographical account of storekeeping during the 1920s.

2413. MAIENSCHEIN, JANE. 100 years exploring life, 1888-1988: the Marine Biological Laboratory at Woods Hole. Boston: Jones & Bartlett, 1989. xvi, 192p. MBAt. *

2414. McLAUGHLIN, JANE A. "The Angelus Bell Tower and Mary Garden in Woods Hole." Spritsail, 6 (Summer 1992), 2-19.
       The tower and Garden of Our Lady were given to St. Joseph's Church by Frances Crane Lillie (lived 1869-1958).

2415. TURKINGTON, FREDERICK T. "From meetinghouse to church and town house." Spritsail, 2 (Winter 1988), 3-15.
       First Congregational Church.

2416. WARBASSE, JAMES P. JR. "From sail to steam to diesel." Spritsail, 4 (Summer 1990), 4-17.
       Ferry service in and out of Woods Hole.

       SEE ALSO entries 236, 1667.

FITCHBURG (WORCESTER CO.)

2417. TAYLOR, ANTHONY R. Fitchburg building traditions. [Fitchburg]: Fitchburg Historical Commission, [198?]. 44p. MWA.

       SEE ALSO entry 1836.

FLORIDA (BERKSHIRE CO.)

2418. COYNE, TERRENCE EDWARD. "The Hoosac Tunnel." Ph.D. dissertation, Clark Univ., 1992. 397p. *
       Abstracted in DAI, 53:4A (1992), 1252.

FOXBOROUGH (NORFOLK CO.)

2419. TRACY, SARAH WHITNEY. "The Foxborough experiment: medicalizing inebrity at the Massachusetts Hospital for Dipsomaniacs and Inebriates, 1833-1919." Ph.D. dissertation, Univ. of Pennsylvania, 1992. viii, 291p. *
       Abstracted in DAI, 53:11A (1993), 4061.

       SEE ALSO entry 1532.

FRANKLIN (NORFOLK CO.)

2420. FRANKLIN, MASS. Historical book: the two hundredth anniversary of the town of Franklin, Massachusetts. [Franklin, 1978] 144p. MWA. *

2421. STRAUSS, ALAN E. "The Beaver Pond archaeological study." MASB, 51 (Spring 1990), 15-33.
       Prehistoric site.

       SEE ALSO entry 41.

GARDNER (WORCESTER CO.)

2422. GREENWOOD, AARON. The diary of Aaron Greenwood. Windsor C. Robinson, ed. Gardner: Gardner Historical Commission, 1983-1991. 3v. M. *
       Covers the years 1857-1863.

GAY HEAD (DUKES CO.)

2423. ATTAQUIN, HELEN AVIS ALYCE. A brief history of Gay Head; or "Aquiniuh." n.p., 1970. 47p. MBChM. *
       "One of two Indian municipalities in Massachusetts."

       SEE ALSO entry 2423.

GILL (FRANKLIN CO.)

2424. GARMAN, JAMES C. "Prehistoric maize at Riverside, Gill." MASB, 52 (Spring 1991), 1-7.

GLOUCESTER (ESSEX CO.)

2425. BROWN, CHANDOS MICHAEL. "A natural history of the Gloucester sea serpent: knowledge, power, and the culture of science in antebellum America." American Quarterly, 42 (Sept. 1990), 402-436.

2426 GLOUCESTER

2426. CLARK, TOM. Charles Olson: the allegory of a poet's life. N.Y.: W.W. Norton, 1991. xi, 403p. MB. *
Lived 1910-1970. See also entry 2434.

2427. CURTIS, NANCY, and RICHARD C. NYLANDER. Beauport: the Sleeper-McCann House. Boston: David R. Godine, 1990. 112p. MB. *
Historic house, belonging to the Society for the Preservation of New England Antiquities.

2428. ERKKILA, BARBARA HOWELL. Village at Lane's Cove. Gloucester: Ten Pound Island Pr., 1989. 212, [10]p. MWA.

2429. GARLAND, JOSEPH E. Eastern Point revisited: then and now, 1899-1989. Gloucester: Association of Eastern Point Residents, 1989. v, 34p. M. *
See also entry 2512.

2430. _____. "The Gloucestermen." Sea History, 49 (1989), 13-15.
Gloucester fishermen, their boats and methods.

2431. JINISHIAN, RUSSELL. "Thomas M. Hoyne: artist of the Gloucestermen." Sea History, 49 (1989), 23-26.
20th century.

2432. MANN, CHARLES EDWARD. The Sargent family and the old Sargent homes. Lynn: Frank S. Whitman, 1919. 64p. MeHi. *

2433. MOSES, MICHAEL. "Mary Blood Mellen and Fitz Hugh Lane." Antiques, 140 (Nov. 1991), 826-836.
Mellen (born 1817) was the artist Lane's student and copyist.

2434. OLSON, CHARLES. Maximus to Gloucester: the letters and poems of Charles Olson to the editor of the Gloucester Daily Times, 1962-1969. Peter Anastas, ed. Gloucester: Ten Pound Island Pr., 1992. xi, 161p. MA. *
See also entry 2426.

2435. SWIDERSKI, RICHARD W. Voices: an anthropologist's dialogue with an Italian-American festival. Bowling Green, Ohio: Bowling Green Univ. Popular Pr., 1986. xiii, 146p. MH. *
St. Peter's Festival.

SEE ALSO entries 1677, 1725.

GOSNOLD (DUKES CO.)

2436. CUTTYHUNK HISTORICAL SOCIETY. Cuttyhunk and the Elizabeth Islands from 1602. Janet Bosworth, ed. Cuttyhunk, 1993. 118p. MWA. *

2437. RAILTON, ARTHUR R. "A puzzling piracy off Tarpaulin Cove." DCI, 33 (Nov. 1991), 97-106.
Naushon Island (1689).

GREAT BARRINGTON (BERKSHIRE CO.)

2438. HAUTANIEMI, SUSAN. "Race, gender, and health at the W.E.B. DuBois boyhood site." MASB, 55 (Spring 1994), 1-7.

GREENFIELD (FRANKLIN CO.)

2439. COPE, KEN. "Sorting out the Goodell companies." CEAIA, 45 (Dec. 1992), 115.
Toolmaking firms (late-19th and 20th centuries).

2440. REID, GERALD F. 150 years: Heritage Bank, 1834-1984. Northampton: Benjamin, [1984]. 94p. MDeeP. *

2441. _____. "The seeds of prosperity and discord: the political economy of community polarization in Greenfield, Massachusetts, 1770-1820." JSH, 27 (Winter 1993), 359-374.

2442. STRECKER, CLARENCE S. History of a New England drug store. New York: Carlton Pr., [1976]. 39p. MDeeP. *
Fiske and Strecker, founded in 1845.

SEE ALSO entries 1688, 1815.

GROTON (MIDDLESEX CO.)

2443. FRANK, DOUGLAS ALAN. The history of Lawrence Academy at Groton, 1792 to 1992. Groton: Lawrence Academy, 1992. xiv, 409p. MBAt. *

2444. SEATON, MICHELLE. "Doctor Betty & Doctor Woody." Yankee, 57 (Mar. 1993), 80-87, 116.
F. Woodward Lewis and Elizabeth Lewis, married physicians, in practice in Groton since 1940.

SEE ALSO entry 1830.

HALIFAX (PLYMOUTH CO.)

2445. GARDNER, RUSSELL HERBERT. "A petroglyph from White's Island, Monponsett Pond, Halifax, MA, and some historical and archaeological notes on the site." MASB, 55 (Spring 1994)), 38-42.

HANCOCK (BERKSHIRE CO.)

2446.   CROSTHWAITE, JANE F. "The spirit drawings of Hannah Cahoon: window on the Shakers and their folk art." Communal Societies, 7 (1987), 1-15.
   Ca. 1850s.

HARVARD (WORCESTER CO.)

2447.   BARTON, CYNTHIA. History's daughter: the life of Clara Endicott Sears, founder of the Fruitlands Museums. Harvard: Fruitland Museums, 1989. ix, 167p. MB. *

2448.   CODE, TREVOR. "Discourses and contexts of power: a New England village preacher as a case study." Australasian Journal of American Studies, 18 (Dec. 1989) 14-24.
   Study of the sermons of the Rev. Stephen Bemis (early-19th century).

2449.   STIER, MARGARET MOODY. "Blood, sweat, and herbs: health and medicine in the Harvard Shaker community, 1820-1855." DubSemPr (1990), 154-167.

HARWICH (BARNSTABLE CO.)

2450.   MONBLEAU, MARCIA J. At home: Harwich, Cape Cod, Massachusetts. [Harwich: Harwich Historical Society, 1993] 184p. MWA. *

HAVERHILL (ESSEX CO.)

2451.   TUCKER, RALPH L. "The Mullicken family gravestone carvers of Bradford, Massachusetts, 1663-1768." Markers IX [1992], 23-57.

2452.   "TWO early poems by Mrs. Elizabeth Palmer Peabody." MHSP, 100 (1988), 40-59.
   Published in the Haverhill Federal Gazette in 1799. Article includes biographical sketch. Megan Marshall, ed.

HAWLEY (FRANKLIN CO.)

2453.   THE HOME to Hawley scrapbook. Tinky Weisblat, ed. [Hawley: Hawley Bicentennial Committee, 1992] 56p. MWA. *

2454.   PARKER, HARRISON. Hawley: the first fifty years, 1770-1820. Amherst: Sara Publishing, 1992. xii, 479p. MDeeP. *

2455.   RIGGS, MAIDA LEONARD. Tales of Hawley. n.p., 1992. [46]p. MDeeP.

SEE ALSO entry 1545.

HEATH (FRANKLIN CO.)

2456.   THE HEATH bicentennial, 1785-1985. Susan B. Silvester, ed. Ashfield: Paideia Publishers, [1989]. 163p. MDeeP. *

SEE ALSO entry 1545.

HINGHAM (PLYMOUTH CO.)

2457.   FOGARTY, EVELYN LINCOLN. "'Old Ship' of Hingham, Massachusetts: New England's unique colonial church." DAR Magazine, 118 (Apr. 1984), 212-213.

2458.   HART, LORENA LAING, and FRANCIS RUSSELL HART. Not all is changed: a life history of Hingham. Hingham: Hingham Historical Society, 1993. xxvi, 509, [46]p. MWA. *

2459.   LEHNER, MONIQUE B., and MINXIE J. FANNIN. "History in towns: Hingham, Massachusetts." Antiques, 136 (Oct. 1989), 812-825.

HOLDEN (WORCESTER CO.)

2460.   HOLDEN, MASS. FIRST CONGREGATIONAL CHURCH. Forward through the ages: the First Congregational Church, United Church of Christ, Holden, 1742-1992. [Holden, 1992] 81p. MWA.

2461.   HOLDEN HISTORICAL SOCIETY. Pictorial history of Holden. Charles T. Skillings, Clare M. Nelson, and Ross W. Beales, comps. and eds. Holden, 1991. 144p. MB. *

SEE ALSO entry 1751.

2462   HOLYOKE

HOLYOKE (HAMPDEN CO.)

2462.   HARTFORD, WILLIAM F. Working people of Holyoke: class and ethnicity in a Massachusetts mill town, 1850-1960. New Brunswick, N.J.: Rutgers Univ. Pr., 1990. 250p. MBAt. *

2463.   WEIR, ROBERT E. "Historian's afterword." Massachusetts Review, 33 (Fall 1992), 377-384.
   The afterword is to a photographic essay (ibid., 361- 376) entitled, "Faces, machines, and voices: the fading landscape of papermaking in Holyoke, Massachusetts."

SEE ALSO entry 1552.

HOPEDALE (WORCESTER CO.)

2464.   SPANN, EDWARD K. Hopedale: from commune to company town, 1840-1920. Columbus: Ohio State Univ. Pr., 1992. xiii, 260p. MWA. *

IPSWICH (ESSEX CO.)

2465.   BROWN, ANNE S. "Visions of community in eighteenth-century Essex County: Chebaco Parish and the Great Awakening." EIHC, 125 (July 1989), 239-262.

2466.   NEWMAN, SIMON P. "Nathaniel Ward, 1580-1652: an Elizabethan Puritan in a Jacobean world." EIHC, 127 (Oct. 1991), 313-326.
   Minister.

2467.   WINSHIP, MICHAEL PAUL. "Encountering providence in the seventeenth century: the experiences of a yeoman and a minister." EIHC, 126 (Jan. 1990), 27-36.
   John Dane and the Rev. John Norton.

SEE ALSO entries 1805, 1809, 1811.

KINGSTON (PLYMOUTH CO.)

2468.   OTTO, BERNARD A. "The Hathaway site, sections 6 and 5, Rocky Nook, Kingston, Massachusetts: a small late woodland and late archaic lithic work site, and a small late archaic shell midden." MASB, 52 (Spring 1991), 18-27.

LAKEVILLE (PLYMOUTH CO.)

2469.   FRENCH, SUSAN ASHLEY. Toys in the sand: recovering childhood memories in Lakeville, Massachusetts. East Freetown, 1989. 286p. WHi. *
   Ca. 1900-1945.

2470.   PRESERVE OUR LAKEVILLE LANDMARKS. Lakeville then and now: a pictorial history. Lakeville, 1993. vi, 72p. M. *

LANCASTER (WORCESTER CO.)

2471.   DAVIS, MARGARET HAIGLER. "Mary White Rowlandson's self-fashioning as Puritan goodwife." Early American Literature, 27:1 (1992), 49-60.
   In her captivity account (1682).

2472.   THOMAS, TERESA A. "For Union, not for glory: memory and the Civil War volunteers of Lancaster, Massachusetts." Civil War History, 40 (Mar. 1994), 25-47.

LAWRENCE (ESSEX CO.)

2473.   CAMERON, ARDIS. Radicals of the worst sort: laboring women in Lawrence, Massachusetts, 1860-1912. Champaign: Univ. of Illinois Pr., 1993. xix, 229p. M. *

2474.   GOLDBERG, DAVID JOSEPH. A tale of three cities: labor organization and protest in Paterson, Passaic, and Lawrence, 1916-1921. New Brunswick, N.J.: Rutgers Univ. Pr., 1989. xiv, 276p. MB. *
   See also this author's Ph.D. dissertation on same subject (Columbia Univ., 1984; entry 6626 in Vol. 8).

2475.   HOOGTERP, MARY C. "'Among my own people': patterns of community in five American cities in the early twentieth century." Ph.D. dissertation, Univ. of California, San Diego, 1990. xiii, 324p. *
   Including Lawrence. Abstracted in DAI, 52:2A (1991), 657.

SEE ALSO entry 438.

LEICESTER (WORCESTER CO.)

2476.   WASHBURN, EMORY. "The Jews in Leicester, Massachusetts." RIJHN, 10 (Nov. 1989), 34-41.
    19th-century historical account of refugees from Newport, R.I., during the American Revolution.

2477.   WHEELER, ROBERT. "Nathaniel Potter: could he be our earliest planemaker?" CEAIA, 46 (Mar. 1993), 3-4.
    Lived 1693-1768.

LENOX (BERKSHIRE CO.)

2478.   KUPFERBERG, HERBERT. Tanglewood. N.Y.: McGraw-Hill, 1976. 280p. MB. *
    History of the Berkshire Symphonic Festival.

2479.   TUCKER, GEORGE H. A history of Lenox. Lenox: Lenox Library Association 1992. viii, 91, 4, 12p. MPB.
    Written ca. 1935-1936.

SEE ALSO entry 1782.

LEXINGTON (MIDDLESEX CO.)

2480.   REINHARDT, ELIZABETH WRIGHT. "Suburbanization and the rural domestic ideal in Lexington, Massachusetts, 1875-1915." Ph.D. dissertation, Boston Univ., 1982. xi, 315p. *
    Abstracted in DAI, 50:6A (1989), 1709-1710.

SEE ALSO entry 1593.

LINCOLN (MIDDLESEX CO.)

2481.   MacLEAN, JOHN C. A rich harvest: the history, buildings, and people of Lincoln, Massachusetts. Portsmouth, N.H.: Peter E. Randall, 1987. xxii, 679p. MWA. *

2482.   MARTIN, MARGARET MUTCHLER. Inheritance: Lincoln's public buildings in the historic district. Lincoln Center: Lincoln Historical Society, 1987. 115, [40]p. M. *

2483.   RAGAN, RUTH MOULTON. Voiceprints of Lincoln: memories of an old Massachusetts town and its unique response to industrial America: an oral history. Lincoln: Lincoln Historical Society, 1991. xxix, 208p. MBAt. *

LONGMEADOW (HAMPDEN CO.)

2484.   HALL, J. R. "William G. Medlicott (1816-1883): an American book collector and his collection." Harvard Library Bulletin, n.s. 1 (Spring 1990), 13-46.

LOWELL (MIDDLESEX CO.)

2485.   ALBERT, FELIX. Immigrant odyssey: a French-Canadian habitant in New England. A bilingual edition of Histoire d'un enfant pauvre. Arthur L. Eno, trans. Orono, Me.: Univ. of Maine Pr., 1991. ix, 179p. VtHi. *
    Albert lived 1843-1924.

2486.   BEAUDRY, MARY C. "The Lowell Boott Mills complex and its housing: material expressions of corporate ideology." Historical Archaeology, 23:1 (1989), 19-32.
    See also next entry.

2487.   _____, and STEPHEN A. MROZOWSKI. "The archeology of work and home life in Lowell, Massachusetts: an interdisciplinary study of the Boott Cotton Mills Corporation." IA, 14:2 (1988), 1-22.
    See also preceding entry and entries 2491-2492, 2501.

2488.   BLEWETT, MARY H. The last generation: work and life in the textile mills of Lowell, Massachusetts, 1910-1960. Amherst: Univ. of Massachusetts Pr., 1990. xxii, 330p. MB. *
    Based on oral history interviews.

2489.   DUBLIN, THOMAS LOUIS. Lowell: the story of an industrial city: a guide to Lowell National Historical Park and Lowell Heritage State Park, Lowell, Massachusetts. Washington, D.C.: U.S. Department of the Interior, 1992. 111p. MWA. *

2490.   FREEMAN, ALLEN. "Lessons from Lowell." Historic Preservation, 42 (Nov./Dec. 1990), 32-38, 68-69.
    Reflections on historic preservation in Lowell.

2491.   GROSS, LAURENCE F. "Building on success: Lowell mill construction and its results." IA, 14, No. 2 (1988), 23-34.
    Boott Cotton Mills. See also next entry.

2492.   _____. The course of industrial decline: the Boott Cotton Mills of Lowell, Massachusetts, 1835-1955. Baltimore: Johns Hopkins Univ. Pr., 1993. xvii, 279p. MWA. *
    See also preceding entry and entries 2486-2487, 2501.

2493.   KENNEY, CHARLES C. Riding the runaway horse: the rise and decline of Wang Laboratories. Boston: Little, Brown, 1992. 323p. MB. *
    Computer company.

2494   LOWELL

2494.   KIANG, PETER NIEN-CHU. "Southeast Asian parent empowerment: the challenge of changing demographics in Lowell, Massachusetts." Vietnam Generation, 2:3 (1990), 5-15.
　　　　Since 1970s.

2495.   LOWELL HISTORICAL SOCIETY. The continuing revolution: a history of Lowell, Massachusetts. Robert Weible, ed. [Lowell], 1991. xii, 430p. MH. *

2496.   MARSTON, SALLIE A. "Neighborhood and politics: Irish ethnicity in nineteenth century Lowell, Massachusetts." Association of American Geographers, Annals, 78 (Sept. 1988), 414-432.

2497.   _____. "Public rituals and community power: St. Patrick's Day parades in Lowell, Massachusetts, 1841- 1874." Political Geography Quarterly [U.K.], 8 (July 1989), 255-269.

2498.   "THE MILL letters of Emeline Larcom, 1840-1842." EIHC, 127 (July 1991), 211-239.

2499.   MILLER, MARC SCOTT. The irony of victory: World War II and Lowell, Massachusetts. Champaign: Univ. of Illinois Pr., 1988. xi, 233p. MBAt. *
　　　　See also this author's Ph.D. dissertation on same subject (Boston Univ., 1978; entry 6719 in Vol. 8).

2500.   NORKUNAS, MARTHA K. "Women, work and ethnic identity: personal narratives and the ethnic enclave in the textile city of Lowell, Massachusetts." Journal of Ethnic Studies, 15 (Fall 1987), 27-48.
　　　　Based on oral history interviews.

2501.   U.S. NATIONAL PARK SERVICE. NORTH ATLANTIC REGIONAL OFFICE. Interdisciplinary investigations of the Boott Mills, Lowell, Massachusetts. Volume II: the Kirk Street agents' house. Mary C. Beaudry and Stephen A. Mrozowski, eds. Boston, 1987. xiv, 166, [34]p. MHi. *
　　　　See also entries 2486-2487, 2491-2492, and entry 6736 in Vol. 8.

　　　　SEE ALSO entries 364, 438, 1652-1653, 1828-1829.

LYNN (ESSEX CO.)

2502.   BIKLEN, SARI KNOPP. "Confiding women: a nineteenth-century teacher's diary." History of Education Review [Australia], 19:2 (1990), 24-35.
　　　　Diary of Mary Mudge (1854).

2503.   CUSHING, ELIZABETH HOPE. The Lynn album: a pictorial history. Norfolk, Va.: Donning, 1990. 192p. MWA. *
　　　　See also entry 2506.

2504.   KARWATKA, DENNIS. "Against all odds." American Heritage of Invention & Technology, 6 (Winter 1991), 50-55.
　　　　Jan Earnst Matzeliger, a black immigrant, became a skilled machinist and a successful inventor in the shoe industry (late-19th century).

2505.   LYNN HISTORICAL SOCIETY. A guide to the manuscripts and special collections. Lynn, 1988. Var. p. MWA. *

2506.   _____. No race of imitators: Lynn and her people; an anthology. Elizabeth Hope Cushing, ed. Lynn, 1992. 234p. MWA. *
　　　　See also entry 2503.

2507.   MULLIGAN, WILLIAM H. JR. "Crispin's daughters: women, work, and technological change in the shoe industry." EIHC, 127 (Oct. 1991), 297-312.
　　　　Prior to 1850.

2508.   SMITH, NANCY A. "The furniture legacy of J. Sanger Attwill." EIHC 126 (Apr. 1990), 67-90.
　　　　The Attwill Furniture Company (established 1926) specialized in museum-quality reproductions and in restoration work.

2509.   VERSLUIS, ARTHUR. "From Transcendentalism to universal religion: Samuel Johnson's orientalism." ATQ, 5 (June 1991), 109-123.
　　　　Johnson lived 1822-1882.

2510.   YAEGER, DAN. "The lady who helped ladies." Yankee, 53 (Sept. 1989), 62-67, 112-114, 116, 118.
　　　　Lydia Pinkham.

　　　　SEE ALSO entries 435, 1635, 1920.

MANSFIELD (BRISTOL CO.)

2511.   MANSFIELD, MASS. ORTHODOX CONGREGATIONAL CHURCH. An observance of 150 years, 1838-1988: the Orthodox Congregational Church (United Church of Christ), Mansfield, Massachusetts. Mansfield, [1987]. 16p. M. *

MARBLEHEAD (ESSEX CO.)

2512.   GARLAND, JOSEPH E. The Eastern Yacht Club: a history from 1870 to 1985. Marblehead: Eastern Yacht Club, 1989. xv, 333, [16]p. MBAt. *
　　　　See also entry 2429.

2513. McCAIN, DIANA ROSS. "A fine romance." Early American Life, 21 (Feb. 1990), 10-13.
Charles Henry Frankland, an English aristocrat, and Agnes Surriage, a fisherman's daughter (1740s and 1750s).

2514. SMITH, LEANNE SEUKELMAN. "'Strange adventures and signal deliverances': narrative masks in John Barnard's Ashton's memorial." NEQ, 63 (Mar. 1990), 60-79.
Compares the experience of Philip Ashton, a Marblehead man captured by pirates, as written by his minister in 1725, with Ashton's autobiographical account (1766). See also next entry.

2515. WILLIAMS, DANIEL E. "Of providence and pirates: Philip Ashton's narrative struggle for salvation." Early American Literature, 24:3 (1989), 169-195.
See also preceding entry.

MARSHFIELD (PLYMOUTH CO.)

2516. KRUSELL, CYNTHIA HAGAR, and BETTY MAGOUN BATES. Marshfield: a town of villages, 1640-1990. Marshfield Hills: Marshfield Research Associates, 1990. 234p. MStuO. *

2517. MOODY, WILLIAM E. "Out from under the bulldozer: salvaging a prehistoric coastal site." MASB, 52 (Fall 1991), 34-43.
Pine Point River site.

SEE ALSO entry 1641.

MASHPEE (BARNSTABLE CO.)

2518. CAMPISI, JACK. The Mashpee Indians: tribe on trial. Syracuse, N.Y.: Syracuse Univ. Pr., 1991. xiv, 174p. MB. *

2519. PETERS, RUSSELL M. The Wampanoags of Mashpee: an Indian perspective on American History. [Somerville: Media Action], 1987. 83p. MWA. *

SEE ALSO entries 14, 212.

MAYNARD (MIDDLESEX CO.)

2520. MULLIN, JOHN R. "Development of the Assabet Mills in nineteenth century Maynard." HJM, 20 (Winter 1992), 64-88.

2521. RIFKIN, GLENN, and GEORGE HARRAR. The ultimate entrepreneur: the story of Ken Olsen and the Digital Equipment Corporation. Chicago: Contemporary Books, 1988. xii, 332p. MB. *
Olsen founded the computer company in 1957.

MIDDLEBOROUGH (PLYMOUTH CO.)

2522. BARDEN, GEORGE M. JR. "1849 revisited." Middleborough Antiquarian, 27 (Sept. 1989), 5, 12-14, 16-17.
Excerpts from the diary of James Gardner Thompson.

2523. _____. "A shoe business, a robbery and a fire." Middleborough Antiquarian, 27 (Dec. 1989), 5, 7, 10.
The Alden, Leonard & Hammond shoe factory was robbed ca. 1880s; the Alden, Walker & Wilde factory was burned in 1904.

2524. BEALS, ROBERT M. "Bay State No. One—Middleboro's first fire pumper." Middleborough Antiquarian, 29 (Spring 1991), 5.
1852.

2525. _____. "'A good man, a great asset.'" Middleborough Antiquarian, 27 (May 1989), 10, 15.
George A. Philbrook (died 1945), longtime superintendent of the Middleboro Gas and Electric Department.

2526. _____. "Isaac Howland, 1649-1724." Middleborough Antiquarian, 29 (Spring 1991), 12-13.
Prominent early settler and soldier in King Philip's War.

2527. _____. "Memories of East Grove Street." Middleborough Antiquarian, 28 (Spring/Summer 1990), 13-14.

2528. _____. "To the rescue!: ladder trucks of the Middleboro Fire Department." Middleborough Antiquarian, 28 (Spring/Summer 1990), 5, 7.

2529. HARLOW, FLORENCE E. "A personal glimpse of the 1920s." Middleborough Antiquarian, 28 (Spring/Summer 1990), 8-9, 11.

2530. JOHNSEN, LEIGH DANA. "Toward pluralism: society and religion in Middleborough, Massachusetts, 1741-1807." Ph.D. dissertation, Univ. of California, Riverside, 1984. xii, 283p. MA. *
Abstracted in DAI, 51:7A (1991), 2498-2499.

2531 MIDDLEBOROUGH

2531. LOPES, JANE. "Cephas Thompson and son—portrait painters to the world." Middleborough Antiquarian, 28 (Fall 1990), 9, 14.
    19th century.

2532. _____. "The Eddy Homestead." Middleborough Antiquarian, 27 (Sept. 1989), 9-10, 15.
    In East Middleborough.

2533. _____. "Massachusetts and the Constitution: the local angle on ratification." Middleborough Antiquarian, 28 (Fall 1990), 7, 10-11.
    1788.

2534. _____. "Middleborough's 'top ten' homes." Middleborough Antiquarian, 27 (Dec. 1989), 8-10.
    Ten houses recommended for preservation by the Middleborough Historical Commission.

2535. MADDIGAN, MICHAEL. "The hats were in the ring: Bull Moose progressivism in Middleboro and the nation." Middleborough Antiquarian, 27 (May 1989), 7-9, 16.
    1912.

2536. PEABODY, MERLE A., and JENNIFER MOTT. "Isaac Thompson, Eqsuire." Middleborough Antiquarian, 27 (Dec. 1989), 13-14.
    Voted to ratify the U.S. Constitution as a Middleborough delegate to the state ratifying convention.

2537. PENNIMAN, ETHEL R. "Houses of North Middleboro." Middleborough Antiquarian, 27 (Dec. 1989), 11-12.

2538. PRATT, LOUISE. "Childhood memories of the Pratt Farm." Middleborough Antiquarian, 27 (Sept.1989), 7-8.
    The author was born in 1887.

2539. SNOW, ELIZABETH J. "Let there be light." Middleborough Antiquarian, 27 (May 1989), 11-15.
    Early lighting devices.

SEE ALSO entry 99.

MILFORD (WORCESTER CO.)

2540. MILFORD TOWN LIBRARY. Milford Town Library, established August 30, 1858; the new Milford Town Library dedication, April 6, 1986. n.p., [1986?]. 43p. MB. *
    Includes historical sketch.

MILLBURY (WORCESTER CO.)

2541. MILLBURY, MASS. OUR LADY OF THE ASSUMPTION CHURCH. Our Lady of the Assumption Parish, Millbury, Mass.: centennial, 1884-1984. Millbury, 1984. Unp. MW.
    Roman Catholic.

SEE ALSO entries 1568-1569.

MILTON (NORFOLK CO.)

2542. CONOVER, JOHN H. The Blue Hill Meteorological Observatory: the first one hundred years, 1885-1985. Boston: American Meteorological Society, 1990. xi, 514p. MB. *

MONTEREY (BERKSHIRE CO.)

2543. CLUTE, SHIRLEY S. "Bidwell's saltbox house." HJM, 21 (Summer 1993), 23-43.
    Built ca. 1750.

2544. GARRETT, WENDELL. "The Manse in Monterey, Berkshire County, Massachusetts." Antiques, 136 (Aug. 1989), 282-291.
    Historic house (built 1750).

SEE ALSO entry 1784.

NAHANT (ESSEX CO.)

2545. PATERSON, STANLEY, and CARL G. SEABURG. Nahant on the rocks. Nahant: Nahant Historical Society, 1991. 431p. MBAt. *

NANTUCKET (NANTUCKET CO.)

2546. ALLEN, JEAN. "Nantucket goes to war." HN, 41 (Spring 1993), 12-16.
    World War II.

2547. ANDERSON, EDGAR A. "Summer of '41." HN, 37 (July 1989), 32-34.
    The author worked in a summer hotel that year.

2548. ANDREWS, J. CLINTON. Fishing around Nantucket. Nantucket: Maria Mitchell Association, 1990. xiv, 77p. MWA.

2549.   ARNOLD, LOUISE STARK. "Memories of sea and sand."
        HN, 40 (Summer 1992), 23-24.
        Recollections of a longtime summer resident.

2550.   BEEGEL, SUSAN. "The Brotherhood of Thieves riot of
        1842." HN, 40 (Fall 1992), 45-48.
        Anti-abolitionist riot.

2551.   _____. "Herman Melville: Nantucket's first tourist?" HN, 39
        (Fall 1991), 41-44.
        1852 visit.

2552.   BERCAW, MARY K. "'A fine, boisterous something':
        Nantucket in Moby-Dick." HN, 39 (Fall 1991), 55-58.

2553.   BURCH, DOUGLAS K. "His work was his hobby." HN, 39
        (Winter 1991), 64-66.
        Dr. Wylie L. Collins (1899-1991), a Nantucket physician.

2554.   _____. "Nantucket: 90 proof." HN, 42 (Winter 1993/1994),
        61-62.
        Bootlegging during Prohibition.

2555.   BURNE, LEE RAND. "The Sconset School of Opinion."
        HN, 41 (Summer 1993), 27-29.
        A "summer school for intellectual discussion."

2556.   CARLSON, CATHERINE C. "Seasonality of fish remains
        from locus Q-6 of the Quidnet site, Nantucket Island,
        Massachusetts." MASB, 51 (Apr. 1990), 2-14.
        Prehistoric site.

2557.   COFFIN, E. W. "Reflections on Tuckernuck." HN, 38
        (Spring 1990), 10-14.
        Tuckernuck Island in the 1920s.

2558.   CRAIG, JOAN PENNOCK. "'Sconset in comparison." HN,
        38 (Fall 1990), 43-44.
        Comparisons between the 1920s-1930s era and the
        present.

2559.   CROSS, ROBERT F. "The day the president came to
        Nantucket." HN, 40 (Summer 1992), 31-34.
        Franklin D. Roosevelt (1933).

2560.   _____. "No reserved seats for the mighty." HN, 41 (Summer
        1993), 24-26.
        Wharf Rat Club.

2561.   DODSON, JAMES. "The ditch that divided Nantucket."
        Yankee, 56 (Apr. 1992), 80-87, 116, 118, 120.
        Illegal attempt to dig a trench between Sesachacha Pond
        and the ocean (1988). See also entry 2596.

2562.   DUNWIDDIE, PETER W. "Forest and heath: the shaping of
        vegetation on Nantucket Island." Journal of Forest History,
        33 (July 1989), 126-133.

2563.   FORTENBERRY, MARK, and DIANE UCCI. "Piecing it
        back together." HN, 38 (Summer 1990), 20-23.
        Restoration of the Jethro Coffin House.

2564.   GAVIN, ALISON M. "Quaker revivals as an organizing
        process in Nantucket, Massachusetts, 1698- 1708." Quaker
        History, 79 (Fall 1990), 57-76.

2565.   GILBRETH, FRANK B. JR. "The Gilbreth 'bug- lights.'"
        HN, 39 (Summer 1991), 20-22.
        Lighthouses.

2566.   GOODE, GLORIA DAVIS. "African-American women in
        nineteenth-century Nantucket: wives, mothers, modistes, and
        visionaries." HN, 40 (Winter 1992), 76-78.

2567.   GORNICK, DOROTHY BOYER. "Maurice W. Boyer,
        Nantucket photographer." HN, 41 (Spring 1993), 7-9.
        Lived 1875-1938.

2568.   HANCE, WILLIAM A. "Naming streets and numbering
        houses: a personal account." HN, 37 (Apr. 1989), 26-31.
        Early 1980s.

2569.   HARING, JACQUELINE KOLLE. "'Captain, the lad's a
        girl!'" HN, 40 (Winter 1992), 72-73.
        1848 incident in which a woman disguised as a man
        shipped out on a whaling voyage.

2570.   HEFFERNAN, THOMAS FAREL. "Moby-Dick and
        Nantucket's Moby Dick: the attack on the Essex." HN, 39
        (Fall 1991), 45-47.
        The sinking of a Nantucket whaleship as a model for
        Herman Melville's novel.

2571.   LACOUTURE, JOHN. "Early aviation on Nantucket." HN,
        40 (Spring 1992), 12-15.

2572.   _____. "Siasconset wireless stations." HN, 38 (Fall 1990),
        36-39.
        1901-1922.

2573.   LAIRD, MARNIE. "Back to the wind." Early American
        Life, 22 (June 1991), 22-29.
        Preservation of an 18th-century saltbox house.

2574.   LAMB, JANE. Wauwinet: as it was, is now, and ever shall
        be! n.p., 1990. vii, 95p. MWA. *
        Village on Nantucket.

2575   NANTUCKET

2575.   LANCASTER, CLAY. "Charles H. Robinson." HN, 38 (Fall 1990), 46-47; (Winter 1990), 52-55.
        Builder (lived 1829-1915), who "erected more structures than any contemporary island builder."

2576.   _____. Holiday island: the pageant of Nantucket's hostelries and summer life from its beginnings to mid-twentieth century. Nantucket: Nantucket Historical Association, 1993. xxii, 241p. MWA. *

2577.   LATHROP, JOHN C. "Camp Sankaty Head." HN, 37 (July 1989), 5-11.
        Caddy camp at Sankaty Head Golf and Beach Club (since 1930s).

2578.   LITTLE, ELIZABETH A. "Shawkemo chapter." MASB, 50 (Oct. 1989), 54-55.
        Massachusetts Archaeological Society.

2579.   LOGUE, BARBARA J. "In pursuit of prosperity: disease and death in a Massachusetts commercial port, 1660-1850." JSH, 25 (Winter 1991), 309-343.

2580.   MEDAGLIA, CHRISTIAN C., ELIZABETH A. LITTLE, and MARGARET J. SCHOENINGER. "Late woodland diet on Nantucket Island: a study using isotope ratios." MASB, 51 (Oct. 1990), 49-60.

2581.   MICHAEL, GAYL. "Celebrating Christmas, a look back." HN, 38 (Winter 1990), 59-61.

2582.   MILLER, RICHARD F. "The Island Guard." HN, 42 (Fall 1993), 46-47.
        Civil War militia unit.

2583.   NORLING, LISA. "Judith Macy and her daybook; or, Crèvecoeur and the Wives of Sherborn." HN, 40 (Winter 1992), 68-71.
        The daybook was for the years 1783-1805. See also entry 2590.

2584.   NYQUIST, CURTIS W. "'By my watch...which was a correct time piece': Gray v. Gardner and the arrival of the ship Lady Adams." Mystic Seaport, Log, 44 (Spring 1992), 3-9.
        Background of an 1821 decision by the state supreme court.

2585.   OGDEN, DAVID M. "My first visit to Nantucket." HN, 37 (Apr. 1989), 21-25.
        The author worked in a summer hotel in 1948.

2586.   PELRINE, DONALD. "The Indian sickness in the town of Miacomet." HN, 39 (Winter 1991), 67-69.
        1764 epidemic, which claimed much of the island's Indian population.

2587.   PHILBRICK, NATHANIEL. Away off shore: Nantucket Island and its people, 1602-1890. Nantucket: Mill Hill Pr., 1994. 300p. MNanHi.

2588.   _____. "'Every wave is a fortune': Nantucket Island and the making of an American icon." NEQ, 66 (Sept. 1993), 434-447.
        Whaling was the icon.

2589.   _____. "'I will take to the water': Frederick Douglass, the sea, and the Nantucket whale fishery." HN, 40 (Fall 1992), 49-51.
        Douglass and Nantucket's tradition of opposition to slavery.

2590.   _____. "The Nantucket sequence in Crèvecoeur's Letters from an American farmer." NEQ, 64 (Sept. 1991), 414-432.
        Published in 1782. See also entry 2583.

2591.   QUINN, WILLIAM P. "Black wake of Argo Merchant." Steamboat Bill, 45 (Fall 1988), 197-200.
        Oil spill following the grounding of a tanker in 1976.

2592.   ROSENTHAL, IRVING. "Nantucket's congregation by the sea." Kfari, 2 (June 1989), 10, 13.
        Congregation Shirat HaYam.

2593.   SHERMAN, HELEN WILSON. "Austin Strong." HN, 37 (Apr. 1989), 13-20.
        Playwright, yachtsman, and commodore of the Nantucket Yacht Club.

2594.   STACKPOLE, EDOUARD A. "The first gubernatorial visit to Nantucket." HN, 37 (July 1989), 25-31.
        Gov. Levi Lincoln Jr. (1825).

2595.   _____. "The Nantucket Historical Association: prelude to the launching." Historic Nantucket 43 (Spring 1994), 75-78.
        Published in commemoration on the society's centennial. Douglas K. Burch, ed.

2596.   TIFFNEY, WESLEY N. JR., and J. CLINTON ANDREWS. "Sesachacha & Sankaty." HN, 38 (Spring 1990), 4-6.
        History of pond, opening to the ocean. See also entry 2561.

2597.   UCCI, DIANE. "Greater Light's rippling reflection." HN, 39 (Summer 1991), 23-25.
        Historic house.

2598.   _____. "Summer rituals: Wauwinet to Tuckermuck." HN, 40 (Summer 1992), 25-27.

2599.   WHITE, BARBARA. "The integration of Nantucket public schools." HN, 40 (Fall 1992), 59-62.
        1840s.

2600.   WOOD, DAVID H. "Clinton Mitchell Ray: the last of the old-time basketmakers." HN, 43 (Spring 1994), 72-73.
        Died 1956.

2601.   WORTH, DAVID D. "One hundred years of water service on Nantucket." HN, 41 (Spring 1993), 4-6.

2602.   YOUNG, ROGER A. "Bicycles and Nantucket." HN, 40 (Spring 1992), 4-8.

        SEE ALSO entries 350, 1608, 1664, 1767, 2381, 2385.

NATICK (MIDDLESEX CO.)

2603.   MANDELL, DANIEL RICHARD. "'To live more like my Christian English neighbors': Natick Indians in the eighteenth century." WMQ, 3 ser. 48 (Oct. 1991) 552- 579.
        See also entry 2605.

2604.   TRAVISANO, THOMAS. "Emerging genius: Elizabeth Bishop and The Blue Pencil, 1927-30." Gettysburg Review, 5 (Winter 1992), 32-47.
        The poet's early writings in a school literary magazine.

2605.   VAN LONKHUYZEN, HAROLD W. "A reappraisal of the praying Indians: acculturation, conversion, and identity at Natick, Massachusetts, 1646-1730." NEQ, 63 (Sept. 1990), 396-428.

        SEE ALSO entries 1532, 1651.

NEW BEDFORD (BRISTOL CO.)

2606.   BLASDALE, MARY JEAN. Artists of New Bedford: a biographical dictionary. New Bedford: Old Dartmouth Historical Society, 1990. xiii, 220p. MB. *

2607.   DAVIS, LANCE EDWIN, ROBERT E. GALLMAN, and TERESA DUNN HUTCHINS. "Call me Ishmael—not Domingo Floresta: the rise and fall of the American whaling industry." Research in Economic History, Supplement 6 (1991), 191-233.
        New Bedford as the center of the industry.

2608.   FRIDAY, ALICE SUE. "The Quaker origins of New Bedford, 1765-1815." Ph.D. dissertation, Boston Univ., 1991. x, 588p. *
        Abstracted in DAI, 52:3A (1991), 972.

2609.   McMULLIN, THOMAS A. "Overseeing the poor: industrialization and public relief in New Bedford, 1865-1900." Social Service Review, 65 (Dec. 1991), 548-563.

2610.   NEW BEDFORD, MASS. ST. HEDWIG'S CHURCH. Commemorative diamond jubilee: St. Hedwig's Church, New Bedford, Massachusetts: October 9, 1983. New Bedford, 1983. [44]p. MB. *
        Roman Catholic.

2611.   PETRO, PAMELA. "The architecture of whaling: New Bedford, Massachusetts." Early American Life, 22 (Oct. 1991), 62-65.

2612.   RODRIGUES, ROSE PEARL. "Occupational mobility of Portuguese males in New Bedford, Massachusetts: 1870 to 1900." Ph.D. dissertation, New School for Social Research, 1990. vii, 248p.
        Abstracted in DAI, 52:2A (1991), 695.

        SEE ALSO entries 350, 1664, 1785.

NEW BRAINTREE (WORCESTER CO.)

2613.   FISKE, JEFFREY H. Wheeler's Surprise: the lost battlefield of King Philip's War. n.p.: Towtaid, 1993. 95p. MStuO. *
        1675 battle.

2614.   ROBBINS, MAURICE. "A copper artifact from New Braintree, Massachusetts." MASB, 52 (Spring 1991), 28-30.
        Indian artifact.

NEWBURY (ESSEX CO.)

2615.   BENES, PETER. "Sleeping arrangements in early Massachusetts: the Newbury household of Henry Lunt, hatter." DubSemPr (1987), 140-152.

        SEE ALSO entry 1641.

2616   NEWBURYPORT

NEWBURYPORT (ESSEX CO.)

2616.   GOODWIN, GEORGE W. (1848-1916). Tall ships of
        Newburyport: the Montana, the Whittier, the Nearchus;
        remembered by George W. Goodwin. Freda M. Abrams, ed.
        Yellow Springs, Ohio: Free Wind Pr., 1989. viii, 63p. M. *

2617.   VINOVSKIS, MARIS A. "Have we underestimated the
        extent of antebellum high school attendance?" History of
        Education Quarterly, 28 (Dec. 1988), 551-567.
            Newburyport (ca. 1860) as a case study.

NEWTON (MIDDLESEX CO.)

2618.   CHASE, JON. The fight for Newton Corner: a story of
        neighborhood development. Newton Corner, 1987. 79p. MB. *

2619.   MILLER, EDWARD DESMOND. "Fulfilling a mission:
        profiles of outstanding student-athletes at Boston College."
        D.Ed. dissertation, Boston College, 1990. 161p.
            Abstracted in DAI, 51:8A (1991), 2651.

2620.   PARKER, FRANKLIN P. "Neare about the falls." Wellesley:
        F.P. Parker, 1988. 101p. MBNEH. *
            Newton Lower Falls.

2621.   WARD, CARMEN WHEELER. "Hetty Shepard Wheeler:
        her leadership role at Pine Manor Junior College, 1916-
        1948." Ed.D. dissertation, Boston Univ., 1993. 242p.
            Abstracted in DAI, 54:2A (1993), 438-439.

        SEE ALSO entry 196, 1532, 1600, 1827.

NORTH ADAMS (BERKSHIRE CO.)

2622.   BURNS, DEBORAH E., and LAUREN R. STEVENS. Most
        excellent majesty: a history of Mount Greylock. n.p.:
        Berkshire County Land Trust and Conservation Fund, 1988.
        xi, 112, [3]p. MPB. *

2623.   BURNS, STEWART. "Capacitators and community: women
        workers at Sprague Electric, 1930-1980." Public Historian,
        11 (Fall 1989), 61-81.

2624.   DAY, JOSEPH C. Dew upon the mountains: a history of St.
        Francis of Assisi Parish, North Adams, Massachusetts. n.p.:
        Capital City Pr., 1989. 371p. MPB. *
            Roman Catholic.

2625.   GABRIELSKY, ROBERT PAUL. "The evolution of the
        Marshall Street mill complex in North Adams." HJM, 19
        (Winter 1991), 24-42.

2626.   SEIDER, MAYNARD. "The CIO in rural Massachusetts:
        Sprague Electric and North Adams, 1937-1944." HJM, 22
        (Winter 1994), 51-73.

2627.   WILNER, ROBERT. "Blackinton remembered." B&M
        Bulletin, 19:3 [1993] 6-11.
            Place in North Adams.

        SEE ALSO entry 1777.

NORTH ATTLEBOROUGH (BRISTOL CO.)

2628.   SHERMAN, RICHARD L. North Attleborough: an
        affectionate history. North Attleborough: Publications
        Committee of the Bicentennial Commission of the Town of
        North Attleborough, 1976. 134p. RHi. *

NORTHAMPTON (HAMPSHIRE CO.)

2629.   BLANCHARD, MICHAEL D. "The politics of abolition in
        Northampton." HJM, 19 (Summer 1991), 175-196.

2630.   CHAMBERLAIN, MARY AVA. "Jonathan Edwards against
        the antinomians and Arminians." Ph.D. dissertation,
        Columbia Univ., 1990. iii, 315p.
            Abstracted in DAI, 52:2A (1991), 572.

2631.   CHASE, LISA. "Imagining utopia: landscape design at
        Smith College, 1871-1910." NEQ, 65 (Dec. 1992), 560-586.
            Landscape architects and the development of the campus
        at Smith.

2632.   CONEY, CHARLES RANDOLPH. "Jonathan Edwards and
        the Northampton Church controversy: a crisis of
        conscience?" Ph.D. dissertation, Univ. of Texas, Arlington,
        1989. vii, 121p. *
            Abstracted in DAI, 50:11A (1990), 3625.

2633.   DILL, DAVID B. JR. "Pliny Earle and the Northampton
        Lunatic Hospital." HJM, 20 (Summer 1992), 143-159.
            Earle was superintendent of the hospital from 1864-
        1885.

2634.   DOWER, CATHERINE. Yella Pessl, first lady of the
        harpsichord: a life of fire and conviction. Lewiston, N.Y.:
        Edwin Mellen Pr., 1992. xv, 211p. MH. *
            Pessl settled in Northampton during the World War II era.

2635. DWYER, MARGARET CLIFFORD. "The U.S. Naval Reserve Midshipmen School, Northampton, 1942-1945." HJM, 22 (Winter 1994), 34-50.
For women reservists.

2636. EDWARDS, JONATHAN. The works of Jonathan Edwards. Perry Miller et al., eds. New Haven, Conn.: Yale Univ. Pr., 1957-. MH. *
10 vols. to date. Note: this item replaces entry 7309 in Vol. 8.

2637. ELLER, GARY STEVEN. "Jonathan Edwards: a study in religious experience and Eriksonian psychobiography." Ph.D. dissertation, Vanderbilt Univ., 1988. iii, 409p. *
Abstracted in DAI, 48:5A (1987), 1106.

2638. FLORENCE, Massachusetts, history, 1895-1985. Janice K. Koleszar, ed. [Northampton]: Book Committee of the Florence Civic and Business Association, 1986. xviii, [150], xxxi p. MW. *

2639. HOLBROOK, CLYDE A. Jonathan Edwards, the valley and nature: an interpretive essay. Lewisburg, Pa.: Bucknell Univ., 1987. 151p. MWA. *

2640. HUSBAND, PAUL EDWARD. "Church membership in Northampton: Solomon Stoddard versus Jonathan Edwards." Ph.D. dissertation, Westminster Theological Seminary, 1990. 297p. *
Abstracted in DAI, 51:5A (1990), 1653.

2641. JENSON, ROBERT W. America's theologian: a recommendation of Jonathan Edwards. N.Y.: Oxford Univ. Pr., 1988. xii, 224p. MWA. *

2642. LESSER, M. X. Jonathan Edwards. Boston: Twayne Publishers, 1988. xv, 153p. MWA. *

2643. LOCKWOOD, ALLISON. Touched with fire: an American community in World War Two. Northampton: Daily Hampshire Gazette, 1993. 179p. MA. *

2644. NOBLES, GREGORY. "The rise of merchants in rural market towns: a case study of eighteenth-century Northampton, Massachusetts." JSH, 24 (Fall 1990), 5-23.

See also entry 146, 576, 1757, 1820, 1824.

NORTHBRIDGE (WORCESTER CO.)

2645. GALEMA, ANNEMIEKE. "Transplanted network: a case study of Frisian migration to Whitinsville, Mass., 1880-1914." European Contributions to American Studies [Netherlands], 20 (1991), 174-194.
Immigrants from Friesland, a region of the Netherlands.

NORTHFIELD (FRANKLIN CO.)

2646. NORTHFIELD MOUNT HERMON NEWS (periodical). Centennial issue. Northfield, [1980?]. 33p. MDeeP.
Includes historical articles about the private school.

2647. NUTTER, KATHLEEN BANKS. "The builder Calvin Stearns: methods of survival in the rural economy." HJM, 18 (Winter 1990), 16-26.
Early-19th century.

NORTON (BRISTOL CO.)

2648. GOODBY, ROBERT G. "Recent research at the G.B. Crane site, Norton, Massachusetts." MASB, 54 (Fall 1993), 61-70.
Prehistoric site.

2649. HELMREICH, PAUL C. "Lucy Larcom at Wheaton." NEQ, 63 (May 1990), 109-120.
Diary, which the poet kept from Nov. 1859-May 1862, while she taught at what is now Wheaton College.

2650. _____. Wheaton College, 1834-1912: the seminary years. Norton: Class of 1949, Wheaton College, 1985. ii, 143p. MWA. *

2651. PERRY, SANDRA A. "Major changes in Wheaton College, 1835-1988: a chapter in American higher education for women." Ph.D. dissertation, Boston College, 1991. 183p.
Abstracted in DAI, 53:1A (1992), 82-83.

NORWELL (PLYMOUTH CO.)

2652. LEVEILLEE, ALAN D., and SUZANNE GLOVER. "An archaeological approach to a suspected 18th and 19th century graveyard: investigations along the North River, Norwell, Massachusetts." MASB, 53 (Fall 1992), 42-52.

2653   OAK BLUFFS

OAK BLUFFS (DUKES CO.)

2653.   "BATHING suits at Cottage City in the late 1800s." DCI, 35 (Aug. 1993), 30-34.

2654.   BAYLIES, HENRY. "The first week in the woods: the first chapter in the history of Martha's Vineyard Camp- meeting." DCI, 33 (Feb. 1992), 129-134.
         Reprint of an article first published in 1872, containing the author's recollections of the first camp meeting on the island in 1835.

2655.   "THE VINEYARD'S first airplane arrivals." DCI, 35 (Aug. 1993), 35-39.
         Hydroplanes (1919).

OAKHAM (WORCESTER CO.)

2656.   LYMAN, RICHARD B. JR. "'What is done in my absence?': Levi Lincoln's Oakham, Massachusetts, farm workers, 1807-20." AASP, 99 (Apr. 1989), 151-187.

SEE ALSO entry 1551.

ORLEANS (BARNSTABLE CO.)

2657.   SCHOFIELD, BILL. "The man who never slept." Yankee, 58 (Jan. 1994), 74-77.
         Bill-Ike Small (died 1939), an insomniac.

PALMER (HAMPDEN CO.)

2658.   CARROLL, MICHAEL. "Sundays in Pulaski Park." Yankee, 54 (July 1990), 44-50, 108-109.
         "Polka capital of New England," in Three Rivers.

PEABODY (ESSEX CO.)

2659.   NORRIS, CURT. "Everyone fell for Jessie Costello." Yankee, 55 (Aug. 1991), 66-71, 118-119.
         Costello was acquitted in a well-publicized trial for the murder of her husband (1933).

2660.   PEDROSA, EDITE CUNHA. "Talking in the new land." New England Monthly, 7 (Aug. 1990), 34-39, 79-81.
         Autobiographical. (The author emigrated from Portugal as a girl.)

PELHAM (HAMPSHIRE CO.)

2661.   BIGELOW, PAUL J. Disowned, disrupted, dissolved: the life and times of the Society of Friends (Quakers) in Pelham, Massachusetts, 1806-1870. 2d ed. Pelham, 1985. vii, 115p. MStuO. *

2662.   _____. Wrights and privileges: the mills and shops of Pelham, Massachusetts, from 1740 to 1937. Athol: Haley's, 1993. xi, 139p. MWA. *

PITTSFIELD (BERKSHIRE CO.)

2663.   NASH, JUNE C. From tank town to high tech: the clash of community and industrial cycles. Albany: State Univ. of New York Pr., 1989. x, 368p. MB. *

2664.   PITTSFIELD, MASS. HOLY FAMILY CHURCH. Holy Family Church, Pittsfield, Massachusetts, 1912-1987. n.p., [1987?]. 100p. MPB.
         Roman Catholic.

SEE ALSO entry 1660.

PLAINFIELD (HAMPSHIRE CO.)

2665.   PLAINFIELD, MASS. Bicentennial celebration: Plainfield, Massachusetts, 1784-1985. Plainfield, 1985. [60]p. M. *

SEE ALSO entry 1545.

PLYMOUTH (PLYMOUTH CO.)

2666.   BEAUDRY, MARY C., and DOUGLAS C. GEORGE. "Old data, new findings: 1940's archeology at Plymouth reexamined." American Archeology, 6:1 (1987), 20-30.

2667.   CAMPBELL, FREDERICK HOLLISTER. "Mrs. Warren's revolution: Mercy Otis Warren's perceptions of the American Revolution before, during and after the event." Ph.D. dissertation, Univ. of Colorado, 1993. 575p.
         Abstracted in DAI, 54:3A (1993), 1068-1069.

2668.   COLE, ADELAIDE M. "Mercy Otis Warren: a woman of substance." DAR Magazine, 119 (Mar. 1985), 180-182.

2669. DONNELLY, MARGUERITE ANNE. "Mercy Otis Warren (1728-1814): satirist of the American Revolution." Ph.D. dissertation, New York Univ., 1988. viii, 158p.
     Abstracted in DAI, 49:8A (1989), 2219.

2670. FRITZ, JEAN. "Mercy Otis Warren." Constitution, 1 (Winter 1989), 58-63.

2671. GEVITZ, NORMAN. "Samuel Fuller of Plymouth Plantation: a 'skillful physician' or 'quacksalver'?" Journal of the History of Medicine and Allied Sciences, 47 (Jan. 1992), 29-48.
     Died 1633.

2672. "GIFTS from our Mr. Spooner." Early American Life, 21 (Dec. 1990), 34-40.
     The Spooner House, an 18th-century dwelling, was left to the town by James Spooner (died 1954); it now belongs to the Plymouth Antiquarian Society.

2673. KIRK-SMITH, HAROLD. William Brewster, "the father of New England": his life and times, 1567-1644. Boston, England: Richard Kay, 1992. ix, 372p. MWiW. *

2674. LOVEJOY, DAVID SHERMAN. "Plain Englishmen at Plymouth." NEQ, 63 (June 1990), 232-248.

2675. MERTZ, ANNE MORRIS. "The saga of a journal: William Bradford's Of Plimoth Plantation." Mayflower Quarterly, 55 (Feb. 1989), 14-16.

2676. PETERSON, MARK ALLEN. "The Plymouth Church and the evolution of Puritan religious culture." NEQ, 66 (Dec. 1993), 570-593.

2677. SNOW, STEPHEN EDDY. Performing the Pilgrims: a study of ethnohistorical role-playing at Plimoth Plantation. Jackson: Univ. of Mississippi Pr., 1993. xxviii, 241p. MWA. *

2678. STEPPING stones: the Pilgrims' own story. Adelia White Notson and Robert Carver Notson, eds. Portland, Ore.: Binford & Mort Publishing, 1987. xxiii, 205p. MB. *

2679. THOMPSON, ROBERT C. "John and Priscilla." Mayflower Quarterly, 55 (Feb. 1989), 20-21.
     John Alden and Priscilla Mullins Alden.

     SEE ALSO entries 1692, 1708.

PROVINCETOWN (BARNSTABLE CO.)

2680. CLARK, EDIE. "Another Rose for Provincetown." Yankee, 53 (Jan. 1989), 68-71, 74, 120-122, 124, 126-127.
     Half-scale model of the racing vessel Rose Dorothea, built by Flyer Santos (1970s).

2681. EGAN, LEONA RUST. Provincetown as a stage: Provincetown, the Provincetown Players, and the discovery of Eugene O'Neill. Orleans: Parnassus Imprints, 1994. xvi, 296p. DLC. *
     1916.

2682. HAMMOND, EDWARD G. "The romantic Provincetown boat." Steamboat Bill, 49 (Spring 1992), 5-11.
     Steamboat service to Provincetown from Boston (1913-1936).

2683. LAPIDES, SUSAN. "Selling Miss Sandy." Yankee, 54 (Dec. 1990), 88-93, 130.
     The Rivers family and commercial fishing in Provincetown (20th century).

2684. ROLBEIN, SETH. "One more tow." Yankee, 55 (Oct. 1991), 66-71, 131-133.
     Sinking of a scallop boat in 1976.

2685. RYDER, RICHARD G. Old Harbor Station, Cape Cod. Norwich, Conn.: Ram Island Pr., 1990. 128p. MWA. *
     Built in Chatham in 1897; moved to Provincetown in 1977.

QUINCY (NORFOLK CO.)

2686. GELLES, EDITH B. "Gossip: an eighteenth-century case." JSH, 22 (Summer 1989), 667-683.
     Royall Tyler's courtship of the younger Abigail Adams (ca. 1782).

2687. MacMAHON, DARCIE A. Archeological collections management at Adams National Historic Site, Massachusetts. Boston: Division of Cultural Resources, North Atlantic Regional Office, National Park Service, U.S. Department of the Interior, 1991. viii, 173p. MWA. *

     SEE ALSO entries 1590, 1604.

2688   RANDOLPH

RANDOLPH (NORFOLK CO.)

2688.   SHAW, STUART BRADLEY. "Mary E. Wilkins Freeman:
realism, sentimentalism, and popular fiction." Ph.D.
dissertation, Univ. of Illinois, 1991. v, 297p. *
    Author Freeman lived 1852-1930. Abstracted in DAI,
52:7A (1992), 2557.

RAYNHAM (BRISTOL CO.)

2689.   WHITE, M. PATRICE. The history of Raynham. Taunton:
Drummond Printing, 1990. 98p. MBNEH. *

SEE ALSO entry 1724.

REHOBOTH (BRISTOL CO.)

2690.   ROBINSON, CHARLES. Asleep beneath the meadows: the
Indian archaeology of Rehoboth, Massachusetts. Providence,
R.I.: Universal Pr., 1992. 134p. RPPC. *

2691.   SNAPE, SUE ELLEN. Rising from cottages. Rehoboth:
Rehoboth Constitutional Bicentennial Committee, 1990. viii,
103p. MBNEH. *
    Rehoboth history.

SEE ALSO entry 147.

REVERE (SUFFOLK CO.)

2692.   FORREY, ROBERT. "The architecture of Americanism: the
Revere Town Hall." EIHC, 126 (July 1990) 148-170.
    Built in 1898.

RICHMOND (BERKSHIRE CO.)

2693.   SILLIMAN, ROBERT H. "The Richmond boulder trains:
verae causae in 19th-century American geology." Earth
Sciences History, 10:1 (1991) 60-72.
    Geological feature that attracted the attention of a number
of leading scientists.

ROCKPORT (ESSEX CO.)

2694.   SCHWARTZ, JONATHAN. "'The quarries are silent': notes
on a Scandinavian community in New England." American
Studies in Scandinavia [Norway], 20:1 (1988), 15-26.

2695.   TWOMBLY, JOHN M. JR. Reflections from Rockport: the
life and accomplishments of artist Joseph L.S. Santoro. n.p.,
1988. 59p. InND. *

ROWE (FRANKLIN CO.)

2696.   WERTH, BARRY. "Windfall." New England Monthly, 6
(Nov. 1989), 38-43, 99.
    Rowe and the Yankee Atomic Electric Company plant.

SEE ALSO entry 1545.

RUTLAND (WORCESTER CO.)

2697.   MEAD, LESLIE A., and SALLY PENDLETON. The
Continental Barracks at Rutland: documentary research in
historical archaeology. [Boston]: Boston Univ. Graduate
School, 1988. iv, 84p. MWA.
    Revolutionary War site.

SEE ALSO entry 1751.

SALEM (ESSEX CO.)

2698.   BEDFORD, HENRY F. "Tenement houses in Salem: a report
for the Bureau of Statistics of Labor, 1873." EIHC, 128 (Jan.
1992), 3-16.

2699.   BESLAW, ELAINE G. "The Salem witch from Barbados: in
search of Tituba's roots." EIHC, 128 (Oct. 1992), 217-238.

2700.   BREMER, FRANCIS JOHN. "Endecott and the red cross:
Puritan iconoclasm in the New World." Journal of American
Studies [U.K.], 24 (Apr. 1990), 5-22.
    Capt. John Endecott's reaction in 1634 to news of a plan
to send a royal governor and establish episcopacy.

2701.   BROWN, DAVID C. "The forfeitures at Salem, 1692."
WMQ, 3 ser. 50 (Jan. 1993), 85-111.
    Legal issues involved in the seizure of property of
persons "accused or convicted of witchcraft."

2702. "THE BUNKIO Matsuki memoir (originally entitled in Japanese 'Moosu to Fenelosa: Bunkio Kaikoroku' ['Morse and Fenollosa: the Bunkio memoir'])." EIHC, 129 (Apr. 1993), 172-187.
Translated by Hina Hirayama. Bunkio Matsuki lived 1867-1940. See also entries 2725, 2730, 2748.

2703. BUTTERWORTH, JEFFREY A. "Simply stupendous: a century of exposition shoes, 1839-1939." EIHC, 127 (Apr. 1991), 138-160.
In the collections of the Essex Institute.

2704. CAHILL, ROBERT ELLIS. The horrors of Salem's witch dungeon (and other New England crimes and punishments). Peabody: Chandler-Smith Publishing House, 1986. 56p. *

2705. CANNON, S. "On parle francais a Salem, Massachusetts." Etudes Canadiennes [France], No. 22 (1987), 103-122.
History of Salem's Franco-American community.

2706. CHASE, THEODORE, and LAUREL K. GABEL. "James Ford (1721/2-81): Salem writing master and stonecarver." Peabody Essex Museum Collections, 130 (Jan. 1994), 5-17.

2707. _____. "John Holliman: eighteenth-century Salem stonecarver." EIHC, 128 (July 1992), 147-161.

2708. CHIPLEY, LOUISE. "'The best instruction of the people': William Bentley on the Congregational clergy and the republic, 1783-1819." EIHC, 127 (July 1991), 194-210.
Congregational minister and diarist.

2709. _____. "'Enlightened charity': William Bentley on poor relief in the early republic, 1783-1819." EIHC, 128 (July 1992), 162-179.

2710. _____. "The financial and tenure anxieties of New England's Congregational clergy during the early national era: the case of William Bentley, 1783-1819." EIHC, 127 (Oct. 1991), 277-296.

2711. COLLISON, GARY L. "Alexander Burton and Salem's 'fugitive slave riot' of 1851." EIHC, 128 (Jan. 1992), 17-26.

2712. COOK, ALBERT B. "Damaging the Mathers: London receives the news from Salem." NEQ, 52 (June 1992), 302-308.
Witchcraft trials (1692).

2713. DAILEY, BARBARA RITTER. "'Where thieves break through and steal': John Hale versus Dorcas Hoar, 1672-1692." EIHC, 128 (Oct. 1992), 255-269.
"Explores the connections between deprivation, theft, and witchcraft accusations."

2714. DAVIS, PATRICIA E. HOWERY. "Siding with the judges: a psychohistorical analysis of Cotton Mather's role in the Salem witchcraft trials." Ph.D. dissertation, Princeton Theological Seminary, 1991. v, 206p. *
Abstracted in DAI, 53:5A (1992), 1556.

2715. DEESE, HELEN R. "The Peabody family and the Jones Very 'insanity': two letters of Mary Peabody." Harvard Library Bulletin, 35 (Spring 1987), 218-229.
1838.

2716. "THE DEVIL hath been raised": a documentary history of the Salem Village witchcraft outbreak of March 1692. Richard B. Trask, ed. West Kennebunk, Me.: Phoenix Publishing, 1992. xxiv, 155p. MWA. *

2717. DEXTER, RALPH WARREN. "The role of E.S. Morse, director of the Peabody Academy of Science, in bringing zoology to Japan (1877-1883)." EIHC, 126 (Oct. 1990), 254-260.

2718. FRUIP, ELOISE, and FRITZ FRUIP. "Witch or saint?: the story of Mary Esty." DAR Magazine, 119 (May 1985), 378-381, 398.
Hanged in 1692.

2719. FYFFE, RICHARD C. "The uses of bibliography: early American imprints at the Essex Institute." EIHC, 125 (Oct. 1989), 274-287.
Article followed by Fyffe's "Catalogue of primarily unrecorded and unlocated American imprints, printed before 1801, in the Essex Institute," ibid., 288-328.

2720. GILDRIE, RICHARD P. "The Salem witchcraft trials as a crisis of popular imagination." EIHC, 128 (Oct. 1992), 270-285.

2721. GOODWIN, LORINDA BETH RODENHISER. "'A stately roof to shelter them': an historical archaeological investigation of the Turner family of eighteenth- century Salem, Massachusetts." Ph.D. dissertation, Univ. of Pennsylvania, 1993. 331p.
The family owned the "House of the Seven Gables." Abstracted in DAI, 54:3A (1993), 983.

2722. GRAGG, LARRY DALE. A quest for security: the life of Samuel Parris, 1653-1720. N.Y.: Greenwood Pr., 1990. xix, 214p. MB. *
Minister in Salem at the time of the witchcraft trials. See also entry 2740.

2723. _____. The Salem witch crisis. Westport, Conn.: Praeger Publishers, 1992. x, 228p. MWalB. *

2724   SALEM

2724.   _____. "'Under an evil hand.'" American History Illustrated, 27 (Mar./Apr. 1992), 54-59.
Witchcraft trials.

2725.   HIRAYAMA, HINA. "Curious merchandise: Bunkio Matsuki's Japanese department." EIHC, 129 (Apr. 1993), 216-231.
Matsuki was "head of the Japanese section of the Almy, Bigelow & Washburn department store in Salem" from 1890-1897. See also entries 2702, 2730, 2748.

2726.   KAMENSKY, JANE. "Words, witches, and woman trouble: witchcraft, disorderly speech, and gender boundaries in Puritan New England." EIHC, 128 (Oct. 1992), 286-307.

2727.   KERN, LOUIS J. "Eros, the devil, and the cunning woman: sexuality and the supernatural in European antecedents and in the seventeenth-century Salem witchcraft cases." EIHC, 129 (Jan. 1993), 3-38.

2728.   KIRBY, BRIAN S. "The loss and recovery of the schooner Amity: an episode in Salem maritime history." NEQ, 62 (Dec. 1989), 553-560.
1785.

2729.   KRIM, ARTHUR J. "Francis Peabody and Gothic Salem." Peabody Essex Museum Collections, 130 (Jan. 1994), 18-35.
Architect (lived 1801-1867).

2730.   LAHIKAINEN, DEAN. "Bunkio Matsuki's Japanese house in Salem, Mass." EIHC, 129 (Apr. 1993), 188-215.
Built 1893-1894. See also entries 2702, 2725, 2748.

2731.   _____. "The Gardner-Pingree House, Salem, Massachusetts." Antiques, 137 (Mar. 1990), 718-729.

2732.   LATNER, RICHARD B. "Witches, history, and microcomputers: a computer-assisted course on the Salem witchcraft trials." History Teacher, 21 (Feb. 1988), 173-194.
Course at Tulane Univ.

2733.   MALONEY, JOAN M. "John F. Hurley: Salem's first hurrah." EIHC, 128 (Jan. 1992), 27-58.
Hurley was the city's first Irish-American mayor (first elected in 1900) and its only mayor "recalled from office by popular vote."

2734.   McCAIN, DIANA ROSS. "The witches of Salem 300 years ago." Early American Life, 23 (Apr. 1992), 10-12, 17-18.

2735.   McCARL, MARY RHINELANDER. "Spreading the news of Satan's malignity in Salem: Benjamin Harris, printer and publisher of the witchcraft narrative." EIHC, 129 (Jan. 1993), 39-61.

2736.   MILLER, EDWIN HAVILAND. Salem is my dwelling place: a life of Nathaniel Hawthorne. Iowa City: Univ. of Iowa Pr., 1991. xviii, 596p. MBAt. *

2737.   MOORE, MARGARET B. "Sarah Savage of Salem: a forgotten writer." EIHC, 127 (July 1991), 240-259.
Early-19th century.

2738.   NYSTEDT, MARK. "A view of St. Peter's (Anglican) Church's first building in Salem, as it was from 1771 to 1833." Peabody Essex Museum Collections, 130 (Jan. 1994), 55-56.

2739.   ODEN, GLORIA. "The black Putnams of Charlotte Forten's journal." EIHC, 126 (Oct. 1990), 237-253.
The family of George Putnam, a hairdresser, was part of Salem's black community from 1845-1869.

2740.   PARRIS, SAMUEL. The sermon notebook of Samuel Parris, 1689-1694. James F. Cooper Jr. and Kenneth P. Minkema, eds. Boston: Colonial Society of Massachusetts, 1993. xii, 323p. MWA. *
See also entry 2722.

2741.   PAYNE, DANIEL G. "Defending against the indefensible: spectral evidence at the Salem witchcraft trials." EIHC, 129 (Jan. 1993), 62-83.

2742.   PESTANA, CARLA GARDINA. "The social world of Salem: William King's 1681 blasphemy trial." American Quarterly, 41 (June 1989), 308-327.
King "claimed to be the son of God."

2743.   RAILTON, ARTHUR R. "Did radical Roger Williams outwit businessman Mayhew?" DCI, 32 (May 1991), 181-187.
Incident during Thomas Mayhew's tenure as an agent for Gov. Matthew Craddock.

2744.   RICHMAN, MIRIAM. "History at home." Early American Life, 20 (Dec. 1989), 28-35.
A number of historic houses in Salem.

2745. ROBINSON, ENDERS A. The devil discovered: Salem witchcraft, 1692. N.Y.: Hippocrene Books, 1991. xvii, 382, [16]p. MB. *
See also next entry.

2746. _____. Salem witchcraft and Hawthorne's House of the seven gables. Bowie, Md.: Heritage Books, 1992. xiv, 374p. MBU. *
See also preceding entry.

2747. SCHAMBERGER, J. EDWARD. "The failure of 'a city upon a hill': architectural images in The scarlet letter." EIHC, 125 (Jan. 1989), 9-24.

2748. SHARF, FREDERIC A. "Bunkio Matsuki: 'Salem's most prominent Japanese citizen.'" EIHC, 129 (Apr. 1993), 135-161.
See also entries 2702, 2725, 2730.

2749. WARD, GERALD W. R. "The democratization of precious metal: a note on the ownership of silver in Salem, 1630-1820." EIHC, 126 (July 1990), 171-200.

2750. WATTERS, DAVID HARPER. "Hawthorne possessed: material culture and the familiar spirit of The house of the seven gables." EIHC, 125 (Jan. 1989), 25-44.

2751. YOOL, GEORGE MALCOLM. 1692 witch hunt: the layman's guide to the Salem witchcraft trials. Bowie, Md.: Heritage Books, 1992. 155p. MB. *

SEE ALSO entries 68, 81, 386-387, 1611, 1684, 1688, 1707, 1884, 1945, 2102, 2119.

SALISBURY (ESSEX CO.)

2752. EARLY Salisbury, Massachusetts: a collection of papers read at the Town Improvement Society, 1869-1900. Newburyport: Parker River Researchers, 1989. 12, 12, 8, 5p. MB. *

2753. WARREN, ROLAND L. Loyal dissenter: the life and times of Robert Pike. Lanham, Md.: University Pr. of America, 1992. 248p. MBU. *
Pike lived ca. 1616-1708.

SANDWICH (BARNSTABLE CO.)

2754. BARLOW, RAYMOND E., and JOAN E. KAISER. The glass industry in Sandwich. Windham, N.H.: Barlow-Kaiser Publishing, 1983-1989. 4v. MWA. *
Note: this item replaces entry 7833 in Vol. 8.

SAUGUS (ESSEX CO.)

2755. MacMAHON, DARCIE A. Archeological collections management at the Saugus Iron Works National Historic Site, Massachusetts. Boston: Division of Cultural Resources, North Atlantic Regional Office, National Park Service, 1988. 224p. MWA. *

SEE ALSO entries 1573, 1635.

SCITUATE (PLYMOUTH CO.)

2756. FREYMANN, JARVIS. Scituate's educational heritage, 1630-1990. Hanover: Scituate Historical Society, 1990. 360p. M. *

2757. SCITUATE, MASS. Scituate's heritage: the people who made it strong. Scituate, [1986?]. 42p. M. *

SHARON (NORFOLK CO.)

2758. WACHS, ELEANOR F. Deborah Sampson Gannett (1760-1827), America's first woman soldier: a source booklet. [Boston]: Office of the Massachusetts Secretary of State, 1990. 36p. M. *
American Revolution.

SHEFFIELD (BERKSHIRE CO.)

2759. COENEN, CHRISTOPHER. Sheffield, 1733-1983: a pictorial recollection. Sheffield: Sheffield 250th Anniversary Committee, 1983. 134p. MPB.

2760. SWAN, JON. "The slave who sued for freedom." American Heritage, 41 (Mar. 1990), 51-52, 54-55.
Mum Bett, slave of John Ashley (1781).

2761   SHREWSBURY

SHREWSBURY (WORCESTER CO.)

2761.   BAKER, ANDREW H., and HOLLY V. IZARD. "New
        England farmers and the marketplace, 1780-1865: a case
        study." Agricultural History, 65 (Summer 1991), 29-52.
            Ward family.

2762.   IZARD, HOLLY V. "The Ward family and their 'helps':
        domestic work, workers, and relationships on a New England
        farm, 1787-1866." AASP, 103 (Apr. 1993), 61-90.

2763.   LARKIN, JACK. "'Labor is the great thing in farming': the
        farm laborers of the Ward family of Shrewsbury,
        Massachusetts." AASP, 99 (Apr. 1989), 189-226

2764.   SMITH, JAMES FERRELL. "Artemas Ward." Harvard
        Magazine, 95 (May-June 1993), 62.
            See also next entry.

2765.   _____. "The rise of Artemas Ward, 1727-1777: authority,
        politics, and military life in eighteenth century
        Massachusetts." Ph.D. dissertation, Univ. of Colorado, 1990.
        vii, 277p. *
            Ward was Washington's second in command at the siege
        of Boston. Abstracted in DAI, 52:3A (1991), 1056.

        SEE ALSO entry 1551.

SOUTH HADLEY (HAMPSHIRE CO.)

2766.   CONFORTI, JOSEPH ANTHONY. "Mary Lyon, the
        founding of Mount Holyoke College, and the cultural revival
        of Jonathan Edwards." Religion and American Culture: a
        Journal of Interpretation, 3 (Winter 1993), 69-89.

2767.   MEEROPOL, ANN KARUS. "A practical visionary: Mary
        Emma Woolley and the education of women." Ed.D.
        dissertation, Univ. of Massachusetts, 1992. xiii, 508p. *
            Woolley (1863-1947) was president of Mount Holyoke.
        Abstracted in DAI, 53:10A (1993), 3459.

2768.   SHMURAK, CAROLE B., and BONNIE S. HANDLER.
        "'Castle of science': Mount Holyoke College and the
        preparation of women in chemistry, 1837-1941." History of
        Education Quarterly, 32 (Fall 1992), 315-342.

        SEE ALSO entries 1820, 1824.

SOUTHBOROUGH (WORCESTER CO.)

2769.   NOBLE, RICHARD E. Fences of stone: a history of
        Southborough, Massachusetts. Portsmouth, N.H.: Peter E.
        Randall, 1990. xvii, 419p. MW. *

SOUTHBRIDGE (WORCESTER CO.)

2770.   CAPILLO, JOE. More tales from Honest Town: memorable
        firsts and compendium of facts. [Peabody: Printed by Kwik
        Kopy, 1993] 32p. MSou.

        SEE ALSO entry 1838.

SOUTHWICK (HAMPDEN CO.)

2771.   HORSTMAN, JUDITH. "The Southwick jog." Yankee, 55
        (Apr. 1991), 57-64, 122, 124, 126.
            Area of the town that owes its inclusion in Southwick to an
        irregularity in the Massachusetts-Connecticut boundary line.

        SEE ALSO entry 1734.

SPENCER (WORCESTER CO.)

2772.   FISKE, JEFFREY H. History of Spencer, Massachusetts,
        1875-1975. Spencer: Spencer Historical Commission, 1990.
        748p. MWA. *

SPRINGFIELD (HAMPDEN CO.)

2773.   COLGLAZIER, GAIL NESSELL. Springfield furniture,
        1700-1850: "a large and rich assortment." Springfield:
        Connecticut Valley Historical Museum, 1990. 56p. MS. *

2774.   CONNECTICUT VALLEY HISTORICAL MUSEUM.
        Springfield fights the Civil War. Guy A. McLain, Martin
        Kaufman, and Joseph Carvalho III, eds. Springfield, 1990.
        214p. MShM. *
            Diaries and essays.

2775.   CONNIFF, RICHARD. "Hungry Hill." Yankee, 54 (Mar.
        1990), 58-64, 130-133.
            Irish neighborhood. Article includes historical
        information.

2776.   DeCESARE, LOUISE M. Archeological collections
management at the Springfield Armory National Historic
Site, Massachusetts. [Boston?]: Division of Cultural
Resources Management, North Atlantic Regional Office,
National Park Service, U.S. Department of the Interior, 1990.
ix, 73p. MWA. *

2777.   DEMERATH, NICHOLAS JAY III, and RHYS H.
WILLIAMS. A bridging of faiths: religion and politics in a
New England city. Princeton, N.J.: Princeton Univ. Pr., 1992.
xvii, 358p. MU. *
    Contemporary sociological study; includes historical
information.

2778.   KONIG, MICHAEL FRANCIS. A study in leadership:
Springfield and its mayors, 1945 to the present. Westfield:
Institute for Massachusetts Studies, Westfield State College,
1990. xiv, 53p. M. *

2779.   O'CONNELL, JAMES C., and MICHAEL FRANCIS
KONIG. Shaping an urban image: the history of downtown
planning in Springfield, Massachusetts. Joseph Carvalho III,
ed. Springfield: Connecticut Valley Historical Museum,
1990. 120p. CtHi. *

2780.   PRETOLA, JOHN P. "Keeping the faith in the west: 150
years of archaeology in Springfield." MASB, 51 (Oct. 1990),
83-85.
    Archaeological collections pertaining to the Connecticut
River Valley in the Springfield Science Museum.

2781.   PUTNAM, WILLIAM LOWELL. A Yankee image: the life
and times of Roger Lowell Putnam. West Kennebunk, Me.:
Phoenix Publishing, 1991. x, 158p. MBAt. *
    Putnam (1893-1972) was a successful businessman, a
public servant at the national level, founder of the Lowell
Observatory, and a mayor of Springfield.

2782.   STATI, PAUL. "Ideology and rhetoric in Erastus Salisbury
Field's The historical monument of the American republic."
Winterthur Portfolio, 27 (Spring 1992), 29-43.
    Painting (1867) in Springfield's Museum of Fine Arts.

2783.   WILLIAMS, RHYS H., and NICHOLAS JAY DEMERATH
III. "Religion and political process in an American city."
American Sociological Review, 56 (Aug. 1991), 417-431.
    See also entry 2777.

SEE ALSO entries 100, 1552, 1568-1569.

STERLING (WORCESTER CO.)

2784.   WHITE, FRANK G. "Sterling, Massachusetts: an early 19th
century seat of chairmaking." CEAIA, 44 (Dec. 1991),
114-115.

STOCKBRIDGE (BERKSHIRE CO.)

2785.   BASS, MILTON. "The Sedgwick pie." Yankee, 53 (June
1989), 74-79.
    Sedgwick family plot in the town cemetery, "laid out in
concentric circles, facing inwards." See also entry 2789.

2786.   CHAPMAN, GERARD. A history of the Red Lion Inn in
Stockbridge, Massachusetts. Bernard A. Drew, ed.
Stockbridge: The Inn, 1987. 52p. MB. *

2787.   FRAZIER, PATRICK. The Mohicans of Stockbridge.
Lincoln: Univ. of Nebraska Pr., 1992. xviii, 307p. MBAt. *
    Stockbridge Indians.

2788.   MILES, LION G. "The red man dispossessed: the Williams
family and the alienation of Indian lands in Stockbridge,
Massachusetts, 1736-1818." NEQ, 67 (Mar. 1994), 46-76.

2789.   SEDGWICK, JOHN. "The eternity club." New England
Monthly, 6 (Sept. 1989), 34-38, 111.
    Sedgwick family burial plot. See also entry 2785.

2790.   STOCKBRIDGE, MASS. The Stockbridge story, 1739-
1989; written and published by the people of Stockbridge,
Massachusetts. Stockbridge, 1989. xvii, 210p. M. *

SEE ALSO entries 1651, 1782.

STURBRIDGE (WORCESTER CO.)

2791.   FOTY, GERALDINE. "Recalling early Thanksgivings in
Sturbridge." On the Common [Sturbridge] (Nov. 1990),
25-26.

2792.   HOWARD, HUGH. "The Village historian." Early American
Life, 23 (Feb. 1992), 36, 65.
    John O. Curtis, then-director of the Curatorial Department at
Old Sturbridge Village, on the restoration of houses at the
Village since the 1960s.

2793.   IZARD, HOLLY V. "Bettering their lot." OSV, 31 (Spring
1991), 4-6.
    The movement of several farm families within the town
(19th century).

2794.   WORRELL, JOHN. "The shape of Pliny Freeman's life."
OSV, 32 (Spring 1992), 4-6.
    Historical archaeology at a farmsite in Sturbridge. (The
Freeman house is at Old Sturbridge Village.)

SEE ALSO entry 1838.

SUDBURY (MIDDLESEX CO.)

2795.   GARFIELD, CURTIS F., and ALISON R. RIDLEY. As
ancient is this hostelry: the story of Wayside Inn. Sudbury:
Porcupine Enterprises, 1988. xiv, 335p. MB. *

2796.   RICHARDSON, EXPERIENCE WIGHT. Diary of
Experience (Wight) Richardson, Sudbury, Mass., 1728-1782.
Ellen Richardson Glueck and Thelma Smith Ernst, comps.
n.p., 1978. 179p. MStuO. *

2797.   SCOTT, LAURA. Sudbury: a pictorial history. Norfolk, Va.:
Donning, 1989. 208p. MeHi. *

SUTTON (WORCESTER CO.)

2798.   BALTER, MARIE, and RICHARD KATZ. Nobody's child:
the Marie Balter story. (1987) Reading: Addison-Wesley,
1991. xxi, 203p. M. *
    Originally published under the title Sing me no sad songs.
Balter (born 1930) recovered from mental illness to become
a social worker in the Sutton State Hospital, where she had
been a longtime patient.

2799.   SMALL, NORA PAT. "Beauty and convenience: the
architectural reordering of Sutton, Massachusetts,
1790-1840." Ph.D. dissertation, Boston Univ., 1994. 329p.
    Abstracted in DAI, 54:7A (1994), 2355.

2800.   SUTTON HISTORICAL SOCIETY. A collection of Sutton
documents, 1720-1778. (1977) Rev. ed., Sutton, 1992. 40p. M. *
    Note: this item replaces entry 8112 in Vol. 8.

SWAMPSCOTT (ESSEX CO.)

2801.   WILKINSON, FRANCES PROCTOR. "The summer Calvin
Coolidge lived next door." Yankee, 55 (Aug. 1991), 84-85.
    At Little's Point (1925).

TAUNTON (BRISTOL CO.)

2802.   LOZIER, JOHN WILLIAM. Taunton and Mason: cotton
machinery and locomotive manufacture in Taunton,
Massachusetts, 1811-1861. N.Y.: Garland Publishing, 1986.
549p. MBU. *
    Published version of author's Ph.D. dissertation (Ohio
State Univ., 1978; entry 8120 in Vol. 8).

SEE ALSO entry 246.

TISBURY (DUKES CO.)

2803.   VAN RIPER, ANTHONY K. "Tisbury deaths and doctors
during the 1860s." DCI, 33 (Nov. 1991), 88-96.

TOPSFIELD (ESSEX CO.)

2804.   BOND, CHARLES LAWRENCE. Houses and buildings of
Topsfield, Massachusetts: an update of "The houses and
buildings of Topsfield, Massachusetts, 1902," by J.H. Towne.
[Topsfield], 1989. viii, 347p. MWA. *
    Towne's work is entry 12520 in the Massachusetts
volume.

TOWNSEND (MIDDLESEX CO.)

2805.   TOWNSEND HISTORICAL SOCIETY. Town of Townsend,
incorporated June 19, 1732: 250th anniversary. Townsend,
1982. Unp. MBNEH. *

TYRINGHAM (BERKSHIRE CO.)

2806.   GILDER, CORNELIA BROOKE. Views of the valley:
Tyringham, 1739-1989. [Tyringham: Hop Brook Community
Club, 1989?] 143p. MPB.

2807.   MYERS, ELOISE. Tyringham, a hinterland settlement. 3d
ed. n.p.: Hinterland Pr., 1989. 122p. M. *
    Note: this item replaces entry 12576 in the Massachusetts
volume.

2808.   SCHULTZ, CHRISTINE. "Remembering the mystery pilot
of Tyringham." Yankee, 54 (Apr. 1990), 90-93.
    Mansell R. James, who disappeared after taking off from
a field in the town in 1919.

UXBRIDGE (WORCESTER CO.)

2809.   ARCHAEOLOGICAL excavations at the Uxbridge
Almshouse burial ground in Uxbridge, Massachusetts.
Ricardo J. Elia and Al B. Wesolowsky, eds. Oxford, England:
British Archaeological Reports, 1991. xiv, 382p. MWA. *

2810.   BELL, EDWARD L. "The historical archaeology of
mortuary behavior: coffin hardware from Uxbridge,
Massachusetts." Historical Archaeology, 24:3 (1990), 54-78.

2811.   ELIA, RICARDO J. "Silent stones in a potter's field: grave
markers at the almshouse burial ground in Uxbridge,
Massachusetts." Markers IX [1992], 133-157.

2812.   MASSACHUSETTS. DEPARTMENT OF
ENVIRONMENTAL MANAGEMENT. Crown and Eagle
Mills: historical preservation feasibility study. n.p., 1980.
14p. MStuO.
   Textile mill complex.

SEE ALSO entry 172.

WALPOLE (NORFOLK CO.)

2813.   McLAUGHLIN, MICHAEL, RUSSELL S. DYNDA, and
WARREN JAMISON. Screw: the truth about Walpole State
Prison by the guard who lived it. Far Hills, N.J.: New
Horizon Pr., 1989. xi, 321p. MB. *
   McLaughlin was the guard.

WALTHAM (MIDDLESEX CO.)

2814.   GLIEDMAN, JOHN A. "Brandeis University: reflections at
middle age." American Jewish History, 78 (June 1989),
513-526.
   The university had recently observed its 40th anniversary.

2815.   GRASS, JOHN. "Kilbourn & Proctor, Inc., 1970-1987."
NAWCCB, 31 (Dec. 1989), 507-509.
   Makers of "quality timepiece movements."

2816.   PETERSEN, KRISTEN A. Waltham rediscovered: an ethnic
history of Waltham, Massachusetts. Portsmouth, N.H.: Peter
E. Randall, 1988. xxix, 629p. MB. *

2817.   SACHAR, ABRAM LEON. A host at last. Boston: Little,
Brown, 1976. 308p. MBU. *
   History of Brandeis Univ.

2818.   TREESE, LORETTA. "The Gores of Gore Place." Early
American Life, 22 (Apr. 1991), 34-41.

SEE ALSO entries 438, 1600, 1828-1829.

WAREHAM (PLYMOUTH CO.)

2819.   RIDER, RAYMOND A. Life and times in Wareham over
200 years, 1739-1939. Wareham: Wareham Historical
Society, 1989. xi, 228p. MWA. *

WARREN (WORCESTER CO.)

2820.   PRETOLA, JOHN P. "The Paquette site: museum salvage
projects, collections and interpretation." MASB, 52 (Fall
1991), 59-67.
   Prehistoric site.

WARWICK (FRANKLIN CO.)

2821.   METCALF, HARLAN GOLDSBURY. Gold on Mount
Grace: boyhood adventures in long-ago Warwick. Athol:
Millers River Publishing, 1985. 63p. MDeeP. *
   Autobiographical account (early-20th century).

WASHINGTON (BERKSHIRE CO.)

2822.   CRANE, JOHN WRIGHT, and BENJAMIN F.
THOMPSON. A history of the town of Washington,
Massachusetts. Pittsfield: Berkshire Family History
Association, 1992. iv, 130p. MPB.
   Written ca. 1918.

2823.   WASHINGTON HISTORICAL COMMISSION.
1777-1977: two hundred years: the history of the town of
Washington, Massachusetts. Louise Elliot, ed. [Pittsfield:
Quality Printing, 1977] 182p. MPB. *

WATERTOWN (MIDDLESEX CO.)

2824.   ANDERSON, ROBERT CHARLES. "Early Watertown land
inventories." NEHGR, 144 (Apr. 1990), 147-150.
   Ca. 1643/1644.

2825 WEBSTER

WEBSTER (WORCESTER CO.)

2825. WEBSTER, MASS. ST. JOSEPH CHURCH. St. Joseph Parish centennial, 1887-1987. Webster, [1987?]. Unp. MB. * Roman Catholic. Text in English and Polish.

WELLESLEY (NORFOLK CO.)

2826. WARNER, PATRICIA CAMPBELL. "The comely rowers: the beginnings of collegiate sports uniforms for women crew at Wellesley, 1876-1900." Clothing and Textiles Research Journal, 10 (Spring 1992), 64-75.

SEE ALSO enty 2621.

WELLFLEET (BARNSTABLE CO.)

2827. ECHEVERRIA, DURAND. A history of Billingsgate. Wellfleet: Wellfleet Historical Society, 1991. iv, 126p. MWA. * Place in Wellfleet.

2828. ELIA, RICARDO J. "The ethics of collaboration: archaeologists and the Whydah project." Historical Archaeology, 26:4 (1992), 105-117.
On the ethics of involvement by archaeologists in a project to salvage the contents of a sunken pirate ship.

2829. McMANAMON, FRANCIS P., JAMES W. BRADLEY, and ANN L. MAGENNIS. The Indian Neck ossuary. Boston: Division of Cultural Resources, North Atlantic Regional Office, National Park Service, U.S. Department of the Interior, 1986. xiv, 183p. MWA. *
Archaeological study of an Indian burial site.

WENHAM (ESSEX CO.)

2830. WENHAM HISTORICAL SOCIETY. Wenham in pictures and prose. [Wenham, 1993] 139p. MWA. *

WEST TISBURY (DUKES CO.)

2831. HOWLAND, JOHN A. "History in a country graveyard." DCI, 30 (May 1989), 122-127.
West Tisbury Cemetery.

2832. "THE SINGING cop found his home here." DCI, 30 (May 1989), 128-129.
Edward J. McNamara, a frequent guest of actor James Cagney, was buried in West Tisbury following his death in 1944.

SEE ALSO entry 1786.

WESTBOROUGH (WORCESTER CO.)

2833. BEALES, ROSS WORN JR. "Literacy and reading in eighteenth-century Westborough, Massachusetts." DubSemPr (1987), 41-50.

2834. _____. "The Reverend Ebenezer Parkman's farm workers, Westborough, Massachusetts, 1726-82." AASP, 99 (Apr. 1989), 121-149.

2835. _____. "'Slavish' and other female work in the Parkman household, Westborough, Massachusetts, 1724-1782." DubSemPr (1988), 48-57.

2836. BRADLEY, JAMES W. "Archaeobotanical clues from Cedar Swamp, Westborough, Mass." MASB, 53 (Spring 1992), 31-39.
See also entry 2839.

2837. HOFFMAN, CURTISS R. People of the fresh water lake: a prehistory of Westborough, Massachusetts. N.Y.: Peter Lang, 1990. xvi, 304p. MW. *

2838. LEAF, JAMES GILLESPIE. "A history of the internal organization of the State Reform School for Boys at Westborough, Massachusetts (1846-1974)." Ed.D. dissertation, Harvard Univ., 1988. ii, 233p. M. *
Abstracted in DAI, 49:9A (1989), 2817.

2839. RHODIN, ANDERS G. J. "Chelonian zooarchaeology of eastern New England: turtle bone remains from Cedar Swamp and other prehistoric sites." MASB, 53 (Spring 1992), 21-30.
See also entry 2836.

SEE ALSO entries 1551, 1621.

WESTFIELD (HAMPDEN CO.)

2840. BROWN, ROBERT T. The rise and fall of the people's colleges: the Westfield Normal School, 1839-1914. Westfield: Institute for Massachusetts Studies, Westfield State College, 1988. xvi, 170p. MWA. *

2841. TAYLOR, EDWARD. The poems of Edward Taylor. Donald E. Stanford, ed. Chapel Hill: Univ. of North Carolina Pr., 1989. xli, 390p. MH. *
   The Puritan minister and poet.

   SEE ALSO entry 189.

WESTPORT (BRISTOL CO.)

2842. BROOKS, AMANDA LEE. "Captain Paul Cuffee (1759-1817) and the crown colony of Sierra Leone: the liminality of the free black." Ph.D. dissertation, Univ. of Chicago, 1988. iii, 315p. *
   Abstracted in DAI, 49:4A (1988), 921.

2843. GILLESPIE, JANET. "Beach plum time." Old RI, 2 (Oct. 1992), 27-29.
   Autobiographical.

WESTWOOD (NORFOLK CO.)

2844. MacMULLAN, JACKIE. "Keeping the streak alive." Yankee, 55 (Dec. 1991), 90-93, 126-127.
   The Westwood High School girls' basketball team and an 18-year winning streak in league play.

WEYMOUTH (NORFOLK CO.)

2845. CUDDY, TOM II, and RONALD W. HARRISON. "'Sowey': Naval Air Station, South Weymouth." American Aviation Historical Society Journal, 33:4 (1988), 282-289.
   Since 1942.

WILBRAHAM (HAMPDEN CO.)

2846. WILLIAMS, MELVIN G. "The ballad of Marcus Lyon: the story lives on." New York Folklore, 14 (Winter- Spring 1988), 123-131.
   1805 song about a famous murder, committed near Wilbraham, for which two Irishmen were later hanged.

WILLIAMSTOWN (BERKSHIRE CO.)

2847. NEWHALL and Williams College: selected papers of a history teacher at a New England college, 1917-1973. Russell H. Bostert, ed. N.Y.: Peter Lang, 1989. xiii, 403p. MB. *
   Richard Ager Newhall.

2848. WHITE, ROBERTA M. "Historical review: the parent movement to improve school nutrition in a New England town." Ed.D. dissertation, Univ. of Massachusetts, 1988. xii, 213p. *
   1946-1986. Abstracted in DAI, 49:8A (1989), 2066- 2067.

   SEE ALSO entry 128.

WILMINGTON (MIDDLESEX CO.)

2849. HILLS, DONALD G. "Lowell Junction, Massachusetts." B&M Bulletin, 17:2 (1990), 20-29.
   Railroad junction.

WINCHESTER (MIDDLESEX CO.)

2850. KNIGHT, ELLEN. "Music in Winchester, Massachusetts: a community portrait, 1830-1925." American Music, 11 (Fall 1993), 263-282.

WINDSOR (BERKSHIRE CO.)

2851. WINDSOR, MASS. Town of Windsor, 200th anniversary, incorporated July 4, 1771. n.p., [1971?]. 128p. M. *

WOBURN (MIDDLESEX CO.)

2852. CLARK, EDIE. "The mother everyone called crazy." Yankee, 54 (Apr. 1990), 84-88, 128, 130-131.
   Anne Anderson's campaign, eventually successful, to link the town's high rate of childhood leukemia to a tainted water supply (1970s and 1980s).

WORCESTER (WORCESTER CO.)

2853. AVERILL, LAWRENCE A. "Recollections of Clark's G. Stanley Hall." Journal of the History of the Behavioral Sciences, 26 (Apr. 1990), 125-130.
   Clark Univ. Reprinted from Oct. 1982 issue of same journal. See also entries 2869, 2877.

2854. BEAGLE, KIMBERLEE L. "How the Worcester County Mechanic's Association brought knowledge to the city of Worcester in 1842." Ph.D. dissertation, Worcester Polytechnic Institute, 1993. 165p. MWA.

2855   WORCESTER

2855.   BEALL, PAMELA E. Artworks in our parks: an inventory of public memorials, Worcester, Massachusetts. [Worcester]: Commonwealth Pr., 1986. 32p. MWA. *

2856.   COHEN, BRUCE. "Labor and the state in Worcester: organization of the metal trades, 1937-1971." HJM, 20 (Summer 1992), 160-177.

2857.   CRAVINS, GEORGES GUILLORY. "Industrial restructuring and its impact on communities and populations of northern mature regions: a case study of Worcester, Massachusetts, 1965-80." Ph.D. dissertation, Clark Univ., 1988. xii, 355p. *
        Abstracted in DAI, 49:7A (1989), 1917.

2858.   "EMERSON and the Worcester Lyceum, 1855-1857: two new letters." NEQ, 52 (June 1992), 290-295.
        Ralph Waldo Emerson. Kent P. Ljungquist and Wesley T. Mott, eds.

2859.   ESTUS, CHARLES W. "A Swedish working-class church: the Methodists of Quinsigamond Village, 1878- 1900." Swedish-American Historical Quarterly, 40 (Jan. 1989), 5-22.

2860.   _____, and JOHN F. McCLYMER. Gå till Amerika: Swedish creation of an ethnic identity for Worcester, Massachusetts. Worcester: Worcester Historical Museum, 1994. 173p. MW.

2861.   FRANKLIN, MARGERY B. "Reshaping psychology at Clark: the Werner era." Journal of the History of the Behavioral Sciences, 26 (Apr. 1990), 176-189.
        Heinz Werner was chairman of the psychology department at Clark Univ. from 1949-1960.

2862.   GAGNON, RICHARD L. Holy Name of Jesus Parish: 100 years in South Worcester. Worcester: D.M.I. Services, 1993. 101p. MWA.
        Roman Catholic.

2863.   GOSLOW, CHARLES BRIAN. "Fairground days: when Worcester was a National League city (1880-82)." HJM, 19 (Summer 1991), 133-154.
        National League of baseball. See also entry 2873.

2864.   HARGROVE, GORDON PAUL. "Changing roles for a settlement house in a New England city, 1965-1990." Ed.D. dissertation, Univ. of Massachusetts, 1992. xii, 235p. *
        Friendly House. Abstracted in DAI, 53:10A (1993), 3675.

2865.   HENDRICKSON, ELISE R. Worcester's gothic revival church tour. [Worcester, 1992] 14p. MWA.

2866.   KENDELL, RALPH R. The history of Pleasant Street Baptist Church: one hundred fiftieth anniversary, Worcester, Massachusetts, 1841-1991. [Worcester: Pleasant Street Baptist Church, 1991] Unp. MWA.

2867.   KOELSCH, WILLIAM ALVIN. "The 'magic decade' revisited: Clark psychology in the twenties and thirties." Journal of the History of the Behavioral Sciences, 26 (Apr. 1990), 151-175.
        Clark Univ.

2868.   KOLESAR, ROBERT J. "The politics of development: Worcester, Massachusetts, in the late nineteenth century." Journal of Urban History, 16 (Nov. 1989), 3-28.

2869.   KUMP, RICHARD JAY. "G. Stanley Hall's quest for excellence: his docent system at Clark University and the Humboldtian ideal." Ph.D. dissertation, Southern Illinois Univ., 1988. viii, 145p. *
        Hall became the founding president of Clark Univ. in 1888. Abstracted in DAI, 50:2A (1989), 373.

2870.   MEYER, WILLIAM B., and MICHAEL BROWN. "Locational conflict in a nineteenth-century city." Political Geography Quarterly [U.K.], 8 (Apr. 1989), 107-122.

2871.   MOYNIHAN, KENNETH J. "Swedes and Yankees in Worcester politics: a Protestant partnership." Swedish-American Historical Quarterly, 40 (Jan. 1989), 23-34.

2872.   O'TOOLE, JOHN M. Tornado! 84 minutes, 94 lives. Worcester: Databooks, 1993. 276p. MW. *
        1953 disaster.

2873.   PHELPS, RICHARD. "When Worcester was Major League; and baseball was in its infancy." Worcester Magazine, 18 (June 8-14, 1994), 14-16.
        Worcester Brown Stockings (late-19th century). See also entry 2863.

2874.   POWERS, VINCENT EDWARD. "Invisible immigrants": the pre-famine Irish community in Worcester, Massachusetts, from 1826 to 1860. N.Y.: Garland Publishing, 1989. xi, 549p. MA. *
        Published version of author's Ph.D. dissertation of same title (Clark Univ., 1976; entry 8439 in Vol. 8).

2875.   SAHAGIAN, ROBERT KREKOR. "Music in Worcester, Massachusetts, from colonial times through the nineteenth century." Ph.D. dissertation, Michigan State Univ., 1988. xii, 193p. MDeeP. *
        Abstracted in DAI, 49:10A (1989), 2860.

2876.   SHORR, MICHAEL J. Worcester's Victorian splendor. [Worcester]: M.J. Shorr, [1990]. 82p. MWA. *
        Victorian architecture.

2877. SOKAL, MICHAEL M. "G. Stanley Hall and the institutional character of psychology at Clark, 1889-1920." Journal of the History of the Behavioral Sciences, 26 (Apr. 1990), 114-124.
    See also entries 2853, 2869.

2878. VOULTSOS, MARY. Greeks in Worcester, Massachusetts. [Worcester]: Curry Printing and Copy Center, 1992. 4v. MWA. *

2879. WHITE, SHELDON H. "Child study at Clark University: 1894-1904." Journal of the History of the Behavioral Sciences, 26 (Apr. 1990), 131-150.

2880. WORCESTER, MASS. BLESSED SACRAMENT CHURCH. Blessed Sacrament Church, 1912-1987. [Worcester]: Heffernan Pr., 1988. 48p. MWA. *
    Roman Catholic.

    SEE ALSO entries 119, 135, 440, 1563, 1836, 2656, 3664.

WORTHINGTON (HAMPSHIRE CO.)

2881. WHITE, FRANK G. "Daniel T. Hewitt's house account." CEAIA, 46 (Mar. 1993), 29-30.
    Account for the building of a house (1820s).

WRENTHAM (NORFOLK CO.)

2882. DeAVILA, RICHARD T. "Ceasor Chelor and the world he lived in." CEAIA, 46 (June 1993), 39-42; (Dec. 1993), 91-97.
    Chelor, a slave, was an 18th-century planemaker.

YARMOUTH (BARNSTABLE CO.)

2883. MANGELINKX, PAUL R. "The Yarmouth Register and the emerging crisis over slavery." HJM, 18 (Winter 1990), 1-15.
    Newspaper (late-1830s and 1840s).

2884. VUILLEUMIER, MARION. The town of Yarmouth, Massachusetts: a history, 1639-1989. [South Yarmouth]: Historical Society of Old Yarmouth, 1989. x, 310p. MWA. *

2885. YARMOUTH, MASS. HISTORICAL COMMISSION. Yarmouth: old homes and gathering places. South Yarmouth, 1989. viii, 144p. MWA. *

New Hampshire

**Entries for the state as a whole
or pertaining to
more than one county**

2886. BAIRD, IRIS W. "Nash Stream: an auto tour of the true North Country with an account of the Sugarloaf Fire Outlook." Magnetic North, 8 (Autumn 1990), 23, 29- 34.

2887. BENNETT, EDWARD. Yankee editor. East Hebron: Pasquaney Pr., 1987. xii, 227p. NhHi. *
    On the author's career since World War II as a New Hampshire newspaper editor and legislator.

2888. BIRKNER, MICHAEL J. Revisiting the legend of Sherman Adams: he wasn't just Ike's gatekeeper. Concord: Concord Monitor, 1993. 5p. NhHi. *
    Former governor and aide to President Dwight Eisenhower. From the Concord Monitor (Apr. 18, 1993).

2889. BROCKWAY, LUCINDA A. "Rural districts: historic preservation as a new planning and management tool for New Hampshire." HNH, 45 (Summer 1990), 136-148.

2890. BROOKS, FRANKLIN. "The education of a New Hampshire philanthropist." HNH, 47 (Spring/Summer 1992), 3-32.
    Philanthropic activities in New Hampshire of Edward Tuck (1842-1938), a graduate of Phillips Exeter and Dartmouth. See also entry 3052.

2891. BROTHERSON, DEIRDRE A. "New Hampshire's statewide Historic Resources Survey Program." HNH, 45 (Summer 1990), 149-202.
    Includes a list of New Hampshire properties on the National Register of Historic Places through January 1990.

2892. BROUDER, EDWARD W. Granite and ether: a chronicle of New Hampshire broadcasting. Bedford: New Hampshire Association of Broadcasters, 1993. 97p. NhHi. *

2893. CALDWELL-HOPPER, KATHI. "The French connection." C&N, 1 (May 1991), 23-24.
    Franco-Americans in New Hampshire.

2894. _____. "Jeremy Belknap: White Mountain explorer." C&N, 2 (Oct. 1992), 60-61.
    Belknap lived 1744-1798.

2895. _____. "Ladies of the club." C&N, 3 (Feb. 1993), 52-53.
    New Hampshire Federation of Women's Clubs.

2896. _____. "The reign of the Wentworths." C&N, 2 (Apr. 1992), 14-16.
    Colonial governors.

2897. _____. "A ride on the snow train." C&N, 1 (Mar. 1991), 26-28.
    Train trips to the ski country (1930s and 1940s).

2898. CALLOWAY, COLIN GORDON. "Wamalancet and Kancagamus: Indian strategy and leadership on the New Hampshire frontier." HNH, 43 (Winter 1988), 264-290.
    Penacook Indian leaders (17th century).

2899. COLE, DONALD B. "The White Mountains in 1845: from the journal of Benjamin Brown French." HNH, 44 (Winter 1989), 202-225.
    Travel diary.

2900. COPELEY, WILLIAM. "Musical instrument makers in New Hampshire, 1800-1960." HNH, 46 (Winter 1991), 231- 248.

2901. CURRIER GALLERY OF ART. New Hampshire clocks, silver and furniture: a salute to Charles S. Parsons. Manchester, 1988. 36p. NhD. *

2902   NEW HAMPSHIRE

2902.   DODGE, TIMOTHY. "Crime and punishment in New Hampshire, 1812-1914." Ph.D. dissertation, Univ. of New Hampshire, 1992. xiv, 623p. NhHi. *
        Abstracted in DAI, 53:4A (1992), 1252.

2903.   DOTY, ROBERT M. By good hands: New Hampshire folk art. Manchester: Currier Gallery of Art, 1989. xii, 122p. MB. *

2904.   DRAVES, DAVID D. Builder of men: life in C.C.C. camps of New Hampshire. Portsmouth: Peter E. Randall, 1992. xiii, 414p. NhU. *
        Civilian Conservation Corps (1930s).

2905.   DUNCAN, DAYTON. Grass roots: one year in the life of the New Hampshire Presidential Primary. N.Y.: Viking, 1991. 436p. Nh. *
        1987-1988.

2906.   GARVIN, DONNA-BELLE, and JAMES LEO GARVIN. On the road north of Boston: New Hampshire taverns and turnpikes, 1700-1900. Concord: New Hampshire Historical Society, 1988. vi, 228p. NhHi. *

2907.   GOETZ, STEPHEN H. "The Ku Klux Klan in New Hampshire, 1923-1927." HNH, 43 (Winter 1988), 245-263.

2908.   GREGG, HUGH. The candidates: see how they run. Portsmouth: Peter Randall, 1990. xvii, 302p. NhD. *
        New Hampshire Presidential Primary. See also next entry.

2909.   _____. A tall state revisited: a Republican perspective. Nashua: Resources of New Hampshire, 1993. 307p. NhHi. *
        New Hampshire Presidential Primary. See also preceding entry.

2910.   HAYES, JAMES H. A select group of diverse New Hampshire historical personalities. Concord: Evans Printing, 1991. [8]p. NhHi.

2911.   HEALD, BRUCE D. Reminisce the valley: the Lakes Region of New Hampshire. Weirs Beach: Weirs Times Publishing, 1992. x, 135p. NhHi. *

2912.   HERITAGE: a North Country sourcebook. Susan B. Hawkins, comp. Gorham: Sun World Printing, 1993. var. p. NhHi.

2913.   HEWES, KIT. "Naming the notches." Magnetic North, 7 (Autumn 1989), 9-11, 14-15.
        Notches in the White Mountains.

2914.   JULYAN, ROBERT HIXSON, and MARY JULYAN. The place names of the White Mountains. (1980) Rev. ed. Hanover: University Pr. of New England, 1993. xix, 175p. Nh. *
        Note: this item replaces entry 8669 in Vol. 8.

2915.   KALKHOFF, RICHARD G. "Toasting the Constitutuion: New Hampshire's celebration of 1788." HNH, 43 (Winter 1988), 291-303.

2916.   LANE, CHARLES STUART. New Hampshire's first tourists in the lakes and mountains. Meredith: Old Print Barn, 1992. 191p. NhHi. *

2917.   LENDA, REX. "Credit and culpability: New Hampshire state politics during the Civil War." HNH, 48 (Spring 1993), 3-84.

2918.   MARVEL, WILLIAM. "Back from the gates of hell: the deadly campaign of the drafted militia." HNH, 44 (Fall 1989), 105-119.
        Civil War. Includes discussion of issues in state politics.

2919.   McCORMACK, MARGARET K. New Hampshire, the Granite State: history and government of New Hampshire. Keene: Ariel Printing, 1990. 83p. NhHi.

2920.   McGRATH, ROBERT. "New Hampshire observed: the art of Edward Hill." HNH, 44 (Spring/Summer 1989), 30-95.
        Catalog of paintings, with text. See also entry 2944.

2921.   McINTOSH, JIM. "And thereby hangs a trail." Magnetic North, 7 (Winter 1989), 19, 22, 24; (Spring 1990), 33-35; 8 (Winter 1990), 8-9, 11-12.
        The naming of ski trails in the White Mountains.

2922.   McINTYRE, FRANCES S. Women artists in the White Mountains, 1840-1940: selected works. Hanover: Dartmouth College, 1990. 16p. NhHi.

2923.   McKENZIE, ALEXANDER A. "Radio in the AMC huts." Appalachia, n.s. 48 (June 15, 1990), 16-29.
        Appalachian Mountain Club (White Mountains).

2924.   METCALF, ERIC NELSON. "In the snows of New Hampshire: rhetorical constructions of the political arena in the 1988 primary." Ph.D. dissertation, Univ. of Massachusetts, 1991. xxvi, 469p. *
        New Hampshire Presidential Primary. Abstracted in DAI, 52:2A (1991), 345.

2925.   MORLEY, LINDA. The western region, New Hampshire: a visual history. Norfolk, Va.: Donning, 1989. 224p. NhHi. *

2926.   MUDGE, JOHN T. B. Mapping the White Mountains: a history of the cartography of the White Mountains of New Hampshire, with reproductions of maps from the 16th to the 20th century. Etna: Durand Pr., 1993. Unp. NhHi. *

2927.   _____. The White Mountains: names, places & legends. Etna: Durand Pr., 1992. xxxiii, 187p. NhHi. *

2928. NEW HAMPSHIRE. BICENTENNIAL COMMISSION ON THE UNITED STATES CONSTITUTION. New Hampshire: the state that made us a nation: a celebration of the bicentennial of the United States Constitution. William M. Gardner, Frank C. Mevers, and Richard F. Upton, eds. Portsmouth: Peter E. Randall, 1989. xx, 273p. NhHi. *

2929. NEW HAMPSHIRE HISTORICAL SOCIETY. New Hampshire collections: a guide to our cultural heritage. Linda Betts Burdick, ed. Concord: New Hampshire Historical Society, 1992. xii, 141p. NhHi. *
    Includes the holdings of a number of institutions.

2930. _____. Shaping the land we call New Hampshire: a land use history. Richard Ober, ed. Concord, 1992. 96p. NhHi. *

2931. "NEW Hampshire chapter of American Institute of Architects." New Hampshire Architect, 4 (Aug. 1952), 7, 15-16.
    Historical sketch of the chapter and its predecessor, the New Hampshire Society of Architects (1934-1948). Includes a list of all members to date.

2932. NEWTON, SUSAN HENDEE. "A case study of the early history of the New Hampshire Alliance for Effective Schools and its school improvement program: the emergence of a state policy initiative." Ph.D. dissertation, Univ. of Connecticut, 1990. vi, 371p. *
    January 1986-January 1988. Abstracted in DAI, 51, No. 10A (1991), 3292-3293.

2933. PALMER, NIALL ANDREW. "The New Hampshire Primary: its role and influence in the American presidential nominating process." Ph.D. dissertation, Univ. of Bristol [U.K.], 1988. 360p.
    Abstracted in DAI, 50:11A (1990), 3726.

2934. PHILBROOK, DANA. "Lake Shore Railroad: the first forty years." B&M Bulletin, 16:4 (1989), 12-27.
    Southern shore of Lake Winnipesaukee.

2935. POPE, LAURA. "Puritan art on high." NHProfiles, 2 (Apr. 1991), 52-54.
    Congregational church steeples.

2936. POTTER, PARKER B. JR. "A way of thinking about historical archaeology in New Hampshire." Archaeology of Eastern North America, 21 (Fall 1993), 111-135.

2937. "RAILROAD collections at the New Hampshire Historical Society." HNH, 45 (Fall 1990), 235-252.
    Richard Schuster, comp.

2938. "REMEMBRANCES of times past." New Hampshire Bar Journal, 32 (Dec. 1991), 209-275.
    Interviews with senior judges and lawyers.

2939. ROBERTS, D. W. "Haunting memories." NHProfiles, 37 (Oct. 1988), 74-75, 131-132.
    Famous New Hampshire hauntings.

2940. SMITH, CHESTER M. JR., and JOHN L. KAY. The postal history of New Hampshire: the post offices and first postmasters from 1775 to 1985. Lake Grove, Ore.: The Depot, 1986. 158p. NhHi. *

2941. STAPLES, WALTER. "Harvesting hardwoods in the north woods." NHPremier, 4 (Feb. 1993), 34-36.
    Sawmills.

2942. THOMSON, MELDRIM. "'Live free or die.'" NHPremier, 1 (Oct. 1990), 44-45.
    John Stark, the Revolutionary War general.

2943. TOWLE, DONALD T. "New Hampshire: birthplace of the spiritual?" HNH, 45 (Winter 1990), 296-316.
    On the historical significance of several tune books of the 1790s and early 1800s, by men who were closely associated with Baptist revivals in the state.

2944. VOGEL, CHARLES. "Edward Hill (1843-1923): artist." HNH, 44 (Spring/Summer 1989), 5-24.
    Article followed by Charles Vogel, "Edward Hill (1843-1923): chronology," 25-29. See also entry 2920.

2945. WILDER, BRAD. History of the New Hampshire federal courts. Concord: [U.S. District Court, New Hampshire District], 1991. vii, 163p. NhHi. *

2946. WILDERSON, PAUL W. Governor John Wentworth & the American Revolution: the English connection. Hanover: University Pr. of New England, 1993. xiv, 364p. NhHi. *

2947. WOODLAND, WOODY. "A look back at primaries past." C&N, 2 (Feb. 1992), 36-38.
    New Hampshire Presidential Primary.

2948. YANKEE BOTTLE CLUB. Yankee glass: a history of glassmaking in New Hampshire, 1790-1886; with a brief history of the Yankee Bottle Club. Keene, 1990. xvi, 76p. NhHi. *

SEE ALSO entries 20, 27, 40, 73, 75-76, 119, 122, 129, 157, 180, 204, 222-224, 226, 230, 238, 245, 345, 347, 349, 353, 358, 388, 420, 430, 438, 465, 487.

New Hamphsire

Entries for Counties†

CHESHIRE COUNTY

2949. CENTRAL square and beyond: historical images of Keene and Cheshire County, by Bion H. Whitehouse. Portsmouth: Peter E. Randall, 1992. xix, 140p. NhHi. *

2950. KEENE STATE COLLEGE. THORNE-SAGENDORPH GALLERY. Elms, trolleys and horseless carriages: Cheshire County photographs (1906-1929) by Bion H. Whitehouse. n.p.: J.A. Wright, 1985. Unp. MDeeP.

2951. LAUFMAN, DUDLEY, and CORINNE NASH. Dick Richardson, old time New Hampshire fiddler. Compiled for the Historical Society of Cheshire County, Keene, New Hampshire. [Canterbury], 1992. viii, 70p. NhHi. *
　　Lived 1893-1981.

COOS COUNTY

2952. ROCKWELL, LANDON H. "Pinkham Notch and above." MtWObNB, 33 (Summer 1992), 43-46; (Fall 1992), 71-73; (Winter 1992), 117-121.
　　Author's recollections of hiking in the Presidential Range (ca. 1930s).

2953. STEARNS, MERTON J. "Experiences on the Berlin and Groveton branches in the early Forties." B&M Bulletin, 17:4 (1991), 6-18.
　　Branches of the Boston and Maine.

SEE ALSO entry 2886.

GRAFTON COUNTY

2954. BAILEY, ABIGAIL ABBOT. Religion and domestic violence in early New England: the memoirs of Abigail Abbot Bailey. Ann Taves, ed. Bloomington, Ind.: Indiana Univ. Pr., 1989. viii, 198p. NhHi. *
　　Bailey lived 1746-1815; her memoirs were first published in the latter year.

2955. CALDWELL-HOPPER, KATHI. "Before the tourists came." C&N, 1 (Nov. 1991), 10-12.
　　Logging camps in Lincoln and Woodstock.

2956. DANIELL, JERE. "Frontier and Constitution: why Grafton County delegates voted 10 to 1 for ratification." HNH, 45 (Fall 1990), 207-229.
　　U.S. Constitution (1788).

2957. FILLION, ROBERT G. Early Haverhill Warren roads: a history of roads between the Pemigewassett and the Connecticut rivers in Grafton County, N.H. Woodsville: Haverhill Heritage Books, 1991. 72p. NhHi. *

2958. HOYT, JOSEPH BIXBY. The Baker River towns. N.Y.: Vantage Pr., 1990. x, 373p. NhHi. *
　　Dorchester, Groton, Plymouth, Rumney, Warren, and Wentworth.

ROCKINGHAM COUNTY

2959. CUMMINGS, OSMOND RICHARD. Trolleys to Beaver Lake: a history of the Chester & Derry Railroad Association, 1891-1928. 2d ed. Forty Fort, Pa.: Harold E. Cox, 1990. 31p. NhHi. *
　　See also entry 1582 in the New Hampshire volume.

2960. WHITTEMORE, KATHARINE. "The shortest coast." Boston Globe Magazine (Sept. 6, 1992), 12-13, 20-24.
　　New Hampshire's seacoast. Article includes historical information.

SEE ALSO entry 346

---

† See the New Hampshire volume in this
series (1979) for a complete list of counties.

* Online Computer Library Center (OLCC) listings for
books and dissertations marked with this symbol may
include additional library locations.

New Hamphsire

Entries for Cities and Towns†

ACWORTH (SULLIVAN CO.)

2961. FRINK, HELEN H. These Acworth hills: a history of Acworth, New Hampshire, 1767-1988. Acworth: Town of Acworth, 1989. xiv, 402p. NhHi. *

ALBANY (CARROLL CO.)

2962. LEAVITT, MARY, and ANN CROTO. The Russell-Colbath House. Barbara G. McKenzie, ed. n.p.: White Mountains Interpretive Association, 1989. ii, 6p. NhAsh-DRuell.
    Historic house, built ca. 1831 and now owned by the U.S. Forest Service.

ALSTEAD (CHESHIRE CO.)

2963. FRINK, HELEN H. Alstead through the years: 1763-1990. Alstead: Alstead Historical Society, 1992. ix, 537p. NhHi. *

ALTON (BELKNAP CO.)

2964. ALTON OLD PHOTOGRAPH COMMITTEE. Alton: a town to remember. Wolfeboro: Kingswood Pr., 1987. 96p. NhAsh- DRuell.

2965. CALDWELL-HOPPER, KATHI. "Early transportion in Alton." C&N, 2 (Feb. 1992), 12-13, 16.

2966. CLARK, EDIE. "Florence Holway's story." Yankee, 57 (Apr. 1993), 90-95, 130-133.
    Elderly victim of a rape committed in 1991.

BARTLETT (CARROLL CO.)

2967. BURBANK, ROB. "Kearsarge firetower: last remaining lookout in the White Mountain National Forest is a link with the past." Appalachia, 49 (June 15, 1992), 34-40.

2968. CARROLL, AILEEN M. Bartlett, New Hampshire: in the valley of the Saco. West Kennebunk, Me.: Phoenix Publishing, 1990. ix, 209p. NhHi. *

2969. MORRELL, ROBERT S. Winds of imagination: Morrell family attraction's flight of fancy. N.Y.: Newcomen Society of the U.S., 1990. 24p. NhHi. *
    Storyland and Heritage New Hampshire.

BENTON (GRAFTON CO.)

2970. BEARDSLEY, HARTNESS. The Moosilauke summit house: with some account of other early mountain houses. n.p., [1992]. 53p. NhHi. *
    Mount Moosilauke. First published in 1937.

2971. BROWN, J. WILLCOX. Forest history of Mount Moosilauke. [Hanover]: Dartmouth Outing Club, 1989. 38p. NhHi. *

2972. CLOUGH, AMOS F. Journal of events whilst on the mountain, 1870. n.p., [1991]. [215]p. NhHi.
    Mount Moosilauke. Autobiographical.

2973. DRAKE, SAMUEL ADAMS. The Moosilauke carriage road. Warren: Warren Historical Society, [1992?]. 12p. NhHi.
    First published in 1882. (See entry 334 in the New Hampshire volume.)

---

† See theNew Hanpshire volume in this series (1979) for a complete list of cities and towns.

* Online Computer Library Center (OLCC) listings for books and dissertations marked with this symbol may include additional library locations.

2974. MOOSILAUKE RAVINE LODGE. Moosilauke Ravine Lodge: 50th anniversary celebration, 1939-1989. n.p., [1989?]. 175p. NhHi. *

BERLIN (COOS CO.)

2975. BOISVERT, RICHARD. "The Mount Jasper Lithic Source, Berlin, New Hampshire: National Register of Historic Places nomination and commentary." Archaeology of Eastern North America, 20 (Fall 1992), 151-165.

2976. ENO, R. D. "Jews of Berlin, New Hampshire: a once thriving community vanishing." Kfari, 2 (June 1989), 8-9.

2977. TAYLOR, WILLIAM L. "Documenting the history of an industrial city: the Brown Company photograph collection of Berlin, New Hampshire." IA, 19:1 (1993), 61-72.
Forest product industries.

SEE ALSO entry 2953.

BETHLEHEM (GRAFTON CO.)

2978. ENO, R. D. "The three faces of Bethlehem." Kfari, 3 (Sept. 1990), 8-10.
Jewish communities in the town.

CANAAN (GRAFTON CO.)

2979. STEARNS, MERTON J. "No. 332 take siding." B&M Bulletin, 19:1 [1993], 38-39.
Train wreck (1949).

CANTERBURY (MERRIMACK CO.)

2980. BORGES, RICHARD CORBIT. "The Canterbury Shakers: a demographic study." HNH, 48 (Summer/Fall 1993), 155-181.
See also next entry.

2981. _____. "The Canterbury Shakers: a demographic study." Ph.D. dissertation, Univ. of New Hampshire, 1988. xii, 237p. *
Abstracted in DAI, 50:6A (1989), 1780-1781.

2982. BOSWELL, MARY ROSE. "Women's work: the Canterbury Shakers' fancywork industry." HNH, 48 (Summer/Fall 1993), 133-154.

2983. CALDWELL-HOPPER, KATHI. "The Canterbury Shakers." C&N, 3 (Mar. 1993), 44-45.

2984. STARBUCK, DAVID R. "Canterbury Shaker Village: archeology and landscape." NHArcheol, 31 (1990), 1-163.

2985. _____. "Those ingenious Shakers!" Archaeology, 43 (July-Aug. 1990), 40-47.

2986. SWANK, SCOTT T., and SHERYL N. HACK. "'All we do is build': community building at Canterbury Shaker Village, 1792-1939." HNH, 48 (Summer/Fall 1993), 99-131.
Construction.

CARROLL (COOS CO.)

2987. SCHILD, GEORG MANFRED. "Bretton Woods and Dumbarton Oaks: American post war planning in the summer of 1944." Ph.D. dissertation, Univ. of Maryland, 1993. iv, 462p. *
The Bretton Woods conference was held in July. Abstracted in DAI, 54:6A (1993), 2300.

CHARLESTOWN (SULLIVAN CO.)

2988. BRUCE, NONA B., and BARBARA BULLOCK JONES. The fort at No. 4, 1740-1760. Charlestown: Old Fort No. 4 Associates, 1990. 14p. NhHi. *

2989. HALL, DONALD. "Carlton Fisk, won't you please come home?" Yankee, 56 (Sept. 1992), 78-82, 110.
Early years of the former Major League catcher.

2990. LATHROP, DONN HAVEN. "Duck soup, hawk stew, and scoggin for breakfast." Upper Valley, 7 (Nov./Dec. 1993), 40-43, 46-47.
On the captivity of Susanna Johnson, taken by Indians in 1754.

2991. "OLD Fort No. 4, Charlestown, N.H." New Hampshire Architect, 12 (Apr. 1961), 21-22.

CHESTER (ROCKINGHAM CO.)

2992. ANDERSON, CINDY. "The town that wouldn't back down." Yankee, 57 (June 1993), 60-65, 118, 120, 122.
Background and aftermath of a 1991 decision by the state supreme court, striking down a local zoning law.

SEE ALSO entry 2959.

CHESTERFIELD (CHESHIRE CO.)

2993.   DOMINICK, ANNE WESTBROOK. "Chesterfield's flamboyant flapper." NHProfiles, 4 (Apr. 1992), 42-44.
Madame Antoinette Sherri, a longtime summer resident, beginning in the 1920s.

COLEBROOK (COOS CO.)

2994.   GIFFORD, WILLIAM H. Colebrook: "a place up back of New Hampshire." (1970) Rev. ed. Colebrook: News and Sentinel, 1993. viii, 386, xv p. NhHi. *
Note: this item replaces entry 2096 in the New Hampshire volume.

CONCORD (MERRIMACK CO.)

2995.   CALDWELL-HOPPER, KATHI. "Concord's own countess." C&N, 1 (Jan. 1991), 26-27.
Sarah Thompson, Countess of Rumford.

2996.   _____. "The Great Emancipator visits Concord." C&N, 2 (Nov. 1992), 52-53.
Abraham Lincoln (1860).

2997.   _____. "A man & his students." C&N, 1 (July 1991), 18-21.
The Rev. Henry A. Coit and St. Paul's School.

2998.   _____. "A spiritual home." C&N, 1 (Mar. 1991), 44-45.
House in which Mary Baker Eddy once lived. See also entry 3011.

2999.   _____. "Upham-Walker House." C&N, 1 (Apr. 1991), 52-54.

3000.   COLBY, VIRGINIA L. Concord eastside: a history of East Concord, N.H. Warren: R.C. Brayshaw, 1993. 72p. NhHi. *

3001.   CONCORD, N.H. WESLEY UNITED METHODIST CHURCH. Wesley United Methodist Church: 25th anniversary, 1960- 1985. [Concord, 1985] [12]p. NhHi.

3002.   CORRIGAN, GRACE GEORGE. A journal for Christa: Christa McAuliffe, teacher in space. Lincoln: Univ. of Nebraska Pr., 1993. xiv, 191p. NhU. *
Killed in the 1986 Challenger explosion.

3003.   DODGE, TIMOTHY. "Hard labor at the New Hampshire State Prison, 1812-1932." HNH, 47 (Fall/Winter 1992), 113-146.

3004.   GARVIN, DONNA-BELLE. "Concord, New Hampshire: a furniture-making capital." HNH, 45 (Spring 1990), 8-87.
Article followed by a listing of "Furniture craftsmen, manufacturers and dealers working in Concord, New Hampshire, prior to 1901," 88-104. Deborah Tapley, comp.

3005.   _____. "Warde's Stone Warehouse: its early history." HNH, 47 (Fall/Winter 1992), 95-111.
Built in 1869-1870; recently acquired by the New Hampshire Historical Society.

3006.   GARVIN, JAMES LEO. "The creation of 'New Hampshire's temple of history.'" HNH, 47 (Spring/Summer 1992), 33-61.
The New Hampshire Historical Society building. See also next entry.

3007.   _____. "From a single stone: the portal sculpture of the New Hampshire Historical Society's building." HNH, 47 (Spring/Summer 1992), 62-84.
See also preceding entry.

3008.   HOWE, DENNIS E. "The origins of the Page Belting Company and nineteenth-century technology." HNH, 49 (Spring 1994), 3-23.
Established 1868. See also next entry.

3009.   _____. "The Page Belting Company: a study of 19th-century power transmission belting." IA, 19:1 (1993), 5-20.
See also preceding entry.

3010.   "JOHN Leach: Concord's first architect." New Hampshire Architect, 6 (Mar. 1955), 10-12.
Architect/builder, who came to Concord ca. 1825.

3011.   MONEYHUN, CHERYL P. "Pleasant View: a home for Mary Baker Eddy." Longyear Museum Quarterly News, 29 (Spring 1992), 433-438.
See also entry 2998.

3012.   SHAW, MARION G. "History of the Rolfe and Rumford Home." New Hampshire Architect, 8 (Sept. 1956), 18.
Home for girls, opened in 1880.

3013.   STARBUCK, DAVID R. "The timber crib dam at Sewall's Falls." IA, 16:2 (1990), 40-61.

3014.   VAN BECK, TODD W. The death and funeral of President Franklin Pierce. Cincinnati: Todd Van Beck, 1990. 35p. NhHi.
1869.

3015.   WHEELING, KEN. "The Abbot-Downing Company's 'Tally Ho' coaches." Carriage Journal, 29 (Spring 1992), 181-183.
19th century.

CONWAY (CARROLL CO.)

3016. BILLINGS, KATHARINE FOWLER. "The long road to save the Green Hills of Conway, New Hampshire: a personal memory of these hills and Anna Stearns." Appalachia, 49 (June 15, 1992), 54-59.

CORNISH (SULLIVAN CO.)

3017. CALDWELL-HOPPER, KATHI. "A little Big Apple." C&N, 1 (Oct. 1991), 14-16.
       Cornish art colony.

3018. VAN BUREN, DEBORAH ELIZABETH. "Landscape architecture and gardens in the Cornish colony: the careers of Rose Nichols, Ellen Shipman and Frances Duncan." Women's Studies [U.K.], 14:4 (1988), 367-388.
       Cornish art colony.

DEERING (HILLSBOROUGH CO.)

3019. JOHNSON, DONALD. Enduring faith: the history of the Deering Community Church, 1789-1989. [Deering], 1991. 371p. NhHi. *

DERRY (ROCKINGHAM CO.)

3020. ALLEN, MEL R. "The disciplined life." Yankee, 55 (Oct. 1991), 72-76, 134-139.
       Astronaut Alan Shepard's early years.

SEE ALSO entry 2959.

DIXVILLE (COOS CO.)

3021. CALDWELL-HOPPER, KATHI. "How a hotel bounced back." C&N, 2 (May 1992), 14-15.
       Balsams Grand Resort Hotel.

3022. TILLOTSON, THOMAS N. Tillotson Rubber Company, Inc.: the power of partnership. N.Y: Newcomen Society of the U.S., 1993. 19p. NhHi. *

DOVER (STRAFFORD CO.)

3023. NASH, ALICE N. "Two stories of New England captives: Grizel and Christine Otis of Dover, New Hampshire." DubSemPr (1989), 39-48.
       Mother and daughter, captured by Indians in 1689.

SEE ALSO entry 346.

DUBLIN (CHESHIRE CO.)

3024. CARVER, JANIE J. "Abbott Handerson Thayer." NHPremier, 4 (May 1993), 47-49.
       Painter (lived 1849-1921).

DURHAM (STRAFFORD CO.)

3025. REESE, K. M. "Lucy Swallow enters college." Chemical & Engineering News, 68 (May 14, 1990), 80.
       First woman student at the Univ. of New Hampshire (1891).

EFFINGHAM (CARROLL CO.)

3026. CALDWELL-HOPPER, KATHI. "Squire Lord's Great House." C&N, 1 (June 1991), 44-46.
       Isaac Lord.

SEE ALSO entry 3147.

ENFIELD (GRAFTON CO.)

3027. CALDWELL-HOPPER, KATHI. "The war of the Dyers." C&N, 1 (Dec. 1991), 10-12.
       Dispute over custody of their children after Mary Dyer left the Enfield Shakers in 1815.

3028. HESS, WENDELL. The Enfield (N.H.) Shakers: a brief history. n.p., 1993. 48p. NhHi.

EPPINGHAM (CARROLL CO.)

3029. HALL, LAWRENCE P. Tales of Eppingham. Gail H. Bickford, ed. Freedom: Freedom Pr. Associates, 1988. vii, 207p. NhHi. *

EPSOM (MERRIMACK CO.)

3030. HUME, PATRICIA W. "The Maurice Yeaton Farm site (NH 38-60)." NHArcheol, 32:1 (1991), 96-105.

FARMINGTON (STRAFFORD CO.)

3031. FARMINGTON, N.H. BICENTENNIAL HISTORY COMMITTEE. The history of Farmington, New Hampshire, from the days of the northwest parish of Rochester to the present time. Farmington: Foster Pr., 1976. 116p. NhHi. *

FITZWILLIAM (CHESHIRE CO.)

3032. DAVIS, LUCILLE PLANTE. A history of the churches of Fitzwilliam, New Hampshire (1765-1985). n.p., [1987?]. 135p. NhKe-Proper.

FRANCESTOWN (HILLSBOROUGH CO.)

3033. THULANDER, O. ALAN. KCO 366: the Francestown Volunteer Fire Department: fifty years of progress and service, a history written by the selfless efforts of countless men and women, 1937-1987. Peterborough: Transcript Printing, [1987?]. 24p. NhHi. *

FRANCONIA (GRAFTON CO.)

3034. McINTOSH, JIM. "Notes toward a history of the Forest Hills Hotel and Franconia College." Magnetic North, 7 (Summer 1989), 56-59, 62.
The college was in operation during the 1960s and 1970s.

FRANKLIN (MERRIMACK CO.)

3035. CALDWELL-HOPPER, KATHI. "The mills of Franklin." C&N, 3 (Jan. 1993), 44-45.
Textile mills.

FREEDOM (CARROLL CO.)

3036. DAVIDSON, GEORGE. A village pastor looks back: a history of the First Christian Church of Freedom, New Hampshire. Freedom: Freedom Press Associates, 1993. 109p. NhHi.

3037. FREEDOM, N.H. FIRST CHRISTIAN CHURCH. The First Christian Church of Freedom, New Hampshire, 1858-1978. n.p., [1978?]. 11p. NhHi.
Includes brief historical sketch.

GILFORD (BELKNAP CO.)

3038. CALDWELL-HOPPER, KATHI. "Story of a New England village." C&N, 2 (July 1992), 44-45.

GILMANTON (BELKNAP CO.)

3039. DODSON, JAMES. "Pandora in blue jeans." Yankee, 54 (Sept. 1990), 92-97, 132-134, 136-137.
Novelist Grace Metalious (author of Peyton place) and Gilmanton.

3040. GEDDES, FLORENCE. Lower Gilmanton church history. n.p.: J.J. Printing, 1977. 12p. NhHi.
History of the First Baptist Church of Gilmanton.

GOFFSTOWN (HILLSBOROUGH CO.)

3041. PERREAULT, ANNE-MARIE. "Edmond Pinard and Pinardville." American-Canadian Genealogist, 17 (Summer 1991), 112-113.

GRAFTON (GRAFTON CO.)

3042. CUSHING, KENNETH R. Isinglass, timber, and wool: a history of the town of Grafton, New Hampshire. Grafton: Kenneth R. Cushing, 1992. 398, [14]p. VtHi. *

HAMPTON (ROCKINGHAM CO.)

3043. RANDALL, PETER EVANS. Hampton: a century of town and beach, 1888-1988. Hampton: Peter E. Randall, 1989. 886p. NhHi. *

SEE ALSO entries 2890, 2960.

HANOVER (GRAFTON CO.)

3044. ALLEN, CHAUNCEY N. "Mem books revisited." DCLB, n.s. 30 (Nov. 1989), 17-26.
Memorabilia scrapbooks of Dartmouth alumni (ca. 1860s-1920s) in the college's special collections.

3045. BEACH, MARY FRAMPTON. "An analysis of the Dartmouth College case and its impact on the founding of American colleges and universities between 1819 and 1839." Ph.D. dissertation, Boston College, 1990. 175p.
Abstracted in DAI, 51:1A (1990), 85-86.

3046. BOOTH, PHILIP E. "Growing up green: a kaleidoscope of heroes." DCLB, n.s. 29 (Nov. 1988), 2-10.
Author was the son of a Dartmouth faculty member (1930s).

3047   HANOVER

3047.   BUCHSBAUM, TAMAR. "A note on antisemitism in admissions at Dartmouth." Jewish Historical Studies, 49 (Winter 1987), 79-84.

3048.   CALDWELL-HOPPER, KATHI. "Eleazar's triumphal failure." Concord North, 3 (Apr. 1993), 36-37.
        Eleazar Wheelock's vision for what became Dartmouth College.

3049.   _____. "A new kind of hospital." C&N, 1 (Aug. 1991), 22-24.
        Mary Hitchcock Hospital, dedicated in 1893.

3050.   COLLINS, JAMES. Mentors: noted Dartmouth alumni reflect on the teachers who changed their lives. Hanover: Dartmouth College, 1991. xi, 83p. NhD. *

3051.   CRAMER, KENNETH C. "Anyone for cricket?" DCLB, n.s. 33 (Nov. 1992), 27-29.
        A 1793 engraving depicts a game of cricket on the grounds of Dartmouth College.

3052.   _____. "Mr. Edward Tuck." DCLB, n.s. 33 (Nov. 1992), 25-27.
        Founding benefactor of Dartmouth's school of business administration. See also entry 2890.

3053.   DANKERT, CLYDE E. "The class of 1776." DCLB, n.s. 29 (Nov. 1988), 11-20.

3054.   DARTMOUTH COLLEGE. Dartmouth. David Bradley and Shelby Grantham, eds. Hanover: University Pr. of New England, 1990. 122p. NhD. *

3055.   DAVIS, ALLEN. "The Leonard cousins go to college: Dartmouth in the 1850s." DCLB, n.s. 31 (Apr. 1991), 50-60.
        Reeves and Leverett Leonard, of Fayette, Mo.

3056.   DODSON, JAMES. "A civil war in the wilderness." Yankee, 55 (June 1991), 80-85, 124-128.
        Dartmouth president James Freedman and the recent "ideological warfare" at the college.

3057.   DOUGLAS, JONATHAN. "Claims to fame." Dartmouth Medicine (Fall 1991), 22-25.
        Dartmouth medicine.

3058.   ENGLE, DEAN. "Rakes who climb." Dartmouth Alumni Magazine, 86 (Feb. 1994), 20-25.
        History of the Dartmouth Mountaineering Club.

3059.   GOLDMAN, SHALOM. "Biblical Hebrew in colonial America: the case of Dartmouth." American Jewish History, 79 (Winter 1989/1990), 173-180.

3060.   GRAHAM, ROBERT B. The Dartmouth story: a narrative history of the college buildings, people, and legends. Hanover: Dartmouth Bookstore, 1990. ix, 250p. Nh. *

3061.   _____. "A firm foundation." Dartmouth Medicine (Fall 1991), 14-21.
        On the history of academic medicine at Dartmouth and the role of the Mary Hitchcock Hospital.

3062.   HOEFNAGEL, DICK. "Benjamin Franklin and the Wheelocks." DCLB, n.s. 31 (Nov. 1990), 2-26.

3063.   _____. "The Paul Room at Baker Library." DCLB, n.s. 33 (Nov. 1992), 20-24.

3064.   _____, and JEFFREY L. HORRELL. "The Sherman Art Library fireplace-mantel: from Paris to Dartmouth." DCLB, n.s. 29 (Apr. 1989), 72-82.

3065.   HOOD MUSEUM OF ART, DARTMOUTH COLLEGE. From Titian to Sargent: Dartmouth alumni and friends collect: Hood Museum of Art, Dartmouth College, September 12-November 1, 1987. Hanover, 1987. xv, 150p. NhHi. *

3066.   JOHNSON, KEN. "The forfeit." Dartmouth Alumni Magazine, 83 (Oct. 1990), 16-18, 20.
        Fiftieth anniversary of a famous moment in Dartmouth football history. See also entry 3076.

3067.   KING, ALLEN L. "Dr. Rowell's clocks." DCLB, n.s. 33 (Nov. 1992), 11-19.
        Collection of clocks at Dartmouth, assembled by Hugh Grant Rowell (lived 1892-1963).

3068.   KLEIN, WOODY. "Glory days." Dartmouth Alumni Magazine, 81 (Nov. 1988), 36-38.
        Dartmouth football (1925).

3069.   LUNARDINI, ROSEMARY. "A century of minutes." Dartmouth Medicine (Winter 1992), 32-41.
        Gleanings from early records of medical faculty meetings.

3070.   MATTHEWS, LOUIS B. "Who was Mary Hitchcock?" Dartmouth Medicine (Spring 1990), 31-33, 49.
        The woman for whom the hospital was named.

3071.   McCORISON, MARCUS A. "Highly personal recollections of Harold Goddard Rugg." Vermont History News, 41 (Nov.-Dec. 1990), 110-114.
        Rugg (1883-1957), a longtime librarian at Dartmouth, was a noted book collector. See also entries 3724, 3839.

3072. MORRISSEY, CHARLES THOMAS. "Who persuaded Robert Frost to matriculate at Dartmouth?: the case of the mysterious alumnus." DCLB, n.s. 29 (Apr. 1989), 46-58.
Frost spent part of a freshman year at Dartmouth in 1892.

3073. PHI BETA KAPPA. ALPHA OF NEW HAMPSHIRE, DARTMOUTH COLLEGE. Alpha of New Hampshire, Phi Beta Kappa bicentennial celebration, 1787-1987. Hanover: Dartmouth College, 1987. 43p. NhD. *

3074. PUTNAM, CONSTANCE E. "George's college." Dartmouth Alumni Magazine, 81 (Feb. 1989), 21-23.
George Putnam's student days at Dartmouth at the beginning of the 20th century.

3075. RAY Nash and the Graphic Arts Workshop at Darmouth College: some reminiscences by his former students. Edward Connery Lathem, ed. Hanover: Friends of the Dartmouth College Library, 1987. 109p. NhD. *
Nash lived 1905-1982.

3076. SHRIBMAN, DAVID. "A matter of honor." Yankee, 54 (Nov. 1990), 90-93, 144-146.
1940 incident, in which Cornell's top-rated football team voluntarily forfeited to Dartmouth after it was found to have scored the winning touchdown on an illegal play. See also entry 3066.

3077. TILLINGHAST, TIG. "Two women, once alive." Dartmouth Alumni Magazine, 85 (Oct. 1993), 23-29.
1991 murder and its aftermath of two graduate students from Ethiopia.

3078. WIDMAYER, CHARLES E. John Sloan Dickey: a chronicle of his presidency of Dartmouth College. Hanover: Dartmouth College, 1991. 317, [8]p. NhD. *
President from 1945-1970.

3079. WILLIAMS, HENRY BEATES. Theatre at Dartmouth, 1769-1914: from Eleazar Wheelock to Walter Wanger. Hanover: Friends of the Dartmouth College Library, 1987. 183, [9]p. NhD. *

SEE ALSO entries 71, 128, 153, 184, 2890.

HARRISVILLE (CHESHIRE CO.)

3080. HAMAN, JAN RATHBUN. "Down by the old mill stream." NHProfiles, 38 (Aug./Sept. 1989), 50-54.
Workers' lives in the Harris Woolen Company; historic preservation of the village.

HAVERHILL (GRAFTON CO.)

3081. FILLION, ROBERT G. Faltering grange: a study of Moosilauke Grange #214, East Haverhill, N.H. [Woodsville], 1987. 39p. NhHi. *
Patrons of Husbandry.

3082. _____. From Number Six to the Oliverian: how East Haverhill came to be. [Woodsville], 1990. 68p. NhHi. *

3083. _____. Haverhill Corner National Historic District. (1988) Rev. ed. Woodsville: Haverhill Heritage Books, 1991. 65p. NhHi. *

3084. _____. Haverhill is 225 years old: in commemoration of the chartering of Haverhill, N.H., May 18,1763-1988. n.p., [1988?]. iv, 58p. NhHi. *

3085. RODGERS, HARRIET CARLETON. Haverhill Corner: reminiscences of Harriet Carleton Rodgers. Robert G. Fillion, ed. Woodsville: Haverhill Heritage Books, 1991. 60p. NhHi. *
Written ca. 1926.

SEE ALSO entries 210, 468, 2954, 2957.

HILL (MERRIMACK CO.)

3086. HILL HISTORICAL SOCIETY. Hill Village on the Pemigewasset: commemorating the 50th anniversary of the relocation of the village of Hill, New Hampshire. Hill, 1991. vi, 149p. NhHi. *

HILLSBOROUGH (HILLSBOROUGH CO.)

3087. "STONE arch bridges of Hillsboro." Granite State Architect, 5 (Feb. 1968), 22-23.

HOPKINTON (MERRIMACK CO.)

3088. HANSON, ROSALIND P. Life and times in Hopkinton, 1735-1970: condensed and updated. n.p., 1989. [89]p. NhHi.
See also Charles C. Lord, Life and times in Hopkinton... (1890; entry 3999 in the New Hampshire volume).

3089. HOPKINTON, N.H. ST. ANDREW'S EPISCOPAL CHURCH. The stained glass windows. Hopkinton, [1993?]. 46p. NhHi.

3090   JAFFREY

JAFFREY (CHESHIRE CO.)

3090.   BEAN, MARGARET C. "Jaffrey's Fortunes." NHPremier, 4 (Aug. 1993), 53-54.
        Amos and Violet Fortune, early black residents.

3091.   HEARING of the grand jury on the death of William K. Dean. Margaret C. Bean, ed. Jaffrey, [1990?]. 351p. Nh. *
        Unsolved murder (1918).

KEENE (CHESHIRE CO.)

3092.   HEFFERNAN, NANCY COFFEY, and ANN PAGE STECKER. Sisters of fortune: being the true story of how three motherless sisters saved their New England home and raised their younger brother while their father went fortune hunting in the California gold rush. Hanover: University Pr. of New England, 1993. xiv, 289p. NhHi. *
        Wilson family.

3093.   LEVIN, ROBERT ALAN. "Preparing elementary teachers: the University of Pittsburgh and Keene State College in historical perspective." D.A. dissertation, Carnegie-Mellon Univ., 1990. iv, 270p. MeU-P. *
        Abstracted in DAI, 51:1A (1990), 94.

        SEE ALSO entry 2949.

KILKENNY (COOS CO.)

3094.   BAIRD, IRIS W. "Mount Cabot and the fire tower." Magnetic North, 7 (Spring 1990), 7-13.

LACONIA (BELKNAP CO.)

3095.   CALDWELL-HOPPER, KATHI. "Glamour of a golden age." C&N, 2 (June 1992), 44-45.
        The Colonial Theatre.

3096.   CONCORD MONITOR (newspaper). Centennial celebration, 100 Laconia: together for tomorrow, 1893-1993. Concord, 1993. 15p.
        Supplement to the issue of May 16, 1993.

3097.   PHILBROOK, DANA. "The rise and fall of Lakeport Yard." B&M Bulletin, 19:1 [1993], 18-19, 22-29.
        Railroad yard.

LEBANON (GRAFTON CO.)

3098.   CALDWELL-HOPPER, KATHI. "Educating the Granite State's girls." C&N, 2 (Aug. 1992), 60.
        Tilden Seminary, West Lebanon (1855-1890).

        SEE ALSO entry 222.

LINCOLN (GRAFTON CO.)

3099.   TAYLOR, WILLIAM L. "Railroad in the wilderness: the East Branch & Lincoln Railroad, 1892-1948." HNH, 48 (Winter 1993), 187-213.
        Logging railroad.

        SEE ALSO entry 2955.

LITTLETON (GRAFTON CO.)

3100.   CALDWELL-HOPPER, KATHI. "History in stereo." C&N, 2 (Jan. 1992), 12-14.
        Kilburn Brothers Stereoscopic View Factory. See also next entry.

3101.   McSHANE, LINDA. "When I wanted the sun to shine": Kilburn and other Littleton, New Hampshire, stereographers. Littleton: Printed by Sherwin Dodge, 1993. vi, 121p. NhHi. *
        Benjamin and Edward Kilburn.

3102.   RAMSEY, FLOYD W. "The day the president came to town." Magnetic North, 7 (Winter 1989), 7-9, 13-15, 17.
        William Howard Taft, campaigning for re-election in 1912.

3103.   WILLEY, WILBUR W. A life that mattered. Lincoln: Glen Pr., 1988. 152p. NhU. *
        Georgia Willey (1892-1985).

3104.   _____. West of Littleton: a short history of the rural communities of Slate Ledge, Partridge Lake, Pattenville, and West Littleton, New Hampshire. Littleton: Wildwood West, 1992. 66p. Nh. *

LIVERMORE (GRAFTON CO.)

3105.   CRANE, PETER JOSEPH. "Glimpses of Livermore: life and lore of an abandoned White Mountains woods community." Ph.D. dissertation, Univ. of Pennsylvania, 1993. 568p.
        Abstracted in DAI, 54:12A (1994), 4546.

LOW AND BURBANK'S GRANT (COOS CO.)

3106. CRANE, PETER JOSEPH. "Madison—the rest of the story." MtWObNB, 30 (Summer 1989), 36-41.
One hundredth anniversary of the first public use of Madison Spring Hut.

LYME (GRAFTON CO.)

3107. THE HALL letters: describing the careers of 19th- century musicians D.C. Hall and Rhodolph Hall of Lyme, New Hampshire. Robert E. Eliason, ed. [Lyme], 1993. x, 428p. NhHi.

3108. OHL, ANDREA. "The Dennis Farm site: late and final woodland utilization in the Connecticut River drainage." NHArcheol, 32:1 (1991), 26-72.

3109. WING, HENRY N. A page from the past. [Lyme]: Lyme Historians, 1989. 17p. NhHi.

3110. WOOD, EVERETT W. Skiway: a Dartmouth winter tale. Hanover: Dartmouth College, 1987. xi, 54p. NhD. *
Dartmouth Skiway.

LYNDEBOROUGH (HILLSBOROUGH CO.)

3111. FLOWERS, CARL JR. "Boom and bust in New Hampshire: the Lyndeborough Glass Company, 1866-1888." HNH, 44 (Fall 1989), 120-137.

MANCHESTER (HILLSBOROUGH CO.)

3112. EATON, AURORE DIONNE. The Currier Gallery of Art: a history, 1929-1989. Manchester: Currier Gallery of Art, 1990. 77p. NhHi. *

3113. _____. A portrait in time: the story of the New Hampshire Insurance Group. n.p., [1989]. [16]p. NhHi.

3114. HAEBLER, PETER. "Nativism, liquor, and riots: Manchester politics, 1858-1859." HNH, 46 (Summer 1991), 67-91.

3115. HENGEN, ELIZABETH DURFEE. "Corporation housing at Amoskeag Manufacturing Company." HNH, 45 (Summer 1990), 117-135.

3116. KLETT, TOM. "A small bite of Manchester's history." NHPremier, 4 (Feb. 1993), 42-43.
The Post Office Fruit and Luncheonette.

3117. MANCHESTER, N.H. ST. RAPHAEL'S CHURCH. Saint Raphael's Church centennial year, 1888-1988, Manchester, New Hampshire. n.p., [1988]. 68p. NhHi.
Roman Catholic.

3118. MANCHESTER, N.H. TEMPLE ADATH YESHURUN. Temple Adath Yeshurun's centennial anniversary journal, 1891-1991. [Manchester, 1991] 100p. NhHi.

3119. NOVAK, MARIAN FAYE. "The men of Battery A." Yankee, 54 (Nov. 1990), 80-85, 152-156.
National Guard unit, one of only a few to be mobilized and sent to Vietnam (1968).

3120. PERREAULT, ROBERT B. The restoration and rededication of Weston Observatory, Oak Hill, Derryfield Park, Manchester, N.H. Manchester: Weston Observatory Restoration Committee, 1978. 31p. NhHi. *

3121. SAMSON, GARY. "Ulric Bourgeois (1874-1963): Franco-American photographer." HNH, 46 (Fall 1991), 131-154.

3122. SULLIVAN, GRACE L. "An analysis of the design, implementation, and utilization of the Manchester Instructional Television Project, Manchester, New Hampshire, 1988-1993." Ed.D. dissertation, Boston Univ., 1994. 283p.
Abstracted in DAI, 54:10A (1994), 3723.

MARLOW (CHESHIRE CO.)

3123. ALLEN, MEL R. "A father's secret." Yankee, 53 (Mar. 1989), 70-75, 122-124, 126, 128, 130-131.
Clifton Chambers's 1988 deathbed confession implicated his son, the local chief of police, in a 1978 murder.

MARTIN'S LOCATION (COOS CO.)

3124. RAMSEY, FLOYD W. "Dolly Copp: beyond the legend." Magnetic North, 6 (Winter 1988), 39-40, 42, 44-50.
See also entry 9642 in Vol. 8.

MEREDITH (BELKNAP CO.)

3125. CALDWELL-HOPPER, KATHI. "Summer on Bear Island." C&N, 1 (Sept. 1991), 10-12.
Popular as a resort (late-19th century).

3126   MEREDITH

3126.   VanVEGHTEN, RUDY. Filling the void: a history of the Meredith Public Library. Meredith: Meredith News, 1989. 112p. NhHi.

MILAN (COOS CO.)

3127.   BAIRD, IRIS W. "Milan Hill: the peripatetic fire tower." Magnetic North, 8 (Summer 1990), 12-16.

MONT VERNON (HILLSBOROUGH CO.)

3128.   MONT VERNON HISTORICAL SOCIETY. Historic Mont Vernon. Volume 1: households, 1750-1957. Freida C. Day, ed. Mont Vernon, 1990. Unp. NhHi. *

MOULTONBOROUGH (CARROLL CO.)

3129.   CALDWELL-HOPPER, KATHI. "The builder of a Castle in the Clouds." C&N, 2 (Sept. 1992), 60-61.
        Thomas Plant and the house he built.

3130.   CLARKE, FRED G. 1903-1993: Camp Tecumseh. West Kennebunk, Me.: Phoenix Publishing, 1994. x, 147p. NhHi. *
        Boys' camp.

3131.   GENNE, WILLIAM H. Geneva Point Center, 1919-1989: an historical appreciation. Moultonborough: Geneva Point Center, 1989. 83p. NhHi.
        Non-denominational religious camp and conference center on Lake Winnipesaukee.

3132.   KELLEY, BARBARA. Kona Farm: a showplace in Moultonborough, New Hampshire. Moultonborough: Harvest Pr., 1989. 60p. NhAsh-MRuell
        Summer estate on Lake Winnipesaukee.

NASHUA (HILLSBOROUGH CO.)

3133.   FLYTHE, JANE M. God's acre: a history of the Old South Burial Ground, Nashua, N.H. [Hollis]: Puritan Pr., 1988. 13p. NhHi.

3134.   GORDON, ROBERT B. "Machine archeology: the John Gage planer." IA, 17:2 (1991), 3-14.
        Ca. mid-19th century.

3135.   "THE INFAMOUS 1980 debate." C&N, 2 (Feb. 1992), 37, 39.
        The debate involved Ronald Reagan, George Bush, and other Republican candidates for president.

3136.   NASHUA, N.H. ST. STANISLAUS CHURCH. 75 years at St. Stanislaus, 1908-1983. Nashua, 1983. [172]p. MB. *
        Roman Catholic. Cover title.

3137.   WINSHIP, STEPHEN. A testiing time: crisis and revival in Nashua. Nashua: Nashua-New Hampshire Foundation, 1989. 208p. NhD. *
        On the rise and decline of the textile industry in Nashua.

        SEE ALSO entry 364.

NELSON (CHESHIRE CO.)

3138.   TOLMAN, F. B. More spit than polish at Tolman Pond. Dublin: Yankee Books, 1987. 144p. NhHi. *
        "An unlikely summer resort in the wilds of Nelson."

NEW BOSTON (HILLSBOROUGH CO.)

3139.   DAVIS, RENA. Under the firehouse roof: 144 years of fire fighting in New Boston, N.H., 1845-1989: a history of the New Boston Fire Department. n.p., [1990]. 68p. NhHi. *

NEW CASTLE (ROCKINGHAM CO.)

3140.   NEW CASTLE, N.H. TRICENTENNIAL CELEBRATION COMMITTEE. New Castle, New Hampshire: tricentennial, 1693-1993. [New Castle], 1993. 36p. NhHi. *

3141.   ST. JOHN, HELEN. From Mrs. Tredick's inn: more reminiscences of New Castle, New Hampshire. Portsmouth: Peter E. Randall, 1987. xii, 108p. Nh. *

3142.   _____. Inalong, outalong, downalong: reminiscences of New Castle, New Hampshire. Portsmouth: Peter E. Randall, 1985. 79p. NhHi. *

        SEE ALSO entries 346, 2960.

NEWBURY (MERRIMACK CO.)

3143.   ANDERSON, DAVID. "Landscape & legacy: the historic Hay estate begins its second century on Sunapee's rocky shore." Forest Notes, No. 187 (Mar./Apr. 1991), 8-11.
        John Hay Wildlife Refuge.

NEWPORT (SULLIVAN CO.)

3144.   GARVIN, DONNA-BELLE. "A 'neat and lively aspect':
Newport, New Hampshire, as a cabinetmaking center."
HNH, 43 (Fall 1988), 202-224.
Early-19th century.

OSSIPEE (CARROLL CO.)

3145.   BRIGDEN, THEODORE H. History of Water Village
Community Church, Ossipee, New Hampshire. Wolfeboro:
Kingswood Pr., 1978. 47p. NhHi.
Originally a Freewill Baptist church, organized in 1870.

3146.   DAVIDSON, GEORGE. The Ossipee Meeting House, 1801:
a brief historical sketch. n.p., 1985. 7p. NhHi.
Ossipee Town Meetinghouse, which became the Second
Congregational Church.

3147.   HIGGINS, MRS. HOWARD B. A history of the First Free
Will Baptist Church of Ossipee, Wakefield and Effingham.
n.p., 1981. 12p. NhAsh-DRuell.

3148.   OSSIPEE BICENTENNIAL BOOK COMMITTEE. Early
Ossipee: a pictorial view. Ossipee: Ossipee Bicentennial
Committee, 1976. [103]p. NhAsh-DRuell.

PETERBOROUGH (HILLSBOROUGH CO.)

3149.   GORDON, BEVERLY S. "From Peterboro to Hollywood."
NHPremier, 2 (Apr. 1992), 36-38.
Actress Bette Davis.

3150.   McGOLDRICK, LINDA CLARK. Nora S. Unwin: artist and
wood engraver. Dublin: William L. Bauhan, 1990. xxii,
183p. NhHi. *
Lived 1907-1982.

3151.   WARNTZ, CHRIS. "Some promises kept: the Peterborough
Town Library." Wilson Library Quarterly, 56 (Jan. 1982),
342-346.
"Oldest tax-supported library in the world."

PLAINFIELD (SULLIVAN CO.)

3152.   CHOICE white pine and good land: a history of Plainfield
and Meriden, N.H. Philip Zea and Nancy Norwalk, eds.
Portsmouth: Peter E. Randall, 1991. xviii, 677p. NhHi. *

PLYMOUTH (GRAFTON CO.)

3153.   CALDWELL-HOPPER, KATHI. "Of baseball & the Babe."
C&N, 1 (June 1991), 22-24.
D&M Baseball Factory, once a leading manufacturer of
baseball equipment.

SEE ALSO entry 2958.

PORTSMOUTH (ROCKINGHAM CO.)

3154.   BRIGHTON, RAY. Tall ships of the Piscataqua, 1830-1877.
Portsmouth: Portsmouth Marine Society, 1989. xx, 390p.
NhHi. *
Portsmouth ships and shipbuilding.

3155.   BROOKE, WILLIAM. "The fatal plunge of Engine 3666."
B&M Bulletin, 18:1 (1991), 38-39.
1939 train wreck.

3156.   CANDEE, RICHARD McALPIN. Building Portsmouth: the
neighborhoods & architecture of New Hampshire's oldest
city. Portsmouth: Portsmouth Advocate, 1992. viii, 200p.
NhHi. *

3157.   _____. "An old town by the sea": urban landscapes and
vernacular building in Portsmouth, NH, 1660-1990: a field
guide for tours of Portsmouth on Tuesday, May 14, 1992.
Portsmouth, 1992. vi, 155p. NhPoA.
See also entry 3177.

3158.   CUNNINGHAM, VALERIE. "The first blacks of
Portsmouth." HNH, 44 (Winter 1989), 181-201.
Dating back to 1645.

3159.   "A DIGNIFIED, well-built type of house." Granite State
Architect, 7 (June 1970), 26, 28-31.
Governor Goodwin House (1811), now a part of
Strawbery Banke.

3160.   ESTHUS, RAYMOND A. Double eagle and rising sun: the
Russians and Japanese at Portsmouth in 1905. Durham,
N.C.: Duke Univ. Pr., 1988. x, 265p. Nh. *
Treaty of Portsmouth.

3161.   GARVIN, JAMES LEO. "The Old New Hampshire State
House." HNH, 46 (Winter 1991), 203-229.
18th-century structure, dismantled in 1990.

3162.   GOSS, NANCY DOUTHAT. Families of the Moffatt-Ladd
House. [Portsmouth], 1993. 137p. NhHi.

3163   PORTSMOUTH

3163. HALL, ALVIN L. "Window to the past." NHProfiles, 37 (Nov. 1988), 45-47.
    Local landscape paintings of Sarah Haven Foster (lived 1827-1900).

3164. HANDLER, MIMI. "The everyday life of Mary Rider." Early American Life, 23 (Aug. 1992), 32-35.
    The home of Rider, a 19th-century Portsmouth resident, had recently been restored at Strawbery Banke.

3165. HARRINGTON, FAITH. "The emergent elite in early 18th century Portsmouth society: the archaeology of the Joseph Sherburne houselot." Historical Archaeology, 23: 1 (1989), 2-18.

3166. KAYE, MYRNA, and BROCK W. JOBE. "Robert Harrold, Portsmouth cabinetmaker." Antiques, 143 (May 1993), 776-783.
    Died 1792.

3167. LEAVENWORTH, STEPHEN. "Surrender in Portsmouth." NHPremier, 4 (Nov. 1993), 44-46.
    Surrender of four German submarines in May 1945, at the end of the war with Germany.

3168. MASURY, ANNE MANKIN. "Landscape and gardens." Antiques, 142 (July 1992), 117-121.
    At Strawbery Banke.

3169. "NEW Hampshire's three coastal forts." NHPremier, 3 (June 1992), 50-51.

3170. OPENO, WOODARD DORR. "The summer colony at Little Harbor in Portsmouth, New Hampshire, and its relation to the Colonial Revival movement." Ph.D. dissertation, Univ. of Michigan, 1990. xv, 278p. NhHi. *
    Colony of summer homes, many of which were owned by Boston residents and families having connections with Harvard Univ. Abstracted in DAI, 51:4A (1990), 1030.

3171. PORTSMOUTH furniture: masterworks from the New Hampshire seacoast. Brock Jobe, ed. Boston: Society for the Preservation of New England Antiquities, 1993. 454p. NhHi. *

3172. "PORTSMOUTH, its houses and its hostels." New Hampshire Architect, 5 (June 1954), 18-19.
    Includes brief historical sketches of some early houses.

3173. PRESERVE and conserve, share and play fair: the grocer and the consumer on the home front battlefield during World War II. Barbara McLean Ward, ed. [Portsmouth]: Strawbery Banke, 1993. 208p. NhPoA. *
    Abbott Store, now at Strawbery Banke.

3174. ROY, CAROLYN PARSONS. "Ceramics and glass." Antiques, 142 (July 1992), 105-109.
    At Strawbery Banke.

3175. ____. "Textiles and clothing." Antiques, 142 (July 1992), 111-115.
    At Strawbery Banke.

3176. SZASZ, FEREN M. "John Lord's Portsmouth." HNH, 44 (Fall 1989), 138-149.
    Lord (1813-1894) was a noted public speaker and the author of the Beacon Lights of History series.

3177. VERNACULAR ARCHITECTURE FORUM. Vernacular Architecture Forum, Tour II: 19th and 20th century landscapes of work, pleasure, and the industrial home. n.p., 1992. 87p. NhPoA.
    See also entry 3157.

3178. WARD, GERALD W. R. "Furnished houses." Antiques, 142 (July 1992), 77-89.
    At Strawbery Banke.

3179. ____. "Three centuries of life along the Piscataqua River." Antiques, 142 (July 1992), 61-66.
    As represented at Strawbery Banke.

3180. ____, and JOHN P. SCHNITZLER. "The buildings." Antiques, 142 (July 1992), 67-75.
    At Strawbery Banke.

3181. WARD, GERALD W. R., and KARIN E. CULLITY. "The furniture." Antiques, 142 (July 1992), 95-103.
    At Strawbery Banke.

3182. WARD, GERALD W. R., and RODNEY D. ROWLAND. "The metals." Antiques, 142 (July 1992), 91-93.
    In the Strawbery Banke collections.

3183. WETHERELL, CHARLES. "The letterbook of George Boyd, Portsmouth, New Hampshire, merchant-shipbuilder, 1773-1775." HNH, 46 (Spring 1991), 3-53; (Summer 1991), 91-125; (Fall 1991), 176-197.

3184. WHEELER, KATHLEEN LOUISE. "The characterization and measurement of archaeological depositional units: patterns from nineteenth-century urban sites in Portsmouth, New Hampshire." Ph.D. dissertation, Univ. of Arizona, 1992. 526p. *
    Abstracted in DAI, 53:11A (1993), 3965-3966.

3185. WINSLOW, RICHARD E. III. "Wealth and honour": Portsmouth during the golden age of privateering, 1775-1815. Portsmouth: Peter E. Randall, 1988. xx, 304p. NhPoA. *

SEE ALSO entries 174, 271-272, 346, 358, 2960.

ROXBURY (CHESHIRE CO.)

3186.   HANSEN, KAREN VYONNE. "'Helped put in a quilt': men's work and male intimacy in nineteenth-century New England." Gender & Society, 3 (Sept. 1989), 334-354.
　　　　The experiences of Brigham Nims (lived 1811-1893). See also entry 215 in this volume and entry 9892 in Vol. 8.

SALEM (ROCKINGHAM CO.)

3187.   BRERETON, CHARLES. "And they're off!" NHProfiles, 2 (June 1991), 44-45.
　　　　History of horse racing at Rockingham Park.

3188.   SYMES, JEFF. "Canobie Lake Park celebrates its 90th season." NHPremier, 2 (July 1992), 7-9.
　　　　Amusement park.

SALISBURY (MERRIMACK CO.)

3189.   SHAW, PAUL S. Historic Salisbury houses: a photographic and descriptive documentation of houses & buildings in Salisbury, New Hampshire. Concord: Town and Country Reprographics, 1993. Unp. NhHi. *

SANDOWN (ROCKINGHAM CO.)

3190.   HOLMES, RICHARD. A view from Meeting House Hill: a history of Sandown, N.H. Portsmouth: Peter E. Randall, 1988. xii, 451p. NhHi. *

SANDWICH (CARROLL CO.)

3191.   O'NEILL, LETITIA. "Family and community in transition: an analysis of three nineteenth century Sandwich, New Hampshire, families." Ph.D. dissertation, Univ. of Cincinnati, 1989. v, 304p. NhHi. *
　　　　Abstracted in DAI, 50:9A (1990), 3036.

3192.   SCRIBNER, JOHN WOODBURY. History of the Freewill Baptist Church of Center Sandwich: four sermons preached by Rev. John Woodbury Scribner, 1884. [Center Sandwich?]: Sandwich Historical Society, 1993. 61p. NhHi.

SARGENT'S PURCHASE (COOS CO.)

3193.   CLOUGH, ISABELLE. "Recollections of a Summit House employee from the late thirties." MtWObNB, 30 (Summer 1989), 43-44.
　　　　Mount Washington.

3194.   COOK, BRUCE. "Summit changes, 1959-1989." MtWObNB, 30 (Winter 1989), 97-98.

3195.   CRANE, PETER JOSEPH. "The death of Private William Stevens." MtWObNB, 33 (Fall 1992), 74-75.
　　　　On Mount Washington (1872). See also entry 3199.

3196.   _____. "Sylvester Marsh's other inventions." MtWObNB, 31 (Fall 1990), 57-61.
　　　　Marsh was the founder of the Mount Washington Cog Railway.

3197.   GORDON, GREG. "The hurricane of '38." MtWObNB, 29 (Fall 1988), 60-62.

3198.   _____. "Twenty years ago: the great blizzard of late February 1969." MtWObNB, 30 (Summer 1989), 48-49.

3199.   "A LATE note on an early mountain victim—the unknown soldier of Mount Washington." MtWObNB, 33 (Summer 1992), 46-50.
　　　　Pvt. William Seely (died 1873). See also entry 3195.

3200.   "LEATHER Lungs Mary." MtWObNB, 33 (Fall 1992), 76.
　　　　Toll collector on Mount Washington (before World War II).

3201.   LEICH, JEFFREY R. "Inside the Summit House." MtWObNB, 32 (Fall 1991), 65-70.

3202.   _____. "Possession of the summit 'a prolific subject of contention.'" MtWObNB, 31 (Summer 1990), 31-38.
　　　　See also entry 3211.

3203.   McKENZIE, ALEXANDER A. "Radio research at the Mount Washington Observatory." MtWObNB, 31 (Winter 1990), 89-93; 32 (Spring 1991), 5-8; (Summer 1991), 34-39.

3204.   NEMETHY, ANDREW. "Nightmare on Mount Washington." Yankee, 57 (Mar. 1993), 64-68, 118-119.
　　　　Winter climbing accident (1991).

3205.   PRESCOTT, PAUL. "Adventuring in 1941." MtWObNB, 30 (Spring 1989), 17-20.
　　　　On Mount Washington.

3206.   PUTNAM, WILLIAM LOWELL. The worst weather on earth: a history of the Mount Washington Observatory. N.Y.: American Alpine Club, 1991. xxi, 265, [32]p. Nh. *

3207.   "RESEARCH studies at the Mount Washington Observatory, 1943-53." MtWObNB, 29 (Winter 1988), 81- 85; 30 (Summer 1989), 34-35.

3208.   "S.B. HATCH, epigrapher." MtWObNB, 34 (Spring 1993), 5-6.
        Hiker, who carved his name on a stone on Mount Washington (1857).

3209.   SMITH, ALAN A. "Mapping the mountain: ten years of cartography on Mount Washington." Appalachia, 48 (Dec. 15, 1990), 18-30; (June 15, 1991), 69-80.

3210.   SPAULDING, J. LLOYD, and IRVING A. SPAULDING. "A second note on David O. Macomber." MtWObNB, 31 (Spring 1990), 9-11.
        First president of Mount Washington Road Company. See also entry 9997 in Vol. 8.

3211.   _____. "The struggle for Mount Washington's summit, 1858-1872: Henry B. Wells vs. Jackson Iron Manufacturing Company." Appalachia, 47 (Dec. 15, 1989), 42-63.
        Struggle over ownership. See also entry 3202.

3212.   WATERMAN, GUY. "Anniversary waltz in Pinnacle Gully: four climbing generations on Huntington Ravine's classic route." Appalachia, 48 (Dec. 15, 1990), 8-17.
        Mount Washington.

SEABROOK (ROCKINGHAM CO.)

3213.   ADAIR, STEPHEN D. "The culture of political economy: a social history of Seabrook Station." Ph.D. dissertation, Northeastern Univ., 1993. 338p.
        The nuclear power plant. Abstracted in DAI, 54:8A (1994), 3210.

3214.   BEDFORD, HENRY F. Seabrook Station: citizen politics and nuclear power. Amherst: Univ. of Massachusetts Pr., 1990. xxii, 224p. Nh. *

3215.   SEABROOK, N.H. FIRST METHODIST EPISCOPAL SOCIETY. 110th anniversary booklet, Smithtown Methodist Church, Smithtown, New Hampshire/First Methodist Episcopal Society of Seabrook, New Hampshire. Smithtown, [1946]. [9]p. NhHi.

3216.   STREAN, RICHARD MICHAEL. "Nuclear power politics." Ph.D. dissertation, Cornell Univ., 1993. 207p.
        Case studies of Seabrook and another nuclear power plant. Abstracted in DAI, 54:11A (1994), 4245.

SEE ALSO entry 2960.

SHARON (HILLSBOROUGH CO.)

3217.   COLLIER, ABRAM T. The secret of Sharon: an overview of the history and character of the town of Sharon, New Hampshire. Sharon: Bicentennial Committee, 1991. x, 68p. NhHi. *

STARK (COOS CO.)

3218.   CALDWELL-HOPPER, KATHI. "POWs at Camp Stark." C&N, 1 (Apr. 1991), 26-28.
        German prisoners (World War II).

STODDARD (CHESHIRE CO.)

3219.   RUMRILL, ALAN F. This silent marble weeps: the cemeteries of Stoddard, New Hampshire. Decorah, Iowa: Amundsen Publishing, 1990. 93p. NhHi. *

STRATHAM (ROCKINGHAM CO.)

3220.   NYLANDER, JANE C. "Provisions for daughters: the accounts of Samuel Lane." DubSemPr (1988), 11-27.
        18th century probate accounts.

TAMWORTH (CARROLL CO.)

3221.   BERGSTROM, RICHARD G. A history of the Chocorua Community Church, in celebration of our 200th anniversary, 1781-1981. n.p., [1981?]. 56p. NhHi.
        Originally a Freewill Baptist church (organized in 1781).

3222.   DAVIES, GERRY, and MARK SMITH. A history of Chocorua Public Library, 1888-1988. n.p., [1988?]. 16p. NhHi. *

3223. EWING, ROBERT, and CHARLES BOLIAN. "Argillite workshops in Tamworth, New Hampshire." NHArcheol, 32:1 (1991), 87-95.
    Prehistoric sites.

3224. TAMWORTH, N.H. Tamworth Old Home Week, 1906: greeting. Cambridge, Mass.: Caustic Claflin, [1906?]. 96p. NhWonO. *
    Includes historical sketches.

3225. _____. Tamworth Old Home Week, 1949. n.p., [1949?]. [28]p. NhWonO.
    Includes historical sketches.

WALPOLE (CHESHIRE CO.)

3226. ADAIR, JAMES R. The man from Steamtown: the story of F. Nelson Blount. Chicago: Moody Pr., 1967. 224p. VtHi. *
    Blount established the railroad museum.

3227. MANTERNACH, JOSIE. "The three faces of Walpole." Forest Notes, No. 197 (Spring/Summer 1993), 10-12, 20.
    History of land use in Walpole.

WASHINGTON (SULLIVAN CO.)

3228. JAGER, RONALD, and SALLY KRONE. "...A sacred deposit": the meetinghouse in Washington, New Hampshire. Portsmouth: Peter E. Randall, 1989. xii, 116p. NhHi. *

WEARE (HILLSBOROUGH CO.)

3229. WEARE HISTORICAL SOCIETY. Weare, New Hampshire: a visual history. Weare, 1990-1992. 4v. NhHi. *

WENTWORTH (GRAFTON CO.)

3230. MUZZEY, FRANCIS A. A history of Wentworth schools. n.p., [1991?]. 381p. Nh. *

3231. _____. Wentworth's reign of terror. n.p., 1992. 16p. NhHi.
    Series of arson-related fires (ca. 1861-1862).

SEE ALSO entry 2958.

WHITEFIELD (COOS CO.)

3232. "THE HOLZES of Whitefield, New Hampshire: sticking to their guns." Kfari, 1 (June 1988), 8-10.
    Oral history interview with proprietors of a gun shop.

WILTON (HILLSBOROUGH CO.)

3233. KENT, MARGARET. "Frye's Measure Mill." Early American Life, 22 (Feb. 1991), 34-37.
    Preservation of a late-19th-century mill and business.

WINCHESTER (CHESHIRE CO.)

3234. KAMMERAAD-CAMPBELL, SUSAN. Doc: the story of Dennis Littky and his fight for a better school. Chicago: Contemporary Books, 1989. xii, 403p. Nh. *
    Principal of Thayer High School.

WOLFEBORO (CARROLL CO.)

3235. AMERICA'S first summer resort: John Wentworth's 18th century plantation in Wolfeboro, New Hampshire. [Concord]: New Hampshire Archeological Society, 1989. iv, 129p. Nh. *
    NHArcheol, 30:1 (1989). David R. Starbuck, ed. See also entry 3238.

3236. FARRELL, JOHN ALOYSIUS. "A novel approach." Boston Globe Magazine (Nov. 17, 1991), 18-22, 24, 26, 28, 30.
    About George V. Higgins's 1991 novel, The Mandeville talent, and the 1962 murder of banker Joseph Melanson.

3237. MOORE, HARRISON. Historical sketch, the First Congregational Church, Wolfeboro, New Hampshire: 150th anniversary (June 17, 1834-June 17, 1984). [Wolfeboro]: First Congregational Church, 1984. 11p. NhHi.
    Organized in 1834.

3238. STARBUCK, DAVID R. "John Wentworth's frontier plantation in Wolfeboro, New Hampshire." HNH, 43 (Fall 1988), 181-201.
    The summer estate of the last royal governor, developed between 1768 and 1775. See also entry 3235.

3239   WOLFEBORO

3239.   WOLFEBORO, N.H. FIRST CHRISTIAN CHURCH. First
Christian Church, Wolfeboro, New Hampshire: one hundred
fiftieth anniversary, 1812-1962. n.p., n.d. [28]p. NhWol.
    Organized in 1812.

3240.   WOLFEBORO, N.H. ST. CECELIA'S CHURCH. History of
St. Cecelia's Catholic Church, Wolfeboro, N.H., presented at
the dedication of the new church, August 32, 1941. n.p.,
[1941?]. [19]p. NhWolHi.
    Since 1890s.

WOODSTOCK (GRAFTON CO.)

3241.   RAMSEY, FLOYD W. The night the bomber crashed: the
story of North Woodstock's famous World War II bomber
crash. n.p., [1990?]. [26]p. NhHi. *

3242.   SIEGER, KIRK. "The Pemi affair." Dartmouth Alumni
Magazine, 85 (Summer 1993), 26-29.
    The author was witness to a shooting in 1981.

SEE ALSO entry 2955.

Rhode Island

**Entries for the state as a whole
or pertaining to
more than one county**

3243. ADLER, EMILY STIER, and J. STANLEY LEMONS. The elect: Rhode Island's women legislators, 1922-1990. Providence: League of Rhode Island Historical Societies, 1990. xi, 262p. RHi. *

3244. _____. "The independent woman: Rhode Island's first woman legislator." RIH, 49 (Feb. 1991), 3-11.
Isabelle Ahearn O'Neill, from Providence, was first elected in 1922.

3245. ANDERSON, HAROLD, and ED. GOLDEN. "Aquatics in Rhode Island over the years." Old RI, 4 (Feb. 1994), 58-61.
Swimming.

3246. "AN ANNOTATED bibliography of materials relating to the history of the Jews in Rhode Island, located in Rhode Island depositories (1967-1989)." RIJHN, 10 (Nov. 1989), 219-275.
Carol J. Frost, comp. See also entry 27 in the Rhode Island volume.

3247. ARCHAMBAULT, FLORENCE. "Lotteries in Rhode Island." Old RI, 3 (Sept. 1993), 59-60.

3248. _____. "Old Home Week." Old RI, 3 (Aug. 1993), 34-37.
Celebrations once held in Newport and other Rhode Island towns.

3249. _____. "Rhode Island's independence day." Old RI, 2 (May 1992), 43.

3250. _____. "The unfortunate Hannah Robinson." Old RI, 4 (Feb. 1994), 17-19.
18th-century love story.

3251. _____. "A Victorian Christmas." Old RI, 3 (Dec. 1993/Jan. 1994), 10-13.

3252. THE ARTISTIC heritage of Newport and the Narragansett Bay: an exhibition and sale to benefit "Save the Bay," southeastern New England's largest environmental organization, July 13-November 30, 1990. Newport: William Vareika Fine Arts, [1990]. Unp. RHi. *

3253. BERNSTEIN, DAVID J. Prehistoric subsistence on the southern New England coast: the record from Narragansett Bay. N.Y.: Academic Pr., 1993. xvi, 188p. RPB. *

3254. _____. "Prehistoric use of plant foods in the Narragansett Bay region." Man in the Northeast, No. 44 (Fall 1992), 1-13.
See also preceding entry.

3255. BERRY, SUSAN J. "The architecture of power: spatial and social order in seven Rhode Island mill villages." Ph.D. dissertation, Univ. of California, Berkeley, 1992. 436p. *
Anthropological study. Abstracted in DAI, 53:10A (1993), 3573-3574.

3256. BOISVERT, DONALD J. "'The agitation of the woman question': Rhode Island women in the early struggle for political equality." Old RI, 4 (Mar. 1994), 20-22; (Apr. 1994), 20-22.

3257. _____. "Christmas in Rhode Island: 1780." Old RI, 2 (Dec. 1992/Jan. 1993), 31-33.

3258. _____. "The day of the great wind remembered, 1938: the hurricane of 1938." Old RI, 2 (Sept. 1992), 6, 8-9, 11-14.

3259. _____. "The great Rhode Island Red caper." Old RI, 2 (Aug. 1992), 32, 35-36, 38.
Rhode Island Red breed of chicken.

* Online Computer Library Center (OLCC) listings for books and dissertations marked with this symbol may include additional library locations.

3260   RHODE ISLAND

3260.   BOISVERT, DONALD J. "Rhode Island and the Civil War." Old RI, 3 (Apr. 1993), 26-30; (May 1993), 38-39; (June/July 1993), 55-59; (Aug. 1993), 55, 57-60; (Sept. 1993), 55-59; (Oct. 1993), 54-58.

3261.   _____. "Rhode Island and the Lincoln connection." Old RI, 3 (Feb. 1993), 16, 18-20.
        Abraham Lincoln.

3262.   _____. "The Rhode Island clambake: a gustatory tribute to Mya arenaria." Old RI, 3 (Sept. 1993), 48- 53.

3263.   _____. "The Rhode Island Greening apple: did it really originate in the Garden of Eden?" Old RI, 3 (Oct. 1993), 30-32.

3264.   _____. "Rhode Island vampires, eerie spirits, and ghostly apparitions." Old RI, 2 (Oct. 1992), 9-13, 15- 16.

3265.   _____. "When George Washington came to call." Old RI, 4 (Feb. 1994), 11-15.
        1781.

3266.   _____. "Youthful winter pleasures of yesteryear." Old RI, 3 (Feb. 1993), 38-39.

3267.   BOTELHO, JOYCE M. Right and might: the Dorr Rebellion and the struggle for equal rights. Providence: Rhode Island Historical Society, 1992. 4v. RHi. *
        1842. See also entries 3279-3280, 3314, 3348, 3350-3351.

3268.   BROWN, HENRY A. L., and HAZEL WADE KENNEDY. Warwick Downs: a sense of place, 1638-1972. Warwick: Priv. Print., 1993. vi, 38p. RHi. *
        In Warwick and Cranston.

3269.   BUHLE, PAUL M. "Vanishing Rhode Island." RIH, 49 (Aug./Nov. 1991), 67-126.
        Changes in the man-made landscape.

3270.   CIPRIANO, LINDA A. "The YWCA of Greater Rhode Island: a proud tradition since 1867." Old RI, 4 (Mar. 1994), 10-14.
        Young Women's Christian Association.

3271.   CLOUETTE, BRUCE ALAN, and MATTHEW ROTH. Historic highway bridges of Rhode Island. Providence: Rhode Island Department of Transportation, 1990. 72p. RHi. *

3272.   _____. Rhode Island historic bridge inventory. Providence: Rhode Island Department of Transportation, 1988. 2v. RHi. *

3273.   COLI, WALTRAUD BERGER, and RICHARD A. LOBBAN. The Cape Verdeans in Rhode Island. Providence: Rhode Island Heritage Commission, 1990. 55p. RHi. *

3274.   CONLEY, PATRICK THOMAS. The Bill of Rights and Rhode Island: Rhode Island: laboratory for the "lively experiment." Madison, Wis.: Madison House Publishers, 1991. 39p. RHi. *

3275.   _____. "The biography of Charles R. Brayton." Old RI, 2 (Oct. 1992), 16-17.
        Brayton (1840-1910) was a Civil War general and for a number of years the powerful chairman of the Republican Party in the state. See also entry 3289.

3276.   _____. "The biography of Nelson W. Aldrich (November 6, 1841-April 16, 1915)." Old RI, 2 (Sept. 1992), 20.
        Prominent U.S. senator from Rhode Island (served 1881-1911). See also entry 3297.

3277.   _____. "Ethnic politics in Rhode Island: the decisive role of the Franco-Americans." Old RI, 3 (June/July 1993), 16-22.

3278.   _____. "Famed Irish leaders from Rhode Island's past." Old RI, 3 (Mar. 1993), 18-20.

3279.   _____. "No tempest in a teapot: the Dorr Rebellion in national perspective." RIH, 50 (Aug. 1992), 67-100.
        See also next entry and entries 3267, 3314, 3348, 3350-3351.

3280.   _____. "Thomas Wilson Dorr (November 5, 1805- December 27, 1854)." Old RI, 2 (Dec. 1992/Jan. 1993), 61-62.
        See also preceding entry.

3281.   COPPA, GREG. "The Verrazano saga." Old RI, 3 (Apr. 1993), 15-17.
        Explorer Giovanni da Verrazano and Rhode Island (1524).

3282.   COREY, STEVEN HUNT. "Rhode Island during King Philip's War: the quest for peace versus the lust for land." NH, 60 (Winter 1987), 13-27.

3283.   DALTON, ED. "First Rhode Island Regiment." Old RI, 2 (June 1992), 17-19.
        Black regiment in the American Revolution.

3284.   _____. "Tempest tales." Rhode Island Monthly, 1 (Sept. 1988), 56-57.
        1938 hurricane.

3285.   _____. "Two hurricane stories." Old RI, 2 (Sept. 1992), 21-23.
        Tragedies of the 1938 hurricane in Galilee and Jamestown.

3286.   D'AMATO, DONALD A. "Aerial history in Rhode Island." Old RI, 4 (Feb. 1994), 34-36; (Mar. 1994), 36, 38-40; (Apr. 1994), 26-29; (June 1994), 24-26.
        To be continued.

3287. D'AMATO, DONALD A. "The audacious Abraham Whipple causes grief for the British navy." Old RI, 3 (June/July 1993), 50-54.
See also entries 3291, 3397, 3586.

3288. _____. "A bold stroke makes revolution complete: Democrats sweep into power." Old RI, 3 (Feb. 1993), 22- 23, 25.
"Bloodless revolution" of 1935, in which Democrats successfully overturned the results of several state senate races and gained control of the legislature.

3289. _____. "Charles R. Brayton: when the fox was sent to guard the chickens." Old RI, 2 (Feb. 1992), 2.
The state's "most notorious political boss during the 19th century." See also entry 3275.

3290. _____. "Early colonial wranglings." Old RI, 2 (Jan. 1992), 14.
Over title to the Shawomet purchase.

3291. _____. "The Gaspee affair." Old RI, 2 (May 1992), 5-6; (June 1992), 15-16; (July 1992), 15-18.
1772. See also entries 3287, 3397.

3292. _____. "General N. Greene: from private to general in one day." Old RI, 2 (Mar./Apr. 1992), 48-49.
Nathanael Greene, the Revolutionary War general.

3293. _____. "A gift of armor proved deadly for Miantonomi." Old RI, 3 (May 1993), 32-34.
Narragansett Indian sachem, killed by Mohegans allied with Massachusetts in 1643.

3294. _____. "Henry B. Anthony used the 'lash of the journal' to control Rhode Island politics." Old RI, 2 (Sept. 1992), 58-59, 61-62.
Anthony (1815-1884), editor and owner of the Providence Journal, rose in politics to become governor and a prominent U.S. senator.

3295. _____. "'King Richard' Greene and Governor Joseph Wanton." Old RI, 3 (Apr. 1993), 58-59, 61.
Revolutionary War Loyalists.

3296. _____. "Licenses to steal in R.I." Old RI, 2 (Mar./Apr. 1992), 6-7.
Early privateering and piracy. See also entry 3299.

3297. _____. "Nelson W. Aldrich: Rhode Island's most powerful politician." Old RI, 2 (Oct. 1992), 58-60; (Nov. 1992), 58-60; (Dec. 1992/Jan. 1993), 58-61; (Dec. 1992/Jan. 1993), 58-61.
Aldrich, a powerful and longtime U.S. senator, was first elected to the post in 1881. See also entry 3276.

3298. _____. "Rhode Island joins in the French and Indian War for patriotism and profit." Old RI, 2 (Feb. 1992), 34-35.

3299. _____. [Series of articles on pirates and piracy in early Rhode Island.] Old RI, 3 (Dec. 1993/Jan. 1994), 26-28, 30-32; 4 (Feb. 1994), 42-45; (Mar. 1994), 49-52; (Apr. 1994), 42-47; (June 1994), 37-41.
To be continued. See also entry 3296.

3300. _____. "The strike of 1922." Old RI, 2 (Nov. 1992), 23-25; (Dec. 1992/Jan. 1993), 23-24, 26.
Textile industry.

3301. _____. "When Rhode Island politicians became the 'laughing stock of the jazz age.'" Old RI, 2 (Aug. 1992), 15, 17-18; (Sept. 1992), 17-19; (Oct. 1992), 23-24.
1920s.

3302. _____. "Why the name Rhode Island?" Old RI, 2 (Jan. 1992), 51.

3303. D'AMATO, JEAN. "Epidemics in old Rhode Island." Old RI, 4 (Feb. 1994), 32.

3304. _____. "'Welfare' in the good old days." Old RI, 3 (Feb. 1993), 17.

3305. DAUGHTERS OF THE AMERICAN REVOLUTION. NATIONAL SOCIETY. Minority military service: Rhode Island, 1775- 1783. [Washington], 1988. viii, 6p. RHi. *

3306. DESBONNET, ALAN, and VIRGINIA LEE. Historical trends: water quality and fisheries, Narragansett Bay. Narragansett: Rhode Island Sea Grant, [1991]. iv, 100p. RHi. *

3307. DIFFILY, ANNE. "Without a trace." Rhode Island Monthly, 1 (July 1988), 40-42.
Six unsolved Rhode Island murders.

3308. DODSON, JAMES. "The battle for the soul of Rhode Island." Yankee, 57 (Sept. 1993), 76-88, 118, 120, 122, 124-133.
Past and present political corruption in the state.

3309. DONOVAN, WILLIAM J. "Crash landing." [Providence] Sunday Journal Magazine (June 7, 1992), 8-9, 11-12, 14, 16, 22.
Investor David F. LaRoche, indicted for bank fraud in 1991.

3310. ELLERY, WILLIAM JR. "Letters of William Ellery, Whig and Federalist." NH, 64 (Summer 1991), 135-146.
Nancy Ellen Giorgi, ed. Ellery (1727-1820) was a legislator, delegate to the Continental Congress, and collector of customs at Newport.

3311. EMLEN, ROBERT P. "The great gale of 1815: artifactual evidence of Rhode Island's first hurricane." RIH, 48 (May 1990), 51-61.

3312   RHODE ISLAND

3312.   FELKER, CHRISTOPHER DANIEL. "Roger Williams's use of legal authority: testing authority in early New England." NEQ, 63 (Dec. 1990), 624-648.

3313.   FERRARO, WILLIAM MICHAEL. "Lives of quiet desperation: community and polity in New England over four centuries: the cases of Portsmouth and Foster, Rhode Island." Ph.D. dissertation, Brown Univ., 1991. xiv, 694p. RHi. *
    "The institution of town meeting government."
    Abstracted in DAI, 52:9A (1992), 3325.

3314.   FORMISANO, RONALD P. "The role of women in the Dorr Rebellion." RIH, 51 (Aug. 1993), 89-104.
    See also entries 3267, 3279-3280, 3348, 3350-3351.

3315.   FOSTER, GERALDINE S. "The Bureau of Jewish Education of Rhode Island." RIJHN, 11 (Nov. 1993), 315-334.

3316.   _____. "The 35th anniversary of the Rhode Island Jewish Historical Notes." RIJHN, 10 (Nov. 1989), 215- 217.

3317.   FOSTER, GERALDINE S., and ELEANOR F. HORVITZ. "Summers along upper Narragansett Bay, 1910-1938." RIJHN, 11 (Nov. 1991), 14-35.
    Vacation sites frequented by Rhode Island Jewish families. See also entries 3330, 3414.

3318.   THE FRENCH in Rhode Island: a brief history. Albert K. Aubin, ed. Providence: Rhode Island Heritage Commission, 1988. 45p. RHi. *

3319.   FULLER, NATHAN. "Roger Williams: without fear of retribution." Old RI, 2 (Nov. 1992), 60-62.
    Williams on liberty of conscience.

3320.   FUOCO, JOE. "The Indians of Rhode Island." Old RI, 2 (Aug. 1992), 11-15.

3321.   GAUSTAD, EDWIN SCOTT. Liberty of conscience: Roger Williams in America. Grand Rapids, Mich.: William B. Eerdmans Publishing, 1991. xiv, 229p. RHi. *

3322.   _____. "Roger Williams: beyond Puritanism." Baptist History and Heritage, 24 (Oct. 1989), 11-19.

3323.   GOLDMAN, SHALOM. "Christians, Jews, and the Hebrew language in Rhode Island history." RIJHN, 11 (Nov. 1993), 344-353.

3324.   GOULD, ELIZABETH BARBER. "Retirement migration of Rhode Islanders, 1967-1979." Ph.D. dissertation, Brown Univ., 1991. ix, 247p. * Abstracted in DAI, 52:9A (1992), 3442.

3325.   GOULD, LEWIS, and KAREN M. LAMOREE. Rhode Island's first ladies. n.p., [1990?]. 58p. RHi. *
    Governors' wives.

3326.   HERNDON, RUTH WALLIS. "Governing the affairs of the town: continuity and change in Rhode Island, 1750-1800." Ph.D. dissertation, American Univ., 1992. xi, 441p. *
    Abstracted in DAI, 53:10A (1993), 3652.

3327.   _____. "On and off the record: town clerks as interpreters of Rhode Island history." RIH, 50 (Nov. 1992), 103-115.
    Town meeting and town council records as edited documents.

3328.   HORVITZ, ELEANOR F. "Cantors, choirs, and choral societies." RIJHN, 11 (Nov. 1993), 335-343.

3329.   _____. "Rhode Island places with Jewish names." RIJHN, 11 (Nov. 1991), 41-45.

3330.   _____, and GERALDINE S. FOSTER. "Summers along lower Narragansett Bay: Block Island and Newport." RIJHN, 11 (Nov. 1993), 275-291.
    See also entry 3317, 3414.

3331.   JONES, DANIEL P. "Commercial progress versus local rights: turnpike building in northwestern Rhode Island in the 1790s." RIH, 48 (Feb. 1990), 21-32.

3332.   _____. The economic and social transformation of rural Rhode Island, 1780-1850. Boston: Northeastern Univ. Pr., 1992. xv, 267p. RHi. *
    Northwestern Rhode Island. See also this author's Ph.D. dissertation on same subject (Brown Univ., 1987; entry 10353 in Vol. 8).

3333.   KAPLAN, LLOYD S., and ROBERT E. PETTERUTI. Who's who in Rhode Island jazz, c.1925-1988. West Greenwich: Consortium Publishing, 1991. 107p. RHi. *

3334.   KELLEY, MILDRED LAXTON. "The original official Rhode Island State Anthem." Old RI, 3 (June/July 1993), 61-62.
    Written by Sarah Taylor and adopted in 1933.

3335.   LAMAR, CHRISTINE. "Revolutionary pension correspondence from Rhode Island archives." NEHGR, 146 (Apr. 1992), 135-142.

3336.   LEONARD, D. W. "The lonely outposts: the patrols of the Life Saving Service." Old RI, 3 (Dec. 1993/Jan. 1994), 24-25.
    Forerunner of the U.S. Coast Guard.

3337. LEVIN, BEATRICE. "Let virtue be a guide to thee: early Rhode Island needlework." Old RI, 2 (Oct. 1992), 25-26.

3338. LEVIN, ZEL. "A century of crime and punishment in Rhode Island." Old RI, 2 (Nov. 1992), 27-29.

3339. _____. "Proud and Polish in Rhode Island." Old RI, 3 (Nov. 1993), 24, 26; (Dec. 1993/Jan. 1994), 34- 36; 4 (Feb. 1994), 28-30; (Mar. 1994), 32-34.

3340. LIND, LOUISE. "'Noel' not always the same as 'Christmas.'" Old RI, 2 (Dec. 1992/Jan. 1993), 16-18.
    Celebration of the holiday by early generations of French Canadians in Rhode Island.

3341. _____. "Rhode Island: a romantic history." Old RI, 3 (Feb. 1993), 12-15.

3342. _____. The Southeast Asians in Rhode Island: the new Americans. Providence: Rhode Island Heritage Commission, 1989. 36p. RHi. *

3343. LOVEJOY, DAVID SHERMAN. "Roger Williams and George Fox: the arrogance of self-righteousness." NEQ, 66 (June 1993), 199-225.

3344. MACAULAY, RUTH. Dull dejection in the countenances of all of them: children at work in the Rhode Island textile industry, 1790-1938. Pawtucket: Slater Mill Historic Site, 1987. 12p. RHi. *

3345. MADEN, SUE. The Jamestown Bridge, 1940-1990: from "the bridge to nowhere" to obsolescence. Jamestown: Jamestown Historical Society, 1990. x, 53p. RHi. *

3346. MILLER, BETTE. "The day of the transient trolley." CrHSN [Nov. 1988], [3-6].

3347. MINETT, TERRY. "Before Providence there was Newport." Old RI, 1 (Dec. 1991), 6-7.

3348. _____. "Dorr's Rebellion: a civil war within Rhode Island." Old RI, 2 (June 1992), 6-7, 10.
    1842. See also entries 3267, 3279-3280, 3314, 3350-3351.

3349. _____. "Rhode Island casts deciding vote in presidential election." Old RI, 2 (Jan. 1992), 42-43.
    1876.

3350. _____. "The trial of Thomas Wilson Dorr: a case of injustice." Old RI, 2 (Jan. 1992), 18, 20; (June 1992), 10, 12-13.
    See also next entry and entries 3267, 3279-3280, 3314, 3348.

3351. _____. "Tyler slams Dorr." Old RI, 1 (Dec. 1991), 20-23.
    President John Tyler's refusal to recognize Thomas Wilson Dorr as governor of Rhode Island in 1842. See also preceding entry.

3352. _____. "Witches, warlocks, & wizardry in the herb garden." Old RI, 2 (Oct. 1992), 6-8.
    Legends and superstitions surrounding Halloween.

3353. MINKIN, TRACEY. "Bruce Sundlun: going it alone." Rhode Island Monthly, 4 (Feb. 1992), 18-24, 77-79.
    The current governor (elected in 1990); article includes biographical information.

3354. MOHANTY, GAIL FOWLER. "Handloom outwork and outwork weaving in rural Rhode Island, 1810-1821." American Studies, 30 (Fall 1989), 41-68.
    See also the next two entries and Gail Fowler's Ph.D. dissertation, "Rhode Island handloom weavers and the effects of technological change, 1780-1840" (Univ. of Pennsylvania, 1984; entry 10202 in Vol. 8).

3355. _____. "Putting up with putting-out: power-loom diffusion and outwork for Rhode Island mills, 1821-1829." Journal of the Early Republic, 9 (Summer 1989), 191-216.

3356. _____. "Rhode Island handloom weavers: a probate perspective." DubSemPr (1987), 86-96.

3357. MOLLOY, DAVID SCOTT JR. "The early turnpikes: from Indian trails to tollgates." Old RI, 4 (Feb. 1994), 20-22.

3358. _____. "Labor Day, September 6, 1993: 100th anniversary of the labor movement in Rhode Island." Old RI, 3 (Sept. 1993), 10-16.

3359. _____. "Motormen, moguls and the machine: urban mass transit in Rhode Island, 1864-1902." Ph.D. dissertation, Providence College, 1991. vii, 493p. RHi. *

3360. _____. "Omnibus in Rhode Island: crucial urban link." Old RI, 4 (Apr. 1994), 31-34.
    A successor to the stagecoach.

3361. _____. "The stagecoach era: symbol of rapid transportation in 1815." Old RI, 4 (Mar. 1994), 28-31.

3362. _____. "Working in Rhode Island." Old RI, 4 (Apr. 1994), 40-41.

3363. MORGENTHAU, RUTH S. Pride without prejudice: the life of John O. Pastore. Providence: Rhode Island Historical Society, 1989. 201p. RHi. *
    The state's first Italian American governor; U.S. senator from 1951 to 1977.

3364   RHODE ISLAND

3364.   MUHLY, FRANK. "A silver lining: twenty-five years of the Rhode Island State Council on the Arts." RIH, 50 (May 1992), 35-64.

3365.   MURPHY, MARTIN J. JR. "The sons of Erin in Rhode Island: 'the field had already been plowed.'" Old RI, 4 (Mar. 1994), 15-19.
        Irish Americans and the Ancient Order of Hibernians.

3366.   ORTIZ, RONALD JOSEPH. "The city-suburb redistribution of selected household types in a changing metropolitan structure: an analysis of the Providence metropolitan area, 1967-1980." Ph.D. dissertation, Brown Univ., 1990. xiv, 330p. *
        Abstracted in DAI, 51:8A (1991), 2884.

3367.   PAGOULATOS, PETER. "Late woodland and contact period land-use patterns in Rhode Island." MASB, 51 (Oct. 1990), 69-82.

3368.   PROVIDENCE PRESERVATION SOCIETY. The Colonial Revival in Rhode Island (1890-1940): a summary of lectures presented as a series entitled "The Colonial Revival phenomenon," Providence Preservation Society, 1989. [Providence], 1989. 14p. RHi. *

3369.   REYNOLDS, RICHARD. "Hockey in the days of long johns, key skates and frozen ponds." Old RI, 4 (Mar. 1994), 42-45.

3370.   RHODE ISLAND HISTORICAL DOCUMENT TRANSCRIPTION PROJECT. Pleas excuse all bad writing: a documentary history of Rhode Island during the Civil War era, 1854-1865. Kris VanDen Bossche, ed. Peace Dale, 1993. 205p. RHi. *

3371.   RHODE ISLAND HISTORICAL SOCIETY. Narragansett Bay—charting its course; an exhibition of graphic and cartographic images tracing the history of Narragansett Bay, September 26, 1991-March 20, 1992. [Providence, 1991.] [8]p. RHi. *
        Pamphlet consists of historical text.

3372.   _____. What a difference a bay makes. Deborah B. Brennan, project director. Providence: Rhode Island Historical Society, 1993. 187p. RHi. *
        Essays relating to the importance of Narragansett Bay in Rhode Island history.

3373.   RHODE ISLAND SCHOOL OF DESIGN. MUSEUM OF ART. The China trade on Narragansett Bay, 1750-1850. Providence, [1992]. 12p. RHi. *
        Cover title for exhibition of Chinese export porcelain.

3374.   SANTORO, CARMELA G. The Italians in Rhode Island: the age of exploration to the present, 1524-1989. Providence: Rhode Island Heritage Commission, 1990. 53p. RHi. *

3375.   SAUNDERS, LAURA S., and JOHN A. SAUNDERS. "Early public transportation to the islands of Rhode Island." Mystic Seaport, Log, 42 (Fall 1990), 70.

3376.   SCANLAN, JAMES J. "Rhode Island coal." Old RI, 3 (Sept. 1993), 26-27.

3377.   SHARPE, ELISABETH K. "Chinese export porcelain with arms of Rhode Island." Antiques, 139 (Jan. 1991), 246-255.

3378.   SILVER, HILARY. "Is industrial policy possible in the United States?: the defeat of Rhode Island's Greenhouse Compact." Politics & Society, 15:3 (1986-1987), 333-368.
        Proposed industrial planning policy (1984).

3379.   SIMMONS, WILLIAM SCRANTON. The Narragansett. N.Y.: Chelsea House Publishers, 1988. 111p. Ct. *
        Narragansett Indians.

3380.   SLACK, NANCY. "'And the beat goes on': over 50 years in Rhode Island." Old RI, 3 (Apr. 1993), 36, 38-39.
        State affiliate of the American Heart Association.

3381.   SOUTH KINGSTOWN, R.I. HIGH SCHOOL. The family in the fifties: hope, & fear, & rock 'n roll; an oral history of Rhode Island in the post-war decade. Written by tenth grade students at South Kingstown High School. [South Kingstown? 1993] 60p. RHi.

3382.   SOUTH KINGSTOWN, R.I. HIGH SCHOOL. HONORS ENGLISH PROGRAM. What did you do in the war, Grandma?: an oral history of Rhode Island women during World War II. Providence: Rhode Island Historical Society, 1989. 60p. RHi. *

3383.   STERLING, JOHN. "Documenting Rhode Island's historical cemeteries." Rhode Island Historical Society, Genealogical News & Notes, 2:2 [1994], [1-3].

3384.   STEVENS, ELIZABETH COOKE. "'From generation to generation': the mother and daughter activism of Elizabeth Buffum Chace and Lillie Chace Wyman." Ph.D. dissertation, Brown Univ., 1993. vi, 474p. RHi. *
        The two lived 1806-1899 and 1847-1929. Abstracted in DAI, 54:10A (1994), 3902.

3385.   STRUM, HARVEY. "Rhode Island and the War of 1812." RIH, 50 (Feb. 1992), 23-32.

3386. SULLIVAN, JOSEPH W. "'A giant of embodied conscience': Joseph M. Coldwell and the Socialist Party in Rhode Island." RIH, 50 (Nov. 1992), 117-129.
"The only Rhode Islander jailed for sedition under the Espionage Act of 1917."

3387. [WALKER, ANTHONY]. Heritage of courage. n.p.: John Peck Rathbun Chapter, Rhode Island Society, Sons of the American Revolution, 1992. iii, 68p. RHi. *
"Deeds of valor" of Rhode Island officers of the Revolution.

3388. WEIL, JEANNE, and JUDITH W. COHEN. "Jews in the jewelry industry in Rhode Island." RIJHN, 10 (Nov. 1989), 286-316.

3389. WIDMER, EDWARD. "Rhode Island miscellany: the men's bars of Rhode Island." RIH, 47 (Feb. 1989), 35-38.

3390. WOLKOVICH-VALKAVICIUS, WILLIAM LAWRENCE. The Lithuanians in Rhode Island: from the Baltic shore to Narragansett Bay. Providence: Rhode Island Heritage Commission, 1992. 43p. RHi. *

3391. WYATT, DONALD W. "The Dexter swindle." Old RI, 2 (Aug. 1992), 24-26.
1809 banking scandal.

3392. _____. "John Chafee's most exciting night." Old RI, 2 (June 1992), 20-23, 25-26.
Winning the Republican gubernatorial nomination in 1962.

3393. _____. "Rhode Island and federalism." Old RI, 3 (Mar. 1993), 50-52, 54.
The "torturous road to ratification."

3394. _____. "Rhode Island's great experiment." Old RI, 2 (July 1992), 21-23, 25.
Prohibition (1880s).

3395. _____. "R.I. nearly missed this war." Old RI, 2 (July 1992), 18-20.
The attempted Fenian attack on Canada in 1870.

3396. _____. "Who was William Peck?" Old RI, 2 (May 1992), 40-41.
First U.S. marshal for Rhode Island.

3397. YORK, NEIL L. "The uses of law and the Gaspee affair." RIH, 50 (Feb. 1992), 3-21.
See also entries 3287, 3291.

SEE ALSO entries 22, 135-136, 166, 191, 200, 246, 249, 280, 296-297, 321, 356-357, 390, 397, 2087, 2180.

Rhode Island

Entries for Counties†

KENT COUNTY

3398. JAMES, SYDNEY VINCENT. "Why is there a Kent County?" RIH, 47 (Aug. 1989), 96-106.

NEWPORT COUNTY

3399. BROCKWAY, LUCINDA A. "The historic designed landscapes of Newport County." NH, 64 (Spring 1991), 61-89.

3400. GILLESPIE, JANET. "Horse and buggy days in Rhode Island." Old RI, 2 (Nov. 1992), 54-56.

3401. _____. "The Sunday afternoon drive." Old RI, 3 (Sept. 1993), 29-31.

3402. SCHNEIDER, STEWART P. "Life on the bay: logs of the Jamestown and Newport ferries." RIH, 48 (Nov. 1990), 113-124.
    Jamestown and Newport Ferry Company.

3403. WALKER, ANTHONY. Wind grist mills on Aquidneck Island. Middletown: Middletown Historical Society, 1992. ix, 78p. RHi. *

PROVIDENCE COUNTY

3404. BERSTEIN, DOROTHY K. "Pawtucket-Central Falls Hadassah: the early years." RIJHN, 10 (Nov. 1991), 503-507.
    Local chapter of the national Jewish organization was organized ca. 1924.

3405. BOISVERT, DONALD J. "The Hope Furnace: founder of cannon for an emerging nation." Old RI, 4 (June 1994), 18-20, 22-23.

3406. CASH, SARAH. "Martin Johnson Heade's 'Thunder Storm on Narragansett Bay.'" Antiques, 145 (Mar. 1994), 422-431.
    Painting (1868), the site of which "is probably near the northern end of the bay."

3407. CONRAD, JAMES LAWSON JR. "Entrepreneurial objectives, organizational design, technology, and the cotton manufacturing of Almy and Brown, 1789-1797." Business and Economic History, 2 ser. 13 (1984), 7-19.

3408. HOFFMANN, CHARLES, and TESS HOFFMANN. Brotherly love: murder and the politics of prejudice in nineteenth-century Rhode Island. Amherst: Univ. of Massachusetts Pr., 1993. xvii, 184p. RHi. *
    Anti-Catholicism as a factor in the trials of members of the Gordon family for the 1843 murder of industrialist Amasa Sprague and the subsequent execution of John Gordon for the crime.

3409. MOLLOY, DAVID SCOTT JR. "Rhode Island's first horsecar: Providence to Pawtucket." Old RI, 4 (June 1994), 42-46.

3410. WILLIAMS, FRANK J. "A candidate speaks in Rhode Island: Abraham Lincoln visits Providence and Woonsocket, 1860." RIH, 51 (Nov. 1993), 107-119.

3411. WYATT, DONALD W. "The tragedy of John Gordon." Old RI, 2 (Nov. 1992), 17-20, 22.
    Gordon, convicted of the 1843 killing of Amasa Sprague, was the last man to be executed in Rhode Island. (See also entry 3408.)

SEE ALSO entries 135, 195, 3331-3332.

WASHINGTON COUNTY

3412. BROWN, CHARLES A. "Wood River Branch Railroad." S'liner, 19:3 (1988), 30-39.
    Short-line railroad between Hope Valley and Wood River (late-19th and early-20th centuries).

† See the Rhode Island volume in this series (1983) for a complete list of counties.

* Online Computer Library Center (OLCC) listings for books and dissertations marked with this symbol may include additional library locations.

3413.   CARPENTER, GEORGE BRADFORD. "War and other reminiscences." RIH, 47 (Nov. 1989), 115-147.
    Reminiscences of a Civil War veteran, written ca. 1912. Carpenter (1842-1914) grew up in Westerly and lived in Ashaway after the war. See also the biographical introduction, by Kris VanDen Bossche, 109-112.

3414.   FOSTER, GERALDINE S., and ELEANOR F. HORVITZ. "Summers along lower Narragansett Bay: Narragansett Pier and nearby areas." RIJHN, 11 (Nov. 1992), 180-214.
    Rhode Island Jews and some of the area's summer resorts (early-20th century). Article followed by three pages of related social news from contemporary issues of The Jewish Herald of Providence. See also entries 3317, 3330.

3415.   MILLER, JOHN. "South County lighthouse[s] still send sailors beaming." Old RI, 2 (Mar./Apr. 1992), 21.

Rhode Island

Entries for Cities and Towns†

BARRINGTON (BRISTOL CO.)

3416.   RHODE ISLAND. HISTORICAL PRESERVATION COMMISSION. Historic and architectural resources of Barrington, Rhode Island. [Providence], 1993. iii, 83p. RHi. *
    Authors: Virginia H. Adams, Richard E. Greenwood, Robert Owen Jones, Pamela A. Kennedy, and Elizabeth Sargent Warren.

BRISTOL (BRISTOL CO.)

3417.   BRAY, MAYNARD, and CARLTON J. PINHEIRO. Herreshoff of Bristol: a photographic history of America's greatest yacht and boat builders. Brooklin, Me.: Wooden Boat Publishers, 1989. xi, 241p. RHi. *

3418.   CANTWELL, MARY. American girl: scenes from a small-town girlhood. N.Y.: Random House, 1992. 209p. RPPC. *
    Autobiographical (1930s and 1940s).

3419.   CONLEY, PATRICK THOMAS. "The Irish in Rhode Island & the Bristol connection." Old RI, 3 (Mar. 1993), 7-13.

3420.   D'AMATO, DONALD A. "General George DeWolf: the man who swindled the whole town." Old RI, 2 (Aug. 1992), 52-54.
    Early-19th century.

3421.   _____. "The nefarious slave trade: 'I would plow the ocean into pea-porridge to make money'—Simeon Potter." Old RI, 2 (May 1992), 50-53.

3422.   DIMOND, F. REGINALD. Life and times of Benjamin Church, 1842-1905: Benjamin Church Home for Aged Men...Bristol, Rhode Island. [Bristol: Benjamin Church Home, 1989] 63p. RHi. *

† See the Rhode Island volume in this series (1983) for a complete list of cities and towns.

* Online Computer Library Center (OLCC) listings for books and dissertations marked with this symbol may include additional library locations.

3423   BRISTOL

3423.   "JAMES de Wolf: one of the 'great folks' of Bristol." Old RI, 2 (July 1992), 6-8.
        Lived 1764-1837.

3424.   LEVIN, BEATRICE. "Colt State Park: the genealogy and the glorious era." Old RI, 3 (May 1993), 6-7, 9, 11-12.

3425.   PINHEIRO, CARLTON J. "Yachting legends in Rhode Island: the Herreshoff Manufacturing Company." Old RI, 3 (Aug. 1993), 8-11; (Sept. 1993), 18-24; (Oct. 1993), 19-23.
        See also entry 3417.

3426.   RHODE ISLAND. HISTORICAL PRESERVATION COMMISSION. Historic and architectural resources of Bristol, Rhode Island. [Providence], 1990. v, 120p. RHi. *
        Authors: Elizabeth Sargent Warren and Pamela A. Kennedy.

SEE ALSO entry 1803.

BURRILLVILLE (PROVIDENCE CO.)

3427.   ONE hundred years ago in Burrillville: selected stories from the local newspapers. Patricia A. Mehrtens, ed. Bowie, Md.: Heritage Books, 1992. vii, 231p. RHi. *

CHARLESTOWN (WASHINGTON CO.)

3428.   VARS, NELSON BYRON (1831-1914). Charlestown, Rhode Island, in the mid-nineteenth century: as seen through the eyes of Uncle Phineas (Nelson Byron Vars). Earl P. Crandall, ed. [Catskill, N.Y.], 1992. 80p. RHi. *
        See also next entry.

3429.   _____. "'Uncle Phineas': recollection of Charlestown, ca. 1840-1886." Old RI, 2 (Sept. 1992), 24-26; (Oct. 1992), 30, 32; (Nov. 1992), 30-32, 35; (Dec. 1992/Jan. 1993), 48, 50-51; 3 (Feb. 1993), 49-52; (Mar. 1993), 48-49; (May 1993), 46-47; (Sept. 1993), 36-37; (Oct. 1993), 52-53.
        Dwight C. Brown, Jr., comp. See also preceding entry.

SEE ALSO entry 3414.

COVENTRY (KENT CO.)

3430.   D'AMATO, DONALD A. Coventry celebration: a pictorial history. Virginia Beach, Va.: Donning, 1991. 192p. RHi. *

3431.   _____. "The history of Coventry." Old RI, 2 (Jan. 1992), 48-49.

3432.   LIND, LOUISE. "Summer fun at Herring Pond in the early 1900's." Old RI, 2 (May 1992), 54.
        Spring Lake.

SEE ALSO entry 3924.

CRANSTON (PROVIDENCE CO.)

3433.   BALDWIN, PETER. "Becoming a city of homes: the suburbanization of Cranston, 1850-1910." RIH, 51 (Feb. 1993), 3-21.

3434.   BOISVERT, DONALD J. "A Rhode Island Thanksgiving, 1856." Old RI, 3 (Nov. 1993), 30-31.

3435.   CRANSTON, R.I. CHURCH OF THE TRANSFIGURATION. Transcentury: the centennial celebration of the Church of the Transfiguration: a history of our church the first one hundred years. [Cranston, 1993?] iv, 73p. RHi. *
        Episcopal

3436.   FUOCO, JOE. "The mills, the row houses of Thornton." Old RI, 2 (Aug. 1992), 40-42.
        Textile industry.

3437.   MILLER, BETTE. "Distinctions of Auburn." CrHSN [Oct. 1989], [4-8].
        Auburn section of Cranston.

3438.   _____. "Edgewood's golden days." CrHSN [Jan. 1990], [4-7].

3439.   _____. "Turning cloth into gold" CrHSN [Nov. 1992], [4-7].
        Sprague mills.

3440.   _____. "We've come a long way, baby!" CrHSN [May 1989], [3-7].
        History of the Cranston Historical Society.

3441.   "THE MYSTERY of Old Spring Road." CrHSN [Sept. 1988], [4-6].

3442.   "SEALED with a kiss: the love letters of Marjorie Gaunt." Yankee, 54 (Sept. 1990), 66-71, 126, 128-129.
        Letters to her husband during World War II.

SEE ALSO entries 3268, 3290, 3405, 3408, 3411.

CUMBERLAND (PROVIDENCE CO.)

3443. LIND, LOUISE. "Lost: a historic grave; anyone seen a box of bones around?" Old RI, 2 (Oct. 1992), 37-40.
On the whereabouts of the Rev. William Blackstone's remains. See also next two entries.

3444. _____. "Who was this William Blackstone, anyway?" Old RI, 2 (Mar./Apr. 1992), 1-3.
See also preceding and following entries.

3445. _____. William Blackstone: sage of the wilderness. Cumberland: Blackstone Valley Tourism Council, 1993. vi, 108p. RHi. *
Blackstone lived 1595-1675.

3446. PALIN, RAYMOND JR. "Revolutionary Cumberland: a note on a historical controversy." RIH, 51 (Nov. 1993), 129-133.
See also next entry.

3447. _____. "Revolutionary Cumberland: Loyalist or patriots?" Old RI, 2 (Dec. 1992/Jan. 1993), 20-23.

3448. RHODE ISLAND. HISTORICAL PRESERVATION COMMISSION. Historic and architectural resources of Cumberland, Rhode Island. [Providence], 1990. v, 71 [4]p. RHi. *
Author: Virginia A. Fitch.

SEE ALSO entry 3384.

EAST GREENWICH (KENT CO.)

3449. BOISVERT, DONALD J. "The Kentish Guards: a Rhode Island tradition." Old RI, 2 (Oct. 1992), 50-51, 53-55.
Originally an independent military company (founded in 1774).

3450. KETTELLE, VIOLET E. The rural roads in East Greenwich in the teens and twenties of 1900: their farms and owners, with some history. East Greenwich, [1990?]. 265p. RHi. *

SEE ALSO entry 3398.

EAST PROVIDENCE (PROVIDENCE CO.)

3451. JOHNSTON, MICHELLE DALLY. Out of sorrow and into hope: the history of the Emma Pendleton Bradley Hospital. East Providence: Bradley Hospital, 1991. 48p. RHi. *

3452. LEARY, THOMAS E. "Men and tongs: the Belgian Rod Mill at the Washburn Wire Company, East Providence, Rhode Island." IA, 18:1-2 (1992), 107-122.

3453. MILLER, BETTE. "A day at Crescent Park was a day to remember." CrHSN [Sept. 1990], [4-7].
In Riverside.

3454. RUMFORD, R.I. NEWMAN CONGREGATIONAL CHURCH. Newman Congregational Church, U.C.C., of Seekonk and East Providence, 1643-1993. [Rumford, 1993?] 39p. RHi. *
Seekonk, Mass.

SEE ALSO entries 147, 3317, 3406.

FOSTER (PROVIDENCE CO.)

3455. BEAMAN, CHARLES C., and CASEY B. TYLER. Early historical accounts of Foster, Rhode Island. Glenview, Ill.: Moshassuck Pr., 1993. viii, 125p. RHi. *
See also entries 1642 and 1644 in the Rhode Island volume.

SEE ALSO entry 3313.

JAMESTOWN (NEWPORT CO.)

3456. LIPPINCOTT, BERTRAM III. Time and tide: a centennial history of the Conanicut Yacht Club, 1892-1992. Jamestown: Conanicut Yacht Club, 1992. ix, 86p. RNHi. *

SEE ALSO entries 3285, 3345, 3376, 3402.

JOHNSTON (PROVIDENCE CO.)

3457. ULLUCCI, LOUIS. "Buses and carts." Johnston Historical Society, Historical Notes, 5 (Sept. 1989), 2-3.
Annual festival at Our Lady of Grace Church (Roman Catholic).

SEE ALSO entry 3660.

3458   LINCOLN

LINCOLN (PROVIDENCE CO.)

3458.   KELLEY, MILDRED LAXTON. "Sleighing tragedy at Lonsdale Crossing." Old RI, 3 (Feb. 1993), 44-46.

3459.   _____. "A story of old Saylesville." Old RI, 2 (July 1992), 40-46, 48.

3460.   REYNOLDS, DOUGLAS M. "Ship's captains, shop's cotton: Wilber Kelly and early American industrialization." RIH, 49 (May 1991), 37-49.
        Mill owner and operator (ca. 1820s).

3461.   SCANLAN, JAMES J. "Bowenite, Rhode Island's mineral." Old RI, 2 (May 1992), 10.
        Discovered by Dr. George Bowen in 1822.

LITTLE COMPTON (NEWPORT CO.)

3462.   RHODE ISLAND. HISTORICAL PRESERVATION COMMISSION. Historic and architectural resources of Little Compton, Rhode Island. [Providence], 1990. ii, 101p. RHi. *
        Author: William McKenzie Woodward.

SEE ALSO entries 3259, 3400.

MIDDLETOWN (NEWPORT CO.)

3463.   BOISVERT, DONALD J. "The nightshirted general." Old RI, 2 (Oct. 1992), 61-62; (Nov. 1992), 51-54; (Dec. 1992/Jan. 1993), 28-30.
        Capture of British Gen. Richard Prescott (1777).

3464.   FULWEILLER, MEGAN. "Paradise lost." Rhode Island Monthly, 1 (Jan. 1989), 41-43, 88-90.
        Van Buren estate.

3465.   MIDDLETOWN HISTORICAL SOCIETY. Middletown, Rhode Island: houses, history, heritage. Middletown, 1990. vii, 107p. RHi. *

NARRAGANSETT (WASHINGTON CO.)

3466.   RANDOLPH, NORRIS. "Cocktail days." New England Monthly, 7 (June 1990), 72-76.
        Recollections of social life in Narragansett.

3467.   RHODE ISLAND. HISTORICAL PRESERVATION COMMISSION. Historic and architectural resources of Narragansett, Rhode Island. [Providence], 1991. v, 80p. RHi. *
        Authors: Walter Nebiker, Robert Owen Jones, and Charlene K. Roice. Pamela A. Kennedy, ed.

SEE ALSO entries 3285, 3414.

NEW SHOREHAM (WASHINGTON CO.)

3468.   BELLANTONI, NICHOLAS FRANK. "Faunal resource availability and prehistoric cultural selection on Block Island, Rhode Island." Ph.D. dissertation, Univ. of Connecticut, 1987. xi, 257p. *
        Based on the excavation of four sites at Great Salt Pond. Abstracted in DAI, 48:11A (1988), 2914.

3469.   BROWN, GEORGE T. "The treasures of Block Island." Old RI, 2 (Sept. 1992), 42-44.
        Longtime resident Frederick J. Benson and the island's Southeast Lighthouse.

3470.   DALY, ERIN. "Block Island's mysterious legend of the Palatine." Old RI, 3 (Apr. 1993), 18-20.
        See also next entry.

3471.   MARTEL, MICHAEL L. "Whatever happened to Block Island's Palatine Light?" Old RI, 4 (Feb. 1994), 38-41.
        Legend relating to an 18th-century shipwreck. See also preceding entry.

3472.   PETRO, PAMELA. "The stumbling block." American Heritage, 39 (Sept./Oct. 1988), 114-117.
        Block Island.

3473.   RHODE ISLAND. HISTORICAL PRESERVATION COMMISSION. Historic and architectural resources of Block Island, Rhode Island. [Providence], 1991. v, 59p. RHi. *
        Author: William McKenzie Woodward.

SEE ALSO entries 3330, 3336.

NEWPORT (NEWPORT CO.)

3474.   ADELMAN, DAVID C. Life and times of Judah Touro: tercentenary address. [Providence]: Touro Fraternal Association, [1936]. 14p. RPJ. *
        1775-1854.

3475.   ARCHAMBAULT, FLORENCE. "Edward King's legacy." Old RI, 3 (Mar. 1993), 14-16.
        Lived 1815-1875.

3476. ARCHAMBAULT, FLORENCE. "Fleet Week, 1910." Old RI, 2 (July 1992), 51, 53.
Celebration occasioned by a visit from the U.S. Navy's White Fleet.

3477. _____. "The Franklin printing press original returns to Newport." Old RI, 3 (May 1993), 22-23, 25.
James Franklin's 18th-century press.

3478. _____. "German sub in Newport Harbor." Old RI, 2 (May 1992), 20-22.
1916.

3479. _____. "Henry Bull's house." Old RI, 2 (Mar./Apr. 1992), 18-19.
17th-century structure.

3480. _____. "Ida Lewis—lightkeeper." Old RI, 2 (Feb. 1992), 18-19.
See also entry 3511.

3481. _____. "The mystery of the crewless vessel." Old RI, 2 (Oct. 1992), 18-19.
1750 incident.

3482. _____. "Newport's city hall." Old RI, 2 (Feb. 1992), 15-16.

3483. _____. "The Ocean House: the rise and fall of a very famous hotel." Old RI, 2 (July 1992), 26, 29-31.

3484. _____. "Peanut Joe." Old RI, 2 (Aug. 1992), 38- 40.
Guiseppe Brangazio, a peanut vendor, who came to Newport ca. 1886.

3485. _____. "Pollock's prize: a love story." Old RI, 3 (Feb. 1993), 8, 10.

3486. _____. "Sarah Osborne." Old RI, 2 (Nov. 1992), 25-26.
See also entries 3516-3517.

3487. ARMS, MEREDITH. "Thomas Worthington Whittredge: home by the sea." Rutgers Art Review, 9-10 (1988), 61- 68.
Landscape and architectural painter (1870s and 1880s).

3488. ARON, MARTIN W. "Religious practices of Newport Jewry prior to the American Revolution." RIJHN, 11 (Nov. 1991), 71-77.

3489. "THE BATTLE of Newport." Old RI, 1 (Dec. 1991), 26-27.
Events surrounding the 1959 Newport Jazz Festival.

3490. BERRY, RICHARD W. "About 1925." NH, 62 (Fall 1989), 145-150.
New England Steamship Company, a "shop installation" serving the vessels of the Fall River Line and other companies. See also entry 3546.

3491. BILZ, ESTHER AUCHINCLOSS NASH. "I remember...reminiscences of Hammersmith Farm." NH, 65 (Spring 1994), 155-163.
Ca. early-20th century.

3492. BOISVERT, DONALD J. "Michel Felice Corne: the first person in America to eat a tomato." Old RI, 3 (June/July 1993), 13-16.
1820s.

3493. "THE BUSINESS of leisure: the Gilded Age in Newport." NH, 62 (Summer 1989), 97-126.

3494. CHERPAK, EVELYN M. "Chester T. Minkler and the development of naval underwater ordnance." NH, 59 (Fall 1986), 155-171.
Civilian employee of the Newport Torpedo Station (World War I era and later). Article followed by "Working in the Torpedo Station: a photographic memoir, " ibid., 172-177.

3495. COLE, JAMES S. "Newport's early circus." NH, 64 (Fall 1991), 175-176.
18th century.

3496. COVELL, VIRGINIA. "In the footsteps of Henry James." NH, 61 (Summer 1988), 69-75.
Observations in James's writings of walking tours in Newport and vicinity. See also entry 3512.

3497. _____. "Newport boarding houses." NH, 64 (Fall 1991), 192-198.

3498. CURRAN, BARBARA A. "An inventory study for the Wanton-Lyman-Hazard House." NH, 62 (Spring 1989), 85- 90.
See also entry 3533.

3499. D'AMATO, DONALD A. "Kings, queens, knaves and jokers in Newport's high society during the Gilded Age." Old RI, 3 (Feb. 1993), 58-59, 61-62.

3500. _____. "The magnificent Newport Casino was built as a result of a grudge." Old RI, 3 (Mar. 1993), 58-59, 61.

3501. _____. "What Alva wants, Alva gets: Alva knew how to shock Newport." Old RI, 3 (Aug. 1993), 18-22; (Sept. 1993), 32, 34-35; (Oct. 1993), 35-39; (Nov. 1993), 54- 55, 57; (Dec. 1993/Jan. 1994), 52-56.
Alva Smith Vanderbilt Belmont. Titles of installments vary. See also entry 3538.

3502. _____. "When Mrs. Astor called the tune in Newport." Old RI, 3 (June/July 1993), 27-29.

3503   NEWPORT

3503.   DRUETT, JOAN. "'My dear wife': the story of John and Henrietta Beblois." NH, 60 (Winter 1987), 5-12.
Correspondence between a 19th-century whaling captain and his wife.

3504.   DUCHESNEAU, JOHN. "The Medal of Honor and Newport." Old RI, 5 (May 1992), 12-13, 15.
Congressional Medal of Honor.

3505.   FICHTNER, MARGARIA. "An heir of mystery." Rhode Island Monthly, 1 (Feb. 1989), 37-39, 69-70.
Doris Duke. Includes biographical information.

3506.   FORD, MARGARET LANE. "A widow's work: Ann Franklin of Newport, Rhode Island." Printing History, 12:2 (1990), 15-26.
18th century.

3507.   FUOCO, JOE. "The strange life of Beatrice Turner." Old RI, 3 (Mar. 1993), 36-40.
Reclusive artist (died 1948).

3508.   GAVAN, TERRENCE. The barons of Newport. Newport: Pineapple Publications, 1988. 88p. RP. *

3509.   "GEORGE Mendonsa: Newport trap fisherman." NH, 64 (Winter 1991), 3-14, 49-53.
Oral history (Mendonsa was born in 1923).

3510.   HAMBRICK-STOWE, CHARLES EDWIN. "The spiritual pilgrimage of Sarah Osborn (1714-1796)." Church History, 61 (Dec. 1992), 408-421.
See also entries 3480, 3516-3517.

3511.   HARRINGTON, FRANCES. "The heroine of Lime Rock: daring rescues in Rhode Island." Oceans, 18 (Nov.-Dec. 1985), 24-27.
Ida Lewis. See also entry 3480.

3512.   HOFFMANN, CHARLES, and TESS HOFFMANN. "Henry James and the Civil War." NEQ, 62 (Dec. 1989), 529-552.
James's views on and relationship to the war, as seen in his Notes of a son and brother (1914). He had been exempted from the draft in Newport in 1863. See also entry 3496.

3513.   HOFLE, ANITA. "'For fear should be caught asleep.'" Old RI, 1 (Dec. 1991), 24-25.
Excerpts from the diary of Mary Gould Almy in August 1778, during the American Revolution.

3514.   "IN his own words: Henry Williams returns to Newport." NH, 65:1 [1993], 35-43.
1844 letter, edited by Ronald M. Potvin.

3515.   JEFFREYS, C. P. BEAUCHAMP. Newport: a short history. Newport: Newport Historical Society, 1992. xiii, 101p. RHi. *
Note: this item replaces entry 2145 in the Rhode Island volume.

3516.   KUJAWA, SHERYL ANNE. "The Great Awakening of Sarah Osborn and the Female Society of the First Congregational Church in Newport." NH, 65 (Spring 1994), 133-153.
See also next entry.

3517.   _____. "'A precious season at the throne of grace': Sarah Haggar Wheaten Osborn, 1714-1796." Ph.D. dissertation, Boston College, 1993. 375p. RHi. *
Abstracted in DAI, 54:6A (1993), 2298.

3518.   KUSINITZ, BERNARD. "The contributions of Newport's colonial Jews to the American way of life." RIJHN, 11 (Nov. 1992), 172-179.

3519.   _____. The history of Judah Touro Lodge of B'nai B'rith, 1924-1979. Newport, 1984. v, 66p. WHi. *

3520.   LAUTH, JOHN P. "History of the Artillery Company of Newport, 1741-1991." Old RI, 2 (Feb. 1992), 20-23.

3521.   LIND, LOUISE. "Was the Western Hemisphere's first Christian Church in Newport?" Old RI, 3 (Apr. 1993), 21-23.
Newport Tower. See also next entry.

3522.   _____. "Who did build Newport's Stone Tower?" Old RI, 3 (Dec. 1993/Jan. 1994), 42-44.
See also preceding entry.

3523.   LIPPINCOTT, BERTRAM III. "The Hutton family of 'Shamrock Cliff.'" NH, 64 (Fall 1991), 163-174.
Historic house.

3524.   LOVELL, MARGARETTA M. "'Such furniture as will be most profitable': the business of cabinetmaking in eighteenth-century Newport." Winterthur Portfolio, 26 (Spring 1991), 27-62.

3525.   LUKER, RALPH E. "'Under our own vine and fig tree': from African unionism to black denominationalism in Newport, Rhode Island, 1760-1876." Slavery & Abolition [U.K.], 12 (Sept. 1991), 23-48.
Study based on the records of the Free African Union Society and other organizations.

3526.   McCRILLIS, JOHN O. C. "Thanks to Susan Braley Franklin, scholar and mentor." NH, 64 (Fall 1991), 183-188.
During the 1920s and 1930s, Franklin helped to shape the author's life and career as a graphic designer.

3527. MECKEL, RICHARD A. "Henrietta Russell: Delsartean prophet to the Gilded Age." Journal of American Culture, 12 (Spring 1989), 65-78.
Instructed "high society" women in "an aesthetic of gesture and expression, which, popularized and expanded, swept the country."

3528. MICHIE, THOMAS S., and CHRISTOPHER P. MONKHOUSE. "Pattern books in the Redwood Library and Athenaeum, Newport, Rhode Island." Antiques, 137 (Jan. 1990), 286-299.
"For architecture, design, and ornament."

3529. MURPHY-SCHLICHTING, MARY. "A summer salon: literary and cultural circles in Newport, Rhode Island, 1850-1890." Ph.D. dissertation, New York Univ., 1992. 270p.
Abstracted in DAI, 53:8A (1993), 2816.

3530. NICOLOSI, ANTHONY S. "The founding of the Newport Naval Training Station, 1878-1883: an exercise in naval politics." American Neptune, 49 (Fall 1989), 291-304.

3531. _____. "The Newport Asylum for the Poor: a successful nineteenth-century institutional response to social dependency." RIH, 47 (Feb. 1989), 3-21.

3532. OCHSNER, JEFFREY KARL, and THOMAS C. HUBKA. "H.H. Richardson: the design of the William Watts Sherman House." Society of Architectural Historians, Journal, 51 (June 1992), 121-145.
1870s.

3533. POTVIN, RONALD M. "The architectural history of the Wanton-Lyman-Hazard House." NH, 62 (Spring 1989). 45-84.
See also entry 3498.

3534. _____. "The rearing of the Quaker faithful: family, meeting and transitions from city to farm." NH, 65:1 [1993], 1-33.
Study of the Obadiah Williams family, which migrated to rural New York State. See also entry 3514.

3535. RAFAEL, ANITA. "Let there be light—at least on Pelham Street." Old RI, 2 (May 1992), 38-39.
1805.

3536. _____. "The merchant prince." Old RI, 2 (Jan. 1992), 2, 4-5.
Aaron Lopez (1731-1782).

3537. _____. "The minister's silkworms." Old RI, 2 (Mar./Apr. 1992), 40-41.
Ezra Stiles's experiment with silkworms (ca. 1763).

3538. RECTOR, MARGARET HAYDEN. Alva, that Vanderbilt woman: her story as she might have told it. [Wickford]: Dutch Island Pr., 1992. 324p. RHi. *
Alva Smith Vanderbilt Belmont (1853-1933).

3539. REYNOLDS, RICHARD. "Richard Canfield: the dashing gambler of Newport." Old RI, 4 (Apr. 1994), 48-50.
Lived 1855-1914.

3540. ROTENBERG, JOSHUA. "Black-Jewish relations in eighteenth-century Newport." RIJHN, 11 (Nov. 1992), 117-171.

3541. SANFORD, DON A. "Entering into the covenant: the history of Seventh Day Baptists in Newport." NH, 66 (Summer 1994), 1-48.

3542. SCHREIER, BARBARA A., and MICHELE MAJER. "The resort of pure fashion: Newport, Rhode Island, 1890-1914." RIH, 47 (Feb. 1989), 22-34.

3543. SCHUMACHER, ALAN T. "Newport's real estate king." NH, 61 (Spring 1988), 36-51.
Alfred Smith (1809-1886), known for "his far-sighted promotion of Newport's most famous and vital thoroughfares—Bellevue (1853) and Ocean (1867) Avenues."

3544. SCOTT, HAROLD L. SR. "Thomas and John Fatkin: 1846 survivors of a disastrous shipwreck near Newport, Rhode Island." NH, 64 (Fall 1991), 177-181.

3545. SELIG, ROBERT A. "A German soldier in New England during the Revolutionary War: the account of Georg Daniel Flohr." NH, 65:2 [1994], 49-65.
Member of the French expeditionary force.

3546. SNYDACKER, DANIEL JR., RICHARD W. BERRY, and EDWARD SMITH JR. "Pride and pleasure in the New England Steamship Company." NH, 62 (Fall 1989), 151-183.
Repair company. See also entry 3490.

3547. SULLIVAN, MARK W. "John F. Kensett at Newport: the making of a luminist painter." Antiques, 138 (Nov. 1990), 1030-1041.
Lived 1816-1872.

3548. TAVERNER, GILBERT Y. "A portfolio of Newport education." NH, 61 (Summer 1988), 95-107.

3549. TILLEY, EDITH JURGENS. "The finest cut 'valley' of the entire year." NH, 64 (Fall 1991), 189-190.
Recollections of a family greenhouse, in business from 1901-1972.

3550   NEWPORT

3550.   WADLEIGH, JOHN R. "1886—a milestone year: Alfred Mahan and McCarty Little come aboard at the War College." NH, 59 (Fall 1986), 149-154.
U.S. Naval War College.

3551.   WOODBRIDGE, GEORGE. "George Washington and Newport." NH, 64 (Summer 1991), 109-133.

3552.   _____. "The Vernon House." NH, 60 (Winter 1987), 28-39.
18th century.

SEE ALSO entries 143, 395, 409, 2476, 3248, 3257, 3265, 3295, 3310, 3330, 3343, 3347, 3402, 3425, 3463.

NORTH KINGSTOWN (WASHINGTON CO.)

3553.   ARCHAMBAULT, FLORENCE. "Gilbert Stuart's birthplace." Old RI, 2 (June 1992), 32, 34-35.
The noted artist (lived 1755-1828).

3554.   BOISVERT, DONALD J. "The Quonset hut: ugly duckling of WWII." Old RI, 3 (Aug. 1993), 60-62.
Building type, developed at the Quonset Point Naval Air Station.

3555.   BRADNER, LAWRENCE H. The Plum Beach Light: the birth, life, and death of a lighthouse. [Wickford: Dutch Island Pr.], 1989. xiii, 196p. RHi. *

3556.   FULLER, NATHAN. "The place of the marked rock." Old RI, 2 (May 1992), 34-36.
Devil's Foot Rock.

3557.   _____. "This is a castle?: The story of Smith's Castle at Cocumscussoc." Old RI, 2 (May 1992), 23, 25- 26.

3558.   McALEER, ALTHEA H., BEATRIX HOFFIUS, and DEBY JECOY NUNES. Graveyards of North Kingstown, Rhode Island. n.p., 1992. 59, [200]p. RHi. *

SEE ALSO entries 1, 3309, 3414.

NORTH PROVIDENCE (PROVIDENCE CO.)

3559.   CANDEE, RICHARD McALPIN. "The 1822 Allendale Mill and slow-burning construction: a case study in the transmission of architectural technology." IA, 15:1 (1989), 21-34.

3560.   DEXTER, VINCENT H. "The colonial powder mill at Centredale." Old RI, 3 (Nov. 1993), 46-49.

3561.   LEONARD, DONALD E. "A house and church in 19th century North Providence." Old RI, 3 (Apr. 1993), 55.
Zachariah Allen House and the Allendale Chapel.

PAWTUCKET (PROVIDENCE CO.)

3562.   BOURCIER, PAUL G. Dolls and duty: Martha Chase and the Progressive agenda, 1889-1925. Providence: Rhode Island Historical Society, 1989. 48p. RHi. *
See also next entry.

3563.   BRADSHAW, MARJORIE A. The doll house: story of the Chase doll. n.p., 1986. 64p. RHi. *
Made by M.J. Chase and Co. See also preceding entry.

3564.   COHEN, PAUL S., and BRENDA H. COHEN. "Slater Mill historic site at Pawtucket, Rhode Island." Journal of College Science Teaching, 22 (Aug. 1993), 381-382.

3565.   D'AMATO, DONALD A. "Rhode Island's race track war: when politicians strained at the bit." Old RI, 3 (Mar. 1993), 22-23, 25-26; (Apr. 1993), 32-34.
Narragansett Racing Association (1937). Second installment entitled "Both Quinn and O'Hara are losers in the 'racetrack war.'"

3566.   JOHNSON, BETTY, and JAMES L. WHEATON. "The first international steamboat muster, on the waterfront." Old RI, 2 (Mar./Apr. 1992), 42-45.
Pawtucket's involvement with early steamboating.

3567.   LAMARRE, BEATRICE. Bean Hill. N.Y.: Vantage Pr., 1988. 138p. RHi. *
Author's recollections of life in a Pawtucket neighborhood since the 1930s.

3568.   PAWTUCKET, R.I. WOODLAWN BAPTIST CHURCH. Woodlawn Baptist Church, Pawtucket, Rhode Island: 1893-1993. n.p., [1994?]. [24]p. RHi. *

3569.   SWANSON, WAYNE R. The Christ child goes to court. Philadelphia: Temple Univ. Pr., 1990. xi, 242p. RPB. *
Case study of a 1984 decision by the U.S. Supreme Court upholding the city's right to display a nativity scene.

SEE ALSO entries 147, 3404, 3407, 3409.

PORTSMOUTH (NEWPORT CO.)

3570.   ALMEIDA, JOYCE FAIRCHILD. The Knights of Hog Island. Warwick: Priv. Print., 1992. x, 84p. RHi. *
Knight family.

3571. CARPENTER, FRANK. "Paradise held: William Ellery Channing and the legacy of Oakland." NH, 65:3 [1994], 91-127.
    Oakland Farm.

3572. CHAMPLIN, NATHANIEL L. "Rhode Island roots of the Champlin Foundation." Old RI, 3 (Mar. 1993), 29-30.

3573. PIERCE, JOHN T. SR. Historical tracts of the town of Portsmouth, R.I. Portsmouth: Hamilton Printing, 1991. vi, 114p. RHi. *

    SEE ALSO entries321, 3313, 3376, 3512.

PROVIDENCE (PROVIDENCE CO.)

3574. ALLEN, MEL R. "The straight shooter." Yankee, 56 (May 1992), 64-69, 122-124.
    The childhood and upbringing of former state attorney general Arlene Violet.

3575. ANTHONY, H. CUSHMAN. "Decoration Day 1916: the happy memories of an old Boy Scout." Old RI, 3 (May 1993), 15-18, 20.

3576. BOISVERT, DONALD J. "The Civil War Soldier's and Sailor's Monument." Old RI, 3 (May 1993), 13-14.

3577. _____. "The house of worship in John Angell's apple orchard." Old RI, 2 (Dec. 1992/Jan. 1993), 6, 10-15.
    First Baptist Meeting House.

3578. _____. "Strike up the band!" Old RI, 3 (Oct. 1993), 60-62.
    David Wallis Reeves and the American Band (late-19th century).

3579. BOURCIER, PAUL G. "Prosperity at the wharves: Providence shipping, 1780-1850." RIH, 48 (May 1990), 35-49.

3580. BROWN, GEORGE T. "'With a voice of singing.'" Old RI, 3 (Mar. 1993), 32, 34.
    History of Providence's University Glee Club.

3581. BROWN, HENRY A. L. John Brown of Providence and his chariot. Providence: Webster Pr., 1989. 12p. RHi. *
    Horse-drawn vehicle.

3582. BROWN UNIVERSITY. FRIENDS OF THE LIBRARY. Special collections at Brown University: a history and guide. Leslie T. Wendel, ed. Providence, 1988. 143p. RPB. *

3583. BRUNKOW, ROBERT DeVRIES. "Individualism and community on the New England frontier: Providence, Rhode Island, in the age of Roger Williams, 1636-1686." Ph.D. dissertation, Univ. of California, Berkeley, 1980. 268p. RHi. *

3584. CANNON, PETER HUGHES. H.P. Lovecraft. Boston: Twayne Publishers, 1989. xv, 153p. RHi. *
    The well-known author (lived 1890-1937).

3585. CARROLL, JOHN M. "A genuine unknown hero." Brown Alumni Monthly, 93 (Oct. 1992), 30-35.
    Fritz Pollard (Brown, class of 1919), an early black football star.

3586. D'AMATO, DONALD A. "Captain Abe Whipple: merchant, privateer, smuggler and hero." Old RI, 3 (May 1993), 50-53.
    Revolutionary era. See also entry 3287.

3587. _____. "John Brown: the cleverest boy in Providence town." Old RI, 2 (June 1992), 50-51.

3588. DALTON, ED. "Rain of fish." Old RI, 2 (July 1992), 12-14.
    Incident that affected parts of Olneyville during a storm in 1900.

3589. DAOUST, NORMA LASALLE. "Housing the poor: the early years of public housing in Providence." RIH, 51 (Feb. 1993), 23-31.

3590. DeSILVA, BRUCE. "The story between the lines." Rhode Island Monthly, 2 (Sept. 1989), 38-42, 86-90, 92, 94-95.
    Includes historical information about the Providence Journal (newspaper).

3591. DESJARLAIS-LUETH, CHRISTINE. "Brown University and academic library history." Libraries & Culture, 25 (Spring 1990), 218-242.

3592. DIFFILY, ANNE. "100 years of women at Brown." Brown Alumni Monthly, 92 (Dec. 1991/Jan. 1992), 18-20, 55.
    See also entry 3662.

3593. DOHERTY, JOE. "H.P. Lovecraft: the scariest man in Rhode Island; weird fiction & dark fantasy." Old RI, 3 (Oct. 1993), 10-14.
    See also entry 3584.

3594. DOWNEY, CHARLOTTE. "Historic names of Providence's waterfront and College Hill." Names, 37 (Dec. 1989), 317-328.

3595. FELLMAN, BRUCE. "Enchanted evenings: Ladd Observatory turns 100." Brown Alumni Monthly, 92 (Mar. 1992), 38-41, 43-45.
    Astronomical observatory at Brown.

3596   PROVIDENCE

3596.   FERGENSON, LARAINE R. "Margaret Fuller as a teacher in Providence: the school journal of Ann Brown." Studies in the American Renaissance (1991), 59-118.
    1837-1838. See also entry 3608.

3597.   FUOCO, JOE. "Italians in Rhode Island: Federal Hill." Old RI, 3 (Apr. 1993), 10-14; (May 1993), 26-29; (June/July 1993), 9, 11-12; (Aug. 1993), 23, 25-27.
    Titles of installments vary.

3598.   GOLDOWSKY, SEEBERT J. A century and a quarter of spiritual leadership: the story of the Congregation of the Sons of Israel and David (Temple Beth-El), Providence, Rhode Island. Providence: Congregation of the Sons of Israel and David, 1989. xiv, 530p. RHi. *
    Synagogue.

3599.   _____. "First Jewish students at Brown University." RIJHN, 11 (Nov. 1993), 296-314.

3600.   _____. "My father and the early labor movement in Rhode Island." RIJHN, 10 (Nov. 1991), 509-510.
    Bernard Manuel Goldowsky (1864-1936), involved in "labor espionage" as a private detective.

3601.   _____. "100th anniversary of Temple Beth-El library." RIJHN, 11 (Nov. 1992), 240-241.
    See also entries 3598, 3605.

3602.   _____. "Society wedding." RIJHN, 10 (Nov. 1989), 317-322.
    Wedding of Flora S. Dimond and Louis Lyons (1892).

3603.   _____. Yankee surgeon: the life and times of Usher Parsons (1788-1868). Boston: Francis A. Countway Library of Medicine, 1988. xvi, 450p. RHi. *

3604.   GOLDSTEIN, MICHAEL. "Alone, a Jew is nothing: Jewish community in Providence in the middle to late nineteenth century." RIJHN, 11 (Nov. 1992), 218-232.

3605.   GOODWIN, GEORGE M. "The design of a modern synagogue: Percival Goodman's Beth-El in Providence, Rhode Island." American Jewish Archives, 45 (Spring/Summer 1993), 31-71.
    Designed between 1947 and 1952. See also entries 3598, 3601.

3606.   GROSSFIELD, LAURA. "A theory of American life: formation of secular identity and community among Providence Jews." RIJHN, 10 (Nov. 1990), 411-431.

3607.   HIMES, CINDY. "From equity to equality." Brown Alumni Monthly, 92 (Dec. 1991/Jan. 1992), 29-34.
    Traces changes in women's physical education and athletics at Brown.

3608.   HOFFMANN, TESS. "Miss Fuller among the literary lions: two essays read at 'the Coliseum' in 1838." Studies in the American Renaissance (1988), 37-53.
    Margaret Fuller. See also entry 3596.

3609.   HOLLERAN, MICHAEL. "Filling the Providence Cove: image in the evolution of urban form." RIH, 48 (Aug. 1990), 65-85.
    Late-19th century.

3610.   HORVITZ, ELEANOR F. "Harry S. Beck and other Jewish printers." RIJHN, 10 (Nov. 1990), 495-502.

3611.   HOWARD-GROH, SUSAN. "A visit from 'father.'" Brown Alumni Monthly, 91 (Oct. 1990), 39-42
    George Washington's visit to Brown in 1790.

3612.   IDA Katherine Colitz: a Providence Jewish clubwoman's diary." RIJHN, 10 (Nov. 1990), 433-441.
    1927-1931.

3613.   JAFFE, BETTY R. "The Miriam Hospital: 65 years of caring." RIJHN, 10 (Nov. 1989), 358-371.

3614.   JAGOLINZER, CARL. "My life in Providence." RIJHN, 10 (Nov. 1990), 487-494.
    Optometrist (born 1897).

3615.   JOHNSON, PEARCE B. Professional football in Rhode Island and its national connections. Richard Reynolds, ed. Providence, 1989. 372p. RHi. *
    The Providence Steam Roller, an early professional team. See also entry 3654.

3616.   KAPLAN, JEREMY. "The Benefit Street and Lippitt Hill Jewish community, 1900-1940." RIJHN, 11 (Nov. 1991), 47-59.
    See also entry 3619.

3617.   KERT, BERNICE. Abby Aldrich Rockefeller: the woman in the family. N.Y.: Random House, 1993. xv, 537p. RHi. *
    Lived 1894-1948. Biography includes Providence background.

3618.   KLYBERG, ALBERT T. "Rhode Island's cabinet of curiosity." Old RI, 3 (Dec. 1993/Jan. 1994), 16-17, 19- 20; 4 (Feb. 1994), 24-27; (Mar. 1994), 24-27.
    History of the Rhode Island Historical Society. Titles of installments vary.

3619.   KRANTZ, FLORENCE ZINN. "Memories of an early childhood near the Benefit Street area." RIJHN, 11 (Nov. 1991), 60-61.
    See also entry 3616.

3620. KRAUSSE, GERALD H. "Metamorphosis of the Providence waterfront: a geographic perspective." RIH, 48 (Nov. 1990), 97-111.

3621. LAMOREAUX, NAOMI R., and CHRISTOPHER GLAISEK. "Vehicles of privilege or mobility?: banks in Providence, Rhode Island, during the age of Jackson." Busines History Review, 65 (Autumn 1991), 502-527.

3622. LANCASTER, JANE. "Encouraging faithful domestic servants: race, deviance, and social control in Providence, 1820-1850." RIH, 51 (Aug. 1993), 71-87.

3623. LEONARD, D. W. "Levi Willard and the Night Watch." Old RI, 3 (Nov. 1993), 22.
Forerunner of police department.

3624. _____. "Mashapaug, Oxen and Hospital ponds." Old RI, 3 (Nov. 1993), 20-21.

3625. LEONARD, DONALD E. "A chain across the harbor." Old RI, 9 (Oct. 1992), 24.
During the American Revolution.

3626. _____. "Doctor Abraham Okie: the Edgar Allan Poe incident." Old RI, 3 (Feb. 1993), 7.
1848.

3627. _____. "George Washington slept here—but only once." Old RI, 3 (Feb. 1993), 43.
Taggart's Tavern (1790).

3628. _____. "One of Providence's outstanding 18th century buildings." Old RI, 2 (Oct. 1992), 20.
First Baptist Meeting House.

3629. _____. "A[n] outstanding woman of Summer Street." Old RI, 2 (Dec. 1992/Jan. 1993), 54-55.
Elleanor Eldridge (born 1785), a well-known black resident.

3630. _____. "Providence's tunnels." Old RI, 3 (Mar. 1993), 31.

3631. _____. "Put your name on the cannon." Old RI, 1 (Dec. 1992/Jan. 1993), 36.
Defense of Providence during the American Revolution.

3632. LISKER, LOWELL S. "The Lamson Oil story." RIH, 51 (Feb. 1993), 33-36.
Lamson Oil Company.

3633. LITTLE, AGNES EASTMAN. One hundredth anniversary of the Home for the Aged in Providence: 1874-1974. (1975) Rev. ed. Providence, [1982]. 51p. RHi. *

3634. McCAUGHEY-SILVIA, REGINA C. "Lectures and discussion questions of the Franklin Lyceum: a guide to attitudes and ideas in nineteenth-century Providence." Ph.D. dissertation, Univ. of Rhode Island, 1991. viii, 436p. *
Ca. 1831-1885. Abstracted in DAI, 53:1A (1992), 140-141.

3635. McLOUGHLIN, WILLIAM GERALD. "Providence: the confident years, 1890-1920." RIH, 51 (May 1993), 39-68.

3636. MILLER, BETTE. "The demise of the giants." CrHSN [May 1991], [3-7].
Large retailers in Providence.

3637. _____. "A gem in the ring of Providence." CrHSN [Feb. 1991], [5-7].
Old Stone Bank building.

3638. _____. "Once there were two arcades." CrHSN [Jan. 1989], [4-6].
Providence Arcade and Bragunn's Arcade, the latter of which was on South Main Street.

3639. _____. "Who is that up there, anyway?" CrHSN [Mar. 1990], [4-8].
"The Independent Man," on top of the State House. See also entry 3657.

3640. MITCHELL, MARTHA. Encyclopedia Brunoniana. Providence: Brown Univ. Library, 1993. 629p. RPB. *
Reference book about Brown.

3641. _____. "Jews at Brown University." RIJHN, 11 (Nov. 1993), 292-295.

3642. NOCERA, JOSEPH. "And then Marvin Barnes got hurt." New England Monthly, 6 (Oct. 1989), 70, 105, 107-109.
The 1973 Providence College basketball team.

3643. PERLMANN, ARI JOEL. "Beyond New York, a second look: the occupations of Russian Jewish immigrants in Providence, R.I., and in other small Jewish communities, 1900-1915." RIJHN, 10 (Nov. 1989), 375-388.

3644. _____. Ethnic differences: schooling and social structure among the Irish, Italians, Jews, and blacks in an American city, 1880-1935. N.Y.: Cambridge Univ. Pr., 1988. xi, 327p. RHi. *

3645. "PERRY Davis, the limping shoemaker who made good." Old RI, 1 (Dec. 1991), 12-13.
Became a manufacturer of patent medicines (19th century).

3646   PROVIDENCE

3646.   PHILLIPS, JANET M. Brown University: a short history. Providence: Office of University Relations, Brown Univ., 1992. 88p. RPB. *

3647.   PROVIDENCE, R.I. FIRST UNITARIAN CHURCH. HISTORY COMMITTEE. Thirty years, 1957-1987, with text and appendices expanded to 1991 and one appendix describing the church's inception and growth to 1931. [Providence, 1991] vii, 87p. RHi. *

3648.   PROVIDENCE COLLEGE. "Providence College: from the beginning": a short history of Providence College. Providence: Providence College Pr., 1992. 30p. RHi. *
        Title page is on inside back cover.

3649.   "THE PROVIDENCE Art Colony, 1850-1920." Sketches: an Art Journal, No. 2 (July 1991), [1-12].
        Authors: Catherine Little Bert and L.J. McElroy.

3650.   RAUB, PATRICIA. "Another pattern of urban living: multifamily housing in Providence, 1890-1930." RIH, 48 (Feb. 1990), 3-19.

3651.   RAUCH, KATHERINE. "The history of Rhode Island Hospital." Old RI, 3 (Nov. 1993), 11-17.

3652.   REILLY, JOSEPH D. "Suburban history: Browntown, Providence, R.I., 1946-1951." Old RI, 4 (Apr. 1994), 23-25.
        Housing development for World War II veterans.

3653.   REYNOLDS, RICHARD. "The Steam Roller story: 1928 NFL champs." Old RI, 3 (Nov. 1993), 58-62.
        See also next entry.

3654.   _____. The Steam Roller story. Providence, 1989. 34p. RHi. *
        Providence Steam Roller (football team). See also entry 3615.

3655.   ROSEN, SAMUEL. "How School House Candy started." RIJHN, 11 (Nov. 1993), 388-393.
        Manufacturer of candy.

3656.   SCANLAN, JAMES J. "The founding of LaSalle Academy." Old RI, 2 (Nov. 1992), 35-36.
        Church school, established ca. 1871.

3657.   _____. "The Independent Man: a crown on the masterpiece." Old RI, 4 (June 1994), 10-14.
        The statue on top of the Rhode Island State House. To be continued. See also entry 3639.

3658.   _____. "The marble of the Rhode Island State House." Old RI, 2 (Sept. 1992), 39.

3659.   _____. "The Smith Street Toll House." Old RI, 3 (Feb. 1993), 54-55.

3660.   _____. "The twelve granite columns of the Arcade Building." Old RI, 2 (July 1992), 55-58.
        From a quarry in Johnston.

3661.   SCHANTZ, MARK SAUNDERS. "Piety in Providence: the class dimensions of religious experience in Providence, Rhode Island, 1790-1860." Ph.D. dissertation, Emory Univ., 1990. 468p. *
        Examines "the relationship between Christianity and capitalism." Abstracted in DAI, 52:4A (1991), 1493.

3662.   THE SEARCH for equity: women at Brown University, 1891-1991. Polly Welts Kaufman, ed. Hanover, N.H.: University Pr. of New England, 1991. 351p. RPB. *

3663.   SELBY, BOB. "Diamonds in the rough: the Providence Grays—the first world champions of major league baseball." [Providence] Sunday Journal Magazine (Apr. 5, 1992), 6-9, 12-15.
        1884 champions.

3664.   SMITH, RONALD A. "Lee Richmond, Brown University, and the amateur-professional controversy in college baseball." NEQ, 64 (Mar. 1991), 82-99.
        Ca. 1880.

3665.   SMOLSKI, CHESTER E. "Waterfronts as a key to city-center development." RIH, 48 (Aug. 1990), 86-94.
        Particularly in Providence.

3666.   STEVENSON, JANIS M. "Eleazer Whipple (1649-1749): Rhode Island's first pensioner." Old RI, 2 (July 1992), 14, 16-17.
        Wounded during King Philip's War, he was granted a sum of money by the town in payment for his expenses.

3667.   SULLIVAN, GEORGE. "When Jim Thorpe ruined the Brown Bruins." Old RI, 2 (Nov. 1992), 41-45, 47; (Dec. 1992/Jan. 1993), 40-44.
        College football game in Providence (1912).

3668.   _____. "When Providence ruled the NFL." Old RI, 3 (Feb. 1993), 40-42.
        Providence Steam Roller, professional football team. See also entries 3615, 3654.

3669.   SULLIVAN, ROBERT J. "The restless landscape: anaylsis of motives for functional change in urban transportation-related buildings." NE-StLVGSPr, 17 (1987), 69-74.

3670.   TESTA, RICHARD LOUIS JR. "Movie exhibition practices and procedures during the Hollywood studio era in Providence, Rhode Island." Ph.D. dissertation, Univ. of Maryland, 1993. viii, 372p. *
        1928-1950s. Abstracted in DAI, 54:5A (1993), 1851.

3671. WALD, MATTHEW. "Memories of deadlines past." Brown Alumni Monthly, 92 (Apr. 1992), 18-19.
Brown Daily Herald, then celebrating its 100th anniversary.

3672. WHITE, RICHARD E. Boys & Girls Clubs of Providence: a history, 1868-1990. [Providence: The Clubs, 1990] [20]p. RHi. *

3673. ZURIER, MELVIN L. "Sons of Zion Synagogue: memories." RIJHN, 11 (Nov. 1992), 235-239.

SEE ALSO entries 135, 249, 371, 3244, 3265, 3280, 3287-3289, 3290, 3294, 3343, 3347, 3350, 3366.

RICHMOND (WASHINGTON CO.)

3674. "STRONG organs of inhabitiveness." Yankee, 57 (June 1993), 100-102, 104.
History of the Octagonal House, in Carolina.

SEE ALSO entry 3412.

SCITUATE (PROVIDENCE CO.)

3675. KRA, SIEGFRIED. "The yellow light." Yankee, 54 (Feb. 1990), 76-81, 107.
Author survived the crash of a small plane on frozen Scituate Reservoir (winter of 1982).

3676. MILLER, BETTE. "The birth of a reservoir." CrHSN [Feb. 1992], [3-7].
Scituate Reservoir.

3677. PROHASKA, SUDA J. "When family breeds contempt." Rhode Island Monthly, 2 (July 1989), 40, 43, 95-96.
Includes historical information about the Joslin family.

SEE ALSO entry 3405.

SMITHFIELD (PROVIDENCE CO.)

3678. LIND, LOUISE. "Smith-Appleby House: a peek at the old days." Old RI, 2 (Aug. 1992), 44-45.

3679. RHODE ISLAND. HISTORICAL PRESERVATION COMMISSION. Historic and architectural resources of Smithfield, Rhode Island. [Providence], 1992. v, 92p. RHi. *
Author: Walter A. Nebiker.

SOUTH KINGSTOWN (WASHINGTON CO.)

3680. CLARKE, WILLIAM CASE. "A boyhood in Wakefield, 1878-1893." Pettaquamscutt Reporter, 25 (Spring 1989), 1-9.
Autobiographical account, written in 1941.

3681. D'AMATO, DONALD A. "The Great Swamp Fight!" Old RI, 2 (Jan. 1992), 6-7.
King Philip's War (1675). See also entry 3687.

3682. GARDNER, THOMAS A. "The early postal services of South Kingstown." Pettaquamscutt Reporter, 25 (Winter 1988/1989), 1-6.
Written in 1923.

3683. "'GET a horse!': the auto comes to town." Pettaquamscutt Reporter, 25 (Winter 1988/89), 9-10.

3684. GOLDMAN, HOWARD A. "That good old man—whoever he was." Old RI, 2 (July 1992), 32, 36-37, 39-40.
Theophilus Whale (died ca. 1720) was thought by many to have been the English regicide Edward Whalley.

3685. LESLIE, JAMES W. "A look at the founding of the University of Rhode Island." Old RI, 2 (May 1992), 29-30.

3686. RAUCH, KATHERINE. "Pettasquamscutt Rock: the Narragansetts and the Atherton Purchase." Old RI, 4 (Apr. 1994), 60-62.
1659.

3687. ROY, MATTHEW. "The Great Swamp massacre." Review: the Magazine for Southern New England (Winter [1990]), 47, 49, 51-55, 68-69.
See also entry 3681.

3688. SCANLAN, JAMES J. "The Cajoot graphite mine." Old RI, 2 (Aug. 1992), 23.

3689. STEDMAN, OLIVER H. "History of the Larchwood Inn." Old RI, 2 (Feb. 1992), 40-41.
In Peace Dale.

3690. TURNBAUGH, SARAH PEABODY, and WILLIAM A. TURNBAUGH. The nineteenth-century American collector; a Rhode Island perspective: selections from the Museum of Primitive Art and Culture, Peace Dale, Rhode Island. Peace Dale: Museum of Primitive Art and Culture, 1991. 62p. RHi. *

3691. YOW, VALERIE RALEIGH. The history of Hera: a women's art cooperative, 1974-1989. Wakefield: Hera Educational Foundation, 1989. 56p. RHi. *

SEE ALSO entry 3414.

3692   TIVERTON

TIVERTON (NEWPORT CO.)

3692.   McLOUGHLIN, WILLIAM GERALD. "Untangling the
        Tiverton tragedy: the social meaning of the terrible haystack
        murder of 1833." Journal of American Culture, 7 (Winter
        1984), 75-84.
            1832 murder of Sarah Maria Cornell, for which the Rev.
        Ephraim K. Avery was tried and acquitted. Additional
        writings on this subject are listed in the Rhode Island
        volume, under Tiverton, and in the Massachusetts volume
        and Vol. 8, under Fall River, Mass.

        SEE ALSO entry 3400.

WARREN (BRISTOL CO.)

3693.   REYNOLDS, RICHARD. "Lizzie Murphy: queen of
        diamonds." Old RI, 4 (Apr. 1994), 11-15.
            Star baseball player (lived 1894-1964).

WARWICK (KENT CO.)

3694.   BRENNAN, DEBORAH B. "Summers on Narragansett Bay:
        amusement parks remembered." Old RI, 2 (May 1992), 44-
        45, 49.
            Rocky Point Park and the American Band.

3695.   D'AMATO, DONALD A. "John Warner called the 'whole
        towne rogues and theeves.'" Old RI, 2 (Feb. 1992), 6-7.
            "Warwick's first town clerk."

3696.   _____. "Rhode Island's 'Crime Castle' exposed in 1935."
        Old RI, 3 (Aug. 1993), 48-49, 51-52; (Sept. 1993), 38-41;
        (Oct. 1993), 40-44; (Nov. 1993), 37-42.
            Carl Rettich and Prohibition-era smuggling and other
        criminal activities. Titles of installments vary.

3697.   _____. Warwick's 350 year heritage: a pictorial history.
        Warwick: Warwick Museum, 1992. 224p. RHi. *

3698.   _____. "Warwick's turbulent, rich, and colorful past." Old
        RI, 2 (June 1992), 28-31; (Nov. 1992), 37- 39.

3699.   GURA, PHILIP F. "Samuel Gorton's commentary on the
        Lord's Prayer." RIH, 51 (Nov. 1993), 121-127.
            Written ca. 1650s.

3700.   KERBER, JORDAN EDWARD. "Conducting 'siteless
        surveys': results from coastal New England." North
        American Archaeologist, 14:1 (1993), 25-42.
            Based on a survey at Potowomut Neck.

3701.   _____. "Saving endangered sites in southern New England:
        public archaeology at Lambert Farm, Warwick, Rhode
        Island." ArcSocConB, No. 53 (1990), 17-24.
            Prehistoric site. See also the next two entries.

3702.   _____, ALAN D. LEVEILLEE, and RUTH L.
        GREENSPAN. "An unusual dog burial feature at the
        Lambert Farm site, Warwick, Rhode Island: preliminary
        observations." Archaeology of Eastern North America, 17
        (Fall 1989), 165-174.
            See also preceding and following entries.

3703.   LEVEILLEE, ALAN D. "Eastern woodland mortuary
        practices as reflected in canine burial features at the Lambert
        Farm site, Warwick, Rhode Island." MASB, 54 (Spring
        1993), 19-24.
            See also the two preceding entries.

3704.   WARWICK Neck: a special portrait of historic resources.
        Bill Nixon, ed. [Warwick Neck]: Warwick Neck
        Improvement Association, 1991. vii, 319p. RHi. *

        SEE ALSO entries 3268, 3290, 3295, 3300.

WESTERLY (WASHINGTON CO.)

3705.   BOISVERT, DONALD J. "The flying horses of Watch Hill."
        Old RI, 2 (Aug. 1992), 6, 8-9.
            Flying Horse Carousel.

3706.   CHICK, LAWRENCE E. The Westerly Band, 1852-1990: an
        informal history. Westerly: Utter, 1989. 68p. RHi. *

3707.   HUMBLE, ROBERTA MUDGE. "Aging, face lifts, and
        community service: the reacquaintance of Westerly with its
        armory." Old RI, 3 (Mar. 1993), 27-28.

3708.   MOORE, PAUL JOHNSON. The search: an account of the
        Fort Road tragedy. Westerly: Sun Graphics, 1989. iv, 100p.
        RHi. *
            The author's sister and stepmother, summer residents of
        Watch Hill, were among the victims of the 1938 hurricane;
        the former's body was recovered after a lengthy search.

3709.   PEABODY, MYRA A. "The survivor." Old RI, 2 (Sept.
        1992), 28-30.
            1938 hurricane.

3710.   PERRY, HARVEY C. II. "Early Rhode Island banking:
        eighth oldest bank in the country." Old RI, 2 (Nov. 1992), 8,
        10-11.
            Washington Trust Company.

3711.   SMITH, ISAAC G. JR. "The Smith Granite Company, Westerly, Rhode Island." Old RI, 2 (Aug. 1992), 19-23.

3712.   UTTER, GEORGE HERBERT. Old pictures of Westerly. Westerly: Utter, 1991. 71, [6]p. RHi. *
        Includes historical text.

        SEE ALSO entry 3413.

        WOONSOCKET (PROVIDENCE CO.)

3713.   ANCTIL, PIERRE. "Brokers of ethnic identity: the Franco-American petty bourgeoisie of Woonsocket, Rhode Island (1865-1945)." Quebec Studies, 12 (1991), 33-48.

3714.   BEIRNE, GERALD. "The Nap Lajoie story: Woonsocket's super star." Old RI, 3 (June/July 1993), 40-45.
        Hall of Fame baseball player (early-20th century).

3715.   BOURGET, PAUL A., and DONALD L. HOARD. Towers of faith and family: St. Ann's Church, Woonsocket, Rhode Island, 1890-1990. Woonsocket: St. Ann's Church, 1990. 312p. RHi. *
        Roman Catholic.

3716.   FOSTER, GERALDINE S. "100th anniversary of B'nai Israel, Woonsocket—1993." RIJHN, 11 (Nov. 1993), 354-358.
        Synagogue.

3717.   GERSTLE, GARY LLOYD. Working-class Americanism: the politics of labor in a textile city, 1914-1960. N.Y.: Cambridge Univ. Pr., 1989. xii, 356p. RHi. *
        See also this author's Ph.D. dissertation on the rise of industrial unionism in Woonsocket, 1931-1941 (Harvard Univ., 1983; entry 10873 in Vol. 8).

3718.   LEVIN, ZEL. "Ethnic diversity key to community strength: a century of Jewish history in Woonsocket." Old RI, 3 (June/July 1993), 23, 25-27.

3719.   _____. "The Frying Pan Club: politics sizzle in Woonsocket." Old RI, 3 (Feb. 1993), 52-54.
        1930s.

3720.   _____. "The religious battle of the century." Old RI, 2 (Dec. 1992/Jan. 1992), 46, 48.
        The Sentinelle Affair in the Roman Catholic Church (1920s).

3721.   LIND, LOUISE. "Fish & chips: a romance, an art, a tradition." Old RI, 3 (Mar. 1993), 58-59.
        Robinson family's restaurant.

3722.   _____. "June 24: big day among Franco-Americans: 'la fete de St. Jean-Baptiste.'" Old RI, 3 (June/July 1993), 7-8.

3723.   MURPHY, JAMES M. "The Gabby Hartnett story: from mill town to Cooperstown." Old RI, 3 (May 1993), 40-45.
        Chicago Cubs catcher, inducted into the Baseball Hall of Fame in 1955. Includes his early life in Woonsocket.

        SEE ALSO entries 3338, 3410.

Vermont

**Entries for the state as a whole
or pertaining to
more than one county**

3724. ABBOTT, PEGGY. "Working with Mr. Rugg's collection."
VtHN, 41 (Nov.-Dec. 1990), 115-116.
The Harold G. Rugg collection of Vermontiana at the
Vermont Historical Society. See also entries 3071, 3839.

3725. ALLEN, ETHAN. The best of Ethan Allen. Benson:
Chaldize Publishers, 1992. 116p. VtU.
Selected writings. See also next entry.

3726. _____, and IRA ALLEN. Ethan and Ira Allen: collected
works. J. Kevin Graffagnino, ed. Benson: Chaldize Pr., 1992.
3v. VtHi. *

3727. ALLEN, LEVI. "The autobiography of Levi Allen." VtH, 60
(Spring 1992), 77-94.
Levi, "the loyalist brother of Ethan and Ira Allen," wrote
this account in 1797. Michael A. Bellesiles, ed. See also
entries 3730, 3820.

3728. BADAMO, MICHAEL. The republic of Vermont, 1777-
1991: a short history. Montpelier: Woodchuck Pr., 1992. 32p.
VtHi. *

3729. BALL, HOWARD. "From 'one town, one [or two] vote[s]'
to 'one person, one vote': the impact of reapportionment on
Vermont, 1777-1992." VtH, 61 (Spring 1993), 85-99.

3730. BANDEL, BETTY. "Levi, language, and people." CCHSB,
25 (Spring 1990), 1-4.
Levi Allen, brother of Ethan and Ira. See also entries
3727, 3820.

3731. BARNETT, BERNICE. "Blazing a trail along the Albany
Post Road." Cracker Barrel, 16 (Fall/Winter 1992-1993),
8-11.
See also next entry.

3732. _____, and B. B. WOODS. Roads in the wilderness. Halifax,
1993. 100p. VtHi. *
A study of two roads—the "very first" in southern
Vermont.

3733. BASSETT, THOMAS DAY SEYMOUR. "Cabin religion in
Vermont, 1724-1791." VtH, 62 (Spring 1994), 69-87.

3734. _____. "Father of a college president: James Buckham
(1795-1886)." CCHSB, 24 (Summer 1989), 4-6.
Congregational minister and father of Matthew H. B.
Buckham, who became president of the Univ. of Vermont in
1871.

3735. _____. The growing edge: Vermont villages, 1840-1880.
Montpelier: Vermont Historical Society, 1992. 232p. VtHi. *
Published version of author's Ph.D. dissertation (Harvard
Univ., 1952; entry 10910 in Vol. 8).

3736. BEACH, ALLEN PENFIELD. Lake Champlain as centuries
pass. Basin Harbor: Basin Harbor Club & Lake Champlain
Maritime Museum, 1994. viii, 115p. VtHi. *

3737. BECK, JANE C. "Traditional folk medicine in Vermont."
DubSemPr (1990), 34-43.

3738. BELLESILES, MICHAEL A. Revolutionary outlaws: Ethan
Allen and the struggle for independence on the early
American frontier. Charlottesville: University Pr. of Virginia,
1993. xi, 428p. VtHi. *
See also this author's Ph.D. dissertation on the same
subject (Univ. of California, Irvine, 1986; entry 10918 in
Vol. 8).

3739. BELLICO, RUSSELL PAUL. "Lake Champlain: a
storehouse of marine history." Scubapro: Diving &
Snorkeling (Spring 1988), 52-55, 74.

---

* Online Computer Library Center (OLCC) listings for books and
dissertations marked with this symbol may include additional
library locations.

3740   VERMONT

3740.   BELLICO, RUSSELL PAUL. Sails and steam in the mountains: a maritime and military history of Lake George and Lake Champlain. Fleischmanns, N.Y.: Purple Mountain Pr., 1992. 393p. VtHi. *

3741.   BERNARD, JEAN-PAUL. "Vermonters and the Lower Canadian rebellions of 1837-1838." VtH, 58 (Fall 1990), 250-263.

3742.   BROWN, ELIZABETH CROCKETT. Historical sketches of Vermont communities. n.p., 1991. x, 134p. VtHi. *

3743.   BRYAN, GEORGE B. A historical who's who of Vermont theatre. Burlington: Center for Research on Vermont, Univ. of Vermont, 1991. v, 77p. VtU. *

3744.   BUEHNER, TERRY L. "Green Mountain women." M.A. thesis, Univ. of Vermont, 1992. ii, 185p. *

3745.   BURLINGTON, DIOCESE OF (ROMAN CATHOLIC). The bishops of Burlington. Burlington, 1992. 20p. VtHi. *

3746.   CALLOWAY, COLIN GORDON. "Surviving the dark ages: Vermont Abenakis during the contact period." VtH, 58 (Spring 1990), 70-81.
        Abenaki Indians. See also next entry.

3747.   _____. The western Abenakis of Vermont, 1600-1800: war, migration, and the survival of an Indian people. Norman, Okla.: Univ. of Oklahoma Pr., 1990. xxv, 346p. VtHi. *
        See also entry 72.

3748.   CARNAHAN, PAUL A., and MICHAEL SHERMAN. "Chandler, Bristol, and Perham photographic collections, Vermont Historical Society Library, Montpelier, Vermont." VtH, 61 (Spring 1993), 100-105.
        Collections of the works of William D. Chandler of St. Albans, R. C. Bristol of Bellows Falls, and Alice Perham of Cambridgeport (late-19th and early-20th centuries).

3749.   CARTER, CHRISTINE. "Sources of women's history at the Vermont State Archives." VtH, 59 (Winter 1991), 30-48.

3750.   CELEBRATING a century of granite art. Gene Sessions, ed. Montpelier: T.W. Wood Art Gallery, 1989. viii, 30p. VtHi. *

3751.   CLEVELAND, RICHARD L., and DONNA BISTER. Plain and fancy: Vermont's people and their quilts as a reflection of America. Gualala, Calif.: Quilt Digest Pr., 1991. 103p. VtHi. *

3752.   CLIFTON, MERRITT. [Baseball in Vermont.] Monroe, Conn.: Samisdat, [1991?]. 3v. VtU. *
        Titles of the volumes vary.

3753.   CLOSE, VIRGINIA L. "Vermont's landmark Act 250." Dartmouth College Library Bulletin, 32 (Nov. 1991), 38-43.
        Background of the state's Land Use and Development Law of 1970.

3754.   COFFIN, HOWARD. "The blue & the gray in Vermont." Vermont Life, 46 (Autumn 1991), 4-13.
        Historic sites associated with the Civil War.

3755.   CROSS, MICHELE A. "Mason S. Stone and progressivism in Vermont public education, 1892-1916." VtH, 62 (Winter 1994), 27-40.

3756.   CROWN POINT ROAD ASSOCIATION. Historical markers on the Crown Point Road. (1965) Rev. ed. Springfield, 1992. xi, 128p. VtHi. *
        Note: this item replaces entry 521 in the Vermont volume.

3757.   CUMMINGS, CHARLES B. "The Vermont war conventions." RHSQ, 19:1 (1989), 3-11.
        Meetings were held in a number of counties in September and October 1917 "to strengthen Vermont's resolve."

3758.   DANN, KEVIN. "From degeneration to regeneration: the Eugenics Survey of Vermont, 1925-1936." VtH, 59 (Winter 1991), 5-29.
        Seeking to improve human genetics, proponents of eugenics sought to identify unfit individuals and discourage or prevent them from reproducing. See also entry 3863.

3759.   _____. "The public and the western Abenaki." CCHSB, 27 (Summer 1993), 1-7.
        The Abenaki as depicted in Burlington's 1909 celebration of the Fourth of July and in the writings of Kenneth Roberts.

3760.   DAVIS, DEANE CHANDLER. Deane C. Davis: an autobiography. Shelburne: New England Pr., 1991. 352p. VtHi. *
        Former governor (lived 1900-1990).

3761.   DEMERITT, DAVID. "Climate, cropping, and society in Vermont, 1820-1850." VtH, 59 (Summer 1991), 133-165.

3762.   DEXTER, WARREN W., and BARBARA C. HANSON. Vermont: wilderness to statehood, 1748-1791. Rutland: Academy Books, 1989. v, 175p. VtHi. *

3763.   DISCOVERING the history and heritage of the Champlain Basin: a resource guide for teachers. Gregory Sharrow and Amy Demarest, comps. Middlebury: Vermont Folklife Center, 1993. 84p. VtHi. *

3764. DOUGLASS, JOHN AUBREY. "The Forest Service, the depression, and Vermont political culture: implementing New Deal conservation and relief policy." Forest & Conservation History, 34 (Oct. 1990), 164-178.

3765. DOW, ELIZABETH H. Treasures gathered here: a guide to the manuscript collection of the Sheldon Museum Research Center. Middlebury: Sheldon Museum, 1991. xxxiii, 167p. VtHi. *

3766. DURFEE, ELEAZER D., and D. GREGORY SANFORD. A guide to the Henry Stevens, Sr., collection at the Vermont State Archives. Montpelier: Vermont State Archives, 1989. x, 162p. VtHi. *
Vermontiana.

3767. ESCHOLZ, PAUL. "The roots of Vermont literature." Vermont Life, 43 (Winter 1988), 10-15.

3768. FASSETT, JOHN. Diary of Captain John Fassett, Jr. (1743-1803), when a first lieutenant of "Green Mountain Boys," September 1st to December 7th 1775. Dorest: Foundation for the Preservation & Protection of Green Mountain Boy History, 1991. 2v. VtHi.
The diary was kept "during trip to Canada and return." One of the two volumes is a facsimile of the manuscript, the other a transcription.

3769. FINBERG, LUISA SPENCER. "The press and pulpit: nativist voices in Burlington and Middlebury, 1853-1860." VtH, 61 (Summer 1993), 156-175.

3770. FISHER, EDWARD W. "The flood of 1927: the myth of the indomitable Vermont." University of Vermont History Review, 4 (Spring 1991), 16-25.

3771. FOX, GERALD B. "Optimism derailed: the economic impact of the Burlington & Lamoille Railroad." M.A. thesis, Univ. of Vermont, 1993. ix, 181p. *

3772. _____. "Vermont's big green machines: the Vermont Transit Lines." University of Vermont History Review, 4 (Spring 1991), 7-15.

3773. GADE, DANIEL W. "Weeds in Vermont as tokens of socioeconomic change." Geographical Review, 81 (Apr. 1991), 153-169.

3774. GALBRAITH, CATHERINE A. "W.W. Atwater: minister, publisher, and crusader against rum." VtHN, 43 (Sept- Oct. 1992), 82-85.
William Warren Atwater (1814-1878), a Methodist minister.

3775. GILLIES, PAUL S. Confronting statehood: a bicentennial series of short stories. Burlington: Center for Research on Vermont, Univ. of Vermont, 1992. ix, 107p. VtU. *
Historical essays.

3776. _____. "Daniel Chipman, first reporter of decisions." Vermont Bar Journal & Law Digest, 17 (Apr. 1991), 14-15, 17-18.
Vermont law reports.

3777. _____. Fifteen and counting: Vermont research, 1974-1989 (and beyond). Burlington: Center for Research on Vermont, Univ. of Vermont, 1989. 11p. VtU. *

3778. _____. "A short history of Vermont corporation law." Vermont Bar Journal & Law Digest, 18 (Apr. 1992), 19-21; (June 1992), 14-16.

3779. GILMORE-LEHNE, WILLIAM JAMES. "Reflections on three classics of Vermont history." VtH, 59 (Fall 1991), 227-249.
Discusses David M. Ludlum, Social ferment in Vermont, 1791-1850 (1939; entry 1291 in the Vermont volume); Lewis D. Stilwell, "Migration from Vermont (1776-1860)" (1937; entry 1912 in the Vermont volume); and Harold F. Wilson, The hill country of northern New England (1936; entry 3599 in Vol. 7).

3780. GRAI·FAGNINO, JONATHAN KEVIN. "'The country my soul delighted in': the Onion River Land Company and the Vermont frontier." NEQ, 65 (Mar. 1992), 24-60.
Ira Allen's role in the company, which was formed in 1773.

3781. _____. "Revolution and empire on the northern frontier: Ira Allen of Vermont, 1751-1814." Ph.D. dissertation, Univ. of Massachusetts, 1993. ix, 481p. VtU. *
Abstracted in DAI, 54:2A (1993), 656-657.

3782. _____. "'Twenty thousand muskets!!!': Ira Allen and the Olive Branch affair, 1796-1800." WMQ, 3 ser. 48 (July 1991), 409-431.
Allen's attempt "to arrange a Franco-American invasion of British Canada and the creation of a democratic republic...as northern neighbor to the U.S."

3783. GREEN MOUNTAIN POWER CORPORATION. Getting power to the people: the first 100 years of the Green Mountain Power Company. South Burlington, 1993. 48p. VtHi. *

3784. GREEN Mountain Horse Association, 1926-1990s; Green Mountain Horse Association Youth Center, 1966- 1990s. South Woodstock: The Association and Youth Center, 1993. 240p. VtHi. *

3785   VERMONT

3785. GUSTAFSON, PETER. "A lost hero of the Green Mountain Boys: remembering Remember Baker." Fort Ticonderoga Museum, Bulletin, 15 (Winter 1988), 15-27.

3786. GUYETTE, ELISE A. "Black lives and white racism in Vermont, 1760-1870." M.A. thesis, Univ. of Vermont, 1992. iv, 156p. *

3787. _____. "The working lives of African Vermonters in census and literature, 1790-1870." VtH, 61 (Spring 1993), 69-84.

3788. HALLOWELL, ANN. "Women on the threshold: an analysis of rural women in local politics (1921-1941)." Rural Sociology, 52 (Fall 1987), 510-521.
    Vermont study.

3789. HAND, SAMUEL BURTON, and PAUL M. SEARLS. "Transition politics: Vermont, 1940-1952." VtH, 62 (Winter 1994), 5-25.

3790. HASTINGS, SCOTT E. JR., and ELSIE R. HASTINGS. Up in the morning early: Vermont farm families in the Thirties. Hanover, N.H.: University Pr. of New England, 1992. 159p. VtHi. *
    Photographs and "first-person recollections."

3791. HAVILAND, WILLIAM A., and MARJORY W. POWER. The original Vermonters: native inhabitants, past and present. (1981) Rev. ed. Hanover, N.H.: Univ. Pr. of New England, 1994. xxi, 338p. VtHi. *
    Note: this item replaces entry 11049 in Vol. 8.

3792. HECKENBERGER, MICHAEL J., JAMES B. PETERSEN, and NANCY ASCH SIDELL. "Early evidence of maize agriculture in the Connecticut River Valley of Vermont." Archaeology of Eastern North America, 20 (Fall 1992), 125-149.

3793. HENSON, BEN. "It was bitter cold in Vermont." Vermont Philatelist, 36 (Feb. 1992), 21-23.
    Summer of 1816.

3794. HEWITT, GEOF. "Hayden Carruth." Vermont Life, 43 (Winter 1988), 17-19.
    Contemporary poet. See also entry 3850.

3795. HIGBEE, WILLIAM WALLACE. Around the mountain: historical essays about Charlotte, Ferrisburg, and Monkton. Charlotte: Charlotte Historical Society, 1991. xxvi, 332p. VtU. *

3796. HILL, WILLIAM C. The Vermont constitution: a reference guide. Westport, Conn.: Greenwood Pr., 1992. xiii, 188p. VtU. *

3797. HINES, TERENCE. "Vermont state revenue stamps." Vermont Philatelist, 30 (Nov.1985), 4-5.

3798. HOFFBECK, STEVEN R. "'Remember the poor' (Galatians 2:10): poor farms in Vermont." VtH, 57 (Fall 1989), 226-240.

3799. HOFFMAN, JON T. "Vermont's first public safety commissioner." VtH, 62 (Summer 1994), 133-147.
    Gen. Merritt A. Edson, appointed in 1947, and the beginning of Vermont's state police force.

3800. HOWES, ALAN B. "The flood of 1927." Hazen Road Dispatch, 17 (Summer 1993), 5-6.

3801. JENNISON, PETER S. Roadside history of Vermont. Missoula, Mont.: Mountain Pr. Publishing, 1989. v, 265p. VtHi. *

3802. JOHNSON, SALLY. "A legacy of music." Vermont Life, 45 (Spring 1993), 16-18.
    The efforts of Helen Hartness Flanders to preserve the musical traditions of Vermont.

3803. JONES, ROBERT WILLOUGHBY. Green Mountains rails: Vermont's colorful trains. Los Angeles: Pine Tree Pr., 1994. 176p. VtHi.

3804. JONES, ROBERT C. Railroads of Vermont. Shelburne: New England Pr., 1993. xviii, 349p. VtHi. *

3805. JORDAN, PHILIP R. Rails beyond the Rutland. Newton, N.J.: Carstens Publications, 1988. 76p. VtHi. *

3806. KASOWSKI, MARGARET ANN, and ELIZABETH BROCK. "Tracing the line: early maps of the southern Quebec border area." Stanstead Historical Society Journal [Canada], 14 (1991), 67-71.

3807. KAYNOR, FAY CAMPBELL. "The golden era of private summer camps." VtHN, 41 (May/June 1990), 46-50.

3808. KERN, ARTHUR, and SYBIL KERN. "James Guild: quintessential itinerant portrait painter." The Clarion, 17 (Summer 1992), 48-57.
    Guild's diary records a number of visits to localities in Vermont between 1818 and 1824.

3809. KIEFER, JOSEPH, and MARTIN KEMPLE. "School gardening in Vermont." VtHN, 40 (May/June 1989), 54-56.

3810. KOTKER, NORMAN. "Hard winters." Vermont Magazine, 3 (Jan./Feb. 1991), 22-26.

3811. KRAMPETZ, NORM. "Recent history of the peace movement in the Deerfield Valley: growing beyond anger." Cracker Barrel, 15 (Spring-Summer 1992), 6-8.

3812. KUNIN, MADELEINE M. Living a political life. N.Y.: Knopf, 1994. x, 396p. VtU. *
   Autobiography of former governor.

3813. _____. "We made a difference": a view of six remarkable years. Montpelier: Editing & Design Publication Services, 1990. 16p. VtHi. *
   On Kunin's recently ended administration.

3814. LAKE CHAMPLAIN TRANSPORTATION COMPANY. I. To seize control: the conflicts over Lake Champlain (1609-1814), a brief history, by Jerry P. Williams. II. Two centuries of ferry boating on Lake Champlain, by Ralph Nading Hill. Burlington: Queen City Printers, 1990. vi, 36p. VtHi. *

3815. LAWLESS, ANN. "Save Outdoor Sculpture!: records, 1992-1993." VtH, 62 (Summer 1994), 166-182.
   As part of a national survey, the state organization documented "242 outdoor sculptures, both publicly and privately owned."

3816. LAWRENCE, GALE. "'Nothing but river valley and hills.'" Vermont Life, 43 (Summer 1989), 56-57.
   Henry David Thoreau's opinion of Vermont.

3817. LECLAIR, ROBYN. "The Abenaki plea for sovereignty." University of Vermont History Review, 4 (Spring 1991), 51-56.
   Abenaki Indians.

3818. LEWANDOSKI, JAN LEO. "The early house in northeastern Vermont: typical and atypical forms, 1770-1830." VtH, 61 (Winter 1993), 18-40.

3819. LUDLUM, DAVID McWILLIAMS. "Vermont weather from 1985 to 1990: a summary." VtHN, 42 (Nov.-Dec. 1991), 95-99.
   See also this author's Vermont weather book (1985; entry 11095 in Vol. 8).

3820. LUGINBUHL, VI. "Levi Allen: the forgotten brother." CCHSB, 25 (Spring 1990), 4-8.
   See also entries 3727, 3730.

3821. MAREK, RICHARD J. "Derelictions and depredations: or five brief notes on Vermont's mails in the 1860's." Vermont Philatelist, 36 (Nov. 1992), 153-157.

3822. MARSHALL, JEFFREY D. "Vilas family papers, 1794-1925." VtH, 62 (Winter 1994), 41-44.
   At the Univ. of Vermont.

3823. MARTIN, CHARLES J. "The Vermont constitution: past, present, and future." Vermont Bar Journal & Law Digest, 17 (Apr. 1991), 7-9; (June 1991), 36-37.

3824. McCORISON, MARCUS ALLEN. "Additions and corrections to Vermont imprints, 1778-1820." AASP, 101 (Oct. 1991), 375-389.
   See also entry 1315 in the Vermont volume and entry 11099 in Vol. 8.

3825. McKNIGHT, JACK. "Ethan Allen, philosopher." Vermont Life, 45 (Winter 1990), 25-28.

3826. MERRILL, PERRY H. Vermont skiing: a brief history of downhill & cross country skiing. Montpelier, 1987. vi, 42p. VtU. *

3827. METRAUX, DANIEL A. "Early Vermont historiography: the career of Pliny H. White." VtHN, 43 (July-Aug. 1992), 63-66.
   Lived 1822-1869.

3828. _____. "Smugglers and bootleggers in the Northeast Kingdom." Hazen Road Dispatch, 15 (Summer 1990), 20-21.

3829. MIDDLEBURY COLLEGE. CHRISTIAN A. JOHNSON GALLERY. Celebrating Vermont: myths and realities. Nancy Price Graff, ed. Hanover, N.H.: University Pr. of New England, 1991. 264p. VtU. *

3830. MILLER, JOHN MORRIS. Deer camp: last light in the Northeast Kingdom. Meg Ostrum, ed. Cambridge, Mass.: MIT Pr., 1992. x, 129p. VtHi. *
   Includes oral histories of experiences in Vermont hunting camps.

3831. MOMMSEN, DURWARD. The Black Jack in Vermont. Lake Oswego, Ore.: La Posta Publications, 1991. vi, 72p. VtU. *
   Postal history.

3832. MOULTON, FAYE SMITH. Adventuring into Vermont's past. Rutland: Academy Books, 1990. vii, 77p. VtU. *

3833. NEILL, MAUDEAN. Fiery crosses in the Green Mountains: the story of the Ku Klux Klan in Vermont. Randolph: Greenhills Books, 1989. viii, 95p. VtHi. *

3834 VERMONT

3834. NIMKE, R W. The Rutland: 60 years of trying. Rutland, Vt., and Walpole, N.H., 1987-1989. 6v. VtHi. *
Rutland Railroad. Note: this item replaces entry 11137 in Vol. 8.

3835. _____. The Rutland: arrivals and departures: train schedules for 1901-1961. Walpole, N.H., 1990. 204p. VtHi. *

3836. NUQUIST, REIDUN D. "The evolution of Vermont History News: reflections of an indexer." VtHN, 45 (Jan.-Feb. 1994), 7-14.
Serial publication of the Vermont Historical Society.

3837. O'BRIEN, CHARLES F. "Aiken and Vietnam: a dialogue with Vermont voters." VtH, 61 (Winter 1993), 5-17.
Sen. George D. Aiken and the Vietnam War (late 1960s and early 1970s).

3838. _____. "The role of Lake Champlain in Canadian-American relations." VtH, 58 (Summer 1990), 150-163.

3839. OSGOOD, WILLIAM E. "The Harold Goddard Rugg collection at the Vermont Historical Society." VtHN, 41 (Nov.-Dec. 1990), 117-120.
See also entries 3071, 3724.

3840. PENDERGAST, JAMES F. "Native encounters with Europeans in the sixteenth century in the region now known as Vermont." VtH, 58 (Spring 1990), 99-124.

3841. PERRIN, NOEL. "Is it Frost or Hard?" Vermont Life, 43 (Winter 1988), 20-21.
The Vermont poetry of Robert Frost and Walter Hard.

3842. PETERSEN, JAMES E. Otter Creek: the Indian road. Salisbury: Dunmore House, 1990. 170p. VtHi. *

3843. PINDELL, TERRY. "Starlight on the rails." Vermont Life, 46 (Winter 1991), 32-35, 70-71.
Recounts some incidents in the state's railroading history.

3844. PLUMLEY, LAVINIA LUCRETIA FLETCHER. Poems. North Montpelier: Driftwind Pr., 1930. 55p. VtU. *
Includes biographical sketch of Plumley (1848-1906).

3845. PODSIADLO, RICHARD J. "Vermont militia uniform regulations for 1837." Military Collector and Historian, 41 (Spring 1989), 14-18.

3846. POTASH, PAUL JEFFREY. "Deficiencies in our past." VtH, 59 (Fall 1991), 212-226.
Historiographical essay.

3847. _____. "Vermont statehood: the first twenty-five years and their echoes today." VtHN, 42 (Mar.-Apr. 1991), 22-28.

3848. PRESERVATION TRUST OF VERMONT. Historic preservation in Vermont. Paul Bruhn, ed. (1982) Rev. ed. Burlington, 1990. 36p. VtHi. *
Note: this item replaces entry 11161 in Vol. 8.

3849. "REPRESENTATIVE Danny Gore's Vermont." VtHN, 43 (Nov.-Dec. 1992), 104-106.
Perennial gubernatorial candidate since 1960s.

3850. ROBBINS, ANTHONY JEROME. "Existentialism and New England: the poetry of Hayden Carruth." Ph.D. dissertation, Louisiana State Univ., 1990. x, 239p. *
Born 1921. Abstracted in DAI, 51:9A (1991), 3075.

3851. RODGERS, ALICE A. "Nineteenth century steamboating on Lake Champlain: pioneering the excursion business." M.A. thesis, Univ. of Vermont, 1993. ii, 88p. *

3852. ROLANDO, VICTOR R. "19th-century charcoal production in Vermont." IA, 17:2 (1991), 15-36.

3853. _____. 200 years of soot and sweat: the history and archeology of Vermont's iron, charcoal, and lime industries. Burlington: Vermont Archaeological Society, 1992. viii, 296p. VtHi. *

3854. _____. "Vermont's 18th- and 19th-century blast furnace remains." IA, 18:1-2 (1992), 61-78.

3855. ROSENFELD, STEVEN. Making history in Vermont: the election of a socialist to Congress. Wakefield, N.H.: Hollowbrook Pub., 1992. xl, 439p. VtHi. *
Bernard Sanders (1990).

3856. ROTH, RANDOLPH ANTHONY. "Wayward youths: raising adolescents in Vermont, 1777-1815." VtH, 59 (Spring 1991), 85-96.

3857. _____. "Why are we still Vermonters?: Vermont's identity crisis and the founding of the Vermont Historical Society." VtH, 59 (Fall 1991), 197-211.

3858. RUSSELL, DICK. "Direct from heaven: the story of Green Mountain granite." Upper Valley, 7 (May/June 1993), 49-53.

3859. SAILLANT, JOHN. "'A doctrinal controversy between the Hopkintonian and the Universalist': religion, race, and ideology in postrevolutionary Vermont." VtH, 61 (Fall 1993), 197-216.
Lemuel Haynes and Hosea Ballou (ca. 1805).

3860. SANFORD, D. GREGORY. "A hardy race: forging the Vermont identity." VtH, 58 (Summer 1990), 201-206.

3861. _____, and PAUL S. GILLIES. "The Vermont Council of Censors." Vermont Bar Journal & Law Digest, 17 (Apr. 1991), 10-12.
See also entry 3878.

3862. SHARROW, GREGORY LEW. "The family farm: an ethnography of dairy farming in Vermont." Ph.D. dissertation, Univ. of Pennsylvania, 1990. ix, 409p. *
Abstracted in DAI, 51:5A (1990), 1724.

3863. SHEPHERD, ELIZABETH H. "Eugenics in the Green Mountain State." University of Vermont History Review, 4 (Spring 1991), 51-67.
See also entry 3758.

3864. SHER, RUTH. And everyone would sashay: the remembrances of the Ed Larkin Contra Dancers. West Topsham: Gibby Pr., 1989. viii, 80p. VtHi. *
Includes a list of performances (1957-1989).

3865. SHERMAN, JOE. "The battle of Valcour Island." Vermont Life, 45 (Summer 1991), 10-14.
Revolutionary War naval battle.

3866. _____. Fast lane on a dirt road: Vermont transformed, 1945-1990. Woodstock: Countryman Pr., 1991. 225p. VtHi. *
Political and economic change.

3867. _____. "The sixties: seedbed of the nineties." Vermont Magazine, 2 (Jan./Feb. 1990), 36-42, 84-86.
Background of 1990s social, cultural, and political attitudes.

3868. SMITH, DONALD L. "Bygone statehood celebrations." Central Vermont Magazine (Summer 1991), 11, 13, 15.

3869. _____, and EARLINE MARSH. "The CCC remembered: Civilian Conservation Corps sixty years ago." Central Vermont Magazine (Winter 1992), 5, 7, 9.

3870. SMITH, ROBERT M. "The Wilson Brothers & Co. in Vermont: a social and architectural history." University of Vermont History Review, 2 (Spring 1988), 19-22.
Philadelphia architectural firm's work in Vermont (late-19th century).

3871. SPRINGSTEAD, EVELYN DeBRUNE. Music in Vermont public schools in the twentieth century. East Montpelier: L. Brown & Sons Printing, 1992. 71p. VtHi. *

3872. STODDARD, GLORIA MAY. Grace & Cal: a Vermont love story. Shelburne: New England Pr., 1989. 159p. VtHi. *
Grace and Calvin Coolidge.

3873. STUART, RALPH, and ROBERT WINKLER. Environmental awareness and chemical right to know in Vermont: 1985-1990. Burlington: MEW Pr., 1992. 38p. VtHi. *

3874. SULLIVAN, ELLEN. A Vermont scrapbook: fifty Vermonters remember. Huntsville, Ala.: Honeysuckle Imprints, 1991. xii, 280p. VtHi. *

3875. TERRY, STEPHEN C. History of Hoff years, 1963-1969. n.p., 1990. 59p. VtHi. *
Gov. Philip H. Hoff.

3876. THOMPSON, ELLIE R. Voices from the hills: 70 years of Vermont broadcasting. n.p.: Vermont Association of Broadcasters, 1989. 48p. VtHi. *

3877. VERMONT. AIR NATIONAL GUARD. Vermont in the air. [Winooski: State of Vermont, Office of the Adjutant General], 1986. 80p. VtHi. *

3878. VERMONT. SECRETARY OF STATE. Records of the Council of Censors of the State of Vermont. Paul S. Gillies and D. Gregory Sanford, eds. Montpelier, 1991. xvii, 817p. VtHi. *

3879. _____. Vermont elections, 1789-1989. Christie Carter, ed. Montpelier, 1989. 362p. VtHi. *

3880. VERMONT. UNIVERSITY. CENTER FOR RESEARCH ON VERMONT. "Lake Champlain: reflections on our past": a bibliography. Burlington, 1989. 90p. VtHi. *
See also entry 11225 in Vol. 8.

3881. _____. University of Vermont graduate theses on Vermont topics, 1975-1992. Kristin Peterson-Ishaq, comp. Burlington, 1993. viii, 246p. VtHi. *

3882. VERMONT. UNIVERSITY. HISTORIC PRESERVATION PROGRAM. Vulnerable Vermont: a study of changes to historic buildings in three Vermont communities. Burlington, 1990. 53p. VtHi. *
Burlington, Fletcher, and Hinesburg.

3883. VERMONT. UNIVERSITY. LIBRARIES. A Vermont 14: commemorative of the two-hundredth anniversary of Vermont's admission to the Union as the nation's fourteenth state, 1791-1991. Edward Connery Lathem and Virginia L. Close, eds. Burlington, 1992. Unp. VtHi. *

3884. VERMONT COMMUNITY FOUNDATION. First years: a report of the people, the funds, and the grants of the Vermont Community Foundation from 1986-1991. Middlebury, 1991. 44p. VtU. *

3885   VERMONT

3885. VERMONT FOLKLIFE CENTER. Many cultures, one people: a multicultural handboook about Vermont for teachers. Gregory Sharrow, ed. Middlebury, 1992. 271p. VtHi. *

3886. VERMONT HISTORICAL SOCIETY. A more perfect union: Vermont becomes a state, 1777-1816. Michael Sherman, ed. Montpelier, 1991. xvi, 223p. VtU. *

3887. _____. We Vermonters: perspectives on the past. Michael Sherman and Jennie Versteeg, eds. Montpelier, 1992. viii, 361p. VtU. *

3888. VERMONT home front, World War II. Ray Zirblis, project coordinator. n.p.: Southern Vermont History Alliance, 1992. Var. p. VtHi.
    Packet of educational materials.

3889. VERMONT'S untold history. Burlington: Public Occurrence, 1976. 21p. VtU. *

3890. VERSTEEG, JENNIE G. "Aspects of the Vermont-Canada forest products relation in the twentieth century." VtH, 58 (Summer 1990), 164-178.

3891. WAGNER, ROBERT. "Vermont currency." Vermont Philatelist, 29 (Feb. 1985), 11-15.

3892. WARNER, MARY (pseud.). "Loyalty Vermont style." VtHN, 44 (Nov.-Dec.1993), 90-92.
    How the author's father and the producers with whom he dealt circumvented the price ceiling on maple syrup during World War II.

3893. WATERMAN, LAURA, and GUY WATERMAN. "Mountain pathways." Vermont Life, 44 (Summer 1990),
    On the history of hiking in the Green Mountains.

3894. WOLKOMIR, JOYCE ROGERS. "Turning points: events that shaped Vermont." Vermont Life, 45 (Winter 1990), 3-13.

3895. WOLTER, CAROL. "The Kelly Stand Turnpike." Cracker Barrel, 15 (Spring-Summer 1992), 16-17.
    In southern Vermont.

3896. WRISTON, JOHN C. JR. "City and village delivery in Vermont." Vermont Philatelist, 34 (Aug. 1990), 56-62.
    Postal service.

3897. _____. "Depot post offices in Vermont—known offices." Vermont Philatelist, 29 (Nov. 1984), 11-14; 30 (Feb. 1985), 3-6; (Aug. 1985), 7-10.

3898. _____. "How the RFD came to Vermont." VtHN, 43 (Mar.-Apr. 1992), 22-26.
    Postal service (rural free delivery), beginning in late 1890s. See also this author's article of same title in Vermont Philatelist, 36 (Aug. 1992), 115-121.

3899. _____. "Trolley mail in Vermont." Vermont Philatelist, 37 (Feb. 1993), 16-21.

3900. _____. "Vermont summer post offices." Vermont Philatelist, 27 (Feb. 1983), 1, 3-7.

3901. _____. Vermont inns and taverns, pre-Revolution to 1925: an illustrated and annotated checklist. Rutland: Academy Books, 1991. vi, 684p. VtHi. *

3902. YALE, ALLEN R. While the sun shines: making hay in Vermont, 1789-1990. Montpelier: Vermont Historical Society, 1991. 79p. VtHi. *

SEE ALSO entries 20, 40, 73, 75, 108, 129, 223-225, 238, 245, 269, 320, 345, 353, 367, 396, 403-404, 406, 420, 487, 3071, 3395.

Vermont

Entries for Counties†

ADDISON COUNTY

3903. PAHL, GREG. "Four miles to the falls: a history of the Beldens Falls Branch Railroad." VtH, 61 (Fall 1993), 217-232.
In New Haven and Middlebury.

3904. POTASH, PAUL JEFFREY. Vermont's burned-over district: patterns of community development and religious activity, 1761-1850. Brooklyn, N.Y.: Carlson Publishing, 1991. xiv, 277p. VtHi. *
Cornwall, Middlebury, and Shoreham.

3905. SHELDON MUSEUM. Addison County heritage: historical studies from the library of the Sheldon Museum. Middlebury, 1987. Unp. VtU. *

3906. VERMONT. DIVISION FOR HISTORIC PRESERVATION. The historic architecture of Addison County: including a listing of the Vermont State Register of Historic Places. Curtis B. Johnson, ed. Montpelier, 1992. 309p. VtHi. *

BENNINGTON COUNTY

3907. MERWIN, JOHN. The Battenkill: an intimate portrait of a great trout river—its history, people, and fishing possibilities. N.Y.: Lyons & Burford, 1993. 190p. VtHi. *

SEE ALSO entry 3811.

CHITTENDEN COUNTY

3908. BANDEL, BETTY. "'I devise and bequeath...'" CCHSB, 26 (Fall 1991), 3-6.
Information about the Hurlbut/Hurlburt family as found in the county probate records.

3909. BEATTIE, BETSY. "Migrants and millworkers: the French Canadian population of Burlington and Colchester, 1860-1870." VtH, 60 (Spring 1992), 91-117.

3910. JERICHO-UNDERHILL BICENTENNIAL COMMITTEE. They left their mark: a collection of sketches of people who helped make history in Jericho and Underhill. n.p., 1992. 60p. VtHi. *

ESSEX COUNTY

3911. HOPPER, GORDON E. The Victory Branch Railroad of Vermont: a spirited lumbering line that helped develop the Northeast. River Forest, Ill.: Heimburger House Publishing, 1989. 32p. VtHi. *
The Victory Branch (1883-1917) of the St. Johnsbury and Lake Champlain Railroad ran between North Concord and Granby.

SEE ALSO entry 3828.

LAMOILLE COUNTY

3912. LIZOTTE, WILLIAM. "Lamoille County postal history—some notes." Vermont Philatelist, 29 (Nov. 1984), 6; 32 (Nov. 1987), 4-6.

SEE ALSO entry 3771.

RUTLAND COUNTY

3913. BOARDMAN, NANCY. "The Welsh revival." Vermont Life, 47 (Winter 1992), 52-54.
Renewed interest in the Welsh heritage of the area's "slate belt."

---

† See the Vermont volume in this series (1981) for a complete list of counties.

* Online Computer Library Center (OLCC) listings for books and dissertations marked with this symbol may include additional library locations.

3914   RUTLAND COUNTY

3914.   "RUTLAND County Stamp Club, Inc." RHSQ, 18:3 (1988), 38-47.
    Since 1934.

3915.   VERMONT. DIVISION FOR HISTORIC PRESERVATION. The historic architecture of Rutland County: including a listing of the Vermont State Register of Historic Places. Curtis B. Johnson and Elsa Gilbertson, eds. Montpelier, 1989. xiv, 498p. VtHi. *

WINDHAM COUNTY

3916.   HURD, JOHN L. Kurn Hattin: the story of home. Westminster: Kurn Hattin Homes, 1989. 190p. VtHi. *
    Homes for boys and girls, in Westminster and Saxtons River respectively.

3917.   PARINI, JAY. "Kipling in Vermont." New England Monthly, 7 (Feb. 1990), 37-39.
    Rudyard Kipling (from 1892-1896).

3918.   WOODS, B. B. "Hamlets of the past: Reid Hollow, Unionville or Bucketville Point, Pleasantville and Slab Hollow." Cracker Barrel, 16 (Fall/Winter 1992-1993), 20-21.

    SEE ALSO entries 3732, 3811.

WINDSOR COUNTY

3919.   SOLLERS, JOHN F. SR. "One gold coach, eighteen farrow hens." VtHN, 44 (Sept.-Oct. 1993), 74-79.
    A 19th-century storekeeper's account book.

3920.   WENDLING, KATHY. From one room school to union high school: the history of Windsor Central Supervisory Union. Kevin Forrest, ed. Woodstock: Windsor Central Supervisory Union, 1989. iv, 146p. VtHi. *

Vermont

Entries for Cities and Towns†

ALBANY (ORLEANS CO.)

3921. HISTORY of Albany, Vermont, 1806-1991. Virginia
Wharton, ed. n.p., [1991?]. v, 322p. VtHi. *

ANDOVER (WINDSOR CO.)

3922. ENO, R. D. "Herb and Miriam Lender: Jewish pioneers in
Vermont." Kfari, 2 (Dec. 1988), 8-10.
Oral history interview.

ARLINGTON (BENNINGTON CO.)

3923. FISHER, DOROTHY CANFIELD. Keeping fires night and
day: selected letters of Dorothy Canfield Fisher. Mark J.
Madigan, ed. Columbia: Univ. of Missouri Pr., 1993. xx,
356p. VtU. *
Writer Fisher lived 1879-1958.

3924. HENRY, HUGH. Arlington along the Battenkill: its pictured
past. Arlington: Arlington Townscape Association, 1993.
144p. VtHi.

3925. MURRAY, STUART, and JAMES McCABE. Norman
Rockwell's four freedoms: images that inspire a nation.
Stockbridge, Mass.: Berkshire House, 1993. xiii, 144p. VtHi. *
The paintings were done in Arlington.

3926. ORAL history of Arlington. Hank Barthel, ed. n.p.:
Matayaya Pr., 1990. 51p. VtHi. *

SEE ALSO entries 3895, 3907.

BAKERSFIELD (FRANKLIN CO.)

3927. WRISTON, JOHN C. JR. "The Bakersfield post office."
Vermont Philatelist, 30 (Aug. 1986), 8-11.

BARNARD (WINDSOR CO.)

3928. KURTH, PETER. "Cassandra in Vermont." Vermont Life, 45
(Winter 1990), 36-39.
Writer Dorothy Thompson as a resident of Barnard.

3929. SLAYTON, THOMAS KENNEDY. Sabra Field: the art of
place. Montpelier: Vermont Life Magazine, 1993. 127p.
VtHi. *
Contemporary printmaker.

BARNET (CALEDONIA CO.)

3930. AMIDON, ROGER LYMAN. Barnet days: a segment of
rural Vermont life now past. 2d ed. Columbia, S.C.: R.L.
Amidon, 1991. 51p. VtHi. *
Note: this item replaces entry 11301 in Vol. 8.

3931. WRISTON, JOHN C. JR. "Barnet post offices." Vermont
Philatelist, 33 (Nov. 1988), 3-8; 34 (Feb. 1989), 3-7.

SEE ALSO entry 222.

BARRE (WASHINGTON CO.)

3932. AUDENINO, PATRIZIA. "Storia de pietra: gli scalpellini di
Barre e l'Aldrich Public Library." Movimento Operaio e
Socialista [Italy], 9:3 (1986), 425-432.
[Stories in stone: the chisels of Barre and the Aldrich
Public Library (1870).]

---

† See the Vermont volume in this
series (1981) for a complete list of cities and towns.

* Online Computer Library Center (OLCC) listings for
books and dissertations marked with this symbol may
include additional library locations.

3933.   BACON, ELISABETH RAMON. Santander to Barre: life in a Spanish family in Vermont. Randolph Center: Greenhills Books, 1988. 68p. VtHi. *
    Autobiographical. (Author was born in Barre in 1921.)

3934.   BLOW, RICHARD H. SR. Barre, Vermont: a time to grow. Barre: Modern Printing, 1990. 187p. VtHi. *
    Autobiographical. (Author was born in Barre in 1920.)
    See also entry 38.

3935.   BOTTAMINI, RICHARD. "The bawdy house murder." Central Vermont Magazine (Winter 1990), 42-43.
    Murder of a prostitute (1919).

3936.   _____. "The case of the headless corpse." Central Vermont Magazine (Summer 1990), 19, 26.

3937.   _____. "Early Barre history: somber, sensational and otherwise." Central Vermont Magazine (Summer 1989), 17-19.

3938.   _____. "How did Barre get its name?" Central Vermont Magazine (Winter 1988), 32-33.

3939.   _____. "Marching past an anniversary." Central Vermont Magazine (Summer 1988), 23-24.
    100th anniversary of the rebuilding of the Barre Congregational Church.

3940.   CLARKE, ROD. Carved in stone: a history of the Barre granite industry. Barre: Rock of Ages Corporation, 1989. 69p. VtHi. *

3941.   COHEN, SYLVIA. "Girls didn't count: recollections of a Chassidic girlhood in Barre, Vermont." Kfari, 3 (Mar. 1990), 8-9, 14.
    Based on an oral history interview by R.D. Eno. (Cohen was born in 1915.)

3942.   DESBIENS, ALBERT, and STEPHEN J. RANDALL. "Granitiers et collectivité: Barre (VT), 1870-1910, une première approche." Histoire sociale/Social History [Canada], 23 (May 1990), 133-152.
    [Granite quarry workers and collective action: Barre, Vermont, 1870-1910: a first approach.]

3943.   GILLANDER, GARY. "Dr. Jacob Spaulding's legacy." Central Vermont Magazine (Summer 1991), 29, 34.
    Spaulding Middle School.

3944.   JONES BROTHERS COMPANY. Four brothers: their contribution to the memorial industry of the United States. Boston, 1942. 31p. VtHi. *

3945.   POPACK, SHMUEL ISAAC. "Rabbi Shmuel Isaac Popack: Chassidic childhood in Barre, Vt." Kfari, 2 (Oct. 1988), 8-10.
    Based on an oral history interview by R. D. Eno.

3946.   RALPH, ELIZABETH. "The Barre Opera House: preserving turn-of-the-century elegance for the future." Central Vermont Magazine (Winter 1991), 11, 13-14.

3947.   RANDALL, STEPHEN J. "Life, labour and death in an industrial city: occupational health of Barre, Vermont, granite workers, 1870-1940." Canadian Review of American Studies, 22 (Fall 1991), 195-209.

3948.   REYNOLDS, ERNEST VENNER. An odyssey of a Vermont country doctor in the twentieth century, 1907-1990. Barre: Modern Printing, 1991. 135p. VtHi. *
    Autobiographical.

3949.   RICHARDSON, WENDY. "'The curse of our trade': occupational disease in a Vermont granite town." VtH, 60 (Winter 1992), 5-28.

3950.   SMITH, DONALD L. "First, last & only: Wildersburgh's representative." Central Vermont Magazine (Summer 1992), 13, 15.
    Nathan Harrington represented the town in 1793 and petitioned for the change of its name to Barre.

SEE ALSO entries 38, 3750.

BELVIDERE (LAMOILLE CO.)

3951.   WRISTON, JOHN C. JR. "Belvidere post offices." Vermont Philatelist, 36 (Nov. 1992), 138-143.

BENNINGTON (BENNINGTON CO.)

3952.   COE, BARBARA LENT. "The Park McCullough House: four generations of social and architectural history." Cracker Barrel, 16 (Spring/Summer 1993), 11-12.

3953.   HALL Park McCullough: Americana collector, 1872- 1966. J. Robert Maguire and J. Kevin Graffagnino, eds. Burlington: Special Collections, Bailey/Howe Library, Univ. of Vermont, 1988. 61p. VtHi. *
    Includes historical sketch.

3954.   HIGGINS, WILLIAM JOHN. Time & place in Bennington: a handbook for the central Bennington historic district. [Bennington: Town of Bennington Historic Preservation Commission], 1990. 129p. VtU. *

3955. JENSEN, OLIVER. "Bennington preserved: a small town on glass." American Heritage, 41 (Nov. 1990), 108- 123.
Preservation of the work of a number of the town's early photographers.

3956. MARVIN, KEITH. Bennington's Wasp. Bennington: Bennington Museum 1987. [18]p. VtU. *
Bennington-built brand of automobile (1920s).

3957. RAVI-BOOTH, VINCENT, EDITH VAN BENTHUYSEN McCULLOUGH, and HALL PARK McCULLOUGH. "Some recollections of the beginnings of Bennington College." Bennington College Bulletin, 35 (June 1957), 7-78.

3958. RESCH, TYLER. Bennington's Battle monument: massive and lofty: an interpretive history. Bennington: Beech Seal Pr., 1993. v, 57p. VtHi. *
Commemorating the Revolutionary War encounter.

3959. _____. "Bennington's monumental monument." Vermont Life, 42 (Summer 1988), 46-50.
See also preceding entry.

3960. _____. Deed of gift: the Putnam Hospital story: a biographical approach. Burlington: Paradigm Pr., 1991. xiv, 139p. VtHi. *

3961. WRISTON, JOHN C. JR. "Thomas Jefferson Tiffany and the Bennington post office." Vermont Philatelist, 37 (Aug. 1993), 102-107.
Late-19th century.

3962. ZOGRY, KENNETH JOEL. "Vermont furniture in the Bennington Museum, 1765-1840." Antiques, 154 (Aug. 1993), 190-201.

3963. ZUSY, CATHERINE. Norton stoneware and American redware: the Bennington Museum collection. Bennington: Bennington Museum, 1991. 79p. VtHi. *

BENSON (RUTLAND CO.)

3964. BARNOUW, ERIK. House with a past. Montpelier: Vermont Historical Society, 1992. v, 106p. VtHi. *
Former Mormon church.

BERKSHIRE (FRANKLIN CO.)

3965. WRISTON, JOHN C. JR. "Berkshire post offices." Vermont Philatelist, 32 (May 1987), 4-10.

BERLIN (WASHINGTON CO.)

3966. BAILEY, MILTON. Memories of Berlin Corners, Vermont. n.p., [1994?]. Unp. VtHi.

3967. BERLIN HISTORICAL SOCIETY. A place to pass through: Berlin, Vermont, 1820-1991. Paul S. Gillies, ed. Berlin, 1992. 163p. VtHi. *

3968. GILLIES, PAUL S. "Murder at Berlin Pond." Central Vermont Magazine (Winter 1991), 36-37.
Ca. 1830s.

BOLTON (CHITTENDEN CO.)

3969. LANE, GARDINER. A history of Bolton. Bolton, 1989. [76]p. VtHi. *

3970. _____. West Bolton at the turn of the century. n.p., [1993?]. 8, [14]p. VtHi. *

BRADFORD (ORANGE CO.)

3971. BRADFORD HISTORICAL SOCIETY. History of the Low Mansion. Bradford, 1991. Unp. VtHi. *

3972. PRATT, MARGARET JENKINS. "The strawberry king of Bradford." VtHN, 44 (July-Aug. 1993), 55-60.
Winfield Smally, the first major grower there (beginning in late 19th century).

BRANDON (RUTLAND CO.)

3973. VISSER, THOMAS D. Historic site review: Smalley-Davenport shop, Forestdale, Vermont. Montpelier: Vermont Division for Historic Preservation, 1992. 40p. VtHi. *
Thomas Davenport patented an electric motor in 1837.

BRATTLEBORO (WINDHAM CO.)

3974. BLACKWELL, MARILYN S. "Growing up male in the 1830s: Thomas Pickman Tyler (1815-1892) and the Tyler family of Brattleboro." VtH, 58 (Winter 1990), 5-23.
Son of Royall and Mary Palmer Tyler. See also next entry.

3975   BRATTLEBORO

3975.   BLACKWELL, MARILYN S. "Love and duty: Mary Palmer Tyler and republican childrearing." M.A. thesis, Univ. of Vermont, 1990. iv, 236p. *
Lived 1775-1866.

3976.   _____. "The republican vision of Mary Palmer Tyler." Journal of the Early Republic, 12 (Spring 1992), 11-35.
As seen in her approach to raising her family, in her writings on childrearing, and in her role in later life as a social leader in her community. See also preceding entry.

3977.   BORN, JOHN F. "Traffic jam at Brattleboro." B&M Bulletin, 19:2 [1993], 6-11.
Railroading incident (1964).

3978.   KEARNEY, SEAMUS. Brattleboro baseball at Island Park, 1911-1915. Brattleboro: Brattleboro Historical Society, 1993. 20p. VtHi.

3979.   MITCHELL, RICHARD M. Pioneer aviation in Brattleboro. Brattleboro: Brattleboro Historical Society, 1991. 20p. VtHi. *

3980.   TORTOLANI, ROBERT. "Brattleboro history." Vermont Philatelist, 33 (Nov. 1987), 7.

SEE ALSO entry 3917.

BURKE (CALEDONIA CO.)

3981.   BURBANK, PHYLLIS. Burke: more than just a mountain. [Burke]: Burke Mountain Club, 1989. 128p. VtHi. *

BURLINGTON (CHITTENDEN CO.)

3982.   BLOW, DAVID J. "Burlington's first black church." CCHSB, 25 (Fall 1989), 5-6.
Church of God in Christ (Black Pentecostal, 1940s-1960s).

3983.   _____. Historic guide to Burlington neighborhoods. Lilian Baker Carlisle, ed. Burlington: Chittenden County Historical Society, 1991. 212p. VtHi. *

3984.   BROOKES, TIM. "Looking back: an oral history of the College of Medicine." Hall A (Winter 1991-1992), 10-15.
Univ. of Vermont.

3985.   BURLINGTON, VT. CHRIST THE KING PARISH. Seventy-second anniversary, Christ the King Parish; fiftieth anniversary, Christ the King Church, October 28, 1979. [Burlington, 1979] Unp. VtU. *
Roman Catholic.

3986.   CARLISLE, LILIAN BAKER. "The Brinsmaids: a New England family's heritage of craftsmanship." Antiques Trader Weekly, 25 (Nov. 1987), 66-69.
Silversmiths.

3987.   COFFIN, HOWARD. UVM: a special place. Virginia Beach, Va.: Donning, 1990. 128p. VtU. *
Univ. of Vermont.

3988.   COHN, ARTHUR B., and MARSHALL MacDONALD TRUE. "The wreck of the General Butler and the mystery of Lake Champlain's sailing canal boats." VtH, 60 (Winter 1992), 29-45.
1876.

3989.   COLLINS, MARY. "Growing up in Burlington." Creating Excellence, 3 (Mar./Apr. 1989), 10-15.
Author's recollections of 1950s and 1960s.

3990.   CONROY, WILLIAM JON. Challenging the boundaries of reform: socialism in Burlington. Philadelphia: Univ. of Pennsylvania Pr., 1990. viii, 264p. VtHi. *
See also this author's Ph.D. dissertation on the 1980s administration of Mayor Bernard Sanders (Fordham Univ., 1987; entry 11373 in Vol. 8); and entries 3990, 4007.

3991.   GOTLIEB, DANIEL B. "A socialist mayor for Burlington?" University of Vermont History Review, 4 (Spring 1991), 43-50.
The election of Bernard Sanders in 1981. See also next entry.

3992.   GUMA, GREG. The people's republic: Vermont and the Sanders revolution. Shelburne: New England Pr., 1989. 199p. VtHi. *
Mayor Bernard Sanders (1980s). See also entries 3988, 4007.

3993.   HOLDEN, ALFRED. "Rails on the roads: trolleys and the growth of Burlington." CCHSB, 27 (Winter 1993), 1-12.

3994.   HOLMES, DAVID R. Stalking the academic communist: intellectual freedom and the firing of Alex Novikoff. Hanover, N.H.: University Pr. of New England, 1989. xii, 288p. VtU. *
Univ. of Vermont (1953).

3995.   JOHNSON, PHILIP. "The bones with no name." VtHN, 44 (Mar.-Apr. 1993), 21-26.
19th-century discovery and controversy over a Vermont fossil whale, now displayed at the Univ. of Vermont.

3996.   JOHNSTONE, DONALD B. Postal history of Burlington, Vermont: the first 100 years. Burlington: Queen City Pr., 1992. 64p. VtHi. *

3997.   _____. "Three War of 1812 letters from Burlington." CCHSB, 28 (Spring 1994), 1-6.

3998.   _____. "Who was the first postmaster of Burlington?" CCHSB, 26 (Fall 1992), 1-3.

3999.   KENT, MARGARET. "Ethan Allen's frontier home." Early American Life, 20 (Oct. 1989), 48-53, 65-68.

4000.   KING, SUZANNE, and PETER SHOEMAKER. "Public history practicum: a look at the history of the Burlington, Vt. Police Department." University of Vermont History Review, 4 (Spring 1991), 68-76.

4001.   MARSHALL, JEFFREY D. Universitas Viridis Montis, 1791-1991: an exhibition of documents and artifacts telling the story of the University of Vermont. Burlington: Bailey/Howe Library, University of Vermont, 1991. 87p. VtHi. *

4002.   MARTIN, MICHEL J. "Organized responses to urban disorder in Burlington, Vermont, 1858-1870." M.A. thesis, Univ. of Vermont, 1992. iv, 76p. *

4003.   MICHAUD, ROBERT B. Salute to Burlington: an informal history of Burlington, Vermont. Lyndonville: Lyndon State College, 1991. ix, 172p. VtHi. *

4004.   MILLS, GORDON. 50 year history of the Sara Holbrook Center. [Burlington: Sara Holbrook Center, 1988] 14p. VtU. *

4005.   "OUR Land Grant colleges: the University of Vermont." The New Englander (April 1960), 12, 59.

4006.   POPECKI, JOSEPH T. The parish of Saint Mark in Burlington, Vermont, 1941-1991. Burlington: Parish of Saint Mark, 1991. v, 100p. VtHi. *
        Roman Catholic.

4007.   "PRESERVING tradition, enduring change: UVM's Old Mill Building." CCHSB, 25 (Fall 1989), 1-4.

4008.   SOIFER, STEVEN DANIEL. "Electoral politics and social change: the case of Burlington, Vermont." Ph.D. dissertation, Brandeis Univ., 1988. 851p. *
        During the administration of socialist mayor Bernard Sanders (1980s). Abstracted in DAI, 49:8A (1989), 2420-2421. See also next entry.

4009.   _____. The socialist mayor: Bernard Sanders in Burlington, Vermont. N.Y.: Bergin & Garvey, 1991. xiv, 285p. VtHi. *

4010.   TAYLOR, BOB PEPPERMAN. "John Dewey in Vermont: a reconsideration." Soundings, 75 (Spring 1992), 175-198.
        Discusses the effects of his background in Vermont on the educator's thinking.

4011.   VERMONT. UNIVERSITY. The University of Vermont: the first two hundred years. Robert V. Daniels, ed. Hanover, N.H.: University Pr. of New England, 1991. 452p. VtHi. *

4012.   WALSH, BRIAN J. "Dreams on hold: Burlington's nineteenth-century Irish." CCHSB, 26 (Winter 1992), 1-15.

4013.   _____. "Dreams realized?: Irish-Americans and progress, Burlington, Vermont, 1830-1910." M.A. thesis, Univ. of Vermont, 1993. v, 154p. *

        SEE ALSO entries 71, 153, 3734, 3759, 3769, 3771, 3855, 3872, 3882, 3909, 4128.

CALAIS (WASHINGTON CO.)

4014.   LARSON, SYLVIA B. Calais, Vermont: the founding of the town: chartered "15 day of August AD. 1781." Bridgewater, Mass.: Research Plus, 1991. 45p. VtHi. *

CASTLETON (RUTLAND CO.)

4015.   LEPPMAN, JOHN A. "Castleton Old Chapel-Medical Building." VtHN, 41 (July-Aug. 1990), 64-67.
        Used by the Castleton Medical Academy (early-19th century); now owned by Castleton State College.

CHARLOTTE (CHITTENDEN CO.)

4016.   CHARLOTTE, VT. CONGREGATIONAL CHURCH. The Charlotte Congregational Church: serving our community for 200 years. Charlotte, 1992. 95p. VtHi.

        SEE ALSO entry 3795.

CLARENDON (RUTLAND CO.)

4017.   DURFEE, HELEN CONGDON. Reflections on my life in Vermont in the early 1900s. n.p., 1993. 31p. VtHi.

4018   COLCHESTER

COLCHESTER (CHITTENDEN CO.)

4018.   FANNY ALLEN HOSPITAL. Walking in the spirit: Fanny Allen Hospital, 1894-1994. Colchester, 1994. 184p. VtU. *

SEE ALSO entry 3909.

CORINTH (ORANGE CO.)

4019.   HOOD, ALICE, and EVERDENE HOOD. History of Corinth, Vermont, 1964-1987: genealogy update. Corinth: Town of Corinth, 1987. viii, 183p. VtHi. *
        See also entry 3950 in the Vermont volume.

CORNWALL (ADDISON CO.)

4020.   GREEN, MARY PEET. Cornwall people and their times. New Haven: Antioch Pr., 1993. 282p. VtHi. *

4021.   WITHERELL, STUART. A history of Cornwall houses and their inhabitants. Cornwall: Cornwall Historical Society, 1989. 72p. VtHi. *

SEE ALSO entry 3904.

CRAFTSBURY (ORLEANS CO.)

4022.   CRAFTSBURY BICENTENNIAL COMMITTEE. Craftsbury, Vermont: chronicle of the bicentennial, 1989. Craftsbury, 1990. 93p. VtHi. *

4023.   CRAFTSBURY HISTORICAL SOCIETY. A Craftsbury album: images of our past. Craftsbury, 1989. vi, 58p. VtHi. *

4024.   DAVIS, ALLEN F. "Craftsbury on my mind." Hazen Road Dispatch, 14 (Summer 1989), 5-7.

4025.   MORRISSEY, CHARLES THOMAS. "Mary Gove Nichols, feminist." Hazen Road Dispatch, 14 (Summer 1989), 12-14.
        19th century.

4026.   SHIELDS, BRUCE P. East Craftsbury's 75th: an illustrated narrative of the United Presbyterian Church on the occasion of the anniversary of its acceptance by the Presbytery of Vermont, 12 July 1906. Craftsbury: East Craftsbury United Presbyterian Church, 1981. 33p. VtHi. *

DORSET (BENNINGTON CO.)

4027.   ARTHUR, ELIZABETH. Looking for the Klondike Stone. N.Y.: Knopf, 1993. 321p. VtHi. *
        Memories of childhood experiences at a summer camp.

4028.   RESCH, TYLER. Dorset: in the shadow of the marble mountain. West Kennebunk, Me: Phoenix Publishing, 1989. xvii, 405p. VtHi. *

DUMMERSTON (WINDHAM CO.)

4029.   DUMMERSTON HISTORICAL SOCIETY. Dummerston: an "equivalent lands" town, 1753-1986. Alice Crosby Loomis and Frances Walker Manix, eds. Dummerston: Dummerston Historical Society, 1990. x, 418p. VtHi. *

SEE ALSO entry 3917.

EAST MONTPELIER (WASHINGTON CO.)

4030.   HILL, ELLEN C., and MARILYN S. BLACKWELL. "Early 20th century business in East Montpelier." Central Vermont Magazine (Winter 1984), 36-39.

ESSEX (CHITTENDEN CO.)

4031.   ESSEX, Vermont: an annotated bibliography to sources in the Brownell, Essex Free, and Essex Junction High School libraries. Penelope D. Pillsbury, comp. Essex: Friends of the Brownell Library, 1992. VtHi.

FAIR HAVEN (RUTLAND CO.)

4032.   OFFENSEND, DOROTHY BACKUS. History of the First Baptist Church, Fair Haven, Vermont. Fair Haven: First Baptist Church, 1992. 20p. VtHi. *

FAIRLEE (ORANGE CO.)

4033.   KAYNOR, FAY CAMPBELL. "The unstoppable Anna Dodge." Vermont Life, 43 (Spring 1989), 12-16.
        Longtime director of Fairlee's Camp Quinibeck.

FERRISBURG (ADDISON CO.)

4034. DANN, KEVIN. "The tale of the lonesome pine." Vermont
Life, 43 (Winter 1988), 23-27.
Rowland E. Robinson, the 19th-century author.

SEE ALSO entry 3795.

FRANKLIN (FRANKLIN CO.)

4035. TOWLE, MARTHA HANNA. A history of Franklin: past
and present, fact or fancy, legend or folksay, 1789-1989.
Franklin: Franklin Historical Society, 1989. viii, 310p. VtU. *

4036. _____. A supplement to "A history of Franklin, 1789-1989."
n.p., 1990. ix, 63p. VtU. *

GEORGIA (FRANKLIN CO.)

4037. GEORGIA, VT. TOWN HISTORY COMMITTEE. Georgia
town history. St. Albans: Regal Art Pr., 1991. 283p. VtHi. *

GRANBY (ESSEX CO.)

4038. GRANBY HISTORICAL GROUP. Thru the woods, down
the river, over the hill, Granby, Vt. Granby, 1990. vi, 322p.
VtHi. *

SEE ALSO entry 3911.

GRAND ISLE (GRAND ISLE CO.)

4039. A HISTORY of the town of Grand Isle as told by the people
of the town. Jan Bender, ed. Grand Isle: Landslide Pr., 1991.
xi, 211p. VtHi. *

4040. VERMONT. UNIVERSITY. CONSULTING
ARCHAEOLOGY PROGRAM. 4,500 years at Gordon's
Landing: archaeology at the Grand Isle Fish Hatchery.
Burlington, 1992. 12p. VtHi. *

GREENSBORO (ORLEANS CO.)

4041. DAVIS, ALLEN F. "Fishing in Greensboro." Hazen Road
Dispatch, 16 (Summer 1991), 1-4.

4042. FISHER, SALLY. "Greta Garbo in Greensboro: facts or
fiction?" Hazen Road Dispatch, 15 (Summer 1990), 1- 3.

4043. _____. "The remarkable C.U. Bears." Hazen Road Dispatch,
16 (Summer 1991), 16-17.
Onetime summer residents.

4044. _____. "That monument on Block House Hill." Hazen Road
Dispatch, 14 (Summer 1989), 29-30.
To the memory of two revolutionary-era soldiers.

4045. GREENSBORO HISTORICAL SOCIETY. The history of
Greensboro: the first two hundred years. Susan Bartlett
Weber, ed. Greensboro, 1990. 281p. VtHi. *

4046. "GREENSBORO then and now: a conversation with
Constance Votey." Hazen Road Dispatch, 16 (Summer
1991), 28-32.
Interviewed by Alan B. Howes.

4047. HILL, LEWIS. Fetched-up Yankee: a New England boyhood
remembered. Chester, Conn.: Globe Pequot Pr., 1990. xii,
206p. VtHi. *
Author was born in 1924.

4048. HILL, NANCY. "Greensboro's bicentennial." Hazen Road
Dispatch, 14 (Summer 1989), 1-4.

4049. HOWES, ALAN B. "The poetess of Elligo." Hazen Road
Dispatch, 16 (Summer 1991), 5-8.
Martha Faulds Coburn (late-19th and early-20th
centuries).

4050. JACKSON, STUART A. "A summer camper, 1938-1945."
Hazen Road Dispatch, 15 (Summer 1990), 4-18.
Autobiographical.

4051. PECK, PENNELL. "A summerhouse heritage." Hazen Road
Dispatch, 18 (June 1993), 31-32.

4052. PECK, RUSSELL H. "Remembering Milt Noyes." Hazen
Road Dispatch, 16 (Summer 1991), 9-12.
Proprietor of a local garage.

4053. SANGREE, GAIL A. "Excerpts from the diary of Jean
Spahr, 1914-1916." Hazen Road Dispatch, 16 (Summer
1991), 21-23.
Summer resident.

4054. TAYLOR, KATRINA V. H., and ELISE V. H. FERBER.
"Notes from the north shore." Hazen Road Dispatch, 18
(Summer 1993), 25-27.
Memories of summers at Caspian Lake (1920s and later).

4055   GUILFORD

GUILFORD (WINDHAM CO.)

4055.   GUILFORD HISTORICAL SOCIETY. Guilford sketches. Dorothy Scott Loos, ed. Guilford, 1991. xi, 214p. VtHi. *

HARDWICK (CALEDONIA CO.)

4056.   ANGELL, ELEANOR. "Glimpses of student life at Hardwick Academy, 1886-1887." Hazen Road Dispatch, 14 (Summer 1989), 8-11.

4057.   DAVIS, ALLEN F. "Taking the waters in Hardwick: Haynesville Springs." Hazen Road Dispatch, 17 (Summer 1992), 20-22.

4058.   DOW, ELIZABETH H. "Early administrative history of the town of Hardwick." Hazen Road Dispatch, 15 (Summer 1990), 10-13.

4059.   _____. "Hardwick on the map, 1895-1915: industrialization in direct democracy." VtH, 58 (Fall 1990), 221-249.
        Woodbury Granite Company.

4060.   "EAST Hardwick's grand old Grange Hall." Hazen Road Dispatch, 16 (Summer 1991), 19-20.

4061.   FISHER, SALLY. "Cobb School researched and remembered." Hazen Road Dispatch, 17 (Summer 1992), 31.

4062.   _____. "Smuggling Chinese into Hardwick." Hazen Road Dispatch, 15 (Summer 1990), 19-20.
        From Canada, after enactment of the Chinese Exclusion Act of 1882.

4063.   HARDWICK [VT.] GAZETTE (newspaper). The Hardwick Gazette, 1889-1989: a century of reporting the news. Ross Connelly, ed. Hardwick, 1989. 64p. VtHi. *

4064.   MITCHELL, JOYCE SLAYTON. "First Congregational Church, East Hardwick, Vermont." Hazen Road Dispatch, 17 (Summer 1992), 8-10.

4065.   _____. "Hardwick's 5 and 10 cent store." Hazen Road Dispatch, 18 (June 1993), 28-30.

HARTLAND (WINDSOR CO.)

4066.   HARTLAND HISTORICAL SOCIETY. In sight of ye great river: history & houses of Hartland, Vermont. Hartland, 1991. x, 258p. VtHi. *

HIGHGATE (FRANKLIN CO.)

4067.   HECKENBERGER, MICHAEL J. et al. "Early woodland period mortuary ceremonialism in the far Northeast: a view from the Boucher Cemetery." Archaeology of Eastern North America, 18 (Fall 1990), 109-144.
        Co-authors: James B. Petersen, Louise A. Basa, Ellen R. Cowie, Arthur E. Spiess, and Robert E. Stuckenrath.

4068.   WRISTON, JOHN C. JR. "Highgate post offices." Vermont Philatelist, 35 (May 1991), 64-69; (Aug. 1991), 109-114; (Nov. 1991), 138-140.

IRA (RUTLAND CO.)

4069.   CHARLES, SHEILA. The history and archeology of the Ira Town Hall site, Ira, Rutland County, Vermont. Montpelier: Vermont Division for Historic Preservation, 1990. 38p. VtHi.

IRASBURG (ORLEANS CO.)

4070.   ORCUTT, MARJORIE A., and EDWARD S. ALEXANDER. A history of Irasburg, Vermont. Rutland: Academy Books, 1989. 162p. VtHi. *

JAMAICA (WINDHAM CO.)

4071.   PATRICK, WARREN S. The history of the Community Church in Jamaica, Vermont. n.p., 1991. ii, 46p. VtU. *

JERICHO (CHITTENDEN CO.)

4072.   GUSTAVSEN, METTE. "Of youth and wonder in Jericho, Vermont: from the 1876-78 diaries of Charles E. Percival." CCHSB, 26 (Spring 1991), 1-10.
        Percival began keeping a diary when he was about 14 years old.

        SEE ALSO entry 3910.

JOHNSON (LAMOILLE CO.)

4073.   GRAFF, NANCY PRICE. Visible layers of time: a perspective on the history and architecture of Johnson, Vermont. Burlington: Univ. of Vermont Historic Preservation Program, 1990. 32p. VtHi. *

4074. TITTERTON, ROBERT J. Julian Scott: a return to Johnson. [Johnson: Dibden Gallery, Johnson State College], 1989. 20p. VtHi. *
Painter (lived 1846-1901).

SEE ALSO entries 3794, 3850.

LONDONDERRY (WINDHAM CO.)

4075. WILEY, EDITH DAVIES. Doings in 'derry: life in a small Vermont town. Londonderry: Londonderry Historical Society, 1992. 239p. VtHi. *

LYNDON (CALEDONIA CO.)

4076. DOWNS, VIRGINIA CAMPBELL. Mansions & meadows: Lyndon the way it was. Lyndon Center: Lyndon Historical Society, 1991. 174p. VtHi. *

MANCHESTER (BENNINGTON CO.)

4077. BUETTINGER, CRAIG. "Sarah Cleghorn, antivivisection, and Victorian sensitivity about pain and cruelty." VtH, 62 (Spring 1994), 89-100.
Cleghorn lived 1876-1959.

4078. LEWIS, PHEBE ANN. The Equinox est. 1769: historic home of hospitality. Manchester: Johnny Appleseed Bookshop, 1993. 64p. VtHi. *
Equinox House.

4079. _____, and ROBERT J. WILSON. The First Congregational Church, Manchester, Vermont: 1784-1984. Manchester: Bicentennital Steering Committee, First Congregational Church, 1984. xi, 138p. VtHi. *

4080. McFARLAND, GERALD W. The "counterfeit" man: the true story of the Boorn-Colvin murder case. N.Y.: Pantheon Books, 1990. xii, 242p. VtHi. *
1812.

4081. "NEIGHBORS: Annie McClure Clarke's reflections on Manchester, Vermont, in 1916." VtHN, 42 (May-June 1991), 42-46.

SEE ALSO entry 435.

MARLBORO (WINDHAM CO.)

4082. GRAFFAGNINO, JONATHAN KEVIN. "'Vermonters unmasked': Charles Phelps and the patterns of dissent in revolutionary Vermont." VtH, 57 (Summer 1989), 133-161.

4083. JOHNSON, PHILIP. "Fish free or die: the Marlboro South Pond case of 1896." VtHN, 43 (May-June 1992), 43-46.
Case involving the right of public access.

4084. NIDO, RUTH E. "The Mathers of Marlboro: one of Vermont's first families." Cracker Barrel, 15 (Fall/ Winter 1991-1992), 12-15.
First published in the Brattleboro Reformer (1939).

4085. SNYDER, JOHN M. Espressivo: music and life at Marlboro. Marlboro: Marlboro Music School and Festival, 1994. 134p. VtHi. *

MARSHFIELD (WASHINGTON CO.)

4086. GOLDBERG, LINDA S. Here on this hill: conversations with Vermont neighbors. Middlebury: Vermont Folklife Center, 1991. 152p. VtU. *
Oral history.

MIDDLEBURY (ADDISON CO.)

4087. BEACHAM, CHRISTINE. If walls could talk: a history of the Waybury Inn. East Middlebury, [1992?]. 51p. VtHi. *
In East Middlebury.

4088. FREEMAN, STEPHEN ALBERT. The Congregational Church of Middlebury, Vermont, 1790-1990: a bicentennial history. Middlebury: Middlebury Congregational Church, 1990. 139p. VtHi. *

4089. "THE ROBINSON years." Middlebury College Magazine, 64 (Spring 1990), 24-29, 31-33.
President Olin Robinson's years at Middlebury (1975-1990). Article signed "T.E." (Tim Etchells).

4090. WHOSE woods these are: a history of the Bread Loaf Writers' Conference, 1926-1992. David Haward Bain and Mary Smyth Duffy, eds. Hopewell, N.J.: Ecco Pr., 1993. vi, 378p. VtHi. *
At Middlebury College.

4091. WRISTON, JOHN C. JR. "History of the Middlebury post offices." Vermont Philatelist, 36 (May 1992), 74-79.

4092   MIDDLEBURY

4092.   YOE, MARY RUTH. "The campus that might have been."
Middlebury College Magazine, 62 (Winter 1988), 16-19.
   Proposed women's campus.

SEE ALSO entries 128, 3765, 3769, 3829, 3903-3904.

MILTON (CHITTENDEN CO.)

4093.   ARCHAEOLOGY CONSULTING TEAM. Discoveries at
the Blue Heron site: an archaeological study in Milton,
Vermont. Essex Junction, 1990. [12]p. VtU. *

MONTGOMERY (FRANKLIN CO.)

4094.   BRANTHOOVER, WILBUR RANDALL, and SARA
TAYLOR. Montgomery, Vermont: the history of a town.
(1976) 2d ed. Montgomery: Montgomery Historical Society,
1991. 192p. VtHi. *
   Note: this item replaces entry 4773 in the Vermont
volume.

4095.   WRISTON, JOHN C. JR. "History of the Montgomery post
offices." Vermont Philatelist, 35 (Nov. 1990), 97-105.

MONTPELIER (WASHINGTON CO.)

4096.   CARTER, PRISCILLA. "A four-year-old's view of the flood
of 1927." Hazen Road Dispatch, 17 (Summer 1992), 7.

4097.   ENO, R. D. "Beth Jacob Synagogue: pluralism in practice."
Kfari, 3 (July 1990), 8-11.

4098.   MONTPELIER, VT. ST. AUGUSTINE CHURCH. The
Church of St. Augustine at Montpelier, Vermont, 1892-1992:
a century of blessings. n.p., 1992. 114p. VtHi. *
   Roman Catholic.

MORRISTOWN (LAMOILLE CO.)

4099.   ENO, R. D. "The Sinows of Morrisville: beset and
embittered, they say shalom to farming." Kfari, 1 (Apr.
1988), 8-11, 13.
   Oral history interview.

4100.   "MORRISTOWN/Morrisville, 1846-54: an identity crisis."
Vermont Philatelist, 36 (Aug. 1992), 109-114.
   Postal history.

MOUNT HOLLY (RUTLAND CO.)

4101.   TARBELL, CARROLL R. History of Mount Holly, Vermont.
n.p., 1987. 306p. VtHi. *

NEWBURY (ORANGE CO.)

4102.   HATHAWAY, RICHARD O. "Hiram Campbell Merrill,
wood engraver (1866-1958)." VtHN, 40 (July/Aug. 1989),
70-73.
   Summer resident.

4103.   STEARNS, MERTON J. "Memories of Wells River,
Vermont." B&M Bulletin, 18:4 [1992], 30-39.
   Author was a railroad telegrapher there (ca. 1944-1945).

4104.   WRISTON, JOHN C. JR. "Newbury post offices." Vermont
Philatelist, 32 (Feb. 1988), 3-5; (May 1988), 3-6; (Aug.
1988), 1, 4-7.

SEE ALSO entry 468.

NEWFANE (WINDHAM CO.)

4105.   CROWELL, ROBERT L., and SUSAN B. CARNAHAN.
Historic Newfane Village: the houses and the people.
Newfane: Moore Free Library, 1989. xi, 256p. VtHi. *

NEWPORT (ORLEANS CO.)

4106.   HAGERMAN, ROBERT L. "Newport's old bears of
baseball." VtHN, 42 (July-Aug. 1991), 62-64.
   Local variation of the game as played in an 1891 match.

4107.   NEWPORT, VT. 75TH COMMITTEE. Newport, Vermont:
200 years since settlement, 75 years since city charter.
Newport, 1993. 72p. VtHi.

NORTHFIELD (WASHINGTON CO.)

4108.   HASSETT, WILLIAM D. While I remember: memories of
Center Village, Northfield, Vermont, and environs.
Northfield: Friends of the Norwich Univ. Library, 1989. xiii,
65p. VtHi. *

NORWICH (WINDSOR CO.)

4109.   LINDHAL, DAVID P. "Development and farmland loss in a Vermont township: separating myth from reality." NE-StLVGSPr, 17 (1987), 33-42.
1939-1980.

4110.   SMALLWOOD, FRANK. "Martin Luther King in Vermont: a recollection." VtHN, 43 (Jan.-Feb. 1992), 114-116.
1962 visit.

SEE ALSO entries 517, 609.

ORWELL (ADDISON CO.)

4111.   HOWE, DENNIS E. "The archaeology of a 1776 cantonment of New Hampshire regiments." NHArcheol, 32 (1991), 1-25.
Continental Army cantonment at Mount Independence.

4112.   STARBUCK, DAVID R. "Building independence on Lake Champlain." Archaeology, 46 (Sept.-Oct. 1993), 60-63.
Excavations at Mount Independence.

4113.   _____. "The general hospital at Mount Independence: 18th-century health care at a Revolutionary War cantonment." Northeast Historical Archaeology, 19 (1990), 50-68.

4114.   _____. Mount Independence and the American Revolution, 1776-1777, Orwell, Vermont. Montpelier: Vermont Division for Historic Preservation, 1991. 16p. VtHi. *

4115.   WICKMAN, DONALD H. "Built with spirit, deserted in darkness: the American occupation of Mount Independence." M.A. thesis, Univ. of Vermont, 1993. v, 168p. *

4116.   WOLKOMIR, JOYCE ROGERS. "The spirit of Mount Independence." Vermont Life, 44 (Summer 1990), 25-28.

PANTON (ADDISON CO.)

4117.   PANTON, VT. STATEHOOD BICENTENNIAL COMMITTEE. Panton—past and present: condensed history of the town of Panton, Vermont, 1761-1991. Lois K. Thurber and Ann Russett, eds. Rev. ed. Panton, 1991. 101p. VtHi.
Note: this item replaces entry 5089 in the Vermont volume.

4118.   STARBUCK, DAVID R. The Ferris site on Arnold's Bay: a research and educational program of the Lake Champlain Maritime Museum. Basin Harbor: Lake Champlain Maritime Museum, 1989. 58p. VtHi. *

PITTSFORD (RUTLAND CO.)

4119.   ANDERSON, GRACE. "Ebenezer Allen, commander of Fort Vigilance, Pittsford, Vermont, 1780." Pittsford Gleanings, 2 (1991), 1-12.

4120.   EARLY cars and Pittsford roads." Pittsford Gleanings, 1 (1989), 13-14.

4121.   HENDEE, CALEB. "General Caleb Hendee." Pittsford Gleanings, 2 (1991), 13-25.
Autobiographical sketch of a militia officer (born 1768).

4122.   NUQUIST, REIDUN D. "Taking the cure at the Vermont Sanatorium, 1917-1918." VtH, 61 (Winter 1993), 41-51.
Letters written by a patient in the Vermont Sanatorium for Incipient Tuberculosis.

4123.   POWERS, CHARLES. [Remarks on the beginning of the "Auto Age" in Pittsford] Pittsford Gleanings, 1 (1989), 1-2.

4124.   PROVIN, LLOYD. "Pittsford and the automobile, truck and farm tractor." Pittsford Gleanings, 1 (1989), 3-8.

4125.   WRISTON, JOHN C. JR. "Pittsford post offices." Vermont Philatelist, 37 (Nov. 1993), 158-165.

PLAINFIELD (WASHINGTON CO.)

4126.   CAPPEL, CONSTANCE. "Utopian colleges: a study of five experimental American educational institutions." Ph.D. dissertation, Union Institute, 1991. 200p.
Goddard College is one of the five. Includes historical information. Abstracted in DAI, 52:12A (1992), 4332.

4127.   PLAINFIELD HISTORICAL SOCIETY. The town of Plainfield, Vermont: a pictorial history, 1870-1940. Plainfield, 1993. 139p. VtHi. *

4128   PLYMOUTH

PLYMOUTH (WINDSOR CO.)

4128.   BUGBEE, SYLVIA. "The Tyson Iron Company papers, 1783-(1835-1868)-1916." VtH, 58 (Summer 1990), 199-201.
The papers are at the Univ. of Vermont.

SEE ALSO entry 3872.

PROCTOR (RUTLAND CO.)

4129.   COOPER, PETER. "Keep the standard high: a history of the Proctor Players Club." RHSQ, 24 (1994), 3-15.
20th-century theatrical group.

4130.   RATTI, GINO. "Coming to America in 1888." RHSQ, 20:3 (1990), 31-45.
Sculptor Cesare Ratti, recruited to work for the Vermont Marble Company.

4131.   RISTAU, ANITA FREGOSI. "'Small beginnings... splendid work': Ada Mayo Stewart (1870-1945) and industrial nursing in Proctor, Vermont." VtHN, 41 (Sept./Oct. 1990), 88-92.
Employed by the Vermont Marble Company.

4132.   _____. "Proctor post office at the turn of the century." Vermont Philatelist, 33 (Aug. 1989), 13-15.

4133.   WRISTON, JOHN C. JR. "Proctor post offices." Vermont Philatelist, 37 (May 1993), 68-73.

PUTNEY (WINDHAM CO.)

4134.   WILSON, FRANK G. Basketville: the autobiography of Frank G. Wilson. N.Y.: Vantage Pr., 1990. 181p. VtHi. *
Retailer.

RICHFORD (FRANKLIN CO.)

4135.   WRISTON, JOHN C. JR, and RHODA BERGER. "Richford post offices." Vermont Philatelist, 30 (May 1986), 5-9.

RIPTON (ADDISON CO.)

4136.   GENTRY, CHISHOLM. "The resurrection of Robert Frost." Vermont Magazine, 2 (Nov./Dec. 1989), 37-43, 91, 98.
Personal recollections of Frost's years at Ripton.

ROCKINGHAM (WINDHAM CO.)

4137.   VERMONT ACADEMY. Vermont Academy: a history of survival and success. Saxtons River, 1989. 128p. VtHi. *
Private school.

SEE ALSO entries 3748, 3916.

ROYALTON (WINDSOR CO.)

4138.   TULLAR, MARTIN. The sermons of Martin Tullar of Royalton, Vermont, with an account of his life, his ancestry, and his progeny. Sage Adams Hall and Madeleine Rowse, eds. n.p., 1992. 215p. VtHi. *
Tullar (1753-1813) was a Congregational minister.

RUPERT (BENNINGTON CO.)

4139.   RUPERT, VT. CONGREGATIONAL CHURCH. BICENTENNIAL COMMITTEE. Two hundred years: Congregational Church, Rupert, Vermont, 1786-1986. Dorothy Sheldon, ed. Rupert, 1986. 126p. VtHi. *

RUTLAND (RUTLAND CO.)

4140.   ANDERSON, THOM. "Rutland Methodist Episcopal Church, 1924-1926." RHSQ, 21:2 (1991), 10-22.
History of the design and construction of the building.

4141.   BURDITT, MARY LOU. "An extraordinary woman of her time." RHSQ, 21:4 (1991), 61-93.
Dr. Emelie Munson Perkins (1890-1986), a physician.

4142.   CARLISLE, LILIAN BAKER. "Rutland, Vermont's 19th century silversmiths." Silver, 21 (Jan./Feb-May 1988), 18-22; (Mar.-Apr. 1988), 8-12.

4143.   [COOPER, PETER]. "A grand tradition: fact and fancy about the Rutland Fair, 1846-1953." RHSQ, 20:2 (1990), 14-27.

4144.   DAVIDSON, JAMES S. "Early settlement and its problems (1770-1775)." RHSQ, 20:1 (1990), 3-9.
Early settlement of Rutland.

4145.   _____. "From frontier foundations to urban beginnings (1770-1791)." RHSQ, 22:1 (1992) 2-15.

4146.   _____. "The new immigration and postwar problems (1779-1791)." RHSQ, 23:1 (1993), 2-15.

4147.   _____. "Revolutionary Rutland (1775-1783)." RHSQ, 21:1 (1991), 2-7.

4148.   EATON, LORRAINE. "Riverside Women's Reformatory." RHSQ, 19:2 (1989), 16-27.
   1921-1970.

4149.   ELWERT, ELEANOR J. "The world of LJE." RHSQ, 18:4 (1988), 51-62.
   Lewellyn J. Egleston (1868-1943) owned the Rutland Business College and served as a state senator and judge of probate. Article describes the contents of his scrapbooks.

4150.   _____, and JAMES P. MONGEON. "Le Sacre Coeur de Marie." RHSQ, 22 (1992), 42-55.
   Immaculate Heart of Mary Church.

4151.   "THE FORTNIGHTLY." RHSQ, 18:2 (1988), 20-34.
   Women' literary society (since 1879) in what is now the Grace Congregational Church. See also entry 4159.

4152.   HANCE, DAWN D. "Early Rutland: the Gove family." RHSQ, 20 (1990), 50-71.

4153.   _____. History of Rutland, Vermont, 1761-1861. Rutland: Rutland Historical Society, 1991. xii, 690p. VtHi. *

4154.   _____. "The Rutland Volunteer Fire Department." RHSQ, 21:3 (1991), 30-55.

4155.   McCOY, LOUISE. "Horace Henry Baxter, 1818-1884." RHSQ, 23:3 (1993), 39-58.
   Businessman.

4156.   McDEVITT, THOMAS B. "Aviation Station/Rutland." Vermont Philatelist, 27 (Nov. 1983), 3-7.
   Postal history.

4157.   PURDY, ELAINE. "Fred R. Patch: his personal recollections of life at Sutherland Falls and the founding of Patch-Wegner Company." RHSQ, 23:2 (1993), 18-35.
   Patch (1853-1938) headed "the largest marble machine tool manufactory in the country."

4158.   ROSS, JEAN C. "The first polio epidemic in the U.S., 1894." RHSQ, 22:4 (1992), 59-71.
   Rutland area. Article discusses the work of and a report by Dr. Charles Solomon Caverly (1856-1918).

4159.   _____. "'First to receive, then to give': the Fortnightly Society of Rutland." VtHN, 40 (Nov./ Dec. 1989), 109-112.
   See also entry 4151.

4160.   "RUTLAND Jewish Center." RHSQ, 19:3 (1989), 30-43.

4161.   "RUTLAND murder mystery, 1874: Daily Globe report." RHSQ, 23 (1993), 63-91.
   James and Helen Davidson, eds. John P. Phair was convicted and executed for the killing of Ann E. Freese.

4162.   SWAN, MARVEL TRUE GUYETTE. Early families of Rutland, Vermont. Dawn D. Hance, ed. Rutland: Rutland Historical Society, 1990. vi, 464p. VtU. *

4163.   "WHERE have all the Ripleys gone?" RHSQ, 19:4 (1989), 46-62.
   Locally prominent family (19th century).

4164.   WICKMAN, DONALD H. "Rutland blacks in the 54th Massachusetts Regiment: their share of the glory." RHSQ, 22 (1992), 18-39.
   The famous Civil War regiment. Article includes the local background of the men.

   SEE ALSO entry 1751.

SHAFTSBURY (BENNINGTON CO.)

4165.   STETSON, FRED. "The Gully years." Vermont Life, 47 (Winter 1992), 18-23.
   Robert Frost in South Shaftsbury.

SHEFFIELD (CALEDONIA CO.)

4166.   SHEFFIELD HISTORICAL SOCIETY. Through hopes, and dreams, and evergreens: the two-hundred year history of Sheffield. Sheffield, 1993. xiii, 184p. VtHi. *

SHELBURNE (CHITTENDEN CO.)

4167.   ASKE, JERRY. History of the Shelburne Shipyard and its shipbuilding activities during World War II and the Korean conflict. Essex Junction: Chittenden County Regional Planning Commision, 1992. 32p. VtHi.

4168.   BRESSOR, JULIE. "Shelburne Farms archives and Webb family collection." VtH, 59 (Summer 1991), 180-183.

4169.   WEBSTER, TRUMAN M. Shelburne: pieces of history. Shelburne: Shelburne Historic Sites Committee, 1994. 133p. VtHi. +

4170   SHELBURNE

4170.   WILSON, LORI. God with us: a history of Trinity Episcopal Church, Shelburne, Vermont, 1790-1990. Shelburne: Trinity Episcopal Church, 1990. 124p. VtHi. *

SHELDON (FRANKLIN CO.)

4171.   YOUNG, STEVE. "Over the hill to the poor farm." Vermont Life, 44 (Spring 1990), 14-19.
        History of the state's last poor farm, closed in 1968.

SHERBURNE (RUTLAND CO.)

4172.   LORENTZ, KAREN D. Killington: a story of mountains and men. Shrewsbury: Mountain Publishing, 1990. xv, 271p. VtU. *

4173.   VARA, JON. "Fire and ice on Killington." Yankee, 56 (Jan. 1992), 58-61, 122-124, 126-127.
        Aftermath of a January 1991 airplane crash.

SHOREHAM (ADDISON CO.)

4174.   PISTORIUS, ALAN. Cutting Hill: a chronicle of a family farm. N.Y.: Knopf, 1990. xv, 279p. VtHi. *
        Treadway family.

4175.   SHOREHAM HISTORICAL SOCIETY. Shoreham: the town and its people. Shoreham, 1988. 104, ix, [56]p. VtHi. *

        SEE ALSO entry 3904.

SOMERSET (WINDHAM CO.)

4176.   BARNETT, BERNICE. "Dam life: stories of life around Somerset Dam." Cracker Barrel, 16 (Spring/Summer 1993), 18-19.

4177.   WOODS, B. B. "Somerset, the town that disappeared." Cracker Barrel, 16 (Spring/Summer 1993), 16-17.

SOUTH BURLINGTON (CHITTENDEN CO.)

4178.   ARCHAEOLOGY CONSULTING TEAM. Discoveries at the Oriole and Cold Crow sites: an archaeological study in South Burlington, Vermont. Essex Junction, 1991. 12p. VtHi. *

SPRINGFIELD (WINDSOR CO.)

4179.   RICHARDSON, FREDERICK WILLIAM. Eighteenth century Springfield: from wilderness to Vermont statehood, 1751-1791; a narrative: a study of the early land records and some of the settlers who lived there. Newport, N.H.: Newport Litho, 1991. xix, 346p. VtHi. *

4180.   _____, and GOLDIE MAY. A touch of history: historic sites and trails, Springfield, Vermont. Lebanon, N.H.: Whitman Pr., 1992. 143p. VtHi. *

4181.   SESSIONS, GENE. "Espionage in Windsor: Clarence H. Waldron and patriotism in World War I." VtH, 61 (Summer 1993), 133-155.
        Waldron, a Baptist minister, was convicted under the Espionage Act.

4182.   SWANSON, JOHN N. "Clare Parker and the Springfield Ice Company." M.A. thesis, Univ. of Vermont, 1991. iii, 119p. *
        20th century.

ST. ALBANS (FRANKLIN CO.)

4183.   FISHMAN, HERTZEL. "A Zionist childhood in St. Albans, Vt." Kfari, 2 (Feb. 1989), 5.
        1920s and 1930s.

4184.   WILSON, DENNIS KENDRICK. Justice under pressure: the Saint Albans raid and its aftermath. Lanham, Md.: University Pr. of America, 1992. 203p. VtHi.
        Civil War incident.

4185.   WOODWARD, JON. "The St. Albans raid: rebels in Vermont! Oct. 19, 1864." Blue & Gray, 8 (Dec. 1990), 8-14, 46-62.
        See also preceding entry.

        SEE ALSO entry 3748.

ST. JOHNSBURY (CALEDONIA CO.)

4186.   CLARK, EDIE. "St. Johnsbury." Yankee, 53 (Oct. 1989), 70-76, 156-158, 160, 162.

4187.   JOHNSON, CLAIRE DUNNE. "I see by the paper...": an informal history of St. Johnsbury. St. Johnsbury, 1987-1989. 2v. VtHi. *
        Note: this item replaces entry 11651 in Vol. 8.

4188. LEE, EDWARD B. East Village portrait: based on the autobiography of Arthusa Hibbard Ayer, 1824-1904. St. Johnsbury, 1988. ix, 93p. VtHi. *

STANNARD (CALEDONIA CO.)

4189. LEWANDOSKI, JAN LEO. "The early history of Goshen Gore and Stannard." Hazen Road Dispatch, 16 (Summer 1991), 14-15.
Goshen Gore was the original name of the town.

STOWE (LAMOILLE CO.)

4190. DAVIS, THOMAS C. "Ski pioneers." Vermont Life, 44 (Winter 1989), 5-8.
Early skiing on Mount Mansfield.

4191. STOWE HISTORICAL SOCIETY. Three Score and Ten Union Society: being autobiographical accounts of the experiences of some early residents of Stowe, Vermont, recorded in 1874-1875. Stowe, 1993. xvi, 84p. VtU. *

STRAFFORD (ORANGE CO.)

4192. SMITH, GWENDA. The Town House. Strafford: Strafford Historical Society, 1992. 200p. VtHi. *
Strafford Town House.

4193. YALE, ALLEN R. "Confirming the oral tradition: the Morrill ice house?" Society for Industrial Archeology, New England Chapter, 9:2 (1989), 19-23.
Justin Morrill Homestead.

STRATTON (WINDHAM CO.)

4194. DAVISON, PETER. "Deep in the blackness of woods: a farewell to Robert Penn Warren." New England Monthly, 77 (Mar. 1990), 37-39.
The novelist and poet, a summer resident of Stratton, was buried there in 1989.

THETFORD (ORANGE CO.)

4195. HUGHES, CHARLES W. The mills and villages of Thetford, Vermont. Thetford: Thetford Historical Society, [1992]. v, 136p. VtHi. *

4196. LATHAM, CHARLES JR. "Church and state in Thetford." VtHN, 45 (Sept.-Oct. 1994), 61-64.

4197. PERRIN, NOEL. Last person rural. Boston: David R. Godine, 1991. xii, 199p. VtHi. *
For related titles by this author, see the Vermont volume (entry 5953) and Vol. 8 (entries 11687-11688).

TINMOUTH (RUTLAND CO.)

4198. ALLEN, MILDRED E. Reflections of Tinmouth. n.p., [198?]. 131p. VtHi. *

TOWNSHEND (WINDHAM CO.)

4199. BRODIE, JOCELYN, J. B. STEARNS, and ANN BRAUDE. Townshend and the founding of Vermont. West Townshend: West Townshend Historical Society, 1991. 40p. VtHi. *

4200. SONNENFELD, MARTHA, and DON LEIGH. The house that became a hospital. Townshend: Grace Cottage Hospital Auxiliary, 1990. vii, lxxx p. VtHi. *
Grace Cottage Hospital.

4201. TUNNELL, TED. "With banner, gun, and sword: Marshall Harvey Twitchell and the 4th Vermont Regiment go to war." VtH, 59 (Spring 1991), 69-84.
Civil War.

UNDERHILL (CHITTENDEN CO.)

4202. AUDETTE, MARY MARGARET MOORE. A history of St. Thomas Church, Underhill Center, Vermont, 1991: on the occasion of its centennial, 1891-1991. [Underhill Center: St. Thomas Parish, 1991?] iv, 66p. VtU. *
Roman Catholic.

4203. WAGNER, CAROL CHRISTINE. "A frontier marriage." VtHN, 41 (Jan./Feb. 1990), 7-10.
Caleb and Polly Campbell Sheldon (early-19th century).

4204. _____. "Town growth, town controversy: Underhill meetinghouses to 1840." VtH, 57 (Summer 1989), 162-179.

4205. _____. "The Underhill Flats: a nutshell history." CCHSB, 25 (Winter 1990), 4-5.

SEE ALSO entry 3910.

4206   VERSHIRE

VERSHIRE (ORANGE CO.)

4206.   STAUNTON, WILLIAM FIELD III. "'Not fit for a dog':
memories of the Ely Copper Mine in 1882." VtHN, 45
(July-Aug. 1994), 50-53.
    The author (lived 1860-1947) was a young engineer at the
time of the strike.

4207.   YOUNGBLOOD, SUSAN. "The Ely war." Vermont Life, 47
(Spring 1993), 44-47, 70.
    On the strike at the Ely Copper Mine.

WARREN (WASHINGTON CO.)

4208.   COMMEMORATION of Warren's bicentennial, 1789-1989.
Katharine Carleton Hartshorn, ed. Waterbury: Buy Monthly
Publishing, [1989]. 64p. VtHi. *

WATERBURY (WASHINGTON CO.)

4209.   KINCHELOE, MARSHA R., and HERBERT G. HUNT JR.
Empty beds: a history of the Vermont State Hospital. Barre:
Northlight Studio Pr., 1988. 245p. VtHi. *

4210.   LAGER, FRED ("Chico"). Ben & Jerry's, the inside scoop:
how two real guys built a business with social conscience and
a sense of humor. N.Y.: Crown Publishers, 1994. xiv, 242p.
VtU. *
    Ben & Jerry's ice cream.

4211.   PALMER, BRIAN. All that hell allows. n.p., 1993. 138p.
VtHi.
    Account of a confinement at Waterbury State Hospital, to
which the author was committed as a violent offender in
1985.

4212.   WATERBURY HISTORICAL SOCIETY. The history of
Waterbury, 1915-1991. James Sabin, ed. Waterbury, 1991. ix,
358p. VtHi. *

WEATHERSFIELD (WINDSOR CO.)

4213.   HUNTER, EDITH FISHER. Weathersfield artists look at
their world, 1777-1989: an exhibit at the Reverend Dan
Foster House, Weathersfield Center, June 21-October 6,
1990. Weathersfield: Weathersfield Historical Society,
[1990?]. 20p. VtHi. *

SEE ALSO entry 1355.

WEST WINDSOR (WINDSOR CO.)

4214.   REICHMAN, CHARLES. "The daily transactions of a 19th
century rural blacksmith." CEAIA, 44 (Dec. 1991), 122-123.
    Charles E. Hastings of Brownsville (1880s).

WESTMINSTER (WINDHAM CO.)

4215.   WRISTON, JOHN C. JR, and CHARLES L. CLARK.
"Westminster post offices." Vermont Philatelist, 31 (Nov.
1986), 4-7; 32 (Feb. 1987), 4-5.

SEE ALSO entry 3916.

WEYBRIDGE (ADDISON CO.)

4216.   WASHINGTON, IDA H. A bicentennial history of the
Weybridge Congregational Church, 1794-1994. n.p., 1994.
87p. VtHi.

4217.   _____. History of Weybridge, Vermont. Weybridge:
Weybridge Bicentennial Committee, 1991. xix, 244p. VtHi. *

WILLIAMSTOWN (ORANGE CO.)

4218.   WILLIAMSTOWN HISTORICAL SOCIETY. A history of
Williamstown, Vermont, 1781-1991. Williamstown:
Williamstown History Book Committee, 1991. xiii, 348p.
VtHi. *

SEE ALSO entry 128.

WILMINGTON (WINDHAM CO.)

4219.   HOYLE, KEVIN. "The grand old dame of Main Street:
Wilmington's Memorial Hall." Cracker Barrel, 16
(Spring/Summer 1993), 6-8.

4220.   LOOK, FRED E. JR. "The Masonic Temple building: 167
years of service." Cracker Barrel, 15 (Spring- Summer 1992),
28-29.

4221.   PRINCE, BONNEY. "Tattingers: history inside and out."
Cracker Barrel, 15 (Spring-Summer 1992), 30-32.
    History of a business location.

4222.   WOODS, B. B. "Berkshire Coal Company to Deerfield Valley Supply: one hundred years of business." Cracker Barrel, 15 (Spring-Summer 1992), 22-23.

SEE ALSO entry 3811.

WINDSOR (WINDSOR CO.)

4223.   BLAISE, SUZANNE HEBERT. Ain't that the truth: a hodgepodge of Windsor memorabilia. Windsor, 1991. 136p. VtHi. *

SEE ALSO entry 465.

WINOOSKI (CHITTENDEN CO.)

4224.   HERRLICH, KATHERINE L. "The origins and manifestations of the labor movement in a textile community: the case of Winooski, Vermont." University of Vermont History Review, 4 (Spring 1991), 26-35.
        See also entry 4224.

4225.   POR amor al pueblo: not guilty! The trial of the Winooski 44. Ben Bradley, Nathan P. Hine, Judith Vollmann, and Nancy Wasserman, eds. White River Junction: Front Porch Publishing, 1986. ix, 176p. VtHi. *
        The defendants had been arrested for illegally trespassing in the Winooski office of Sen. Robert Strafford in 1984 while protesting U.S. policy in Central America.

4226.   STRAUSS, ROBERTA. "Unionization battle in Winooski: fifty year anniversary." CCHSB, 27 (Spring 1993), 1-7.
        Textile Workers Union of America. See also entry 4222.

SEE ALSO entry 3734.

WOODBURY (WASHINGTON CO.)

4227.   BECK, JANE C. Memories touched by fancy: the paintings of Bessie Drennan, Vermont artist. Middlebury: Vermont Folklife Center, 1990. 40p. VtHi. *
        Lived 1862-1961.

WOODFORD (BENNINGTON CO.)

4228.   WOODS, B. B. "Woodford in the early days." Cracker Barrel, 15 (Fall/Winter 1991-1992), 6-7.

WOODSTOCK (WINDSOR CO.)

4229.   FILANOVA, NATASHA. "It happened in Woodstock: terrible tales from the past." Woodstock Common, 9 (Summer 1991), 14-20.

4230.   HALL, KAREN. "Oh, those long summer baseball nights." Woodstock Common, 9 (Summer 1991), 9-11.

4231.   WOODSTOCK AREA CHAMBER OF COMMERCE. Old days, new ways: Woodstock and its neighbors. Woodstock, 1986. 40p. VtHi.

SEE ALSO entries 3784, 3920.

Index

This index lists authors, editors, and compilers, as well as subjects and places. The references are to entry numbers, not pages. Library of Congress subject headings have usually been preferred. If there is a bibliography for a particular subject, it is listed as the first subheading under that subject. Vital dates and other data are provided when needed to distinguish persons with identical names.

Headings are listed in word-by-word rather than letter-by-letter order (East Windsor before Easthampton). Corporate names divided by a period (such as Connecticut. State University) precede the names of institutions and organizations not so divided (such as Connecticut Humanities Council).

The only geographical names in this index are those that are subjects of writings listed in the bibliography. See the six state volumes in this series for complete lists of counties, cities, and towns. The indexes to the state volumes also identify a number of other place names.

Headings with many entries, such as "Churches, Congregational," are usually subdivided by states. In other cases, the best way to find material about a particular subject in one state or locality is first to become familiar with the range of entry numbers for that state or locality.

1308, 1337, 1353, 1364, 1366-1367, 1383, 1389, 1452, 1499;
Massachusetts, 2306, 2371, 2411, 2429, 2545, 2547, 2549, 2551,
2558, 2575-2576, 2585, 2602, 2653, 2682; New Hampshire, 2897,
2960, 2978, 3021, 3034, 3043, 3125, 3138, 3170, 3193-3194;
Rhode Island, 3268, 3317, 3330, 3414, 3432, 3438, 3466-3467,
3473, 3483, 3493, 3497, 3499, 3501-3502, 3529, 3538, 3542, 3705;
Vermont, 4041-4043, 4051, 4054, 4057, 4172
Restaurants, see Hotels and restaurants
Retail trade, 187, 268, 316, 762, 819, 823, 945, 975, 1183, 1466,
1492, 1691, 1833, 1965, 2327, 2339, 2412, 2702, 2725, 2748,
3004-3005, 3173, 3232, 3484, 3549, 3632, 3636, 4030, 4065, 4134,
4221
Rettich, Carl, 3696
Revere, Paul, 1593, 2113
Revere, Mass., 2692
Revivals, 35, 104, 116-117, 260, 559, 578, 585, 877, 1570, 1654,
1798, 2130, 2465, 2564, 2654, 2943, 3516-3517, 3904
Revolution, American, 63, 689, 702, 798, 929, 1033, 1077, 1810,
2113, 3291, 3738, 4114, 4146-4147; diaries, 757, 1751; economic
conditions, 558; French participation, 216, 3257, 3265, 3545;
German mercenaries, 1751; historic buildings and sites, 2697, 4118;
historiography, 389, 482, 2667, 2669; intellectual life, 540;
Loyalists, 576, 853, 1632, 1650, 2176, 3295, 3446-3447, 3727,
3820; military, 67, 75, 361, 517, 538, 598, 609, 734, 909, 1040,
1575, 1593, 1661, 1751, 1855, 1886, 2173, 2697, 2758, 2764-2765,
2942, 3283, 3292, 3305, 3335, 3387, 3449, 3463, 3551, 3631, 3768,
3785, 3958-3959, 4044, 4111-4116, 4119; monuments, 3958, 3959;
and nationalism, 1951; naval operations, 2385, 3185, 3287, 3586,
3625, 3865; newspapers, 250; ordnance, 3405; physicians, 1751;
politics and government, 96, 422, 556, 558, 1339, 1548, 1587-1588,
1590, 1601, 1613, 1617, 1630, 1633, 1638, 1681, 1818, 1823, 2173,
2764-2765, 2946, 3249, 3310, 3393, 3447, 3727, 3738, 3762, 3781,
4082; prisoners of war, 757, 1751; and religious life, 96, 260, 404,
520, 2530; social conditions, 466, 558, 858, 1131, 1139, 1548,
1576, 1751, 1834, 2476, 2760, 3053, 3513, 4082; spies, 19, 2120,
2176; and the arts, 576, 909; traitors, 517, 609, 734
Reynolds, Bill, 2131
Reynolds, Douglas M., 390-391, 3460
Reynolds, Ernest Venner, 3948
Reynolds, Richard, 3369, 3539, 3615, 3653-3654, 3692
Reynolds, Thomas Hedley, 1326-1327
Reynolds family, 731
Rhetoric, 4, 16, 299, 329, 764, 1711, 2123, 2161, 2924
Rhode Island, 22, 135-136, 166, 191, 200, 246, 249, 280, 296-297,
321, 356-357, 390, 397, 2087, 2180, 3243-3397; bibliographies,
102, 203, 3246
Rhode Island. Attorney General, 3574
Rhode Island. General Assembly, 3243-3244, 3288, 3301
Rhode Island. Historical Preservation Commission, 3416, 3426, 3448,
3462, 3467, 3473, 3679
Rhode Island. National Guard, 3707
Rhode Island. State Anthem, 3334
Rhode Island. State Archives, 3335
Rhode Island. State Council on the Arts, 3364
Rhode Island. State House, Providence, 3639, 3657-3658
Rhode Island Greening (variety of apple), 3263
Rhode Island Historical Document Transcription Project, 3370
Rhode Island Historical Society, Providence, 3371-3372, 3618
Rhode Island Hospital, Providence, 3651
Rhode Island Jewish Historical Notes (periodical), 3316

Rhode Island Red (breed of chicken), 3259
Rhode Island School of Design. Museum of Art, Providence, 3373
Rhodin, Anders G. J., 2839
Ribicoff, Abraham, 612
Rice, Molly Craig, 2406
Rice, Ray, 1481
Richards, Bruce B., 1371
Richards, David, 1110
Richards, Kenneth G., 1839
Richards, Phillip M., 2132
Richards family, 1280
Richardson, Eleanor Motley, 1367, 1495
Richardson, Experience Wight, 2796
Richardson, Frederick William, 4179-4180
Richardson, Halton J. Sr., 2951
Richardson, Henry Hobson, 2367, 3532
Richardson, Ralph W., 392
Richardson, Wendy, 3949
Richford, Vt., 4135
Richman, Miriam, 2744
Richmond, J. Lee, 3664
Richmond, Me., 1455
Richmond, Mass., 2693
Richmond, R.I., 3412, 3674
Richter, Paula Bradstreet, 1808
Rickard, Timothy J., 726
Ricketson, William F., 1697
Riddle, Lyn, 1511
Rider, Christine, 393
Rider, Mary, 3164
Rider, Raymond A., 2819
Rider-Wood House, Portsmouth, N.H., 3164
Ridgefield, Conn., 909-911; battle of (1777), 909
Ridley, Alison R., 2795
Rieke, Alison, 865
Rifkin, Glenn, 2521
Riggs, Maida Leonard, 2455
Riley, Stephen T., 1681
Ring, Betty, 394, 2133
Ring, Elizabeth, 1011, 1330
Riots, 1392, 1902, 2011, 2550, 3114
Ripley, David B., 613
Ripley, George, 1594
Ripley family, 4163
Ripton, Vt., 4136
Ristau, Anita Fregosi, 4131
Ritchie, Mrs. Wallace, 1285
Rivard, Paul E., 1111-1112
Rivers family, 2683
Riverside, place in East Providence, R.I., 3453
Riverside National Register District, Gill, Mass., 2424
Riverside Women's Reformatory, Rutland, Vt., 4148
Roads (see also Streets), 525, 643, 648-650, 820, 938, 1163, 1227,
2906, 2957, 2973, 3210, 3331, 3357, 3441, 3450, 3659, 3731-3732,
3756, 3895, 4120
Robb, Carol, 1911
Robbins, Anthony Jerome, 3850
Robbins, Marjorie B., 721
Robbins, Maurice, 1872, 2614
Robbins Museum of Archaeology, Attleboro, Mass., 1872